RECENT VIEWS ON
BRITISH HISTORY

RECENT VIEWS ON BRITISH HISTORY

ESSAYS ON HISTORICAL WRITING SINCE 1966

edited for the Conference on British Studies
by Richard Schlatter

Rutgers University Press
New Brunswick, New Jersey

Library of Congress Cataloging in Publication Data
Main entry under title:

Recent views on British history.

Bibliography: p.
Includes index.
1. Great Britain—Historiography—Addresses, essays,
lectures. I. Schlatter, Richard Bulger, 1912–
II. Conference on British Studies.
DA1.R4   941'.0072   81–23557
ISBN 0–8135–0959–9   AACR2

096716

Contents

Preface

In 1957 the Conference on British Studies decided to sponsor a series of essays on the most significant developments in the field of British history since about 1939. The emphasis was to be on new interpretations and on problems still needing investigation. These articles were first printed in various learned journals. Then the Publication Committee of the Conference, under the chairmanship of Samuel Clyde McCulloch, decided to reprint the articles in one volume, and the result was *Changing Views of British History*, edited by Elizabeth Furber (Cambridge, Harvard University Press, 1966).

In 1978, the Publication Committee, now headed by Peter Stansky, decided that a new edition was needed and asked me to organize it and be the editor. But this time it was stipulated that all the essays should be prepared especially for the new volume and not be reprints of articles previously published elsewhere.

Otherwise the present volume follows the pattern set in 1966. The editors of the volumes did not wish to impose a rigid scheme of approach on the various authors, each one a recognized expert in his or her field. Consequently here, as in 1966, some authors have treated their period in broad strokes, emphasizing only the peaks, and others have gone into more detail, analyzing periodical literature and collections of source materials. The essays on the earlier periods tend to be shorter, reflecting the obvious fact that less is being done, for example, in early medieval history than in the twentieth century. The essays also vary somewhat in their chronological coverage. The original idea was to discuss publications of the period from 1966 to 1978: the deadline for completion of the articles was set at December 1979. Some authors met that deadline, but others were delayed and, finishing their chapters only late in 1981, were able to include material published since 1978. Even so, we managed better this time than last; our predecessors began in 1957 and published their volume in 1966 while we began in 1978 and made it by 1984! Finally, and this to the present editor is a source of much satisfaction since it adds to the liveliness of a volume which could be dully encyclopedic, the essays show very clearly the different styles and personal attitudes toward history of their authors.

Lawrence Stone has said that the last forty years have been the most fruitful and creative period in the whole history of the profession. The present essays, together with those in the 1966 volume, demonstrate that this is true for the special field of British history as well. But one note of pessimism about the future sounds on several occasions here; after the great increase in the number of professional and academic historians in the 1950s and the 1960s, the number of students has, for well-known reasons, dropped catastrophically. It is possible that the most able students are the ones who have left history for fairer fields. "If this happens the past twenty-five years will come to be seen as something of a heroic phase in the evolution of historical understanding, squeezed in between two periods of quiet consolidation of received wisdom" (Stone, *The Past and the Present*, Boston and London, 1981, xi). For the moment, however, we can be reasonably well satisfied. The field of British history flourishes and shows new strengths and new approaches which prove that it is alive and well.

Some names which were often cited with awed respect in the 1966 volume have been superseded—for example, G. M. Trevelyan, A. F. Pollard, Sir George Clark and the *Oxford History of England*, Conyers Read, Wallace Notestein, and most notably of all, Sir Lewis Namier and the Namierite school he founded. New authorities have come to the fore; some of the most frequently mentioned in this new volume are G. R. Elton, E. P. Thompson, Peter Laslett and the Cambridge Group, J. H. Plumb, Keith Thomas, Alan McFarlane, and Lawrence Stone. A few, including J. H. Hexter, Ragnild Hatton, and Christopher Hill, figure prominently in both volumes; and perhaps only three of the historians of the more distant past continue to inspire students: Maitland, Powicke, and Neale.

The traditional fields such as political, diplomatic, religious, and military history are still being cultivated, but they continue to lose ground, comparatively, to the newer fields, as predicted in 1966. The impression these essays give is that the most flourishing of all fields in all periods is economic history. At the time when the study of economic theory is in complete disarray, economists appear to have turned to the study of history in the hope, perhaps, that they may learn how to deal with our present discontents.

The most striking of the new continues to be social history. Studies of the family, urban and rural society, crime, the everyday life of ordinary people, and quantitative studies of such things as disease and population have proliferated, in the process developing new techniques and uncovering unsuspected sources of information. While most of the essays in the 1966 volume began with a discussion of new work in political history, several of the new essays begin with social history, and three of the essays begin by discussing work in historical demography.

Two trends which were just beginning to interest historians of Britain twenty years ago have failed to develop: the early enthusiasm for the *Annales* school across the Channel has declined, and psychohistory and psychobiography have found few advocates. On the other hand, biography flourishes; it attracts numerous professional scholars as well as gifted amateurs and is the brand of history which appeals to the widest nonprofessional audience. The only exception to the prominent place of biography in all periods is in the earlier Middle Ages, where, as Bryce Lyon points out, material for the study of individual lives is missing. It becomes available only in the fifteenth century.

From these essays, the reader gets the general impression that medieval history is being less intensively studied than it was twenty years ago, has been less innovative, and still relies on many of the authorities of two or three generations back. It is also less overwhelmed with materials, although those materials are more intractable and may discourage would-be students. Medievalists cannot pursue demographic studies satisfactorily because the sources are deficient; indeed, D. C. Moore maintains that no really sound demographic studies can be done before 1838, when the first accurate survey of population was made, a conclusion which would hardly be accepted by Laslett and the Cambridge Group.

Beginning with the Tudor century, materials become more copious, and the social historians can begin to pursue their interests with greater assurance. (Incidentally, historians of the period, including G. R. Elton, are attempting to begin the Tudor period with Henry VIII and Thomas Cromwell and push Henry VII back into the Middle Ages, the kind of revision in periodization that is rarely successful in the traditional discipline of history). Then, in the nineteenth and twentieth centuries, the materials begin to overwhelm the student, and the later essays in this volume, inevitably, become longer. Robert Smith points out that three thousand books and articles on the reign of George III alone have been published since 1966.

There is some evidence here to support the conclusion that those periods of history which have a present-day reference are the most flourishing. The period of the English Civil War in the seventeenth century continues to enlist the interest of modern radicals, liberals, and conservatives and serves as a, for the most part, genteel arena for their academic battles. By contrast, the medieval period, the later Stuart reigns, and the reigns of the first two Georges are somewhat lacking in contemporary reference and tend to seem a little dull and pedestrian. But the nineteenth and twentieth centuries are close enough to make what historians say about them of immediate concern to all of us. The problems of an industrial and technological age, of war and diplomacy, of representative government are our problems, too.

Perhaps the influence of contemporary events upon the study of history is most dramatically illustrated by the last three essays in this volume. Scottish nationalism and the terrible troubles in Ireland have led to a more intensive and extensive study of those areas, and our authors tell us, surprisingly, that the quality of that historical study has been improving in spite of (or because of?) the passions involved. But the most dramatic is Robin Winks's description of the explosion in empire history. The end of the empire has caused more interest than its previous history. For the first time the points of view and actions of the colonial subjects as well as those of the rulers are being investigated, and the idea of a Third World born out of former empires has come to be a commonplace of present-day study. The result is, not only a proliferation of publications which almost makes the study of the history of the empire as a single field impossible, but a revolution in methods and points of view so complete what Winks can find nothing reported by his distinguished predecessor, Philip Curtin, in the 1966 volume of any interest for the present-day student.

Several of the authors of these essays point to a decline, not only in history in general, but in British history especially. This decline is, no doubt, more marked in the United States, where our essayists reside, than in Britain; and it should be noted that, as we learn from the recent survey *The Past Before Us*, edited by Michael Kammen (Ithaca, N.Y., and London, 1980), British remains the most popular of all foreign histories studied in the United States.

But there has been a declination, and that has something to do, perhaps, with the fate of the Whig interpretation of history. British and American historians once assumed that what really mattered in world history was the forward march of human liberty—political, legal, constitutional, and economic. Britain was the model case history and also the mother of American liberty. Magna Carta, the common law, Parliament, the revolutions of 1648, 1688, and 1776, the Industrial Revolution, social welfare legislation, bills of rights, the American Constitution, and the British Commonwealth of Nations seemed to be the cornerstones of modern history, which was itself the history of progress. But historians have lost faith in that satisfying scenario and, as a consequence, faith in the preeminent importance of British history.

But perhaps that is too strong a statement. In the Whig interpretation, the main event was always revolution, and certainly the study of the revolutionary crises of the seventeenth century has continued to attract a very large number of eminent scholars. Moreover, the left wing of the Whig perspective has joined with the Marxists to produce the spectacular rise of social history and the notable popularity of E. P. Thompson, both in England and in the United States, where his influence on the writing of American history has been compared to that formerly wielded by F. J. Turner.

But in spite of all this, British history does seem less important than it once did. We may suspect that this has to do, not only with the loss of faith in Whig liberalism, but with the fact that Britain has shrunk from being the world's largest, richest, and most powerful empire to a small, impoverished island, a minor partner in the liberal European alliance. Other areas of the world—the Far East, Africa, South America—are more important to most people. A seventeenth-century historian would have thought the histories of Spain and of the Netherlands as interesting as the history of Britain. If we today do not give much attention to those histories in our university curriculum, is it not because those countries have ceased to be major powers? Perhaps British history will eventually be crowded out by Russian, Chinese, Islamic, and Third World histories. If so, the next edition of this volume will, alas, be thinner and poorer.

THE NORTH AMERICAN CONFERENCE
ON BRITISH STUDIES

In 1980 the North American Conference on British Studies celebrated its thirtieth anniversary with a gala event hosted by the British Embassy in Washington, D.C.

The North American Conference is the official organization in the United States and Canada of scholars working in the field of British history and culture. Its status as such is recognized by the American Historical Association, of which it is an affiliate. Its nearly eight hundred members are drawn from fifty states and five provinces. The Conference meets once a year, in the autumn, usually with one of the regional conferences.

The Conference has fostered the growth of regional conferences: the Pacific Coast Conference, the Pacific Northwest Conference, the Rocky Mountain Conference, the Midwest Conference, the Southern Conference, the Mid-Atlantic Conference, and the New England Conference. Each of these active and autonomous associations has its own officers, programs, and other activities.

The North American Conference awards prizes for books published by American and Canadian scholars. It also sponsors a considerable publications program. It publishes the *Journal of British Studies* at the University of Illinois at Chicago Circle; *Archives in British History and Culture*, a series devoted to the publication of documents, at West Virginia University, Morgantown; and *Current Research in British Studies*, a quadrennial survey of research in progress in the United States and Canada, at Kansas State University, Manhattan. The Conference also sponsors a newsletter, the *British Studies Intelligencer*, published three times a year at the University of California, Irvine; and a series of short monographs, *Studies in British History and Culture*, edited at Wittenberg University, Springfield, Ohio. Under the aegis of the Conference, a biographical series is being published, and Cambridge University Press continues to publish a bibliographical series. *Albion*, an independent quarterly of British Studies, is sent to all members of the Conference. It prints the proceedings of the regional conferences and the North American Conference. *Albion* is published by Appalachian State University, Boone, North Carolina.

Richard Schlatter

Abbreviations

AHR   American Historical Review
BIHR   Bulletin of the Institute of Historical Research
BJRL   Bulletin of the John Rylands Library
EcHR   Economic History Review
EHR   English Historical Review
HJ   Historical Journal
HLQ   Huntington Library Quarterly
IHS   Irish Historical Studies
JBS   Journal of British Studies
JEcH   Journal of Economic History
JMH   Journal of Modern History
LQR   Law Quarterly Review
PP   Past and Present
SHR   Scottish Historical Review
SPCK   Society for Promoting Christian Knowledge
Studies   Studies: An Irish Quarterly Review
TRHS   Transactions of the Royal Historical Society
VS   Victorian Studies

Change or Continuity
Writing since 1965
on English History before
Edward of Caernarvon

Bryce Lyon

In the early 1960s when I first surveyed and assayed the writing on that period of English history from Roman Britain to the accession of Edward II, I dealt with a corpus published between 1939 and 1965.[1] A question then often on the lips of those occupied with medieval English history was the effect of World War II upon the study of the distant past. Some scholars, convinced that the war and modernization had damaged the cause of medievalism, even accused that recognized bellwether of English history, the *English Historical Review*, of printing fewer articles on the period before Bosworth Field. Repudiating this nasty charge, the editor garnered statistics that proved medieval history was holding on to its traditional share of space.

But how has it fared since 1965? Although this question has not been programmed, the following brief quantification will both save space and inform the reader that the author is aware of historical quantification and of its present vogue. From 1965 through 1978 the fourteen volumes of the *English Historical Review* printed 125 articles on pre-1485 England and 206 articles on post-1485 England. Let us hope that this trend toward fewer medieval articles is not serious or long term. But what about other English and non-English journals? In the *Transactions of the Royal Historical Society*, usually half of the articles concern medieval history. Only once, in 1976, was there an alarming drop, when but 1 out of 10 articles was on a medieval subject. Medieval history has also remained bullish in the *Bulletin of the Institute of Historical Research* and continued to receive its due not only in *History* but even in that avant-garde publication *Past and Present*.[2] In *Speculum*, the leading journal on medieval studies in North America, where obviously all the contributions are on subjects medieval, only 57, or roughly 17 percent, of the 326 articles on history appearing since 1965 concern English history. The *Canadian Historical Review* has decided to limit itself solely to Canadian history. In the *American Historical Review*, articles on medieval, and particularly English medieval, history appear less and less frequently. In the more specialized journals such as *Traditio* and the *Journal of British Studies*, not only are the contributions on English medieval history less frequent but they are also inferior to the others. For better or worse, English medieval history no longer evinces the strength that has been its trademark in North America.

On the Continent in the non-English-speaking world there is a dearth of articles as well as books on medieval England. Seldom do British scholars publish in the continental journals, and rare is the continental scholar whose interest is medieval England. Seldom is medieval England the subject of an article in *Historische Zeitschrift*, *Le moyen âge*, *La revue historique*, or *Annales*, a condition that has worsened since just before and after World War II, when scholars such as Mitteis, Kienast, Perroy, and Fawtier were still making valuable contributions to English medieval history.

In journals specializing in kinds rather than in periods or areas of history, no medieval history fares well. Since 1965 scarcely a fifteenth of the articles in the *Economic History Review* have concerned medieval England, and the *Journal of Economic History* has printed only five articles on medieval subjects. In the *Journal of Ecclesiastical History* published at Cambridge, the English medieval church fares better, but less well than formerly. *Isis*, the journal of the history of science, rarely includes an article on a medieval subject, and when one does appear it usually concerns Roger Bacon or Grosseteste. Nor is medieval history well represented in the many journals that have sprouted up during the past twenty years as a forum for new historical interests and methodologies. While occasionally an article on early medieval history appears in a highly specialized journal such as *Britannia*, founded ten years ago to promote interest in Romano-British studies, any view of medieval England just about sinks from sight in those journals catering to psychohistory, quantification, comparison, theory, methodology, urban development, modernization, and the peasantry. Because medieval records rarely produce the kinds of evidence needed for such research, this is not surprising, but the content of these journals as well as those on economic history underlines the great proliferation of historical interests and often their remoteness from medieval history. Moreover, even the leading legal journals which regularly used to publish articles on legal history by F. W. Maitland, Paul Vinogradoff, W. S. Holdsworth, T. F. T. Plucknett, G. A. Holmes, C. H. McIlwain, and G. E. Woodbine seldom offer anything on the common law, let alone on subjects medieval. What appears in law reviews and historical journals today reflects modern society with its emphasis on technology, its rapid increase in population, its new legal problems, and its demand for the practical and relevant. A loser has been English medieval history.

This crude exercise in quantification with its figures, percentages, and generalized statements on bulk or production has been less than revealing on kinds of history and completely silent on quality. Here what is needed is not quantification but assessment and, yes, impression. To place in perspective the bits and pieces of the discussion that follows, let it first be said that historical writing on medieval England has become less and less comprehensive, broad, and integrated despite all the talk about comparative history and the utilization of affiliated disciplines. For at least a decade, writing has mostly been concentrated on limited time periods and specific problems, few encompassing long spans of time. Research has become microscopic. In 1965 W. A. Pantin, writing a memorial to Frederick Maurice Powicke (1879–1963) for the *English Historical Review*, was impressed with Powicke's dislike of rigidly breaking up and pigeonholing of history into periods, themes, and types. That almost all of Powicke's major books aimed at weaving the totality of history into a continuous narrative meant studying the whole spectrum of history so as to obtain a complete picture. Although Powicke's preference came to be religious and intellectual history, it never blotted out other history or ever hindered him in his other aim—to get inside people. Like Powicke, who was his contemporary and who died but a few years earlier, F. M. Stenton was equally devoted to the complete historical picture.[3] Today few are the medievalists who write like Powicke and Stenton. R. W. Southern is the exception rather than the rule. History, like so many of the humanistic disciplines, moves in patterns of style. One can but hope that the present style will be a necessary period of research and readjustment involving critical scrutiny of traditional syntheses and approaches to history that will result in the knowledge and perspective essential for the formulation of other new syntheses and interpretations.[4]

Although bibliographical guides; books on such disciplines as paleography, diplomatics, numismatics, prosopography, place names, and geography; catalogs of coins, historical monuments, and archaeological findings; reference works on dates; facsimiles of documents; editions and calendars of records; and translations may not pierce the frontiers of knowledge or set new directions in historical writing, without such endeavors no new historical knowledge and ideas could emerge. While it must suffice to say here that such work continues on about the same scale as in the past, it would be remiss not to mention a few publications of special value.[5] One, the inestimable guide of Charles Gross on the primary and secondary sources of medieval England has been a handbook of medievalists on both sides of the Atlantic since 1900. It was revised in 1915, but thereafter scholars had to leaf through journals or occasional guides published on limited periods and subjects in order to keep up to date. Then in 1975, under the sponsorship of the Royal Historical Society, the American Historical Association, and the Mediaeval Academy of America, a new edition by E. B. Graves appeared.[6] Most welcome, this edition, following the traditional organization, includes 7,225 entries, double the number in the 1915 edition; unfortunately its entries stop with 1970, which means that already it is more than ten years out of date. To supplement it are the Bibliographical Handbooks being compiled under the auspices of the Conference on British Studies, of which there are now two volumes covering the period from 1066 to 1377.[7]

Without getting bogged down in the citation of records recently published, it should be noted that all the official acts of the Norman kings have now been edited. The appearance of the third volume dealing with Stephen's reign completes a solid documentation for the study of this period so fundamental for the political and institutional development of medieval England.[8] Also happily concluded for the period of the Middle Ages are the translations in the English Historical Documents inaugurated by D. C. Douglas in 1953, a series that allies an extraordinarily broad selection of sources on every facet of English history with intelligent commentaries and bibliographical references.[9] Armed with these volumes and the new edition of Gross, one need not wander aimlessly among the mountains of sources of medieval England, the likes of which do not exist on the Continent. Scholars of church history during the reigns of Henry II and John should be aware that A. Morey and C. N. L. Brooke have edited all the letters and charters of Gilbert Foliot, that important bishop and bitter opponent of Becket, and that C. R. and M. G. Cheney have calendared the letters of Innocent III dealing with England and Wales from 1198 to 1216 with an appendix of the most valuable texts.[10] Now the investiture struggle can be studied in greater depth, and an attempt can be made to describe the range of Innocent's business with England and to assess the effectiveness of his interventions.

Perhaps the two most significant editions and translations concern the two most famous judges and legal writers of the twelfth and thirteenth centuries. For his edition and translation of Glanville's treatise on the laws of England, the first medieval textbook on the subject, G. D. G. Hall must be congratulated.[11] It is most useful to have an edition that is an improvement over that of G. E. Woodbine and a complete translation that so accurately renders the meaning of the twelfth-century legal vocabulary. Hall's introduction places the treatise into proper relation with contemporary thought and legal study and also traces the revival of legal study and the practice of law in the twelfth century. The part most interesting but debatable is his attempt to prove that Glanville was not the author of this celebrated treatise, a matter left open by Maitland almost a hundred years ago. Rather, Hall sees the author as Geoffrey de Lucy, a possible choice but one that has not convinced Doris Stenton, who has proposed instead that a number of royal justices may have collaborated with Glanville and commissioned a clerk to do the writing. A ghost writer, however, is no more convincing than Geoffrey de Lucy, and J. C. Russell has argued from internal evidence that a common thread of style and thought points to Glanville as the author.[12] No one can be certain, any more than was Maitland, and it is premature to uncouple Glanville from *De legibus*.

In a task even more ambitious S. E. Thorne has edited and translated the famous treatise of Bracton on the common law of medieval England.[13] All that scholars possessed until Woodbine produced his edition in three volumes between 1915 and 1942 was the very deficient edition and translation of Travers Twiss, which appeared in six volumes of the Rolls Series between 1878 and 1883. Woodbine's edition stimulated an exceptional flurry of Bractonian scholarship that not only questioned the authorship but, by revisions to the text, instigated debate over Bracton's knowledge and use of Roman law. A new look at Bracton was in order, but nothing could be done without a revision of Woodbine and an accurate translation. Thorne has provided both, a considerable achievement, as all legal historians know, and in the process has advanced the study of Bracton.

Since the time of Maitland, who believed Bracton responsible for both the treatise and the celebrated *Notebook*, there has been continuous debate over authorship, a debate Thorne has joined. In his introduction to volume 3 Thorne suggests that parts of *De legibus* go back to the 1220s and 1230s, making them too early to have been composed by Bracton. He contends that revisions and additions were made to these early portions to bring them up to date and that about 1236 Bracton became associated with this work; further, that in 1256 some editor abridged the swollen text into *De legibus* as we know it. But what was the *Notebook* and what was its connection with *De legibus*? Thorne argues that clerks of the bench copied cases from the court rolls for study, that some five hundred of these cases were cited in *De legibus*, and that the *Notebook*, therefore, was a collected edition of such earlier compilations made from transcripts with annotations by some person having no immediate connection with *De legibus*. There was, so Thorne believes, a common force behind all these works and activity, and it was not Bracton but Justice William de Ralegh, whom Thorne calls "the prime mover behind the *De legibus*." As Ralegh's most famous clerk, Bracton had been associated with all these efforts. Independent, ambitious, and soundly educated in the law, he was typical of the clerks who served Ralegh and who produced the *Notebook* for their own use and then the *De legibus* for the instruction of themselves and the members of the growing legal establishment of the thirteenth century. Quite plausible, Thorne's argument will nevertheless surely be challenged by Bractonian experts. Arrayed against him is the late H. G. Richardson, who argued in one of his last books that Bracton was an Oxford man, had learned his Roman law there, and had never gotten around to a final draft of *De legibus*, which explains the inconsistencies identified by modern scholarship. One should also recall that Maitland was convinced that Bracton's clerks copied materials from rolls to leaves, which then became the treatise. Doris Stenton agrees that Bracton had not completed a rough draft of *De legibus* when he retired from the king's bench in 1257 but doubts that he had gone to Oxford and learned his law there.[14] As is evident, the question is so prickly that is too early to deprive Bracton of the authorship. Thorne is so persuasive, however, that ultimately scholars may well be convinced that Bracton was but one collaborator in a common effort.

That the interests of historians have become increasingly specialized is attested to by the paucity of comprehensive works. Even the best of the textbooks and surveys that have appeared are not intended to create new currents of thought. At most they but digest and present the results of past and recent scholarship. That only Anglo-Saxon history has been synthesized leads to the sad conclusion that, no matter the kind of history, the large, comprehensive work seems relegated to the past. Some titles suggest that the contents are horizontally and vertically comprehensive, but this rarely proves to be the case. As the following evidence reveals, no Stubbs, Maitland, Tout, Powicke, or Knowles seems to be writing at the moment.

Of three good books on Anglo-Saxon history, none tells the complete story. D. P. Kirby writes well on historical geography and most interestingly on the church in the tenth century. D. J. V. Fisher concentrates on ecclesiastical and political history with insights on Alfred the Great and Edward the Confessor. P. H. Sawyer has recently brought out a well-informed survey strong on kingship, government, and the effect of Christianity. Strangely, not one delves far into social and economic history, long a favorite subject of articles and currently of great interest to Anglo-Saxon scholars. To obtain a broad coverage of the pre-1066 period, albeit without learning much about social and economic developments, all three volumes must be read.[15] While revising F. M. Stenton on certain points, these books in no way supplant him.

As for the histories of kings and their times, the work of H. R. Loyn reflects the learning of one of the foremost authorities on Anglo-Norman history. Here is a well-proportioned picture of Alfred and his achievements that makes no attempt to create a new image, a happy decision given the tendency of most authors of this genre to destroy old reputations and then to construct new ones.[16] In an ambitious book on Edward the Confessor, F. Barlow has this much-maligned king parting company with Ethelred the Unready to become a realistic and shrewd politician responsible for considerable achievements during the twilight of Anglo-Saxon history. So unrecognizable is Edward that Barlow's book looks like an attempt at apotheosis. No wonder Barlow finds it easy to explain why Edward became a saint in the twelfth century. Evidently a master at making and unmaking royal reputations, Barlow does a complete reversal in a short study of William the Conqueror that appeared a few years earlier. In it, he portrays the great man to be what he was: a bastard. William is scaled down to the level of ordinary men, life size, or a little less so. This pot-bellied and bloodstained warrior had no more political intuition than the next man and could no better read the future.[17] Comparing this portrait with the encomiums lavished upon William and the Norman achievements by D. C. Douglas, one becomes slightly bewildered. Good, old-fashioned common sense triumphs, however, to determine Edward a loser and William a winner. In the gallery of the great, the portrait of William Rufus is, as always, turned to the wall, awaiting a historian who will turn it about and retouch it into the creative brother who paved the way for the institutional achievements of Henry I.[18]

A modern evaluation of Henry I, though promised, is long overdue. Meanwhile Stephen has been the concern of two. The more comprehensive, that of R. H. C. Davis, adheres to the traditional unfavorable view of Stephen and downgrades Stephen's administration even though the level of chancery records dips but 10 percent below those for the reign of Henry I. It would seem that Davis, having edited the acts of Stephen's reign, must speak with authority. But one is discombobulated in reading the book by H. A. Cronne, the coeditor of Stephen's acts, which states that Stephen was rather good at government. Perhaps this impression emerges because Cronne concentrates on the royal household, government, and revenue at the expense of politics and church affairs.[19] Henry II has finally received a modern assessment in the large book by W. L. Warren that rests upon solid documentation and deep understanding. Scorning any attempt to debunk Henry's achievements, Warren gives Henry the traditional high marks for innovative government, a reasonable stand on church–state relations, and a successful policy on the Continent. Though up to date, this book will neither change interpretations nor better inform about Henry, which is, of course, the weakness of such books on medieval kings; the sources simply do not permit them to get inside their subjects. This is so evident in the tiny book of L. F. Salzman on Edward I, where, despite emphasis on the importance of the individual in history, Edward fails to emerge as an individual; nor is much said about his considerable achievements.[20] Not until the later fifteenth century are the records adequate for even a rough facsimile of biography.

To complement these general works on England down to 1307 are two on Scotland. A good one by A. A. M. Duncan dealing with Scottish history down to 1286 shows that Scotland remained mostly on the periphery of European civilization, producing in this period no notable thinkers or churchmen. G. W. S. Barrow in his study of Robert Bruce constructs the theme that at this time in Scotland there evolved a concept of *communitas regni Scotie*, a political entity presaging a nation. Though a novel idea for Scotland, obviously borrowed from what historians have said about thirteenth-century England, it rests upon evidence much shakier for Scotland than for England.[21]

Turning now to history not primarily concerned with lives and times, it is the case that, although the constitutional history of Stubbs no longer holds the floor and that although Tout's administrative history is less influential than it was twenty years ago, legal history is alive and well, owing perhaps to Maitland, whose wide interests appeal to the devotees of the present vogue of social, intellectual, and comparative history. Maitland remains modern because he approached the study of medieval England with a touch of the sociologist, the historian of ideas, and the good European. He was aptly described by H. Brunner in 1907: "He has brought England out of an isolation which is by no means 'splendid' and plunged her into the mainstream of European thought."[22] While evident in various fields of research, Maitland's enduring appeal glows brightest in legal history, a fact recognized by the reissue of his *History of English Law* in paperback edition with an intelligent introduction by S. F. C. Milsom showing Maitland's influence on legal study and the ways in which he has been revised.[23] A recognized authority on English medieval law, Milsom has also written a most useful and interpretive account of the foundation of the common law. Asking how a system of law, a system of ideas with the hypothesis that rules are constant, can adapt itself to a changing world, he argues that immediate needs of clients and practitioners change the law, that the common law survived because of the increasing abuse of its elementary ideas, which means that the formal rules are under continual though variable pressure. In another work on the common law R. C. van Caenegem skillfully traces the development of royal courts from the Conqueror to Glanville, detailing the growth of royal writs, procedure, and juries, and compares the common law to continental law. He concludes that the common law triumphed because its continental rivals arrived too late.[24]

For a concise survey of legal history from Alfred the Great to the fifteenth century, there is a book by A. Harding with the thesis that, after the *curia regis* and eyre system centralized royal justice, the eyre disintegrated under Edward I so that power and initiative returned to local courts and the justices of the peace assumed legal functions formerly performed by the justices in eyre.[25] H. G. Richardson and G. O. Sayles, in a stimulating and iconoclastic book not always successful in converting one to its various conclusions (a kind of companion volume to their notorious *Governance of Mediaeval England*), examine the chief legal and legislative records from Ethelbert to Magna Carta, challenging interpretations of other scholars and even the authenticity of such records as the Assizes of Clarendon and Woodstock. Sayles has also summed up his well-known ideas on parliament and defended his thesis in a short and highly readable volume.[26]

Other kinds of history evince a want of synthesis and overview. Financial history, frequently the subject of articles and monographs, awaits a book that embraces a long period of time. The study by B. Lyon and A. E. Verhulst deals only with financial institutions from the early Middle Ages into the thirteenth century and is primarily a comparison of English financial institutions with those of the neighboring states of Flanders, Normandy, and Capetian France. H. M. Jewell's history of local administration covers the whole medieval period with an approach that studies local administration through the functions of local officials.[27] Military history is the concern of various studies but almost always in the context of feudal service, its replacement by nonfeudal methods, and the finance of war. Only the book by J. Beeler attempts to discuss war from 1066 to 1189, with results not all that satisfactory because it is a book of bits and pieces never tied together. It hardly supersedes what C. W. C. Oman wrote about England and cannot match the study of J. F. Verbruggen.[28] Economic history, though spotty, fares better. In an economic history of England from the Norman period to the late medieval period, M. M. Postan expands his well-known ideas, which are, by the way, set forth in greater depth in his chapter on English medieval agrarian history in *The Cambridge Economic History*, of which he is an editor, and in two volumes of his collected works on agriculture, trade, and finance. English urban history has little interested scholars since the days of James Tait. Nevertheless there are two books that provide general accounts of English towns. C. Platt, concentrating upon the topographical and structural features of the town rather than on the more abstract constitutional and economic issues, contends that study of excavation sites has done more than documents to advance knowledge of urban development. On the other hand, Susan Reynolds, emphasizing economic and social phenomena, argues that overseas trade and the wool industry were less important influences on urban growth and economy than regional economic conditions. She also attacks the prevailing view that the towns were controlled by a small, self-perpetuating merchant patriciate, a view subscribed to by May McKisack, whose conclusions still seem preferable. Although Reynolds makes a few references to urban history on the Continent, there is little comparison, a deficiency of most books on English towns.[29]

Though the ambitious survey of English agriculture edited by H. P. R. Finberg will eventually cover a vast expanse of time, it involves collaboration, with the inevitable variation in approach and conclusions, as is so evident in the volume covering the thousand years between A.D. 43 and 1042.[30] S. Appelbaum in his section on Roman Britain argues that there is no connection between the shapes of fields and the types of soil and ploughs. He also accepts the eventual collapse of Romano-British agriculture. Finberg, writing on the Anglo-Saxon period, sees, however, a continuity of agrarian methods and of the estates. With the evidence so miserable, debate over this difficult question will continue, but present research would appear to support Applebaum's position.

On church history, two books have appeared, each with a special theme. That by R. E. Rodes discusses ecclesiastical administration from the Anglo-Saxons to the Reformation. Though compressed, his sections on canon law; papal government; and provincial, diocesan, and parish organization are enlightening. C. H. Lawrence has edited a book with six contributions on relations between the English church and the papacy from Celtic times to the fifteenth century. The contributions are commendable, but unfortunately some are redundant when disproving the old view of Stubbs that the English church was not wholly committed to papalism, a view long ago disproved by Maitland. A refreshingly different study of church history is R. C. Finucane's book on miracles, popular beliefs, and pilgrims, which tells why certain saints became popular and describes the function of their shrines in medieval society.[31] Despite the urging of Southern that there was important work to be done, cultural history has almost drawn a blank during the past twelve years. The one general treatment is a discussion of chroniclers from 550 to 1307 by A. Gransden.[32]

So much for the general terrain of historical writing on pre-1307 England. Let me now explore the more specialized studies with the aim of drawing a kind of mental map on a large scale that will highlight the headwaters, rivulets, streams, eddies, dams, high and low areas, and rich and poor lands of scholarship. The intensive archaeological work since 1945 on early Britain has begun to show profit. A fine example is S. Frere's formidable study of Roman Britain, the first comprehensive work since the classic book of R. G. Collingwood in 1936 and one that replaces much of Collingwood on the basis of evidence provided by archaeology.[33] According to Frere: the third and fourth centuries were a more fortunate period in Roman Britain than hitherto believed, perhaps because of Britain's distance from the Roman troubles on the Continent; when, however, ties with Rome were severed, as they definitely were in 410, they were never renewed—a thesis long supported by J. B. Bury and his disciples. Along with Frere should be read J. Wacher's work on Roman towns. Archaeologically it studies all the Roman sites that classical historians call cities (*coloniae* and *municipia*) but not the smaller places known as *oppida*. Wacher feels that Roman Britain did not survive the "Dark Ages" of the fifth and sixth centuries, that there was no urban continuity into the Anglo-Saxon period.[34]

From Roman Britain one plunges into that no-man's-land that followed, a period when there may or may not have been a Celtic revival and when the Angles, Saxons, and Jutes were making their initial inroads. So poor are the sources and so different the conclusions of the experts that it is virtually impossible to determine in which direction the prevailing historical winds are blowing. In a book on Celtic Britain, M. Dillon and Nora Chadwick look at events in the fifth century from a very Celtic viewpoint, concluding that, for a period, Britain was independent and that the Anglo-Saxon presence was minimal. Experts like

J. N. L. Myres disagree. E. John sees Roman institutions surviving through this period and influencing the Anglo-Saxon states of the seventh century, a continuity and influence that seem to be exaggerated.[35]

Omnipresent in this period is Arthur, who has literally caused an epidemic of books. That children and laymen want to believe in the heroic Arthur is understandable, but why so many professionals do defies any empirical explanation. Is it that, after so many centuries of hegemony, Britain, once again an island without much power beyond its coasts, now is nostalgic for that age when Arthur courageously stemmed the continental tide? Or is it that modern Britain seeks a hero untainted by modern history? Or is it that to have heroes has for so long been démodé that now they are again desired? For whatever reasons, the cult of Arthur is flourishing. Typical is a book by J. Morris dealing with Arthur as a historical figure who was "the last Roman Emperor; but he ruled as the first medieval king" (p. 506). Strangely, Roman Britain seems to have survived into and after Arthur's time, thus giving him a dual personality. As counterweight to this historical romance is a careful analysis of the so-called sources for Arthur by D. N. Dumville, who shows their deficiency and the misunderstanding of them. He disposes of the "no smoke without a fire" school of historians with this conclusion, to which many historians would say amen: "The fact of the matter is that there is no historical evidence about Arthur; we must reject him from our histories and, above all, from the titles of our books" (p. 188).[36] This fine piece of critical scholarship deserves reading.

Early Anglo-Saxon history is also dominated by the findings of the archaeologist. A work edited by D. M. Wilson provides a good survey by a group of specialists, of which the studies on coins and towns are outstanding. The only questionable part of the book is Wilson's statement that archaeology gives no clues to political history. H. M. and J. Taylor have produced a survey of every building that can be ascribed to a date before 1066. The doyen of such specialists, J. N. L. Myres, has written two works on Anglo-Saxon pottery that show how, between 400 and 650, pottery provides *excellent* evidence for political and cultural history.[37] The most dramatic research remains that on the Sutton Hoo Ship burial. Progress on this tantalizing piece of evidence has been slow, but there has appeared a first volume evaluating it by that acknowledged authority R. Bruce-Mitford. Probably the finest historical archive for the early Anglo-Saxon age, the ship has been the subject of argument as to the date of its burial and its significance for cultural history. Despite arguments that the person buried in the ship was not a king, Bruce-Mitford, using extensive numismatic evidence, concludes that the subject of burial was Raedwald, king of East Anglia, and proposes 624–625 as the date of burial. This supports the suggestion made by H. M. Chadwick in 1940 but does not really answer why there are no remnants of the body. Bruce-Mitford believes that the body was decomposed by the acidic

soil, whereas Myres suggests that it was later removed for proper Christian burial and that all the apparel and jewels were left behind.[38]

If one turns from the Anglo-Saxon artifact to the written sources, rather than
parting with uncertainty, one simply finds more of it. The problem is that more
written sources have been discovered but that they are relatively few and difficult
to fathom, a situation that produces honest differences of opinion, some of which
inevitably stem from subjective feelings. Debate, while not extensive, continues
to be sharp over the nature of early Anglo-Saxon society. Was it free or aristocratic and what relation does the structure of a society have to agrarian patterns and
political institutions? Notwithstanding the slim evidence to support their view of
an early free society, the "Germanist" school still prevails. D. A. Bullough has
emphasized the social and economic mobility of the ceorl, arguing that it was
quite possible for a ceorl to become a thegn. G. C. Homans sees evidence of an
open-field system as early as the seventh century and attributes this to a continuity
between the English field system and those on the Continent. He is certain that
a communal system was brought to Britain by the Germans. T. M. Charles-
Edwards has contended that Anglo-Saxon kinship was like that of the Continent,
where a corporate kindred group supplied its kinsmen with a standard holding so
as to uphold their status as normal freemen. This standard holding may or may
not have been the mysterious hide determined by recent scholarship to have been
a fiscal unit or assessment.[39] In opposition are E. John, who sees no free peasantry
coming across the North Sea to Britain, and H. Vollrath-Reichelt, who denies
the existence of communities of free peasants and detects no special insular character to Anglo-Saxon society.[40]

Opinion on Anglo-Saxon political history remains as fluid as ever. Perhaps the
most striking effort at revision is that of V. I. Evison, who argues that Britain
was not taken over gradually after 449 by small bands of Anglo-Saxons but was
reduced by a single, coordinated invasion after 449 involving much of the southern coast. Unfortunately the archaeological evidence mustered to support this
view has been riddled by reliable archaeologists.[41] Despite the mischievous attempt of the late V. H. Galbraith to raise doubts about the authenticity of Asser,
Doris Whitelock does seem to have shown that such a person lived at the time of
Alfred and wrote his life. While Asser and the *Anglo-Saxon Chronicle* state that
Pope Leo IV annointed Alfred in 853, J. L. Nelson is certain that this was impossible and explains the references to this event as the work of Alfred, who had
them inserted because he wished to develop an aura about his person and to provide a prestigious Christian sanction like that enjoyed by the Carolingians.
H. R. C. Davis has developed the interesting interpretation that Alfred, though
not actually writing the *Anglo-Saxon Chronicle*, was in a general sense its author
because he made certain that points of view and accomplishments flattering to him
and his subjects were emphasized in order to instill confidence in his people, to

shore them up in the struggle against the Danes. This part of the *Chronicle* was in effect a kind of propaganda sheet.[42]

Opinion still seesaws on the significance of the contact between the Anglo-Saxons and the Danes. M. W. Campbell has suggested that Edward the Confessor was able in 1051 to force Earl Godwin to pledge his support of Duke William of Normandy as the next king of England because at this particular point Godwin was politically weak. The most interpretive view of Anglo-Saxon government has come from J. Campbell, who portrays an extremely strong Anglo-Saxon state, unified, sophisticated, and innovative, that probably contained the precedents for Domesday Book. England may ultimately have avoided the fate of the ancien régime in Europe because its society rested upon a much older and successful regime. What Englishman could take umbrage over this flattering view of his country?[43] All this is slippery ground upon which not much change has occurred. Indeed, there may even have been some historical backsliding.

The church has fared better. H. Mayr-Harting's book on the early days of Christianity from 597 to 750 has excellent assessments of Gregory the Great, Wilfred, and Bede and informative details about early forms of prayer and worship. In a study of Irish Christianity, Kathleen Hughes shows the Irish church to be resilient as late as the ninth and tenth centuries and demonstrates its influence on artistic and architectural instincts of early Irish society. Also instructive is her introduction to the sources of Irish Christianity. Adding to the plethora of studies on St. Patrick, R. P. C. Hanson develops the novel view that Patrick received all his ecclesiastical training in England, an idea requiring further evidential support.[44]

That cultural history was but another aspect of church history in the early Middle Ages is manifest by the continuing interest in Bede. There has been revision of Charles Plummer's exceptional edition of and commentary on Bede's history that appeared in 1896 but no new edition until 1969. The analysis of the manuscripts by R. A. B. Mynors is excellent, but unhappily the high quality of the translation by B. Colgrave is marred by his notes, which are deficient, which means that Plummer cannot be disregarded. M. Miller has explained how Bede used Gildas for his account of post-Roman Britain, and J. N. Stephens so interprets Bede's history that it becomes a history of England rather than just of the church. The study of C. P. Wormald on Anglo-Saxon literacy is an antidote to those who dwell too much on figures like Bede and who praise the precosity of Anglo-Saxon culture. He is convinced that literacy was extremely limited, most of it being a monopoly of the clergy, and that not even the efforts of Alfred increased lay literacy. He even thinks that there was more lay literacy across the Channel.[45]

The nine-hundredth anniversary of the Norman conquest in 1966, which spawned ceremonies, speeches, papers, and a flurry of books and articles, does not solely account for the amazing volume of work devoted to Norman England, a period upon which more has been written than on any other prior to 1307. Certainly 1066 and all that had fundamental consequences for the historical development of England, but what explains this tremendous preoccupation with the Norman period? Could it be that the work of such as J. H. Round, Maitland, Vinogradoff, F. M. Stenton, C. H. Haskins, D. C. Douglas, and V. H. Galbraith dealt with such extraordinarily basic problems and opened up so many exciting streams of investigation that the present efforts are but a continuation of what these distinguished historians inaugurated? Could it be that these historians became exemplars for younger historians or that, conversely, the younger historians, unhappy at living with the interpretations of the older, are striving to emancipate themselves by seeking new perspectives on the Norman conquest and its consequences? All this, while possible, is belied by the thrust of works produced. Except for a study here and there, there are no surprises, no new paths hewn. Had one taken a long sleep like Rip Van Winkle, unlike Rip, one would have awakened to perceive no change in Norman scholarship. It has trodden the same paths and, beset with myopia, focused upon the same problems, ever more microscopic in scope. Did those earlier pioneers in Norman history plough the field so thoroughly that only a few balks and headlands were left for later tillers? Enough for impressions and speculations.

H. R. Loyn gives the broadest coverage of the conquest, but it differs little from his more substantial book on Anglo-Saxon England and the Norman conquest published in 1962. A book by R. A. Brown is very Roundish and, disposing of the Anglo-Saxon state as weak and in need of an injection, denies Anglo-Saxon fiefs and feudal continuity, considers Norman tactics and castles new, and credits the Normans with reforming the church and bringing England into the mainstream of continental history. In one study R. H. C. Davis has the efficient Normans exploiting a very useful Anglo-Saxon government, and in another he tries to discover what the Normans thought of themselves, concluding from a reading of the Norman chroniclers that they had a kind of collective image of themselves that changed over centuries. It would have been interesting to know what others thought of the Normans. R. W. Finn has decided that the Norman conquest resulted in a vast redistribution of land.[46] Except for the Davis book on the Norman image, all of this is old stuff reminiscent of Round and Douglas. No sooner had Kurt-Ulrich Jäschke demonstrated the *Carmen de Hastingae Proelio* to be an authentic source composed in 1067 and consequently the earliest source on the conquest, than doubts raised by R. H. C. Davis made it very unlikely. Seemingly the *Carmen* is neither an original source nor a poem by Guy of Amiens used by Orderic Vitalis but simply a literary curiosity, an exercise written by an anonymous pen in one of the schools of northern France or Flanders between 1125 and 1140.[47]

The Norman state, according to J. Le Patourel in what he calls an essay in reinterpretation, was a complex of lands that all the Norman rulers attempted to keep unified. Aware that a united Normandy and England afforded more political and economic options, the Conqueror did not cut William Rufus into the spoils until, on his deathbed, circumstances forced him to do so. Convinced that the conquest wrought change in England and that the evidence shows Henry I and Stephen also doing what they could to keep England and Normandy unified, Le Patourel has written a book persuasive in the thesis that English and Norman history can be understood only when studied together.[48] E. King has provided a plausible reinterpretation of the anarchy under Stephen by suggesting that the aristocracy behaved badly because they had lived with three strong kings and could not adjust to a weak ruler. Uncertain of the future, they became political trimmers like the aristocracy of the fourteenth and fifteenth centuries described by K. B. McFarlane and, in fact, longed for stable government, which did not come until Henry II.[49] Writings on Norman government mostly replay the old refrain. C. W. Hollister and J. W. Baldwin have done a comparative study of administration under Henry I and Philip Augustus and concluded that both kings instituted vice-regencies, exchequers, or central accounting procedures; improved records; and itinerant officials but that the *curiales* of Henry I consisted of great and lesser men, whereas those of Philip Augustus were limited to a few of his creatures. Though some details in this comparison are new, the main conclusions are not. Other works simply deal with key figures such as Odo of Bayeux and Roger of Salisbury or with technical aspects of administration, all in all, not too much to talk about.[50]

The work on Domesday Book reminds one of the parable of the loaves and the fishes: there is ever more of it; in fact, a surfeit. V. H. Galbraith's final book skillfully sums up his earlier work on Domesday Book, especially that which revised Round's famous explanation of Domesday's compilation. The one interesting addition is his observation that the present-day Anglo-Saxon adherents have assumed the posture of an antihistorical camp.[51] As to the compilation of the famous record, B. Dodwell disputes Galbraith's conclusion that there were no preliminary records drawn up by hundreds and villages. She argues, from a different interpretation of the evidence, that preliminary geographical records existed. S. P. J. Harvey has also made a case for preliminary records. Defined as lists of the holdings of large fiefs or records of county fiscal assessments, they were kinds of hidage lists that those on the circuits could check and then incorporate into Domesday Book. Harvey also contends that Domesday Book was the idea of Ranulf Flambard.[52]

Domesday Book and feudalism go together like pork and beans. One seldom mentions one without the other, and of feudalism there continues to be ample talk. C. W. Hollister continues to do business with both the Anglo-Saxons and

Normans. Though not consistently a continuity man, he sees the scutage and fyrd as Norman derivatives of Anglo-Saxon precedents and downgrades Norman knight service with the argument that much military service was, in fact, mercenary.[53] R. A. Brown and J. C. Holt have proclaimed their adherence to the Norman view of Round and F. M. Stenton. So the classic debate drones on like the trench warfare of World War I, a few feet gained and a few lost by both sides.[54] The rest of the research on feudalism is highly technical, and Holt has caused a storm with his argument that, from the outset in 1066, the fiefs granted by the Normans were heritable in accordance with the heritable custom of Normandy and the Continent. E. King and S. D. White do not see succession this way. Neither sees heritability at this point, whether the evidence be legal or political.[55] Beyond these debates, all that needs reporting is a book by D. F. Benn that is good in its updating of Armitage's book on Norman castles published in 1912, except for its failure to distinguish royal from private castles.[56]

Reflecting the general excellence of work on legal history are the few studies on Norman legal developments. In a book on English justice, Doris Stenton devotes much space to Norman innovations. After noting the Anglo-Saxon legal inheritance, she argues forcefully against the position of R. C. van Caenegem that there was a gradual judicialization of writs between the *Leges Primi* of Henry I and Glanville. She sees the judicial writ as the innovation of Henry II. But in a recent article on the origin of the presenting jury, van Caenegem appears to have the better of the argument in that he adduces more evidence for his position and does so with constant reference to similar procedures on the Continent. The intent of his article is to refute N. D. Hurnard's explanation of the origin of the presenting jury by showing that, as early as the reigns of Henry I and Stephen, criminals were prosecuted by royal officials, chiefly justices, a judicial procedure leading to the indicting jury. Van Caenegem also contends that a similar process of accusation by archdeacons was successfully opposed by Henry II. This important article, printed in a *Festschrift*, should not be overlooked.[57] To be read with the van Caenegem article is one by W. T. Reedy, Jr., who sees the general eyres of Henry II developing from ad hoc judicial commissions and localized eyres of Henry I's reign. T. S. Green has investigated attitudes of society toward liability for homicide, concluding that, from the late Anglo-Saxon period, society made a distinction between murder and homicide and that the local communities resisted royal twelfth-century law demanding death for homicide as well as for murder.[58]

Like the Anglo-Saxon church, the Norman church is the subject of studies with the potential for stirring up the vintage interpretations, studies to be read only after finishing the good survey by M. Brett on the church under Henry I, which concentrates on the secular church and its organization. C. Morris, denying that the famous Ordinance of 1076 immediately separated spiritual and secular courts, contends that separation of jurisdiction came gradually, that in any event the Ordinance did not introduce an unknown principle because Anglo-Saxon England, like Normany, was familiar with the concept of a separate spiritual jurisdiction. M. Gibson refreshingly reinterprets Lanfranc and his scholarship, particularly his commentaries on the Pauline Epistles. Against R. W. Southern, who portrayed Anselm as an ivory-tower scholar bereft of political ability, S. N. Vaughn has filed the interesting brief that Anselm was an astute politician who always achieved his ends, as when receiving the arch-bishopric of Canterbury free from simony and obtaining the banishment of lay investiture. In another revisionary article, D. L. Bethell asserts that the Benedictines yielded no ground to the seculars in the early twelfth century but continued to dominate and be elected to important ecclesiastical posts until the end of the century. The article of H. Mayr-Harting on the functions of a recluse reminds one that church history is not simply ecclesiastical politics and struggles over investiture. It contends that the *Life of Wulfric (1090–1150)* written by John of Ford in 1180, had a moral as well as an academic purpose, that it was intended to illustrate the virtues of the good life and to note the miracles of healing. Mayr-Harting feels that the recluse resolved tensions and fulfilled many societal needs, even inspiring art and symbolizing the ideal of monasticism.[59]

Except for legal and church historians, others have ignored or slighted the Angevin period even though in 1965 the English-speaking world celebrated the 750th anniversary of Magna Carta. Three of medieval England's most colorful kings, one of whom was her greatest, have been curiously neglected. The Warren book mentioned earlier is the only extensive treatment of the period, but within the limits of Henry II's reign. A view not popular among Englishmen is Le Patourel's that the Angevin empire was based on the continental possessions and controlled by men who saw them as the primary interests. Essentially this is what Haskins said early in this century. F. J. West, writing on the justiciarship, provides a convenient survey but scarcely inquires into why such an office was needed. Hubert Walter, that figure so influential under Richard and John and certainly comparable to Wolsey, has finally received his due, a comprehensive study by C. R. Cheney and another by C. R. Young that is less good than Cheney's but in agreement on Walter's decisive role in Angevin administrative innovations. C. Duggan sketches that loyal Angevin administrator Richard of Ilchester as a person better at execution than at creation. J. E. Lally concludes that Henry II did not reward his royal servants as lavishly as Henry I and that, when he did, it was by marriages and wardships. J. C. Holt has done the principal study on Magna Carta, the first comprehensive one since McKechnie's in 1905. In analyzing the clauses as historian rather than lawyer, Holt argues that the charter was too imprecise thereby causing the civil war, and that the barons were the culprits with their unrealistic demands upon John, who emerges as a hero. We must still await a study that integrates Magna Carta into the politics of John's

reign with the same evenhanded treatment of the legally oriented McKechnie book.[60]

Ranking after the books on Glanville and Bracton by Hall and Thorne is that
by S. F. C. Milsom on those writs of Henry II which, he argues, were devised
to make feudal courts fulfill their purpose but succeeded rather in destroying
them and insuring the triumph of the common law. A difficult book, it seriously
challenges Maitland's explanation of the possessory assizes. It argues that the
royal court proceedings developed in the 1150s whereby, through a writ, a de-
mandant might compel a lord to accept a new tenant he did not want, began a
breach of feudal autonomy that shattered the lords' control over their fiefs and
courts. Where Maitland was inclined to see this process as deliberate on the part
of Henry II and his advisers, Milsom regards it as unintentional. D. W. Sutherland's book on the assize of novel disseisin beginning with Henry II and extending
over the centuries shows how the idea that novel disseisin must be recent was
abandoned in order to make the assize ever more useful. Eventually the rightful
owner did not have to exercise his claim at once, and ultimately a person did not
have to be in possession to make a claim.[61]

Briefly but convincingly, M. T. Clanchy has traced how written law gradually
supplanted oral custom and became authoritative with Henry II and how hence-
forth written evidence prevailed over the oral in the courts. In his studies on the
courts, R. V. Turner sees Magna Carta as making a difference. The court of exchequer declined in jurisdiction; there was less arbitrary disseisin, less disseisin
on technical grounds, and less sale of justice. Turner also contends that the judges
of John were mainly laymen rather than clerics, that their instruction in the law
was at most elementary, and that they began their careers in the financial service
of John and then moved up. Skeptical of van Caenegem's conclusion that the
court of exchequer was separate from that of common pleas in the later twelfth
century, B. Kemp marshals evidence supporting the stand of Richardson, Sayles,
West, and Harding that they were not then separate courts and dates their separation as 1197/1198. N. D. Hurnard pleads strongly that juries acquitted those
they considered not capitally liable, a conclusion supported by the article of
J. M. Kaye. Today such persons would be tried for manslaughter.[62]

New appraisals of the cause célèbre of Henry II's reign, his struggle with
Becket, invoke no reversal of opinion on the principals and their motives.
D. Knowles's book on Becket repeats what he has said previously and but reiterates his feeling that Becket had deficiencies of character. B. Smalley offers a most
insightful study of the opinions of contemporary and near-contemporary theo-
logians on the Becket dispute and concludes that political realities rather than theological and intellectual reasons determined their positions. C. R. Cheney ac-
cords rough treatment to Pope Innocent III, whom he sees as an opportunist in
political relations, less capable in canon law than thought to be, who used his

intellectual ability, pastoral concern, ready wit, and an incisive tongue primarily to build papal power. He it was who forced the monks of Canterbury to choose Langton as archbishop. Examining the sermons of this famous archbishop, P. B. Roberts has noted the spurious ones, described the techniques of sermon making, and concluded that Langton's opinions were conventional ones learned at Paris.[63]

Leaving high-church circles for the quieter atmosphere of monasticism, I welcome A. Squire's biography of Aelred of Rievaulx, a very careful work though devoid of novel revelations. A. Gransden has unearthed evidence of Benedictine bickering that hints of democratic movements in the abbeys to restrict the power of the abbots. V. M. Lagorio reveals how the monks of Glastonbury Abbey developed the legend associating St. Joseph of Arimathea with the founding of the abbey.[64]

Even with diligence, a quest of recent studies in intellectual history has ended with but a clutch of articles. The 750th anniversary of the death of Gerald of Wales evoked some writing about Gerald. M. Richter has examined Gerald's personality and thought, suggesting that his attitudes on issues and people changed with age and disappointment in his career. A. A. Goddu and R. H. Rouse have shown that Gerald's knowledge of classical authors stemmed largely from an anonymous collection of extracts from ancient and patristic letters and orations compiled at Orléans during the second half of the twelfth century. In a stimulating article describing the ability of twelfth-century writers to observe and realistically describe the world about, A. Gransden shows that some could vividly describe buildings and natural phenomena. According to M. T. Clanchy, individuals accused of being *moderni* were likely those trained in law, medicine, and theology.[65]

Work on agrarian history can be more profitably discussed when evaluating the research on the thirteenth and early fourteenth centuries. For the twelfth century, not much has been done, a statement also true for urban history, which consists wholly of local studies. W. Urry, looking at Canterbury, has found that, by 1200, the monks were lords of half the property of Canterbury, which produced 5 percent of their total income. He argues that the rights of urban self-government existed long before the mid-twelfth century. S. Reynold, in an article on London scolding those who cling to the outmoded views of Stubbs, Round, Tait, and G. A. Williams on borough history, believes it impossible to say whether the leading citizens derived more wealth from land or trade, from distant or local trade. She would drop usage of the term *patrician* because she does not perceive such a clear-cut class dominating the political and economic structure of twelfth-century London. The nicest of these little studies is by E. M. Carus-Wilson on the borough of Stratford-upon-Avon, in which she traces the growth of a classic *ville neuve* granted the customs of Breteuil.[66]

Writings on the thirteenth century proclaim historians to be quixotic and trendish. There is little political, administrative, military, and diplomatic history and but a mite more constitutional history. Is it that historians have become satiated by such history, or have they declared a moratorium, a time to take stock before proceeding on? Legal history has done better, mostly because of the work recently completed on Bracton. There is nothing to say about church history, and a few lines will suffice to highlight the impoverishment of intellectual history. Except for one aspect of social and economic history, it, too, has languished. Even trade, finance, industry, and urban development have drawn little interest. There are no good explanations for this trend. Even if such history was richer and more significant on the Continent in the thirteenth century, much remains to be done for England. But in agrarian history there has literally been an explosion. A rough count produces close to fifty books and articles. It is almost as though English historians have said to *Annales* history and particularly to M. Bloch, R. Boutruche, and G. Duby, "We also can do it." But why has the thirteenth century been the focus of close to 85 percent of such writing? Richer sources may be one answer, but probably a better reason is that M. M. Postan has produced a number of hypotheses on thirteenth-century agrarian history that have kindled the interest of younger scholars in the land and its exploitation and spurred them to buttress or to undermine his suggestions. But I return later to these concerns.

A *tour d'horizon* of history other than agrarian can and should be rapid and highly selective. M. T. Clanchy boldly asserts that Henry III, despite everything said to the contrary, had a royal policy with an exalted view of kingship and government and concludes that "Henry contributed to the foundation which upheld the English monarchy for generations: a divine kingship and sovereign judicature, superior to ecclesiastical and lay magnates alike" (p. 214). Supporting this iconoclasm, J. R. Studd portrays Henry as keeping tight control over the Lord Edward. H. M. Colvin has amassed a mine of information showing Henry as a great builder.[67] From M. Prestwich comes an integrated picture of royal administration, war, politics, and finance along with advocacy for Tout's conclusion that the wardrobe dominated Edwardian finance and that the exchequer lost control over the wardrobe in the later years of Edward.[68] Though the book of J. M. W. Bean studies the decline of feudalism from 1215 to 1540, the part on the thirteenth century gives details on the exactions and evasions of the feudal incidents.[69] What must be a definitive study by J. P. Trabut-Cussac on the governance and administration of Gascony under Henry III and Edward I has now made possible comparison of the English and Gascon systems of administration.[70]

Parliament has been the interest of P. Spufford, who has assembled records pertinent to its origins accompanied by a succinct introduction, of G. Cuttino, and of E. B. Fryde and E. Miller, who have assembled two volumes of basic studies. Comparative study of representative institutions has been abetted by A. Marongiu's superb book and another by A. R. Myers on representative assembles down to 1789. A study by B. Lyon on Edward I and Philip IV of France suggests why Edward failed and Philip prevailed in struggling to keep their prerogative powers unrestricted. G. L. Harriss, in the best study done on Parliament, emphasizes the role of the commons in providing supply to kings needing it for the safety of the realm. With evidence obtained by tracing the evolution of fiscal imposts from the Angevins into the fourteenth century, Harriss counters the view of G. O. Sayles downgrading this role.[71] Other welcome contributions to constitutional history chiefly provide information honing a story well studied.[72]

Having discussed the status of Bractonian studies, I turn here to other legal subjects. Most informative is C. R. Cheney's book on notaries public, those professionals who were never prominent in England or recognized by the common law. Cheney has been able to identify but two prior to 1279 and emphasizes that, when there were more, they worked for the courts of the church and chancery. In a fascinating study investigating the county year book reports of the general commissions of assize at the close of the Trinity Term for Warwickshire, R. C. Palmer describes the kinds of cases, the individuals who presided, and the legal qualifications of those who pleaded. He shows what can be done with the legal dramatis personae on a level away from the central courts. A well-argued and important article by W. E. Brynteson contends that the practice of making law existed already in the early Middle Ages, that it did not first develop in the twelfth and thirteenth centuries.[73] N. D. Hurnard explains the occasions and need for royal pardons of homicide. All sorts of accidents required equity; occasionally money influenced the kings; and Edward I set a precedent in 1294 by pardoning criminals if they would serve with him in Scotland. In a quantitative study of homicide in seven counties over a period of seventy-four years, J. B. Given has found that there were 3,492 deaths, for which 2,434 persons were accused, most from the humble ranks. He concludes that there was a high rate of homicide but that also a high proportion of the accused—two-thirds—were acquitted, perhaps because the only punishment was death. R. B. Pugh looks into the reasons for imprisonment and into the types of gaols but does not relate his rich factual data to the social values and mentality of the age.[74]

From a short detour into intellectual history that turns up but three scholars, all interested in thirteenth-century thinkers who wrote on tides and optics,[75] I turn to the area of social and economic history. Studies on economic activities and developments not directly connected with the land mostly reinforce previous interpretations and conclusions. So P. D. A. Harvey's picture of the inflation beginning in the late twelfth century and causing a catastrophic fall in the value of silver confirms the view of rising prices in the thirteenth century. Likewise M. Prestwich's examination of Edward I's monetary policies, which shows that, in the two recoinages of 1279 and 1300, there was little or no debasement, confirms the long-held teaching that English sterling was a sounder currency than most of the debased continental ones. Mavis Mate has looked into the indebtedness of Canterbury Cathedral Priory and found that the borrowing was to cover extraordinary expenditures and never to increase production of the estates. She also expands our knowledge about the mechanics of borrowing and confirms Postan's argument that landlords did not invest for greater production.[76] More information on the Italian bankers comes from a book by R. W. Kaeuper on the financial relations of the Ricccardi of Lucca with Edward I. M. W. Beresford has studied the foundation of new towns but only clarifies, particularly for Gascony, this interesting economic expansion. A study by E. Miller, on the wool industry, ends with conclusions different from those of previous studies. Rather than seeing the English acquire a supremacy in wool manufacturing in the fourteenth century, as did Carus-Wilson, he sees this supremacy acquired in the late thirteenth century, when the severe political, economic, and social troubles of Flanders gave England the advantage.[77]

Since most of the writing on agrarian history revolves around some of Postan's hypotheses, let me note them. He suggests that expanding markets influenced lords to cease farming out their estates as they had in the twelfth century in favor of taking over their management and to cease commuting labor services of the peasants in favor of reimposing them in order to maximize their profits. The decline of the "gentry" in the thirteenth century Postan attributes to the small landholders losing their land to the great magnates in the scramble for land. He also perceives a considerable land market among the peasantry. Finally, he believes that, in the later thirteenth century, the economy no longer expanded but that the population did, thereby making rural society poorer in 1300. These ideas, conveniently found in his collected papers published in 1973, have been attacked by only a few scholars, chiefly A. R. Bridbury. In a review of Postan's essays, Bridbury calls them disappointing in that none produces evidence to support the hypotheses, evidence Postan has promised to produce for some forty years. Bridbury finds no data on manorial profits and observes that Postan has backpedaled on the chronology of labor services, obviously because the evidence does not exist, and reverted to the older explanation of an unfree peasantry gradually becoming free. Bridbury himself has recently zeroed in on the chronology of labor services, arguing that the thirteenth-century landlord had little incentive to manage his own estate, that there is no evidence for increased thirteenth-century landlord management, that the twelfth-century system of farming out estates continued, and that only later did movements in prices and costs force lords to surrender their lands to the peasants. His conclusions are, of course, a reversion to the older interpretation and agree with what Bloch and others have found on the Continent.[78] E. King has doubted the crisis of the "gentry" and has proposed a compromise. He finds that, while some gentry families did disappear when they badly managed their lands and incomes and some magnates thereby benefited, other gentry families with more acumen bought the land of their less able brethren, thereby profiting and strengthening their position. P. R. Hyams does not find the buying and selling of land by peasants to the same extent as Postan: instead he finds peasants leasing lands and sometimes losing them, on which occasion, a lord or perhaps another peasant would purchase the land. In a shrewd study of merchet, S. Scammell concludes that payment of merchet in the thirteenth century did not mean that the peasants were sinking to a more unfortunate position. Merchet was essentially a test of unfreedom in the royal courts little related to social and legal condition.[79]

A majority of scholars have jumped on Postan's bandwagon. In an extensive view of rural society, J. Z. Titow confirms the Postan views and argues against making too much of technological progress, which he does not see, and lack of which limited opportunities of landlords for investment. From a quantitative study of Winchester lands, Titow finds that grain yields were low and declined in the last quarter of the century. By a perceptive study of a regional society at the end of the thirteenth century, R. H. Hilton has concluded that landlords and royal courts denied free status to anyone holding in villeinage, that the towns served local and regional markets and did not specialize in what they produced, and that the great estates of some of the churches pooled their produce for sale at a central market. For the village of Cuxham, P. D. A. Harvey finds pressure on tenants in the late thirteenth century to be pushed back into villeinage, a conclusion reached also by A. N. May for the Winchester estates.[80] In another article based on the Pipe Rolls between 1150 and 1250, Harvey sees a shift from farming the demesnes to direct management, as do also B. Harvey for the estates of Westminster Abbey, E. Searle for Battle Abbey, and S. Raban for the estates of Thorney and Crowland. In an essay on the twelfth and thirteenth centuries, E. Miller accounts for this shift from farming the demesne to management.[81] Through a case study of Sir Geoffrey de Langley, P. R. Coss sees a crisis of the "gentry." Examining the struggle for control of parochial patronage, J. E. Newman decides that the old gentry lost out to the great magnates and to a rising class of career men. Finally, in a comprehensive book on Canterbury, F. R. H. Du Boulay finds knights holding extremely small fiefs, some with only a dozen tenants, a smallness that could spell trouble for men he hesitates to call knights. His details on estate management are excellent and show that the peasants of Kent had more freedom and paid fewer labor rents.[82] From this brief précis of writing stimulated by the ideas of Postan, the fact emerges that, while he himself never produced the evidence to substantiate his ideas, scholars supporting them may well be digging up the necessary evidence in their research on estates scattered over England.

To give the impression that only the above problems have been of recent concern to historians is a distortion. H. E. Hallam's study has illuminated land reclamation and colonization in the fenlands, described utilization of land in the twelfth and thirteenth centuries, and provided data on the peasant population. A. C. Chibnall's work on Sherington has almost reconstructed the landscape of this village, furrow by furrow. Also not to be ignored is the work on field systems.[83] Studies edited by A. H. R. Baker and R. A. Butlin update the seminal work of H. L. Gray and the Orwins. R. A. Dodgshon questions the classic Orwin explanation on the subdivision of fields into strips of furrows, an explanation that takes into account the heavy plough and the direction of the fields, preferring instead a modified version of the Vinogradoff explanation of shareholding going back to an early tribal basis. He believes that shares were equitably divided according to the lay of the land and its fertility and sees evidence for this extending back to the Anglo-Saxons.[84]

My evaluation fifteen years ago of the writing done between 1939 and 1965 on English history prior to 1307 led me to the following conclusions. Scholarly production was impressive, with at least 80 percent from English pens. Too much of the research concerned minutiae and the piling up of details on political, constitutional, administrative, and legal history. The interpretive synthesis was too rare. Except for agrarian history, there was not much attention to social and economic phenomena. Religious history had ploughed new furrows and produced needed syntheses. Intellectual history was almost nonexistent. Regrettably, little of the writing was in any sense comparative. Whether the subject was Germanic law, feudalism, the investiture struggle, or representative institutions, all were English. The English historian who glanced across the Channel was a phenomenon.

What are my impressions now? First, not much has changed. Scholarly production has declined slightly, with less coming from American and continental scholars, who are increasingly turning to other historical interests, and with about 90 percent now coming from English pens. Although new journals devoted to new fields and methodologies have provided more space for medieval scholarship, little seems occupied by things medieval. Excessive attention is given to minutiae, Domesday Book, feudalism, and agrarian history, while the traditional preoccupation with constitutional and administrative history seems to have ended without even any stocktaking or reinterpretation of these fields. The high quality of legal history speaks well of its present practitioners and of its founder Maitland, *primus inter pares*. Religious history has declined in quality and dug into scattered problems. Intellectual history is even poorer than before, with only the Anglo-Saxon period receiving any major attention. Conceivably, the intellectual revival, scholasticism, the introduction of Aristotle, and the rise of universities bypassed medieval England, but this is not likely. R. W. Southern's plea of long ago for intellectual history yet goes unheeded. Interest in industry, trade, banking, business techniques, and urban history is still minimal. The eyes of social and economic historians, ever myopic, remain glued to the agrarian history of the late twelfth and thirteenth centuries. I hope that significant conclusions will someday emerge from this extremely detailed and localized research now in progress, but given the insularity of the historiography on medieval England, it is my hunch that the conclusions will not be in accord with those found for the Continent. This leads me to the dearth of comparative history. Was medieval England so insular that its whole society was different? Research teaches one to be alert to regional differences and to beware the generalization, but can the conclusions of historians for agrarian history in the thirteenth-century France be so different from those now being formed for thirteenth-century England?

Although some refreshing research has sprung from the *Annales* methodology that has begun to influence the writing of English social and economic history, fortunately English historians have been level-headed enough to understand that the *Annales* approach has special limitations with medieval history. Both the *Economic History Review* and *Past and Present* serve good portions of *Annales* history, and both cater more to historical debate. One could but wish that *Past and Present* would encourage kinds of history other than social and economic. With its articles, notes, and documents on the minutiae, the grand old *English Historical Review* has unfortunately become dull and gray. *History*, which seems to encourage articles concerned with interpretation and research on fundamental problems, is delightfully refreshing. Congratulations to its board of editors!

Over a century ago, Stubbs put his finger on why so many medievalists wrote about political, social, economic, religious, and intellectual institutions rather than people. Sources on institutions were available, offering a chance of understanding them. With people, this was rarely the case, as is so evident from the books on such major figures as kings, justiciars, and leading churchmen, whose characters, personalities, motivations, and emotions are at best only vaguely and hazily perceived, while their accomplishments and failures can be clearly discerned. The inability to deal with people in a way possible for the modern historian has ever been a major problem with writing medieval history, causing it generally to be unbalanced, deficient in the human dimension, less many-splendored and whole. Perhaps, knowing this, Powicke strove to use his talents in all kinds of history in an attempt to get inside people as well as their society and institutions and to create, as in his later books, a large historical portrait that spoke to the reader. If the examples of Powicke and Maitland (he could make dead facts come alive) are not heeded, English medieval history may well become a stygian world forbidding to those who would study and learn about it.

NOTES

1. "From Hengist and Horsa to Edward of Caernarvon: Recent Writing on English History," in E. C. Furber, ed., *Changing Views on British History: Essays on Historical Writing since 1939*, Cambridge, Mass., 1966, 1–57.

2. Obviously, articles on medieval history continue to do well in the publications of the numerous local English historical and antiquarian societies.

3. *EHR* 80: 1–9. For some of F. M. Stenton's most significant contributions, see Doris Stenton, ed., *Preparatory to Anglo-Saxon England: Being the Collected Papers of Frank Merry Stenton*, Oxford, 1970.

4. An article of David Knowles's summarizes what is familiar to all historians about medieval scholarship from the last quarter of the nineteenth century to 1945 but makes slight attempt to evaluate recent trends ("Some Trends in Scholarship, 1868–1968, in the Field of Medieval History," *TRHS* 19, 1969: 139–157).

5. Various series of records in the Public Record Office continue to appear, as do the sources published by such organizations as the Pipe Roll Society and the Royal Historical Society.

6. E. B. Graves, *Gross's A Bibliography of English History to 1485*, Oxford, 1975.

7. M. Altschul, *Anglo-Norman England, 1066–1154*, London, 1969; B. Wilkinson, *The High Middle Ages in England, 1154–1377*, Cambridge, 1978.

8. H. A. Cronne and R. H. C. Davis, eds., *Regesta Regum Anglo-Normannorum, 1066–1154*, vol. 3, *Regesta Regis Stephani ac Mathildis Imperatricis ac Gaufridi et Henrici Ducum Normannorum, 1135–1154*, Oxford, 1968. In 1969 facsimiles of original charters and writs appeared in vol. 4 of this series. Some two hundred charters and writs are reproduced from vol. 3.

9. For the period covered in this essay, see H. Rothwell, *English Historical Documents, 1189–1327*, London, 1975. About three-fifths of the documents concern political history and royal government. See also P. Chaplais, *English Royal Documents: King John–Henry VI, 1199–1461*, New York, 1971.

10. A. Morey, ed., *Gilbert Foliot and His Letters*, Cambridge, 1965; C. N. L. Brooke, ed., *The Letters and Charters of Gilbert Foliot*, Cambridge, 1967; and C. R. Cheney and M. G. Cheney, eds., *Letters of Pope Innocent III (1198–1216) concerning England and Wales*, Oxford, 1967. Another significant edition and translation is that by M. Chibnall of *The Ecclesiastical History of Orderic Vitalis*, Oxford, 1969.

11. G. D. G. Hall, ed. and trans., *The Treatise on the Laws and Customs of the Realm of England Commonly Called Glanvill*, Edinburgh, 1965, which appeared in that most useful series Nelson's Medieval Classics.

12. "Ranulf de Glanville," *Speculum* 45, 1970: 69–79. While discussing legal sources of the twelfth century, one should note that, although the new edition and translation of the *Leges Henrici Primi*, Oxford, 1972, by L. J. Downer, is a considerable improvement over the older ones, it is questionable that Downer is justified in the assertion that the *Leges* "emerge as a genuine document of their times."

13. S. E. Thorne, *Bracton on the Laws and Customs of England*, 4 vols, Cambridge, Mass., 1968–1977. For a discussion of Roman law in the twelfth and thirteenth centuries, see R. V. Turner, "Roman Law in England before the Time of Bracton," *JBS* 15, 1975: 1–25.

14. H. G. Richardson, *Bracton: The Problem of His Text*, London, 1965. See also the articles printed as "A Bracton Symposium," *Tulane Law Review* 43, 1968: 455–602.

15. D. P. Kirby, *The Making of Early England*, 1967; D. J. V. Fisher, *The Anglo-Saxon Age*, 1973; P. H. Sawyer, *From Roman Britain to Norman England*, 1978. For a reliable survey see J. R. Lander, *Ancient and Medieval England: Beginnings to 1509*, New York, 1973.

16. H. R. Loyn, *Alfred the Great*, Oxford, 1967.

17. F. Barlow, *Edward the Confessor*, 1970; idem, "Edward the Confessor's Early Life, Character and Attitudes," *EHR* 80, 1965: 225–251; idem, *William I and the Norman Conquest*, 1965. Cf. D. C. Douglas, *The Norman Achievement*, 1969; idem, *The Norman Fate*, *1100–1154*, 1976. For the post-1066 period see also G. W. S. Barrow, *Feudal Britain: The Completion of the Medieval Kingdoms*, *1066–1314*, 1972.

18. E. Mason has argued that William Rufus effectively developed his father's policies, making possible the more publicized but essentially imitative work of Henry I. The reputation of William has suffered because of the hostile Henrician historiography ("William Rufus: Myth and Reality," *Journal of Medieval History* 3, 1977: 1–20).

19. R. H. C. Davis, *King Stephen*, London, 1967; H. A. Cronne, *The Reign of Stephen*, London, 1970.

20. W. L. Warren, *Henry II*, London, 1973; L. F. Salzman, *Edward I*, London, 1968. See also C. W. Hollister and T. K. Keefe, "The Making of the Angevin Empire," *JBS* 12, 1973: 1–25. Richard I has been the subject of two books which necessarily devote considerable attention to Richard's role in the Third Crusade; see J. A. Brundage, *Richard Lion Heart: A Biography*, New York, 1974, and John Gillingham, *The Life and Times of Richard I*, London, 1973. Recently Gillingham has produced evidence that Richard did not die before a castle at Chalûs in his quest for treasure trove but was in this area to subdue a revolt of Aimar of Limoges and Audemar of Angoulême. No sporting adventure but a serious military expedition was the cause of Richard's death ("The Unromantic Death of Richard I," *Speculum*, 54, 1979: 18–41).

21. A. A. M. Duncan, *Scotland, the Making of the Kingdom*, vol. 1, Edinburgh, 1975; G. W. S. Barrow, *Robert Bruce and the Community of the Realm of Scotland*, London, 1965.

22. *LQR* 23, 1907: 143.

23. F. W. Maitland, *History of English Law*, Cambridge, 1968. See also C. H. S. Fifoot, *Frederic W. Maitland: A Biography*, Cambridge, Mass., 1971, and H. F. Bell, *Maitland: A Critical Examination and Assessment*, London, 1965.

24. S. F. C. Milsom, *Historical Foundations of the Common Law*, London, 1969; R. C. van Caenegem, *The Birth of the Common Law*, Cambridge, 1973. See also J. H. Baker, *An Introduction to English Legal History*, London, 1971.

25. A. Hardine, *The Law Courts of Medieval England*, London, 1973; cf. idem, *A Social History of English Law*, London, 1966.

26. H. G. Richardson and G. O. Sayles, *Law and Legislation from Aethelberht to Magna Carta*, Edinburgh, 1966; idem, *Governance of Medieval England*, Edinburgh, 1963; G. O. Sayles, *The King's Parliament of England*, London, 1975.

27. B. Lyon and A. E. Verhulst, *Medieval Finance: A Comparison of Financial Institutions in Northwestern Europe*, Ghent and Providence, 1967; H. M. Jewell, *English Local Administration in the Middle Ages*, London, 1972. See also H. Hearder and H. R. Loyn, eds., *British Government and Administration: Studies Presented to S. B. Chrimes*, Cardiff, 1974.

28. J. Beeler, *Warfare in England*, *1066–1189*, Ithaca, N.Y., 1966; J. F. Verbruggen, *The Art of Warfare in Western Europe during the Middle Ages*, Amsterdam, 1978.

29. M. M. Postan, *The Medieval Economy and Society: An Economic History of Britain 1100–1500*, Berkeley, 1973; idem, "Medieval Agrarian Society at Its Prime: England," in *The Cambridge Economic History of Europe: The Agrarian Life of the Middle Ages*, 2d ed., Cambridge, 1966, 1: 549–659; idem, *Essays on Medieval Agriculture and General Problems of the Medieval Economy*, Cambridge, 1973; and idem, *Essays on Medieval Trade and Finance*, Cambridge, 1973; C. Platt, *The English Medieval Town*, 1976; Susan Reynolds, *An Introduction to the History of English Medieval Towns*, Oxford, 1977. See the local study of C. Platt, *Medieval Southampton: The Port and Trading Community*, A.D. *1000–1600*, 1973.

30. H. P. R. Finberg, ed., *The Agrarian History of England and Wales*, A.D. *43–1042*, vol. 1, pt. 2, Cambridge, 1972.

31. R. E. Rodes, *Ecclesiastical Administration in Medieval England*, Notre Dame, Ind., 1977; C. H. Lawrence, *The English Church and the Papacy in the Middle Ages*, 1965; R. C. Finucane, *Miracles and Pilgrims: Popular Beliefs in Medieval England*, Totowa, N.J., 1978; idem, "The Use and Abuse of Medieval Miracles," *History* 60, 1975: 1–10. Other short but useful studies are J. Scammell, "The Rural Chapter in England from the Eleventh to the Fourteenth Century," *EHR* 86, 1971: 1–21, and E. Mason, "The Role of the English Parishioner, 1100–1500," *Journal of Ecclesiastical History* 27, 1976: 17–29. See also N. Orme, *Education in the West of England, 1066–1548*, Exeter, 1976.

32. A. Gransden, *Historical Writing in England c. 550–c. 1307*, 1974.

33. S. Frere, *Britannia: A History of Roman Britain*, 1967; R. G. Collingwood, *Roman Britain and the English Settlements*, (Oxford, 1936). Unfortunately *Britain in the Roman Empire*, 1968, by J. Liversidge, bears no comparison to the Frere book. In his study of the northern military areas of Roman Britain, P. Salvay provides information on the civilian society and the relations of the Romans with the natives (*The Frontier People of Roman Britain*, Cambridge, 1965).

34. J. Wacher, *The Towns of Roman Britain*, London, 1975.

35. M. Dillon and Nora Chadwick, *The Celtic Realms*, London, 1967; E. John, *Orbis Britanniae and Other Studies*, Leicester, 1966. The views of J. N. L. Myres appear regularly in his reviews in the *EHR*.

36. J. Morris, *The Age of Arthur: A History of the British Isles from 350 to 650*, London, 1973; D. N. Dumville, "Sub-Roman Britain: History and Legend," *History* 62, 1977: 173–192. Cf. R. W. Hanning, *The Vision of History in Early Britain*, New York, 1966.

37. D. M. Wilson, *The Archaeology of Anglo-Saxon England*, London, 1976; H. M. Taylor and J. Taylor, *Anglo-Saxon Architecture*, 2 vols., Cambridge, 1965; J. N. L. Myres, *Anglo-Saxon Pottery and the Settlement of England*, Oxford, 1969; idem, *A Corpus of Anglo-Saxon Pottery of the Pagan Period*, 2 vols., Cambridge, 1978.

38. R. Bruce-Mitford, *The Sutton Hoo Ship-Burial*, vol. 1, London, 1975. This massive work is splendidly illustrated and can be supplemented by Bruce-Mitford's less scholarly book, *The Sutton Hoo Ship-Burial: A Handbook*, London, 1968. For an interesting argument that the person commemorated was not royal, see J. O. Prestwich, "King Aethelhere and the Battle of the Winwaed," *EHR* 83, 1968: 89–95. Numismatic evidence in this period largely comes from archaeological efforts. Recent numismatic studies have centered on the question of volume of Anglo-Saxon coinage and the wealth of Anglo-Saxon England. See especially H. B. A. Petersson, *Anglo-Saxon Currency, King Edgar's Reform to the Conquest*, Lund, Sweden, 1969; P. H. Sawyer, "The Wealth of England in the Eleventh Century," *TRHS* 15, 1965: 145–164; D. M. Metcalf, "How Large Was the Anglo-Saxon Currency?" *EcHR* 18, 1965: 475–482; P. Grierson, "The Volume of Anglo-Saxon Coinage," *EcHR* 20, 1967: 153–160.

39. D. A. Bullough, "Anglo-Saxon Institutions and Early English Society," *Annali della Fondazione italiana per la storia amministrativa* 2, 1965: 647–659; G. C. Homans, "The Explanation of English Regional Differences," *PP*, no. 42, 1969: 18–34; T. M. Charles-Edwards, "Kingship, Status and the Origin of the Hide," *PP*, no. 56, 1972: 3–33. On the hide, see A. R. H. Baker, "The Kentish Iugum: Its Relationship to Soils at Gillingham," *EHR* 81, 1966: 74–79; J. F. McGovern, "The Hide and Related Land-tenure Concepts in Anglo-Saxon England," *Traditio* 28, 1972: 101–118; C. Hart, "The Tribal Hidage," *TRHS* 21, 1971: 133–157.

40. John, *Orbis Britanniae*; H. Vollrath-Reichelt, *Königsdanke und Königtum bei den Angelsachsen bis zur Mitte des 9 Jahrhunderts*, Cologne, 1971. In connection with these studies it is interesting to note that J. M. Wallace-Hadrill has aruged that one must view western Europe as a whole in

order to interpret its history and that Anglo-Saxon England can never be understood in isolation (*Early Medieval History*, Oxford, 1975).

41. V. I. Evison, *The Fifth-century Invasions South of the Thames*, London, 1965; cf. D. P. Kirby, "Problems of Early West Saxon History," *EHR* 80, 1965: 10–29.

42. Doris Whitelock, *The Genuine Asser*, Reading, 1968; J. L. Nelson, "The Problem of King Alfred's Royal Annointing," *Journal of Ecclesiastical History* 18, 1967: 145–163; H. R. C. Davis, "Alfred the Great: Propaganda and Truth," *History* 56, 1971: 169–182.

43. On the Danes, see H. R. Loyn, *The Vikings in Britain*, New York, 1977: A. P. Smyth, *Scandinavian Kings in the British Isles, 850–880*, Oxford, 1978; D. M. Wilson, "Scandinavian Settlement in the North and West of the British Isles—An Archaeological Point-of-View," *TRHS* 26, 1976: 95–113; E. John, "War and Society in the Tenth Century: The Maldon Campaign," *TRHS* 27, 1977: 173–195. For the other studies, see M. W Campbell, "Earl Godwin of Wessex and Edward the Confessor's Promise of the Throne to William of Normandy," *Traditio* 28, 1972: 141–158; J. Campbell, "Observations on English Government from the Tenth to the Twelfth Century," *TRHS* 25, 1975: 39–54; W. A. Chaney, *The Cult of Kingship in Anglo-Saxon England: The Transition from Paganism to Christianity*, Berkeley, 1970.

44. H. Mayr-Harting, *The Coming of Christianity to Anglo-Saxon England*, London, 1972; Kathleen Hughes, *The Church in Early Irish Society*, London, 1966; idem, *Early Christian Ireland: Introduction to the Sources*, London, 1972; R. P. C. Hanson, *Saint Patrick, His Origins and Career*, Oxford, 1968. For a good collection of specialized studies see M. W. Barley and R. P. C. Hanson, eds., *Christianity in Britain, 300–700*, Leicester, 1968.

45. Charles Plummer, *Beda Venerabilis, 673–735*, Oxford, 1896; B. Colgrave and R. A. B. Mynors, *Bede's Ecclesiastical History of the English People*, Oxford, 1969; M. Miller, "Bede's Use of Gildas," *EHR* 90, 1975: 241–261; J. N. Stephens, "Bede's Ecclesiastical History," *History* 62, 1977: 1–14; C. P. Wormald, "The Uses of Literacy in Anglo-Saxon England and Its Neighbours," *TRHS* 27, 1977: 95–114. For an excellent study of chronology which vindicates Bede's contributions, see K. Harrison, *The Framework of Anglo-Saxon History to A.D. 900*, Cambridge, 1976. In his investigation of ecclesiastical calendars, C. Hart has concluded that the Danes obliterated much Anglo-Saxon scholarship in the ninth century ("The Ramsey Computus," *EHR* 85, 1970: 29–44). See also P. H. Blair, *The World of Bede*, New York, 1970.

46. H. R. Loyn, *Anglo-Saxon England and the Norman Conquest*, London, 1962; idem, *The Norman Conquest*, London, 1965; R. A. Brown, *The Normans and the Norman Conquest*, London, 1968; idem, "The Norman Conquest," *TRHS* 17, 1967: 109–130; R. H. C. Davis, "The Norman Conquest," *History* 51, 1966: 279–286; idem, *The Normans and their Myth*, 1976, R. W. Finn, *The Norman Conquest and Its Effects on the Economy, 1066–1086*, 1971. See also D. Whitelock et al., *The Norman Conquest: Its Setting and Impact*, 1966; G. W. Keeton, *The Norman Conquest and the Common Law*, New York, 1966.

47. Kurt-Ulrich Jäschke, *Wilhelm der Eroberer: Sein doppelter Herrschaftsantritt im Jahr 1066*, Sigmaringen, 1977; R. H. C. Davis, "The Carmen de Hastingae Proelio," *EHR* 93, 1978: 241–261.

48. J. Le Patourel, *The Norman Empire*, Oxford, 1977; idem, "The Norman Succession, 996–1135," *EHR* 86, 1971: 225–250; idem, "What Did not Happen in Stephen's Reign," *History* 58, 1973: 1–17. Cf. C. W. Hollister, "The Anglo-Norman Civil War: 1101," *EHR* 88, 1973: 315–334.

49. E. King, "King Stephen and the Anglo-Norman Aristocracy," *History* 59, 1974: 180–194.

50. C. W. Hollister and J. W. Baldwin, "The Rise of Administrative Kingship: Henry I and Philip Augustus," *AHR* 83, 1978: 867–905; C. W. Hollister, "The Origins of the English Treasury," *EHR* 93, 1978: 262–275; D. R. Bates, "The Character and Career of Odo,

Bishop of Bayeux (1049/50–1097)," *Speculum* 50, 1975: 1–20; E. J. Kealey, *Roger of Salisbury, Viceroy of England*, Berkeley, 1972.

51. V. H. Galbraith, *Domesday Book: Its Place in Administrative History*, Oxford, 1974. Galbraith has suggested that the royal chaplain Samson was employed at Winchester in the compilation of Domesday Book ("Notes on the Career of Samson Bishop of Worcester [1096–1112]," *EHR* 82, 1967: 86–101).

52. B. Dodwell, "The Making of the Domesday Survey in Norforlk: The Hundrèd and a Half of Clacklose," *EHR* 84, 1969: 79–84; S. P. J. Harvey, "Domesday Book and Its Predecessors," *EHR* 86, 1971: 753–773; idem, "Domesday Book and Anglo-Norman Government," *TRHS* 25, 1975: 175–193. See also R. W. Finn, *Domesday Studies: The Eastern Counties*, London, 1967; H. C. Darby and R. W. Finn, *The Domesday Geography of South-West England*, Cambridge, 1967; R. Lennard, "The Composition of the Domesday Caruca," *EHR* 81, 1966: 770–775; B. P. Wolffe, *The Royal Demesne in English History*, Athens, Ohio, 1971.

53. C. W. Hollister, *The Military Organization of Norman England*, Oxford, 1965; idem, "1066: The 'Feudal Revolution,'" *AHR* 73, 1968: 708–723. Cf. M. Chibnall, "Mercenaries and the Familia Regis under Henry I," *History* 62, 1977: 15–23.

54. R. A. Brown, *Origins of English Feudalism*, London, 1973; J. C. Holt, "The Carta of Richard de La Haye, 1166: A Note on Continuity in Anglo-Norman Feudalism," *EHR* 84, 1969: 289–297. See also W. E. Wightman, *The Lacy Family in England and Normandy, 1066–1194*, Oxford, 1966; E. King, "The Peterborough 'Descriptio Militum' (Henry I)," *EHR* 84, 1969: 84–101; S. P. J. Harvey, "The Knight and the Knight's Fee in England," *PP*, no. 49, 1970: 3–43; J. Scammell, "The Origin and Limitations of the Liberty of Durham," *EHR* 81, 1966: 449–473.

55. J. C. Holt, "Politics and Property in Early Medieval England," *PP* 57, 1972: 3–52; idem, "Politics and Property in Early Medieval England: A Rejoinder," *PP* no. 65, 1974: 127–135; E. King, "Politics and Property in Early Medieval England: The Tenurial Crisis of the Early Twelfth Century," ibid., 110–117; S. D. White, "Succession to Fiefs in Early Medieval England," ibid., 118–127.

56. D. F. Benn, *Norman Castles in Britain*, London, 1968.

57. Doris Stenton, *English Justice between the Norman Conquest and the Great Charter, 1066–1215*, Philadelphia, 1964; R. C. van Caenegem, in C. Brooke, ed., *Church and Government in the Middle Ages: Essays Presented to C. R. Cheney on His Seventieth Birthday*, Cambridge, 1976.

58. W. T. Reedy, Jr., "The Origins of the General Eyre in the Reign of Henry I," *Speculum* 41, 1966: 688–724; T. S. Green, "Societal Concepts of Criminal Liability for Homicide in Medieval England, ibid. 47, 1972: 669–694. See also R. V. Turner, "The Origin of the Medieval English Jury: Frankish, English, or Scandinavian?" *JBS* 7, 1968: 1–10; idem, "The Medieval English Royal Courts: Problems of Their Origins," *Historian* 27, 1965: 471–497; R. B. Pugh, *Itinerant Justices in English History*, Exeter, 1967.

59. M. Brett, *The English Church under Henry I*, 1975; C. Morris, "William I and the Church Courts," *EHR* 82, 1967: 449–463; M. Gibson, *Lanfranc of Bec*, Oxford, 1978; F. Barlow, "A View of Archbishop Lanfranc," *Journal of Ecclesiastical History* 16, 1965; S. N. Vaughn, "St. Anselm of Canterbury: The Philosopher-Saint as Politician," *Journal of Medieval History* 1, 1975: 279–305; D. L. Bethell, "English Black Monks and Episcopal Elections in the 1120's," *EHR* 84, 1969: 673–698; H. Mayr-Harting, "Functions of a Twelfth-century Recluse," *History* 60, 1975: 337–352. For a study of another principal churchman of the early twelfth century, see D. Nicholl, *Thurstan, Archbishop of York (1114–1140)*, York, 1964. See also R. V. Turner, "Clerical Judges in English Secular Courts: The Ideal versus the Reality," *Medievalia et Humanistica* 3, 1972: 75–98. In the closest attempt at cultural history, C. Clark has done two articles on language and names. She concludes that, although English as a lan-

guage received competition after 1066, it was not superseded, as is shown by its continued use for place names. Her study of women's names after the Conquest suggests that Norman women played a very minor part in the post-Conquest settlement of England. See "People and Languages in Post-conquest Canterbury," *Journal of Medieval History* 2, 1976: 1–33; "Women's Names in Post-conquest England: Observations and Speculations," *Speculum* 53, 1978: 223–251.

60. J. Le Patourel, "The Plantagenet Dominions," *History* 50, 1965: 289–308; F. J. West, *The Justiciarship in England, 1066–1232*, Cambridge, 1966; C. R. Cheney, *Hubert Walter*, 1967; C. R. Young, *Hubert Walter, Lord of Canterbury and Lord of England*, Durham, N.C., 1968; C. Duggan, "Richard of Ilchester, Royal Servant and Bishop," *TRHS* 16, 1966: 1–21; J. E. Lally, "Secular Patronage at the Court of King Henry II," *BIHR* 49, 1976: 159–184; J. C. Holt, *Magna Carta*, Cambridge, 1965. Holt has suggested that Magna Carta was publicized to the community at large by means of French translations ("A Vernacular-French Text of Magna Carta, 1215," *EHR* 89, 1974: 346–364). See also J. C. Holt, *Magna Carta and the Idea of Liberty*, New York, 1972; I. Jennings, *Magna Carta and Its Influence in the World Today*, London, 1965; V. H. Galbraith, "Runnymede Revisited," *Proceedings of the American Philosophical Society*, 1966.

61. S. F. C. Milsom, *The Legal Framework of English Feudalism*, Cambridge, 1976; D. W. Sutherland, *The Assize of Novel Disseisin*, Oxford, 1973.

62. M. T. Clanchy, "Remembering the Past and the Good Old Law," *History* 55, 1970: 165–176; R. V. Turner, *The King and His Courts: The Role of John and Henry III in the Administration of Justice, 1199–1240*, Ithaca, N.Y., 1968; idem, "The Judges of King John: Their Background and Training," *Speculum* 51, 1976: 447–461; B. Kemp, "Exchequer and Bench in the Later Twelfth Century—Separate or Identical Tribunals?" *EHR* 88, 1973: 559–573; N. D. Hurnard, *The King's Pardon for Homicide*, Oxford, 1969; J. M. Kaye, "Early History of Murder and Manslaughter," *LQR* 83, 1967. For a challenge to Maitland's definition of frankalmoin, see A. W. Douglas, "Frankalmoin and Jurisdictional Immunity: Maitland," *Speculum* 53, 1978: 26–48. See also W. M. McGovern, "Contract in Medieval England: The Necessity for Quid pro Quo and a Sum Certain," *American Journal of Legal History* 13, 1969: 173–201.

63. D. Knowles, *Thomas Becket*, London, 1970; B. Smalley, *The Becket Conflict and the Schools: A Study of Intellectuals in Politics*, Oxford, 1973; C. R. Cheney, *Pope Innocent III and England*, Stuttgart, 1976; P. B. Roberts, *Studies in the Sermons of Stephen Langton*, Toronto, 1968. See also J. W. Alexander, "The Becket Controversy in Recent Historiography," *JBS* 9, 1970: 1–26; R. Foreville, "Mort et survie de saint Thomas Becket," *Cahiers de Civilisation Médiévale* 14, 1971: 21–38. For informative studies on the church courts and law, see J. E. Sayers, *Papal Judges Delegate in the Province of Canterbury, 1198–1254*, 1971; idem, "Canterbury Proctors at the Court of 'Audientia Litterarum Contradictarum,'" *Traditio* 22, 1966: 311–331; C. Morris, "From Synod to Consistory: The Bishops' Courts in England, 1150–1250," *Journal of Ecclesiastical History* 22, 1971: 115–123. See also M. G. Cheney, "The Recognition of Pope Alexander III: Some Neglected Evidence," *EHR* 84, 1969: 474–497; F. D. Logan, *Excommunication and the Secular Arm in Medieval England*, Toronto, 1968.

64. A. Squire, *Aelred of Rievaulx*, 1969: A. Gransden, "A Democratic Movement in the Abbey of Bury St. Edmunds in the Late Twelfth and Early Thirteenth Centuries," *Journal of Ecclesiastical History* 26, 1975: 25–39; V. M. Lagorio, "The Evolving Legend of St. Joseph of Glastonbury," *Speculum* 46, 1971: 209–231. See also E. Searle, "Battle Abbey and Exemption: The Forged Charters," *EHR* 83, 1968: 449–480; W. R. Jones, "Patronage and Administration: The King's Free Chapels in Medieval England," *JBS* 9, 1969: 1–23.

65. M. Richter, "Gerald of Wales: A Reassessment on the 750th Anniversary of His Death," *Tra-*

ditio 29, 1973: 379–390; A. A. Goddu and R. H. Rouse, "Gerald of Wales and the Florilegium Angelicum," *Speculum* 52, 1977: 488–521; A. Gransden, "Realistic Observations in Twelfth-century England," ibid. 47, 1972: 29–51; M. T. Clanchy, "Moderni in Education and Government in England," ibid. 50, 1975: 671–688.

66. W. Urry, *Canterbury under the Angevin Kings*, 1967; S. Reynolds, "The Rulers of London in the Twelfth Century," *History* 57, 1972: 337–357; E. M. Carus-Wilson, "The First Half-century of the Borough of Stratford-upon-Avon," *EcHR* 18, 1965: 46–63. See also R. H. Britnell, "English Markets and Royal Administration before 1200," *EcHR* 31, 1978: 183–196.

67. M. T. Clanchy, "Did Henry III Have a Policy?" *History* 53, 1968: 203–214; J. R. Studd, "The Lord Edward and King Henry III," *BIHR* 50, 1977: 4–19; H. M. Colvin, *Building Accounts of King Henry III*, Oxford, 1971. For other studies of this period, see R. F. Walker, "Hubert de Burgh and Wales, 1218–1232," *EHR* 87, 1972: 465–494; M. T. Clanchy, "The Franchise of Return of Writs," *TRHS* 17, 1967: 59–82; J. W. Alexander, "New Evidence on the Palatinate of Chester," *EHR* 85, 1970: 715–729; D. A. Carpenter, "The Decline of the Curial Sheriff in England, 1194–1258," *EHR* 91, 1976: 1–32; M. Altschul, *A Baronial Family of Medieval England: The Clares, 1217–1314*, Baltimore, 1965.

68. M. Prestwich, *War, Politics and Finance under Edward I*, 1972; T. F. Tout, "Exchequer and Wardrobe in the Later Years of Edward I," *BIHR* 46, 1973: 1–10. See also B. F. Byerly and C. R. Byerly, *Records of the Household and Wardrobe, 1285–1286*, London, 1977; A. Z. Freeman, "A Moat Defensive: The Coast Defense Scheme of 1295," *Speculum* 42, 1967: 442–462.

69. J. M. W. Bean, *The Decline of English Feudalism, 1215–1540*, Manchester, 1968. Cf. J. S. Critchley, "Summonses to Military Service Early in the Reign of Henry III," *EHR* 86, 1971: 79–95.

70. J. P. Trabut-Cussac, *L'administration anglaise en Gascogne sous Henri III et Edouard I de 1254 à 1307*, Geneva, 1972.

71. P. Spufford, *Origins of the English Parliament*, 1967; G. Cuttino, "Mediaeval Parliament Reinterpreted," *Speculum* 41, 1966: 681–687; E. B. Fryde and E. Miller, eds., *Historical Studies of the English Parliament*, 2 vols., Cambridge, 1970; A. Marongiu, *Medieval Parliaments: A Comparative Study*, London, 1968; A. R. Myers, *Parliaments and Estates in Europe to 1789*, London, 1975; B. Lyon, "What Made a Medieval King Constitutional?" in *Essays in Medieval History Presented to Bertie Wilkinson*, Toronto, 1969, 157–175; G. L. Harriss, *King, Parliament and Public Finance in Medieval England to 1369*, Oxford, 1975.

72. H. G. Richardson and G. O. Sayles, "The Earliest Known Official Use of the Term 'Parliament,'" *EHR* 82 1967: 747–749; J. H. Denton, "The Crisis of 1297 from the Evesham Chronicle," *EHR* 93, 1978: 560–579; N. Pronay and F. Taylor, "The Use of the 'Modus Tenendi Parliamentum' in the Middle Ages," *BIHR* 47, 1974: 11–23; W. R. Jones, "Bishops, Politics, and the Two Laws: The *Gravamina* of the English Clergy, 1237–1399," *BIHR* 41, 1966: 209–249; J. S. Illsley, "Parliamentary Elections in the Reign of Edward I," *BIHR* 49, 1976: 24–40. See also C. H. Knowles, *Simon de Montfort, 1265–1965*, 1965; K. B. McFarlane, "Had Edward I a 'Policy' towards the Earls?" *History* 50, 1965: 145–159; J. S. Roskell, "A Consideration of Certain Aspects and Problems of the English *Modus Tenendi Parliamentum*," *BJRL* 50, 1967/1968: 411–442.

73. C. R. Cheney, *Notaries Public in England in the Thirteenth and Fourteenth Centuries*, Oxford, 1972; R. C. Palmer, "County Year Book Reports: The Professional Lawyer in the Medieval County Court," *EHR* 91, 1976: 776–801; W. E. Brynteson, "Roman Law and Legislation in the Middle Ages," *Speculum* 41, 1966: 420–437. See also J. S. Critchley, "The Early History of the Writ of Judicial Protection," *BIHR* 45, 1972: 196–213; D. A. Crowley, "The Later History of Frankpledge," *BIHR* 48, 1975: 1–15; P. R. Hyams, "The Proof of Villein

Status in the Common Law," *EHR* 89, 1974: 721–749; G. J. Hand, *English Law in Ireland, 1290–1324*, Cambridge, 1967.

74. N. D. Hurnard, *The King's Pardon for Homicide before A.D. 1367*, Oxford, 1969; J. B. Given, *Society and Homicide in Thirteenth-century England*, Stanford, Calif., 1977; R. B. Pugh, *Imprisonment in Medieval England*, Cambridge, 1968.

75. B. S. Eastwood, "Mediaeval Empiricism: The Case of Grosseteste's Optics," *Speculum* 43, 1968: 306–321; D. C. Lindberg, "Lines of Influence in Thirteenth-century Optics: Bacon, Witelo, and Pecham," ibid. 46, 1971: 66–83; R. C. Dales, "Adam Marsh, Robert Grosseteste, and the Treatise on the Tides," ibid. 52, 1977: 900–901.

76. P. D. A. Harvey, "The English Inflation of 1180–1220," *PP* 61, 1973: 3–30; M. Prestwich, "Edward I's Monetary Policies and Their Consequences," *EcHR* 22, 1969: 406–416; Mavis Mate, "The Indebtedness of Canterbury Cathedral Priory 1215–95," *EcHR* 26, 1973: 183–197. See also idem, "A Mint of Trouble, 1279 to 1307," *Speculum* 44, 1969: 201–212.

77. R. W. Kaeuper, *Bankers to the Crown: The Riccardi of Lucca and Edward I*, Princeton, N.J., 1973; M. W. Beresford, *New Towns of the Middle Ages: Town Plantations in England, Wales and Gascony*, London, 1967; E. Miller, "The Fortunes of the English Textile Industry during the Thirteenth Century," *EcHR* 18, 1965: 64–82. For a good account of the financial transactions of the Jews in the thirteenth century, see V. D. Lipman, *The Jews of Medieval Norwich*, London, 1967.

78. A. R. Bridbury, "The Farming Out of Manors," *EcHR* 31, 1978: 503–511. For Postan's response, see "A Note on the Farming Out of Manors," *EcHR* 31, 1978: 521–525.

79. E. King, *Peterborough Abbey 1086–1310: A Study in the Land Market* (Cambridge, 1973; idem, "Large and Small Landowners in Thirteenth-century England: The Case of Peterborough Abbey," *PP*, no. 47, 1970: 26–50; P. R. Hyams, "The Origins of a Peasant Land Market in England," *EcHR* 23, 1970: 18–37; S. Scammell, "Freedom and Marriage in Medieval England," *EcHR* 27, 1974: 523–537. For church participation in the land market, see S. Raban, "Mortmain in Medieval England," *PP*, no. 65, 1974: 3–26.

80. J. Z. Titow, *English Rural Society, 1200–1350*, London, 1969; idem, *Winchester Yields: A Study in Medieval Agricultural Productivity*, Cambridge, 1972; R. H. Hilton, *A Medieval Society: The West Midlands at the End of the Thirteenth Century*, London, 1967; P. D. A. Harvey, *A Medieval Oxfordshire Village, Cuxham, 1240 to 1400*, London, 1965; A. N. May, "An Index of Thirteenth-century Peasant Impoverishment? Manor Court Fines," *EcHR* 26, 1973: 389–402. See also B. Dodwell, "Holdings and Inheritance in Medieval East Anglia," *EcHR* 20, 1967: 53–66. For the reasons landlords did not invest, see M. M. Postan, "Investment in Medieval Agriculture," *JEcH* 27, 1967.

81. P. D. A. Harvey, "The Pipe Rolls and the Adoption of Demesne Farming in England," *EcHR* 27, 1974: 345–359; B. Harvey, *Westminster Abbey and Its Estates in the Middle Ages*, Oxford, 1977; E. Searle, *Lordship and Community: Battle Abbey and Its Banlieu, 1066–1538*, Toronto, 1974; S. Raban, *The Estates of Thorney and Crowland: A Study in Medieval Monastic Land Tenure*, Cambridge, 1977: E. Miller, "England in the Twelfth and Thirteenth Centuries: An Economic Contrast?" *EcHR* 24, 1971: 1–14. See also J. Maddicott, *The English Peasantry and the Demands of the Crown, 1294–1341*, Oxford, 1974.

82. P. R. Coss, "Sir Geoffrey de Langley and the Crisis of the Knightly Class in Thirteenth-century England," *PP*, no. 68, 1975: 3–37; J. E. Newman, "Greater and Lesser Landowners and Parochial Patronage: Yorkshire in the Thirteenth Century," *EHR* 92, 1977: 280–308; F. R. H. Du Boulay, *The Lordship of Canterbury: An Essay on Medieval Society*, London, 1966.

83. H. E. Hallam, *Settlement and Society: A Study of the Early Agrarian History of South Lincolnshire*, Cambridge, 1965; A. C. Chibnall, *Sherington: Fiefs and Fields of a Buckinghamshire*

Village, Cambridge, 1965. See also W. O. Ault, "The Village Church and the Village Community in Medieval England," *Speculum* 45, 1970: 197–215; C. Platt, *The Monastic Grange in Medieval England*, London, 1969.

84. A. H. R. Baker and R. A. Butlin, *Studies of Field Systems in the British Isles*, Cambridge, 1973; R. A. Dodgshon, "The Landholding Foundations of the Open-field System," *PP*, no. 67, 1975: 3–29.

Centuries of Transition
England in the Later
Middle Ages

Barbara A. Hanawalt

"At the close of the Middle Ages, a sombre melancholy weighs on people's souls."[1] In 1924 Johan Huizinga thus expressed not only the mood of the late medieval writers but also that of medievalists at the time, who looked upon the period as a sad disintegration of a once lustrous and integrated culture. The subtle brilliance of his manipulation of chronicles, in addition to artistic and literary evidence, in *The Waning of the Middle Ages* left readers smelling the sickly sweet odor of decay. Huizinga represented a long tradition of disdain for the later Middle Ages. Readers of William Stubbs's *Constitutional History* were told in volume 3 that the events of the fifteenth century would force even "the most enthusiastic admirer of medieval life" to admit that "all that was good and great in it was languishing even to death."[2] The very forbidding aspect of the later Middle Ages has probably been one of the factors tempting modern medievalists to rush to the study of the fourteenth and fifteenth centuries. Rather than being repulsed by Huizinga's grim picture of cultural decline, historians in the last ten years have eagerly sought out more information on morbidity, mortality, warfare, and political intrigue. A taste for social and cultural disintegration, however, is not the only factor that has given rise to the recent popularity of the Middle Ages.

If nature abhors a vacuum, historians abhor gaps in historical knowledge.[3] The periods preceding the fourteenth and fifteenth centuries have received thorough study for years, but many classic works, like F. W. Maitland's great study of legal history, end with the death of Edward I in 1307.[4] The rest of the fourteenth century was treated sporadically. Parliamentary developments, taxation, the Hundred Years' War, the Peasant Revolt, some monarchs, and aspects of economic history were studied for the fourteenth century. By 1959 May McKisack had sufficient secondary work at her disposal to write a comprehensive, analytical narrative of the fourteenth century for the Oxford History of England series,[5] but E. F. Jacob had a much harder task for the fifteenth century.[6] Now the records for study are available, and the major historical questions have been posed; hence, medievalists trained in paleography and at home in the archives and who are looking for untilled ground have tended to stake their claims in the wilderness of the later Middle Ages.

The increasingly thorough study of the sixteenth and seventeenth centuries has also spurred research in the preceding period. Early modernists, anxious to trace the roots of changes in government, warfare, and social institutions back into the fifteenth century, often found that the documents were decidedly medieval in character and too daunting to read. Medievalists were needed to provide the answers, and they are beginning to do so. Furthermore, medievalists frequently feel piqued by the categorical claims of early modernists about what the Middle Ages was really like and how different the modern period is. Thus Philippe Ariès's thesis that people in the Middle Ages, unlike their more modern descendants, lacked sentimentalized notions about childhood,[7] or Lawrence Stone's contention that the modern family is nuclear whereas the medieval family was open lineage and extended,[8] have raised the hackles of medievalists and have forced them to look for counterexamples.

Historians' fascination with the birth of a new culture—the great transition periods in history—has also stimulated research on the terra incognita between 1307 and 1485. In a sense this approach takes the coin of Huizinga and earlier writers and turns it to the obverse. What they saw as signs of decaying medieval culture become promises of the brave new world that will take its place. Viewed in this context, the period of 1350 to roughly 1500 is one of those great watershed periods in England comparable to the Norman Conquest and the Industrial Revolution. The Black Death, the Hundred Years' War, the Peasants' Revolt of 1381, the tensions between kings and subjects all brought major shifts in social perceptions and political and economic institutions. Accompanying these changes were dislocations in the religious and intellectual realms, epitomized by the challenge of Ockham and the teachings of Wyclif and the Lollards. No less important was the development of general systems of taxation, extended bureaucracies, and foot-soldier armies. While no medievalist would deny that these transformations represent the progressive destruction of the medieval world order, many now find excitement in tracing the change from the old world view to a more modern one.

Apart from its appeal as a neglected area of study, the late Middle Ages is also well suited for investigating the questions raised by the so-called new social history that has swept all fields of historical inquiry in the last decade. The emergence of demography as one of the major areas of research has meant for the fourteenth and fifteenth centuries a number of studies on the effects of the Black Death. But historians have also been interested in the composition of social classes and their evolution over the two centuries. Like Tudor historians, medievalists have scrutinized the power and wealth of the aristocracy, the rise of the gentry, and the condition of the peasantry. Not content to describe these social classes, scholars have looked at intraclass relationships and the tensions between social strata. Historians of medieval governmental institutions have investigated not only taxation, warfare, and changes in the administration of justice, but the effects of these institutions on the populace. The publication of Marc Bloch's books in English and the general vogue for the *Annales* school has stimulated medievalists as well as other historians to contribute to social and cultural research.

Although increasingly influenced by the social history issues preoccupying other fields, medievalists can look back to a long tradition of their own in this area. Historians at the turn of the twentieth century had been profoundly interested in the social organization of medieval England. Thus, Maitland's great contributions to legal history were not dry studies of one statute after another or one court case after another, but rather were thoroughly grounded in the origins of laws, their social functions, and their modifications in the face of changing society. As influential and inspiring today as in its own time, his social history approach to legal studies was followed by Bertha Haven Putnam, Nellie Neilson, T. F. T. Plucknett, and Helen Cam. For all of his anti-Catholic prejudices, another pioneer, George G. Coulton, also made substantial and lasting contributions to our knowledge of English social history. The years between the wars and immediately after World War II saw some break in this tradition as historians understandably became more interested in the rise of democratic institutions and the roots of political stability in England. Continuity was preserved, however, in the work of economic historians such as Eileen Power, M. M. Postan, Sylvia Thrupp, and E. M. Carus-Wilson.

Source materials for the late Middle Ages have responded well to the application of both traditional and new methodologies. It used to be that archaeological investigation was reserved for Roman and Anglo-Saxon sites, but over the last ten years and more, the late medieval towns and villages have seen major excavations. Aerial photography and more careful attention to topography and place-names have done much to help explain both agricultural practices and village layouts. Finally, the computer has made it possible to analyze information in the vast volumes of account rolls, tax lists, court rolls, wills, and other such records. Although a few patient scholars such as J. E. Thorold Rogers and William Beveridge had employed them systematically for price and wage series, most earlier historians had been able to use these materials only for rather limited studies or to extract anecdotal material. The computer has become a convenient tool both for quantification and for textual analysis.

Not only has the late Middle Ages received increased attention in the last ten years, but the boundary dates of the period have also been stretched. Several recent political narratives have experimented with removing the old divisions. C. S. L. Davies's *Peace, Printing and Protestantism*, D. M. Loades's *Politics and the Nation, 1450–1660*, and Anthony Goodman's *A History of England from Edward II to James I* all argue that the roots of Tudor government were in the later Middle Ages and that there was more continuity than change through the Tudor period.[9] No one, including any of these three authors, has set definitive dates for this new periodization, but there is concurrence in all areas of historical inquiry that regnal dates no longer offer useful breaking points. Hence, rather than attempt a survey of publications chronologically in this essay, I discuss the material topically, taking into account the varying time periods covered by current use of the term *late medieval history*.

One may break into what Maitland called the "seamless web of history" at any point and follow out the strands,[10] but it seems appropriate to begin with demographic changes, since their influence was pervasive in the English population, from peasants to kings. Much research of the last decade has focused on M. M. Postan's thesis about the alleged Malthusian conditions in England in the first quarter of the fourteenth century. While the thesis appeared long before 1966, his essays on the topic have recently been collected into a volume, *Essays on Medieval Agriculture and General Problems of the Medieval Economy*.[11] Postan has argued that the population of England expanded more or less steadily through the thirteenth century but that, during the latter part of that time in some places, and certainly from 1300 to 1325 in most parts of England, the population became too large to be supported by its agricultural production. Widespread famine resulted, lowering the population of England significantly even before the Black Death. Postan contends that part of the crisis in food supply resulted from soil exhaustion of marginal lands that had been brought into cultivation in the thirteenth century. Further study has indicated that grain production may also have decreased because the weather became substantially worse in the fourteenth century.[12] There were repeated bad harvests, but the Great Famine of 1315–1317 was the most devastating. As northern Europe was beginning to recover from it, another severe famine struck in the early 1320s. Ian Kershaw has dealt with the problem of these cold, wet years in northern European history and has shown that there was increased mortality not only from the Great Famine but from accompanying illness. He shows that animals as well as people died from disease in those years.[13] It was the loss of herds to murrain that made economic recovery so slow. Postan and Titow's article on heriots demonstrates the close relationship between poor grain crops and increased deaths in the first quarter of the fourteenth century.[14] Although there have been some quarrels with the thesis,[15] evidence from local studies, such as Zvi Razi's demographic study of the court rolls of Halesowen,[16] support it.

Predictably famine had its most severe effects on the poor. The nobles, wealthy merchants, and even the well-to-do peasants escaped starvation. The Black Death, on the other hand, killed the healthy and well-fed as readily as the poor. The experience of the Black Death had a profound influence on England and Europe as a whole, not only because mortality was so high, but because the scourge did not follow class lines. While Huizinga was fascinated by the cultural effects of the devastation, modern historians have tried to assess, first of all, the extent of the losses.

The precise extent of mortality from the plague is impossible to determine. There have been studies of the plague in London, among the clergy, and even on some manors, that help to form estimates. These materials have been summarized and evaluated by John Hatcher in *Plague, Population, and the English Economy, 1348–1530*.[17] But even after his careful sifting of evidence, Hatcher selects the figure of one-third of the population lost largely because it falls between the high estimate of one-half and a lower one of a quarter. Because there are no records reliable enough to establish either the population before the plague or the mortality attributable to it, the guess of one-third to one-half must stand. Hatcher's book is of great value to the general reader for its careful critique of such earlier works as J. C. Russell, *British Medieval Population*, T. H. Hollingsworth, *Historical Demography*, and J. F. D. Shrewsbury, *A History of Bubonic Plagues in the British Isles, 1348–1670*, as well as a number of more specialized studies.[18]

The plague was a particularly destructive disease because it revisited about every generation, causing death among young people of childbearing age who had escaped earlier plagues. As Sylvia Thrupp once commented, the fifteenth century was the "golden age for bacteria" if for nothing else.[19] Had the disease problems been limited to plague, the population might have recovered. By analyzing wills, an unorthodox source for demography, but one of the few available for fifteenth-century England, Robert S. Gottfried has shown that plague, dysentery, smallpox, influenza, and other diseases were as prevalent in England as on the continent.[20] Because of the prevalence of plague and other diseases, the population of England did not begin to recover its preplague proportions until the 1470s. Population continued to increase through the sixteenth century. Norman J. G. Pounds, in *An Economic History of Medieval Europe*, has conveniently summarized the population trends in graphic form.[21]

The wider use of archaeology and aerial photography have contributed greatly to our knowledge about the contraction of population and the destruction of some communities over the century following the first visitation of the Death. K. J. Allison, M. W. Beresford, J. G. Hurst, and others in *The Deserted Villages of Northamptonshire*[22] and M. W. Beresford and J. G. Hurst in *Deserted Medieval Villages* have documented the disappearance of some villages and the contraction of others as a result of population decline.[23]

The drastic fluctuation in population in the fourteenth through fifteenth cen-

turies had a profound effect on the general economy of England. Postan's interpretation of its effects may be found in his contribution to the new agricultural
history volume of *The Cambridge Economic History of Europe*.[24] Edward Miller
and John Hatcher, in *Medieval England: Rural Society and Economy, 1086–
1348*, have refined his arguments and added some of their own work in primary
sources.[25] Basing their argument on the assumption that the economy followed
population trends, they contend that the thirteenth century, with its abundant
population and improved farming techniques, was the height of demesne farming.
As resources became tighter in the early fourteenth century, lords released some
demesne land to peasants because the great demand for land from a hungry population meant that landowners could do as well from rents as from direct farming.
Even with the easing of the pressure on land and food supplies after 1325, the
lords continued to rent out portions of their land. For those who survived the
famines, the years between 1325 and 1348 were fairly prosperous. Excess profits
were spent on industrial products so that trade and towns prospered during
this period.

Study of the century and a half following the Black Death and its subsequent
visitations has raised the question of whether the population losses stimulated the
economy or brought about a general recession for England. M. M. Postan argues that the late fourteenth and fifteenth centuries saw declining trade, abandonment of demesne farming, and retreat from urban development.[26] Harry A.
Miskimin, writing generally on the European economy, has presented a similar
pessimistic view in *The Economy of Early Renaissance Europe, 1300–1460*.[27] For
some years it appeared that A. R. Bridbury, in *Economic Growth: England in the
Later Middle Ages*, was a voice alone in claiming that England's economy did not
suffer decay in the late Middle Ages but instead experienced a shift in areas of
prosperity.[28] Evidence for a resolution of this difference of interpretation is not
yet completely assembled, so that it is best to look at the studies that have been
done so far and assess the tenor of the debate.

Those who would argue that the later Middle Ages was a period of prosperity
for England point to the changes in wool production. The wool trade has always
been a popular area of investigation in economic history, but T. H. Lloyd's recent work has shown that the whole story has not been presented. First in *The
Movement of Wool Prices in Medieval England* and more recently in *The English
Wool Trade in the Middle Ages*, he has explored the shifts in the market for English wool and woolen cloth.[29] The sale of wool abroad was very much tied to the
international politics of the day. Lloyd shows the progressive hold that the Commons was able to exert over the Staple and wool taxation as it played its part in
funding the Hundred Years' War. As the market for wool shrank in response to
the weavers' revolt in Flanders, the English turned increasingly to the production

of cloth. The decline in Flanders meant that there was an open market for cloth on the Continent, so that while wool exports declined, cloth exports rose. Lloyd has also discussed the increased home market for woolen cloth as a spur to the transition.

The woolen cloth industry, like other industries, did not experience steady growth; there were always major troughs of recession. John Hatcher, in *English Tin Production and Trade before 1500*, has shown that in Cornwall, the chief area of mining and smelting, prosperity was high in the 1330s, but the region could not sustain this level of production with its decreased population after 1349.[30] There were simply not enough wage workers available for mining. By 1385 to 1420 the industry had made a remarkable recovery to preplague levels but later went into decline again. Apart from the work of Lloyd on wool production and that of Hatcher on tin, there has been little published on crafts, craft guilds, or industries in the last decade.[31]

The evidence that is available on English trade and manufacture shows that changes in demand and the technology of production (increased use of water mills) meant a relocation of prosperity. Thus while some of the traditional centers of wool production such as York or Warwick were suffering major setbacks in the late fourteenth and fifteenth centuries, places such as Coventry and Lavenham were experiencing a boom. One of the current debates, therefore, is about an overall assessment of the fate of cities in the wake of population decline. Intensifying the impact of decreased population on the economic viability of cities, the Hundred Years' War had devastating effects on some of the port cities of the south. Although some urban centers managed to hold their own, most historians feel that there was a general decay, the dating of which is a matter of debate. C. Phythian-Adams and R. B. Dobson put the urban crisis in the period 1450–1570, whereas P. Clark and P. Slack move it forward to 1500–1700.[32]

After a long lull in activity, urban history has again become a major research area. London has always attracted researchers,[33] but the most interesting innovation in the field has been Colin Platt's combination of written records with extensive archaeological evidence in *Medieval Southampton*.[34] Archaeological evidence shows much about how merchants lived, what they ate, and how they updated their housing. Written records discuss what they traded and with whom. Another comprehensive study of a major urban center is C. Phythian-Adams's work on Coventry.[35] His investigation of the total community and its cultural life makes this book fascinating reading. Two very good surveys of current knowledge about towns have also been published recently. Colin Platt's *The English Town* uses a number of published studies, archaeological diagrams, and primary sources to illustrate town planning, the quality of life in medieval cities, and the problems of growth and causes of decay in the late Middle Ages.[36] It is a fine introduction to urban studies. Susan Reynolds has also produced a survey, *An Introduction to the History of English Medieval Towns*, covering material from the Roman era through the fifteenth century.[37] While her work is mostly descriptive, she emphasizes the thesis that conflicts arose in towns because the economic elite who controlled them abused their power through overtaxation and self-promotion. Urban conflict tended to be between the taxers and the taxed.

Before a final verdict can be reached on the health of town economies in the later Middle Ages, more studies will have to be done on the market and fair towns. While large and well-documented cities such as London and York inevitably attract scholars' attention, most people's contact with trade and town life was the local market center. If these smaller trade centers were prospering, then one could argue for a shift rather than a decline of town importance. J. C. Russell's *Medieval Regions and Their Cities*, which argues that a region was composed of a network of villages, small towns, and cities that drew upon each other's resources, is on the right track, if too generally executed.[38] More detailed studies are addressed to the problem of market towns and fairs and their regions.[39]

The international crises of the fourteenth and fifteenth centuries played a major role in England's economy in the later Middle Ages, as already noted for the wool trade. England's continental trade has received considerable attention over the last decade. One of the major imports from Gascony and other areas was wine, and that trade has been analyzed in a series of essays by Margery Kirkbridge James, *Studies in the Medieval Wine Trade*.[40] Hostilities with France were occasionally a severe hindrance to the importation of wines, but there was a continuance of trade, with English shippers doing an increased amount of the hauling. Nevertheless, James's figures show that imports failed to reach the pre-1337 levels again; perhaps the number of consumers had also declined after the Black Death. Wend R. Childs's *Anglo-Castilian Trade in the Later Middle Ages, 1254–1485* presents a similar picture of dogged persistence on the part of merchants in the face of political interference and warfare.[41] Spain and England developed a complementary trade in the mid-fourteenth century. England exported her finished cloth to Spain and in turn imported wool, olive oil, and iron. The profitable trade with Spain also flagged in the fifteenth century, but Childs, in a nicely stated epilogue, cautions against taking this apparent drop in volume of trade as conclusive evidence of recession. She maintains that the loss was commensurate with the decline in population and may, therefore, be regarded more as a balanced adjustment to the new realities than as a recession.

One of the continual problems that hindered trade in the fourteenth and fifteenth centuries was that of bullion shortages and tampering with currency in order to meet the expenses of war. One of the very good chapters in Lloyd's book on wool trade is that on the currency problems of the early years of the war. Among a number of other historians who have given this problem prominence,

John H. Munro, in *Wool, Cloth and Gold: The Struggle for Bullion in the Burgundian Trade, 1340–1478*, has made it the major thrust for his interpretation.[42]

Turning from trade and urban centers to the effects of population loss on the economy and society of the countryside, one finds that the past decade has produced a number of studies of all facets of rural life, both pre- and postplague. Dorothea Oschinsky's edition of Walter Henley's treatise on estate management, along with other similar manuals of advice, has been a great contribution.[43] There has also been a series of monographs studying, over the centuries, the fortunes of various estates. Barbara Harvey, in *Westminster Abbey and Its Estates in the Middle Ages*; Eleanor Searle, in *Lordship and Community: Battle Abbey and Its Banlieu, 1066–1538*; Ian Kershaw, in *Bolton Priory: The Economy of a Northern Priory*; and F. D. H. DeBoulay, in *The Lordship of Canterbury*, all discuss ecclesiastical estates, whereas John Hatcher, in *Rural Economy and Society in the Duchy of Cornwall, 1300–1500*, studies lay estates.[44] Some generalizations about profitability and land use emerge from these studies. All show that in the thirteenth century there tended to be direct cultivation of the demesne because of the availability of cheap labor. As the pressure of population increased, before the Black Death, some land was rented. The real changes, however, took place at the end of the fourteenth century, when the greatly reduced population made it impossible for landlords to get cheap labor. Although they passed and tried to enforce the repressive Statute of Labourers, landlords could not keep wages to the pre-1349 level. Cultivation of the demesne became impossible on a large scale and by the 1420s, or earlier demesne was rented or leased in copyhold. Some landlords turned increasingly to grazing, which was considerably less labor intensive. The shift to rents rather than direct exploitation of the demesne had varying effects on the prosperity of the estates. Hatcher has found that the Cornish estates, with a diversified economy including boroughs and tin production, weathered the change. In general, however, Cornwall was atypical, for as Harvey's and other studies show, proceeds from the rents could not support the monastic houses in quite the luxury they had known. They reached stability by the fifteenth century, but at reduced standards.

The old saying "It is an ill wind that blows no good" is very apt in discussing the effects of population reduction on the peasantry. Two books by R. H. Hilton serve well for a discussion of their fortunes, although there are a number of other studies as well.[45] In *A Medieval Society: The West Midlands at the End of the Thirteenth Century*, Hilton sets the stage by describing the economic and social conditions of the peasantry in the late thirteenth century at the period of intensive demesne farming and before the calamities of the fourteenth century.[46] In his Ford Lectures of 1973, published under the title *The English Peasantry in the Later Middle Ages*, he demonstrates how the peasant's lot had changed dramatically.[47] Following the population decline, those peasants who survived famine and disease were, for the first time, able to sell their labor competitively and to rent lands readily. The fifteenth century was, therefore, a period of prosperity and new opportunities for the peasantry.

Both lords and lesser landholders began to shift to grazing and thus to enclosing the champion country in the fifteenth century. J. A. Yelling, in *Common Field and Enclosure in England*, 1450–1850, has found that while there was some enclosure of the champion country and conversion to grassland from 1450 to 1550, grain production still predominated.[48] After 1550 the conversions became more noticeable, and champion country actually began to change its character.

Before leaving the topic of economic history, some special features of recent research in the area should be noted. I have already remarked on Colin Platt's use of archaeological research for urban history. He has also used it creatively in an informative general work, *Medieval England: A Social History and Archaeology from the Conquest to 1600 A.D.*[49] Other historians have also made effective use of archaeology, as did Hilton in discussing peasant housing in *A Medieval Society*. The number of medieval excavations is growing, and the results are readily available in *Medieval Archaeology* and in a number of books such as Guy Beresford, *The Medieval Clay-land Village: Excavations at Glotho and Barton Blount*.[50] Careful scrutiny of the physical remains, attention to folklore, and historical geography have also added to the sophistication of the local history studies.[51] W. G. Hoskins was the leader in this field, and his work has influenced a number of other historians. J. R. Ravensdale, in *Liable to Floods: Village Lands Cope on the Edge of the Fens*, A.S. 450–1850, has written a fine study of this type, interweaving a number of sources of information.[52] Finally, a feature of recent research is that whole regions rather than just villages have been the subject of analysis. Thus Hatcher studied all of Cornwall, Hilton investigated the West Midlands, and H. E. Hallam, in *Settlement and Society*, studied the fenland region.[53] The regional studies point up the interconnections between the different classes of society and the lines of communication across the land. They also show how different one region was from another, depending on its original settlement patterns and its ecology.

Having looked at both demography and the economy, it is now appropriate to turn to the living conditions of the various strata in the society. A great deal of creative work has been done in the last decade on studying peasant communities.[54] From such studies we have learned much about economic matters, such as the land market, but also about community regulation, the experience of the plague and famines, and family life. W. O. Ault has done two very fine books on the bylaws communities developed to police themselves: *Open-field Husbandry and the Village Community: A Study of Agrarian By-laws in Medieval England* and *Open-field Farming in Medieval England: A Study of Village By-laws*.[55] Medieval English villages in the champion country appear in his books as little commonwealths that developed their own rules of economic and social control and their own strong village identities.

The work on village social dynamics has been pushed even further with village reconstruction studies based on manorial court rolls. This approach was pioneered by J. Ambrose Raftis and his students and is one of the major recent contributions to medieval social history. The groundwork for what has been called the "Toronto school" of village studies was laid in Raftis's book, *Tenure and Mobility: Studies in the Social History of a Medieval English Village*, and his two articles, "Social Structures in Five East Midland Villages," and "The Concentration of Responsibility in Five East Midland Villages."[56] The method is to reconstruct a village's population by grouping all references from manorial court rolls under family surnames. The work of Raftis and his students has inspired others to look again at these records for fresh insights into village dynamics. R. M. Smith has been working on Suffolk villages, and Zvi Razi, as I have already mentioned, used village reconstruction for a demographic study of a manner in Worcestershire.[57] These two scholars have been critical of Raftis's approach and have attempted to refine the methodology. The differences should not cloud the remarkable fact that their conclusions all point in the same direction. The next step in this type of study will be to link village records to external court rolls: royal, ecclesiastical, and county.

The studies by Raftis and others have shown that we can no longer assume that the only social distinctions were the legal ones between free and unfree peasants. Because the active land market and intermarriage blurred these legal categories, they were less meaningful than earlier historians assumed. More important in establishing status was the wealth of the family and its ability to hold the major offices in the village. Although the labels differ from study to study, there were clearly three basic groups in the village. The upper status group were families with substantial landholdings, long residence in the village, and control over such offices as juror, reeve, capital pledge, and ale taster. The second group had less land, held major village offices less frequently, but were long established village residents. The third group, cottagers, had little land and consequently had to rely on wages for part of their income; they never held village office.

The population decline following 1349 gradually altered the social structure of the village communities. For instance, Raftis found that in the village of Upwood in Huntingdonshire the mortality from the plague brought a profound shift in village politics. The old power structure broke up, and increasingly land was held by a few wealthy and powerful villagers, sometimes newcomers rather than members of the old village elite.[58] The same process occurred in Cuxham in Oxfordshire and in Holywell-cum-Needingworth.[59] As demesne lands were released for rent, the process accelerated. Those peasant proprietors who had families to work the land and money to rent new lands became the yeomen of the fifteenth century. They ceased to identify with the village community and instead took more interest in county politics. The old system of community social control began to break down, and enforcement of the by-laws began to die out as manorial courts lost their significance.

By the middle of the fifteenth century, serfdom in England was nearly dead. The court rolls show that peasants continued to pay their rents, but they allowed payment in lieu of work services to fall into arrears. Often manorial officials made little or no effort to collect what was due. Hilton has discussed the destruction of the old village community in his Ford lectures and also in *The Decline of Serfdom in England*.[60] There has been some debate in *Past and Present* about why French and English peasants experienced different fates in the fifteent century. In England the peasants left the land for wage work or accumulated more land to become yeomen. In France the peasantry held on to traditional family landholdings under the domination of the lord.[61] Alan Macfarlane, in *The Origins of English Individualism: The Family, Property, and Social Transition*, has argued that England was different from the Continent and did not have a classic peasantry.[62] Therefore, there was no major transition in social organization from the thirteenth to the seventeenth centuries. His is a provocative book with an unusual definition of peasantry; it deserves attention from medievalists working in peasant studies because of the questions he raises about manorial court sources.

One would expect that intensive work on the social dynamics of peasant communities would by now have produced a fresh interpretation of the revolt of 1381, but it has not yet appeared. There have been two new studies trying new approaches but using the already familiar facts. Michel Molat and Philippe Wolff, in *Ongles bleus, Jacques, et Ciompi: Les revolutions populaires en Europe aux XIVe et XVe siècles*, have experimented with the comparative approach but needed more space to draw meaningful conclusions.[63] Hilton, in *Bond Men Made Free: Medieval Peasant Movements and the English Rising of 1381*, has applied a Marxist interpretation to the revolt and the earlier resistance to seignorial control.[64] Some of the most interesting new information on the narrative may be found in E. B. Fryde's lengthy introduction to an edition of Charles Oman's *The Great Revolt of 1381*.[65] Perhaps one of the reasons that the revolt has attracted little study is that current research on fifteenth-century rural conditions makes the revolt appear more and more as simply one violent incident in an inexorable process of social change.

The long-standing debate over the gentry among Tudor historians is at last beginning to spur medievalists to investigate the origins of that social group. The economic fortunes of knights in the late thirteenth and early fourteenth centuries have been the subject of several studies. Postan has argued that the booming land market at the turn of the fourteenth century benefited the barons but was a disaster for knights who lost land. Hilton has found the same pattern for the West Midlands, as has P. R. Cross.[66] Edmund King, in *Peterborough Abbey, 1086– 1310: A Study in the Land Market*, has shown that, while some of the knightly class declined in fortunes, others rose.[67] Those who lost their status lacked sufficient income from lands to maintain their social position and keep themselves distinct from prosperous peasant neighbors or merchants who bought estates in the countryside. To make up for their economic deficiencies, they either mortgaged their lands and eventually lost them to creditors or sided with various nobles and political factions hoping for reward and, having chosen the wrong side, were ruined. Similar patterns may be seen in later centuries as well.[68] In contrast, Katherine S. Naughton, in *The Gentry of Bedfordshire in the Thirteenth and Four- teenth Centuries*, has found stability among the ranks of the gentry families.[69] Those names which disappeared did so, she found, because of the absence of male heirs.

By the late fourteenth century the gentry were becoming more numerous and politically powerful. Their ranks were swelled by newcomers who rose through trade or manufacture, profits of war, or service to kings and lords, even by very successful peasants. The Paston family, among the most studied of these rising gentry because of the rich archive of letters they left, are even more accessible now with Norman Davis's new edition, *Paston Letters and Papers of the Fifteenth Century*.[70] The open market for land and the renting of demesne gave this group economic opportunities for investment in the countryside. As money from war, trade, and law were invested in the countryside, the political power of the inves tors rose as well. These were the people who filled the Commons in the fourteenth century and extended its control over taxation. As Alan Harding shows in *The Law Courts of Medieval England*, the extension of a permanent status to the jus- tices of the peace gave the gentry a very tangible source of power in their commu- nities and in the counties.[71] The power of the gentry can be overemphasized, however, and it is worth remembering that they often owed their political posi- tions to an aristocratic patron.

Recent studies of the upper class, especially K. B. McFarlane's *The Nobility of Later Medieval England*, show that aristocrats were very successfully consolidat- ing their wealth and power in the late fourteenth and fifteenth centuries.[72] Rather than relying on feudal vassals, they increasingly surrounded themselves with spe- cialized household staffs drawn from gentry, clerks, lawyers, and soldiers and divided into financial officers, advisers, and fighting men. As the previously mentioned work on estate management indicates, the household (*familia*) could be very efficient. In matters of administering justice and securing rights over the subject tenants, the household was also indispensable; and in times of war or when the lord was traveling, the fighting component accompanied him. To dis- tinguish members of his household, the lord dressed them in his livery and provided them with a living and money. The political implications of livery and maintenance are discussed later.

The abandonment of direct cultivation of the demesne by the early fifteenth century implies that the nobility were experiencing some economic losses in the late fourteenth and fifteenth centuries. The class did become a smaller elite group by the end of the fourteenth century. J. R. Lander, in *The Crown and Nobility, 1450–1488*; Joel T. Rosenthal, in *Nobles and the Noble Life, 1295–1500*; and J. M. W. Bean, in *The Decline of English Feudalism*, have discussed this transition.[73] By the end of the fourteenth century the aristocrats of England were identified by their summons to Parliament. The size of the parliamentary peerage ranged from fifty to sixty families. The attrition rate of male heirs through war, execution, or natural causes was about 25 percent over twenty-five years, but the peerage was replenished by families rising through marriage, wealth, or service. Bean has examined the legal tools aristocratic families employed to keep inheritances intact.

In general, the elite maintained their wealth and even increased it during the late Middle Ages. Leading families acquired additional lands through marriage alliances and from royal gifts. While some may have made fortunes on the Hundred Years' War, more recent research suggests that many spent their own resources in war and often waited in vain for compensation from the king.[74] There are a number of recent studies on the aristocratic families that show their successes and failures both economically and politically.[75]

By the end of the fourteenth century the peers had been decisively transformed from feudal lords into aristocrats. They built large country residences designed for comfort rather than defense. They became patrons of the arts, book collectors, founders of colleges, and even wrote literary works themselves. Their clothing, entertainments, and feasts were costly and sumptuous. F. R. H. DuBoulay, in *An Age of Ambition*, has caught some of the flavor of their lives.[76] The nobles were equally magnificent in their charitable contributions and endowment of chantries, as Joel T. Rosenthal has shown in *The Purchase of Paradise*.[77]

Apart from the general study of social structures, medievalists have devoted relatively little attention to the family and women, areas very much in vogue in other periods. Many social historians have touched on the medieval family and its internal relationships in connection with village studies or biographies, and there have been some fine articles on inheritance patterns.[78] But we still do not know whether the late medieval family was extended or nuclear, what role servants played in households, and how children were regarded. Richard H. Helmholtz has written an excellent and very readable book on divorce and marriage as they appeared in the ecclesiastical court records in *Marriage Litigation in Medieval England*. But neither his study nor Michael Sheehan's outstanding articles can answer definitively whether the family unit was a close and cohesive one or one in which there was a very small emotional component.[79] The challenges of Ariès and Stone, therefore, have not been met.

The economic and legal position of women both within and outside marriage is beginning to receive attention. Eileen Power, of course, has had a long interest in the topic, and recently M. M. Poston has edited and published a series of her essays under the title *Medieval Women*.[80] There have been several collections of essays and some debate over the payment of merchet, a fee to the lord extracted from peasant women when they married.[81]

The antisocial behavior of medieval people has been studied as well as their social organization.[82] While by-laws helped to regulate daily contacts, tensions within villages often led to thefts and homicides. The court cases available for studying these matters are best treated quantitatively, since reading for interesting cases inevitably distorts the broader picture. James B. Given, in *Society and Homicide in Thirteenth-century England*, has done a quantitative analysis of eyre rolls that explores the relationship of homicide to types of inheritance in particular regions and to economic development of the thirteenth century.[83] He has dealt particularly well with the role of women both as victims and as accused. Barbara A. Hanawalt, in *Crime and Conflict in English Communities, 1300–1348*, deals with all felonies and surveys eight counties.[84] The evidence shows a society in which people from all walks of life turned readily to crime to supplement their incomes or to secure their dominance in power struggles. Rather than going short in the lean years of famine, Englishmen turned even more readily than usual to illegal acquisition of goods. The search for a historic Robin Hood goes without success, although a very good edition of the fifteenth-century poems, together with a fine historical introduction has been produced by R. B. Dobson and J. Taylor: *Rymes of Robyn Hood: An Introduction to the English Outlaw*.[85]

Political historians have been in a state of outright revolt against the old style of constitutional and administrative history, if one may judge from introductions to recent books and from book reviews. G. L. Harriss's review in the *English Historical Review* of Bertie Wilkinson's *The Later Middle Ages* sums up the difference of approach.[86] Harriss feels that an impasse has been reached between the old school and the new in doing political history. The old school looked at history primarily as a series of constitutional conflicts. Their generally Whiggish approach left out much political activity that did not reflect the progress of constitutional development and sometimes ignored or deemphasized setbacks. The current approach sees political change in a historical context that takes into consideration patronage systems, local power struggles, and marriage and dynastic policies.

K. B. McFarlane has been the inspiration for much of the new political history. While he was not a prolific publisher during his lifetime (he was too exacting a scholar to rush into print), he had a strong influence on his students and colleagues, and they have edited many of his unpublished essays since his death. McFarlane was particularly anxious to try to assess the human element in political events. In *The Nobility of Later Medieval England*, his Ford Lectures of 1953, he laid the groundwork for the recent discussion of the nobility and their role as political power brokers. He has dispelled the myth that the nobles of the late fourteenth and fifteenth centuries were "over-mighty" subjects who stood in the way of a constitutional reform that the Lancastrian kings, together with the Commons, could otherwise have brought about. He explored the organization and function of the barons' councils and the implications of the concept of "good lordship." The connection between the lord and members of his council or the gentry in his patronage sphere was just as honorable, he argued, as the earlier form of feudalism. Both systems were based on assumptions of benefits the lord would give to his clients in return for their support. In "good lordship," both sides were expected to honor their commitments in courts and on the battlefield.

His work has inspired a number of studies of the patronage system and the role of the aristocracy in government. One of the best of the new detailed studies has been that of Carole Rawcliffe, in *The Staffords*.[87] Her series of estate records are remarkably complete and enable her to suggest the hypothesis that the gentry who ran the estates were more concerned with preserving the dukes' network of systematic patronage than with making a profit. Two collections of essays have brought together much of the new material in a readily accessible form: *Patronage, Pedigree and Power in Later Medieval England* and *Fifteenth-century England: Studies in Politics and Society*.[88] The various articles address the problem of the extent to which the nobility used their councils and their patronage networks to influence the composition of Commons, interfere with the judicial system, and procure preferment in office for their clients. The work completed so far does not permit conclusive answers to these interesting problems, but what has been done shows great promise in explaining fifteenth-century local and national politics.

The fourteenth and fifteenth centuries were times of nearly continuous warfare, and the subject has produced some excellent studies. Michael Prestwick, in *War, Politics and Finance under Edward I*, overturns the earlier image of Edward as the "English Justinian."[89] He shows how Edward was able to use his nobility for military service; how he was forced to tax heavily in order to carry out extensive wars in Wales and Scotland; and how he got loans. Prestwick also analyzes the indirect costs of the war in such matters as alienating the country from the monarchy through heavy taxation, frittering away the lands of the Crown in gifts to the nobility in order to gain their cooperation, and allowing the disorder and lawlessness in the countryside to continue while Edward occupied himself with warfare.

Problems of recruitment and taxation for war and their effects on the populace have received attention for other periods as well. Herbert J. Hewitt, in *The Or-*

ganization of War under Edward III, 1338–1362, has done an excellent book on the armies of Edward: supplies and pillage, return of veterans from the wars, felons in the forces, free captains and mercenaries.[90] J. R. Maddicott, in *The English Peasantry and the Demands of the Crown, 1294–1341*, carries the work of Prestwick further into the fourteenth century.[91] He has found that in parts of England taxation and purveyances ruined the peasantry. Another book in this group is G. L. Harriss's *King, Parliament and Public Finance in Medieval England to 1369*.[92] The conclusion that one reaches from these studies is that the modern state with a centralized government consisting of a strong monarchy and an increasingly assertive Parliament was accomplished through oppressive taxation of the populace. This process, which Whig historians saw as a positive evolution to twentieth-century democracy, is now viewed as unreasonable demands on the part of the monarchy, sometimes with the complicity of Commons, on an overburdened peasantry.

Another by-product of prolonged warfare was the increased use of diplomacy in the later Middle Ages. The practice of day-to-day diplomacy, treaty negotiation, and the working out of terms of ransoms produced, as Maurice H. Keen has shown in *The Laws of War in the Later Middle Ages*, a rudimentary form of international law.[93] Because these negotiations occurred between monarchs or their representatives, international law strengthened the position of kings. The diplomatic history of the Hundred Years' War has also received close attention. John Ferguson has written about England's diplomatic attempts in the mid-fifteenth century so surround and isolate France, and J. J. N. Palmer has tried to show that the two countries wanted a lasting peace at the end of the fourteenth century but that Gascony revolted upon discovering that the price of a treaty would be to have John of Gaunt as lord.[94] The latter is an interesting thesis, but the evidence adduced is insufficient to bear its weight.

As McFarlane has made clear, the king governed with the aid of his nobility. They provided armies for his wars and diplomats for his negotiations. Even though they no longer were bounded by feudal service, they did much of the financing for war and became leaders of campaigns. The king would naturally turn for political and military advice to the peers on whom he was so reliant, who were related to him by ties of class and blood. One cannot say, however, that the alliance was always a congenial one or that the bonds of loyalty prevented the formation of factions.

Edward II experienced major insurrections and finally was deposed by his discontented nobles. Two recent books, Maddicott's on Thomas of Lancaster and Phillips's on Aylmer of Valence, analyze not only the wealth and estates of these nobles but their motivations for resisting Edward II. R. M. Haines, likewise, has investigated the career of Adam Orleton and his role in the killing of the king.[95] The biographies try to make the actions of these powerful nobles and bishop more comprehensible, but even a dispassionate history of their activities does not clear them of conspiracy charges. Natalie Fryde has written, in *The Tyranny and Fall of Edward II, 1321–1326*, about the Despenser period.[96] She makes some interesting points about Edward's greed leading him to make the Exchequer more efficient in his last years. More than most scholars, she has been able to make a medieval character, the younger Despenser, come alive.

For the most part, Edward III worked successfully with his nobility, but problems again became severe under Richard II. Various aspects of Richard II's reign and the activities of the Lords Appellant have received attention. An excellent survey of the relationship of Richard and his barons may be found in Anthony Tuck's *Richard II and the English Nobility*.[97] He gives credit to Richard for having a consistent policy aimed at concentration of power in the Crown. In pursuit of it, his harshness drew baronial hostility that led to his deposition.

The major focus for political historians in the last ten years has been on the relationship between kings and nobility in the fifteenth century. K. B. McFarlane had spent considerable effort investigating Henry IV, and in *Lancastrian Kings and Lollard Knights* there is an outline of his conclusions.[98] He presents Henry as a man of personal ambition, an opportunist rather than a monarch of vision and a firm constitutional sense. Because he was financially weak, Henry could not exercise the autocracy that Richard II had but instead had to compromise with Commons to get money. These accommodations left Commons with the right to demand accountability in financial matters, and this right became a precedent to be cited in later centuries. McFarlane was skeptical about interpretations stressing a special Lancastrian commitment to working with the Commons against the nobility. John L. Kirby, in his biography of Henry, however, upholds this older view.[99]

Henry V has remained safety a hero figure, but Henry VI has not been rehabilitated, nor has there even been a major biography of him, partly because he appears to be such an unappealing subject and partly because there are still relatively few administrative studies of his reign. His relations with his barons, however, have been the subject of revisionist interpretation. J. R. Lander has argued that the skirmishes of the Wars of the Roses were not as disruptive as once believed.[100] He points out that the Lancastrian kings enjoyed remarkable loyalty from the majority of the aristocracy, considering their ineptitude as rulers. Part of the complacency came from the nobles' disinterest in the reverses in France, where they were no longer making a profit on war in any case. They were being successful in increasing their wealth and power through marriage alliances and generous royal gifts of land to buy their loyalty.

The Yorkist period has received fairly extensive study because the administrative changes made during those years are now seen as the beginning of the "new monarchy." C. D. Ross has published a biography of Edward IV for the Methuen series on English monarchs that covers every aspect of his reign.[101] Ross concludes that Edward's worst mistake was the Woodville marriage alliance. Because of the numerous in-laws that had to be married and rewarded, Edward upset the marriage market of the nobility, and in the end the Woodvilles bear prime responsibility for the fall of his dynasty.

Historians now see the financial arrangements of Edward's reign as leading directly to the major changes in government after 1461 and into Henry VIII's reign. Edward IV promised that he would live on money generated from royal estates rather than ask Commons for a subsidy. By a series of accidents and some successes of policy, he was able to keep his promise. With the Hundred Years' War over and Edward's good fortune in staying out of renewed war, he did not need tax money. Where Henry VI had given away the confiscated estates of rebels, Edward IV kept them in the hands of the Crown. Bertram P. Wolffe has studied the role of the Crown lands in two books: *The Crown Lands, 1461 to 1536: An Aspect of Yorkist and Early Tudor Government* and *The Royal Demesne in English History: The Crown Estate in the Governance of the Realm from the Conquest to 1509.*[102] While he is perhaps overstating the case, that only with the Yorkists were the kings asked to "live on their own," the fact that they did brought about major changes in administration. Rather than using the cumbersome Exchequer system for keeping track of the demesne revenues, financial managers similar to a lord's council handled the revenues. The king's council became increasingly important in government.

If Commons played less of a role under the Yorkists, it had already matured into an institution with important rights and privileges. The Ford Lectures of J. G. Edwards provide a series of insightful reflections on the development of Parliament in the fourteenth century.[103] George Holmes has done a study of the Good Parliament that supports his overall conclusions for one instance.[104] Both these writers see the financial activity of the Commons as the most outstanding feature and the one that ultimately gave them their power. During the fourteenth century they experimented with various forms of taxation, settling on the subsidy—an assessed tax on movable property—as the only viable one. After the Revolt of 1381 they were understandably reluctant to try a poll tax again. But not only did they determine the type of tax; they also were finally able to make the king's officials accountable to them for the revenues raised from the Staple and subsidies.

Legal and administrative history have had a sporadic record of scholarly production in the last decade, perhaps because of the reaction against Tait. One hopes these areas will not continue to be neglected, for they are fundamental to understanding the changes that were taking place in the administration of justice. Two surveys have been published that should serve as pathbreakers, but as yet there have been no followers.[105] Two monographs have added to our knowledge of courts and procedures, but one is at the very beginning of the period and the other at the very end. Naomi D. Hurnard's *The King's Pardon for Homicide before A.D. 1307* is a comprehensive study based on careful analysis of existing court-roll information.[106] She finds varying standards of judgment applied in such matters as the age of minors, the culpability of mothers in infanticide, and the types of self-defense that were excusable. Marjorie Blatcher, in *The Court of King's Bench, 1450–1550: A Study in Self-help*, has shown how that court declined and common law itself sank in importance because the chancery courts became more efficient.[107] King's Bench was saved along with common law because of changes in procedure that made it more efficient. She also found that courts catered to those who were successful in pursuing their cases through using their influence—a long-standing tradition of self-help that Edward I bemoaned in his statutes.

Legal historians are chipping away at the procedural and administrative problems by following Maitland's lead and using information from the abundant plea rolls.[108] Some of the studies are flawed because the researchers have treated plea-roll cases like precedent cases. In doing so, they are reflecting their training as lawyers rather than as historians, who meticulously consider the nature of their sources. Cases selected from the plea rolls at random, or worse, because they look interesting, will provide a very unrepresentative picture of procedure.

Two aspects of the history of the church have received special attention in the last decade: the administration and politics of bishops and popular religion. Bishops and archbishops played an important role in the politics of the fourteenth and fifteenth centuries, and like magnates, they are apt subjects for biography. I have already mentioned that Bishop Orleton's career during the reign of Edward II has been studied, but so, too, have those of Thomas Arundel and Archbishop William Courtnay in the late fourteenth century, and Archbishop Henry Chichele in the fifteenth century.[109] Bishops of this rank remained wealthy and powerful, but some of the ecclesiastical estates, both bishoprics and monasteries, suffered some economic stagnation in the fifteenth century.[110]

Perhaps the most interesting work on the church is in the area of parish life and popular religion. Peter Heath's *The English Parish Clergy on the Eve of the Reformation* discusses the living conditions, training, and employment of the local clergy.[111] He has found that, very likely, more of the fifteenth-century clergy were educated than previously thought. Thus inadequacy of clerical preparation would not have caused demands for the reform of religion. The lay piety of the later Middle Ages was partly responsible for the support of educated clergy in the private chantries and guild chapels.[112] Popular expressions of religious fervor remained strong. Ronald C. Finucane, in *Miracles and Pilgrims: Popular Beliefs in Medieval England*, has written about the cult of saints.[113] He is overly concerned with examining the physical basis of miracle cures, but the book is a fine study of popular piety. On the local level, Dorothy Owen's *Church and Society in Medieval*

Lincolnshire reconstructs the differing religious experiences of bishops, parish priests, and parishioners.[114] Her discussion of the clergy's complicity in the folk beliefs of the populace is particularly effective, giving the full flavor of popular religion. This aspect is too often overlooked in discussions of medieval religion.

Wyclif's heresy continues to draw comment, although in general Lollardy has received more attention than the theology or political thinking of Wyclif himself. Gordon Leff has studied Wyclif in the context of the general problem of heresy in the later Middle Ages and in reference to the influence of universities. He emphasizes the fundamental criticisms of the church leveled by the Spiritual Franciscans and Wyclif's espousal of a realist, as opposed to a nominalist, metaphysics.[115] The study does not supplant J. A. Robson's earlier work that put Wyclif in the tradition of Thomas Bradwardine, Thomas Buckingham, and Richard FitzRalph. Both he and Beryl Smalley identified Wyclif's realist position with his idea of the invisible church and the importance of the authority of the Bible.[116]

Wyclif's political theory continues to intrigue historians because of his attack on the political power of the church. He has often appeared as an early advocate for the division of church and state, but modern research has found him to be a conservative in the tradition of the Gelasian theory of the two swords. His rebellion against the church has been seen as an outgrowth of disappointments in his own career ambitions.[117]

An active debate continues over the influence of Lollardy on English politics. The current consensus is that Lollardy had limited influence. In *Lancastrian Kings and Lollard Knights*, McFarlane found that support among the upper classes lessened after Oldcastle's unsuccessful revolt. Margaret Aston, in "Lollardy and Sedition, 1381–1431," has questioned the role of Lollardy as revolutionary ideology. She argues that Lollards were essentially conservatives in their views of royal authority and that the movement was, in any case, a theological rather than a social one.[118] Lollardy continued to be a religious force in England, but after the early fifteenth century and a few martyrdoms, it was less in evidence publicly.

William of Ockham challenged traditional intellectual truths just as Wyclif did religious ones. There is no question that his philosophical contribution represented a major departure from tradition, but there are still strong emotions about whether it was for the better. Those who feel that the thirteenth-century philosophy and theology, dominated by Aquinas, was the high point of the medieval synthesis continue to regard Ockham as a destroyer of the golden age of philosophy.[119] Other writers have been desirous of tracing the roots of modern scientific thinking and skepticism to Ockham's logic.[120] Gordon Leff, in *The Dissolution of the Medieval Outlook*, will not go so far as those who claim that Ockham was the first great modernist in philosophy, but he does argue that Ockham made substantial contributions in logic while remaining a traditionalist in outlook.[121]

Ockham's intellectual contribution encompassed religious disputes of the day centering on the charge of heresy against the Spiritual Franciscans and attacks on the papacy. A. S. McGrade, in *The Political Thought of William of Ockham: Personal and Institutional Principles*, argues that Ockham wanted the pope to de-emphasize the secular aspects of his office and become predominantly a spiritual leader, believing the state should take over the punishment of wrongdoers and heretics.[122] McGrade has emphasized Ockham's strong intolerance for heresy and his accusation against some popes of being heretics themselves.

Since printing was not a major component of medieval English culture in the late Middle Ages, Elizabeth Eisenstein's *The Printing Press as an Agent of Change: Communications and Cultural Transformations in Early-Modern Europe* will influence future discussion mostly on the wider issues it raises about the role of literacy in society.[123] V. J. Scattergood, in *Politics and Poetry in the Fifteenth Century*, has shown that verse was used in various public protests including workers' wage revolts.[124] That literacy was becoming more widespread may be guessed at from Nicholas Orme's *Education in the West of England, 1066–1548*.[125] He notes that there were a number of schools available to promote elementary literacy in the towns. The age span at such institutions was seven to twenty, and there was no distinction between reading schools and song schools. Teachers came from the group of trained clergy that Heath discussed. One can perhaps assume a larger literate public in the fifteenth century in view of the role that propaganda, particularly in historical writing, was beginning to play in establishing the legitimacy of new regimes.[126]

Society did not suddenly become literate and forget its oral traditions. Folklore has become increasingly important in our attempt to understand society in the later Middle Ages, especially for the experiences of those people who could not leave written remains.[127] Formal oral traditions also continued, and medieval historians should be aware of the excellent work that is being done in theater history, particularly in regard to the gild plays.[128]

A short review of the writings in late medieval English history over the past ten years necessarily leaves out much and reflects the particular interests of the reviewer. There are, fortunately, a number of bibliographical guides that can provide more complete listings. One should start with Margaret Hastings's essay "High History or Hack History: England in the Later Middle Ages," which appeared in *Changing Views of British History*. M. D. Knowles has written a survey of scholarship in medieval history, taking a sweeping overview from 1868 to 1968. There is also the Cambridge bibliographical handbook for the fifteenth century, compiled by DeLloyd Guth.[129] By far the greatest aid to researchers in the field is Edgar B. Graves, *A Bibliography of English History to 1485*.[130] In all fields of British history we are indebted to the Royal Historical Society for the *Annual Bibliography of British and Irish History* under the general editorship of G. R. Elton. One of the very valuable aspects of this bibliography is that it lists the separate articles in *festschriften* and collections of essays. It also lists articles and publications of local records and archaeological societies.

The theme of Karl F. Morrison's review of recent writing on medieval history for the American Historical Association was that there are no grand synthetic works but, rather, a series of specialized studies.[131] While this observation holds true for the study of late medieval England, there are legitimate reasons for this lack of the sweeping analysis. First, as historians we have become very particular about careful documentation of historical interpretations. We know much more about both the types of sources available and the range of questions that should be asked than did Stubbs or Tait. Historical research has become too sophisticated to accept simplistic generalizations, unicausal theories, or insufficiently documented assertions. This trend is all to the good.

As Margaret Hastings pointed out in her summing up of earlier writings on the late Middle Ages, research on the fourteenth and fifteenth centuries is still in an early stage compared to that of the twelfth and thirteenth centuries. There remain many gaps in our knowledge about fundamental aspects of the period. It is better to wait for these to be filled than venture too quickly into generalization.

But to say that generalized studies are premature is not to imply that the majority of historians of late medieval England have been working on minutiae of historical inquiry. Their research does not generally partake of the worst aspects of the fragmentation that Morrison observes in "medievalism." While there are pockets of historians working on trivial, or seemingly trivial, issues, in general they are not busy writing footnotes to hallowed works of the past. In part, they are spared this temptation because of the scarcity of such grand works to footnote. But also the approach of most scholars in the field, from political historians to demographers, is dedicated to taking a broader look at particular historical phenomena. The history of Parliament, for instance, is now studied in the context of economic history and patronage systems rather than simply as isolated incidents of confrontation or accommodation between kings, nobles, and Commons.

Medievalists writing since 1966 have not been reluctant to extend the boundaries of their studies. The old chronological barriers of 1307 and 1485 are disappearing. Archaeology has proved useful for economic, social, and even political history. Computers are not regarded as a threat to humanistic tradition but as a practical tool, like microfilm and Xerox, for furthering scholarly inquiry where appropriate. The supplementing of old with new methodologies means that in the future we will be able to use information heretofore literally buried in the earth or excluded because of the overwhelming bulk of the documents.

Are historians of the late Middle Ages still a melancholy group studying Huizinga's picturesque three Ds: death, decadence, and decline? My survey indicates a general optimistic trend in the recent interpretations of late medieval events. Although Postan has been identified with the pessimistic view of the postplague period, for the early fourteenth century, where his own research has been concentrated, he has argued that after 1325 the survivors of famine enjoyed a period of prosperity. While the fifteenth century was devastating for population growth, Hilton has seen the period as something of a golden age for the peasantry. Land was plentiful, wages high, and serfdom all but disappeared. Not until wages declined as population rose in the late fifteenth and sixteenth centuries did the laboring class again face deprivation and famine. Historians working on urban, industrial, and trade history are also cautiously optimistic. Export of raw wool fell, but production and sale of cloth increased—never to the old level of wool sales, but to a respectable level. Some urban centers declined, but others prospered, at least until the early modern period. Childs's cautious optimism may well sum up the current thinking. If trade was declining, the contraction was commensurate with the shrinking consumer market. In political history as well there is a feeling that the War of the Roses has been pictured as worse than it actually was and that the shiny "new monarchy" begins in the fifteenth century.

It appears from the research surveyed that the optimists will carry the day. But Huizinga and the demographers must not be pushed aside as distasteful naysayers. With population at best stable and held at a low level because of disease, death was ever present. A peasant might rise to yeoman only to find that he had no surviving sons to whom to pass on his proud new status. An Age of Ambition and rampant upward social mobility may seem like a fine thing to our democratic perspective, but such trends could be very disruptive in the fifteenth century as the traditional hierarchical society disintegrated. In sumptuary legislation, books of morals and manners, and literary pieces, people were urged to keep their proper places so that peace and good order could be maintained as they had been in the past. Even the increased power of Commons and its challenges to the king could appear to be threatening and dangerous to those caught up in the events, rather than yet another constitutional triumph. Certainly, the recent histories of war finance have shown that medieval warfare was hell, especially for noncombatants and taxpayers. Finally, some optimists are dangerously close to the Whiggish interpretations of history that they reject. Too often there is an unstated assumption that all transition periods are for the good because they are a step toward our modern world. If we are to follow McFarlane's injunction to try to understand medieval history from the viewpoint of participants, the pessimistic view must also have its day.

Because the questions have been so well posed by recent scholarship and tantalizing new evidence is within reach, the period of late medieval English history will continue to be an exciting area of research. While there may not be books presenting a grand theory to explain how the medieval world view changed, there will be comprehensive theses on such subjects as the role of aristocrats and patronage in the political system, the influence of demography on trade and serfdom, peasant social systems before and after the Black Death, and the structure of late medieval English families.

NOTES

1. Johan Huizinga, *The Waning of the Middle Ages* (reprint), New York, St. Martin's, 1942, 31.
2. William Stubbs, *The Constitutional History of England*, Oxford, Clarendon, 1878, 3:613.
3. Bernard S. Cohn, "History and Anthropology: The State of Play," *Comparative Studies in Society and History* 22, 1980: 198–221.
4. S. F. C. Milsom wrote the introduction for a new paperback edition of F. Pollock and F. W. Maitland, *The History of English Law*, Cambridge, the University Press, 1966.
5. May McKisack, *The Fourteenth Century*, Oxford, Clarendon, 1959.
6. E. F. Jacob, *The Fifteenth Century, 1399–1485*, Oxford, Clarendon, 1961.
7. Philippe Ariès, *Centuries of Childhood: A Social History of Family Life*, trans. Robert Baldick, New York, Random House, Vintage, 1972.
8. Lawrence Stone, *The Family, Sex and Marriage in England, 1500–1800*, New York: Harper & Row, 1977.
9. C. S. L. Davies, *Peace, Printing and Protestantism*, St. Albans, Paladin, 1977; D. M. Loades, *Politics and the Nation, 1450–1660*, London, Collins, Fonatana, 1974; Anthony Goodman, *A History of England from Edward II to James I*, London, Longman, 1977.
10. Pollock and Maitland, *English Law*, 1:2.
11. M. M. Postan, *Essays on Medieval Agriculture and General Problems of the Medieval Economy*, Cambridge, the University Press, 1973. A statement of the thesis may also be found in the articles in which it originally appeared: M. M. Postan, "Medieval Agrarian Society at Its Prime: England," in idem, ed., *The Cambridge Economic History of Europe*, 2d ed., Cambridge, the University Press, 1966 1:549–659, and "Some Economic Evidence of Declining Population in the Later Middle Ages," *EcHR*, 2d ser., 2, 1950: 221–246. J. Z. Titow has presented a very lucid summary plus much more information in *English Rural Society, 1200–1350*, Cambridge, the University Press, 1972.
12. J. Z. Titow, *Winchester Yields: A Study in Medieval Agricultural Productivity*, Cambridge, the University Press, 1972, deals not only with the influence of weather but with population and other factors.
13. Ian Kershaw, "The Great Famine and the Agrarian Crisis in England, 1315–1322," PP, no. 59, 1972: 3–50.
14. M. M. Postan and J. Z. Titow, "Heriots and Prices on Winchester Manors," *EcHR*, 2d ser., 11, 1959: 392–411.
15. Not all scholars have accepted this thesis. Edward Miller, "The English Economy in the Thirteenth Century: Implications of Recent Research," *PP*, no. 28, 1964: 21–48, and idem, "England in the Twelfth and Thirteenth Centuries: An Economic Contrast?" *EcHR*, 2d ser., 24, 1971: 1–14 have put the economic decline back into the thirteenth century. Barbara Harvey, "The Population Trend in England between 1300–1348," *TRSH*, 5th ser., 16, 1966: 23–42, and D. G. Watts, "A Model for the Early Fourteenth Century," *EcHR*, 2d ser., 20, 1967: 543–547, have argued that Postan's price evidence was inconclusive and that good harvests and a healthy land market continued up until the Black Death. W. C. Robinson, "Money, Population and Economic Change in Late Medieval Europe," *EcHR*, 2d ser., 12, 1959: 63–67 has argued that the influx of bullion rather than overpopulation caused price fluctuations in the first half of the century. Both economic evidence, such as shrinkage of land under civilization

and increased wages, and direct evidence of reduction in replacement rates argue for Postan's theory.

16. Zvi Razi, *Life, Marriage and Death in a Medieval Parish: Economy, Society and Demography in Halesowen, 1270–1400*, Cambridge, the University Press, 1980.

17. John Hatcher, *Plague, Population, and the English Economy, 1348–1530*, London, Macmillan, 1977.

18. J. C. Russell, *British Medieval Population*, Albuquerque, N.M., University of New Mexico Press, 1948; T. H. Hollingsworth, *Historical Demography*, Ithaca, N.Y., Cornell University Press, 1969; J. F. D. Shrewsbury, *A History of Bubonic Plagues in the British Isles, 1348–1670*, Cambridge, the University Press, 1970. See also J. M. W. Bean, "Plague, Population, and Economic Decline in England in the Later Middle Ages," *EcHR*, 2d ser., 15, 1962/1963): 423–437; Christopher Morris, "The Plague in Britain," *Historical Journal* 14, 1971: 205–215; J. C. Russell, "Effects of Pestilence and Plague, 1315–1385," *Comparative Studies in Society and History* 8, 1966: 464–473; Sylvia L. Thrupp, "Plague Effects in Medieval Europe," *Comparative Studies in Society and History* 8, 1966: 474–483; A. R. Bridbury, "The Black Death," EcHR, 2d ser., 26, 1973: 557–592.

19. Raymond Grew and Nicholas H. Steneck, eds., *Society and History: Essays by Sylvia Thrupp*, Ann Arbor, University of Michigan Press, 1977, contains both her published articles and a few previously unpublished pieces.

20. Robert S. Gottfried, *Epidemic Disease in Fifteenth-century England: The Medical Response and the Demographic Consequences*, New Brunswick, N.J., Rutgers University Press, 1978. He concludes that, although other diseases were present, plague remained the chief killer throughout the century.

21. Norman J. G. Pounds, *An Economic History of Modern Europe*, London, Longmans, Green, 1974. Information on population size and ways of deriving it may be found in a variety of places: A. R. H. Baker, "Changes in the Later Middle Ages," in H. C. Darby, ed., *New Historical Geography of England*, Cambridge, the University Press, 1977, 186–247; J. D. Chambers, *Population, Economy and Society in Pre-industrial England*, Oxford: the University Press, 1972; John Krause, "The Medieval Household: Large or Small," *EcHR*, 2d ser., 9, 1957: 420–432; Joel T. Rosenthal, "Medieval Longevity and the Secular Peerage, 1350–1550," *Population Studies* 27, 1973: 287–294; and E. A. Wrigley, *Population and History*, London: Weidenfeld & Nicolson, 1969. For a summary of the current literature, see R. S. Scofield, "Historical Demography: Some Possibilities and Some Limitations," *TRHS*, 5th ser., 22, 1971: 119–132.

22. K. J. Allison, M. W. Beresford, J. G. Hurst, et al., *The Deserted Villages of Northamptonshire*, Leicester, the University Press, 1966.

23. M. W. Beresford and J. G. Hurst, *Deserted Medieval Villages*, London: Lutterworth, 1971.

24. Postan, "Medieval Agrarian Society."

25. Edward Miller and John Hatcher, *Medieval England: Rural Society and Economy, 1086–1348*, London, Longmans, Green, 1978.

26. M. M. Postan, *Essays on Medieval Trade and Finance*, Cambridge, the University Press, 1973; idem, *The Medieval Economy and Society: An Economic History of Britain in the Middle Ages*, London, Weidenfeld & Nicolson, 1972.

27. Harry A. Miskimin, *The Economy of Early Renaissance Europe, 1300–1460*, Cambridge, the University Press, 1969.

28. A. R. Bridbury, *Economic Growth: England in the Later Middle Ages*, 2d ed., London, Harvester, 1975. A summary of current debates may be found in J. L. Bolton, *The Medieval Economy, 1150–1500*, London, Dent, 1980.

29. T. H. Lloyd, *The Movement of Wool Prices in Medieval England*, Cambridge, the University

Press, 1973; idem, *The English Wool Trade in the Middle Ages*, Cambridge, the University Press, 1977.

30. John Hatcher, *English Tin Production and Trade before 1500*, Oxford, Clarendon, 1973. For an anthropological theory on the role of wage labor in peasant mining communities, see Ian S. W. Blanchard, "The Miner and the Agricultural Community in Later Medieval England," *Agricultural History Review* 20, 1972: 93–106, and idem, "Labour Productivity and Work Psychology in the English Mining Industry, 1400–1600," *EcHR*, 2d ser., 31, 1978: 1–24.

31. J. Harvey, *Medieval Craftsmen*, London, Batsford, 1975; H. E. Jean Le Patourel, "Documentary Evidence and the Medieval Pottery Trade," *Medieval Archaeology* 12, 1968: 101–126.

32. Charles Phythian-Adams, "Urban Decay in Late Medieval England," in P. Adams and E. A. Wrigley, eds., *Towns in Societies: Essays in Economic History and Historical Sociology*, Cambridge, the University Press, 1978, 159–185. R. B. Dobson, "Urban Decline in Late Medieval England," *TRHS*, 5th ser., 27, 1977: 1–22. M. Palliser, "A Crisis in English Towns? The Case of York," *Northern History* 14, 1978: 108–125. P. Clark and P. Slack, eds., *Crisis and Order in English Towns, 1500–1700*, London, Routledge & Kegan Paul, 1972, would put the crisis as late as 1570.

33. Timothy Baker, *Medieval London*, New York: Praeger, 1970, has provided a popular account of the city. A. E. J. Hollaender and William Kellaway, eds., *Studies in London History Presented to Philip Edward Jones*, London, Hodder & Stoughton, 1969, is a collection of essays on London including administrative history as well as social and economic history. Caroline M. Barron, *The Medieval Guildhall in London*, London, Corporation of London, 1974; David J. Johnson, *Southwark and the City*, London, Corporation of London, 1974.

34. Colin Platt, London, *Medieval Southampton*, Routledge Kegan Paul, 1973.

35. Charles Phythian-Adams, *Desolation of a City: Coventry and the Urban Crisis of the Late Middle Ages*, Cambridge, the University Press, 1979.

36. Colin Platt, *The English Town*, London, Secker & Warburg, 1976.

37. Susan Reynolds, *An Introduction to the History of English Medieval Towns*, Oxford, Clarendon, 1977. There are now some further aids in helping with the study of towns: Maurice Beresford, *New Towns of the Middle Ages*, London, Lutterworth, 1967; M. D. Lobel, ed., *Historic Towns: Maps and Plans of Towns and Cities in the British Isles, with Historical Commentaries, from Earliest Times to Circa 1800*, 2 vol. to date, Oxford, Lovel Johns, 1969, 1972; Alan Everitt, ed., *Perspectives in English Urban History*, New York, Barnes & Noble, 1973.

38. J. C. Russell, *Medieval Regions and Their Cities*, Bloomington, Indiana University Press, 1972.

39. Ellen Wedemeyer, "Social Groupings at the Fair of St. Ives (1275–1302)," *Medieval Studies* 32, 1970: 27–59; A. F. Butcher, "The Origins of the Romney Freemen, 1433–1523," *EcHR*, 2d ser., 27, 1974: 16–27; J. P. Cooper, "The Social Distribution of Land and Men in England, 1436–1700," *EcHR*, 2d ser., 20, 1967: 419–440.

40. Margery Kirkbridge James, *Studies in the Medieval Wine Trade*, ed. E. M. Veale, Oxford, the University Press, 1971. Some of the essays in the book have been published previously, and some are new.

41. Wend R. Childs, *Anglo-Castilian Trade in the Later Middle Ages, 1254–1485*, Manchester, the University Press, 1978. See also Alison Hanham, "Foreign Exchange and the English Wool Merchant in the Late Fifteenth Century," *BIHR* 40, 1973: 160–175; D. C. Coleman and A. H. John, eds., *Trade, Government, and Economy in Pre-industrial England: Essays Presented to F. J. Fisher*, London, Weidenfeld & Nicolson, 1976; Elspeth M. Veale, *The English Fur Trade in the Later Middle Ages*, Oxford, Clarendon, 1966.

42. John H. Munro, *Wool, Cloth and Gold*, Toronto, University of Toronto Press, 1972;

Thomas F. Reddaway, "The King's Mint and Exchange in London, 1343–1543," *EHR* 82, 1967: 1–23; N. J. Mayhew, ed., *Edwardian Monetary Affairs*, Oxford, British Archaeological Reports, 1977. Also on trade and banking, see Richard W. Kaeuper, *Bankers to the Crown: The Riccardi of Lucca and Edward I*, Princeton, N.J., Princeton University Press, 1973.

43. Dorothea Oschinsky, ed., *Walter of Henley and Other Treatises on Estate Management and Accounting*, Oxford, Clarendon, 1971.

44. Barbara Harvey, *Westminster Abbey and Its Estates in the Middle Ages*, Oxford, Clarendon, 1977; Eleanor Searle, *Lordship and Community*, Toronto, Pontifical Institute of Medieval Studies, 1971; Ian Kershaw, *Bolton Priory*, London, Oxford University Press, 1973; F. D. H. DeBoulay, *The Lordship of Canterbury*, London, Thomas Nelson, 1966; John Hatcher, *Rural Economy and Society in the Duchy of Cornwall, 1300–1500*, Cambridge, the University Press, 1970. See also Colin Platt, *The Monastic Grange in Medieval England: A Reassessment*, London, Macmillan, 1969; P. F. Brandon, "Cereal Yields on the Sussex Estates of Battle Abbey during the Later Middle Ages," *EcHR*, 2d ser., 25, 1972: 403–20; M. M. Postan, "Investment in Medieval Agriculture," *JEcH* 17, 1967: 576–587; Barbara Harvey, "The Leasing of the Abbot of Westminster's Demesne in the Later Middle Ages," *EcHR*, 2d ser., 22, 1969: 17–27; Mavis Mate, "Prices in Early Fourteenth-century England: Causes and Consequences," *EcHR*, 2d ser., 28, 1975: 1–16; Robert Rees Davies, "Baronial Accounts, Incomes and Arrears in the Later Middle Ages," *EcHR*, 2d ser., 21, 1968: 211–219; A. J. Pollard, "Estate Management in the Later Middle Ages: The Talbots and Whitchurch," *EcHR*, 2d ser., 25, 1972: 553–556. There are further articles in local history journals.

45. Individual village studies, discussed later, contain a great deal of information on the changes. Barbara Dodwell, "Holdings and Inheritance in Medieval East Anglia," *EcHR*, 2d ser., 20, 1967: 63–66; Christopher Dyer, "A Redistribution of Incomes in Fifteenth-century England," *PP*, no. 39, 1968: 11–33; Barbara J. Harris, "Landlords and Tenants in the Later Middle Ages: The Buckingham Estates," *PP*, no. 43, 1969: 146–150; Douglas C. North and Robert P. Thomas, "The Rise and Fall of the Manorial System: A Theoretical Model," *JEcH* 31, 1971: 777–803. A reply to the North and Thomas article by Andrew Jones is in *JEcH* 32, 1972: 934–944; see also idem, "Land and People at Leighton Buzzard in the Later Fifteenth Century," *EcHR*, 2d ser., 25, 1972: 18–27.

46. R. H. Hilton, *A Medieval Society: The West Midlands at the End of the Thirteenth Century*, New York, Wiley, 1966.

47. R. H. Hilton, *The English Peasantry in the Late Middle Ages*, Oxford, Clarendon, 1974.

48. J. A. Yelling, *Common Field and Enclosure in England, 1450–1850*, London, Macmillan, 1977.

49. Colin Platt, *A Social History and Archaeology from the Conquest to 1600 A.D.*, New York: Scribner's, 1978.

50. Guy Beresford, *The Medieval Clay-land Village: Excavations at Glotho and Barton Blount*, Society for Medieval Archaeology, ser. 6, London, 1975.

51. There are some further publications to aid in this type of research: Brian K. Roberts, *Rural Settlement in Britain*, Folkstone, Dawson, Archon, 1977; F. W. B. Charles, *Medieval Cruck Building and Its Derivatives*, London, Society for Medieval Archaeology, 1967; M. J. Swanton, ed., *Studies in Medieval Domestic Architecture*, London, Royal Archaeological Institute Monographs, 1975; Eric Mercer, *English Vernacular Houses*, London, Her Majesty's Stationery Office, 1975; A. R. H. Baker and R. A. Butlin, *Studies of Field Systems in the British Isles*, Cambridge, the University Press, 1973; H. C. Darby, ed., *New Historical Geography of England*, Cambridge, the University Press, 1973.

52. J. R. Ravensdale, *Liable to Floods: Village Lands Cope on the Edge of the Fens*, Cambridge, the University Press, 1974.

53. H. E. Hallam, *Settlement and Society*, Cambridge, the University Press, 1967.

54. There are many village studies, and many more will appear in the future. See, for instance, Albert C. Chibnall, *Sherington: Fiefs and Fields of a Buckinghamshire Village*, Cambridge, the University Press, 1965; idem, *Beyond Sherington: The Early History of the Region of Buckinghamshire Lying to the North-east of Newport Pagnell*, Chichester, Phillimore, 1979; Margaret Spufford, *A Cambridgeshire Community: Chippenham from Settlement to Enclosure*, Occasional Papers, no. 20, Leicester, the University Press, 1965.

55. W. O. Ault, *Open-field Husbandry and the Village Community: A Study of Agrarian By-laws in Medieval England*, Philadelphia, American Philosophical Society, 1965; idem, *Open-field Farming in Medieval England: A Study of Village By-laws*, London, Allen & Unwin, 1973.

56. J. Ambrose Raftis, *Tenure and Mobility: Studies in the Social History of a Medieval English Village*, Toronto, Pontifical Institute of Medieval Studies, 1964; idem, "Social Structures in Five East Midland Villages," *EcHR*, 2nd ser., 18, 1965: 83–100; idem, "The Concentration of Responsibility in Five East Midland Villages," *Mediaeval Studies* 28, 1966: 92–118. For other studies, see Raftis's recent book, *Warboys: Two Hundred Years in the Life of an English Medieval Village*, Toronto, Pontifical Institute of Medieval Studies, 1974, and those of his students: Edwin B. DeWindt, *Land and People in Holywell-cum-Needingworth*, Toronto, Pontifical Institute of Medieval Studies, 1974; Edward Britton, *The Community of the Vill*, Toronto, Macmillan of Canada, 1977. The latter two books deal with land tenure, mobility, family, and village dynamics in the late thirteenth and fourteenth centuries. All three monographs required the painstaking task of village reconstitution. See also Anne DeWindt, "Peasant Power Structures in Fourteenth-century King's Ripton," *Medieval Studies* 38, 1976: 236–267. Barbara A. Hanawalt, "Community Conflict and Social Control: Crime in the Ramsey Abbey Villages," *Mediaeval Studies* 39, 1977: 402–423, combines material from the Regional Data Bank with criminal court records.

57. R. M. Smith, "Kin and Neighbors in a Thirteenth-century Suffolk Community," *Journal of Family History* 4, 1979: 219–256. See Zvi Razi, "Review Article: The Toronto School's Reconstitution of Medieval Peasant Society, A Critical View," *PP*, no. 85, 1980: 141–157; and his book on Halesowen, idem, *Life, Marriage and Death*.

58. J. Ambrose Raftis, "Changes in an English Village after the Black Death," *Mediaeval Studies* 29, 1967: 158–177.

59. P. D. A. Harvey, *A Medieval Oxfordshire Village, Cuxham 1240–1400*, Oxford, Clarendon, 1965; DeWindt, *Holywell-cum-Needingworth*.

60. R. H. Hilton, *The Decline of Serfdom in England*, Studies in Economic History, London, 1969.

61. Robert Brenner, "Agrarian Class Structure and Economic Development in Pre-industrial Europe," *PP*, no. 70, 1976: 30–74, has taken a Marxist point of view, arguing that demography did not play a substantial role but peasant capitalism did. The demographic explanation, the "neo-Malthusian" position, was defended by Emmanuel LeRoy Ladurie, "A Reply to Professor Brenner," *PP*, no. 79, 1978: 55–59. See also Guy Bois, "Against the Neo-Malthusian Orthodoxy," ibid., 60–69, and Arnost Klima, "Symposium: Agrarian Class Structure and Economic Development in Pre-industrial Europe," *PP*, no. 85, 1979: 49–66.

62. Alan MacFarlane, *The Origins of English Individualism: The Family, Property, and Social Transition*, Cambridge, the University Press, 1978.

63. Michel Molat and Philippe Wolff, *Ongles bleus, Jacques, et Ciompi: Les revolutions populaires en Europe aux XIVᵉ et XVᵉ siècles*, Paris, Calmann-Lèvy, 1970.

64. R. H. Hilton, *Bond Men Made Free: Medieval Peasant Movements and the English Rising of 1381*, London, Temple Smith, 1973. In general Marxist theory has played very little role in analysis of late medieval social or political history.

65. E. B. Fryde, "Introduction," in Charles Oman, The Great Revolt of 1381, Oxford, Claren-
    don, 1969. R. B. Dobson, ed., *The Peasants' Revolt of 1381*, London, Macmillan, 1970, is a
    useful collection of documents. See also Eleanor Searle and Robert Burghart, "The Defense of
    England and the Peasants' Revolt," *Viator* 3, 1972: 365–388 and R. H. Tillotson, "Peasant
    Unrest in the England of Richard II: Some Evidence from Royal Records," *Historical Studies*,
    16, 1974: 6–21.
66. P. R. Cross, "Sir Geoffrey de Langley and the Crisis of the Knightly Class in Thirteenth-
    century England," *PP*, no. 68, 1975: 3–37; see also J. E. Newman, "Greater and Lesser
    Landlords and Parochial Patronage: Yorkshire in the Thirteenth Century," *EHR* 92, 1977:
    280–308.
67. Edmund King, *Peterborough Abbey, 1086–1310: A Study in the Land Market*, Cambridge, the
    University Press, 1973; see also idem, "Large and Small Landowners in Thirteenth-century
    England," *PP*, no. 47, 1970: 26–50.
68. N. Denholm-Young, *The Country Gentry in the Fourteenth Century*, Oxford, Clarendon, 1969;
    Scott L. Waugh, "The Profits of Violence: The Minor Gentry in the Rebellion of 1321–22,"
    Speculum 52 1977: 843–869. K. B. McFarlane's books on the nobility, discussed later, should
    also be consulted. See Sally Harvey, "The Knight and the Knight's Fee in England," *PP*,
    no. 49, 1970: 3–43. G. E. Mingay, *The Gentry: The Rise and Fall of a Ruling Class*, New
    York, Longmans, Green, 1976, extends his summary back into the fifteenth century.
69. Katherine S. Naughton, *The Gentry of Bedfordshire in the Thirteenth and Fourteenth Centuries*,
    Occasional Papers, 3rd ser., no. 2, Leicester, the University Press, 1976.
70. Norman Davis, *Paston Letters and Papers of the Fifteenth Century*, 2 vols., Oxford, Clarendon,
    1971, 1976. See also Alison Hanham, ed., *The Cely Letters, 1472–1488*, London, Early En-
    glish Text Society, 1975.
71. Alan Harding, *The Law Courts of Medieval England*, New York, Barnes & Noble, 1973.
72. K. B. McFarlane, *The Nobility of Later Medieval England*, Oxford, Clarendon, 1973.
73. J. R. Lander, *The Crown and Nobility, 1450–1488*, Montreal, McGill-Queen's University
    Press, 1976; Joel T. Rosenthal, *Nobles and the Noble Life, 1295–1500*, New York, Barnes &
    Noble, 1976; J. M. W. Bean, *The Decline of English Feudalism*, Manchester, the University
    Press, 1968.
74. D. Hay, "The Division of Spoils of War in Fourteenth-century England," *TRHS*, 5th ser., 4,
    1954: 91–109; K. B. McFarlane, "England and the Hundred Years' War," *PP*, no. 22,
    1962: 3–13; M. M. Postan, "The Cost of the Hundred Years' War," *PP*, no. 27, 1964:
    34–53. This debate has remained without a conclusion, but evidence on individual nobles in-
    dicates that they spent a considerable amount of their own revenue on the war.
75. J. R. Maddicott, *Thomas Lancaster, 1307–1322*, Oxford, Clarendon, 1970; J. R. S. Phil-
    lips, *Aymer de Valence, Earl of Pembroke, 1307–1324*, Oxford, Clarendon, 1972; Carole
    Rawcliffe, *The Staffords, Earls of Stafford and Dukes of Buckingham, 1394–1521*, Cambridge,
    the University Press, 1978. R. R. Davies, *Lordship and Society in the March of Wales,
    1282–1400*, Oxford, Clarendon, 1978, has shown how different lordship was in Wales,
    where local custom gave the lords considerably more control over their peasantry and where the
    king's control was limited.
76. F. R. H. DuBoulay, *An Age of Ambition*, London, Nelson, 1970.
77. Joel T. Rosenthal, *The Purchase of Paradise*, London, Routledge & Kegan Paul, 1970.
78. Dodwell, "Holdings and Inheritance"; Rosamond J. Faith, "Peasant Families and Inheritance
    Customs in Medieval England," *Agricultural History Review* 14, 1966: 77–95; C. Howel,
    "Peasant Inheritance Customs in the Midlands, 1280–1700," in J. Goody, J. Thirsk, and
    E. P. Thompson, eds., *Family and Inheritance: Rural Society in Western Europe*, Cambridge,
    the University Press, 1976, 112–155; Ivy Pinchbeck and Margaret Hewitt, *Children in En-

glish Society, 2 vols., London, Routledge & Kegan Paul, 1969, 1973; Barbara A. Hanawalt, "Childrearing among the Lower Classes of Late Medieval England," *Journal of Interdisciplinary History* 8, 1977: 1–22; Richard H. Helmholtz, "Infanticide in the Province of Canterbury during the Fifteenth Century," *History of Childhood Quarterly* 2, 1975: 382–389.

79. Richard H. Helmholtz, *Marriage Litigation in Medieval England*, Cambridge, the University Press, 1974; Michael M. Sheehan, "The Formation and Stability of Marriage in the Fourteenth Century: Evidence of an Ely Register," *Mediaeval Studies* 33, 1971: 228–264; idem, "Marriage Theory and Practice in the Conciliar Legislation and Diocesan Statutes of Medieval England," *Mediaeval Studies* 40, 1978: 408–460. See also Sue Sheridan Walker, "The Marrying of Feudal Wards in Medieval England," *Studies in Medieval Culture* 4, 1974: 209–233; Ann S. Haskell, "The Paston Women on Marriage in Fifteenth-century England," *Viator* 4, 1973: 459–472.

80. M. M. Postan, *Medieval Women*, Cambridge, the University Press, 1975. See also Susan Moser Stuart, ed., *Women in the Middle Ages*, Philadelphia, University of Pennsylvania Press, 1976; Derek Baker, ed., *Medieval Women: Dedicated and Presented to Professor Rosalind M. T. Hill*, Oxford, Clarendon, 1978.

81. J. Schammell, "Freedom and Marriage in Medieval England," *EcHR*, 2d ser., 27, 1974: 523–537; idem, "Wife-Rents and Merchet," *EcHR*, 2d ser., 29, 1976: 487–490; Eleanor Searle, "Freedom and Marriage in Medieval England: An Alternative Hypothesis," ibid., 482–486; idem, "Seigneurial Control of Women's Marriage: The Antecedents and Function of Merchet in England," *PP*, no. 82, 1979: 3–42. Schammell has argued that the merchet was a tax on people, whereas Searle has suggested that it was a tax on chattels. Another issue is the extent to which the lords interfered with peasant marriages.

82. J. G. Bellamy, *Crime and Public Order in the Later Middle Ages*, London, Routledge & Kegan Paul, 1973, has written mostly about upper-class criminals. See also Carl Hammer, Jr., "Patterns of Homicide in a Medieval University Town: Fourteenth-century Oxford," *PP*, no. 78, 1978: 1–23; R. B. Pugh, "Some Reflections of a Medieval Criminologist," *Proceedings of the British Academy* 59, 1973. Pugh's book, *Imprisonment in Medieval England*, Cambridge, the University Press, 1968, discusses the administration of medieval prisons and shows that their grim reputation was deserved.

83. James B. Given, *Society and Homicide in Thirteenth-century England*, Palo Alto, Calif., Stanford University Press, 1977.

84. Barbara A. Hanawalt, *Crime and Conflict in English Communities, 1300–1348*, Cambridge, Mass., Harvard University Press, 1979.

85. R. B. Dobson and J. Taylor, *Rymes of Robinhood*, London, Heinemann, 1976.

86. G. L. Harriss, Review, *EHR* 86, 1971: 122–125; Bertie Wilkinson, *The Later Middle Ages*, London, Longmans, Green, 1969. See Wilkinson's eloquent reply to the new political history: "The Later Middle Ages in England: Continuity, Transitions, or Decline?" *Transactions of the Royal Society of Canada* 11, 1973: 243–254.

87. See also John G. Edwards, "The Huntingdonshire Parliamentary Elections of 1450," in T. A. Sandquist and Michael R. Powicke, eds., *Essays in Medieval History Presented to Bertie Wilkinson*, Toronto, University of Toronto Press, 1969, 383–395; Patricia Jalland, "The Influence of the Aristocracy on Shire Elections in the North of England, 1450–1470," *Speculum* 47, 1972: 483–507; K. B. McFarlane, "Parliament and 'Bastard Feudalism,'" in R. W. Southern, ed., *Essays in Medieval History*, London, Macmillan, 1968, 240–263; Alan Rogers, "Parliamentary Elections in Grimsby in the Fifteenth Century," *BIHR* 45, 1973: 95–101; J. R. Maddicott, "The County Community and the Making of Public Opinion in Fourteenth-century England," *TRHS*, 5th ser., 29, 1978: 27–43.

88. Charles Ross, ed., *Patronage, Pedigree and Power in Later Medieval England*, London, Sutton,

1979; S. B. Chrimes, C. D. Ross, and R. A. Griffiths, eds., *Fifteenth-century England: Studies in Politics and Society*, Manchester, the University Press, 1972.

89. Michael Prestwick, *War, Politics and Finance under Edward I*, Totowa, N.J., Rowman & Littlefield, 1972.

90. Herbert J. Hewitt, *The Organization of War under Edward III, 1338–1362*, Manchester, the University Press, 1966.

91. J. R. Maddicott, *The English Peasantry and the Demands of the Crown, 1294–1341*, Past and Present Society Supplements, vol. 7, Oxford, 1975.

92. G. L. Harriss, *King, Parliament and Public Finance in Medieval England to 1369*, Oxford, Clarendon, 1975.

93. Maurice H. Keen, *The Laws of War in the Later Middle Ages*, London, Routledge and Kegan Paul, 1965.

94. John Ferguson, *English Diplomacy, 1422–1461*, Oxford, Clarendon, 1972; J. J. N. Palmer, *England, France and Christendom, 1377–1399*, Chapel Hill, University of North Carolina Press, 1972. For more on the Hundred Years' War, see Malcolm G. A. Vale, *English Gascon, 1399–1453*, Oxford, Clarendon, 1970; Kenneth Fowler, ed., *The Hundred Years' War*, London, Macmillan, 1971; Christopher Lloyd, *The British Seamen, 1200–1860: A Social Survey*, London, Rutherford, 1968; Philip Warner, *Sieges of the Middle Ages, 1066–1485*, London, Bell, 1968; C. F. Richmond, "English Naval Power in the Fifteenth Century," *History* 52, 1967: 1–15; Timothy J. Runyan, "Ships and Mariners in Later Medieval England," *JBS* 16, 1977, 1–17; James W. Sherborne, "The English Navy: Shipping and Manpower 1369–1389," *PP*, no. 37, 1967: 1–17; John Barnie, *War in Medieval English Society: Social Values in the Hundred Years' War, 1337–1339*, Ithaca, N.Y., Cornell University Press, 1974; C. T. Allmand, ed., *War, Literature and Politics in the Late Middle Ages: Essays in Honour of G. W. Coopland*, Liverpool, the University Press, 1976. The last-mentioned has a series of essays that discuss the decay of feudal armies and their replacement with foot soldiers.

95. R. M. Haines, *The Church and Politics in Fourteenth-century England: The Career of Adam Orleton, c. 1275–1345*, Cambridge, the University Press, 1978.

96. Natalie Fryde, *The Tyranny and Fall of Edward II, 1321–1326*, Cambridge, the University Press, 1979. For a short survey, see Michael Prestwick, *The Three Edwards: War and State in England, 1272–1377*, New York, St. Martin's, 1980.

97. Anthony Tuck, *Richard II and the English Nobility*, London, Arnold, 1973. See also Anthony Goodman, *The Loyal Conspiracy: The Lords Appellant under Richard II*, London, Routledge & Kegan Paul, 1971; Richard H. Jones, *Royal Policy of Richard II: Absolutism in the Later Middle Ages*, Oxford, Blackwell, 1968; Caroline M. Barron, "The Tyranny of Richard II," *BIHR* 41, 1968: 1–18; F. R. H. DuBoulay and Caroline M. Barron, eds., *The Reign of Richard II: Essays in Honour of May McKissack*, London, Athlone, 1971. Gervase Mathew, *The Court of Richard II*, New York, Norton, 1968, writes on the cultural activities and literary patronage of the court. Louisa D. Duls, *Richard II in the Early Chronicles*, The Hague: Mouton, 1975, tries to find the origins of the sixteenth-century views of Richard.

98. K. B. McFarlane, *Lancastrian Kings and Lollard Knights*, Oxford, Clarendon, 1972.

99. John L. Kirby, *Henry IV of England*, London, Constable, 1970.

100. J. R. Lander, *Crown and Nobility*, London, Hutchinson, 1969; idem, *Conflict and Stability in Fifteenth-century England*, London, Hutchinson, 1969. See also essays in Chrimes, Ross, and Griffiths, eds., *Fifteenth-century England*; Bertie Wilkinson, "Fact and Fancy in Fifteenth-century English History," *Speculum* 42, 1967: 837–892; Ralph A. Griffiths, "Local Rivalries and National Politics: The Percies, the Nevilles, and the Duke of Exeter, 1452–1455," *Speculum* 43, 1968: 589–632; Alfred L. Brown, "The King's Councillors in Fifteenth Century England," *TRHS*, 5th ser., 19, 1969: 94–118; Roger Virgoe, "The Composition of the

King's Council, 1437–1461," *BIHR* 43, 1970: 134–160; William Huse Dunham, Jr. and Charles T. Wood, "The Right to Rule in England: Depositions and the Kingdom's Authority, 1327–1485," *AHR* 81, 1976: 838–861.

101. Charles D. Ross, *Edward IV*, London, Methuen, 1974. See also D. A. L. Morgan, "The King's Affinity in the Polity of Yorkist England," *TRHS*, 5th ser., 23, 1972: 1–25. There are a variety of other articles on the topic.

102. Bertram P. Wolffe, *The Crown Lands, 1461 to 1536: An Aspect of Yorkist and Early Tudor Government*, New York, Barnes & Noble, 1970; idem, *The Royal Demesne in English History: The Crown Estate in the Governance of the Realm from Conquest to 1509*. London, Allan & Unwin, 1971.

103. J. G. Edwards, *The Second Century of the English Parliament*, ed. J. A. Roskell, Oxford, Clarendon, 1979. G. O. Sayles, *The King's Parliament of England*, London, Arnold, 1975, has only one brief chapter on the fourteenth and fifteenth centuries.

104. George Holmes, *The Good Parliament*, Oxford, Clarendon, 1975.

105. S. F. C. Milsom, *Historical Foundations of the Common Law*, London, Butterworth, 1969; Alan Harding, *A Social History of English Law*, Baltimore, Penguin, 1966.

106. Naomi D. Hurnard, *The King's Pardon for Homicide before A.D. 1307*, Oxford, Clarendon, 1969.

107. Marjorie Blatcher, *The Court of King's Bench, 1450–1550: A Study in Self-help*, London, Athlone, 1978.

108. There are a number of specialized articles; These are representative of the type of research being done: Margaret E. Avery, "An Evaluation of the Effectiveness of the Court of Chancery under the Lancastrian Kings," *LQR* 86, 1970: 84–97; Thomas A. Green, "Societal Concepts of Criminal Liability for Homicide in Medieval England," *Speculum* 47, 1972: 669–694; J. M. Kaye, "The Early History of Murder and Manslaughter," *LQR* 83, 1967: 365–395; S. F. C. Milsom, "Account Stated in the Action of Debt," *LQR* 82, 1966: 534–545. See also John G. Bellamy, *The Law of Treason in England in the Later Middle Ages*, Cambridge, the University Press, 1970. The research on ecclesiastical law has been particularly fine and has already been discussed under the topic of women and family history. The social histories of crime also have information on judicial procedure.

109. Joseph Damus, *William Courtenay, Archbishop of Canterbury*, University Park, Pennsylvania State University Press, 1966, a study also very valuable for studying the suppression of Wyclif; Margaret Aston, *Thomas Arundel: A Study of the Church in the Reign of Richard II*, Oxford, Clarendon, 1967; Joel T. Rosenthal, *The Training of an Elite Group: English Bishops in the Fifteenth Century*, Philadelphia, American Philosophical Society, 1970.

110. R. M. Haines, *The Administration of the Diocese of Worcester in the First Half of the Fourteenth Century*, London, Church Historical Society, 1965; R. B. Dobson, *Durham Priory, 1400–1450*, Cambridge, the University Press, 1973.

111. Peter Heath, *The English Parish Clergy on the Eve of the Reformation*, London: Routledge & Kegan Paul, 1969.

112. K. L. Wood-Legh, *Perpetual Chantries in Britain*, Cambridge, the University Press, 1965; William R. Jones, "English Religious Brotherhoods and Medieval Lay Piety: The Inquiry of 1388–89," *History* 36, 1974: 646–659; Warren O. Ault, "The Village Church and the Village Community in Medieval England," *Speculum* 45, 1970: 197–215.

113. Ronald C. Finucane, *Miracles and Pilgrims: Popular Beliefs in Medieval England*, Totowa, N.J., Roman & Littlefield, 1977. See also Donald J. Hall, *English Medieval Pilgrimage*, London, Routledge & Kegan Paul, 1966.

114. Dorothy Owen, *Church and Society in Medieval Lincolnshire*, Lincoln, Lincolnshire Local History Committee, 1971.

115. Gordon Leff, *Heresy in the Later Middle Ages*, 2 vols., Manchester, the University Press, 1969; see also his essay, "Heresy and the Decline of the Middle Ages," *PP*, no. 20, 1969: 36–51. His other works have also touched on the problem of Wyclif and other heresies in England: *Paris and Oxford in the Thirteenth and Fourteenth centuries*, New York, Wiley, 1968; *The Dissolution of the Medieval Outlook: An Essay on Intellectual and Spiritual Change in the Fourteenth Century*, New York, Harper & Row, 1976.

116. J. A. Robson, *Wycliff and the Oxford Schools*, Cambridge, 1961; Beryl Smalley, "The Bible and Eternity: John Wyclif's Dilemma," *Journal of the Warburg and Courtauld Institutes* 27, 1965: 73–89.

117. L. J. Daly, "Wyclif's Political Theory: A Century of Study," *Medievalia et Humanistica* 4, 1973: 177–187, provides a convenient summary. See also M. J. Wilks, "The Early Oxford Wyclif: Papalist or Nominalist?" *Studies in Church History* 5, 1969: 69–99; idem, "Predestination, Property and Power: Wyclif's Theory of Domination and Grace," *Studies in Church History* 2, 1965: 220–236.

118. Margaret Aston, "Lollardy and Sedition, 1381–1431," *PP*, no. 17, 1973: 1–40. See also Ann Hudson, "The Examination of Lollards," *BIHR* 46, 1973: 145–159.

119. Armand A. Maurer, *Medieval Philosophy*, New York, Random House, 1975.

120. Ernest A. Moody, *Studies in Medieval Philosophy, Science and Logic*, Berkeley and Los Angeles, University of California Press, 1975; James A. Weisheipl, "Ockham and Some Mertonians," *Mediaeval Studies* 30, 1968: 163–213. History of science has been an active field of research over the decade. See, for instance, Edward Grant, *Physical Science in the Middle Ages*, New York, Wiley, 1971.

121. See also Gordon Leff, *William of Ockham: The Metamorphosis of Scholastic Discourse*, Totowa, N.J., Roman & Littlefield, 1975.

122. A. S. McGrade, *The Political Thought of William of Ockham: Personal and Institutional Principles*, Cambridge, the University Press, 1974.

123. Elizabeth Eisenstein, *The Printing Press as an Agent of Change*, Cambridge, the University Press, 1979. See also G. D. Painter, *William Caxton: A Quincentenary Biography of England's First Printer*, London, Chatto & Windus, 1976; N. F. Blake, *Caxton: England's First Publisher*, New York, Barnes & Noble, 1976.

124. V. J. Scattergood, *Politics and Poetry in the Fifteenth Century*, London, Blandford, 1971.

125. Nicholas Orme, *Education in the West of England, 1066–1548*, Exeter, the University Press, 1976. See also Margaret Aston, "Lollardy and Literacy," *History* 62, 1977: 347–371; M. T. Clanchy, "Modernity in Education and Government in England," *Speculum* 50, 1975: 671–688; J. J. G. Alexander and M. T. Gibson, eds., *Medieval Learning and Literature: Essays Presented to Richard William Hunt*, Oxford, Clarendon, 1976.

126. A. Gransden, "Propaganda in English Medieval Historiography," *Journal of Medieval History* 1, 1975: 24–40; A. Hanham, *Richard III and His Early Historians, 1483–1535*, Oxford, Clarendon, 1975; Paul E. Gill, "Politics and Propaganda in Fifteenth-century England: The Polemical Writings of Sir John Fortesque," *Speculum* 46, 1971: 333–347.

127. Dorothy Hartley, *Lost Country Life*, New York, Pantheon, 1981.

128. Stanley J. Kahrl, *Traditions of Medieval English Drama*, London, 1974. The Records of Early English Drama at the University of Toronto has a major new publication series; see, for example, Lawrence Clopper, ed., *Chester*, Toronto, University of Toronto Press, 1979.

129. Margaret Hastings, "High History or Hack History: England in the Later Middle Ages," in Elizabeth Chapin Furber, ed., *Changing Views on British History*, Cambridge, Mass., Harvard University Press, 1966, 58–100; M. D. Knowles, "Some Trends in Scholarship, 1868–1968, in the Field of Medieval History," *TRHS*, 5th ser., 19, 1969: 139–157; De-

Lloyd J. Guth, ed., *Late Medieval England, 1377–1485*, Cambridge, the University Press, 1976.

130. Edgar B. Graves, *A Bibliography of English History to 1485*, Oxford, Clarendon, 1975.

131. Karl F. Morrison, "Fragmentation and Unity in 'American Medievalism,'" in Michael Kammen, ed., *The Past Before Us: Contemporary Historical Writing in the United States*, Ithaca, N.Y., Cornell University Press, 1980.

Recent Writings
on Tudor History

Wallace MacCaffrey

The modern historiography of the Tudor age took shape in the last years of the nineteenth century and the early years of the twentieth and not surprisingly came to reflect the preoccupations of that generation. Politics and religion were the dominant themes, the first colored strongly by a strident nationalism and the second reflecting a liberal-Protestant bias (or alternatively a militantly defensive Catholicism). One single historian played a disproportionately large role in the writing of Tudor history in the first generation of this century: A. F. Pollard of the University of London. Very much a child of his age, he saw the Tudors as the builders of the modern English state and interpreted the Reformation from a secularized Protestant angle of view. These circumstances led to a historiographical tradition somewhat more conservative in its range of interests and the kind of questions it sought to deal with than those traditions which took their rise when historians were more attuned to the newer social sciences.

Robert A. Smith, writing in *Changing Views of British History*, had occasion to remark on the erosion of Pollardian stereotypes which was already setting in at that time. Since then the process has proceeded apace.[1] Not only has there been large-scale rewriting of Tudor political history but the horizons of Tudor historians have—a little belatedly—expanded. Whole ranges of questions, whole universes of phenomena, which had been ignored altogether have come under the historian's lens. As a result, the whole structure of sixteenth-century historical studies of England has assumed new and much larger dimensions. Some of the new wings in the edifice are not much more than bare frameworks, but others are in at least a semifinished condition.

This essay is divided into several parts. The first concerns itself with traditional subjects of political history, treated in chronological order. In this section much of the text is an account of revisions. The rejection of the old sharply limned historical portraits of our predecessors in favor of canvases much more ambiguous in line and color—and often unfinished—reflects the difference between the self-confident world of the early twentieth century, with its unwavering certainties about the meaning of the past, and our questioning generation, skeptical of even the modest generalization and doubtful as to any certain assertions about the historical past. The later portions of the essay, beginning with the discussion of foreign policy, are topically arranged. One of them, that on religious history, again recounts a revisionary phase, but others such as the discussion of economic and social history have much to say of new ground broken.

Before launching into a discussion of historical writing, it is worth saying a little about the continuing publication of source materials. The volume is considerable; only a few items are singled out here. Two old series are *The Calendar of State Papers relating to Scotland and Mary, Queen of Scots 1547–1603*, the final volume of which, covering 1597 to 1603, appeared in Edinburgh in 1969. *The Calendar of Patent Rolls, Elizabeth I* is now complete to 1572 (vol. 4, London, 1964; vol. 5, London, 1966). The proclamations of the Tudor sovereigns have been edited with full texts by Paul L. Hughes and James F. Larkin (*Tudor Royal Proclamations*, 3 vols., New Haven, Conn., 1964–1969). (There have been two exhaustive commentaries on the proclamations, R. W. Heinze, *The Proclamations of the Tudor Kings* (London, 1976) and F. A. Youngs, *The Proclamations of the Tudor Queens* (London, 1976). Local record societies continue to issue new documents in a quantity too large to be dealt with here. One major collection of Tudor family papers, perhaps the largest such collection after the Cecils', has been cataloged recently, *A Calendar of the Shrewsbury and Talbot Papers in Lambeth Palace Library and the College of Arms*, edited by G. R. Batho (London, 1971).

Smith was able to point to the fading magic of the year 1485, which had so long stood as a watershed between "medieval" and "modern" England. Nothing so aptly illustrates the final abandonment of Bosworth as an "utterly memorable" event in English history as a comparison of two general survey works by the same author. G. R. Elton, in *England under the Tudors* (London, 1955), began with the hallowed date of 1485. His new volume, *Reform and Reformation: England 1509–1558* (London, 1978) opens, as the title indicates, not with the accession but with the death of Henry VII. The latter event marks the end of an era; the accession of his son coincides with a whole new set of problems, which were to preoccupy Englishmen not only until 1558 but until the end of the century. Implicit in the choice of starting date is the assumption that Henry VII was the last "medieval" king—certainly not the innovating absolutist who founded a "new monarchy." But a statement of this level of generality has only a very limited usefulness since it lumps the first Tudor with almost a dozen generations of his predecessors.

If one focuses on a narrower perspective, Henry VII's reign is seen as the culmination of a phase—the final phase—of medieval monarchy. Some sixty years earlier the unlucky chance of heredity had brought the hapless Henry VI to the throne. In his listless grasp, political order dissolved and paralysis of the administrative apparatus followed. Civil war brought the Yorkists to the throne, but Edward IV's hold on power was for a long time an uncertain one. After 1470 he was able to accomplish much in the reestablishment of royal authority, but his premature death opened the way for two coups d'etat that seemed to presage an English "Time of Troubles" hardly less bizarre in character and almost as threatening to the monarchy as that of seventeenth-century Russia.

In a series of recent works, the history of the decades from 1450 to 1509 has been rewritten. R. L. Storey's *The End of the House of Lancaster* (London, 1966) displays the Wars of the Roses, not so much as a struggle between two rival dynastic factions, but rather as the crack-up of a system of noble politics which demanded the constant mastery of a strong and willful sovereign, at once leader and umpire. The first Yorkist's struggle to fill this role is treated at length in Charles Ross's biography, *Edward IV* (London, 1974). The career of his ultimate successor, the first Tudor, is explored with similar thoroughness by S. B. Chrimes, *Henry VII* (London, 1972). Both these biographies not only deal with the personality and the political career of their subjects but also examine the functioning of major institutions—Council, Parliament, the law courts, the Exchequer—and relations with the church. Some of their conclusions rest on the extended work of J. R. Lander, whose collected essays on this era are assembled in *Crown and Nobility 1450–1509* (Montreal, 1976). The biographies also make extensive use of the work of B. P. Wolffe, whose research is summarized in two works *The Royal Demesne in English History* (London, 1971) and *The Crown Lands 1461 to 1536* (London, 1970). These books give us a full understanding of the Chamber finance practiced by both Edward and Henry, of their land-management policy, and of the renovated administrative structure which Wolsey (and Cromwell) inherited.[2]

What emerges from these studies is a long process of reconstruction, lasting half a century or more, interrupted (and diverted) by the melodrama of Richard III. Edward IV wins high marks, but the bad luck of his premature death placed his work in jeopardy, and Henry was compelled to duplicate at least part of his predecessor's accomplishment. Edward was, however, that rare bird, an administrator-king, the exacting but efficient bureaucrat for whom no detail was too small. Both monarchs were "medieval" in the sense that they sought to reconstruct rather than consciously to innovate, but it is clear that by 1509 the strength of the Crown vis-à-vis the great nobles was far greater than it had been during the early fifteenth century. Henry VIII inherited a greater freedom of action and a larger margin of control over the nobility than any predecessor for many generations back. If he chose to use it, he had a great reservoir of power at his disposal.

These studies, by their thoroughness and accuracy, have taught us much that we had not seen before, and yet the picture now in front of us is far more blurred, full of ambiguities, and haunted by uncertainties than the sharply etched views they replaced. We understand a little, but far too little, of the actual functioning of those institutions on which the Tudor monarchy rested—above all the activities of Council in all its protean forms. Council was clearly at one of those pregnant moments in its long history when it was giving birth to numerous offspring, some abortive, some destined for long and vigorous careers. At least one important start has been made in sorting out this tangled story with J. A. Guy's *The Cardinal's Court: The Impact of Thomas Wolsey in Star Chamber* (Hassocks, Sussex, 1977), which describes for us the opening phase of that great court's history.

The work of the last twenty years has laid the foundations for a new synthesis of the half century that ended with the death of Henry VII and has provided a fair amount of agreement as to its main aspects. For the age which follows—the four decades of Henry VIII—there has been abundant and vigorous scholarship that has radically altered our conception but probably less agreement among historians as to the nature of the Henrician regime. Three seminal works have tackled the personality and the career of the second Tudor on a grand scale. J. J. Scarisbrick's *Henry VIII* (London, 1968) is both a study of the man and an interpretation of the reign; G. R. Elton's considered views on these years are contained in his *Reform and Reformation* as well as in his more specialized studies, particularly *Policy and Police: The Enforcement of the Reformation in the Age of Thomas Cromwell* (London, 1972) and *Reform and Renewal: Thomas Cromwell and the Common Weal* (London, 1973). L. B. Smith has written a discriminating and subtle analysis of the royal personality in his *Henry VIII: the Mask of Royalty* (London, 1971). In their differing ways, all these studies go far to diminish the reputation of Henry as statesman or even as a politician. Scarisbrick goes least far; his Henry is a wayward and self-indulgent playboy who, however, never loses his grasp of power to the cardinal-minister and, in the crisis of the divorce, grows under the pressure of events into a master strategist. Smith's Henry is a man ridden by inner insecurities; Elton's, a prince who can be manipulated by his servants, one of whom, Cromwell, is seen as the real initiator of policy and shaper of a new religiopolitical order. Scarisbrick gives Wolsey credit for a degree of humanist-inspired statesmanship which was thwarted by his royal master's adolescent longing for glory. In Elton's various studies,[3] Thomas Cromwell is seen not only as an astute political manager but as a statesman of uncommon vision whose boldest and most original schemes for fundamental reform were crushed by the stupidity and insensitivity of the royal egotist and who was ultimately destroyed by the intrigues of a squalid court faction who frightened a too susceptible king with the bogy of Cromwell's heterodoxy.[4]

All this has gone far to destroy the myth of Henry VIII as a great ruler, although it has not diminished the impact of his unrestrained willfulness upon the world in which he lived. But even more than in the case of his father, these revisions of the received interpretation leave a complex and blurred picture. One may see the king as a conventional dynast who somehow rose to sufficient understanding of contemporary ideals of reform to manipulate them to his own ends. Or one can perceive him as the unwitting agent of change whose idiosyncratic impulses could be bent sufficiently to serve the ends of radical reformers of the English commonweal. In both versions, the first phase of the English Reformation is seen as containing genuine reformist elements, albeit sadly deformed by the interventions and interdictions of the royal autocrat. These reformist impulses, so far as they are manifest in actual policy decisions, were moderate, Erasmian, and even more specifically Marsilian in nature rather than straightforwardly Lutheran. They may have incorporated some considerable element of Lollard belief and practice, although this is almost impossible to measure accurately. (The study of religious history is dealt with separately below.)

The most important act of resistance to the Henrician reforms was the Pilgrimage of Grace in 1537. There was a long hiatus in serious study of this major episode after the two-volume work of Madelein H. Dodds and Ruth Dodds, *The Pilgrimage of Grace 1536–1537*, London, 1915. Recently a whole series of important articles have begun a systematic revision of the received tradition. These include A. G. Dickens, "Secular and Religious Motivation in the Pilgrimage of Grace" (*Studies in Church History* 4, 1967, C. S. L. Davies, "The Pilgrimage of Grace Reconsidered" (*PP*, no. 41, 1968); M. L. Bush, "The Problem of the Far North: A Study of the Crisis of 1537 and Its Consequences" (*Northern History* 6, 1971); two articles on the Lincolnshire rising, one by Mervyn James, "Obedience and Dissent in Henrician England: The Lincolnshire Rebellion, 1536" (*PP*, no. 48, 1970), and the other by Margaret Bowker, "Lincolnshire 1536: Heresy, Schism or Religious Discontent?" (*Studies in Church History* 9, 1972); and (on the second northern rising) Mervyn James, "The Concept of Order and the Northern Rising of 1569" (*PP*, no. 60, 1973).

Besides these major revaluations of the Henrician years, the debate on the nature of Henrician government opened by G. R. Elton in his *Tudor Revolution in Government* (London, 1953) has continued. Elton argued for a fundamental shift from "household" to bureaucratic government under the vigorous direction of Cromwell. The most important critique of the Eltonian thesis was that of G. L. Harriss and Penry Williams (*PP*, 25 July 1963). Harriss in particular attacked Elton's distinction between household and bureaucracy, arguing that the latter underestimates the maturity of medieval bureaucracy. He also insisted that the great changes of the 1530s in practice and in theory owe more to medieval precedent than Elton would allow and represent a much less significant degree of change than the latter argues for. It is this line of argument that the studies of Wolffe cited earlier follow when they suggest that the Chamber administration of Yorkist and early Tudor times was an emergency measure designed to deal with a breakdown in the functioning of royal bureaucracy. The Henrician years are seen as an era in which there was a gradual return to Exchequer control, modified in some practices by Chamber innovations. In such a view, this phase of administrative history from about 1470 to 1555 is not a revolutionary one but, rather, a long period of construction marked by some important innovations which were hewn out in the very process of repair.

Recent historians of Henry VIII's reign have been at work revising earlier formulations. But the reigns of his two immediate successors had not been the subject of full-scale and serious scholarly study since Froude's time. The one exception to this statement is of course Pollard's study of the Protector Somerset (published in 1900), and his views of the duke had long held the field.[5] This neglect has been remedied during the last thirty years by a spate of new and important work on the reign of Edward VI which is likely to change radically our views of those years.

The most considerable study of the Edwardian epoch is to be found in the two-volume work of W. K. Jordan (*Edward VI, Vol. 1, The Young King: The Protectorship of the Duke of Somerset*, Cambridge, Mass., 1968, and *Vol. 2, The Threshold of Power: The Dominance of the Duke of Northumberland*, Cambridge, Mass., 1970). These two encyclopedic volumes give a detailed narrative of the reign, enriched by topical chapters on economic, religious, and social history. The general interpretation of Somerset's career does not differ widely from that of Pollard; both authors see the duke as a flawed idealist—a man of principle, ill-endowed with political skill. In Jordan's work the young king is viewed as an increasingly important actor in the latter years of his short reign. This interpretation has come under heavy fire in two recent books. M. L. Bush, in *The Government of the Protector Somerset* (London, 1975), perceives a much more pragmatic and self-serving duke whose policy was shaped largely by the exigencies of the Scottish war and whose social and religious views were secondary elements of his policymaking. D. E. Hoak, in *The King's Council in the Reign of Edward VI* (London, 1976), studies in detail the power structure within the Council; he gives very high marks to Northumberland as a politician and administrator and sees the young king as a negligible factor.[6] These two works concentrate on the high politics of the reign; the crisis of peasant revolt in the summer of 1549 is reexamined in Julian Cornwall's *Revolt of the Peasantry* (London, 1977), a mildly revisionist critique of Jordan's narrative.

The politics of Mary's reign still await the kind of attention given to her brother's. A useful account of one major aspect is found in David Loades's *Two Tudor Conspiracies* (1975), and a solid biography of one leading Marian councillor, the first Lord Paget, was published in 1973 by Samuel R. Gammon (*Statesman and Schemer, William Paget, First Lord Paget, Tudor Minister*, Newton Abbot and Hamden, Conn., 1973). Cardinal Pole and the whole character of the Catholic restoration still lack the full-scale study the importance of the subject demands.[7]

The political history of the last forty years of the century has recently been studied largely in the form of biography. A formidable list of lives of Tudor statesmen has appeared. There is a useful one-volume biography of William Cecil by B. W. Beckingsale, *Burghley: Tudor Statesman 1520–1598* (London, 1967). Lives of privy councillors include F. G. Emmison's *Tudor Secretary of State: Sir William Petrie at Court and at Home* (London, 1961), Stanford E. Lehmberg's *Sir Walter Mildmay and Tudor Government* (Austin, Tex., 1964), Neville Williams's *Thomas Howard, Fourth Duke at Norfolk* (New York, 1964), R. Tittler's *Nicholas Bacon, the Making of a Tudor Statesman* (London, 1976), Robert W. Kenny's *Elizabeth's Admiral: The Political Career of Charles Howard, Earl of Nottingham, 1536–1624* (Baltimore, 1970), and Mary Dewar's *Sir Thomas Smith: A Tudor Intellectual in Office* (London, 1964). Amos Miller's *Sir Henry Killigrew* (Leicester, 1963) and Joan Rees's *Fulke Greville, Lord Brooke, 1554–1628* (London, 1971) deal with lesser notables. Robert Lacey has written lively accounts of two late Elizabethan favorites, *Robert Earl of Essex* (London, 1971) and *Sir Walter Raleigh* (London, 1974).[8] A good study of a second-level figure, more civil servant than politician, is A. G. R. Smith's *Servant of the Cecils: The Life of Sir Michael Hicks, 1543–1612* (London and Totowa, N.J., 1977). These are all important additions to our biographical knowledge of Elizabeth's reign but do not substantially alter the received views of it. An attempt at a fresh view of the reign's early years is to be found in Wallace T. MacCaffrey's *The Making of the Elizabethan Regime* (Princeton, N.J. and London, 1968).[9] But Elizabethan studies are still overshadowed by the work of earlier writers, especially that of J. E. Neale. It is probably time for some reevaluations of a reign the historiography of which is still dominated by the conceptions of a generation or more ago.

So far this essay has dealt with studies primarily chronological or biographical in focus. In the balance of this survey the orientation is topical. The first subject dealt with is, in a sense, an aspect of political history: foreign relations. This is a topic which has received surprisingly little specialized treatment by Tudor historians. Of course, the biographers of the first two Tudors necessarily gave much space to the foreign policy of those rulers, but there is little work specifically and separately devoted to England's relations with her neighbors as such. The most important such study is R. B. Wernham's *Before the Armada: The Emergence of the English Nation, 1485–1588* (London, 1966), a synthetic work which, how-ever, rests on the author's intimate knowledge of State Papers, Foreign. It is a brief work to cover so much ground, and the reader seeks fuller bibliographical references to support the large generalizations in which the book abounds. A survey of Tudor foreign policy, based on secondary works, was written by F. C. Crowson (*Tudor Foreign Policy*, London, 1973). Charles Wilson has brought Elizabeth's policy in the Low Countries under attack in his *Queen Eliza-beth and the Netherlands* (London, 1970). But detailed study of Elizabethan for-eign policy has not been substantially advanced since the work of Conyers Read.[10]

Another corollary to the study of political history is the analysis of political institutions. In this area there was much important activity in the years after the Second World War. J. E. Neale's ground-breaking volumes on Parliament were paralleled by authoritative monographs on the Court of Wards and the Council in the Marches of Wales. In recent years there have been fewer such studies. Two volumes on the Henrician parliaments from 1529 to 1547 add measurably to our knowledge; we still await the same thorough investigation of the Edwardian and Marian houses.[11] The authority of J. E. Neale as the historian of the Elizabethan parliaments has until very recently stood unchallenged.[12] The publication of the long-awaited and long-delayed biographical volumes of the History of Parlia-ment Trust should stimulate further work;[13] in the meantime a challenge has been thrown down by G. R. Elton in a preliminary skirmish—"Parliament in the Sixteenth Century: Functions and Fortunes" (*HJ* 22, 1979). What is perhaps most needed at this point is a study of the Tudor Parliament which focuses on its function as understood by contemporaries. How did they perceive the purposes and the everyday working of the institution? Until there is a clearer answer to the questions, much of the discussion about the parliamentary breakdown of the sev-enteenth century will continue to be muddled.[14]

Other major political institutions have not fared well. The whole history of Council, in its protean manifestations, still remains to be investigated. Aside from Guy's study of early Star Chamber and Hoak's examination of the Council in the unusual circumstances of a royal minority, there has been only one mono-graph on the Council—Michael Pulman's *The Elizabethan Privy Council in the Fifteen-seventies* (Berkeley and Los Angeles, 1971). Admittedly the very scope of conciliar activity, its undefined limits, and the great gaps in the sources make a full-scale study of even a short period a daunting task. Probably a more oblique topical approach such, for instance, as a study of conciliar regulation of the econ-omy may prove more fruitful. The Council's agents were, of course, the justices of the peace, and of that important corps we need to know much more than we do yet. The most considerable recent work has been that of J. H. Gleason in *The Justices of the Peace in England, 1558 to 1640* (London, 1969). There is an illuminating study of one important county, A. Hassell Smith's *County and Court: Government and Politics in Norfolk, 1558–1603* (London, 1974), which offers a model to be imitated for other regions since, in exploring the important interaction of royal government and squirearchy, it probes the limits of effective royal power.[15]

Legal history has continued to receive a good deal of attention. Our knowledge of Chancery and of the prerogative courts has been advanced, but it is in the study of common law that the most original work has been done. W. J. Jones's *The Elizabethan Court of Chancery* (London, 1967) is an authoritative study of the great court;[16] Sir Julius Caesar's account of the Court of Requests, *The Ancient State, Authorities and Proceedings of the Court of Requests* (London, 1975) has been edited by L. M. Hill. But Star Chamber, except for Guy's book mentioned above, still remains to be explored.[17]

The common law is still full of mysteries. J. H. Baker has explained some of the reasons for this in an essay, "The Dark Age of English Legal History" (in D. Jenkins, ed., *Legal History Studies*, (London, 1972), and more recently done a great deal to remedy the situation in a four-hundred-page introduction to volume 2 of *The Reports of Sir John Spelman* (Publications of the Selden Society, vol. 94, for the year 1977, London, 1978). This is a comprehensive survey of the development of legal thought, legal practice, and legal institutions during the first half of the Tudor century and helpful for understanding later developments. Light is thrown on special aspects by J. S. Cockburn's *History of English Assizes 1558–1714* (London, 1972) and Wilfrid R. Prest's *The Inns of Court under Elizabeth I and the Early Stuarts 1590–1640* (London, 1972).[18]

Crime and the criminal law have come in for long-overdue examination. A good introduction to the historical study of crime is *Crime in England 1550–1800* edited by J. S. Cockburn (London, 1977). Major procedural changes in criminal law are the subject of J. H. Langbein's *Prosecuting Crime in the Renaissance: England, Germany, France* (Cambridge, Mass., 1974), while Joel Samaha, *Law and Order in Historical Perspective: The Case of Elizabeth Essex* (New York and London, 1974) pinpoints the administration of justice in a single county.[19] These should be harbingers of things to come, especially since the publication of calendars of existing assize records for Elizabeth now provides easily accessible sources for an intensive study of criminal justice.[20] Other specific problems within the common law have been studied by Gareth Jones in *History of the Law of Charity 1532–1827* (London, 1969) and John Bellamy in *The Tudor Law of Treason, an Introduction* (London, 1979).[21]

Legal institutions loomed large in the affairs of Tudor England; military institutions—the navy apart—were generally negligible. Nevertheless there has been a respectable body of publication on Tudor military history in the last two decades. Lindsay Boynton's *The Elizabethan Militia 1558–1638* (Toronto, 1967) studies an institution to which increasingly serious attention was given during Elizabeth's reign. Individual campaigns have been examined in detail in C. G. Cruickshank's *Army Royal: Henry VIII's Invasion of France, 1513* (London, 1969), in his *The English Occupation of Tournai 1513–1519* (London, 1971), and in Howel A. Lloyd's *The Rouen Campaign 1590–92* (London, 1973). A contemporary soldier's account of his career and profession is now available in *The Works of Sir Roger Williams* edited by John X. Evans (London, 1972).[22] The development of the Tudor navy is broadly treated as the first part of G. J. Marcus's *A Naval History of England: The Formative Centuries* (London, 1961).[23]

The distance between political and religious (or at least ecclesiastical) history has never been great in Tudor studies, and this mingling of piety and politics has worked to the disadvantage of religious studies. Not enough serious attention has been given to the reshaping of the religious consciousness and sensibilities, especially of English lay men and women. The history of the English Reformation has suffered also from the denominational biases of most of its historians, an effect which has continued far into the present century. Within the last two decades the influences of secularism and of ecumenicism have gone far toward alleviating both the problems. More attention is being given to the theological and intellectual history of the age and scholars of whatever persuasion approach its problems with less heat and more dispassion. A good example of this change in outlook is A. G. Dickens's one-volume survey, *The English Reformation* (London, 1964). Beginning with an account of late medieval religious practice and the emergence of Lollardy, it concludes with the Elizabethan settlement. Although the author is an Anglican clergyman, the tone throughout is one of careful scholarly objectivity. Much the same tone pervades most of the works mentioned below.

One of the least-studied aspects of the English Reformation has been the state of grass-roots religion, the practice and faith of the individual parish, in the generations before Luther. Some useful light has been cast on that subject by two books. One by Peter Heath, *The English Parish Clergy on the Eve of the Reformation* (London, 1969), is a general survey; the other, Margaret Bowker's *The Secular Clergy in the Diocese of Lincoln, 1495–1520* (London, 1968), is limited to a single vast diocese. An important question about which we still know so tantalizingly little is the relations between native English heresy (Lollardy) and the imported Lutheran influences after 1517. Two important articles throw some light: Margaret Aston's "Lollardy and the Reformation: Survival or Revival?" (*History* 2, 1964), and A. G. Dickens's "Heresy and the Origins of English

Protestantism" (in J. H. Bromley and E. H. Kossmann, eds., *Britain and the Netherlands*, vol. 2, Groningen, 1964).

There is a substantial study of the first generation of Henrician radicals who consciously repudiated the Roman past. William A. Clebsch, in *England's Earliest Protestants 1520–1535* (New Haven, Conn., 1964), has made an intensive investigation of the careers and the thought of the religious radicals who defied state and church in the decades before Henry's own impulses drove him into a reluctant cooperation with them. He argues that even in this era there were distinctively national strands in English Protestant thought which separate it in some respects from mainstream continental Lutheranism. Sir Thomas More continues to attract the attention of a host of writers, but probably the most important development in Moreana has been the steady flow of volumes in the Yale University Press edition of his complete works.[24] More's fellow martyr Bishop Fisher is the subject of a book by Edward Surtz, *The Works and Days of John Fisher* (Cambridge, Mass., 1967).

Scarisbrick has some careful and informative chapters on the personal religious views of Henry VIII and their influence on the legislation of the 1530s. The Erasmian piety which so powerfully influenced the Henrician court is the subject of J. K. McConica's *English Humanists and Reformation Politics under Henry VIII and Edward VI* (London, 1965), a comprehensive survey of the impact of the Dutch humanist on the English reform movement. The more pragmatic side of the Henrician reformation is carefully examined by both Elton and Scarisbrick; there have been some useful articles on particular aspects of these years.[25]

The vexed question of the monastic dissolution which in past generations produced so much heat was magisterially dealt with by David Knowles in the third volume of *The Religious Orders in England* (London, 1959). Recent work has shifted to the administrative and economic aspects of this great transformation in English life. Joyce Youings's *The Dissolution of the Monasteries* (London, 1971) provides a carefully selected group of relevant documents and an authoritative introduction to the unfolding process of the dissolution.[26] Another study, by Allan Kreider, investigates in detail a neglected but important aftermath of the monastic dissolution in his *English Chantries: The Road to Dissolution* (Cambridge, Mass., 1979), which emphasizes not only the economic side of this episode but its impact upon popular piety.

The religious history of the decade between Henry's death and Elizabeth's accession stands in sharp contrast to its political history. As I have said, a whole spate of important studies is transforming our perception of Edwardian politics; very little new work has been done on the radical Protestant phase from 1547 to 1553 or on the Catholic reaction under Mary. An authoritative biography of the first Protestant archbishop has been provided by Jasper Ridley (*Thomas Cranmer*, London, 1962), following upon this author's earlier life of Nicholas Ridley. Jordan's work surveys extensively the formal changes in religion under Edward VI, but what is needed is a study which explores the underlying shift in religious sensibilities between 1520 and 1560, a cultural transformation of the first importance. The religious revolution needs also to be placed more fully in its long-term English context as well as in the whole movement of the Reformation in Western Europe. And, as suggested above, a study of Cardinal Pole's primacy and his efforts to initiate a Catholic Reformation should be high on the agenda of future research. The one significant exception to the barrenness of Marian studies is David Loades's *The Oxford Martyrs* (London, 1967), a work of wider scope than the title suggests, for it examines the dilemma posed for Protestants by a lawful but ungodly prince.

When one turns from the mid-Tudor years to the Elizabethan epoch, the richness of recent historical studies in religion stands in sharp contrast to the earlier period. The volume of such work is large; more important are the fresh perspectives opened up by these books. Several general surveys look at large landscapes. Claire Cross, in her *Church and People, 1540–1660: The Triumph of the Laity in the English Church* (London, 1976), picks up a central thread of the English Reformation, its fundamental laicism, and follows it through to the Restoration of the Stuarts. The first volume of Horton Davies's study of Protestant worship and theology in England, *Worship and Theology in England, from Cranmer to Hooker 1534–1603* (Princeton, N.J., 1970), deals with this century. Two collections of essays edited by Felicity Heal and Rosemary O'Day investigate the institutional history of the Church of England during a period of major transformations. Their emphasis on particular problems in local settings is a very useful shift in direction.[27]

Two books require special mention because of the impact they have had on our understanding of Puritanism. One is the wide-ranging and learned work of Patrick Collinson, *The Elizabethan Puritan Movement* (London, 1967).[28] This book reveals a movement more complex and inwardly riven than earlier, less sophisticated studies suggested. It also highlights the tension between the *politique* and the evangelical wings of the English reform movement; both equally ardent in their rejection of the old faith, they gradually drifted apart once the Protestant regime was firmly in the saddle. A second book of equal importance is William Haller's *The Elect Nation: The Meaning and Relevance of Foxe's Book of Martyrs* (New York, 1963), which very vividly reveals the emotional power of the evangelical faith, not only as a religious phenomenon but in broader cultural terms, and specifically in providing a potent historical myth which served both the Protestant and the English national imagination. The large history of the whole dissenting tradition is dealt with in Michael R. Watt's *The Dissenters from the Refor-*

mation to the French Revolution (London, 1978), of which the first part gives a useful survey of the years 1532–1640.

Specific aspects of the Puritan tradition are examined by Paul Seaver in *The Puritan Lectureships* (Stanford, Calif., 1970), which deals with Puritan strategies of proselytism. S. J. Knox has written the life of a major Puritan leader in his *Walter Travers* (London, 1962), and John C. Coolidge has explored an aspect of Puritan theology in *The Pauline Renaissance in England: Puritanism and the Bible* (London, 1970). An even more radical figure has been dealt with in Donald J. McGinn's study *John Penry and the Marprelate Controversy* (New Brunswick, N.J., 1966).

The completion of *Elizabethan Nonconformist Texts* edited by Leland H. Carlson (vols. 3–4, London, 1962–1970) makes available the writing of the major radicals, particularly in the later volumes, Barrow and Greenwood. It makes easier a judgment of the thesis advanced most persuasively in B. R. White's *English Separatist Tradition from the Marian Martyrs to the Pilgrim Fathers* (London, 1971) that separatism should be seen not so much as an outgrowth of Puritanism but as another, independent movement with its own roots in the earliest phase of the English Reformation.

Studies of the life of the church established by law have also gone forward. Besides the collected essays edited by Heal and O'Day already mentioned, there have been other specialized works. V. K. J. Brook's *Life of Archbishop Parker* (London, 1962) supersedes earlier biographies of the first Elizabethan primate. W. P. Haugaard's *Elizabeth I and the English Reformation* (London, 1968) examines in close detail the first years of the new order, particularly the crucial Convocation of 1562; and Claire Cross has handled the same subject more broadly in *The Royal Supremacy in the Elizabethan Church* (London, 1969), a collection of documents with a useful and lengthy introduction. Bishop Jewel is the subject of a monograph by W. M. Southgate, *John Jewel and the Problem of Doctrinal Authority* (Cambridge, Mass., 1962), while the career of Whitgift's coadjutor and successor, Bancroft, is examined in another work, S. B. Babbage's *Puritanism and Richard Bancroft* (London, 1962).[29] Although these are useful books, they have not given to studies of the establishment the kind of impulse which has done much to transform our understanding both of Elizabethan Puritanism and Catholicism. One work, standing alone at present, points a direction which other scholars might profitably follow. This is Phyllis Hembry's *The Bishops of Bath and Wells, 1540–1640* (London, 1967), a history of the temporalties of that see in the Reformation century, a study valuable in itself and a topic which should be explored for other English bishoprics.[30]

The history of English Catholicism has long been the preserve of Catholic scholars working within their tradition; it has produced works of meticulous scholarship but often of limited perspectives. A real breakthrough to broader ground has been achieved in the work of John Bossy. His essay in *Past and Present* (April 1962), "The Character of Elizabethan Catholicism," set the problem of the English Catholics in a larger and more inclusive framework—that of the embattled minority, familiar enough in many other historical settings.[31] This shift in perspective was exploited more fully in his book *The English Catholic Community 1570–1850* (London, 1975). Although only the first section deals with Tudor times, its theme—the transformation from church to sect—reorders older visions of the problem in a definitive way.

Other works in recusant history have moved along more traditional lines. William Trimble's *The Catholic Laity in Elizabethan England* (Cambridge, Mass., 1964) is something of an exception in that it draws attention to the shifting circumstances which gave the laity an unaccustomed importance in the affairs of their faith. Marvin O'Connel has written a life of one of the most articulate of the early exiles, *Thomas Stapleton and the Counter Reformation* (New York, 1964). Albert J. Loomie has studied in detail the careers of the Catholic exiles at the court of Spain in *The Spanish Elizabethans* (New York, 1963).[32] Thomas S. Clancy has dealt with the polemics of the English Catholics in *Papist Pamphleteers: The Allen Persons Party and the Political Thought of the Counterreformation in England 1572–1615* (Chicago, 1964). The link between anti-Catholic and anti-Spanish sentiment is the subject of William S. Maltby's *The Black Legend in England: The Development of Anti-Spanish Sentiment* (Durham, N.C., 1971).[33]

The Reformation has been largely studied as a national phenomenon; scholars were aware that the rate and character of change had important regional differences, but only recently have close investigations of these manifestations begun. Roger B. Manning, in *Religion and Society in Elizabethan Sussex: A Study of the Enforcement of the Religious Settlement 1558–1603* (Leicester, 1969), deals with a somewhat isolated southern county, while C. A. Haigh, in *Reform and Resistance in Tudor Lancashire* (London, 1975), covers much the same ground in a remote northern shire. James E. Oxley, in *The Reformation in Essex* (London, 1965), limits himself to the period up to 1558. R. C. Richardson's *Puritanism in Northwest England: A Regional Study of the Diocese of Chester to 1642* (London, 1972) and K. R. Wark's *Elizabethan Recusancy in Cheshire* (Manchester, 1971) explore two sides of the coin, the two modes of dissent. It would be a profitable exercise for a future historian to explore one of the populous dioceses (or counties) of the Midlands, the Thames Valley, or East Anglia.

These have been twenty fruitful and transforming years in the study of sixteenth-century religious problems in England. The damping down of ancient religious passions which so long colored all such studies has brought to the fore a generation of scholars drawn from different traditions who have approached the subject with larger and clearer vision and have quite measurably raised the standards of historical writing in this field. We are in a fair way to leave behind us a conception of the English Reformation which was often parochial, partisan, and antiquarian and to move on to a more truly historical understanding.

Our understanding of political and religious history has been appreciably deepened by the new work of the past two decades, yet that achievement seems almost modest when measured against the strides taken in the field of social and economic history. This was an area in which substantial individual studies had appeared, some of them such landmarks as Tawney's *Agrarian Problem in the Sixteenth Century* (London, 1912) or W. R. Scott's massive three volumes on the joint stock companies (1912). There had been studies of particular industries, such as J. U. Nef's account of the coal industry (1932); but in general work in the field was spotty, with large areas quite untouched or only treated in a very amateur way. More important still was a general lack of direction, the absence of integrative impulses which aimed at obtaining some view of the whole movement of the English economy between 1500 and 1700. English historians of this era were perhaps slower to respond to the new and potent impulses, many of them, but not all, continental in origin, which were transforming all studies of the Western European economy and society. What has happened in the last twenty years is a vigorous, albeit somewhat belated, response to those new stimuli. There has of course been a proliferation of titles, but much more significant is the opening up of whole new areas of investigation. New questions have been asked; bodies of data which had lain ignored have been tapped. Large dimensions have been added to our total historical vision of the age. Bold new attempts are being made to understand overall tendencies in the movement of society and economy in this and in the succeeding century.

As the previous sentence suggests, economic history does not fall tidily within the boundaries set by political events. Much of the work discussed below spills over into the Stuart age. A good place to begin is the compendious volume 4 of *The Agrarian History of England and Wales*, edited by Joan Thirsk (London, 1967), which deals with the century 1540–1640 (volume 3 has not yet appeared). Nearly a dozen essays by different experts survey a whole range of problems: landlordship, farm labor, markets, prices, and housing, as well as such special topics as enclosure. These essays provide an authoritative and comprehensive account of our present understanding of what was by far the largest sector of the Tudor economy. They reflect not only the accumulation of knowledge but increased sophistication of method and a more purposeful organization of research around focal questions. Much of what is written in this volume pivots on an essential fact, of which we are much more acutely aware than our predecessors: the growth of English population in the sixteenth century. The long upswing of the demographic curve carried England out of the postplague doldrums of the fifteenth century and doubled the population before leveling off about 1650. This augmentation of the population created many obvious problems, not the least of which was finding food and work for so many newcomers in a world of limited and relatively inflexible technology.

While the brute fact of population growth is now taken for granted, solid information about demographic matters—comparative rates of growth, total population, geographical or age distribution—is still in scarce supply for the Tudor age. The bulk of our all-too-sparse data comes from tax records, muster rolls, or ecclesiastical censuses, usually fragmentary and local in character and requiring very careful interpretation. So far, no one has been bold enough to attempt anything so ambitious as J. C. Russell's *British Medieval Population* (Albuquerque, N.M., 1948). Julian Cornwall's article "English Population in the Early Sixteenth Century" (*EHR*, 2d ser., 23, 1970) seeks to establish some general limits for total population, but most writers have not done more than make estimates for local areas where some lucky chance provides a data base from which to work.[34]

Nevertheless, the assumption that the population did double in this century underlies all discussion of its economic history. The awkward question as to how this vast increase was fed has naturally engaged considerable attention. The most ambitious book to tackle this problem is Eric Kerridge's *The Agricultural Revolution* (London, 1967), which argues, in radical disagreement with his predecessors, that the major changes in agricultural technique—such as up-and-down husbandry, new fertilizers, and new crops—appeared on the scene a full century earlier than the dates traditionally assigned. It was this increase in production which helped to tide over what seemed to be a threatening Malthusian crisis. Another angle of approach to the problem of increased population is used by Joan Thirsk in *Economic Policy and Projects: The Development of a Consumer Society in Early Modern England* (London, 1979). Here she describes at length those innovating "projects" such as new crops like woad or new techniques like the knitting frame, which found work for many more hands and at the same time reduced dependence on imports.[35]

On the related subject of enclosures, over which so much ink has been spilled by modern historians, Thirsk offers a brisk summary of contemporary views in *The Agrarian History*. Kerridge, once again an iconoclast, in his *Agrarian Problems in the Sixteenth Century and After* (London, 1969), attacks the basic notion of tenurial insecurity, which presumably had given the enclosers the necessary leverage for their operations. These studies underline the complexities of the whole agrarian economy, in which regional, and even local, differences of soil, climate, and custom affected agricultural practice and social relationships in contrasting and sometimes contradictory ways.[36]

There is no general history of either industry or commerce on the scale of *The Agrarian History*.[37] There have been several surveys of the whole economy in the early modern period, of which P. H. Ramsey's *Tudor Economy Problems* (London, 1963), D. C. Coleman's *The Economy of England 1450–1750* (London, 1977), and L. A. Clarkson's *The Pre-industrial Economy in England 1500–1750* (London, 1971) are excellent examples.[38]

Any such general study faces a methodological problem in finding a focus and a shape. Medieval economic history has been shaped by the exploration of the rise and transformation of the manorial economy and the emergence of an urban sector; studies of the post-1750 economy have pivoted on the industrial revolution. The very ambiguity of the term *preindustrial*, so frequently used for the sixteenth and seventeenth centuries, suggests the problem of giving a general character to the economy of this era. Clearly it was a time not only of population growth but also of increased and diversified production, both in agriculture and industry, of widening markets, and of a more complex distribution system. But it was not a period in which radical alteration in the basic institutions of the economy took place. Change came slowly and almost imperceptibly, eroding but not destroying the ancient molds of manor, gild, markets, fairs within which production and distribution went on. Contemporaries, although often disturbed by conditions around them, were very slow to articulate or to analyze economic phenomena, at least to the end of the sixteenth century. A sophisticated attempt to deal with these difficulties is found in S. M. Jack's *Trade and Industry in Tudor and Stuart England* (London, 1977). This book makes intelligent use of the questions and the techniques used by economic historians studying more modern societies.

Studies of individual trades and services continue to be published. Peter J. Bowden has written a thorough account of the wool trade; E. S. Godfrey has studied glassmaking.[39] What is striking is the absence of a full-scale study of cloth making—surely the most important of all early-modern English industries. Aspects of it are dealt with in studies of other topics, but this great industry itself, so central to the economy of the Tudors, remains substantially unexamined for the period after 1500.

Communications are studied by T. S. Willan in *The Inland Trade: Studies in English Internal Trade in the Sixteenth and Seventeenth Centuries* (Manchester, 1976).[40] Ralph Davis's *The Rise of the English Shipping Industry in the Seventeenth and Eighteenth Centuries* (London, 1962) has useful material on the Elizabethan merchant marine. Several aspects of English expansion overseas in the Tudor era have been treated by historians. David B. Quinn's numerous essays on the earliest explorers and the first attempts at settlement are collected in *England and the Discovery of America, 1481–1620* (London, 1974); the phase of organized piracy is the subject of Kenneth R. Andrews's *Elizabethan Privateering* (London, 1964), while the problem of investment in overseas ventures is explored in detail by Theodore K. Rabb in *Enterprise and Empire: Merchant and Gentry Investment in the Expansion of England, 1575–1630* (Cambridge, Mass. 1967). This book, making use of the computer, compiles and analyzes massive information on the several thousand investors who backed a wide variety of overseas enterprises in these decades.

The very complex problems of prices, inflation, and currency have been given much more sophisticated analysis in recent work. Y. S. Brenner's article, "The Inflation of Prices in Early Sixteenth Century England" (*EHR*, 2d ser., 14, 1961) has been reprinted along with other important articles on the subject in *The Price Revolution in Sixteenth Century England*, edited by P. H. Ramsey (London, 1971). R. B. Outhwaite's pamphlet in the Economic History Society's series, *Inflation in Tudor and Early Stuart England* (London, 1971) is a useful introduction. Two major works have very carefully examined central aspects of money supply: C. A. Challis's *The Tudor Coinage* (Manchester, 1978) and J. D. Gould's *The Great Debasement: Currency and the Economy in Mid-Tudor England* (London, 1970). The latter work breaks new ground and carries our understanding of the Tudor economy forward to a new degree of subtlety and depth.

These last two books display the government as a major participant in the English economy. But even more important were the endless interventions of the government in the general regulation of the economic, and of the social, order. The most superficial acquaintance with sources makes clear how frequent and how wide-ranging were the attempts of Parliament, Council, and the latter's agents at the local level to lessen the frictions and strains which, to these anxious men, seemed perpetually to threaten basic social order.[41] Prices, wages, the movement of commodities, the flow of labor, the plight of the unemployed and the helpless were all subjects to which they devoted long hours of effort. We have piecemeal knowledge of all this important activity, but we still lack a large-scale study (or series of studies) on what, from a contemporary point of view, was probably the most significant aspect of the state's business. We still do not have a satisfactory assessment of the intentions of the Tudor Crown, nor the scope and relative success (or failure) of its strenuous efforts to regulate the affairs of the commonwealth. Aside from this major undone enterprise, there is also need for a new and thorough study of royal finance in all its branches, and, in a larger sense, of the royal administrative system, particularly in the latter half of the century.[42] Someone should attempt for the Elizabethan era what G. R. Elton did for early Tudor administration in his *Tudor Revolution in Government*.

The study of Tudor economic history during the past two decades has been built upon a substantial foundation of earlier work. But those scholars working in what is somewhat loosely called "social history" had a harder task. These historians took as their subject a whole range of institutions which are neither strictly political nor economic in character, such as social classes, family, or schools. They were striking out in most cases into virtually unexplored territory. Certainly the kinds of questions they were asking and the techniques of investigation they were using were unfamiliar to earlier Tudor historians, and they were exploring data which in the past had largely lain neglected. They have varied, of course, in the angle of their approach. Some have singled out a single institution or class for study on a national scale. Others have adopted a "total history" approach, examining both intensively and comprehensively the whole life of a particular community—town, county, or parish.

In the 1950s W. K. Jordan's monumental studies of English philanthropy in the sixteenth and seventeenth centuries opened up one such line of investigation. His successors in more recent decades have pushed ahead on other fronts. Two seminal works have been produced by Lawrence Stone, both of them spilling over into the seventeenth or later centuries. The first of these, *The Crisis of the English Aristocracy, 1560–1640* (London, 1965), owed something of its genesis to the "storm over the gentry." This dispute concerned the fortunes of the landowning classes in the generations just before the Civil War and their relation to its causes. But the book extends far beyond the bounds suggested by that problem. It is a massive study of the whole social economy of the English ruling elite in these eighty years. It includes in its topics their income and expenditure, their land-management practices, education, religion, and their behavior as local magnates, courtiers, and politicians. A book of such scope challenges further studies of the elite in other periods and of the fortunes of other social strata.[43]

Stone's second work, no less massive in size and scope, studies a central social institution. *The Family, Sex and Marriage in England 1500–1800* (New York and London, 1977) lays out very boldly a grand schema of family structure and of the sentiments and habits on which it rested over a three-century span. He sees the sixteenth and early seventeenth centuries as marked by a radical shift away from the open-lineage family of the Middle Ages, founded on kin and community, to a more limited circle, focused on the father; this in turn would give way, later in the seventeenth century, to a yet more restricted grouping in what he calls the "closed domesticated nuclear family." How far these hypotheses will be accepted by the learned community is yet to be tested, but for the first time we have a framework of articulated conceptions within which the history of the English family can be seriously examined.

Another work of broad scope which, like Stone's books, has opened up a new dimension in sixteenth-century studies is Keith Thomas's *Religion and the Decline of Magic* (London, 1971). Witchcraft itself has been the subject of occasional study by English historians in the past, but Thomas has placed it in a much larger context so that his work really embraces the whole range of popular belief about the supernatural (apart from formal Christian doctrine). Besides the vast body of information which the book contains, it raises very important questions about the fundamental nature of the conceptual world in which the great mass of Tudor Englishmen lived.[44] It ought to make all historians of religion in the period think again about their basic assumptions. There has been a too-facile acceptance of formal Protestant (and Catholic) piety as embodying the Englishman's whole view of the moral and spiritual universe. Thomas's book is a healthy corrective; it is also a pointer to one direction for future research: the popular culture of Tudor England.

Thomas's work is very appositely complemented by another study, Alan Mac-Farlane's *Witchcraft in Tudor and Stuart England: A Regional and Comparative Study* (London, 1970), which is based largely on an exhaustive examination of witchcraft cases in the Essex assize and ecclesiastical courts from 1560 to 1680. Drawing heavily for its interpretative analysis on contemporary anthropological approaches, this book lays out in pragmatic detail popular belief and practice. Together these books expand our understanding of the world of subliterate English men and women. They should stimulate an expansion of historians' horizons so as to make use of the techniques and knowledge anthropology places at our disposal.

Both these works encompass English society at large. At the other end of the spectrum are the numerous studies which take as their subject some small entity—town, county, or parish. Of these there is considerable variety, although the sixteenth century has not been so well served as the seventeenth, where the Civil War has served as a magnet around which many local studies have clustered.

Probably the easiest communities to examine are towns. Their communal life is embodied in legal institutions and in formal records; the structure of relationships is more visible than in rural society. Urban history is a well established historical discipline in England; there have been notable additions to the corpus in the last twenty years. A useful introduction to the present state of early-modern urban studies is to be found in Peter Clark and Paul Slack's *English Towns in Transition 1500–1700* (London, 1976), which briefly surveys the main features of urban life in these centuries. A similar book, written from a historical geographer's point of view, is John Patten's *English Towns 1500–1700* (London, 1978). Both works illustrate the difficulties of generalization about English urban life in an age when different towns experienced very diverse turns of fortune. Some leading medieval towns were in decay or struggling through painful cycles of readjustment to changing economic circumstances; others were laying the foundations of new prosperity; overall direction of movement is not easy to discern. As with economic history at large, this was an age of flux rather than of easily definable change.

Studies of individual cities have continued to appear. Sixteenth-century Winchester and Worcester have both been the subjects of book-length studies which explore not merely the formal legal categories but the whole spectrum of community life: A. D. Dyer's *The City of Worcester in the Sixteenth Century* (Leicester, 1973) and Tom Atkinson's *Elizabethan Winchester* (London, 1963). Peter Clark and Paul Slack have edited a volume of essays on various aspects of town life, *Crisis and Order in English Towns, 1500–1700* (London, 1972). The essays are original in character and suggest some important new ways in which urban historians might seek to explore their subject. What is conspicuously missing is a large-scale study of Tudor London; without such a history, the keystone of urban studies is still lacking. G. D. Ramsay's monograph *The City of London in International Politics at the Accession of Elizabeth Tudor* (Manchester, 1975) is a useful account of one episode in the metropolis's history.[45] Neither Bristol nor Norwich, the leading provincial centers of the age, has yet been adequately examined.

The counties have received some attention, although not so much as from Stuart historians. Yorkshire, as befits its size, has been the subject of two studies, R. B. Smith's *Land and Politics in the England of Henry VIII: The West Riding of Yorkshire, 1530–46* (London, 1970) and J. T. Cliffe's *The Yorkshire Gentry from the Reformation to the Civil War* (London, 1969). Two other northern counties have been the subject of books: Mervyn James, *Family, Lineage, and Civil Society, a Study of Society, Politics and Mentality in the Durham Region, 1500–1640* (Oxford, 1974) and S. J. Watts, *From Border to Middle Shire: Northumberland, 1586–1625* (Leicester, 1975).[46] A more politically oriented work, that of A. Hassell Smith on Norfolk, is mentioned above. Perhaps the most ambitious county study to date is Peter Clark's *English Provincial Society from the Reformation to the Revolution: Religion, Politics and Society in Kent 1500–1640* (Hassocks, 1977). These somewhat cumbrous titles reveal the ambition of the authors, influenced directly or indirectly by the *Annales* school, to include the intangible as well as the tangible aspects of the community life in their work. The uneven, often spotty, character of local sources often makes the achievement of this goal difficult. Moreover, the underlying assumption of these studies—that the county is truly a society as well as a legal and political entity—may or may not hold in every case; certainly it is an assumption that needs to be further tested.

Some of the most interesting and original work in local history has been devoted to the smallest communities, village and parishes. A model for such work was W. G. Hoskins's *The Midland Peasant* (London, 1957); some of his shorter studies are collected in *Provincial England* (London, 1963). His work spans a longer period than the sixteenth century; several recent books concentrate on the Tudor-Stuart epoch. Although materials are sparse, and their largely legal and administrative character limits the historian to a rather skeletonlike reconstruction, it is possible, at least in some instances, to achieve a richer and fuller picture. One such book is Margaret Spufford's *Contrasting Communities: English Villagers in the Sixteenth and Seventeenth Centuries* (London, 1974). By a skillful selection of three Cambridgeshire villages (one in the fens, another on the clay uplands, and the third on the chalk), she is able to show the important differences in development among three communities in one small county. She illuminates not only such traditional topics as crops and land distribution or the size of holdings but also literacy and religion. Another work of the same genre, David Hey's *An English Rural Community: Myddle under the Tudors and Stuarts* (Leicester, 1974), chooses as its subject a single Shropshire parish. The chance survival of a local antiquarian's work (dated about 1700) enables him to enrich the usual archival sources and to give an interestingly detailed picture of one of the thousands of parishes which were the basic social units of early-modern English society.[47]

Returning to works which take the national rather than the local scene for their subject brings me to one of the most important topics in social history: education. This was one of Stone's major themes in his study of the aristocracy. He has pursued it in a larger way as the editor of a collection of essays, *The University in Society* (Princeton, N.J., 1974), of which the first volume is given over to Oxford and Cambridge from the fourteenth to the nineteenth centuries. Education in our century (at every level from dames' schools to the universities) has been the subject of two books, Joan Simon's *Education and Society in Tudor England* (London, 1966) and Kenneth Charlton's *Education in the Renaissance, England* (Toronto, 1965).[48] Both are attempts to do much more than merely catalog information about educational matters. Both explore the increasingly self-conscious relation between society at large and the schools to which it gave increasingly large resources in this century. They seek to interpret the humanist ideology which articulated the concern for education as well as the more pragmatic impulses which sent university enrollments soaring and led to the founding of new schools in many communities all over the country.[49]

That opportunities for formal education increased in this century has been generally accepted, but the actual effects upon society at large are harder to estimate. One obvious test is the degree of literacy in Tudor society. Here an interesting start in exploring an extremely difficult problem has been made by David Cressy in a series of articles: "Literacy in Pre-industrial England" (*Societas* 4, 1974); "Educational Opportunity in Tudor and Stuart England" (*History of Education Quarterly*, 1976); and "Levels of Illiteracy in England 1530–1730" (*HJ* 20, 1977).

The topic of education brings me to a border area where the interests of historians encounter those of other scholars, particularly those concerned with the history of ideas, taken in the largest sense. Two areas have traditionally engaged the attention of Tudor historians: political and social thought and literature. The latter has been pretty largely the preserve of scholars expert in that discipline, and it is they, rather than professional historians, who have explored the political and social content of contemporary literature. A good example of such a study is David Bevington's *Tudor Drama and Politics: A Critical Approach to Topical Meaning* (Cambridge, Mass., 1968). From the historian's side, A. L. Rowse has continued his multivolume account of Elizabethan England with two volumes on general cultural history, *The Elizabethan Renaissance: The Life of the Society* (London, 1971) and *The Elizabethan Renaissance: The Cultural Achievement* (London, 1972). A stimulating series of essays which touches on all the arts and their relations to general cultural patterns is John Buxton's *Elizabethan Taste* (London, 1964).[50]

Sixteenth-century English political thought lacks the seminal writers, such as Bacon, Hobbes, Milton, or Locke, who play so large a role in the whole history of the next century. Nevertheless, there has been an established tradition of interest in Tudor political and social thought, and several notable books on the subject have appeared within the last two decades. Arthur B. Ferguson's *The Articulate Citizen and the English Renaissance* (Durham, N.C., 1965) is an important book, for it authoritatively surveys the whole tradition of social criticism in England, beginning well back in the Middle Ages and ending in the middle of the Tudor century. It affords an excellent introduction to the group who have usually been known as the "Commonwealth men." These writers are the subject of a book by Whitney R. D. Jones, *The Tudor Commonwealth 1529–1559* (London, 1970), but the received tradition to which the Jones book pretty well adheres has been attacked in a recent article by G. R. Elton, "Reform and the 'Commonwealth-Men' of Edward VI's Reign" (in P. Clark, A. G. R. Smith, and N. Tyacke, eds., *The English Commonwealth*, Leicester, 1979).[51]

A lucid survey of the major political writers of the Tudor century is found in Christopher Morris's *Political Thought in England: Tyndale to Hooker* (reprint, London, 1965). A series of books have explored the civic consciousness of the Tudor age, of which the Commonwealth tradition is only one aspect. W. H. Greenleaf, in *Order, Empiricism and Politics: Two Traditions of English Political Thought, 1500–1700* (London, 1964), and Donald W. Hanson, in *From Kingdom to Commonwealth: The Development of Civic Consciousness in English Political Thought* (Cambridge, Mass., 1970), have both argued for underlying tensions within the received—but ill-articulated—political conceptions of the English ruling classes.[52] It took the Civil War to bring these to the surface of full consciousness. An original and stimulating study is Michael Walzer's *Revolution of the Saints: A Study in the Origins of Radical Politics* (Cambridge, Mass., 1965), which casts the radical Puritan preachers in a seminal role as the first practitioners of a whole new mode of political behavior.[53] The English reception of the great Italian pragmatist Machiavelli is chronicled in Felix Raab in *The English Face of Machiavelli: A Changing Interpretation, 1500–1700* (Toronto, 1964).

This was an age which often found it easier to express its underlying political and social conceptions in symbol or ritual than in words. Long neglect of such manifestations by English historians has been remedied by several works of recent years. The exploitation of spectacle and pageantry by the first Tudors was explored by Sydney Anglo, *Spectacle, Pageantry and Early Tudor Policy* (London,

1969). The Elizabethan age has been treated in two outstanding books. Frances Yates's *Astraea: The Imperial Theme in the Sixteenth Century* (London, 1975) illuminates the abundant use of symbol by portraitists and engravers in their projection of Elizabeth's imperial role. Similar themes are taken up by Roy Strong in *The Cult of Elizabeth: Elizabethan Portraiture and Pageantry* (London, 1977). He has also exploited the same kinds of materials in R. C. Strong and J. A. VanDorsten's *Leicester's Triumph* (London, 1977), the subject of which is that earl's reception in the Low Countries in 1586. The less splendid but no less significant pageantry of the English towns is studied by David Bergeron in *English Civic Pageantry 1558–1642* (London, 1971). Works like these, by opening up the world of the Tudor imagination, expand our understanding of the way in which the political and social order was conceived by contemporaries.

A special corner of intellectual history which is of particular interest to the professional historian is the work of their predecessors in the art. Two large-scale studies in recent decades have been devoted to historiography in our century. Both of them aim at much more than a catalog of Tudor historical writing; each is a serious essay in intellectual history. F. Smith Fussner's *The Historical Revolution: English Historical Writing and Thought 1580–1640* (London, 1962) reveals by its title the author's argument that the historians of this age are radical innovators, the founders of a new historiographical tradition. F. J. Levy's *Tudor Historical Thought* (San Marino, Calif., 1967) covers a somewhat different time span and makes fewer claims for the innovatory character of the Tudor historians. May McKisack, in *Medieval History in the Tudor Age* (London, 1971), is concerned with a more limited topic but one which illuminates both the ages with which she deals.[54]

∝℘

These thirty years of Tudor historical studies have been fruitful ones. In the traditional areas of investigation—politics, political institutions, and religion—a vigorous revisionism has fundamentally altered our received views of these topics. What we have now is not a new set of stereotypes to replace the old but a stronger sense of the complexity and the ambiguities of the age. Even more important than these revisions is the minor explosion which has taken place in social and economic history. The new methodologies and the new concepts generated in these fields of study on the Continent, in Britain, and in America are now penetrating the study of the English sixteenth century; much remains to be done, but the pioneers have pushed the frontiers forward. The new ground which needs to be broken is visible enough; the great problem—certainly in America—is that of finding the hands for the work. The acute depression which afflicts the academic workplace is choking off the supply of young scholars to such an extent that a real generation gap, as severe as that produced by war in the past, faces the profession.

NOTES

1. Two useful bibliographical aids for Tudor historians have appeared within the last decade or so. The volume *Tudor England 1485–1603*, London, 1968, in the Bibliographical Handbooks issued by the Conference on British Studies was edited by Mortimer Levine. A new series, issued annually, began appearing in 1975 under the sponsorship of the Royal Historical Society, *Annual Bibliography of British and Irish History*, general editor, G. R. Elton, Hassocks and Atlantic Highlands, N.J., 1975–

2. See also G. L. Harriss, "Aids, Loans, and Benevolences," *HJ* 6, 1963.

3. See G. R. Elton's collected essays in *Studies in Tudor and Stuart Politics and Government*, 2 vols., London, 1974.

4. For a study of one of Cromwell's protégé's, see A. J. Slavin, *Politics and Profit: A Study of Sir Ralph Sadler 1507–47*, London, 1966.

5. See Elton's reply *PP*, no. 29, 1964: 26–49; J. P. Cooper in *PP*, no. 26, 1963: 110–112; Harriss and Williams in *PP*, no. 31, 1965: 87–96; and Elton in *PP*, no. 32, 1965: 103–109.

6. See also B. L. Beer, *Northumberland: The Political Career of John Dudley, Earl of Warwick and Duke of Northumberland*, Kent, Ohio, Kent State University Press, 1973.

7. One useful article is that by R. H. Pogson, "Reginald Pole and the Priorities of Government in Mary Tudor's Church," *HJ* 18, 1975.

8. Another book on Raleigh is A. L. Rowse, *Sir Walter Raleigh: His Family and Private Life*, London, 1962.

9. See also Mortimer Levine, *The Early Elizabethan Succession Question 1558–1568*, Stanford, Calif. 1966. Joel Hurstfield has written an illuminating essay, "Queen and State: The Emergence of an Elizabethan Myth," in J. S. Bromley and E. H. Kossmann, eds., *Britain and the Netherlands*, vol. 5, London, 1975.

10. See N. M. Sutherland, "Queen Elizabeth and the Conspiracy of Amboise," *EHR* 81, 1966, and Roger Howell, "The Sidney Circle and the Protestant Cause in Elizabethan Foreign Policy," *Renaissance and Modern Studies* 19, 1975.

11. Stanford E. Lehmberg, *The Reformation Parliament 1529–1536*, London, 1977; idem, *The Later Parliaments of Henry VIII 1536–1547*, London, 1977. See also Goronwy Edwards, "The Emergence of Majority Rule in the Procedure of the House of Commons," *TRHS*, 5th ser., 15, 1965.

12. An exception to this generalization is to be found in the work of Joel Hurstfield. His valuable essays on Elizabethan history are included in the collection *Freedom, Corruption and Government*, London, 1973.

13. V. F. Snow's edition of John Hooker's manual, *Parliament in Elizabethan England: John Hooker's Order and Usage*, New Haven, Conn., 1977, makes available an important source for parliamentary history.

14. For a thoughtful analysis of the problems confronting historians of Tudor institutions, see the three-part presidential address of G. R. Elton, "Tudor Government: The Points of Contact," *TRHS*, 5th ser., 24, 25, 26, 1974–1976. They deal successively with Parliament, Council, and Court.

15. See also the biography by Wilbur Dunkel, *William Lambarde, Elizabethan Jurist*, New Brunswick, N.J., 1964, and R. M. Warnicke, *William Lambarde: Elizabethan Antiquary*, Chichester, 1973.

16. See also Stuart Prall, "The Development of Equity in Tudor England," *American Journal of Legal History*, 1964, and W. H. Bryson, *The Equity Side of the Exchequer: Its Jurisdiction, Administration, Procedures and Records*, London, 1975.

17. But see Thomas G. Barnes, "Due Process and Slow Process in the Late Elizabethan–Early Stuart Star Chamber," *American Journal of Legal History*, 1962. L. A. Knafla, *Law and Politics in Jacobean England: The Tracts of Lord Ellesmere*, 1977, although largely concerned with seventeenth-century affairs, has a valuable account of the career of Elizabeth's last lord keeper. See also idem, "Conscience in the English Common Law Tradition, "*University of Toronto Law Journal* 26, 1976.

18. See also A. W. B. Simpson, "The Early Constitution of the Inns of Court," *Cambridge Law Journal*, 1970.

19. See also A. L. Beier, "Vagrants and the Social Order in Elizabethan England," *PP*, no. 64, 1974.

20. J. S. Cockburn, ed., *Calendar of Assize Records*, London, 1975–

21. See also G. R. Elton, "The Law of Treason in the Early Reformation," *HJ* 2, 1968.

22. See also Thomas Esper, "The Replacement of the Longbow by Firearms in the English Army," in *Technology and Culture*, London, 1975, and C. S. L. Davies, "Provisions for Armies: Effectiveness of Early Tudor Government," *Economic History Review*, 2d ser., 17, 1964.

23. See also C. S. L. Davies, "The Administration of the Royal Navy under Henry VIII: The Origins of the Navy Board," *EHR* 80, 1965.

24. R. S. Sylvester, ed., *Complete Works of St. Thomas More*, New Haven, Conn., 1963– . They now include *The History of Richard III; Translations of Lucian; Utopia; Responsio ad Lutherum; The Confrontation of Tyndale's Answer*. Note especially J. H. Hexter's introduction to *Utopia*. See also J. D. M. Derrett, "The Trial of Sir Thomas More," *EHR* 79, 1964; L. Miles, "Persecution and the Charges against Thomas More," *JBS* 5, 1965; and R. Pineas, *Thomas More and Tudor Polemics*, Bloomingdale, Ind., 1968.

25. See Margaret Bowker's two articles, "The Supremacy and the Episcopate: The Struggle for Control 1534–1540," *HJ* 18, 1975, and "The Henrician Reformation and the Parish Clergy," *BIHR* 50, 1977; Michael Kelly, "The Submission of the Clergy," *TRHS*, 5th ser., 15, 1965. Also N. D. Tjernagel, *Henry VIII and the Lutherans: A Study in Anglo-Lutheran Relations from 1521 to 1547*, St. Louis, 1965.

26. See also G. W. O. Woodward, *The Dissolution of the Monasteries*, London, 1966.

27. F. Heal and R. O'Day, eds., *Church and Society in England, Henry VIII to James I*, London, 1977, and R. O'Day and F. Heal, eds., *Continuity and Change: Personnel and Administration of the Church of England, 1500–1642*, Leicester, 1976.

28. Patrick McGrath, *Papists and Puritans*, New York, 1967, surveys a briefer period.

29. For a biography of an eminent lay Puritan, see Claire Cross, *The Puritan Earl: The Life of Henry Hastings, Third Earl of Huntingdon, 1536–1595*, London, 1966. See also Peter Cable, "Matthew Hutton, a Puritan Bishop?" *History*, June 1979.

30. See also Claire Cross, "The Economic Problems of the See of York: Decline and Recovery in the Sixteenth Century," *Agricultural History Review* 18, 1970, suppl.

31. See also Bossy's article, "Rome and the Elizabethan Catholics: A Question of Geography," *HJ* 1, 1964.

32. See also L. Hicks, *An Elizabethan Problem: Some Aspects of the Careers of Two Exile-Adventurers*, New York, 1963.

33. For a special aspect of the recusant problem, see A. de C. Parmiter, "Elizabethan Popish Recusancy in the Inns of Court," *BIHR*, suppl. 11, 1976.

34. See also Ian Blanchard, "Population Change, Enclosure and the Early Tudor Economy," *EHR*, 2d ser., 23, 1970. A study focused on this same problem is Victor Skipp's *Crises and Development: An Ecological Case Study of the Forest of Arden, 1570–1674*, London, 1978.

35. See also Eric Kerridge, *The Farmers of Old England*, London, 1973.

36. See also A. B. Appleby, "Agrarian Capitalism or Seigneurial Reaction? The Northwest of England 1500–1700," *AHR* 80, 1975.

37. See D. C. Coleman's sixty-page summary in *Industry in Tudor and Stuart England*, London, 1975.

38. See also W. G. Hoskins, *The Age of Plunder, King Henry's England, 1500–1547*, New York and London, 1976; B. A. Holderness, *Pre-industrial England, Economy and Society 1500–1750*, London and Totowa, N.J., 1976; R. O'Day, *Economy and Community: Economic and Social History of England, 1500–1700*, London, 1975.

39. Peter J. Bowden, *The Wool Trade in Tudor and Stuart England*, London, 1962; E. S. Godfrey, *The Development of English Glassmaking 1560–1640*, London, 1976.

40. See also J. Crofts, *Packhorse, Waggon and Post: Land Carriage and Communications under the Tudors and Stuarts*, Toronto, 1968. For maritime affairs, see Ralph Davis, *English Overseas Trade 1500–1700*, London, 1973, and G. V. Scammell, "Shipowning in the Economy and Politics of Early Modern England," *HJ* 15, 1972.

41. For an introduction to conciliar intervention, see Vincent Ponko, Jr., "The Privy Council and the Spirit of Elizabethan Economic Management, *1558–1603*, *Transactions of the American Philosophical Society*, n.s., 58, pt. 4, 1968.

42. See two useful articles by R. B. Outhwaite that open up the problems of Elizabethan finance: "Royal Borrowing in the Reign of Elizabeth I: The Aftermath of Antwerp," *EHR* 86, 1971, and "Who Bought Crown Lands? The Pattern of Purchase 1589–1603," *BIHR*, 1971.

43. See also Lawrence Stone, *Family and Fortune*, London, 1973, a book more largely concerned with the Stuart era than the Tudor; Alan Simpson, *The Wealth of the Gentry, 1540–1660: East Anglian Studies*, Chicago, 1961, a regional study; and the following articles: Roger S. Schofield, "The Geographical Distribution of Wealth in England, 1334–1649," *EHR*, 2d ser., 18, 1965; F. M. L. Thompson, "The Social Distribution of Landed Property in England since the Sixteenth Century," *EHR*, 2d ser., 19, 1966; J. P. Cooper, "The Social Distribution of Land and Men in England 1436–1700," *EHR*, 2d ser., 20, 1967.

44. For a study of magic in a more sophisticated and learned setting, see Peter J. French, *John Dee: The World of an Elizabethan Magus*, London, 1972.

45. See, however, F. J. Fisher, "London as an 'Engine of Economic Growth,'" in J. S. Bromley and E. H. Kossmann, eds., *Britain and the Netherlands*, vol. 4, chap. 7, The Hague, 1971, and Helen Miller, "London and Parliament in the Reign of Henry VIII," *BIHR*, 1962. See also, for one facet of London life, Frank F. Foster, *The Politics of Stability: A Portrait of the Rulers of Elizabethan London*, Royal Historical Society Studies in History 1, 1977.

46. See also G. A. J. Hodgett, *Tudor Lincolnshire*, Lincoln, 1975.

47. See also P. A. J. Pettit, *The Royal Forests of Northamptonshire, 1558–1714* London, 1968.

48. See also A. C. F. Beales, *Education under Penalty: English Catholic Education from the Reformation to the Fall of James II, 1547–1689*, London, 1963.

49. See also Hugh Kearney, *Scholars and Gentlemen: Universities and Society in Pre-industrial Britain 1500–1700*, London, 1970.

50. See also J. A. VanDorsten, *The Radical Arts: First Decade of an Elizabethan Renaissance*, London, 1970.

51. Mary Dewar's new edition of *A Discourse of the Commonweal of this Realm of England*, Char-

lottesville, Va., 1969, gives an authoritative text for a key work which, she argues strongly, was written by Sir Thomas Smith rather than John Hales.

52. See also Brenden Bradshaw, "The Tudor Commonwealth: Reform and Revision," *HJ* 22, 1979.

53. For a critique of Walzer's position, see Quentin Skinner, *Foundations of Modern Political Thought*, 1978, 2:322–323.

54. See also F. S. Fussner, *Tudor History and the Historians*, London, 1970.

New Ways and Old
in Early Stuart History

David Underdown

In a *Times Literary Supplement* issue devoted to "new ways in history" in 1966, Keith Thomas outlined an agenda for British historians. It was time, he thought, for them to show greater conceptual precision, use quantitative techniques to test explicitly formulated theoretical models, and broaden their scope to encompass the total society, applying appropriate insights from sociology and anthropology. Thomas looked forward to the "dethronement of politics" by social history in the manner already achieved by the *Annales* school in France. The new history would be concerned with demography, marriage and the family, popular religion and culture, and other topics relating to the lives of ordinary people. Some of the "new ways" were already being followed by 1966, but the process was still only in its early stages.[1]

By 1978 it is clear that, although not all of Thomas's predictions have been fulfilled, some items from his agenda have indeed greatly changed prevailing views of early seventeenth-century English history. The relevant essays in *Changing Views* almost automatically began with political history.[2] This time, such an order of priorities is unthinkable. The greatest advances since the early 1960s have been in social history, and although more traditional branches of the discipline have retained their vitality, even there, important advances have resulted from that broadening of the historian's vision which Thomas advocated. No longer can the political historian ignore the work of colleagues trying to penetrate the mists shrouding the lives of the common people. Selection of the most significant themes from the mass of recent writing on the period 1603–1660 is a daunting task, but it is with demographic and social history that one naturally begins.

It is only a slight exaggeration to say that systematic study of English demographic history dates from the foundation of the Cambridge Group for the History of Population and Social Structure in 1964.[3] With the aid of an army of local

99

researchers, serious investigation of parish registers and similar sources was begun. Demographic historians tend to be interested in centuries rather than decades, and this, along with the greater survival of usuable records for later periods, means that work specifically concerned with the years 1603–1660 is limited in quantity. But many of the longer studies throw some light on the period, and at least the broad outline of English population growth has been established. The population explosion of the sixteenth century appears to have continued into the first two decades of the seventeenth, with some deceleration by the 1630s and markedly slower growth after mid-century.

The earliest publicist of demographic history was Peter Laslett, whose study of two Leicestershire villages (Clayworth and Cogenhoe) had already shown some of its possibilities. In *The World We Have Lost*, Laslett provided a sort of manifesto for the Cambridge Group, though he has denied that this was his intention.[4] Laslett's sweeping claims for the "new" history, his static conception of pre-industrial society, and his sallies against historians who saw the Civil War as the result of social conflict, all provoked sharp criticism.[5] Yet the book at least brought the subject of quantitative demographic history before a wide public. It was followed by *An Introduction to English Historical Demography*, edited by E. A. Wrigley, in which the two most favored techniques, aggregative analysis and family reconstitution, were carefully explained.[6]

The pioneering study originating in the Cambridge Group, from which others have perhaps been too quick to generalize, was Wrigley's of the village of Colyton.[7] Around 1646, Wrigley shows, Colyton entered a period of much slower population growth than it had experienced in the previous century. The average age at marriage, especially for women, rose perceptibly, and the deliberate practice of birth control appears to have been adopted. Wrigley sees these developments as occurring more or less autonomously, but David Levine, in *Family Formation in an Age of Nascent Capitalism*, argues that they were the result of local economic decline.[8] Although no other village has yet provided such a wealth of data, the vitality of demographic history is obvious. Other major contributions include Laslett's work on household size in England, and a variety of studies of bridal pregnancy, illegitimacy (both declining in the seventeenth century), and similar topics. A new journal, *Local Population Studies*, serves as an outlet for the flood of information.[9] And lest it be thought that the historians of population deal only with the nameless multitudes, it might be noted that T. H. Hollingsworth's "The Demography of the British Peerage" was published just prior to the first efforts of the Cambridge Group.[10] Demographic history is no longer in its infancy, though many more refinements of method and formulations of new questions can be expected as it further matures.

The relevance of the demographers' work to other branches of history is not always easy to see, but it is very clear in one important topic: mortality, especially in relation to disease and famine. There have been several illuminating local studies. Ian Sutherland's survey of mortality in London suggests that the 1603 and 1625 plagues may have been worse than the more famous one of 1665.[11] Andrew B. Appleby shows that in underdeveloped Cumberland and Westmorland sharp increases in mortality often attributed to epidemics were in fact temporary subsistence crises. Elsewhere, however, the same author questions the relationship of mortality to environmental factors. In London the death rate actually declined as the city became more crowded, and there appears to be little correlation between death and food prices.[12] While the connections between disease, diet, and the environment thus remain unclear, progress has been made on the political consequences of food shortages. John Walter and Keith Wrightson find that grain riots posed little threat to the social order, thanks to the operation of the "moral economy" and effective ameliorative measures by the authorities.[13] There was, though, a high incidence of popular violence in this period. The subject is discussed, with appropriate continental comparisons, in two articles by C. S. L. Davies.[14] There was also some connection between retaliation against enclosers and grain dealers and similar action against villagers who violated local norms of sexual or family behavior; thus E. P. Thompson's analysis of "skimmingtons" and other local rituals has important implications, even if much of the evidence comes from later times.[15]

All these are new directions, but on the subjects of poor relief and vagrancy, historians are treading more familiar paths. The years covered by this essay begin with the completion of Wilbur K. Jordan's massive studies of English philanthropy. Flawed as Jordan's work may have been by his refusal to take into account population growth and inflation and by his exaggeration of the role of the private sector, one aspect withstands challenge: the "changing pattern of social aspirations" from religious to secular concerns.[16] More recently, analyses of poor relief in Salisbury by Paul Slack (a remarkable instance, this, of Puritan reform imposed by a reluctant community), and in Warwickshire by A. L. Beier, have continued the revision of older notions that the paternalist monarchy had a more generous poverty program than the allegedly individualistic Puritans.[17] As for vagrancy, it is an old subject now scarcely recognizable as the one that inspired the picturesque "rogues and vagabonds" approach. Vagrancy is now subject to quantification and is viewed in the general context of geographical mobility and of subsistence migration by the poor in search of work. A good example is an article by Slack which defines the nature and extent of vagrancy and suggests that it was most characteristic of unstable woodland and pasture communities.[18] Others have found these same wood-pasture regions, along with towns and industrial parishes, to be significant sources of emigration to North America.[19] Immigration, on the other hand, has received little attention. In spite of the recent growth of black history, there is almost nothing on blacks in England in this period to complement the superb illumination of English racial attitudes in the first chapter of Winthrop D. Jordan's *White over Black*.[20]

Another of the demographers' main concerns, the history of the family, has attracted others besides the statistically minded. There are beginnings for three components of the family: women, children, and the aged. Roger Thompson, in *Women in Stuart England and America*, summarizes previous research and suggests some promising hypotheses, but is stronger on America than on England.[21] Ivy Pinchbeck and Margaret Hewitt's *Children in English Society*, volume 1, is informative on public provision for poor children but lacks any theoretical base of the kind that Phillipe Ariès has proposed.[22] Articles by Steven R. Smith question Ariès's contention that the concept of the next phase, adolescence, had not yet developed in the seventeenth century, but like the same author's survey of writings on the problems of aging, leave much room for further study.[23] Child rearing, birth control, and sex are also being investigated, although until very recently one could point to no more than a few pioneering efforts.[24] A successful case study that covers many of these topics, however, is Alan Macfarlane's *The Family Life of Ralph Josselin, a Seventeenth-century Clergyman*.[25] Macfarlane applies the perspectives of social anthropology in analyzing Josselin's voluminous diary, throwing much interesting light on family and neighborhood ties, local rituals, and attitudes to public affairs, religion, and economic activity. Unfortunately Josselin's reticence deprives us of information on the diarist's sex life and other important matters.

All these aspects of the history of the family are brought together in a highly individual synthesis in Lawrence Stone's massive *The Family, Sex and Marriage in England, 1500–1800*.[26] Like so much of Stone's work, this is history on the grand scale, drawing on a vast range of sources, both quantifiable and literary. Reduced to its essentials, Stone's thesis is that during these three centuries occurred the transition from the distant, deferential family relations of the late medieval era to the "affective individualism" of modern times. By 1600 the earlier "open lineage" type, in which the nuclear family was subsumed in the wider kinship network, was being supplanted by the "restricted partriarchal nuclear" type, in which kinship ties were weaker than national or religious ones but patriarchal authority over the nuclear unit was stronger than ever. The third, "closed domesticated nuclear" type, Stone sees just originating around 1640. This ambitious book incorporates much important information on value systems, sexual behavior, parent–child relations, and the like. It also shows great awareness of the complexities of social structure and of differences in the pace of change at various social levels. New familial patterns, Stone argues, originated near the top; affective individualism appeared first among the gentry and wealthy bourgeoisie and percolated upward to the court aristocracy and downward to the lower orders. Some may find this a rather elitist conception, but for the present Stone provides the best synthesis of all previous output on the subject.

Beyond the family, another unit of concern to social historians has been the local community. Work in this field often derives much inspiration from those earlier masters H. P. R. Finberg and W. G. Hoskins. Alan Everitt has followed in their footsteps, identifying several significant themes which emerge from the bewildering diversity of the localities: the contrast between fielden and pastoral or forest regions, for example.[27] Many of the more politically oriented county studies I discuss later contain useful information, and one county has been the subject of a separate social and economic history: C. W. Chalklin's *Seventeenth-century Kent*.[28] Two books reach down to the village level. Margaret Spufford's *Contrasting Communities* painstakingly uses wills and other local records to penetrate the social, economic, and religious life of three Cambridgeshire villages and to show the striking differences between communities only a few miles apart—in educational opportunities, for instance. David G. Hey's *An English Rural Community* is less comparative but is able to use the fascinating reminiscences of a local man, Richard Gough, to bring the villagers to life.[29]

At the other end of the scale, the nation, the best starting point is Lawrence Stone's framework for the study of English social structure. His article examines changes in the hierarchies of status, income, and power and tries to define the nature and causes of social mobility at all levels. Even for a historian of Stone's breadth this is a tall order for a single article, but numerous hypotheses are proposed for others to test or challenge. An obvious need is for detailed investigation of the various status groups composing this structure. Stone has set an impressive example in *The Crisis of the Aristocracy 1558–1641* (also discussed later for its contribution to political history).[30] There is no comparable work on the gentry, although there have been several local studies, including J. T. Cliffe's excellent *The Yorkshire Gentry*.[31] No full-scale analysis of any other group has been attempted, though the London population has been studied in suggestive articles by Steven Smith on the apprentices and R. G. Lang on the merchants. The latter questions J. H. Hexter's contention that merchants were recruited from, and if successful rejoined, the gentry.[32]

The only general social history concentrating on this period that has been written since the early 1960s is Carl Bridenbaugh's *Vexed and Troubled Englishmen 1590–1642*. In some respects this book departs from the prevailing trends in social history. Bridenbaugh has little interest in theory or sociological models and discusses demographic and economic themes without benefit of quantification. But in other ways it follows the pattern: "history from below"—in this case, of a descriptive rather than an analytical mode. No previous historian provides as complete a picture of the life of the ordinary people of England and of the communities, urban as well as rural, in which they lived.[33]

⟨⟨⟩⟩

    Separation of economic from social history is somewhat artificial, particularly in what still has many of the hallmarks of "Tawney's century." The outstanding recent achievement, *The Agrarian History of England and Wales*, volume 4, *1500–1640*, edited by Joan Thirsk, certainly shows Tawney's influence, along with that of the Leicester "local-particularist" school of Finberg and Hoskins. Chapters on regional differences, farming methods, marketing arrangements, prices and profits, landlords, laborers, and much else, provide an incomparable survey of rural life. Perhaps of most general significance is Thirsk's chapter, "The Farming Regions of England," which sets out a typology of contrasting field and forest or pasture communities which has important implications for other kinds of history besides the economic. Thirsk and Everitt have both developed the contrast elsewhere: the more rapid population growth, industrialization, and social instability of the wood-pasture regions, compared with the tighter manorial control and closer bonds of neighborhood of the usually nucleated fielden settlements.[34] Forest societies and economies have been studied in several other works, including Philip A. J. Pettit's *The Royal Forests of Northamptonshire: A Study in their Economy, 1558–1714* and Victor Skipp's *Crisis and Development: An Ecological Case Study of the Forest of Arden 1570–1674*.[35] Skipp combines economic and demographic analysis to show how Arden adjusted to the disturbance of "ecological equilibrium" caused by earlier population growth.

    Tawney's work in agrarian history has had one severe critic. Eric Kerridge, in *Agrarian Problems in the Sixteenth Century and After*, argues that enclosure was socially desirable, attacks (excessively legalistically) Tawney's contention that the law gave peasants scant protection against encroachments on their common rights, and deplores Tawney's socialist principles. As in the famous debate over the standard of living during the Industrial Revolution, the issue ranges against each other two fundamentally opposed political and moral attitudes toward early capitalism. Appleby attempts a reconciliation in a case study of the northwestern counties, concluding that Tawney was right in that, after 1603, the peasants lost security of tenure but that Kerridge is also right in that the resulting agrarian capitalism was beneficial to the region.[36]

    Kerridge makes a less contentious revision of chronology in his *The Agricultural Revolution*. Here he successfully questions the traditional association of the new agricultural techniques with the era of "Turnip" Townshend, Robert Bakewell, and Jethro Tull in the eighteenth century. In fact, Kerridge shows,

new crops (even the famous turnip), the use of water meadows, more sophisticated crop rotations, and other improvements were all well established by 1660.
The steady inroads of capitalist methods thus make this period a crucial stage in
the process of modernization.[37]

There have been several other notable contributions to the history of agriculture and landownership. Output may have been increasing and inflation de-
celerating, but two articles by W. G. Hoskins show the continuing short-term
fluctuations caused by the weather. H. J. Habakkuk discusses the impact of the
Civil War on landlords, confirming Thirsk's earlier conclusion that they suffered
less than used to be supposed. Much information on inheritance customs is presented in a volume edited by Jack Goody and others, in which Thirsk and
J. P. Cooper make continental comparisons, while Spufford and Cicely Howell
show the familiar seventeenth-century decline in middle-sized peasant holdings.
Finally, R. Machin has proposed an important revision of Hoskins's thesis about
the "great rebuilding": a complex process, Machin suggests, differing in date
from region to region, but more common in the years around 1700 than a century earlier.[38]

Industrial history has produced less innovative work during the years under
review. Not much is left of J. U. Nef's argument for 1540–1640 as a period of
dynamic industrial growth, though it survives in J. W. Gough's otherwise unre-
markable *The Rise of the Entrepreneur* and is subjected to criticism in Sybil M.
Jack's useful survey, *Trade and Industry in Tudor and Stuart England.* Nef's thesis
also colors William Rees's *Industry before the Industrial Revolution,* an immensely
detailed work on the coal and iron industries, especially in Wales and the border
counties.[39] There are some new ideas, however, in an article by G. Hammersley
which questions assumptions that the iron industry was depleting its woodland
fuel supplies by the seventeenth century. Elsewhere Hammersley has traced the
brief flickering of the copper industry in the century before 1640, and several
other industries have been examined: leather by L. A. Clarkson, glass by Eleanor S. Godfrey, and most impressively, shipping by Ralph Davis.[40] Two contributions by Cooper argue that the English Revolution was not really a watershed
separating an earlier age of government regulation from a later one of laissez-
faire.[41] Such industrial development as occurred demanded new attitudes toward
time and work, a subject brilliantly explored in E. P. Thompson's "Time,
Work-Discipline, and Industrial Capitalism."[42] Much of this deals with later
years, but as is Thompson's habit, he suggests valuable insights for our period.

Commerce and investment have been more fruitful in provoking fresh hypotheses, especially on their political aspects. The new techniques of econometrics
have had little impact, though two studies of investment make effective use of the
computer. Theodore K. Rabb, in *Enterprise and Empire: Merchant and Gentry
Investment in the Expansion of England, 1575–1630,* distinguishes between the

types of investment the two groups in his title tended to prefer, with some heavy doses of methodology. Karl S. Bottigheimer, in *English Money and Irish Land: The 'Adventurers' in the Cromwellian Settlement of Ireland*, performs a similar operation on the mainly London investors who speculated in Irish lands during the Civil War.[43]

More directly concerned with overseas trade is K. N. Chaudhuri's solid *The English East India Company*. Other aspects of commerce have been treated in articles on the African, Polish, and Spanish trades.[44] Harland Taylor and J. S. Kepler both demonstrate the stimulus the Thirty Years' War gave to the English carrying trade, while Kepler has also examined the free port which flourished for a time at Dover during the war. The war's impact on the English economy is also visible in W. B. Stephens's analysis of cloth exports from the outports in the 1620s, which shows the highly variable effects of war and depression from port to port.[45] To economic as well as social historians, local differences seem increasingly important.

Generalizing about the national economy is made easier, however, by the overwhelming predominance of London. Wrigley's "simple model" of the capital's socioeconomic importance deals with the century after 1650 but is also relevant to the earlier period.[46] The huge gulf between the wealth of merchants in London and the provinces is demonstrated by Richard Grassby, while the Londoners' influence on government after 1649 is explored by James Farnell in an article on the pressures behind the Navigation Act and the first Dutch War.[47] Robert Brenner proposes a general interpretative framework for the interaction of commerce and politics, identifying three successively dominant mercantile groups, each associated with a phase of government: the old Merchant Adventurers, the Levant–East Indies group, and the new American and Caribbean interests. The second and third he roughly equates with the crown and Parliament respectively. The equation was really less clear-cut, as Robert Ashton points out, in that the American interests were not the only ones to oppose the crown before 1640, with elements of both trading groups being involved in court politics.[48] In the long run, though, as Ernst Schulin's survey of opinions on trade and national policy shows, the Civil War made a crucial difference in that, after it, merchants were no longer impeded by a hostile or indifferent government. Indeed, the more wide-ranging analysis of tracts and pamphlet literature by Joyce O. Appleby in her *Economic Thought and Ideology in Seventeenth-century England* argues that English writers at this time developed the first clear conception of the free-market economy.[49]

Much of this discussion assumes that London's main concentration was on foreign trade. Although this was of course eventually to be the case, R. G. Lang reminds us not to antedate this development: in James I's reign more than half of the aldermen were primarily engaged in domestic trade.[50] Internal trade has re-

ceived less attention than foreign, but aspects of it are dealt with in Peter J. Bowden's *The Wool Trade in Tudor and Stuart England*, much of which is also useful
for the cloth industry, and in sections of T. S. Willan's *The Inland Trade: Studies
in English Internal Trade in the Sixteenth and Seventeenth Centuries*. J. Crofts's
*Packhorse, Waggon and Post: Land Carriage and Communications under the Tudors
and Stuarts*, is a descriptive survey of land transport, informative on the hitherto
neglected carriers.[51] For all aspects of trade, movements of prices and profits are
central. Discussion of the former has generally focused on the sixteenth century,
but Y. S. Brenner has pursued the great inflation down to 1650, rejecting mone-
tarist explanations in favor of population growth, as most modern opinion does.
After constructing his own price series, however, Robert A. Doughty combines
the two explanations: population growth for the secular upward movement, currency manipulation for the occasional accelerations.[52] As for profits, Grassby's argument, from admittedly imperfect evidence, that the level of trading profits actually fell during the seventeenth century, has yet to be assimilated.[53]

There have been several useful general surveys of the economy, which usually
include 1603–1660 in the longer development of preindustrial England.[54] The
most thorough descriptive surveys are in *A New Historical Geography of England*,
edited by H. C. Darby.[55] F. V. Emery's chapter, "England *circa* 1600," complements (in less detail) Thirsk's chapter on agricultural regions in the *Agrarian
History* but also has much on towns, industry, and transport. Darby's own chapter, "The Age of the Improver," covers developments after 1600. Constrained by
the nature of their sources, early Stuart economic historians have followed to only
a limited extent the recent trend toward sophisticated quantification of the subject.
But the relationship of economic change to social developments, to the lives of
ordinary people, especially in the rural sector, has been steadily illuminated.

⤛⤜

The new agenda has also left its mark on the still heavily traveled paths of
politics and government. Three recent themes are particularly noticeable: a continuing effort to relate political conflict to the changing balance between aristocracy and gentry; a preoccupation with the Court–Country polarity, which in turn
has directed attention to the local gentry communities of which the "Country" was
composed; and less commonly but still significantly, an attempt to go beyond Parliament and Court and beyond even the local elites, to the investigation of popular
politics. Social change, regional diversity, and the total community: all are important items of the new agenda.

The need to find a satisfactory explanation of the English Revolution has naturally preoccupied nearly all historians of this period. The great debate over the
gentry which raged through the 1950s has now subsided,[56] but work has pro-

ceeded on the specialized studies so often demanded by despairing protagonists. An early example is Alan Simpson's *The Wealth of the Gentry, 1540–1660*, a series of case histories which illustrate, and often modify, earlier stereotypes.[57] Other local, county studies are also useful, but it is the peerage rather than the gentry on which the definitive work has been done. Stone's *Crisis of the Aristocracy* has already been noted for its significance as social history; its importance as a bridge to political history is just as great. Having overcome the financial crisis that afflicted them in the later years of Elizabeth's reign, Stone argues, the peers fell victim to a crisis of confidence. Measures of improved estate management by which they remedied those earlier financial difficulties weakened the ties of paternalism and deference between them and their tenants; officeholding and the "inflation of honors" linked them to a corrupt, unpopular Court; and their failure to compensate for loss of military power by acquiring techniques of political management created a vacuum at the summit of society. Reviewers have subjected Stone's statistics on the landed wealth of the peers to critical scrutiny, but the book's masterly depiction of the aristocratic life-style more than compensates for whatever statistical deficiencies it may contain.[58]

Although this massive work offers more insight into the causes of the revolution of 1640–1660 than anything else published in recent years, it is not a complete analysis of that subject. Room for such an analysis remained even after the appearance of Perez Zagorin's *The Court and the Country: The Beginning of the English Revolution*.[59] This book provides a detailed political analysis of the events leading to civil war. But Zagorin's "Country" is not far removed from the national opposition party of traditional historiography, and its local dimensions are not fully explored. At the same time, Zagorin's assumptions about the stability of the underlying structure enable him to dismiss the possible connection of political to social change.

The necessary synthesis is attempted in Stone's *The Causes of the English Revolution 1529–1642*.[60] Stone's analysis of the conflict summarizes the work of an entire generation. Preconditions of revolution balance considerations of power (the Tudors' failure to establish the monarchy on sound financial, military, and bureaucratic foundations); social change (a rising gentry filling the gap left by the temporarily weakened peerage); and politics (an opposition with the rudiments of an ideology based on Puritanism, "Country" values, and the common law). All contributed to a broadened crisis of confidence in the three pillars of monarchy: the aristocracy, the church, and the Court. Stone employs such social-scientific concepts as *status anxiety* and *relative deprivation*, but his narrative also stresses the contingent events which brought revolution from mere possibility to actuality. In a short book covering such complex themes, there are bound to be matters with which experts will quibble, but this remains the most challenging survey of the central issues of the period.

Alas, history never stands still. The whole conception of the English Revolution as an event with deep-seated social causes is again being questioned. The debate over the gentry has been followed by another, happily less acerbic, debate over the aristocracy. As long ago as 1961 G. R. Elton proclaimed that "the political troubles of the early seventeenth century were not in the main social at all" but amounted to "struggles within a homogeneous 'ruling class.'"[61] In the 1970s that ruling class has come under scrutiny in a way that emphasizes not its decline, but its effective survival.

The effects of aristocratic decline, Conrad Russell wrote in 1973, were "not visible to the naked eye of a political historian working on the 1620s." Stone, he also complained, had explained "events which did not happen [a revolution in 1640–1642] in terms of a social change for which the evidence remains uncertain."[62] While attributing the outbreak of the Civil War to short-term circumstances, Russell leaves room for social causes in the later "revolution from below." Others have been less circumspect. James Farnell sees the peers still in charge of Parliament's affairs throughout the war and reduces even the city of London to a state of clientage. In a general attack on Stone's "conflict" model, Paul Christianson resurrects an older paradigm of seventeenth-century society, based on surviving notions of order and hierarchy. In such a society one might certainly expect to find the peers in control, and that is indeed what Christianson discovers in the first months of the Long Parliament.[63] The causes of revolution, in this view, must be sought in the ambitions of opposition leaders and the king's failure to gratify them.

Others have seen the role of the aristocracy in ways different from both Stone and his critics. Brian Manning's "The Aristocracy and the Downfall of Charles I" also stresses the leadership of the "Country" peers in 1640–1641.[64] Manning, however, clearly does not suppose that the Civil War erupted in an England still dominated by hierarchy and deference: indeed, he has gone further than anyone in identifying it as a social crisis. From a very different standpoint, J. H. Hexter rejects both the "aristocratic cabal" explanation and Stone's thesis of social disequilibrium. In a sharp rebuttal of the Farnell-Christianson position, Hexter appeals for a return to an older tradition of historical inquiry: for a reexamination of the political debates of the seventeenth century, along with the neglected issues of law and liberty.[65]

Law and liberty may recently have been neglected, but other aspects of politics have not. Parliamentary elections have continued to receive much attention. John K. Gruenfelder studies both Strafford's electoral patronage and the Short Parliament elections, finding that by 1640 the older contests for prestige and preeminence were giving way to a more issue-oriented politics. David Underdown finds much the same development in the 1645–1648 by-elections.[66] The most fruitful line of research has been into the broadening of the political nation.

Richard L. Bushman pointed the way in a suggestive article in 1963, and later J. H. Plumb demonstrated the expansion of the electorate throughout the entire century. The subject has now been thoroughly investigated in Derek Hirst's *The Representative of the People? Voters and Voting in England under the Early Stuarts.*[67] Plumb's thesis is amply confirmed: Hirst estimates that in 1640 the electorate comprised between a quarter and 40 percent of the adult male population, which is another startling reminder that historians can no longer confine their attention to the elite. The expansion was encouraged by groups in the Commons who wished to promote the electorate's independence of the control of both Crown and peers. The extent to which voters were in fact directed by landlords and patrons is less clear, but Hirst's cautious account suggests that it was increasingly difficult to control them.[68]

Elections beget parliaments. Here again change is in the air, and the oppositional character of the Parliaments of the entire 1604–1629 period is in question. Elton insists that they were not oppositional at all and urges even Stuart historians to regard Parliament as the Crown's partner in governing the nation. Setting an example, he disputes the reputation of the 1604 Apology as a constitutional landmark, arguing that it was merely the abortive work of a minority.[69] Contributions by Russell point in the same direction. While accepting the reality of financial and other grievances in the 1620s, Russell depicts a Commons less reluctant to vote supplies or to make them conditional on redress of grievances than often supposed. Even foreign policy, he suggests, was not really an opposition issue.[70] This, and the complementary view of parliamentary politics as an extension of Court faction, amounts to a frontal attack on the old orthodoxy of Wallace Notestein's "winning of the initiative" thesis. Although not a direct product of this reappraisal, Elizabeth Read Foster's work on clerks of the Parliament and House of Lords procedures also involves aspects of parliamentary history hitherto neglected.[71]

The three major studies of particular parliaments that have appeared in recent years show relatively few signs of these revisionist ideas. Notestein's posthumous *The House of Commons 1604–1610* provides a faithful account of procedures and debates. But it lacks the incisive quality of this great master's earlier work and is excessively preoccupied with the origins of later disputes. Robert Zaller's less substantial *The Parliament of 1621: A Study in Constitutional Conflict* follows the same paths, as the subtitle makes clear. Robert E. Ruigh's more thorough *The Parliament of 1624: Politics and Foreign Policy* provides an excellent account of the foreign policy debates. Although Ruigh carefully examines patronage networks, none of these three books contains a detailed Namierite analysis of MPs, which remains as a task for future historians. Another task will be reexamination of the crucial 1628/1629 Parliament, now made possible by the publication of a superb edition of its debates.[72]

Even in the 1620s Parliament was only an occasional institution; the executive branch of government was the permanent one. G. E. Aylmer's earlier fine study of the Caroline bureaucracy still preempts this field before 1640, though Michael Hawkins's essay "The Government: Its Role and Aims" is a useful overview; and in 1961 Penry Williams presented the best account of the Council in the Marches of Wales in this period.[73] Recent historians have been more concerned with the corrupting effects of power than with institutions. Joel Hurstfield has discussed early Stuart corruption, judiciously avoiding the anachronistic application of later norms.[74] That there was a decline in standards under James I remains the common view, though Linda L. Peck tries to modify it by identifying Northampton, one of the notorious Howard clique, as a reformer. Reformers or no, the Howards did well enough out of government, as is clear in Stone's *Family and Fortune: Studies in Aristocratic Finance in the Sixteenth and Seventeenth Centuries*, which also shows the mind-boggling profits made by the first earl of Salisbury.[75]

Early Stuart government can also be studied through biographies. There are a good many of these, though few offer dramatically new insights: certainly not John Bowle's *Charles I*. Mark L. Schwarz thinks it time for a more favorable assessment of James I, though that remains to be written. Of James's ministers, Robert Carr has rightly inspired nothing more than an article, but Lionel Cranfield is the subject of a thorough study by Menna Prestwich, to supplement Tawney's earlier book on his business career.[76] Most of the numerous works on Francis Bacon belong to intellectual history, but Joel J. Epstein's rather conventional *Francis Bacon: A Political Biography* is an exception.[77] The most important work on any of Charles I's ministers is C. V. Wedgwood's *Thomas Wentworth, First Earl of Strafford, 1593–1641: A Revaluation*, more realistic than her 1935 biography, thanks to the opening of the Wentworth papers. Other worthwhile Caroline biographies include Martin J. Havran's of Cottington (stronger on the diplomat than the chancellor of the Exchequer) and Anthony F. Upton's of the financial adventurer Sir Arthur Ingram.[78] The "opposition" side has been less productive, although there have been several studies of Ralegh (the most interesting is Stephen J. Greenblatt's, on Ralegh the role player), and others of the first Lord Brooke and John Hampden.[79] By far the most detailed is Vernon F. Snow's *Essex the Rebel*.[80] The biographical gaps are obvious: still no full studies of Buckingham and Warwick, for instance, though both may soon be on the way.[81]

From prewar politics and government, I proceed to the years of revolution, of which Ivan Roots's *The Great Rebellion 1642–1660* is a survey of the traditional kind. Wedgwood's two earlier volumes under that same title have not yet been followed by a third to carry the narrative beyond 1647. A brief monograph, *The Trial of Charles I*, however, displays her customary stylish elegance. In works of this kind, there is little sign that political history is being dethroned.[82]

Nor is there any sign of it in the continuing stream of writing on the Long

Parliament. Here an important source of inspiration has been the earlier work of J. H. Hexter, identifying a "middle group" between the war and peace parties, and undermining religion as the basis for the later Presbyterian–Independent party division.[83] Christopher Thompson traces the origins of the "middle group" back to the 1620s, while Valerie Pearl shows that it survived Pym's death and again resurfaced as the Royal Independents after the war.[84] Lawrence Kaplan's *Politics and Religion during the English Revolution: The Scots and the Long Parliament 1643–1645*, an account of the process by which the Scots became allies of the peace group instead of the war party, is also in the Hexter mold.[85] David Underdown, in *Pride's Purge: Politics in the Puritan Revolution*, combines the influence of Hexter (in arguing that the revolution of 1648–1649 occurred when the Independents split between their "middle group" and radical wings) with that of Namier (in attempting a statistical analysis of MPs). The book also relates the revolution at Westminster to developments in the provinces. The sequence of reappraisals of the Long Parliament is completed by Blair Worden's definitive *The Rump Parliament, 1648–1653*, which provides a splendidly detailed analysis of this often maligned assembly.[86]

The Hexter approach has not, however, gone unquestioned. Mark Kishlansky argues against seeing even early Civil War parliamentary politics in adversary, "party" terms.[87] A series of articles by Lotte Glow Mulligan challenges the "middle group" interpretation, while in 1969 Stephen Foster tried (and failed) to resurrect religion as the determinant of party allegiances.[88] Finally, John R. Mac-Cormack, in *Revolutionary Politics in the Long Parliament*, returns to a two-party version of Long Parliament politics, but again without success.[89]

National affairs after the expulsion of the Rump have been less intensively studied, although Austin Woolrych effectively reexamines "The Calling of Barebone's Parliament," George D. Heath takes a fresh look at the Instrument of Government, and Roots surveys the legislative process and achievements of the Protectorate Parliaments.[90] By far the most significant work on government in the 1650s, however, is G. E. Aylmer's *The State's Servants: The Civil Service of the English Republic, 1649–1660*, a worthy sequel to the same author's definitive study of Charles I's bureaucracy.[91] Again supported by a massive weight of documentation, statistics, and case histories, Aylmer shows that the revolution had a limited, but none the less real, impact on both the personnel of government and attitudes to public service. The concept of service to the impersonal state rather than to the personal ruler was slowly emerging.

Biography has been as popular a genre for the Interregnum as for the earlier part of the century. There have been acceptable studies of the Puritan Lord Wharton and of General George Monck, on the younger Sir Henry Vane as a naval administrator (less useful on Vane as politician or theorist), and a rather uncritical account of the lawyer Bulstrode Whitelocke.[92] K. H. D. Haley, *The*

First Earl of Shaftesbury is useful for Ashley Cooper's career before, as well as after, 1660.[93] Oliver Cromwell continues to fascinate historians, if perhaps not to quite the same extent as in earlier years. The most thorough recent study is Antonia Fraser's *Cromwell: Our Chief of Men*; the most interesting, Christopher Hill's *God's Englishman: Oliver Cromwell and the English Revolution*, which presents a complex Cromwell who is, among other things, the personification of English Protestant imperialism.[94]

The political history surveyed so far, important as much of it is, has been of a more or less traditional kind. But in the past twenty years a strikingly different conception of the English Revolution has been made possible by two somewhat more innovative approaches: first by the study of its local, county dimensions; and more recently through investigation of the political behavior of the common people.

The first of the new county studies was Thomas G. Barnes's *Somerset 1625–1640: A County's Government during the 'Personal Rule.'* This book is still the best analysis of a county's institutional structure before the Civil War, and it also skillfully explores factional politics in the county. Far removed from the old tradition of parochial antiquarianism, it illuminates national history in many important ways, particularly in respect to resistance by the "Country" to Court centralization. Thus pioneered by Barnes, the localist approach came of age with the publication of Alan Everitt's *The Community of Kent and the Great Rebellion, 1640–60.* Everitt provides the conceptual model for many later county studies: the "county community," defined and unified by bonds of kinship, neighborhood, and local tradition. County loyalties, Everitt shows, were often stronger than national ones, and they explain the gentry's opposition to the personal rule, their general preference for neutrality during the Civil War, and their reaction against Parliament when they found that they had exchanged one threat to local independence for a worse one. The Civil War was thus as much about centralization and localism as about the competition of king and Parliament. Everitt's book also includes a fine account of local administrative developments during the war, but its enduring value resides in its brilliant formulation of the concept of the "county community."[95] Subsequent historians have pursued both the localist and neutralist facets of the model: Underdown on Somerset, J. S. Morrill on Cheshire, Anthony Fletcher on Sussex (in a book whose merits include thorough coverage of the prewar years), and B. G. Blackwood on Lancashire.[96] All these authors emphasize local priorities over national ones; Clive Holmes, in his admirable *The Eastern Association in the English Civil War*, is almost alone in resisting the trend.[97]

A bewildering variety of social structures, economies, and political traditions can be observed in these county studies. It might be tempting to conclude that general theories about the revolution ought to be avoided precisely because of these differences. Morrill, however, successfully constructs a theory out of the diversity in his *The Revolt of the Provinces: Conservatives and Radicals in the English Civil War 1630–1650.*[98] Like Everitt, Morrill identifies localism as a basic element in resistance both to the Crown in the 1630s and to Parliament in the following decade. Localism impinged on national politics as the "Country" mentality, but Morrill's "Country" is very different from Zagorin's national opposition movement. Morrill distinguishes between the "official" Country, a group of politicians with a program; and the "pure" Country, the far more numerous localists who successively supported and rejected them. Morrill's "Country" is socially more inclusive than Everitt's gentry elite, encompassing also the equally localist yeomen and lesser folk who surfaced briefly as the neutralist Clubmen in 1645.

Towns have been less well served than counties, although London naturally has not been ignored. Valerie Pearl has followed her earlier *London and the Outbreak of the Puritan Revolution: City Government and National Politics, 1625–43* with two notable articles on the interaction of London and Westminster politics in the postwar period. James Farnell has delineated the role of London Baptists and other radicals in the events leading to Barebone's Parliament.[99] The best general view of provincial urban politics is the introduction to *Crisis and Order* edited by Clark and Slack. A prevailing trend toward municipal oligarchy is evident, although according to John T. Evans, Norwich may have been an exception to this. Clark and Slack also find localism to be as characteristic of urban as of rural societies, here relying on the one really thorough study of a provincial town during the Interregnum: Roger Howell's *Newcastle upon Tyne and the Puritan Revolution: A Study of the Civil War in North England.*[100]

Everitt's county community was a community of gentry, but in county as in electoral politics, signs of a broadening of the inquiry have recently become evident. An example is Clark's *English Provincial Society from the Reformation to the Revolution: Religion, Politics and Society in Kent 1500–1640*, an ambitious attempt to connect gentry politics with the social and economic life of the county. Clark's community is a good deal less united than Everitt's harmonious society, and he discovers in Kent a more widespread and popular Puritan movement than his predecessor depicted. An increasing interest in people below the elite is apparent in several of the county histories noted earlier, and Morrill's emphasis on the sort of peasant conservatism represented by the Clubmen is also significant. Very different in its approach to popular politics is Brian Manning's *The English People and the English Revolution, 1640–1649*. Manning shows the relevance of earlier social and economic tensions to the Civil War and accumulates much evidence of popular initiative in support of Parliament in London and in several regions of protoindustrialization. But the book relies heavily upon what many will regard as an anachronistic model of class struggle and ignores altogether the Clubmen, the biggest popular movement of the entire period. Manning has, however, analyzed peasant conservatism elsewhere, and the example he has set in exploring popular politics deserves to be followed by other historians with different viewpoints, for it is obvious that much remains to be done.[101]

The theme of popular politics brings me to a more familiar subject: the Levellers and the radical sects which succeeded them. Manning's book contains a stimulating treatment of the Levellers, but the most complete account of the movement is still H. N. Brailsford's posthumous and somewhat discursive *The Levellers and the English Revolution*, edited by Christopher Hill. When this was published, C. B. Macpherson's argument that the Levellers would still have denied the vote to servants and wage earners was generally accepted. Subsequent discussion has tended to restore the Levellers' democratic credentials; the matter is best clarified in Keith Thomas's essay "The Levellers and the Franchise."[102] The traditional view of the Levellers' strength in the New Model Army, and indeed the entire notion of a radical army before 1647, has been challenged in an important article by Mark Kishlansky.[103] Another aspect of the radical scene is covered in Patricia Higgins's essay on women in Civil War politics, which describes the striking, though sporadic, claims made for equality of the sexes.[104] There have been many works on the religious and political ideas of the radical sects. These are considered in their place, but even without them, the inordinate length of this survey confirms that politics has not been dethroned. It has, though, been immensely broadened and enriched.

The dethronement of constitutional history, on the other hand, took place long before the 1960s. From the slim harvests of the past few years, there is little that demands attention.[105] Two exceptions focus on the revival of the impeachment process: Clayton Roberts's *The Growth of Responsible Government in Stuart England*, more concerned with the post-1660 period, but useful earlier; and Colin G. C. Tite's *Impeachment and Parliamentary Judicature in Early Stuart England*, which clarifies differences between the 1621 cases and later ones. The resumption of the House of Lords' other judicial powers is discussed in an article by Jess Stoddart Flemion, who shows that in the 1620s there were sound reasons for providing swifter justice.[106]

Already I am drifting from constitutional into the adjacent field of legal history, where there are greater signs of a revival. J. S. Cockburn's *A History of English Assizes 1558–1714* illuminates procedures and the organization of the circuits and has valuable chapters on the courts' administrative and political functions. Essays by J. H. Baker and Thomas G. Barnes are informative on the criminal justice system and Star Chamber procedures respectively.[107] No full study of the justice of the peace system has appeared, but Barnes's *Somerset* is indispensable for Charles I's reign, while J. H. Gleason's *The Justices of the Peace in England, 1558–1640* analyzes the composition of the Commission of the Peace in six selected counties.[108]

The most significant recent trend in legal history is toward the exploration of social and political themes. The interest shown by historians of the sixteenth and eighteenth centuries in the social context of crime is now spreading into the early Stuart period. This is evident in *Crime in England 1550–1800*, edited by J. S. Cockburn, a collection including several essays that show the strong influence of the new social history. Several other books occupy the frontiers between law, society, and politics. Wilfred R. Prest's *The Inns of Court under Elizabeth I and the Early Stuarts* is a splendid study of the Inns' social composition and political affiliations as well as of the legal education they provided. W. J. Jones, in *Politics and the Bench: The Judges and the Origins of the English Civil War*, concisely surveys the connections between law and politics, while the outlook of one important lawyer is examined in Louis A. Knafla's *Law and Politics in Jacobean England: The Tracts of Lord Chancellor Ellesmere*. Another valuable work is Brian P. Levack's *The Civil Lawyers in England, 1603–1641: A Political Study*, which Namierizes the members of Doctors' Commons. Not surprisingly, most of them emerge as dutiful servants of church and crown. A survey of Protectorate judges by Stephen F. Black is an exception to the general dearth of work on the Interregnum. The campaign to reform the law, however, has been covered in books by Stuart Prall and Donald Veall and in an excellent article by Mary Cotterell.[109]

Military, naval, and foreign affairs have been almost as much in eclipse as constitutional history during the past two decades, for reasons probably sufficiently obvious. The best work on military history, Lindsay Boynton's *The Elizabethan Militia 1558–1638*, is as much administrative as military, but it is good on the decay and attempted reform of the local forces under the first two Stuarts.[110] Hostility to the military and its political implications are described by Lois G. Schwoerer, *"No Standing Armies!" The Antiarmy Ideology in Seventeenth-century England*.[111] Interest in Civil War campaigns remains high but has produced little of more than antiquarian significance, apart from coverage of the fighting in the county histories already noted. In keeping with the move toward "history from below," however, the war's impact on the civilian population is beginning to receive attention, for instance in an article by Ian Roy on Gloucestershire.[112] Biographies of Sir Ralph Hopton and Sir William Waller also deserve mention, although neither is a well-rounded study.[113] As for naval history, J. R. Powell's *The Navy in the English Civil War* and the same author's *Robert*

Blake, General-at-Sea are the only major offerings, and both are largely confined to maritime antiquarianism.[114]

The study of foreign policy has been slightly more productive, although less so than one might expect during years in which Britain at last became part of Europe.[115] Most of the recent work deals with the Jacobean and Cromwellian periods, and the intervening years have been neglected. Maurice Lee, Jr., has surveyed Anglo-French relations before 1610 and has also examined the quality of James I's diplomats.[116] Anglo-Spanish relations are discussed by K. R. Andrews, Albert J. Loomie, and Charles H. Carter, the last-named in an important revision of older views about Gondomar's influence.[117] The Protestant component in English policy weakened in this period, but one champion of it has received a solid biography in Michael J. Brown's *Itinerant Ambassador: The Life of Sir Thomas Roe.* As for the Protectorate, Charles P. Korr's *Cromwell and the New Model Foreign Policy: England's Policy toward France, 1649–1658* is diplomatic history of the traditional kind: informative, but perhaps less interesting than recent suggestions that policy was formed by the pressures of competing interest groups.[118]

The same mixture of old and new themes is evident in work on religious history. A major study in the older mode is Horton Davies's *Worship and Theology in England,* volume 2, *From Andrewes to Baxter and Fox, 1603–1690.* Like the earlier volumes of Davies's massive series, this is "internal" church history, enlightening on the forms and setting of worship, but with little on the church's place in the community or on the social function of its rituals. Also written from the top down is Paul A. Welsby's conscientious but unexciting biography of Laud's Calvinist predecessor, George Abbot. On the other bishops, Arthur P. Kautz takes a more favorable view of James I's appointments than some recent writers, while Peter King shows that the Laudian system could work if operated by a determined bishop and also surveys the episcopate during the 1640s.[119]

At the same time, a broadening of the subject continues as historians address themselves to the church as a social, economic, and legal institution. Claire Cross's *Church and People 1450–1660: The Triumph of the Laity in the English Church* is a useful brief survey which shows the increasing success of influential laymen in controlling the church through both political institutions and a variety of patronage devices. Cross wisely defines the laity as Protestant and downplays the loaded term *Puritan.* Patronage is also discussed in two suggestive articles by Rosemary O'Day and in a major book on lectureships by Paul Seaver, which I considered below.[120] The church's financial situation long ago received definitive treatment in Christopher Hill's *Economic Problems of the Church,* and there is less left to be said on that subject; but Phyllis Hembry's *The Bishops of Bath and Wells, 1540–1640: Social and Economic Problems* is a sound local study, showing the diocese's partial recovery after 1603 from earlier depredations.[121] Finally, the church's place in the legal system is described in Ronald A. Marchant's *The Church under the Law: Justice, Administration and Discipline in the Diocese of York 1560–1640*, the best existing account of the structure and operation of the ecclesiastical courts.[122]

The Catholic laity have been the subject of two major works, both treating the seventeenth century in a longer time span. J. H. C. Aveling's *The Handle and the Axe: The Catholic Recusants in England from Reformation to Emancipation* builds on the author's numerous Yorkshire studies but eschews documentation and lacks the social insight of John Bossy's masterly *The English Catholic Community, 1570–1850*.[123] Both stress Catholic resilience under a persecution which (except at Court) was no less severe under Charles I than under his predecessor, as Martin J. Havran and Keith Lindley also confirm. Lindley, too, endorses earlier suggestions that only a minority of Catholics actively supported Charles in the Civil War.[124]

Puritanism remains a topic of obsessive interest, and few seemed inclined to adopt C. H. George's heroic remedy for its confusions: to jettison the whole concept. George's "Puritanism as History and Historiography" is essential reading, not least for its warning against elevating Weberian abstractions into historical realities.[125] His earlier (with Katherine George) *The Protestant Mind of the English Reformation, 1570–1640* remains of value in spite of its tendency to beat some dead horses at excessive length. Its persuasive argument that the Jacobean period was one of relative concensus is complemented by Nicholas Tyacke's fine discussion of the conflict caused by Arminian innovations in the 1630s.[126]

Yet even though before 1640 mainstream Puritans *were* Anglicans, the habit of creating antithetical ideal types persists. Two books which do so are John F. H. New's *Anglican and Puritan: The Basis of Their Opposition, 1558–1640* and J. Sears McGee's *The Godly Man in Stuart England: Anglicans, Puritans and the Two Tables, 1620–1670*. Neither is as provocative as Michael Walzer's *The Revolution of the Saints: A Study in the Origins of Radical Politics*. Walzer sees Puritanism both as a prototype of later revolutionary movements and as the response of alienated intellectuals and "masterless men" to a world collapsing into disorder. One of several problems about "Puritanism as a Revolutionary Ideology," however, is that many of Walzer's Puritans turn out to be distinctly unrevolutionary in the 1640s.[127]

Historians invariably respond to theoretical difficulties by demanding more monographic studies. Given the elusiveness of Puritanism, Paul S. Seaver's *The Puritan Lectureships: The Politics of Religious Dissent 1560–1662* is an appropriate enterprise, carefully analyzing the most effective means of disseminating Puritan teachings.[128] Another fruitful approach has been by way of local studies. Two good examples are Marchant's earlier *The Puritans and the Church Courts in the Diocese of York 1560–1642* and R. C. Richardson's *Puritanism in North-west England: A Regional Study of The Diocese of Chester to 1642*, which shows the continuing Puritan survival within the church.[129] Those allegedly backward northern regions attracted much evangelistic attention from Puritans; the subject has been treated with his customary insight by Christopher Hill.[130]

Most of these authors tend to minimize denominational distinctions, except of course the fundamental one between mainstream Puritans and the sects. Murray Tolmie, in *The Triumph of the Saints: The Separate Churches of London, 1616–1649*, insists, however, on the separate identity of Independents and Baptists (of both particular and general varieties) and provides a useful survey of their activities.[131] The most ambitious and significant work on the more radical sects is Hill's *The World Turned Upside Down*, which I discuss under political ideas. One of these sects has received very thorough treatment in B. S. Capp's *The Fifth Monarchy Men: A Study in Seventeenth-century English Millenarianism*; the Quakers have been even more popular. Hugh Barbour, in *The Quakers in Puritan England*, offers only a brief narrative but usefully considers such topics as regionality, the conversion experience, and Quakers' debates with orthodox clergy. Richard T. Vann, in *The Social Development of English Quakerism, 1655–1755*, argues that early Friends were less plebian than usually supposed and that their social composition roughly corresponded to that of the country at large, though another study by Judith J. Hurwich casts some doubt on this.[132]

The theme to have received the heaviest recent emphasis is millenarianism. This has been elevated to a central position, not only among the sects, as in Capp's book, but among mainstream Puritans as well. John F. Wilson, in *Pulpit in Parliament: Puritanism during the English Civil Wars 1640–1648*, finds much millenarian content in the official sermons of "establishment" preachers.[133] William M. Lamont, in *Godly Rule: Politics and Religion 1603–60*, repeats the argument of his *Marginal Prynne*, that before 1640 Puritans were strong theoretical supporters of monarchy, but he also undertakes an exploration of millenarianism. This, Lamont finds not only in Puritan thought but also, more surprisingly, in that of the Laudians as well. So broad a conception of millenarianism reduces its analytical value, as Capp points out.[134] Others besides Lamont have investigated or used it in a variety of different ways, however: for instance, the contributors to *Puritans, the Millennium and the Future of Israel: Puritan Eschatology 1600 to 1660*, edited by Peter Toon, and Tai Liu, *Discord in Zion: The Puritan Divines and the Puritan Revolution*. Christopher Hill traces a related concept, *Antichrist in Seventeenth-century England*, through several successive mutations to its eventual internalization. All these millenarian studies appeared within a few years after 1968; the connection with the prevailing political mood seems inescapable.[135]

Fertile in new hypotheses as many of them are, the works surveyed thus far do not really confront the religious beliefs and practices of ordinary people, as distinct from those of clerics and educated laymen. Hill's *World Turned Upside Down* comes closest to doing so but is concerned solely with the radical minority.[136] Some of the local studies mentioned earlier explore popular mentalities, notably Spufford's *Contrasting Communities*; and a few other avenues leading into the subject have been pursued. One promising approach might be through the study of iconoclasm, of which there were major outbreaks in the 1640s. John Phillips's *The Reformation of Images: Destruction of Art in England, 1535–1660* provides a brief chronological survey but is superficial and weak in social analysis. Another manifestation of popular religion, anti-Catholic feeling, is examined with more insight by Robin Clifton, who finds that although there were only sporadic outbursts in the prewar years, during the revolution it provided the basic "popular political vocabulary."[137]

The most productive approach to popular religion has been through the study of witchcraft. Older accounts of the subject tend either to concentrate on its intellectual history or to explain its apparently spasmodic outbreaks as responses to specific social crises caused by plague or war. The application of anthropological methods has dramatically transformed the situation. The pioneering work is Alan Macfarlane's *Witchcraft in Tudor and Stuart England*, based on an analysis of witchcraft prosecutions in Essex. Witchcraft in Essex villages, Macfarlane shows, was not a sporadic response to crisis but endemic throughout the period. Its persistence is related to the breakdown of older notions of community and hospitality, leaving residual feelings of social guilt, which were typically projected upon deviant or unprotected villagers as scapegoats for misfortune. Witchcraft beliefs thus turn out to be less religious than social phenomena. Whether the regularity of accusations in Essex was typical of the whole country, however, remains to be tested.[138]

Macfarlane's interpretation of witchcraft is incorporated along with much else in Keith Thomas's magnificent *Religion and the Decline of Magic: Studies in Popular Beliefs in Sixteenth and Seventeenth Century England*.[139] Space, alas, permits only a sadly inadequate indication of the content of this rich and highly original study. Breaking through the familiar world of Catholic and Protestant, Anglican and Puritan, to the world of folk beliefs, magical remedies, wizards, witches, and cunning men, it provides an incomparable picture of popular religion. Thomas shows how limited was the impact of formal religion (though not its ritualized externals) at the grass-roots level. Witchcraft is placed in the context of a vast range of supernatural explanations for misfortune and the unknown, and we encounter a more convincing popular mentality than in any earlier book on this period. *Religion and the Decline of Magic* brilliantly implements one part of the program its author mapped out in 1966, with which this essay began. The need for regional studies to investigate the possibility of local cultural variations is obvious. Thomas provides the starting point and points the way to what will surely be a significant preoccupation of the next twenty years: the further exploration of popular religion and culture.

⮰⧖⮳

The history of culture has customarily been concerned with the literate: who wrote, and what did they write? There is no dearth of recent work of this traditional kind on early Stuart England; but in keeping with the trend of the times, historians are beginning to turn the question round: who read, and what did they read? The initial step is thus to define the extent of literacy. Both because it is easier to discover who could write (or at least sign) than who could read, and because the usable sources raise formidable difficulties, much of the discussion has inevitably been methodological, as in R. S. Schofield's preliminary article in 1968.[140] Lawrence Stone's trial balloon soon afterward surveyed literacy and education in the centuries after 1640, raising further important questions about the sources and their employment.[141] The Cambridge Group has subsequently accumulated much data on literacy, and some of the results are now available. An important series of articles by David Cressy relates variations in literacy rates to changing levels of educational opportunity. Less optimistic about the early seventeenth century than some, Cressy suggests a decline of literacy around 1600, after a dramatic earlier improvement under Elizabeth, and deduces from this a temporary contraction of educational opportunities. In 1642 male illiteracy still averaged 70 percent for the whole country. Debate continues over whether this figure is too high and over possible regional variations, but real progress has been made.[142]

Thanks to an earlier article by Stone, the phenomenon of an "educational revolution" in the century 1540 to 1640 is now historical orthodoxy. Primary and secondary schooling has not been neglected, but more attention has been directed to the universities, especially to their social composition. Earlier contentions about increasing gentry dominance are refuted for Cambridge by Joan Simon, who shows instead a marked growth in the representation of bourgeois and professional families. Stone's analysis of Oxford, however, indicates an increase in gentry matriculants, at least after 1625.[143] Another familiar theme, localism, is explored by Victor Morgan, who concludes (from Cambridge) that the universities were not necessarily a force for national integration, for they often reinforced the sense of regional or county identity.[144]

While it is becoming clearer who was educated, what use people made of their education is less apparent. Hugh Kearney, in *Scholars and Gentlemen: Universities and Society in Pre-industrial Britain, 1500–1700*, notes a revival of curricular conservatism in the early seventeenth century, though Mark H. Curtis sides with Thomas Hobbes in arguing that the universities contributed to civil strife by producing an excess of unemployable, and hence alienated, intellectuals. Even if this was true, it made them no more popular with radicals in the 1650s, as Christopher Hill has shown.[145] The whole subject of Baconian, Puritan, and other projects for educational reform is conscientiously surveyed by Richard L. Greaves in *The Puritan Revolution and Educational Thought: Background for Reform*.[146]

Below the elite level there are only preliminary studies. Peter Clark and R. C. Richardson have assembled evidence about book ownership, but the absence of other comparable studies makes it difficult to evaluate it.[147] H. S. Bennett's *English Books and Readers, 1603 to 1640*, offers only indirect guidance on what was read at the popular level, being (as its subtitle makes clear) a history of the book trade.[148] Gordon J. Schochet, however, in *Patriarchalism in Political Thought: The Authoritarian Family and Political Speculation and Attitudes Especially in Seventeenth-century England*, examines the transmission of doctrines of obedience to the illiterate and marginally literate through such means as household manuals and catechisms. Schochet also considers such familiar figures as Sir Robert Filmer, but his attempt to use the new studies of the family to illuminate political attitudes is distinctly innovative.[149] Why authority needed to reiterate this message of obedience has been convincingly explained by Christopher Hill. Another vehicle of the printed word, less likely to sustain conservative values, has received detailed treatment in Joseph Frank's *The Beginnings of the English Newspaper, 1620–1660*. But the study of popular literature clearly demands further attention.[150]

More traditional intellectual historians have also been preoccupied with problems of order and obedience. W. H. Greenleaf, in *Order, Empiricism and Politics: Two Traditions of English Political Thought, 1500–1700*, sees the rise of empiricism at the heart of the declining faith in the "Great Chain of Being." The final chapters of Donald W. Hanson's *From Kingdom to Commonwealth: The Development of Civic Consciousness in English Political Thought* create one abstraction, civic consciousness, to explain the disappearance of another, "double majesty," in the mid-seventeenth century. Corinne C. Weston, in *English Constitutional Theory and the House of Lords, 1556–1832*, on the other hand, thinks the prevailing paradigm was "mixed monarchy" and heavily stresses its use in Charles I's answer to the Nineteen Propositions.[151] Whatever the paradigm, people had to choose between competing theories of allegiance; some of the uncomfortable dilemmas faced by moderates are described in Irene Coltman's *Private Men and Public Causes: Philosophy and Politics in the English Civil War*. Also concerned with moderates is John M. Wallace's *Destiny His Choice: The Loyalism of Andrew Marvell*, which contains a useful analysis of the "Engagement" controversy of the early 1650s.[152]

The Engagement debate is seen by Quentin Skinner, in three important articles, as being central to the context of Thomas Hobbes's thought.[153] Hobbes has been the subject of a variety of reassessments. C. B. Macpherson relates him, as well as the Levellers and Harrington, to the market economy, while Keith Thomas is more impressed by the patriarchal and other precapitalist survivals in his outlook. Others to stress Hobbes's relationship to the past rather than the future include Willis B. Glover and J. G. A. Pocock, who thus advance the now well-established process of viewing him in a Christian tradition.[154]

Next to Hobbes, the most prominent theorist to have been reconsidered is James Harrington. He looms large in Macpherson's work but is perhaps more convincingly established as the English spokesman for ideas of civic humanism derived from Machiavelli, in Felix Raab's posthumous *The English Face of Machiavelli: A Changing Interpretation, 1500–1700*. J. G. A. Pocock amplifies and explores this thesis with great profundity in *The Machiavellian Moment: Florentine Political Thought and the Atlantic Republican Tradition*, in several essays, and in the introduction to his edition of *The Political Works of James Harrington*.[155] Harrington, Pocock argues, was responsible for a Kuhnian "paradigm-shift" in which English republicanism abandoned the ancient constitution as its legitimizing base in favor of the virtuous independent citizen.

The only other separate studies of parliamentarian thinkers are Margaret A. Judson's brief *The Political Thought of Sir Henry Vane the Younger* and Christopher Hill's vastly more complex *Milton and the English Revolution*.[156] Hill's determination to place Milton in the context of his times may not please literary scholars, but historians may find his characterization of the great poet of a revolution that failed more persuasive. The book is also a splendid introduction to the radical thought of the Interregnum. This subject receives more general treatment in Hill's *The World Turned Upside Down*, a penetrating analysis of the radical spectrum of the 1650s, from "True Levellers" to Quakers. Especially in the discussion of the Ranters there are clear echoes of the "counterculture" of the late 1960s.[157] Once again we encounter the concern for the lives and ideas of the powerless.

Hill's examination of the revolution's intellectual consequences had been preceded by another major work on its antecedents, *Intellectual Origins of the English Revolution*.[158] Three central strands emerge: Sir Walter Ralegh's new conception of history, Sir Edward Coke's adaptation of the common law to the needs of a commercial society, and the exposure of the London "middling sort" to applied science and mathematics. All three stimulated the questioning of authority and thus prepared the way for the revolution.

Intellectual Origins contains a restatement of Robert Merton's argument for a connection between science and Puritanism. This provoked a lively debate in which opinion at first tended to question the relationship. Margery Purver's *The Royal Society: Concept and Creation* provided further ammunition against Hill by stressing the Wilkins circle at Oxford as the society's forerunner, rather than the Puritan Gresham College group. Other critics, like Douglas Kemsley and (more persuasively) Barbara J. Shapiro, reversed Hill's argument by detecting an Anglican or Latitudinarian affinity with science, while Richard P. Ross compromised by accepting that commercial needs gave an initial impetus to mathematics but contending that after 1600 the discipline developed autonomously.[159] Recently, however, the Puritan-science connection has been powerfully rehabilitated in Charles Webster's *The Great Instauration*. Webster's wide-ranging work shows how Puritan millenarianism combined with Baconian ideas to produce the expectant mood of 1640, and it emphasizes the importance of Samuel Hartlib's circle, with their ambitious projects for technological, educational, and social reform.[160]

More technical contributions to the history of science have also opened up new perspectives. The significance of Thomas Hariot's work, for example, is highlighted in Robert H. Kargon's *Atomism in England from Hariot to Newton* and in several essays in *Thomas Hariot, Renaissance Scientist*, edited by John W. Shirley. There has been no major separate work on Bacon's scientific theory, but Lisa Jardine's *Francis Bacon: Discovery and the Art of Discourse* analyzes its ultimate basis, his system of logic. Two important studies of William Harvey have appeared: Sir Geoffrey Keynes's leisurely *The Life of William Harvey* and Gweneth Whitteridge's detailed account of the process of discovery, *William Harvey and the Circulation of the Blood*.[161] As for medical practice, R. S. Roberts provides a useful introduction to the composition and organization of the profession,[162] while Thomas, in *Religion and the Decline of Magic*, reminds us of the deficiencies of available medical services and hence the widespread resort to folk remedies. Hilda Smith shows how sexual stereotypes affected the treatment of women's diseases and also led the physicians to attack the professional status of midwives.[163] Convenient reviews of recent scholarship in medical history are included in *Medicine in Seventeenth-century England*, edited by Allan G. Debus.[164]

Aspects of the history of science formerly dismissed as superstitious dead ends have also received refreshingly unprejudiced attention. Frances Yates continues to advocate the centrality of hermeticism to scientific progress, though her *The Rosicrucian Enlightenment* is less convincing than her earlier work. Others to follow this path include P. M. Rattansi and Allan G. Debus.[165] Astrology has also attained a new respectability, notably in Thomas's great book, but also in studies of its use for propaganda purposes during the Civil War.[166]

A survey of intellectual and cultural history ought properly to include coverage of the arts, but it is impossible here even to summarize the mass of often innovative work that has been done by literary scholars. To the historian, perhaps the most interesting recent development is the growing recognition of the cultural component of the early seventeenth-century conflict. David M. Bergeron, in *English Civic Pageantry 1558–1642*, shows how royal progresses and lord mayor's shows were used to convey the conventional messages of order and authority, messages also preached to the converted in court masques. Judith Hook's *The Baroque Age in England* has useful chapters on the implications of court taste and patronage of the visual arts for the Court–Country division.[167] On music she is only brief and suggestive, but two articles by G. A. Philipps indicate the different patronage patterns of Court and Country.[168] In literature, the cultural conflict is amply demonstrated in Hill's *Milton* and in a fine essay by P. W. Thomas.[169]

During the past two decades many new vistas have opened for Stuart historians. It has been a period of great creativity. Stone's *Crisis of the Aristocracy*, Thomas's *Religion and the Decline of Magic*, and Hill's *World Turned Upside Down*, to name only a few of the works all too hurriedly surveyed in this essay, are among the outstanding historical achievements of recent times. In fertility of hypothesis and willingness to confront new questions, Stuart historians continue to display a vigorous originality.

Much has been done to implement the program outlined by Keith Thomas in 1966. We have observed rapid progress in the study of demography and the history of the family, and significant movement on such related topics as the local community, literacy, and education. Although much remains to be done in these areas, historians of politics, religion, and culture have begun to reach down from the elite to the common people. What is still needed, among much else, is a continuing effort to work from social history to politics: the investigation, for example, of possible connections between the social and economic structures of communities and their political behavior and popular mentalities. Besides the regional differences that will undoubtedly continue to preoccupy scholars, the effects of social and economic change on the various sorts and conditions of men and women also deserve further study. What impact, for instance, did the spread of a market economy have on the lives of women and on their roles in the family and community?

Nowhere are the opportunities more obvious than in the study of popular culture. Apart from Thomas's work, this still remains an almost untilled field. Historians of later centuries are beginning to take seriously the topics of sport and leisure, for example; yet apart from Dennis Brailsford's preliminary survey, *Sport and Society: Elizabeth to Anne*, almost nothing has been done for the early Stuart period.[170] Community festivals and rituals, and the implications of possible regional variations in their survival or disappearance, should also be of interest to future historians. In all such explorations it is reasonable to expect borrowing of methods and models from such adjacent disciplines as sociology, anthropology, and folklore.

In the light of the growing concern for "history from below," some recent trends in political history seem somewhat regressive: notably the reaction against social causation in interpretations of the English Revolution. Yet even here one can take comfort in the existence of a healthy disrespect for current orthodoxies. Politics, to repeat, has not been entirely dethroned, even if it has been largely replaced by social history as the keystone which holds the discipline together.

Formidable problems confront historians of this, as of other, periods— problems connected with the continuing decline of Britain in the modern world (why study the history of a bankrupt offshore island?); with the disenchantment of much of history's former nonacademic public; with the attraction of students to rival disciplines. But the historian's perspective remains distinctive and vital. Anyone who has the good fortune to be aware of the quality of younger scholars now waiting in the wings is bound to be optimistic about the future course of British studies. Commemorations of the death of the past are premature; we await further exploration of the total life of English society.

NOTES

1. Keith Thomas, "The Tools and the Job," *Times Literary Supplement*, no. 3,345, 1966: 275– 276. See also idem, "History and Anthropology," *PP*, no. 24, 1963: 3–24.
2. Perez Zagorin, "English History, 1558–1640: A Bibliographical Survey"; P. H. Hardacre, "Writings on Oliver Cromwell Since 1929," both in Elizabeth C. Furber, ed., *Changing Views on British History*, Cambridge, Mass., 1966, 119–159.
3. For an indication of the previous state of the subject, see the section on population in Mary F. Keeler, ed., *Bibliography of British History: Stuart Period, 1603–1714*, Oxford, 1970, 310–311, which lists practically nothing relating to the early seventeenth century.
4. Peter Laslett and John Harrison, "Clayworth and Cogenhoe," in H. E. Bell and R. L. Ollard, eds., *Historical Essays 1600–1750 Presented to David Ogg*, London, 1963, 157–184; also (with revisions) in Peter Laslett, ed., *Family Life and Illicit Love in Earlier Generations*, Cambridge, 1977, 50–61; idem, *The World We Have Lost*, New York, 1965.
5. For example by Christopher Hill in *History and Theory* 6, 1967: 117–127, and Harold Perkin in *EHR* 82, 1967: 323, 417–418.

6. E. A. Wrigley, ed., *An Introduction to English Historical Demography*, London, 1966.

7. E. A. Wrigley, "Family Limitation in Pre-industrial England," *EcHR*, 2d ser., 19, 1966: 82–109; also in Orest Ranum and Patricia Ranum, eds., *Popular Attitudes towards Birth Control in Pre-industrial France and England*, New York, 1972, 53–99. See also idem, "Mortality in Pre-industrial England: The Example of Colyton, Devon, over Three Centuries," *Daedalus* 97, 1968: 546–580; also in D. V. Glass and Roger Revelle, eds., *Population and Social Change*, London, 1972, 243–285.

8. David Levine, *Family Formation in an Age of Nascent Capitalism*, New York, 1977.

9. Peter Laslett, "Size and Structure of the Household in England over Three Centuries," *Population Studies* 23, 1969: 199–223; also (with revisions) in Peter Laslett and Richard Wall, eds., *Household and Family in Past Time*, Cambridge, 1972, 125–158; P. E. H. Hair, "Bridal Pregnancy in Rural England in Earlier Centuries," *Population Studies* 20, 1966–1967: 233–243; idem, "Bridal Pregnancy in Earlier Rural England Further Examined," ibid. 24, 1970: 59–70; Peter Laslett and K. Oosterveen, "Long Term Trends in Bastardy in England," ibid. 27, 1973: 255–286; also (with revisions) in Laslett, *Family Life and Illicit Love*, 102–159. Among numerous possible examples of work in *Local Population Studies*, E. A. Wrigley's "The Changing Occupational Structure of Colyton over Two Centuries," vol. 18, 1977: 9–21 (a reply to Levine) might be noted.

10. T. H. Hollingsworth, "The Demography of the British Peerage," *Population Studies*, 18, 1964, suppl.

11. Ian Sutherland, "When was the Great Plague? Mortality in London, 1563 to 1665," in Glass and Revelle, *Population and Social Change*, 287–320.

12. Andrew B. Appleby, "Disease or Famine? Mortality in Cumberland and Westmorland, 1580–1640," *EcHR*, 2d ser., 26, 1973: 403–431; idem, "Nutrition and Disease: The Case of London, 1550–1750," *Journal of Interdisciplinary History* 6, 1975–1976: 1–22. I regret that Appleby's *Famine in Tudor and Stuart England*, Stanford, Calif., 1978, appeared too late for comment. See also David Palliser, "Dearth and Disease in Staffordshire 1540–1670," in C. W. Chalklin and M. A. Havinden, eds., *Rural Change and Urban Growth 1500–1800: Essays in English Regional History in Honour of W. G. Hoskins*, London, 1974, 54–75.

13. John Walter and Keith Wrightson, "Dearth and the Social Order in Early Modern England," *PP*, no. 71, 1976: 22–42. See also Peter Clark, "Popular Protest and Disturbance in Kent, 1558–1640," *EcHR*, 2d ser., 29, 1976: 365–381.

14. C. S. L. Davies, "Les revoltes populaires en Engleterre (1500–1700)," *Annales* 24, 1969: 24–60; idem, "Peasant Revolt in France and England: A Comparison," *Agricultural History Review* 21, 1973: 122–34.

15. E. P. Thompson, "'Rough Music': Le Charivari Anglais," *Annales* 27, 1972: 285–312.

16. W. K. Jordan, *The Charities of Rural England, 1480–1660: The Aspirations and the Achievements of the Rural Society*, New York, 1961; idem, *Social Institutions in Kent, 1480–1660: A Study of the Changing Patterns of Social Aspirations*, Ashford, Kent, 1961; idem, *The Social Institutions of Lancashire: A Study of the Changing Patterns of Aspirations in Lancashire, 1480–1660*, Manchester, 1962. For recent discussion of Jordan's omission of the inflation factor, see W. G. Bittle and R. T. Lane, "Inflation and Philanthropy in England: A Re-assessment of W. K. Jordan's Data," *EcHR*, 2d ser., 29, 1976: 203–210; J. F. Hadwin, "Deflating Philanthropy," *EcHR*, 2d ser., 31, 1978: 105–117, and ensuing exchanges on 118–128.

17. Paul Slack, "Poverty and Politics in Salisbury 1597–1666," in Peter Clark and Paul Slack, eds., *Crisis and Order in English Towns 1500–1700*, London, 1972, 164–203; A. L. Beier, "Poor Relief in Warwickshire 1630–1660," *PP*, no. 35, 1966: 77–100.

18. Paul Slack, "Vagrants and Vagrancy in England, 1598–1664," *EcHR*, 2nd ser., 27, 1974:

360–379. For other examples, see Peter Clark, "The Migrant in Kentish Towns 1580–
    1640," in Clark and Slack, *Crisis and Order*, 117–163, and Julian Cornwall, "Evidence of
    Population Mobility in the Seventeenth Century," *BIHR* 40, 1967: 143–152.

19. T. H. Breen and Stephen Foster, "Moving to the New World: The Character of Early Mas-
    sachusetts Immigration," *William and Mary Quarterly*, 3d ser., 30, 1973: 189–222; David
    Souden, "'Rogues, Whores and Vagabonds'? Indentured Servant Emigrants to North America
    and the Case of Mid-seventeenth-century Bristol," *Social History* 3, 1978: 23–38.

20. Winthrop D. Jordan, *White over Black*, Chapel Hill, N.C., 1968. Several works by James
    Walvin, including *Black and White: The Negro and English Society 1555–1945*, London,
    1973, touch on the early seventeenth century, but too briefly to be enlightening. Folarin Shyl-
    lon, *Black People in Britain 1555–1833*, London and New York, 1977, is polemic, not
    history.

21. Roger Thompson, *Women in Stuart England and America: A Comparative Study*, London and
    Boston, 1974. For gentry attitudes to marriage, see Mirian Slater, "The Weightiest Business:
    Marriage in an Upper-gentry Family in Seventeenth-century England," *PP*, no. 72, 1972:
    25–54.

22. Ivy Pinchbeck and Margaret Hewitt, *Children in English Society*, vol. 1, *From Tudor Times to
    the Eighteenth Century*, London, 1969.

23. Steven R. Smith, "The London Apprentices as Seventeenth-Century Adolescents," *PP*, no. 72,
    1972: 25–54; idem, "Religion and the Conception of Youth in Seventeenth Century En-
    gland," *History of Childhood Quarterly* 2, 1974–1975: 493–516; idem, "Growing Old in
    Early Stuart England," *Albion* 8, 1976: 125–141. Also suggestive on adolescence is Bernard
    Capp, "English Youth Groups and *The Pinder of Wakefield*," *PP*, no. 76, 1977: 127–133; and
    on aging, Peter Laslett, "The History of Aging and the Aged," in idem, *Family Life and Illicit
    Love*, 174–213.

24. Joseph Illick, "Childrearing in Seventeenth-century England and America," in Lloyd De-
    Mause, ed., *The History of Childhood*, New York, 1974, 303–350. Robert V. Schnucker,
    "Elizabethan Birth Control and Puritan Attitudes," *Journal of Interdisciplinary History* 5,
    1974–1975: 655–667; idem, "La position puritaine à l'égard de l'adultère," *Annales* 27,
    1972: 1379–1388. G. R. Quaife, "The Consenting Spinster in a Peasant Society: Aspects of
    Premarital Sex in 'Puritan' Somerset, 1645–1660," *Journal of Social History* 11, 1977–1978:
    228–244.

25. Alan Macfarlane, *The Family Life of Ralph Josselin, a Seventeenth-century Clergyman*, Cam-
    bridge, 1970.

26. Lawrence Stone, *The Family, Sex and Marriage in England, 1500–1800*, New York, 1977.

27. Alan Everitt, "Social Mobility in Early Modern England," *PP*, no. 33, 1966: 56–73; idem,
    Change in the Provinces: The Seventeenth Century, Leicester, 1969.

28. C. W. Chalklin, *Seventeenth-century Kent*, London, 1965. James Whetter, *Cornwall in the
    17th Century: An Economic History of Kernow*, Padstow, Cornwall, 1974, though mainly eco-
    nomic, is also useful on social history.

29. Margaret Spufford, *Contrasting Communities: English Villagers in the Sixteenth and Seventeenth
    Centuries*, London and New York, 1974; David G. Hey, *An English Rural Community: Myddle
    under the Tudors and Stuarts*, Leicester, 1974.

30. Lawrence Stone, "Social Mobility in England, 1500–1700," *PP*, no. 33, 1966: 16–55; also
    in Paul S. Seaver, ed., *Seventeenth-century England: Society in an Age of Revolution*, New York,
    1976, 26–70; idem, *The Crisis of the Aristocracy 1558–1641*, Oxford, 1965.

31. J. T. Cliffe, *The Yorkshire Gentry from the Reformation to the Civil War*, London, 1969. A less
    successful example is Howell A. Lloyd, *The Gentry of South-west Wales, 1540–1640*, Cardiff,
    1968.

32. S. R. Smith, "The Social and Geographical Origins of the London Apprentices, 1630–1660," *Guildhall Miscellany* 4, 1971–1973: 195–206; R. G. Lang, "Social Origins and Social Aspirations of Jacobean London Merchants," *EcHR*, 2d ser., 27, 1974: 28–47; J. H. Hexter, "The Myth of the Middle Class in Tudor England," in *Reappraisals in History*, New York, 1961.

33. Carl Bridenbaugh, *Vexed and Troubled Englishmen 1590–1642*, New York, 1968. General surveys which include early seventeenth-century social history within longer periods are: Charles Wilson, *England's Apprenticeship, 1603–1763*, New York, 1965; Christopher Hill, *Reformation to Industrial Revolution: British Economy and Society, 1530–1780*, London, 1967.

34. Joan Thirsk, ed., *The Agrarian History of England and Wales*, vol. 4, *1500–1640*, London, 1967. See also idem, "Seventeenth-century Agriculture and Social change," in idem, ed., *Land, Church, and People: Essays Presented to Professor H. P. R. Finberg*, Reading, 1970, 148–177, also in Seaver, *Seventeenth-century England*, 72–110. Everitt, "Social Mobility", idem, *Change in the Provinces*.

35. Philip A. J. Pettit, *The Royal Forests of Northamptonshire*, Gateshead, Durham, 1968; Victor Skipp, *Crisis and Development: An Ecological Case Study of the Forest of Arden, 1570–1674*, Cambridge, 1978.

36. Eric Kerridge, *Agrarian Problems in the Sixteenth Century and After*, London and New York, 1969; Andrew B. Appleby, "Agrarian Capitalism or Seigneurial Reaction? The N.W. of England, 1500–1700," *AHR* 80, 1975: 574–594.

37. Eric Kerridge, *The Agricultural Revolution*, London, 1967. See also idem, *The Farmers of Old England*, Totowa, N.J., 1973, for a brief, popular restatement of his thesis.

38. W. G. Hoskins, "Harvest Fluctuations and English Economic History, 1480–1619," *Agricultural History Review* 12, 1964: 28–96; ibid., "1620–1759," 16, 1968: 15–31; H. J. Habakkuk, "Landowners and the Civil War," *EcHR*, 2d ser., 18, 1965: 130–151; Jack Goody, Joan Thirsk, and E. P. Thompson, eds., *Family and Inheritance: Rural Society in Western Europe, 1200–1800*, Cambridge, 1976; R. Machin, "The Great Rebuilding: A Reassessment," *PP*, no. 77, 1977: 33–56.

39. J. W. Gough, *The Rise of the Entrepreneur*, London, 1969; Sybil M. Jack, *Trade and Industry in Tudor and Stuart England*, London, 1977. For a worthwhile study of an individual projector, see J. W. Gough, *Sir Hugh Myddleton, Entrepreneur and Engineer*, Oxford, 1964. William Rees, *Industry before the Industrial Revolution*, 2 vols., Cardiff, 1968.

40. G. Hammersley, "The Charcoal Iron Industry and Its Fuel, 1540–1750," *EcHR*, 2d ser., 26, 1973: 593–613; idem, "Technique or Economy? The Rise and Decline of the Early English Copper Industry, ca. 1550–1660," *Business History* 15, 1973: 1–31; L. A. Clarkson, "The Organization of the English Leather Industry in the Late Sixteenth and Seventeenth Centuries," *EcHR*, 2d ser., 13, 1960–1961: 245–56; idem, "The Leather Crafts in Tudor and Stuart England," *Agricultural History Review* 14, 1966: 25–39; Eleanor S. Godfrey, *The Development of English Glassmaking 1560–1640*, Chapel Hill, N.C., 1975; Ralph Davis, *The Rise of the English Shipping Industry in the Seventeenth and Eighteenth Centuries*, London and New York, 1962.

41. J. P. Cooper, "Economic Regulation and the Cloth Industry in Seventeenth-century England," *TRHS*, 5th ser., 20, 1970: 73–99; idem, "Social and Economic Policies under the Commonwealth," in G. E. Aylmer, ed., *The Interregnum: The Quest for Settlement 1646–1660*, London, 1972, 121–42.

42. E. P. Thompson, "Time, Work-discipline, and Industrial Capitalism," *PP*, no. 38, 1967: 56–97.

43. Theodore K. Rabb, *Enterprise and Empire*, Cambridge, Mass., 1968; Karl S. Bottigheimer, *English Money and Irish Land*, Oxford, 1971.

44. K. N. Chaudhuri, *The English East India Company: The Study of an Early Joint-Stock Company*, *1600–1640*, London, 1965; R. Porter, "The Crispe Family and the African Trade in the Seventeenth Century," *Journal of African History* 9, 1968: 57–77; Jan K. Federowicz, "Anglo-Polish Commercial Relations in the First Half of the Seventeenth Century," *Journal of European Economic History* 5, 1976: 359–378; Harland Taylor, "Price Revolution or Price Revision? The English and Spanish Trade after 1604," *Renaissance and Modern Studies* 12, 1968: 5–32.

45. Harland Taylor, "Trade, Neutrality, and the 'English Road,' 1630–1648," *EcHR*, 2d ser., 25, 1972: 236–260; J. S. Kepler, "Fiscal Aspects of the English Carrying Trade during the Thirty Years War," ibid., 261–283; idem, *The Exchange of Christendom: The International Entrepot at Dover, 1622–1651*, Leicester, 1976; W. B. Stephens, "The Cloth Exports of the Provincial Ports, 1600–1640," *EcHR*, 2d ser., 22, 1969: 228–248; and exchange with J. D. Gould, 249–257.

46. E. A. Wrigley, "A Simple Model of London's Importance in Changing English Society and Economy 1650–1750," *PP*, no. 37, 1967: 44–70. See also F. J. Fisher, "London as an 'Engine of Economic Growth,'" in J. S. Bromley and E. H. Kossmann, eds., *Britain and the Netherlands*, vol. 4, *Metropolis, Dominion and Province*, The Hague, 1971, 3–16.

47. Richard Grassby, "The Personal Wealth of the Business Community in Seventeenth-century England," *EcHR*, 2d ser., 23, 1970: 220–234. James E. Farnell, "The Navigation Act of 1651, the First Dutch War, and the London Merchant Community," *EcHR*, 2d ser., 16, 1963–1964: 439–454.

48. R. Brenner, "The Social Basis of English Commercial Expansion, 1550–1650," *JEcH* 32, 1972: 361–384; idem, "The Civil War Politics of London's Merchant Community," *PP*, no. 58, 1973: 53–107; Robert Ashton, "Conflicts of Concessionary Interest in Early Stuart England," in D. C. Coleman and A. H. John, eds., *Trade, Government and Economy in Pre-industrial England: Essays Presented to F. J. Fisher*, London, 1976, 113–131.

49. Ernst Schulin, *Handelsstaat England: Das politische Interesse der Nation am Aussenhandel vom 16. bis ins frühe 18. Jahrhundert*, Wiesbaden, 1969; Joyce O. Appleby, *Economic Thought and Ideology in Seventeenth-century England*, Princeton, N.J., 1977.

50. R. G. Lang, "London's Aldermen in Business: 1600–1625," *Guildhall Miscellany* 3, 1969–1971: 242–264.

51. Peter J. Bowden, *The Wool Trade in Tudor and Stuart England*, London and New York, 1962; T. S. Willan, *The Inland Trade*, Manchester and Totowa, N.J., 1976; J. Crofts, *Packhorse, Waggon and Post*, London and Toronto, 1967.

52. Y. S. Brenner, "The Inflation of Prices in England, 1551–1650," *EcHR*, 2d ser., 15, 1962–1963: 266–284; Robert A. Doughty, "Industrial Prices and Inflation in Southern England, 1401–1640," *Explorations in Economic History* 12, 1975: 177–187.

53. Richard Grassby, "The Rate of Profit in Seventeenth-century England," *EHR* 84, 1969: 721–751.

54. For example, L. A. Clarkson, *The Pre-industrial Economy in England, 1500–1750*, London, 1971, and Donald C. Coleman, *The Economy of England, 1450–1750*, London and New York, 1977.

55. H. C. Darby, ed., *A New Historical Geography of England*, Cambridge, 1973.

56. For a useful introduction to the controversy, see the selections in Lawrence Stone, ed., *Social Change and Revolution in England, 1540–1640*, London, 1965.

57. Alan Simpson, *The Wealth of the Gentry, 1540–1660: East Anglian Studies*, Chicago, 1961.

58. One measure of the importance of a book is the number of wide-ranging reviews it provokes. On Stone's *Crisis*, see for example, those by Aylmer, *PP*, no. 32, 1965: 113–125; Coleman, *History* 51, 1966: 165–178; Ashton, *EcHR*, 2d ser., 22, 1969: 308–322; and above all,

J. H. Hexter, "The English Aristocracy, Its Crises, and the English Revolution, 1558–1660," *JBS* 8, no. 1, 1968: 22–78.

59. Perez Zagorin, *The Court and the Country: The Beginning of the English Revolution*, London, 1969.

60. Lawrence Stone, *The Causes of the English Revolution 1529–1642*, London and New York, 1972.

61. G. R. Elton, "Stuart Government," *PP*, no. 20, 1961: 80.

62. Conrad Russell, review of Stone, *Causes*, *EHR* 88, 1973: 859; idem, ed., *The Origins of the English Civil War*, London and New York, 1973, Intro., 7.

63. James E. Farnell, "The Aristocracy and Leadership of Parliament in the English Civil Wars," *JMH* 44, 1972: 79–86; idem, "The Social and Intellectual Basis of London's Role in the English Revolution," *JMH* 49, 1977: 641–660; Paul Christianson, "The Causes of the English Revolution: A Reappraisal," *JBS* 15, no. 2, 1976: 40–75; idem, "The Peers, the People, and Parliamentary Management in the First Six Months of the Long Parliament," *JMH* 49, 1977: 575–599.

64. In Brian Manning, ed., *Politics, Religion and the English Civil War*, London, 1973, 37–80.

65. J. H. Hexter, "Power Struggle, Parliament, and Liberty in Early Stuart England," *JMH* 50, 1978: 1–50. For further criticisms, see Derek M. Hirst, "Unanimity in the Commons, Aristocratic Intrigues and the Origins of the English Civil War," ibid., 51–71.

66. John K. Gruenfelder, "The Electoral Patronage of Sir Thomas Wentworth, Earl of Strafford," *JMH* 49, 1977: 557–574; idem, "The Election to the Short Parliament, 1640," in Howard S. Reinmuth, ed., *Early Stuart Studies: Essays in Honor of David Harris Willson*, Minneapolis, 1970, 180–230; David Underdown, "Party Management in the Recruiter Elections, 1645–1648," *EHR* 83, 1968: 235–264.

67. Richard L. Bushman, "English Franchise Reform in the Seventeenth Century," *JBS* 3, no. 1, 1963: 36–56; J. H. Plumb, "The Growth of the Electorate in England from 1600 to 1715," *PP*, no. 45, 1969: 90–116; Derek Hirst, *The Representative of the People?* Cambridge, 1975.

68. For a qualification of his own view of Commons' control over their returns, see Derek Hirst, "Elections and the Privileges of the House of Commons in the Early Seventeenth Century: Confrontation or Compromise?" *HJ* 18, 1975: 851–862.

69. G. R. Elton, "A High Road to Civil War?" in Charles H. Carter, ed., *From the Renaissance to the Counter-reformation: Essays in Honour of Garrett Mattingley*, New York, 1965, 325–347; also in idem, *Studies in Tudor and Stuart Politics and Government: Papers and Reviews 1946–1972*, Cambridge, 1974, 2:164–182, and see also 3–18, 155–163.

70. Conrad Russell, "Parliament and the King's Finances," in idem, *Origins of the English Civil War*, 91–116; idem, "Parliamentary History in Perspective, 1604–1629," *History* 61, 1976: 1–27; idem, "The Foreign Policy Debate in the House of Commons in 1621," *HJ* 20, 1977: 289–309. Russell's forthcoming *Parliaments and English Politics 1621–1629* will provide a systematic exposition of these arguments.

71. Wallace Notestein, *The Winning of the Initiative by the House of Commons*, London, 1924, Elizabeth Read Foster, *The Painful Labour of Mr. Elsyng*, Philadelphia, 1972; idem, "Procedure in the House of Lords during the Early Stuart Period," *JBS* 5, no. 2, 1966: 56–73. See also Sheila Lambert, "The Clerks and Records of the House of Commons, 1600–1640," *BIHR* 43, 1970: 215–231, and for politics in the Lords, Jess Stoddart Flemion, "The Struggle for the Petition of Right in the House of Lords: The Study of an Opposition Party Victory," *JMH* 45, 1973: 193–210; idem, "The Nature of Opposition in the House of Lords in the Early Seventeenth Century: A Reevaluation," *Albion* 8, 1976: 17–34.

72. Wallace Notestein, *The House of Commons, 1604–1610*, New Haven, Conn., 1971; Robert Zaller, *The Parliament of 1621: A Study in Constitutional Conflict*, Berkeley and Los Angeles,

1971; Robert Ruigh, *The Parliament of 1624*, Cambridge, Mass., 1971, Robert C. Johnson, Mary Frear Keeler, Maija Jansson Cole, and William B. Bidwell, eds., *Commons Debates 1628*, New Haven, Conn., 1977–

73. G. E. Aylmer, *The King's Servants: The Civil Servants of Charles I*, 1625–1642, London, 1961; Michael Hawkins, "The Government: Its Role and Aims," in Russell, *Origins of the English Civil War*, 35–65; Penry Williams, "The Activity of the Council in the Marches under the Early Stuarts," *Welsh Historical Review* 1, 1960–1963: 133–160.

74. Joel Hurstfield, "Political Corruption in Modern England: The Historian's Problem," *History* 52, 1967: 16–34; idem, "The Political Morality of Early Stuart Statesmen," *History* 56, 1971: 235–243; both reprinted in idem, *Freedom, Corruption and Government in Elizabethan England*, Cambridge, Mass., 1973, 137–162, 183–196.

75. Linda Levy Peck, "Problems in Jacobean Administration: Was Henry Howard, Earl of Northampton, a Reformer?" *HJ* 19, 1976: 831–858; Lawrence Stone, *Family and Fortune*, Oxford, 1973.

76. John Bowle, *Charles I: A Biography*, London, 1975; Marc L. Schwarz, "James I and the Historians: Toward a Reconsideration," *JBS* 13, no. 2, 1974: 114–134. P. R. Seddon, "Robert Carr, Earl of Somerset," *Renaissance and Modern Studies* 14, 1970: 48–68; Menna Prestwich, *Cranfield: Politics and Profits under the Early Stuarts*, Oxford, 1966.

77. Joel J. Epstein, *Francis Bacon: A Political Biography*, Athens, Ohio, 1977.

78. C. V. Wedgwood, *Thomas Wentworth, First Earl of Strafford, 1593–1641*, London, 1961; Martin J. Havran, *Caroline Courtier: The Life of Lord Cottington*, London, 1973; Anthony F. Upton, *Sir Arthur Ingram, c. 1565–1642: A Study of the Origins of an English Landed Family*, Oxford, 1961.

79. Stephen J. Greenblatt, *Sir Walter Ralegh: The Renaissance Man and His Roles*, New Haven, Conn., 1973; Ronald A. Rebholz, *The Life of Fulke Greville, First Lord Brooke*, Oxford, 1971; John Adair, *A Life of John Hampden the Patriot (1594–1643)*, London, 1976, a popular biography, without documentation.

80. Vernon F. Snow, *Essex the Rebel: The Life of Robert Devereux, the Third Earl of Essex, 1591–1646*, Lincoln, Neb., 1970.

81. Warwick's brother, Holland, has been the subject of an article: Barbara Donagan, "A Courtier's Progress: Greed and Consistency in the Life of the Earl of Holland," *HJ* 19, 1976: 317–353.

82. Ivan Roots, *The Great Rebellion 1642–1660*, London, 1966; C. V. Wedgwood, *The Great Rebellion*, 2 vols., London, 1966; idem, *The Trial of Charles I*, London, 1964.

83. J. H. Hexter, *The Reign of King Pym*, Cambridge, Mass., 1941; idem, "The Problem of the Presbyterian Independents," *AHR* 44, 1938–1939: 29–49.

84. Christopher Thompson, "The Origins of the Politics of the Parliamentary Middle Group, 1625–1629," *TRHS*, 5th ser., 22, 1972: 71–86; Valerie Pearl, "Oliver St. John and the 'Middle Group' in the Long Parliament: August 1643–May 1644," *EHR* 81, 1966: 490–519; idem, "The 'Royal Independents' in the English Civil War," *TRHS*, 5th ser., 18, 1968: 69–96.

85. Lawrence Kaplan, *Politics and Religion during the English Revolution*, New York, 1976.

86. David Underdown, *Pride's Purge*, Oxford, 1971; idem, "The Independents Reconsidered," *JBS* 3, no. 2, 1964: 57–84; and exchange with George Yule in *JBS* 7, no. 2, 1968: 11–32, and *JBS* 8, no. 1, 1968: 83–93. An attempt to computerize Long Parliament MPs by Steven D. Antler—"Quantitative Analysis of the Long Parliament," *PP*, no. 56, 1972: 154–157—met with little success: see R. S. Schofield's comments in *PP*, no. 68, 1975: 124–129. Blair Worden, *The Rump Parliament, 1648–1653*, Cambridge, 1974.

87. Mark Kishlansky, "The Emergence of Adversary Politics in the Long Parliament," *JMH* 49, 1977: 617–640.

88. See especially Lotte Glow, "Political Affiliations in the House of Commons after Pym's Death," *BIHR* 38, 1965: 48–70, and Lotte Glow Mulligan, "Peace Negotiations, Politics and the Committee of Both Kingdoms, 1644–1646," *HJ* 12, 1969: 3–22. Stephen Foster, "The Presbyterian Independents Exorcized: A Ghost Story for Historians," *PP*, no. 44, 1969: 52–75; and see also exchanges between Foster and others in *PP*, no. 47, 1970: 116–146.

89. John R. MacCormack, *Revolutionary Politics in the Long Parliament*, Cambridge, Mass., 1974; Two other useful articles on Long Parliament politics are Patricia Crawford, "The Savile Affair," *EHR* 90, 1975: 76–93, and A. N. B. Cotton, "Cromwell and the Self-denying Ordinance," *History* 62, 1977: 211–231.

90. Austin Woolrych, "The Calling of Barebone's Parliament," *EHR* 80, 1965: 492–513; George D. Heath, "Making the Instrument of Government," *JBS* 6, no. 2, 1967: 15–34; Ivan Roots, "Cromwell's Ordinances: The Early Legislation of the Protectorate," in Aylmer, *Interregnum*, 143–164; idem, "Lawmaking in the Second Protectorate Parliament," in H. Hearder and H. R. Loyn, eds., *British Government and Administration: Studies Presented to S. B. Chrimes*, Cardiff, 1974, 132–143.

91. G. E. Aylmer, *The State's Servants*, London and Boston, 1973.

92. G. F. Trevallyn Jones, *Saw-Pit Wharton*, Sydney, 1967; Maurice Ashley, *General Monck*, London, 1977; Violet A. Rowe, *Sir Henry Vane the Younger: A Study in Political and Administrative History*, London, 1970; Ruth Spalding, *The Improbable Puritan: A Life of Bulstrode Whitelocke 1605–1675*, London, 1975.

93. K. H. D. Haley, *The First Earl of Shaftesbury*, Oxford, 1968.

94. Antonia Fraser, *Cromwell*, London, 1973; Christopher Hill, *God's Englishman*, London, 1970; An excellent introductory life is Roger Howell, Jr., *Cromwell*, Boston, 1977.

95. Thomas G. Barnes, *Somerset, 1625–1640*, Cambridge, Mass., 1961; Alan Everitt, *The Community of Kent and the Great Rebellion, 1640–60*, Leicester, 1966. See also idem, "The County Community," in E. W. Ives, ed., *The English Revolution 1600–1660*, London, 1968, 48–63; idem, *The Local Community and the Great Rebellion*, London, 1969.

96. David Underdown, *Somerset in the Civil War and Interregnum*, Newton Abbot, Devon, 1973; J. S. Morrill, *Cheshire 1630–1660: County Government and Society during the English Revolution*, London and New York, 1974; Anthony Fletcher, *A County Community in Peace and War: Sussex 1600–1660*, London and New York, 1975; B. G. Blackwood, *The Lancashire Gentry and the Great Rebellion 1640–60*, Manchester, 1978. Another excellent study of the prewar period is Mervyn E. James, *Family, Lineage, and Civil Society: A Study of Society, Politics, and Mentality in the Durham Region, 1500–1640*, Oxford, 1974. S. J. Watts and Susan J. Watts, *From Border to Middle Shire: Northumberland, 1586–1625*, Leicester, 1975, is useful on local factions but lacks the county-community concept.

97. Clive Holmes, *The Eastern Association in the English Civil War*, Cambridge, 1975.

98. J. S. Morrill, *The Revolt of the Provinces*, London and New York, 1976.

99. Valerie Pearl, *London and the Outbreak of the Puritan Revolution*, London, 1961; idem, "London Puritans and Scotch Fifth Columnists: A Mid-seventeenth-century Phenomenon," in A. E. J. Hollaender and William Kellaway, eds., *Studies in London History Presented to Philip Edmund Jones*, London, 1969, 517–551; idem, "London's Counter-revolution," in Aylmer, *Interregnum*, 29–56; James E. Farnell, "The Usurpation of Honest London Householders: Barebone's Parliament," *EHR* 82, 1967: 24–46.

100. John T. Evans, "The Decline of Oligarchy in Seventeenth-century Norwich," *JBS* 14, no. 1, 1974: 46–76. Roger Howell, *Newcastle upon Tyne and the Puritan Revolution*, Oxford, 1967.

For urban politics in Kent in the 1620s, see Peter Clark, "Thomas Scot and the Growth of Urban Opposition to the Early Stuart Regime," *HJ* 21, 1978: 1–26.

101. Peter Clark, *English Provincial Society from the Reformation to the Revolution*, Hassocks, Sussex, 1977; Brian Manning, *The English People and the English Revolution, 1640–1649*, London, 1976; idem, "The Peasantry and the English Revolution," *Journal of Peasant Studies* 2, 1974–1975: 133–158. Other articles on popular politics are: idem, "Religion and Politics: The Godly People," in idem, ed., *Politics, Religion and the English Civil War*, London, 1973, 83–123; Joyce L. Malcolm, "A King in Search of Soldiers: Charles I in 1642," *HJ* 21, 1978: 251–273; and J. S. Morrill, "Mutiny and Discontent in English Provincial Armies 1645–1647," *PP*, no. 56, 1972: 49–74.

102. H. N. Brailsford, *The Levellers and the English Revolution*, Stanford, Calif., 1961. Keith Thomas, "The Levellers and the Franchise," in Aylmer, *Interregnum*, 57–78. See also J. C. Davis, "The Levellers and Democracy," *PP*, no. 40, 1968: 174–180, and Roger Howell and David E. Brewster, "Reconsidering the Levellers: The Evidence of *The Moderate*," *PP*, no. 46, 1970: 68–86; both reprinted in Charles Webster, ed., *The Intellectual Revolution of the Seventeenth Century* London and Boston, 1974, 70–100.

103. Mark Kishlansky, "The Case of the Army Truly Stated: The Creation of the New Model Army," *PP* 81, 1978: 51–74. Kishlansky's forthcoming *Rise of the New Model Army* will further amplify the argument.

104. Patricia Higgins, "The Reactions of Women, with Special Reference to Women Petitioners," in Manning, *Politics, Religion* 179–222.

105. A recent selection of documents is J. P. Kenyon, ed., *The Stuart Constitution: Documents and Commentary*, Cambridge, 1966.

106. Clayton Roberts, *The Growth of Responsible Government in Stuart England*, Cambridge, 1966; Colin G. C. Tite, *Impeachment and Parliamentary Judicature in Early Stuart England*, London, 1974; Jess Stoddart Flemion, "Slow Process, Due Process, and the High Court of Parliament: A Reinterpretation of the Revival of Judicature in the House of Lords in 1621," *HJ* 17, 1974: 3–16.

107. J. S. Cockburn, *A History of English Assizes 1558–1714*, Cambridge, 1972; J. H. Baker, "Criminal Courts and Procedure at Common Law 1550–1800," in J. S. Cockburn, ed., *Crime in England 1550–1800*, Princeton, N.J., 1977, 15–48; Thomas G. Barnes, "Due Process and Slow Process in the Late Elizabethan–Early Stuart Star Chamber," *American Journal of Legal History* 6, 1962: 221–249, 315–346. Another study of procedure is Edith G. Henderson, *Foundations of English Administrative Law: Certiorari and Mandamus in the Seventeenth Century*, Cambridge, Mass., 1963.

108. J. H. Gleason, *The Justices of the Peace in England, 1558–1640: A New Eirenarcha*, Oxford, 1969.

109. J. S. Cockburn, ed., *Crime in England 1550–1800*, Princeton, N.J., 1977; Wilfred R. Prest, *The Inns of Court under Elizabeth I and the Early Stuarts*, London, 1972; W. J. Jones, *Politics and the Bench*, London, 1971; Louis A. Knafla, *Law and Politics in Jacobean England*, Cambridge, 1977; See also idem, "Ellesmere and Politics, 1603–1617," in Reinmuth, *Early Stuart Studies*, 11–63; and G. W. Thomas, "James I, Equity and Lord Keeper John Williams," *EHR* 91, 1976: 506–528. Brian P. Levack, *The Civil Lawyers in England, 1603–1641*, Oxford, 1973; Stephen F. Black, "*Coram Protectore:* The Judges of Westminster Hall under the Protectorate of Oliver Cromwell," *American Journal of Legal History* 20, 1976: 32–64. Useful on an often-neglected court is D. E. Kennedy, "The Establishment and Settlement of Parliament's Admirality, 1642–1648," *Mariner's Mirror* 48, 1962: 276–291. Stuart Prall, *The Agitation for Law Reform during the Puritan Revolution, 1640–1660*, The Hague, 1966; Donald Veall, *The Popular Movement for Law Reform, 1640–1660*, Oxford, 1970;

Mary Cotterell, "Interregnum Law Reform: The Hale Commission of 1652," *EHR* 83, 1968: 689–704.

110. Lindsay Boynton, *The Elizabethan Militia 1558–1638*, London, 1967. See also Stephen J. Stearns, "Conscription and English Society in the 1620s," *JBS* 11, no. 2, 1972: 1–23.

111. Lois G. Schwoerer, *"No Standing Armies!"* Baltimore, 1974.

112. Ian Roy, "The English Civil War and English Society," *War and Society* 1, 1973: 24–43.

113. F. T. R. Edgar, *Sir Ralph Hopton: The King's Man in the West (1642–1652)*, Oxford, 1968; John Adair, *Roundhead General: A Military Biography of Sir William Waller*, London, 1969.

114. J. R. Powell, *The Navy in the English Civil War*, Hamden, Conn., 1962; idem, *Robert Blake, General-at-Sea*, London, 1972.

115. J. R. Jones, *Britain and Europe in the Seventeenth Century*, New York, 1966, is a useful but very brief introduction to the subject. G. M. D. Howat, *Stuart and Cromwellian Foreign Policy*, New York, 1974, should be avoided.

116. Maurice Lee, Jr., *James I and Henri IV: An Essay in English Foreign Policy 1603–1610*, Urbana, Ill., 1970; idem, "The Jacobean Diplomatic Service," *AHR* 72, 1966–1967: 1264–1282.

117. K. R. Andrews, "Caribbean Rivalry and the Anglo-Spanish Peace of 1604," *History* 59, 1974: 1–17; Albert J. Loomie, *Toleration and Diplomacy: The Religious Issue in Anglo-Spanish Relations, 1603–1605*, Philadelphia, 1963; idem, "Sir Robert Cecil and the Spanish Embassy," *BIHR* 42, 1969; 30–57; idem, "Gondomar's Selection of English Officers in 1622," *EHR* 88, 1973: 574–581; Charles H. Carter, "Gondomar: Ambassador to James I," *HJ* 7, 1964: 189–208. See also idem, *The Secret Diplomacy of the Hapsburgs, 1598–1628*, New York, 1964, chaps. 9–10.

118. Michael J. Brown, *Itinerant Ambassador*, Lexington, Ky., 1970; Charles P. Korr, *Cromwell and the New Model Foreign Policy*, Berkeley and Los Angeles, 1975. See also R. C. Thompson, "Officers, Merchants and Foreign Policy in the Protectorate of Oliver Cromwell," *Historical Studies Australia and New Zealand* 12, 1965–1967: 149–165; Bernd Martin, "Aussenhandel und Aussenpolitik Englands unter Cromwell," *Historische Zeitschrift* 218, 1974: 571–592.

119. Horton Davies, *Worship and Theology in England*, vol. 2, *From Andrewes to Baxter and Fox, 1603–1690*, Princeton, N.J., 1975; Paul A. Welsby, *George Abbot, the Unwanted Archibishop 1562–1633*, London, 1962; Arthur P. Kautz, "The Selection of Jacobean Bishops," in Reinmuth, *Early Stuart Studies*, 152–179; Peter King, "Bishop Wren and the Suppression of the Norwich Lecturers," *HJ* 11, 1968: 237–254; idem, "The Episcopate during the Civil Wars, 1642–1649," *EHR* 83, 1968: 523–537. See also Andrew Foster, "The Function of a Bishop: The Career of Richard Neile, 1562–1640," in Rosemary O'Day and Felicity Heal, eds., *Continuity and Change: Personnel and Administration of the Church in England 1500–1642*, Leicester, 1976, 33–54.

120. Claire Cross, *Church and People 1450–1660*, Atlantic Highlands, N.J., 1976; Rosemary O'Day, "The Reformation of the Ministry, 1558–1642," in O'Day and Heal, *Continuity and Change*, 55–75; idem "Ecclesiastical Patronage: Who Controlled the Church?" in Felicity Heal and Rosemary O'Day, eds., *Church and Society in England: Henry VIII to James I*, London, 1977, 137–155.

121. Christopher Hill, *Economic Problems of the Church*, Oxford, 1956; Phyllis Hembry, *The Bishops of Bath and Wells, 1540–1640*, London, 1967. See also C. Haigh, "Finance and Administration in a New Diocese: Chester, 1541–1641," in O'Day and Heal, *Continuity and Change*, 145–166.

122. Ronald A. Marchant, *The Church under the Law*, Cambridge, 1969.

123. J. H. C. Aveling, *The Handle and the Axe*, London, 1976; John Bossy, *The English Catholic Community 1570–1850*, London, 1975. Among several local studies by Aveling, note his

Northern Catholics: The Catholic Recusants of the North Riding of Yorkshire 1558–1790, London and Dublin, 1966.

124. Martin J. Havran, *The Catholics in Caroline England*, Stanford, Calif., 1962; Keith J. Lindley, "The Lay Catholics of England in the Reign of Charles I," *Journal of Ecclesiastical History* 22, 1971: 199–221; idem "The Part Played by the Catholics," in Manning, *Politics, Religion*, 127–176.

125. C. H. George, "Puritanism as History and Historiography," *PP*, no. 41, 1968: 77–104.

126. C. H. George and Katherine George, *The Protestant Mind of the English Reformation, 1570–1640*, Princeton, N.J., 1961; Nicholas Tyacke, "Puritanism, Arminianism and Counter-Revolution," in Russell, *Origins of the English Civil War*, 119–143.

127. J. F. H. New, *Anglican and Puritan*, Stanford, Calif., 1964; J. Sears McGee, *The Godly Man in Stuart England*, New Haven, Conn., 1976; Michael Walzer, *The Revolution of the Saints*, Cambridge, Mass., 1965; idem, "Puritanism as a Revolutionary Ideology," *History and Theory* 3, 1963–1964: 59–90.

128. Paul S. Seaver, *The Puritan Lectureships*, Stanford, Calif., 1970. See also W. J. Sheils, "Religion in Provincial Towns: Innovation and Tradition," in Heal and O'Day, *Church and Society*, 156–176.

129. R. A. Marchant, *The Puritans and the Church Courts in the Diocese of York 1560–1642*, London, 1960; R. C. Richardson, *Puritanism in North-west England*, Manchester, 1972. See also idem, "Puritanism and the Ecclesiastical Authorities: The Case of the Diocese of Chester," in Manning, *Politics, Religion*, 3–33. An older study, which takes the opposite position by stressing deprivations of Puritan clergy, is Stuart B. Babbage, *Puritanism and Richard Bancroft*, London, 1962.

130. Christopher Hill, "Propagating the Gospel," in Bell and Ollard, *Historical Essays*, 25–59; idem, "Puritans and 'the Dark Corners of the Land,'" *TRHS*, 5th ser., 13, 1963: 77–102. These two articles are reprinted together under the latter title in Christopher Hill, *Change and Continuity in Seventeenth Century England*, London, 1974, 3–47.

131. Murray Tolmie, *The Triumph of the Saints*, Cambridge, 1977. Recent biographies of Puritan ministers include Keith L. Sprunger, *The Learned Doctor William Ames: Dutch Backgrounds of English and American Puritanism*, Urbana, Ill., 1972; and Peter Toon, *God's Statesman: The Life and Work of John Owen*, Exeter, 1973.

132. B. S. Capp, *The Fifth Monarchy Men*, London, 1972; Hugh Barbour, *The Quakers in Puritan England*, New Haven, Conn., 1964; Richard T. Vann, *The Social Development of English Quakerism, 1655–1755*, Cambridge, Mass., 1969; idem, "Quakerism and the Social Structure in the Interregnum," *PP*, no. 43, 1969: 71–91; Judith Jones Hurwich, "The Social Origins of the Early Quakers," *PP*, no. 48, 1970: 156–161; and reply by Vann, 162–164.

133. John F. Wilson, *Pulpit in Parliament*, Princeton, N.J., 1969; For a more political analysis of these sermons, see Hugh Trevor-Roper, "The Fast Sermons of the Long Parliament," in idem, ed., *Essays in British History Presented to Sir Keith Feiling*, London and New York, 1964, 85–138; also in idem, *Religion, the Reformation and Social Change*, London, 1967, 294–344.

134. William M. Lamont, *Godly Rule: Politics and Religion, 1603–60*, London, 1969; idem, *Marginal Prynne*, London, 1963; idem, "Puritanism as History and Historiography: Some Further Thoughts," *PP*, no. 44, 1969: 133–146; Bernard S. Capp, "Godly Rule and English Millenarianism," *PP*, no. 52, 1971: 106–117. William M. Lamont, "Richard Baxter, the Apocalypse and the Mad Major," *PP*, no. 55, 1972: 68–90; Bernard S. Capp, "The Millenium and Eschatology in England," *PP*, no. 57, 1972: 156–162. The last three articles are reprinted in Webster, *Intellectual Revolution*, 386–434.

135. Peter Toon, ed., *Puritans, the Millenium and the Future of Israel*, Cambridge, 1970; Tai Liu,

Discord in Zion, The Hague, 1973; Christopher Hill, *Antichrist in Seventeenth-century England*, London, 1971.

136. Christopher Hill, *The World Turned Upside Down: Radical Ideas during the English Revolution*, London, 1972.

137. John Phillips, *The Reformation of Images*, Berkeley and Los Angeles, 1973; Robin Clifton, "The Popular Fear of Catholics during the English Revolution," *PP*, no. 52, 1971: 23–55; idem, "Fear of Popery," in Russell, *Origins of the English Civil War*, 144–167.

138. Alan Macfarlane, *Witchcraft in Tudor and Stuart England: A Regional and Comparative Study*, London, 1970. See, for an example of the further work needed, Philip Tyler, "The Church Courts at York and Witchcraft Prosecutions, 1567–1640," *Northern History* 4, 1969: 84–109.

139. Keith Thomas, *Religion and the Decline of Magic*, New York, 1971.

140. R. S. Schofield, "The Measurement of Literacy in Pre-industrial England," in Jack Goody, ed., *Literacy in Traditional Societies*, Cambridge, 1968, 311–325.

141. Lawrence Stone, "Literacy and Education in England 1640–1900," *PP*, no. 42, 1969: 69–139.

142. David Cressy, "Literacy in Pre-industrial England," *Societas* 4, 1974: 229–240; idem, "Educational Opportunity in Tudor and Stuart England," *History of Education Quarterly* 16, 1976: 301–320; idem, "Levels of Illiteracy in England, 1530–1730," *HJ* 20, 1977: 1–23; idem, "Literacy in Seventeenth-century England: More Evidence," *Journal of Interdisciplinary History* 8, 1977–1978: 141–150. See also Richard T. Vann, "Literacy in Seventeenth-century England: Some Hearth-Tax Evidence," ibid. 5, 1974–1975: 287–293, and Spufford, *Contrasting Communities*, chaps. 6–8.

143. Lawrence Stone, "The Educational Revolution in England, 1540–1640," *PP*, no. 28, 1964: 41–80. Joan Simon, "The Social Origins of Cambridge Students, 1603–1640," *PP*, no. 26, 1963: 58–67; Lawrence Stone, "The Size and Composition of the Oxford Student Body, 1580–1909," in idem, ed., *The University in Society*, vol. 1, *Oxford and Cambridge from the 14th to the Early 19th Century*, Princeton, N.J., 1974, 3–110.

144. Victor Morgan, "Cambridge University and 'The Country' 1560–1640," in Stone, *University in Society*, 183–245.

145. Hugh Kearney, *Scholars and Gentlemen*, Ithaca, N.Y., 1970; Mark H. Curtis, "The Alienated Intellectuals of Early Stuart England," *PP*, no. 23, 1962: 25–43; Christopher Hill, "The Radical Critics of Oxford and Cambridge in the 1650s," in idem, *Change and Continuity*, 127–148.

146. Richard L. Greaves, *The Puritan Revolution and Educational Thought*, New Brunswick, N.J., 1969; providing a much broader context is Charles Webster's *The Great Instauration: Science, Medicine and Reform, 1626–1660*, London, 1975.

147. Peter Clark, "The Ownership of Books in England, 1560–1640: The Example of Some Kentish Townfolk," in Lawrence Stone, ed., *Schooling and Society: Studies in the History of Education*, Baltimore, 1976, 95–111; R. C. Richardson, "The Diocese of Chester: Religion and Reading in the Late Sixteenth and Early Seventeenth Centuries," *Local Historian* 11, 1974: 14–17.

148. H. S. Bennett, *English Books and Readers, 1603 to 1640: Being a Study in the History of the Book Trade in the Reigns of James I and Charles I*, Cambridge, 1970.

149. Gordon J. Schochet, *Patriarchialism in Political Thought*, Oxford, 1975. See also idem, "Patriarchalism, Politics and Mass Attitudes in Stuart England," *HJ* 12, 1969: 413–441.

150. Christopher Hill, "The Many-headed Monster," in Carter, *Renaissance to the Counter-reformation*, 296–324; also in Hill, *Change and Continuity*, 181–204; Joseph Frank, *The Be-*

ginnings of the English Newspaper, 1620–1660, Cambridge, Mass., 1961. A good study of a journalist is P. W. Thomas, *Sir John Berkenhead 1617–1679: A Royalist Career in Politics and Polemics,* Oxford, 1969.

151. W. H. Greenleaf, *Order, Empiricism and Politics,* London and New York, 1964; Donald W. Hanson, *From Kingdom to Commonwealth,* Cambridge, Mass., 1970; Corinne C. Weston, *English Constitutional Theory and the House of Lords, 1556–1832,* London, 1965.

152. Irene Coltman, *Private Men and Public Causes,* London, 1962; John M. Wallace, *Destiny His Choice,* Cambridge, 1968.

153. Quentin Skinner, "History and Ideology in the English Revolution," *HJ* 8, 1965: 151–178; idem, "The Ideological Context of Hobbes's Political Thought," ibid. 9, 1966: 286–317; idem, "Conquest and Consent: Thomas Hobbes and the Engagement Controversy," in Aylmer, *Interregnum,* 79–98.

154. C. B. Macpherson, *The Political Theory of Possessive Individualism, Hobbes to Locke,* Oxford, 1962; idem, "Hobbes's Bourgeois Man," in K. C. Brown, ed., *Hobbes Studies,* Oxford, 1965, 169–183; Keith Thomas, "The Social Origins of Hobbes's Political Thought," in ibid., 185–236; Willis B. Glover, "God and Thomas Hobbes," in ibid., 141–68; J. G. A. Pocock, "Time, History and Eschatology in the Thought of Thomas Hobbes," in J. H. Elliott and H. G. Koenigsberger, eds., *The Diversity of History: Essays in Honour of Sir Herbert Butterfield,* Ithaca, N.Y., 1970, 149–198.

155. Felix Raab, *The English Face of Machiavelli,* London, 1964; J. G. A. Pocock, *The Machiavellian Moment,* Princeton, N.J., 1975; idem, ed., *The Political Works of James Harrington,* Cambridge, 1977. See also idem, "Machiavelli, Harrington, and English Political Ideologies in the Eighteenth Century," *William and Mary Quarterly,* 3d ser., 22, 1965: 549–583, idem, "James Harrington and the Good Old Cause: A Study of the Ideological Context of his Writings," *JBS* 10, no. 1, 1970: 30–48.

156. Margaret A. Judson, *The Political Thought of Sir Henry Vane the Younger,* Philadelphia, 1969; Christopher Hill, *Milton and the English Revolution,* New York, 1978.

157. For whom, see also A. L. Morton, *The World of the Ranters: Religious Radicalism in the English Revolution,* London, 1970.

158. Christopher Hill, *Intellectual Origins of the English Revolution,* Oxford, 1965.

159. Margery Purver, *The Royal Society,* Cambridge, Mass., 1967. It seems unnecessary to list all the contributions to the complex initial debate between Hill, Kearney, Gweneth Whitteridge, and Raab, which continued in *PP,* nos. 27–33, 1964–1966. The relevant articles are reprinted in Webster, *Intellectual Revolution,* 160–196, 218–285. See also Douglas S. Kemsley, "Religious Influences in the Rise of Modern Science: A Review and Criticism, particularly of the 'Protestant-Puritan Ethic' Theory," *Annals of Science* 24, 1968: 199–226; Barbara J. Shapiro, *John Wilkins, 1614–1672: An Intellectual Biography,* Berkeley and Los Angeles, 1969; idem, "Latitudinarianism and Science in Seventeenth-century England," *PP,* no. 40, 1968: 16–41; also in Webster, *Intellectual Revolution,* 286–316; idem, "The Universities and Science in Seventeenth Century England," *JBS* 10, no. 2, 1971: 47–82; Richard P. Ross, "The Social and Economic Causes of the Revolution in the Mathematical Sciences in Mid-seventeenth Century England," *JBS* 15, no. 1, 1975: 46–66. An effort by Lotte Mulligan to restate the Anglican-science connection, in "Civil War Politics, Religion and the Royal Society," *PP,* no. 59, 1973: 92–116 (also in Webster, *Intellectual Revolution,* 317–346), contains glaring weaknesses which are pointed out by Shapiro in *PP,* no. 66, 1975: 133–138.

160. See also Charles Webster, ed., *Samuel Hartlib and the Advancement of Learning,* London, 1970, Intro.; also idem, "New Light on the Invisible College: The Social Relations of English Science in the Mid-seventeenth Century," *TRHS,* 5th ser., 24, 1974: 19–42. Also on the Hart-

lib circle is Hugh Trevor-Roper, "Three Foreigners: The Philosophers of the Puritan Revolution," in idem, *Social Change*, 237–293.

161. Robert H. Kargon, *Atomism in England from Hariot to Newton*, Oxford, 1966; John W. Shirley, ed., *Thomas Hariot, Renaissance Scientist*, Oxford, 1974; Lisa Jardine, *Francis Bacon*, Cambridge, 1974; Sir Geoffrey Keynes, *The Life of William Harvey*, Oxford, 1966; Gweneth Whitteridge, *William Harvey and the Circulation of the Blood*, London and New York, 1971.

162. R. S. Roberts, "The Personnel and Practice of Medicine in Tudor and Stuart England," *Medical History* 6, 1962: 363–382; ibid. 8, 1964: 217–234.

163. Hilda Smith, "Gynaecology and Ideology in Seventeenth-century England," in Berenice A. Carroll, ed., *Liberating Women's History: Theoretical and Critical Essays*, Urbana, Ill., 1976, 97–114.

164. Allan G. Debus, ed., *Medicine in Seventeenth-century England: A Symposium Held at U.C.L.A. in Honor of C. D. O'Malley*, Berkeley and Los Angeles, 1974.

165. Frances Yates, *The Rosicrucian Enlightenment*, London and Boston, 1972; P. M. Rattansi, "Paracelsus and the Puritan Revolution," *Ambix* 11, 1963: 24–32; idem, "The Social Interpretation of Science in the Seventeenth Century," in Peter Mathias, ed., *Science and Society, 1600–1900*, Cambridge, 1972, 1–32; Allan G. Debus, *The English Paracelsians*, London, 1965.

166. Harry Rusche, "*Merlinia Anglici:* Astrology and Propaganda from 1644 to 1651," *EHR* 80, 1965: 322–333; idem, "Prophecies and Propaganda, 1641 to 1651," *EHR* 84, 1969: 752–770.

167. David M. Bergeron, *English Civic Pageantry 1558–1642*, London, 1971; Judith Hook, *The Baroque Age in England*, London, 1976.

168. G. A. Philipps, "Crown Musical Patronage from Elizabeth I to Charles I," *Music and Letters* 58, 1977: 29–42; idem "John Wilbye's Other Patrons," *Music Review* 38, 1977: 81–93

169. P. W. Thomas, "Two Cultures? Court and Country under Charles I," in Russell, *Origins of the English Civil War*, 168–193.

170. Dennis Brailsford, *Sport and Society*, London, 1969.

The Later Stuarts
1660–1714

Stephen B. Baxter

A generation ago, when Professor Walcott surveyed this period of English history, he bemoaned its traditional character. Sir George Clark, G. M. Trevelyan, and David Ogg were still commanding figures, as they had been for many years. Interpretations were, on the whole, traditional too. Perhaps it may have been because this period was generally considered a backwater in English political history, perhaps because it was also thought to be the most reactionary of generations. For one reason or another, there was not very much going on. Even the younger people seemed to be doing very traditional work, when they did anything at all.

A world which had Purcell for its composer, Wren for its architect, Newton for its physicist, Dryden for its poet, Congreve and Wycherley for its playwrights; Defoe and Addison and Steele for its journalists, cannot have been a backwater and in fact never was one. To a large extent the historians were not looking in the right places for their subject matter. Many of the good things went by default to the literature faculties, while quite a few of the rest were abandoned to specialists in the history of science or the history of economics. Naturally enough, the dregs the historians did keep for themselves were not terribly exciting. The English Revolution was over by 1660, and such things do not happen every day. If most of us are ready to agree that the Industrial Revolution, with capital letters, comes after 1780, then the Restoration is perforce a part, and not the most exciting part either, of something horrid called Preindustrial England. The name itself is enough to frighten people away.

Twenty years on, therefore, the era of the later Stuarts may still be one of the less crowded fields of English history, if only because the historians have defined it too narrowly. Superficially it may appear that not much has happened in the past generation. The commanding figures, now J. H. Plumb and Ragnhild Hatton, are conservative in their techniques. But in the course of their long and brilliant careers Professors Plumb and Hatton and their friends have trained a new generation to carry on the tradition of high old-fashioned scholarship expressed in limpid prose. Others have been experimenting with new techniques in the field of social history. If some of this new work fails as sociology or anthropology as well as history, some of it is both interesting and important. Computer studies for an age before the census of 1851 are pretty unreliable affairs. Sampling techniques can be even more unreliable. Reconstruction studies seem to offer promise of greater reliability, though at prohibitive cost in time and in money.

Surely it is to the good that so much is being done at the point where local and social history intersect. One risk is that older kinds of history will be abandoned in favor of the fashionable novelty of the moment. That by itself is not too serious, for such trends tend to be self-correcting. If legal and constitutional and religious history are unfashionable at one moment, they will return to favor at another. At any given time there will always be specialities in which no work—or even worse, bad work—is being done. Those are the specialties which can provide dissertation topics for the next generation of research students, if there is someone left to train them. That is a second and greater risk. So many positions are going to the computer specialist or, say, to the African historian, that soon there may be no one left to train people in the older disciplines. At best, the later Stuart period may be dissolved in a larger pool known as early-modern, or pre-industrial, England. At worst, the world that existed before the census of 1851 may be abandoned entirely while history becomes the younger brother of the social sciences.

It is undoubtedly true that some of the most important work of the past twenty years had been done in publishing original sources. The magnificent work of A. Rupert Hall and his friends in publishing *The Correspondence of Isaac Newton* and *The Correspondence of Henry Oldenburg* has opened up entirely new vistas in the history of science and spawned something of a Newton industry.[1] Henry L. Snyder's edition of *The Marlborough-Godolphin Correspondence* (3 vols., New York 1975) has a few too many printing errors, but it is still a work of absolutely fundamental importance for the reign of Queen Anne. The indefatigable E. S. de Beer has edited the first five volumes of *The Correspondence of John Locke* (Oxford, 1976) with his usual exemplary skill and learning, and we are promised three more volumes. The splendid edition of *The Diary of Samuel Pepys*, by Robert Latham and William Matthews is just as welcome to historians as it may be to our literary friends.[2] Maurice F. Bond's edition of *The Diaries and Papers of Sir Edward Dering Second Baronet, 1644 to 1684* should be of general interest.[3] I was permitted to read some of the manuscripts many years ago and found them helpful. J. R. Powell and E. K. Timings edited *The Rupert and Monck Letter Book, 1666, Together with Supporting Documents* for the Navy Record Society (London, 1969). The publication of Thomas Isham's diary, covering a period when the boy was between thirteen and fifteen, may have been something of a joke and was certainly a nonevent.[4] More important was C. H. Josten's edition of the correspondence and notes of Elias Ashmole.[5] Another interesting and useful contribution has been made in a lesser compass by Philip Roberts with his publication of *The Diary of Sir David Hamilton, 1709–1714* (Oxford 1975). Sir David, who at one time had some difficulty in persuading the world that he was more than merely a man midwife, was Queen Anne's physician during the last five years of the reign. His notes on the events of July 1714 are of particular importance.

General works on the period tend to be ephemeral and one-sided. Professor Hatton, a generous soul, divides the world into those who are good at domestic history and those who are good at diplomatic history. Unfortunately there are those who are good at neither one nor the other. Thus Paul Langford's *The Eighteenth Century, 1688–1815* (London, 1976) is a superficial study of foreign policy, presumably intended for English students reading for their A levels. John Carswell, whose work can be weak, did a better job than usual with his *From Revolution to Revolution: England 1688–1776* (London, 1973). Even so, there is, it seems to me, a clear line between the good amateur job and the general work done by a professional. One would, perhaps, expect that Christopher Hill would devote most of his energy to the period before the Civil War. Some two-fifths of his *The Century of Revolution, 1603–1714* (Edinburgh, 1961), however, is concerned with the later Stuarts. J. P. Kenyon has contributed two works in this area. His *The Stuarts: A Study in English Kingship* (New York, 1959) was thought to be one of his slighter works. Recently he has published a new book on *Stuart England* (New York, 1978). Kenyon writes very well, and the book is a perceptive general study. Whether this or Christopher Hill's book can be made to work in an American classroom is another question. Paul S. Seaver's *Seventeenth Century England: Society in an Age of Revolution* (New York, 1976) is not a general work but, rather, a collection of four interesting essays with social history as the general theme. Such books tend to get lost, and even more so the individual papers in the various books; but collections of essays are certainly on the increase. One of the more useful ones was *Historical Essays, 1600–1750: Presented to David Ogg* (H. E. Bell and R. L. Ollard, eds., London, 1963).

One way to take a look at the political history of a given period is to write a royal biography. This is unfortunately a genre that attracts hack writers, and it is sometimes difficult to distinguish the hacks from the scientific biographers without a scorecard. Most of the time, the work of Maurice Ashley is negligible, and sometimes it is dangerous. But his *Charles II* had a better reception than his *James II*.[6] The first readers of the latter thought that it was a dreary book, very dull, and one which made virtually no use of new source materials. Such works are dangerous when they spoil the market for something better. Fortunately in this instance the market was not spoiled for John Miller, whose *James II: A Study in Kingship* (Hove, 1978) is being very well received. At times it is possible to tell that some works are based on the original manuscripts and others not. Thus neither Nesca A. Robb nor Henri and Barbara van der Zee appear to have been permitted to work through the Archives of the Queen of the Netherlands at The Hague, where the papers of William III are preserved. This did not prevent them from writing biographies, and they made skillful use of other materials, but it could not help being something of a handicap.[7] Stephen B. Baxter was permitted to use the Royal Archives at The Hague for his *William III and the Defense of European Liberty* (New York, 1966.)

David Green wrote a popular life of Queen Anne (London, 1970). This is a field which has more traps than most, for Queen Anne did not date her letters, and their correct order is a matter of some importance. Edward Gregg solved many problems and made a real contribution with his *Queen Anne* (London, 1979). Gregg was fortunate in being able to rely on the editorial work of Henry Snyder and Philip Roberts, but much of the credit belongs to himself. Making a real woman and, indeed, a statesman of Queen Anne involves more than putting the duchess of Marlborough and Mrs. Masham in their places. It involves a reassessment of all the individuals and all the institutions with which she had to work. Students will need time to digest Gregg's book, and on reflection they may not be able to digest all of it, for the author is a partisan of his heroine even at her least amiable moments. Even so, we now have for the first time a serious biography of the last of the Stuarts. Although he did not become king until 1714, it is impossible to pass by the magnificent *George I, Elector and King* (Cambridge, Mass., 1978) of Ragnhild Hatton. For many years it had been the received doctrine that there were no letters or related personal correspondence or accounts, nothing in fact on which to base a scientific study. Professor Hatton went out and found the materials herself and has now put them together into a masterful work. Although its chief importance, naturally enough, lies in a later period, George I was born in 1660, and her earlier pages have much fascinating material about England in Europe during the years 1660–1714.

Sovereigns tend to be less parochial than their subjects, for the simple reason that very few Englishmen ever read the foreign dispatches or took much of an interest in continental affairs. Occasionally a war might intrude, forcing the English to pay some attention. P. G. Rogers described one such incident in *The Dutch in the Medway* (London, 1970), a popular work. For the rest, apart from some of the royal biographies cited above, there has been very little work on the general area of Britain in Europe. J. R. Jones wrote a general book, *Britain and Europe in the Seventeenth Century* (London, 1966), while M. S. Anderson concentrated on *Britain's Discovery of Russia, 1553–1815* (London, 1958). Ragnhild Hatton and M. S. Anderson combined to edit a volume of piety in *Studies in Diplomatic History: Essays in Memory of David Bayne Horn* (Hamden, Conn., 1970). An even more important collection of papers had appeared two years earlier with the title *William III and Louis XIV: Essays by and for Mark A. Thomson*.[8] These two books had a better reception than did the two relevant volumes of *The New Cambridge Modern History*, which appeared in 1961 and 1970. Volume 5 was thought to be both dull and inaccurate; volume 6, when it finally did appear, was thought not even to reach the level of a reference work.[9] There was too much repetition; several of the authors of individual chapters disagreed with each other; and so on. It was certainly unfortunate that volume 6 was delayed for so many years. By the time it came out, several of the chapters were out of date. But there does seem to have been an unnecessarily harsh tone to the reviews. Several of the papers in each volume have real merit and are still being used. A happier series has been that with the general title *Britain and the Netherlands*.[10] By no means all of the papers in these volumes refer to this chronological period, but there are some that do.

On the domestic scene, nonroyal biography has not been a particularly successful medium in recent years. Maurice Ashley contributed a study of *General Monck* (Totowa, N.J., 1977), and much of the other work of this type has not been very much better. Dorothy H. Somerville's *The King of Hearts: Charles Talbot, Duke of Shrewsbury* (London, 1962) was a disappointment. Robert Harley continues to defeat all comers.[11] G. F. Trevallyn Jones achieved a sprightly title, at least, with his *Saw-Pit Wharton: The Political Career from 1640 to 1691 of Philip, Fourth Lord Wharton* (Sydney, 1967). George Hilton Jones tried unsuccessfully to defend both his hero and James II in his book *Charles Middleton: The Life and Times of a Restoration Politician* (Chicago, 1967.) Middleton was not "in the secret" as secretary of state, so that all the dirt reached James II through the channel of the other secretary, Sunderland. All that Middleton received were innocent-looking ostensibles. If one reads only those, it is possible to think that James II was a victim. Substantially the only work of this type that is worth study is K. H. D. Haley's *The First Earl of Shaftesbury* (Oxford, 1968). Of two older biographies with the same title, Haley's fine book replaces the study by Louise Fargo Brown completely. It does not quite do so much to the 1871 book by W. D. Christie, since Christie printed documents to which Haley merely refers. For the rest, it can be considered a definitive work.

Most recent work has concentrated not so much on individuals, royal or otherwise, as on Parliament. Of these, the most important is J. H. Plumb's *The Origins of Political Stability: England, 1675–1725*.[12] The title was not, perhaps, entirely fortunate, for the half century that began in 1675 was one of great instability, caused by the gradual apprehension that the heir to the throne was a papist. In the most recent work to appear on the Glorious Revolution, there is an increasing measure of agreement on the importance of the religious factor. Now if the cause of instability was, to begin with, a series of conversions to Rome in the royal family, then may not the hearty Protestantism of the early Hanoverians have something to do with the achievement of stability in the mid-1720s? Or the success of George I in foreign affairs? Or the mere weight of his German fortune and army? It seems to some readers that the role of Robert Walpole was exaggerated by Plumb, but we shall not really know until he gives us the final volumes of his magisterial *Life* of the statesman.

Other general works on the politics of the period are pale by comparison. Maxwell P. Schoenfeld gave us a little book on *The Restored House of Lords* (The Hague, 1967). There is some relevant material in John Cannon's *Parliamentary Reform, 1640–1832* (New York, 1973), though not very much. Clayton Roberts wrote an attractive book in *The Growth of Responsible Government in Stuart England* (Cambridge, 1966), but it has, perhaps, aged more than many of the works published at roughly the same time. To a considerable extent, Parliament was captured by the executive after 1688 as a matter of ordinary practice. In constitutional theory the Revolution subjected the executive to the authority of Parliament; but on a day-to-day basis the executive was normally in control on the issues which mattered. Again and again one sees Cabinet memoranda on a particular topic, dated as much as two years before the topic is raised in the House of Commons. It was always tremendously difficult for a body of 513, or 558, men to act spontaneously. Thus the executive, by careful planning, was often able to get its way. A 1969 book by Douglas R. Lacey seems to be a happier effort, and an important one too.[13]

To turn to more specific studies, D. T. Witcombe made a useful contribution with his *Charles II and the Cavalier House of Commons, 1663–1674* (New York, 1966). Maurice Lee, Jr., took his eye off Scotland for a moment to write a good book on *The Cabal*. J. P. Kenyon's *The Popish Plot* was a good piece of work, as everything from that author is, but it was not perhaps one of his major achievements.[14] More important was J. R. Jones, *The First Whigs: The Politics of the Exclusion Crisis, 1678–1683* (London, 1961). That is a work which has established itself as something of a classic. In 1972 there appeared two works which should be read together. J. R. Western's *Monarchy and Revolution: The English State in the 1680s* (London) should be compared and contrasted with J. R. Jones's *The Revolution of 1688 in England* (London). Professor Kenyon tends to prefer the Western book, while others see more in Jones; but the two works together are surely a winning combination. In 1963 Professor Kenyon published his *The Nobility in the Revolution of 1688* (Hull, 1963), a delightful shorter study. David H. Hosford followed through with *Nottingham, Nobles, and the North: Aspects of the Revolution of 1688* (Hamden, Conn., 1976). It may be said in passing that no enthusiast for William III, however frantic, would argue that the prince conducted the Revolution of 1688 in a vacuum. It was an English revolution in which the noblesse participated and in which the people at least acquiesced. But far too many people tend to forget the very great contributions of

the royal family, not merely William, but Mary and Anne as well, to the successful outcome of that revolution. Nor did the contributions of the Dutch Republic,
and Brandenburg too, hurt the cause one little bit. John Carswell wrote a slight
and inaccurate book on this topic, while George L. Cherry wrote a study of the
Convention Parliament of 1689.[15]

For the years after the Revolution we have at least some division lists, which
makes a new level of sophistication possible in analyzing political life. A number
of guides have been made available in recent years, though there is still hope of
further discoveries in one archive or another.[16] Some of the best work in this
rather technical field has been done by Henry Horwitz. His *Revolution Politicks:
The Career of Daniel Finch, Second Earl of Nottingham, 1647–1730* was successful if viewed as a series of essays rather than the biography it did not try to be.
His more recent *Parliament, Policy and Politics in the Reign of William III* is a
precise work of meticulous scholarship although it is not, perhaps, a book for
beginners.[17] Dennis Rubini was less successful. His *Court and Country 1688–
1702* (London, 1967), good as it is, seems slight and thin by comparison with the
work of Horwitz.

The best work in this field, rivaling that of Plumb, is *British Politics in the Age
of Anne* by Geoffrey Holmes (London, 1967). Holmes does work of a quality
equal to that of Horwitz and writes well into the bargain, which is something of a
relief. He has also edited *Britain after the Glorious Revolution, 1689–1714*
(London, 1969) and more recently has given us a good study of *The Trial of
Doctor Sacheverell* (London, 1973). W. A. Speck has done important work on
the electorate in his *Tory and Whig: The Struggle in the Constituencies, 1701–1715*
(London, 1970). By comparison, the work of James O. Richards, *Party Propaganda under Queen Anne* (Athens, Ga., 1972), is not impressive. P. W. J. Riley
published a small work, *The English Ministers and Scotland, 1707–1727,*[18]
which is in fact mostly concerned with the years 1707–1710. In 1979 the Manchester University Press published his *The Union of England and Scotland: A
Study in Anglo-Scottish Politics of the Eighteenth Century* (Manchester), a work of
much broader scope. B. W. Hill's *The Growth of Parliamentary Parties, 1689–
1742* (Hamden, Conn., 1976) presents some problems. There are quite a few
small factual errors, and it is not quite clear that the Tories were as healthy in
1742 as Hill makes them appear. That particular issue does not concern me here.
A more satisfying book is J. P. Kenyon's *Revolution Principles: The Politics of
Party, 1689–1720* (Cambridge, 1977). Kenyon emphasized the centrality of the
religious issue in this period and took an almost Tory view of the world. If he had
it would not have been wrong, for there were more Tories than Whigs. He raised
again the point made earlier by Gerald M. Straka, that Anglicans did not rely
on John Locke in the first generation after his work was published; they had
their own justifications for the Revolution.[19] Lois G. Schwoerer discussed the ha-

tred of Englishmen for the new world that was developing around them in *"No Standing Armies!" The Antiarmy Ideology in Seventeenth-century England* (Baltimore, 1974.)

Administrative history may not be particularly exciting to the general reader, but it does have its uses. For the research student, it provides a number of manageable dissertation topics. Of wider import is the fact that England was very much better governed under the later Stuarts than she had been under the earlier ones, and also that she was very much better governed than the peoples of contemporary Holland, France, and Germany by 1714. Without the remarkable development of administrative skills that in fact took place, it is difficult to see how the English could possibly have overtaken the Dutch in commerce or the French in warfare and in diplomacy. D. B. Horn's *The British Diplomatic Service, 1689–1789* (New York, 1961) was highly praised when it came out. Since then, reflective readers have noted that Professor Horn took perhaps an excessively Scottish view of the world. He also tended to antedate the achievement of professionalism in the diplomatic service. There was a continuing problem in obtaining men rich enough to be able to ignore the low and irregularly paid wages of the period, men who were also able to meet the social and linguistic requirements of continental courts. Phyllis S. Lachs discussed an earlier generation in her *The Diplomatic Corps under Charles II and James II* (New Brunswick, N.J., 1965.) I am not yet convinced that there was a professional diplomatic service, with regular pay and a standard *cursus honorum*, before the death of George II. Other departments have not fared terribly well. Henry Roseveare's *The Treasury: The Evolution of a British Institution* seems unsatisfactory for the period covered by this essay.[20] Ming-Hsun Li has discussed *The Great Recoinage of 1691 to 1699*, while I. K. Steele's book on the Board of Trade was not especially well received. Bernard Pool discussed Navy board contracts, while Thomas C. Barrow took up the American customs service.[21] Of these works, Barrow's was much the most successful. Perhaps the most important administrative study published in recent years was J. R. Western's *The English Militia in the Eighteenth Century: The Story of a Political Issue, 1660–1802*.[22] Western, whose premature death was a sad loss to the profession as well as to his friends, demonstrated the collapse of the militia during the later years of the Restoration and showed why it could not be called out in 1688 to defend the monarchy.

O. F. G. Hogg's substantial two-volume work *The Royal Arsenal: Its Background, Origin, and Subsequent History* (New York, 1963) is really a contribution to military history. So, too, perhaps is the recent book by H. L. Blackmore, *The Armouries of the Tower of London*, volume 1, *Ordnance* (London, 1978). Military and naval history attract more readers than other forms of administrative history. In the past they have also attracted numbers of scholars of the lowest description, a problem that has not been completely remedied in our own generation. Recent work in the field has included the useful book by John L. Childs, *The Army of Charles II*.[23] R. E. Scouller wrote on *The Armies of Queen Anne*, while David Chandler discussed their leader in *Marlborough as Military Commander*.[24] Two rather narrow monographs have appeared on specific aspects of the Nine Years' War. The title of Edward B. Powley's *The Naval Side of King William's War* (Hamden, Conn., 1972) is misleading; it covers the period down to June 1690 only. K. Danaher and J. G. Sims have edited *The Danish Force in Ireland, 1690–1691* for the Irish Manuscripts Commission (Dublin, 1962). Richard Ollard wrote a rather weak book about Admiral Holmes, while Patrick Crowhurst contributed a more disappointing discussion of an important topic in his book on merchant shipping in wartime. R. D. Merriman compiled a book of documents on Queen Anne's navy.[25] One of the most useful contributions of recent years in any area of administrative history, civilian or military, has been the *Office-holders in Modern Britain* series, for which we all owe many thanks to J. C. Sainty. Four volumes have appeared in the series since 1972.[26]

Legal and constitutional history has not fared terribly well in the last twenty years. Currently there is increasing interest in the history of crime, and J. S. Cockburn has edited *Crime in England 1550–1800* (London, 1978). Howard Nenner made an interesting contribution with his *By Colour of Law: Legal Culture and Constitutional Politics in England, 1660–1689* (Chicago, 1977). Jennifer Levin took up *The Charter Controversy in the City of London, 1660–1688, and Its Consequences*.[27] G. W. Keeton did what he could to make the odious Jeffreys a human being in his *Lord Chancellor Jeffreys and the Stuart Cause* (London, 1965). Michael Landon's *The Triumph of the Lawyers: Their Role in English Politics, 1678–1689* (University, Ala., 1970) chose seven Whig lawyers not including Somers as representative figures. The work was generally considered unsound. William H. Sachse bravely undertook an impossible task in his *Lord Somers: A Political Portrait* (Madison, Wis., 1975). As the title indicates, Professor Sachse was more interested in the statesman than in the chancellor. His book, although like everything Sachse ever wrote it is good work, demonstrates the impossibility of writing the biography of someone whose papers have been destroyed. Gareth Jones undertook a more topical approach in his *History of the Law of Charity, 1532–1827*.[28] This is a sound work, based on the cases themselves and not just on a superficial reading of the statutes. It is especially good on the development of *cy-près* doctrine, which also interested David Owen in his *English Philanthropy, 1660–1960* (Cambridge, Mass., 1964). Professor Owen's book was a severe disappointment, at least in the chapters dealing with the seventeenth and eighteenth centuries. Another topical study is John H. Langbein's *Torture and the Law of Proof: Europe and England in the Ancien Régime* (Chicago, 1978). There was, of course, more torture in England before the Civil War than afterward, despite the revival of the Council of the Marches of Wales for the period 1660–1689. But it remained a part of the law of Scotland even after the union of 1707.

There has been even less activity in the field of constitutional history. A useful compilation by E. N. Williams was *The Eighteenth Century Constitution 1688–1815: Documents and Commentary* (Cambridge, 1960). This was followed in 1966 by J. P. Kenyon's *The Stuart Constitution 1603–1688: Documents and Commentary* (Cambridge, 1966) in the same series. Of the two, Kenyon's is the more valuable work.

Twenty years ago the age of Norman Sykes was just drawing to a close with the publication of his Ford Lectures, *From Sheldon to Secker: Aspects of English Church History, 1660–1768* (New York, 1959). Except for Sykes's books, there had been very little written on English church history since World War I, even less that was much good. He was a brilliant lecturer, not something very common at Cambridge in those days, and he did attract some students. G. V. Bennett and J. D. Walsh edited a volume of essays in his memory which appeared in 1966.[29] Since then, Professor Bennett has given us an exceptionally important book on Francis Atterbury.[30] G. F. A. Best told the story of Queen Anne's Bounty in his fine book *Temporal Pillars*.[31] Horton Davies has written five good volumes on *Worship and Theology in England*, of which volume 2, *From Andrewes to Baxter and Fox, 1603–1690*, was thought to be relatively weak (Princeton, N.J., 1975). Although the entire work was greeted as a masterful survey of the field, this particular volume was thought to be slightly dated and also to be weak on theology. Those who feel this way can refer to H. R. McAdoo's *The Spirit of Anglicanism: A Survey of Anglican Theological Method in the Seventeenth Century* (New York, 1965). It remains the case that religious history in general and the history of the Church of England in particular is a neglected field. There has been some controversy about the work of R. S. Bosher, whose book of 1951 on the Restoration Settlement has been attacked both by George R. Abernathy, Jr., and more recently by I. M. Green.[32] For the rest, there has been very little, and especially little on the ordinary parish clergy. This makes the two books of Alan Macfarlane on Ralph Josselin all the more welcome.[33]

There has been scarcely more activity in the field of nonconformist history, especially in the area of Old Dissent. Considerable interest has, however, been shown in recusant history, and the quality of this work has been excellent. In 1963 A. C. F. Beales published *Education under Penalty: English Catholic Education from the Reformation to the Fall of James II, 1547–1689* (London). Hugh Aveling followed with *Northern Catholics: The Catholic Recusants of the North Riding of Yorkshire, 1558–1790* (New York, 1966), which is, among other things, a substantial contribution in the field of local history. John Miller's *Popery and Politics in England, 1660–1688* (New York, 1973) was perhaps more involved with politics than religion, if the two can be separated. His strictures on James II were considered severe at that time, although his recent biography of the king is being well received. Another excellent study of the recusants is John Bossy's *The English Catholic Community, 1570–1850* (New York, 1976). Richard T. Vann has done some first-class work with another unpopular sect, this time the Quakers. His *The Social Development of English Quakerism, 1655–1755* (Cambridge, Mass., 1969) was greeted with enthusiasm when it appeared. Professor Vann tells me that a project is now underway with a view to reconstituting the entire Quaker community down to the year 1800. This will be a major contribution in not one but a number of fields, when it appears. A less happy work was D. Elton Trueblood's *Robert Barclay* (New York, 1968), a weak study of an important figure. In the absence of more work by specialists in religion, it is almost ironic that it is the political historians who have had to remind us of the importance of religious issues in this period. They were indeed the predominant issues, and until they were settled, England could not hope to achieve anything approaching political stability.

The magnificent editions of the correspondence of Newton and of Oldenburg have accompanied, and to some extent inspired, a flowering in the area of the history of science. The older generation in this field, sound in itself but dating from before the flood of publications by A. R. Hall, is perhaps typified by Richard S. Westfall, whose *Science and Religion in Seventeenth-century England* (New Haven, Conn., 1958) came out just before the first volume of the Newton. Margery Purver discussed the Royal Society in her *The Royal Society: Concept and Creation* (Cambridge, Mass., 1967). Barbara J. Shapiro wrote about one of its first fellows in her book *John Wilkins, 1614–1672: An Intellectual Biography* (Berkeley and Los Angeles, 1969). Since Wilkins was also bishop of Chester, his career should be of some interest to those who date the complete opposition of science and Christianity to 1660. Michael Hunter's *John Aubrey and the Realm of Learning* (New York, 1975) falls more easily into the history of science than into general intellectual history. Naturally enough, more has been done on Newton than on the lesser men. As it happens, very little psychobiography has been attempted within the chronological limits of this period. Frank E. Manuel entered the lists with *A Portrait of Isaac Newton* (Cambridge, Mass., 1968) and returned with *The Religion of Isaac Newton* in 1974 (Oxford). Reviewers found both books troubling. The first was held to present a pretty dark picture, while the Freudian interpretation given in the second was considered to be of dubious validity. Both works, however, are firmly based on original sources, and both of them are impressive pieces of scholarship. Now that the *Correspondence* is complete, there will of course be other Lives, and there is already something of a Newton industry. Fortunately, a guide to this material has been prepared by Peter and Ruth Wallis.[34] Among the recent works in this field, that of Henry John Steffens, *The Development of Newtonian Optics in England* (New York, 1977), is chiefly concerned with the period after Newton's death. Something of a stir has been caused by the more general work of Margaret C. Jacob, *The Newtonians and the English Revolution, 1689–1720* (Ithaca, N.Y., 1976). In some quarters, the book has been received with high praise. In others, the author has been attacked for making a Marxist analysis and for gravely overstating the importance of the Latitudinarians. Were they the source of Newtonian natural philosophy, which would of course make them crucial figures in European intellectual history, or were they merely placemen?

By contrast, there has been something of a holiday in Locke studies, one which might prudently continue until the fine edition of his *Correspondence* is finished. The Straka thesis, that Locke's writings were not adopted by Anglicans during the reign of William III, has been elaborated by J. P. Kenyon in his *Revolution Principles: The Politics of Party, 1689–1720*. In the same year (1977) H. T. Dickinson published his important *Liberty and Property: Political Ideology in Eighteenth-century Britain* (New York). The two works should be read together, since they do not always agree. Other contributions in the field dominated by the name of Locke include W. H. Greenleaf's *Order, Empiricism, and Politics: Two Traditions of English Political Thought, 1500–1700* (Oxford, 1964). John Dunn discussed *The Political Thought of John Locke* (Cambridge, 1969), while Gordon J. Schochet took up the work of those whom Locke hated in his *Patriarchalism in Political Thought* (New York, 1975).

In other areas, it is startling to realize that Caroline Robbins published *The Eighteenth-century Commonwealthman* more than twenty years ago.[35] In this fundamental work, whose importance has only gradually been realized, Robbins demonstrated the continuity of liberal thought from the Interregnum to the American Revolution and showed how it survived, more or less by going underground. George L. Cherry was less happy with his *Early English Liberalism: Its Emergence through Parliamentary Action, 1660–1702* (New York, 1962). Robbins, in a severe review, felt that the Cherry book added nothing to our knowledge of the period, except perhaps confusion to our already confused concepts of liberalism. A much more important work, though contentious enough in its own way, was C. B. MacPherson's *The Political Theory of Possessive Individualism, Hobbes to Locke* (Oxford, 1962). MacPherson's Marxist analysis has had a better reception from philosophers and political scientists than it has from historians, which may say more about history faculties than about the book. Another important contribution which has not, perhaps, had all the reception it deserved is Felix Raab's *The English Face of Machiavelli: A Changing Interpretation, 1500–1700* (Toronto, 1964).

It is generally held, at least by non-Catholics, that the second condemnation of Galileo marked the end of Catholic intellectual life. The muses fled north of the Alps precisely in 1633, never to return. In *The Problem of Certainty in English*

Thought, 1630–1690 (The Hague, 1963), Henry van Leeuwen found that Anglicanism was less doctrinaire than Rome, as a system, and that its relative flexibility was more congenial to the development of scientific thought. There is of course considerable argument over just how congenial the English universities, at least, were to the development of scientific thought. Hugh Kearney's book on the universities was not received with uniform applause, nor was the larger work by Lawrence Stone.[36] Much of the work being done at the universities, and it was good work too, was in history or in linguistics; Newton, however, did do his work at Cambridge, though he may have been lonely there. Oxford did not have Newton, but it did have Dr. Fell. Shortly after his death, and thanks to his efforts, something that we may think of as the Oxford University Press appeared in about 1690.[37] If more was going on in the metropolis or at least away from Oxford and Cambridge, not all of that activity was sound by any means. Joseph M. Levine has written about John Woodward, a credulous polymath who assembled a collection of curiosities. His "Roman" shield was in fact of sixteenth-century provenance. Can one take seriously the claim that Dr. Woodward was a serious pioneer in the field of paleontology? Katherine S. Van Eerde discussed another minor figure, the cartographer John Ogilby. Ogilby's poems are now forgotten, and so too are his translations of Virgil, Homer, and Aesop. His maps, with the exception of the important *Britannia* of 1675, were not all that much better than his poems. He did well as a bookseller, however, and it was in this field that he had his most important successes. It is possible that the muses were lured north of the Alps by the development of a market for their wares—by royal patronage in France and by middle-class buying power in England—rather than that they fled in horror at the treatment of Galileo? Perhaps both motives were operative.[38] A good deal of the best work was done, not at the universities by dons, but at Court or in solitude by courtiers. John M. Wallace discussed Andrew Marvell in his *Destiny His Choice: The Loyalism of Andrew Marvell* (New York, 1968), while Royce Macgillivray took up a broader topic in the useful *Restoration Historians and the English Civil War* (The Hague, 1974).

Surprisingly little has been done with illustrated works and in particular with art history in the last twenty years, apart from coffee-table books. The cost of illustrations continues to rise, so that mere historians are soon priced out of the market. One fine work that few of us could afford to buy was Jeanette Black's edition of *The Blathwayt Atlas*, whose two volumes came to 575 dollars.[39] We shall not soon see reproductions of that quality again, at any price. Michael Foss wrote an amusing little book about a time when collecting was more reasonable. His *The Age of Patronage: The Arts in England, 1660–1750* (Ithaca, N.Y., 1972) was not felt to be up to date, nor scholarly; but it was entertaining. Bryan Little's biography of *Sir Christopher Wren* was also a disappointment to some.[40] Much more successful is the magnificent *A History of York Minster* (Oxford, 1978)

edited by G. E. Aylmer and Reginald Cant. One of the great buildings of the
Western world has apparently received a treatment worthy of it. Mark Girouard
has written an important and charming book in *Life in the English Country House:
A Social and Architectural History* (New Haven, Conn., 1978). David Burnett
has addressed himself to the question of the history of Longleat, one of the most
important of the great houses.[41] Less successful was Judith Hook's *The Baroque
Age in England* (London, 1976), an exercise in reductionism which went so far
as to approach nullity. Peter Thornton has given us an admirable account of
Seventeenth-century Interior Decoration in England, France and Holland (New
Haven, Conn., 1979). A. A. Tait has made good use of aerial photography in
his work *The Landscape Garden of Scotland, 1735–1835* (Edinburgh, 1980).

It is a short distance from the country houses to those who lived in them.
T. H. Hollingsworth made a noble attempt at demographic analysis by class in
his "The Demography of the British Peerage."[42] This is a fundamental problem,
for the peerage seem to have set fashions for lesser mortals to follow a generation
later; but those who have labored in this particular vineyard tell me that Hollingsworth was careless with his details. His book may be thought of as a pioneer
effort in a field that is sure to grow. Ivy Pinchbeck and Margaret Hewitt worked
with young people of all classes in their *Children in English Society* (2 vol., London, 1969). G. E. Mingay gave the clear-sighted an account of the gentry in his
The Gentry: The Rise and Fall of a Ruling Class (London, 1976). His traditional
and conservative tone is probably correct, however unfashionable it may be. Unfortunately the book was published in very small type, so that older readers may
not bother to give it the attention it deserves. Other separate groups have fared
less well. Roger Thompson had some good ideas when he wrote *Women in Stuart
England and America: A Comparative Study* (Boston, 1974), but he was weak on
his facts and with his research techniques. As it happens, most of the comparative
work that has been done in recent years has been quite uneven. In this age of
specialization there are few indeed who can discuss two societies with equal
weight. Folarin Shyllon's *Black People in Britain 1555–1833* (Oxford, 1978)
has some later Stuart material. So does David B. Davis, *The Problem of Slavery in
Western Culture* (Ithaca, N.Y., 1966). This monumental study, of which only the
first volume is of concern here, deserves great praise and has received it in the
years since it came out. Specialists were rather surprised, however, to see the author confuse serfdom with slavery, while they were startled by his attempts to
portray English colonial slavery as being no worse than the Latin variety. Was
not manumission easier in countries which used the Roman law? A very small,
special group was discussed by T. D. Whittet in his *The Apothecaries in the Great
Plague of London 1665.*[43]

The last twenty years have seen the appearance of a large number of excellent
works in the field of economic history. Of these, the most attractive is Charles

Wilson's brilliant *England's Apprenticeship*, *1603–1763* (New York, 1965), which should be required reading even for those who are frightened of the dismal science. Wilson writes with as much skill as does J. K. Galbraith, without being tendentious. Technical studies which have appeared in the journals since 1965 would indicate that the Dutch were losing their mastery over the English in one field after another well before 1763; but it does seem to be the case that London interest rates danced to the tune played at Amsterdam until the end of the Seven Years' War, while a threat that the Dutch might not make their usual loans during the year 1759 had to be taken very seriously indeed. In the period with which I am concerned, the Dutch—and the French, Italians, and Saxons too, for that matter—were unquestionably ahead of the English in certain specific areas. Again and again the English adopted a continental technique and in time, made it work for a relatively mass market.

Two institutional studies of the first class should be read together. C. D. Chandaman's *The English Public Revenue*, *1660–1688* (New York, 1975) was written many years before it was published, so that it fits in with P. G. M. Dickson's *The Financial Revolution in England: A Study in the Development of Public Credit*, *1688–1756* (New York, 1967) better than might be imagined. Chandaman's tables have been greeted by the profession with applause, and his book as a whole is a significant contribution to the field. Unfortunately he did become involved in an argument with the ghost of W. A. Shaw, whose introductions to the various volumes of the *Calendar of Treasury Books* were slightly more royalist than was Charles II himself. Shaw felt that Parliament had cheated the king of money that was rightfully his. Chandaman's figures are certainly much more nearly exact than were Shaw's. Unfortunately they do not prove, as Chandaman claims that they do, that Parliament kept its promises. For the period with which P. G. M. Dickson was concerned, the question of promises was less important. Once the money market could get away from the concept of the king as an individual client, rather more apt than most to default on his obligations, and begin to think of a national debt those interest payments, at least, were absolutely certain, then it was possible for interest rates to fall from 10 percent in the reign of Charles II to 8 in William's time, to 5 in Anne's and ultimately to 4 percent in the days of the early Hanoverians. A very substantial portion of the diplomatic, and indeed of the military, history of the eighteenth century comes down to the basic fact that there was enough public confidence to support a Bank of England from 1694 and not enough to support a Bank of France until after the end of the ancien régime. Dickson's massive and admirable book describes and explains the building of the credit structure which helped so much in making England the world's greatest power.[44]

For technical reasons, the study of foreign trade is easier to document than is the life of the domestic economy. Therefore our knowledge of English economic history is skewed, with excessive emphasis being placed on foreign trade. We must always remember that agriculture was the largest industry in the country and that domestic service came next; that manufacture was more important than trade in terms of hands employed; and that the domestic market was larger and more important in most ways than the sum of the foreign ones. Of general works, *The Cambridge Economic History of Europe* can be recommended. Volume 4, *The Economy of Expanding Europe in the Sixteenth and Seventeenth Centuries*, edited by E. E. Rich and C. H. Wilson, appeared in 1967. An important survey by an individual scholar was B. H. Slicher van Bath's *The Agrarian History of Western Europe, A.D. 500–1850*.[45] For one reason or another, Slicher van Bath does not make very easy reading, but he must be read even so. Joan Thirsk wrote work of high quality as prose and scholarship too. Her *English Peasant Farming: The Agrarian History of Lincolnshire from Tudor to Recent Times* (London, 1957) made use of probate inventories and was therefore a pioneer work in the area of the new social history now being pursued at Leicester. Eric Kerridge has given us two important books. His *The Agricultural Revolution* of 1967 is perhaps the more important, and at the same time rather less popular in tone, than his *The Farmers of Old England* of 1973.[46] Both works argue, in my opinion correctly, that the agricultural revolution took place for the most part before 1760. This is of course harsh doctrine for the friends of Arthur Young and Coke of Norfolk, but it is supported by the findings of William Albert, whose *The Turnpike Road System in England 1663–1840* (Cambridge, 1972) is a good but unduly neglected book. Albert argued that a substantial portion of the transport revolution had already taken place before the 1750s, when the turnpike mania is supposed to have begun. By, say, 1751 the main arteries were already in place, and if they were, then clearly agricultural produce could move from farm to market over the new roads. As an individual, I find the arguments of Kerridge and Albert persuasive. Over the next few years other specialized studies can be expected to settle the matter.

Serious work on the economy is impossible without reference to Phyllis Deane and W. A. Cole's *British Economic Growth, 1688–1959: Trends and Structure*.[47] Individual industries have been the focus of a number of worthy studies. D. C. Coleman wrote a good book, *The British Paper Industry, 1495–1860: A Study in Industrial Growth*. Julia De Lacy Mann described *The Cloth Industry in the West of England from 1640 to 1880*.[48] In 1963 D. C. Coleman published another good book with his *Sir John Banks, Baronet and Businessman: A Study of Business, Politics and Society in Later Stuart England* (Oxford). M. W. Flinn used the vehicle of an industrial dynasty to make a significant contribution with his *Men of Iron: The Crowleys in the Early Iron Industry*.[49] T. S. Willan's *The Inland Trade: Studies in English Internal Trade in the Sixteenth and Seventeenth Centuries* (Totowa, N.J., 1976) is not without flaws. It does contain some Restoration material. More or less popular surveys are available in L. A. Clarkson's *The*

Pre-industrial Economy in England, 1500–1750 and in Peter Earle's *The World of Defoe.*[50] Clarkson's book is useful, but it is by no means of the stature of Charles Wilson's work. Peter Earle's study is also useful, especially in its discussion of Defoe's economics. Clarkson has turned to the darker side of the picture in his *Death, Disease and Famine in Pre-industrial England.*[51] Another rather gloomy picture is presented by Jürgen Kuczynski in his *Darstellung der Lage der Arbeiter in England von 1640 bis 1760.* Although Kuczynski based his work on secondary materials and employed a Marxist framework, his study is both provocative and skillful. Some readers felt that he antedated the development of class cleavage and the triumph of capitalism.[52]

So far as foreign trade is concerned, it must of course move by water. Ralph Davis's *The Rise of the English Shipping Industry in the Seventeenth and Eighteenth Centuries* was not, perhaps, appreciated at its true value when it first appeared in 1962. It has proved to be a helpful work. An admirable and outstanding contribution was made by Jacob M. Price in his *The Tobacco Adventure to Russia: Enterprise, Politics, and Diplomacy in the Quest for a Northern Market for English Colonial Tobacco, 1676–1722* (Philadelphia, 1961). Price has a knack for picking the large topic that someone else might not think of and then for treating it so well that it need not be done again. His work will stand the test of time. So will that of K. N. Chaudhuri, whose *The Trading World of Asia and the English East India Company 1660–1760* (Cambridge, 1978) is full of good things. Although some of the argument is on the technical side, it is not necessary to have calculus to read the book, which is based on thorough computer studies as well as a wide range of manuscript sources. R. W. K. Hinton has discussed *The Eastland Trade and the Common Weal in the Seventeenth Century*, while W. E. Minchinton edited *The Growth of English Overseas Trade in the Seventeenth and Eighteenth Centuries.*[53] A. D. Francis, who had the good fortune to know Portuguese as well as Dutch, wrote well about *The Methuens and Portugal, 1691–1708.* H. E. Fisher took a slightly broader topic and carried it further in his valuable book on *The Portugal Trade: A Study of Anglo-Portuguese Commerce 1700–1770.*[54] Further east, Paul Cernovodeanu took up the question of *England's Trade Policy in the Levant and Her Exchange of Goods with the Romanian Countries under the Later Stuarts (1660–1714)* (Bucharest, 1972). Older works on the Levant trade are wholly inadequate and are badly in need of replacement; but this book is not, perhaps, the answer to our needs. English trade with the Danubian Principalities was negligible in quantity, and it is doubtful whether there was very much policy involved, either. Gedalia Yogev's *Diamonds and Coral: Anglo-Dutch Jews and Eighteenth Century Trade* (Leicester, 1978) promises to be more useful. Indian gentlemen would buy coral, though they had very little use for most other things coming from Europe, and in time the Jewish community came to handle most of this trade as well as that in Indian diamonds for European consumption.

It is a matter of some dismay that there are so few regional studies covering the period of the later Stuarts, when there have been so many good ones for the period before the outbreak of the Civil War. Two welcome exceptions have appeared recently. Of these, *Seventeenth-century Norwich: Politics, Religion, and Government 1620–1690* (Oxford, 1979) by John T. Evans, bridges the gap that so often is found between the first and second halves of the century. The second, a compilation of sources rather than merely a book, is the *Records of an English Village: Earls Colne 1400–1750*, (Cambridge, 1980), edited by Alan Macfarlane and others, which has been published in microfiche. This is a work that will be particularly welcome, since so much of the recent secondary literature has been based on the Earls Colne data. Now, that literature can be tested against the sources. For the most part, however, the second half of the century has suffered, at least relatively, from neglect. To some extent this may reflect structural changes in the economy itself. With the coming of the turnpike in the 1690s, regions, one by one, would have been absorbed into the national mainstream. But that change, a very gradual one, is not an adequate explanation for the present state of the literature. We are at present badly handicapped by the lack of good works on London, the West, the North, and so on. Thus Peter Clark and Paul Slack's edition of *Crisis and Order in English Towns, 1500–1700: Essays in Urban History* (Toronto, 1972) is mostly concerned with the period before 1660. It is a good book, but it is not of much help to the student of the Restoration years. Their more recent *English Towns in Transition, 1500–1700* (New York, 1976) is in effect a progress report on the work of the last generation, quite a little of it their own. But we need a great deal more in the way of urban history than we have at the moment. The regions have done even less well. One interesting contribution is Peter Earle's *Monmouth's Rebels: The Road to Sedgemoor, 1685* (New York, 1978). Earle studied the men of 1685 and found them to be of the better sort, nonconformist in their religion. Perhaps this is where Christopher Hill's people are to be found after the Restoration, in the West of England. For Wales there is Geraint H. Jenkins's *Literature, Religion and Society in Wales 1660–1730* (Cardiff, 1978). Jenkins noted an increase in Welsh-language publication during this period. Essentially this was a middle-class phenomenon, although it did have some aristocratic patronage. The aristocrats had to use English themselves, to protect their estates and careers, while the peasants were illiterate. If there was an increase in publication, there is likely also to have been an increase in the size and prosperity of the Welsh middle class.

So far as the colonies were concerned, the English after 1660 knew less than before and cared very little indeed. That at least was the argument of Gustav H. Blanke's *Amerika im Englischen Schrifttum des 16. und 17. Jahrhunderts.*[55] There had been a certain amount of visiting back and forth in the years before the Restoration, and there would be a resumption roughly coinciding with the foundation of Georgia in 1732; but there was relatively little physical contact between the colonies and the mother country in the seventy years that followed the executions of Hugh Peters and Henry Vane. Considering their fates, perhaps it is not quite that surprising after all. One scholar who has been working on the relationship between the two cultures is Alison Gilbert Olson, who published two books on the subject in 1970.[56]

Ireland is in fact the only one of the regions to have been given much attention, save for Scotland which is treated separately in this volume. And it may be impious to think of Ireland as a region, rather than as the dependant but separate kingdom it was in theory. Most Englishmen, even before the enactment of the Sixth of George I, did not bother with constitutional niceties; and as the horizons of the English economic world expanded, it did come to act as the successor to the smaller regions of the period before 1642. For English purposes, there is much to be learned from looking at the distorting mirror known as Ireland. In the past, its history has been bedeviled by partisan and confessional tract writing. That very fact made J. C. Beckett's *The Making of Modern Ireland, 1603–1923* (New York, 1966) all the more important. Here was good work, impartial work, in a convenient compass. R. Dudley Edwards made his own contribution in *A New History of Ireland* (Toronto, 1972). Anglican in tone, but still useful if the reader is aware of the possibility of bias, is Francis Godwin James's *Ireland in the Empire, 1688–1770: A History of Ireland from the Williamite Wars to the Eve of the American Revolution.*[57] In 1976 there finally appeared the massive and authoritative third volume of *A New History of Ireland, Early Modern Ireland 1534–1691*, edited by T. W. Moody, F. X. Martin, and F. J. Byrne (Oxford, 1976). This is not a work for beginners, and even those with some experience may want to use Beckett or Edwards as a guide to the more detailed study. Separate monographs include the slight and weak book of Carolyn A. Edie, *The Irish Cattle Bills: A Study in Restoration Politics.*[58] A better book by a better scholar is J. G. Simms's *Jacobite Ireland, 1685–1691.*[59]

Publication dates do not always reflect anything more significant than the publisher's schedule. J. D. Chambers was, as it happens, one of the first of the postwar demographers. His *Population, Economy, and Society in Pre-industrial England*, however, did not appear until 1972.[60] Thus pride of place in the demographic parade may belong to D. V. Glass and D. E. Eversley, the editors of *Population in History: Essays in Historical Demography*, which appeared in 1965.[61] The year 1965 was a banner one for the profession in many ways, and perhaps a revolutionary one. In September the National Endowments for the Arts and Humanities came into existence with initial budgets of ten million dollars apiece. Their work and that of other agencies such as the Canada Council has been of fundamental importance since then, as progressive inflation has robbed the income of many of the older private foundations of much of their buying power. The coincidence of dates is intriguing, although it does not apply to Britain. It is of course obvious that students of demography must have begun their work long before 1965 if they were to publish in that year. In 1966 the Cambridge Group for the History of Population and Social Structure burst on the scene with its first book, *An Introduction to English Historical Demography: From the Sixteenth to the Nineteenth Century.*[62] In the same year Peter Laslett published his more popular work *The World We Have Lost* (New York, 1966). Laslett's book has had an uneven press. Designed for an English popular audience, it did not have the scholarly tone of the works by Glass and Eversley, or by Wrigley. Nor did it travel too well. When Americans tried to assign it in their courses, student reaction ranged from boredom to outright dismay. However true it may be that the word *class* was used in its modern sense for the first time during the French Revolutionary Wars, it was difficult to persuade students that Laslett was correct when every word of Defoe contradicted him. So too, the idea that there were no grandparents in the seventeenth century seemed unlikely at the time, and it seems even less likely now, after a good deal of more careful research.

Much of the criticism of Laslett seems to have been rather unfair. He wrote, deliberately, a popular book, one that called attention to what might otherwise have remained an abstruse and remote specialty. That book was not merely popular; it was exciting and provocative as well. Doubtless, history should come as close as possible to being an exact science. But it should also be fun, and for everyone except the poor American undergraduates, *The World We Have Lost* was and is fun. It is clear that in this field both techniques and findings are in need of a good deal of refinement. In 1972 Peter Laslett edited another work with the extraordinary title *Household and Family in Past Time: Comparative Studies in the Size and Structure of the Domestic Group over the Last Three Centuries in England, France, Serbia, Japan and Colonial North America, with Further Materials from Western Europe.*[63] It is difficult for the student of English history to take the Serbian or Japanese family very seriously, even on a comparative basis. The differences in climate, health conditions, and social structure may be superable for the anthropologist, but they are and should be insuperable for the historian. Once again, however attractive the concept of comparative history may be, it does not seem to work out very well in practice.

There may be times, then, when the new specialty may seem to be a flawed jewel. This has been the case more than once with the work of Lawrence Stone. Professor Stone is an exceptionally talented and distinguished scholar, a man of very big ideas. It is unfortunate that he presents them prematurely, at least on occasion. His broad ideas have great merit. The details will be refined by others, in time. But the broad ideas do not have quite the impact they should, when they appear in less than polished form.[64] It seems a pity. More enduring work, and work of the highest quality, is being done by a remarkable woman named Margaret Spufford. Her *A Cambridgeshire Community: Chippenham from Settlement to Enclosure* was a model piece of scholarship.[65] A slightly less happy but still useful work was that of David G. Hey, *An English Rural Community: Myddle under the Tudors and Stuarts* (Leicester, 1974). Dr. Hey's study has the advantage of being about a part of the world well removed from the east coast. Others have noted already what an exceptional emphasis is being placed on a few easily accessible counties such as Essex, thanks perhaps to the devoted labors of its archivist, Emmison. Myddle is in Shropshire. Surely we need to know even more than we do now about the valley of the Severn and the Wye before we have anything like a balanced view of the country as a whole. Some of the more recent volumes published in the Victoria County History series are a help, but in general the older volumes in the series are not particularly useful to the present generation.

Other recent work has sometimes taken the form of a guide, designed to help researchers or perhaps even to lure them into the field. T. H. Hollingsworth published his *Historical Demography* (Ithaca, N.Y.) in 1969. An even more remarkable book was published by W. B. Stephens four years later with the title *Sources for English Local History* (Totowa, N.J., 1973). John Richardson's *The Local Historian's Encyclopedia* had a less warm reception when it appeared in 1975 (New Barnet). Some portions of the Richardson book were considered very good; parts were disappointing, and thin as well. Recently Alan Macfarlane and his friends have entered the field of guidebooks with an important handbook on reconstitution.[66] Of course the tie between demography and local history can be broken. Professor Vann has been using reconstitution techniques in his work on the Society of Friends, as Professor Stone has been using demographic ones in his work on marriage and the family.

Taken as a whole, this new field does present some fairly serious problems. Very very few of the ten thousand–odd parishes of early modern England had all the records which the modern researcher requires, especially if they are needed for long time spans. If one goes after a particular community, a great deal of very hard work may not in the end prove very much. We think, for example, that life expectancy declined sharply, almost catastrophically, in the seventy years after about 1590. It may have declined by almost 25 percent. But that thought is based on the records of three or four villages, and we simply do not know whether those villages were typical. So too, in those three or four villages which have been studied in detail, the population was remarkably mobile. Would this have been true of the bulk of the country, and especially of those villages which were not served either by a road or by a navigable river? We do not know. And for all the mathematical precision in which the specialists clothe their new findings, we never shall.

When a village or a group of them is found with the proper kinds of records, then there is cause for rejoicing. Certainly the work of the Cambridge Group and the Leicester Department of Local History has given us a new world. Much of the older social history of the period before 1965 seems puerile in the light of these more recent studies. But it must be remembered that the survival of documentation is accidental and that its survival in the correct types and quantities is exceptionally rare. Years ago Sir John Habakkuk used to take three counties and compare them in a wondrous and compelling fashion. Yet one was left with the uneasy feeling that his three counties might not be significant, or representative, or balanced; they might merely be the three counties whose records were in the best shape at the time Sir John undertook his researches. Extrapolating from that kind of material in order to come up with general laws is daring, it is breathtaking; but it is also very possibly unsound. What is needed are many more such studies, each of which will act as a control on the others. Gradually, study by study, details will emerge which will make the broader picture more reliable. Unfortunately Dr. Spufford, in a recent review, has pointed out that reconstitution—the most trustworthy of the new techniques—is almost prohibitively expensive both in time and in money. She feels that Essex has been overdone. But who is going to volunteer to spend twenty years on one of the other counties? And who will pay that volunteer for his time during the twenty years that he is assembling his materials? That is one of the things that academic tenure is meant to take care of, to provide the time the researcher must have for a major work. But one will still have to discover able young people, with both the quality and the patience that Dr. Spufford has demonstrated in her own work, if very much is to be achieved. Some of these young scholars are now coming forward, and it is in this field that some of the most exciting work of the next twenty years will be done.

What of the future? The past twenty years have seen real progress, yet important gaps remain. We need the History of Parliament volumes, a good history of London, a new history of the Levant Company, and something up to date on England in the Mediterranean. A general work on the gradual shift westward of England's economic center of gravity would be helpful, as would a reassessment of the relative parts played by Ireland, the American colonies, and the slave trade in the growing prosperity of the western ports. More regional studies should be undertaken. It may well be true that the consumption of spirits doubled in the reign of William III and doubled again in the reign of Anne, inaugurating the Gin Age, but was this a London or a national phenomenon? It would be helpful if the demographers would do more than they have done so far in breaking down their material by class and by region. Scientific biographies of Charles II and of Clarendon, among his ministers, would be of considerable usefulness, if only to underline the importance of the administrative and diplomatic history that some of the political specialists tend to forget. We need much more good work devoted to integrating religious and other types of specialty history into the mainstream. We need, in short, more of everything, including readers. The best historians remember that, and take pains with their writing. Only so can the period of the later Stuarts avoid being a backwater in English history.

NOTES

This chapter is designed to be a sequel to Robert Walcott, "The Later Stuarts (1660–1714): Significant Work of the Last Twenty Years (1939–1959)," *AHR* 67, 1962: 352–370 and reprinted in Elizabeth Holden Furber, ed., *Changing Views on British History*, Cambridge, Mass., 1966. For a more recent survey see the fine article by Richard R. Johnson, "Politics Redefined: An Assessment of Recent Writings on the Late Stuart Period of English History, 1660 to 1714," *William and Mary Quarterly*, 3d ser., 35, 1978: 691–732. That article includes references to unpublished dissertations and articles, not merely to books. See also William L. Sachse, ed., *Restoration England, 1660–1689*, Conference on British Studies Bibliographical Handbooks, New York, 1971, and the forthcoming volume in the same series, *Augustan England, 1689–1760*, by Stephen B. Baxter.

1. A. Rupert Hall et al., eds., *The Correspondence of Isaac Newton*, 7 vols., New York, 1959–1978; A. Rupert Hall and Maria Boas Hall, eds., *The Correspondence of Henry Oldenburg*, 11 vols. to date, Madison, Wis., 1965–
2. Berkeley and Los Angeles, 9 vols., 1970–1976.
3. House of Lords Record Office, Occasional Publications, no. 1, London, 1976.
4. *The Diary of Thomas Isham of Lamport (1658–81), Kept by Him in Latin from 1671 to 1673 at His Father's Command.* Translated from the original by Norman Marlow, with introduction, appendices, and notes by Sir Gyles Isham, together with a preface by Sir George Clark, Farnborough, 1971.
5. *Elias Ashmole (1617–1692): His Autobiographical and Historical Notes, His Correspondence, and Other Contemporary Sources Relating to his Life and Work*, 5 vols., New York, 1966.
6. Maurice Ashley, *Charles II: The Man and the Statesman*, London, 1971; idem, *James II*, London, 1978.
7. Nesca A. Robb, *William of Orange: A Personal Portrait*, 2 vols., London, 1963–1966; Henri van der Zee and Barbara van der Zee, *William and Mary*, London, 1973. Robb at least tried to write a serious work; the van der Zees wrote journalism.
8. Ragnhild Hatton and J. S. Bromley, eds., Toronto, 1968.
9. *The New Cambridge Modern History:* Vol. 5, F. L. Carsten, ed., *The Ascendancy of France, 1648–88*, Cambridge, 1961; vol. 6, John S. Bromley, ed., *The Rise of Great Britain and Russia, 1688–1715–25*, Cambridge, 1970.
10. J. S. Bromley and E. H. Kossmann, eds., 5 vols. to date, London, 1960–1975.
11. For example, Elizabeth Hamilton, *The Backstairs Dragon: A Life of Robert Harley, Earl of Oxford*, London, 1970; Angus McInnes, *Robert Harley: Puritan Politician*, London, 1970; and Sheila Biddle, *Bolingbroke and Harley*, New York, 1974.
12. Boston, Mass., 1967. Reprinted 1969 as *The Growth of Political Stability in England, 1675–1725*, Baltimore.
13. Douglas R. Lacey, *Dissent and Parliamentary Politics in England, 1661–1689: A Study in the Perpetuation and Tempering of Parliamentarism*, New Brunswick, N.J., 1969.

14. Maurice Lee, Jr., *The Cabal*, Urbana, Ill., 1965; J. P. Kenyon, *The Popish Plot*, New York, 1972.

15. John Carswell, *The Descent on England: A Study of the English Revolution of 1688 and Its European Background*, London, 1969; George L. Cherry, *The Convention Parliament 1689: A Biographical Study of Its Members*, New York, 1966. It is a continuing nuisance that the History of Parliament volumes for this period have not been published.

16. For example, J. C. Sainty and D. Dewar, compilers, *Divisions in the House of Lords: An Analytical List, 1685 to 1857*, House of Lords Record Office, Occasional Publications, no. 2, London, 1976, I. F. Burton, P. W. J. Riley, and Edward Rowlands, eds., *Political Parties in the Reigns of William III and Anne: The Evidence of Division Lists*, London, 1968; and Aubrey Newman, ed., *The Parliamentary Lists of the Early Eighteenth Century: Their Compilation and Use*, Leicester, 1973.

17. New York, 1968, and Newark, Del., 1977, respectively.

18. University of London Historical Studies, No. 15, London, 1964.

19. Gerald M. Straka, *Anglican Reaction to the Revolution of 1688*, Madison, Wis., 1962. This work has not yet received the attention it deserves.

20. London, 1969. It is only fair to say that Roseveare is himself unhappy with Stephen B. Baxter, *The Development of the Treasury 1660–1702*, Cambridge, Mass., 1957.

21. Ming-Hsun Li, *The Great Recoinage of 1691 to 1699*, London, 1963; I. K. Steele, *Politics of Colonial Policy: The Board of Trade in Colonial Administration, 1696–1720*, New York, 1968; Bernard Pool, *Navy Board Contracts, 1600–1832*, Hamden, Conn., 1966; Thomas C. Barrow, *Trade and Empire: The British Customs Service in Colonial America, 1660–1775*, Cambridge, Mass., 1967.

22. Studies in Political History, Toronto, 1965.

23. Studies in Social History, Buffalo, 1976.

24. R. E. Scouller, *The Armies of Queen Anne*, Oxford, 1966; David Chandler, *Marlborough as Military Commander*, New York, 1973.

25. Richard S. Ollard, *Man of War: Sir Robert Holmes and the Restoration Navy*, London, 1969; Patrick Crowhurst, *The Defence of British Trade 1689–1815*, Folkestone, 1977; R. D. Merriman, *Queen Anne's Navy: Documents Concerning the Administration of the Navy of Queen Anne, 1702–1714*, London, 1961.

26. J. C. Sainty, compiler, *Office-holders in Modern Britain*: vol. 1, *Treasury Officials, 1660–1870*, London, 1972; vol. 2, *Officials of the Secretaries of State, 1660–1782*, London, 1973; vol. 3, *Officials of the Board of Trade, 1660–1780*, London, 1974; vol. 4, *Admiralty Officials, 1660–1780*, London, 1975.

27. University of London Legal Series (under the auspices of the Institute of Advanced Legal Studies), no. 9, London, 1969.

28. Cambridge Studies in English Legal History, New York, 1969.

29. G. V. Bennett and J. D. Walsh, eds., *Essays in Modern English Church History in Memory of Norman Sykes*, New York, 1966.

30. *The Tory Crisis in Church and State, 1688–1730: The Career of Francis Atterbury, Bishop of Rochester*, Oxford, 1975.

31. G. F. A. Best, *Temporal Pillars: Queen Anne's Bounty, the Ecclesiastical Commissioners, and the Church of England*, Cambridge, 1964.

32. R. S. Bosher, *The Making of the Restoration Settlement: The Influence of the Laudians 1649–1662*, 1951; George R. Abernathy, Jr., *The English Presbyterians and the Stuart Restoration, 1648–1663*, Transactions of the American Philosophical Society, n.s., 55, pt. 2, Philadelphia, 1965; I. M. Green, *The Re-establishment of the Church of England 1660–1663*, Oxford, 1978.

33. Alan Macfarlane, *The Family Life of Ralph Josselin, a Seventeenth-century Clergyman: An Essay in Historical Anthropology*, New York, 1970; his full edition of *The Diary of Ralph Josselin, 1616–1683*, London, 1976, replaces the abbreviated version published by the Camden Society in 1908.

34. *Newton and Newtoniana 1672–1975: A Bibliography*, Folkestone, 1978.

35. Caroline Robbins, *The Eighteenth-century Commonwealthman: Studies in the Transmission, Development and Circumstance of English Liberal Thought from the Restoration of Charles II until the War with the Thirteen Colonies*, Cambridge, Mass., 1959.

36. Hugh Kearney, *Scholars and Gentlemen: Universities and Society in Pre-industrial Britain, 1500–1700*, Ithaca, N.Y., 1970; Lawrence Stone, ed., *The University in Society*, 2 vols., Princeton, N.J., 1974.

37. Not in 1478. See Harry Carter, *A History of the Oxford University Press*, vol. 1, *To the Year 1780*, New York, 1975.

38. Joseph M. Levine, *Dr. Woodward's Shield: History, Science, and Satire in Augustan England*, Berkeley and Los Angles, 1978; Katherine S. Van Eerde, *John Ogilby and the Taste of His Times*, Folkestone, 1976.

39. Providence, R.I., 1970–1975.

40. *Sir Christopher Wren: A Historical Biography*, London, 1975.

41. David Burnett, *Longleat: The Story of an English Country House*, London, 1978.

42. *Population Studies*, 25, Suppl., 1965.

43. The Sydenham Lectures for 1965, Ewell, Epsom, Surrey, n.d.

44. An earlier work by J. Keith Horsefield, *British Monetary Experiments, 1650–1710*, Cambridge, Mass., 1960, may also be consulted.

45. Olive Cornish, trans., New York, 1963.

46. Eric Kerridge, *The Agricultural Revolution*, New York, 1967; *The Farmers of Old England*, Totowa, N.J., 1973.

47. University of Cambridge, Department of Applied Economics, Monograph no. 8, New York, 1967.

48. New York, 1958, and Oxford, 1971, respectively.

49. Edinburgh University Publications in History, Philosophy and Economics, no. 14, Edinburgh, 1962.

50. New York, 1972, and London, 1976, respectively.

51. New York, 1975.

52. *Die Geschichte der Lage der Arbeiter unter dem Kapitalismus, vol. 22, pt. 2, Die Geschichte der Lage der Arbeiter in England, in den Vereinigten Staaten von Amerika und in Frankreich*, Berlin, 1964.

53. New York, 1959, and London, 1967, respectively.

54. New York, 1966, and London, 1971, respectively.

55. Beitrage zur englischen Philologie, no. 46. Bochum-Langendreer, 1962.

56. Alison Gilbert Olson, *Anglo-American Politics 1660–1775: The Relationship between Parties in England and Colonial America*, New Brunswick, N.J., 1970; Alison G. Olson and Richard M. Brown, eds., *Anglo-American Political Relations, 1675–1775*, New Brunswick, N.J., 1970.

57. Harvard Historical Monographs 68, Cambridge, Mass., 1973.

58. Transactions of the American Philosophical Society, n.s., 60, pt. 2, Philadelphia, 1970.

59. Studies in Irish History, 2d ser., 5, Toronto, 1969.

60. Edited, with a preface and introduction, by W. A. Armstrong, New York, 1972.

61. Chicago, 1965.

62. E. A. Wrigley, ed., New York, 1966.

63. New York, 1972.
64. Lawrence Stone, *The Family, Sex and Marriage in England 1500–1800*, London, 1977.
65. Leicester, 1965.
66. Alan Macfarlane with Sarah Harrison and Charles Jardine, *Reconstructing Historical Communities*, Cambridge, 1978.

Early Georgian England

Henry L. Snyder

The early Hanoverian period has traditionally received rather less attention from historians than it deserves. A relatively quiescent half century politically, it appeared to lack the excitement and novelty of the late Stuart period which preceded it or the reign of George III which followed. The War of the Austrian Succession or the early part of the Seven Years' War did not change so profoundly and markedly the course of European history as did the War of the Spanish Succession or the Napoleonic wars. Political parties seemed to hibernate, recuperating from the excesses of Anne's reign, in preparation for the new national and popular character they were to take on in the age of Edmund Burke, John Wilkes, and Charles James Fox. Whether writing on the economy, the society, or the church, historians stressed stability, continuity, tranquility in preference to other more stirring qualities. The politicians and certainly the sovereigns were treated as dull mediocrities. The taciturn George I was hardly a rival for the debonair Charles II or the eccentric but vigorous George III. The supposed motto of the most influential politician of the period, Sir Robert Walpole, was Quieta non Movere. The most long-tentured minister, the duke of Newcastle, was easily dismissed as a bumbler and a hack.

Much of the inattention which characterizes the historian's response to the period may be attributed to the relative dearth of materials. With two notable exceptions (the earl of Hardwicke and the duke of Newcastle), the papers of all the major political figures have by and large disappeared. Hardly a scrap survives in the hand of George I. Conversely the Newcastle papers, by virtue of their great bulk and his near-indecipherable handwriting, have discouraged scholars until recently from making a close study of them. Sir Lewis Namier was a notable exception. This dearth of materials extends to printed sources. The great Public Record Office calendars run out at the beginning of the eighteenth century. The row upon row of memoirs and correspondence that appeared regularly in the nineteenth century deal primarily with figures active after 1760. It is not surprising, therefore, that the range of publications treated in this section may appear at first glance not so impressive as those in other sections. Yet it is most rewarding to report that both the quantity and quality of historical writing for the early Hano-

verians has been noteworthy and praiseworthy. Furthermore, historians have
tackled some of the most formidable topics—for example, public credit and
Newcastle—and have treated them in a most successful manner.

I can begin with the survey works that provide both general and specialized
coverage of the period. For a general treatment, Dorothy Marshall's *Eighteenth-
century England* (1st ed., London, 1962; 2d ed., London, 1974) remains unsur-
passed. Reflecting her background as a social historian, it is the most balanced
and sympathetic account. The latest edition is little modified, though it does reflect the recent work of G. Holmes and J. H. Plumb on the vitality of parties in
place of its previous reliance on the work of Robert Walcott. Aside from added
footnotes, the other additions deal mainly with the nature of specific ministries,
drawing upon such works as P. Langford on the Rockingham administration and
J. Cannon on the Fox-North coalition. John Owen's traversal of *The Eighteenth
Century 1714–1815* (Totowa, N.J., 1975) appeared at the same time as Marshall's second edition. It proves to be a disappointment, for it is essentially a
conventional political history though with useful diplomatic coverage. Social,
economic, and intellectual topics are treated cursorily in summary chapters.
Eighteenth-century politics and constitutional developments receive more sophisticated analysis in two separate chapters. Yet Owen clings too closely to his
Namierite origins and seems curiously out of touch with research subsequent to
his own admired *Rise of the Pelhams* (London, 1957). Both in his downplaying of
the role of parties after 1714 and in his neglect of popular politics, his approach
is old-fashioned and out of date. His treatment of such figures as George I and
Newcastle repeats the usual clichés. Another, briefer survey by John Carswell,
From Revolution to Revolution, 1688–1776 (London, 1973), is interesting for
some illustrative material but falls between two stools: it is too brief and elementary for scholars and yet presupposes too much background for the student. It is a
not wholly satisfactory synthesis of standard secondary works.

The finest contribution in general surveys is William A. Speck's *Stability and
Strife: England, 1714–1760* (Cambridge, Mass., 1977). Divided into two main
sections, the first analyzes the structure of society and the changes that took place
within it and the economy during the early Hanoverian period. There is no better
introduction for the advanced student. Speck draws on an impressive array of
contemporary printed materials and has carefully mastered the secondary literature. At once up to date and abreast of the most recent published research, he
nevertheless uses his material with caution and is always judicious in his treatment. Besides a detailed breakdown of the social structure, he anatomizes the political structure and treats the church and the economy in comparable detail. A
beginning student might find the diet overrich, but students at any stage can read
this work with profit. The second portion of the text is devoted to a narrative
history, almost wholly political in character and focused on the central govern-

ment. It suffers from the limited space allotted and provides only a summary account.

The most sophisticated and important political survey to appear which extends into the period covered in this volume is J. H. Plumb's *The Growth of Political Stability in England, 1675–1725* (London, 1967). Though only the last of the six chapters, "The Triumph of the Venetian Oligarchy," is devoted to the Hanoverian period, the work is essential for understanding the eighteenth-century political establishment, here characterized as "two processes, the development of oligarchy and the growth of executive" (p. 65). According to Plumb, the destruction of the Tory party was due in part to internal dissensions, the hostility of George I, and finally, the taint of Jacobitism, manipulated so masterfully by Sir Robert Walpole. Above all, it was the political wizardry of Walpole and his centralization of patronage that were responsible for one-party rule. His control of the House of Lords and his manipulation of the House of Commons were complemented by the success of the Whig oligarchs in wresting control of the constituencies away from the minor landowners, a subject also treated in Plumb's "Growth of the Electorate in England, 1600–1715" (*PP*, no. 45, 1969).

Another dimension of English party politics is treated in *Anglo-American Politics 1660–1775: The Relationship between Parties in England and Colonial America* (Oxford, 1973). Alison Gilbert Olson contends that a close working relationship between English and colonial political leaders developed in the late Stuart period. While London helped to settle disputes, the colonial factions found it useful to develop ties with English counterparts for resolving problems and promoting their interests. The disintegration of the Tories and the alliance of Walpole's opposition with London merchants hostile to colonial interests undermined this relationship, which gradually disappeared. Mid-century English politicians who reawakened concern for the colonies did so in paternal, rather than fraternal, fashion, which was sure to provoke a hostile reaction. Another element in the breakdown of communication was the consequence of Newcastle's long tenure in the secretary of state's office, according to James Henretta in his *'Salutary Neglect': Colonial Administration under the Duke of Newcastle* (Princeton, N.J., 1972). By hamstringing the commissioners of trade and reserving for himself the management of colonial patronage while yet taking little active interest in the direction of colonial affairs, Newcastle undercut the power of the colonial governors and allowed the colonists to drift away from English control.

The most important new reference work for Parliament is the massive two-volume set *The House of Commons 1715–1754* (New York, 1970) prepared by Romney Sedgwick and associates for the History of Parliament Trust. The central feature of the work is the invaluable set of biographies of members of Parliament, which is based upon both voluminous manuscripts and printed sources. It is a mine of information that, with the volumes for the succeeding period edited by Sir Lewis Namier and John Brooke (*The House of Commons, 1754–1790*, 3 vols., London, 1964) will be quarried by generation of scholars to come. The work also includes an extensive analysis and history of each individual constituency. It is preceded by a useful introductory survey that deals with procedure and provides a narrative history of parliamentary parties in which the Jacobite element is given great weight. Though this emphasis is not supported by many scholars, the various lists (especially the important Worsley list, which analyzes the membership of the 1714 and 1716 parliaments) and biographies make the volumes indispensable for scholars working in the period.[1]

Parliamentary procedure is dealt with in much greater detail and with impressive documentation in two major works which have appeared in the past decade. Thanks to the efforts of Peter D. G. Thomas, we finally have in his *House of Commons in the Eighteenth Century* (Oxford, 1971) a full and informed account of the organization and conduct of the business in the House. He treats exhaustively such topics as the arrangement of business, attendance of members, seating, conduct of debate, procedure, committees, and the role of the Speaker. His work is complemented by Sheila Lambert's *Bills and Acts: Legislative Procedure in Eighteenth Century England* (Cambridge, 1971). Lambert provides an even more exhaustive discussion of the preparation and progress of legislation through the House. Above all, Lambert provides us with an informed account of private-bill procedure. Her work is based upon the collection of private bills in the British Library that she has identified as the papers of Robert Harper. Harper, a private conveyancer, drew up more than a third of the private bills which passed into legislation between 1731 and 1762. The critical role of the chairman of ways and means is described as well as the role and working membership of committees. She includes a valuable chapter on treatises and handbooks of parliamentary procedure. But it is in her chapters on enclosure bills, estate bills, and local bills that the full value of her contribution becomes evident. She has taken an obscure yet important subject and brought extraordinary illumination to it. Her initial objective had been to prepare her *List of House of Commons Sessional Papers 1701–1750* (London, 1968), which appeared under the aegis of the List and Index Society. In the process she discovered that the standard collection of eighteenth-century sessional papers assembled by Luke Hansard on the order of Speaker Abbott at the turn of the nineteenth century was far less complete than scholars had assumed. By her indefatigable efforts she has tracked down what must be virtually all the surviving printed documents—bills, reports, accounts, and papers—for publication in this country by Scholarly Resources. The Abbott set was particularly defective for the 1714–1760 period, the earliest bill dating only from 1740. Lambert's compilation fills nineteen substantial volumes for this period alone. It is supplemented by an index volume which identifies all relevant documents ordered to be printed and which contains references to the journals or

elsewhere where the documents are to be found in print. The separately published items are reproduced by photo offset. They are a mine of information for
scholars, especially valuable for the social and economic historian. In sum, the
volumes of Sedgwick, Thomas, and Lambert have wrought a revolution in our
knowledge about the House of Commons in the first half of the eighteenth century, its membership, organization, and business.

The past twenty-five years have seen a notable increase in interest in party history in the late seventeenth and early eighteenth centuries in contrast to the near-
exclusive focus on the George III period in the previous quarter century or
more. Brian W. Hill has attempted a synthesis of recent research in his *Growth of
Parliamentary Parties 1689–1742* (London, 1976). Although weighted to the
later Stuarts, it carries the survey up to the fall of Walpole. Hill stresses the vitality and continuity of party throughout the period. He makes a particular point
of separating the Whig and Tory elements in the opposition groupings of the
1720s and the 1730s, and he insists that the Whigs retain their party identity
even after going into opposition. He believes that lack of trust between the two
groups and the basic commitment of opposition Whigs to Whig principles shared
with the government led them to desert their Tory counterparts in critical divisions, thus insuring the survival of Walpole's ministry. Hill also attaches little
importance to the Jacobite element among the Tories. Taking up where Hill left
off, J. C. D. Clark treats "The Decline of Party, 1740–1760" (*EHR* 93,
1978).[2] Not accepting either of the currently prevailing theories, that the two-
party system existing in Anne's reign declined rapidly after (a) the Hanoverian
Succession or (b) the fall of Walpole, Clark maintains "that the 1750s witnessed
the destruction of Whig and Tory parties surviving in direct descent from those
of Anne's reign, and the supersession of one party system by another" (p. 500).
The intense competition for office among the leaders of the Old Corps of the
Whigs in 1754–1757 was one cause. Another was the demise of Jacobitism. The
last plot collapsed in 1753; the last invasion attempt failed in 1759. Clark contends that the Tory party was dominated by Jacobites until the 1750s and that
Jacobitism was a major issue in English politics until mid-century.

Clark is only one of a number of historians who have attempted to identify the
Tories closely with the exiled Stuarts. The most devoted adherent of this point of
view is Eveline Cruickshanks, who wrote (without acknowledgment) the third
chapter in Sedgwick's History of Parliament Trust volumes in which she stressed
this theme. More recently she has devoted a whole volume to this subject, *Political Untouchables: The Tories and the '45* (New York, 1979). She makes the case as
eloquently as she can for identifying the Tory party as Jacobite between 1715 and
1745. Her contention that the Tories (Jacobites) refused to cooperate with the
opposition Whigs at crucial moments, thus saving Walpole, is contested by Brian
Hill, as noted above. The real issue is whether or not those who corresponded

with the Pretender were prepared to support military action against the first two Georges. The actual number who would even commit themselves in writing is not great. Moreover, none were prepared to act without direct military support from France. Dr. Cruickshanks has performed a useful service in identifying those Tories with Jacobite sympathies and chronicling their negotiations. But to brand the whole Tory party as Jacobite on the basis of harmless flirtations and negative evidence presses the case too far.

The threat of Jacobitism is also taken seriously by Paul Fritz in *The English Ministers and Jacobitism between the Rebellions of 1715 and 1745* (Toronto, 1975). He contends that the English ministers, above all Walpole, were obsessed by it. Walpole devoted inordinate attention and resources to spies and surveillance measures designed to nullify its threat and alert the government to Jacobite plans. The most useful contribution of the study is its explication of Walpole's intelligence system, based upon the Cholmondeley manuscripts and the Stuart papers, a topic also treated by Fritz in "The Anti-Jacobite Intelligence System of the English Ministers, 1715–45 and the Rise of Walpole" (*HJ* 16, 1973). A contrary view is taken by Gareth V. Bennett in "Jacobitism and the Rise of Walpole," in *Historical Perspectives: Studies in English Thought in Honour of J. H. Plumb* (London, 1974), edited by Neil T. McKendrick.

Bennett maintains that Walpole used the threat of Jacobitism to rout his political rivals and secure his hold on the king. George I, concerned for the security of his throne, responded gratefully to Walpole's exposure of the Christopher Layer conspiracy and the Atterbury plot, though Bennett shows these were largely manufactured threats. Layer, a half-crazed conspirator, was not in touch with the main Jacobite leadership, and Atterbury had already decided against an attempt at that time (1722).

Some students of parliamentary politics contend that the role of principle is too often forgotten. The Namier contention about the absence of real principle and conviction as a motivating element for politicians has not been accepted for the earlier period. The most important work on ideology is J. P. Kenyon's *Revolution Principles: The Politics of Party 1689–1720* (Cambridge, 1977). In this seminal work, he contends that the radical justifications of the Revolution propounded by the Whigs were unpopular and by and large unacceptable. Only the accident of the Hanoverian succession and the collapse of the Tories made it possible for the Whigs, increasingly a minority party, to enter and retain control of the ministry. By the 1720s they had jettisoned most of their radical ideas. The Whigs became oligarchic and mercenary, with no thought for reform, toleration, or popular participation in government (p. 203). His views were first set forth in "The Revolution of 1688: Resistance and Contract," in McKendrick's *Historical Perspectives*. Isaac Kramnick extends the discussion of political ideology into the 1730s in his *Bolingbroke and His Circle: The Politics of Nostalgia in the Age of Wal-*

pole (Cambridge, Mass., 1968). A study in the history of ideas, it is a stimulating treatise devoted essentially to an examination of the Country principles enunciated by Bolingbroke and his friends and allies. It gives, perhaps, rather short shrift to their counterpart, the Court program of Walpole and his supporters; and it is intended as an antidote (perhaps excessive) to the attitude that ideology played little if no role in the 1720s and 1730s. In "The Principles and Practice of Opposition: The Case of Bolingbroke versus Walpole," also in *Historical Perspectives*, Quentin Skinner maintains that the Tories strove hard to make opposition respectable and acceptable to the political electorate. They did so by employing "Old Whig" arguments against Walpole, "denouncing the size of the land forces and the Ministry's devices for controlling the House of Commons" (p. 124). The need to justify opposition to the king's government also explains their "professed principle of patriotism" (p. 127). It is a neat thesis, though perhaps overworked in this article.

Elections and election returns, a subject treated at some length by Sedgwick, is also the subject of a number of separate pieces. In "Party Configurations in the Early Eighteenth-century House of Commons" (*BIHR* 45, 1972), Henry L. Snyder uses unpublished analyses of election returns to determine party allegiances of MPs from 1698 to 1722 and the party composition of each Parliament from 1701 to 1715. His evidence suggests clear party identification and consistent party allegiance for most MPs. W. A. Speck, in "The General Election of 1715" (*EHR* 90, 1975), contends that the thorough-going purge of Tory officeholders after the accession of George I resulted in greater unity for the party than at any time since 1710.[3] Based on their performance in the previous seven elections, they tasted victory once more. Although Crown influence told against them in the smaller boroughs, ideological issues and concern for the Protestant succession were decisive, outweighing fears for the church.

Political biography continues to attract scholars. Pride of place must go to the most recent, *George I: Elector and King* by Ragnhild Hatton (Cambridge, Mass., 1978). It is noteworthy in many respects. Professor Hatton has managed to draw a convincing and rounded portrait in spite of the almost total absence of any surviving personal or official papers. She has combed successfully archives both on the Continent and in England.[4] Not only the Hanover archives but the papers of two of George's Hanoverian ministers, Andreas Gottlieb von Bernstorff and Friedrich Wilhelm von Görtz, have yielded important new evidence for the king's conduct. George emerges as an able, affectionate, enlightened ruler with a taste for music and art that belies the usual caricatures that have passed for character sketches of this hitherto enigmatic figure. Hatton has classified his relationship to Melusine von der Schulenburg (his mistress from 1691 and possibly his morganatic wife) and their three daughters, never acknowledged as such by either parent. She establishes that Sophia Charlotte von Kielmansegg, also pre-

sumed to be his mistress, was in fact his half-sister, the natural daughter of his
father. George I's intense interest in continental diplomacy and his policies both
as elector and king receive full due from the author, who is herself a master diplomatic historian. Hatton makes it clear that George remained in firm control of
his government until his death. Although Walpole ultimately gained the king's
confidence by his expert handling of the Treasury and the Parliament, he had
little voice in foreign affairs until the next reign. And the king continued to consult his German ministers as well as their English counterparts on Hanoverian
and Imperial affairs even after 1720. The vexed question of his linguistic abilities
is handled expertly. He did know some English and by the later part of his reign
was able to both read and write it. Altogether, this book is a most notable
achievement.

The number of substantial biographies is disappointingly small. H. T. Dickinson's *Walpole and the Whig Supremacy* (London, 1973) adds nothing to the state
of knowledge on this topic and is not without factual error. His biography
Bolingbroke (London, 1970) is more substantial and successful. Dickinson traces
Bolingbroke's long career with impressive mastery and is equally at home describing the intense party rivalries of Anne's reign or the Country opposition
coached by Bolingbroke against Walpole. Although he may at times put his subject's conduct in the best light (e.g., on the flight to France in 1715), his is a well-
researched and valuable study and has no real competition. "The Pardon of Lord
Bolingbroke" (*HJ* 14, 1971), by Henry L. Snyder, describes the efforts of the
earls of Stanhope and Sunderland to effect Bolingbroke's return to England.
They hoped to use him to mobilize Tory support for the government against the
dissident Whigs led by Walpole and Charles Townshend. A draft in the Sunderland papers indicates that he considered a full pardon in 1721.

The Pelham brothers have both received monograph-length treatment. The
elder, Thomas, duke of Newcastle, has fared best. The most comprehensive account is *The Duke of Newcastle* (New Haven, Conn., 1974) by Reed Browning.
Browning has treated Newcastle with care and understanding. He has not altered
the standard view of his character, that of a fussy, mediocre politician with an
immense appetite for work and a possessive, jealous nature. Yet he gives him
credit for those areas in which he excelled, notably his management of patronage,
and he provides a detailed examination of his foreign policy, an examination that
is necessarily complex and extended, given the three decades the duke held a secretaryship of state. Withal, the personality of the man fails to emerge, though one
cannot fault Browning for his expert handling of domestic and foreign affairs.

Browning's biography is neatly complemented by Ray Kelch's *Newcastle: A
Duke without Money* (Berkeley and Los Angeles, 1974). More limited in its objectives, it fills them nicely. To treat the financial vicissitudes of a great nobleman
in such detail is a challenging, rarely attempted task. Kelch demonstrates that the

duke's supposed vast wealth has been overrated; that, rather, Newcastle consistently lived beyond his means; and that in his later years he was forced to subsist on a reduced income to avoid bankruptcy. Moreover, he was unusually honest by contemporary standards and did not enrich himself at the public expense, though his four decades in office gave him ample opportunity. Rather, it was his life-style and the expense of maintaining his own personal base in the constituencies that undid him. In "The Duke of Newcastle and the Financing of the Seven Years War" (*JEcH* 31, 1971), Reed Browning contends that Newcastle was a more-than-competent financial minister and illustrates his point by a step-by-step analysis of the revenue-raising process employed to finance the war.

John Wilkes's biography of Henry Pelham, *A Whig in Power* (Evanston, Ill., 1964) is disappointing. It makes no real advance upon Archdeacon Coxe's long admired two-volume study, *Memoirs of the Administration of the Right Honourable Henry Pelham, Collected from the Family Papers, and Other Authentic Documents* (London, 1829). Although Wilkes seems to have made extensive use of manuscript material, the study has little new information and contains both errors of fact and interpretations not borne out by the work of other scholars. It is desirable to have a modern life of Pelham, and this biography is at least serviceable for student purposes; but it promises more than it delivers. A minor but far more fascinating figure is the subject of Robert Halsband's *Lord Hervey: Eighteenth-century Courtier* (Oxford, 1973). An observer rather than a principal, and of interest to historians primarily as a memoirist, Hervey receives sympathetic treatment in this account and as full an analysis as the subject warrants or the material permits.

William Pitt, earl of Chatham, has been the focus of two biographies. Neither one fills the need for the major, modern assessment of his career that will replace the honored but now out-dated study by Basil Williams *The Life of William Pitt, Earl of Chatham* (2 vols., London, 1913). The most satisfying is Stanley Ayling's *The Elder Pitt* (London, 1976). It is not a work of original scholarship; it is a very well-written, sympathetic, and credible portrait. Avoiding the idolatry of Williams and the hostility of A. von Ruville's *William Pitt, Earl of Chatham* (3 vols., trans. H. J. Chaytor and Mary Morison, London and New York, 1907), Ayling provides a plausible and full account of Pitt's career. Though he does not provide a complete explanation of Pitt's idiosyncracies, a task probably impossible of fulfillment, he does provide comment which puts Pitt's behavior in perspective. It is the most balanced account yet attempted. Reasonably well-grounded on modern scholarship, it summarizes recent interpretations if it provides no new ones. The kind of restudy one would like to find is not attempted.

The life of Peter D. Brown, *William Pitt, Earl of Chatham: The Great Commoner* (London, 1978), is less satisfactory, perhaps because one expects more from a professional academic historian. It is essentially a political and diplomatic history of Chatham's life and times. It makes no attempt to provide a full portrait and is singularly terse on his health and his family life. Drawing upon the diary of the fourth duke of Devonshire, it provides some new insights on Chatham's relations with his Cabinet colleagues during his great ministry. Other than this source, it uses little new material and makes no advance upon previous scholarship. The Ayling volume is superior as a study of the man and his career. In "William Pitt and Public Opinion, 1757" (*EHR* 88, 1973), Paul Langford comments on the fluctuations in Pitt's popularity during the winter of 1756/ 1757. He contends that they were the consequence first of a Pitt-Tory alliance which inspired pro-Pitt addresses, then of anti-Pitt sentiment because of his support of John Byng, and that his return to office was the result of a well-run out-of-doors campaign.

A book of unique value is John M. Beattie's *The English Court in the Reign of George I* (Cambridge, 1967). There is nothing comparable to the kind of insight and information it provides. Consequently, though the analysis and comments are directed to the early Hanoverian period, they have a wider value for scholars trying to understand the Court, its composition, and its influence from the Restoration down to the end of the eighteenth century. Not until the ministry of the younger Pitt were serious inroads made into the nature and perquisites of places, and even then the impact of his reforms was slow in being realized. Beattie emphasizes "the organization that provided for the personal needs of the monarch and created the social setting in which he lived" (p. ix). The separation of the household from the central government had taken place long before. But places in the household often had the advantage of bringing the occupant into frequent if not daily contact with the king. Their greatest value was, however, for the profits and honor they brought to the holder. The patronage value for the ministry was also not overlooked.

A valuable series of handbooks on officeholders in the eighteenth century has been edited by J. C. Sainty and published in London under the auspices of the Institute of Historical Research. It includes: *Treasury Officials 1660–1870* (1970), *Officials of the Secretaries of State 1660–1782* (1973), *Officials of the Board of Trade 1660–1870* (1974), and *Admiralty Officials 1660–1870* (1975).

One of the great political upheavals of the first half of the eighteenth century has been expertly dissected by Paul Langford in *The Excise Crisis: Society and Politics in the Age of Walpole* (Oxford, 1975). The explosiveness of this issue and Walpole's own shortcomings in handling it have never been fully explained. Langford assures us that Walpole did miscarry. He held the bill until the last session of the Parliament because he thought it would help, not hinder, the government cause in the upcoming elections. The soundness of the scheme is not doubted. But it drew vociferous complaints from the shopkeepers and tradesmen who feared and resented the intrusive and inquiring excisemen who would be charged with collecting the tax. Their complaints were picked up by the opposition and carried to the palace itself. George II momentarily wavered in his support of his prime minister, and this ambivalence was sensed by the courtiers and communicated to the Parliament. Not only did the government majority evaporate in the Commons, but even Walpole's hold on the Lords was threatened. The prime minister was forced to withdraw the bill to save his office. He never quite regained the same unchallenged authority after this episode.

Paul Langford's *The Eighteenth Century 1688–1815* (London, 1976) now joins the David Horn survey *Great Britain and Europe in the Eighteenth Century* (Oxford, 1967) to provide the interested reader with an informed and eminently readable survey of British foreign policy in the eighteenth century. Whereas Horn examines Britain's relations with European powers on a country-by-country basis, Langford treats the subject in a more traditional chronological framework that essentially considers the whole of Europe at once. John J. Murray's *George I: The Baltic and the Whig Split of 1717* (Chicago, 1969) is a work to be avoided, for it is a mass of ill-digested data. Much of it is of questionable value because of his own limited understanding of the topic and his egregious errors in handling foreign names and texts. He is unable to weld his material into a comprehensive or comprehensible analysis. An example of proper expertise in handling this material is to be found in Derek McKay's "The Struggle for Control of George I's Northern Policy, 1718–1719" (*JMH* 45, 1973). McKay explains that Stanhope and Sunderland had to force the Hanoverian Bernstorff to give up control of the king's northern diplomacy to prevent his undermining their whole foreign policy. In "The Duke of Newcastle and the Origins of the Diplomatic Revolution" (in J. H. Elliott and H. C. Koenigsberger, eds., *The Diversity of History: Essays in Honor of Sir Herbert Butterfield*, London, 1970), D. B. Horn states that Newcastle was as responsible as Kaunitz for the shift to Franco-Austrian, Anglo-Prussian alliances. Newcastle had pursued a foreign policy which annoyed France and Austria and had refused a Russian alliance until it was too late to keep Austria's friendship. Another useful piece for students is Stephen Baxter's "The Myth of the Grand Alliance in the Eighteenth Century" (in *Anglo-Dutch Cross Currents in the Seventeenth and Eighteenth Centuries*, Los Angeles, 1976). Baxter contends that the old alliance between England, the Dutch Republic, and the emperor became increasingly untenable after the death of William III. That it survived as long as it did was chiefly due to the vanity of George II, who was intent upon playing the kind of role in European affairs played by William III. This same determination resulted in the king making many more personal decisions about the conduct of his government than historians have been willing to credit. John Owen takes a similar view of the king in "George II Reconsidered" (in J. T. Bromley and P. G. M. Dickson, eds., *Statesmen, Scholars, and Merchants: Essays in Eighteenth-century History Presented to Dame Lucy Sutherlund*, Oxford, 1974). He contends that the grandfather exercised as much as or more authority than did his grandson, George III. In the selection and retention of ministers, appointments in the church and army, and the conduct of foreign affairs, his influence was never negligible and often decisive. The accession of George III was hardly so critical for the constitution as historians have insisted.

For students of England's foreign commerce, John J. McCusker, in "The Current Value of English Exports, 1697 to 1800" (*William and Mary Quarterly*, 3d ser., 28, 1971) and Jacob M. Price, in "New Time Series for Scotland's and Britain's Trade with the Thirteen Colonies and States, 1740–1791" (*William and Mary Quarterly*, 3d ser., 32, 1975) improve on trade figures in Charles Whitworth's *State of the Trade of Great Britain* (London, 1776). McCusker concludes from his analysis of customs ledgers that random errors tend to balance out but that systematic distortions are more of a problem (for example, smuggling caused official figures to understate the volume of some imports). The main problem is the ledgers' use of official instead of current values, which he tackles by giving a "systematic conversion of the constant value series of exports from England, Wales, and Scotland into a current value series through the mechanism of a commodity price index" (p. 607). Price gives tables of Scottish and British (England plus Scotland) exports and imports to and from each of the thirteen colonies or states. In *Money and Exchange in Europe and America, 1600–1775: A Handbook* (Chapel Hill, N.C., 1978), McCusker provides copious data on the value of coins and the rates of exchange for the seventeenth and eighteenth centuries, often on a year-by-year basis, with helpful commentaries. This should provide a reference tool of considerable value and will spare the scholar tedious and time-consuming searches for monetary information.

In *The Portugal Trade: A Study of Anglo-Portuguese Commerce 1700–1770* (London, 1971) H. E. S. Fisher studies the early history of one of the longest standing commercial alliances enjoyed by Britain. This is emphatically an economic study. Drawing heavily on manuscript sources in both England and Portugal, Fisher charts the steady expansion of the trade until 1760, its rapid contraction thereafter. The trade was based upon wine shipments and bullion to England in return for textiles, grain, and manufactures. The prosperity of the trade was due in no small measure to the wealth the Portuguese derived from Brazil and the role Portugal played as an entrepot between Britain and Brazil. The contraction came from the decline in grain exports from England as English domestic demand took up the supply and from a decline in income in Portugal and its colony. The importance of the trade for English economic development is especially noted. One aspect of this trade receives more detail in A. D. Francis's *The Wine Trade* (New York, 1973). Francis notes how the Louis XIV wars depressed the wine trade with France and how the Methuen treaties of 1703 gave the Portuguese wines the tariff advantage that led to their gradual domination of the English market. Although English taste gradually shifted to hard spirits and native products, population increases maintained the level of the wine trade. Trade to the other end of the Mediterranean is the subject of *Aleppo and Devonshire Square: English Traders in the Levant in the Eighteenth Century* (London, 1967) by Ralph Davis. Dealing primarily with the Radcliffe family, who were leading Levant merchants in the first half of the eighteenth century, he documents a relatively obscure but steady exchange of goods. English broadcloths were the principal outward cargo; silk from Persia and Syria filled the holds on the return voyage.

The study of trade with Ireland has undergone a transformation at the hands of L. M. Cullen in *The Anglo-Irish Trade 1660–1800* (Manchester, 1968). In this important revisionist work, he destroys one shibboleth after another. The prohibition against Irish woolens was not nearly so injurious to Ireland as historians have traditionally stated. Rather, there was a steady overall increase, with Irish linen the most important commodity. Between 1720 and 1760 the trade increased fivefold. In terms of tonnage, coal was the most important English export; but hops, manufactures, and above all, colonial produce figured prominently in the statistics. As Francis G. James explains, one reason for the relative prosperity of Ireland was "The Irish Lobby in the Early Eighteenth Century" (*EHR* 81, 1966), a pressure group directed by the lord lieutenant and the Irish Parliament which enjoyed considerable success at Westminster. Of related interest is J. C. D. Clark's "Whig Tactics and Parliamentary Precedent: The English Management of Irish Politics, 1754–1756" (*HJ* 21, 1978). Clark maintains that it is necessary to treat England and Ireland as a single political unit in the 1750s. English ministers formed assumptions, particularly about party and its role in government, based on their experiences in Irish political management. Trends and developments, particularly in the breakdown of the party system, occurred earlier or anticipated similar developments in England. The management techniques which the English politicians perfected to meet these changes were then applied, by Newcastle specifically, in the management of the British House of Commons.

In the realm of domestic economic history, the most important work to appear in recent years is P. G. M. Dickson's *The Financial Revolution in England: A Study in the Development of Public Credit 1688–1756* (London and New York, 1967). Though we have had excellent studies on the Treasury by Stephen Baxter and on the public revenue by C. O. Chandaman for the Restoration period, the early eighteenth century has been less well served. Historians have relied chiefly upon the long series of calendars of treasury books edited by W. A. Shaw for the Public Record Office (London, 1897–1903). Yet this series barely extends into George I's reign, and Chandaman has demonstrated that Shaw's interpretations

and summaries are unreliable. Dickson repairs this omission in part. His theme
is the transformation in government finance wrought by the new credit experiments pursued by the government after the Revolution. Vast new sums of money
on an unprecedented scale had to be raised for the Louis XIV wars. Lord God-
olphin's management of the short-term debt provided the means to reduce France
and maintain stability after the war. The sources of domestic credit, the nature of
the London money market, and the importance of foreign investors all receive
due notice. By his assiduous sifting of printed manuscript sources, Dickson has
provided a definitive treatment of one side of the treasury for the first half of the
eighteenth century. B. L. Anderson proposes that the situation in the counties
varied from that in London in his "Provincial Aspects of the Financial Revolution of the Eighteenth Century" (*Business History* 11, 1969). The private sector
was more important in the counties, as opposed to the public sector, which was
the principal outlet for funds in London.

In *Deceleration in the Eighteenth-century British Economy* (London, 1976), Anthony J. Little develops the thesis of a period of stagnation or recession, if not
decline, in economic growth during the second quarter of the eighteenth century
in contrast to long periods of increase from the time of the Restoration and again
after 1750. He gives as a primary cause low prices, especially for grain, which
depressed the home market. His argument is essentially a theoretical one, based
upon the relationships among prices, profits, and investments. It does not square
with evidence adduced by other scholars suggesting substantial growth in a number of sectors of the economy in the 1725–1750 period. The book is provocative,
but the evidence to sustain it is hardly conclusive.

One area in which there was a definite upsurge in activity is in turnpikes,
treated by William Albert in *The Turnpike Road System in England 1633–1840*
(Cambridge, 1972). Though covering a broad period, this study is particularly
important for the first half of the eighteenth century, for it reveals much more
activity than historians have hitherto recognized. Dividing his study into four
periods, Albert considers the period 1663–1750 as the first. Noting first the thirteen main routes leading from London, he finds that nine hundred miles out of
total route mileage of fifteen hundred had been turnpiked by 1730, fourteen hundred by 1750, leaving hardly more than ten turnpikes to be completed after mid-
century. Up to 1720, 37 acts were passed, then 115 in the next thirty years.
Thereafter the pace quickened, with 184 acts passed in the decade 1750–1760.
Sidney and Beatrice Webb's contention that turnpike development was "scattered"
and "unconnected" in the first half of the eighteenth century is handsomely
refuted.

The first three chapters of Charles K. Hyde's *Technological Change and the
British Iron Industry, 1700–1870* (Princeton, N.J., 1977) deal with the industry
in the first half of the eighteenth century. Until 1720 England was self-sufficient

in pig iron, used mainly for casting, but imported bar iron, used for hardware and small arms, owing to increased demand and the superior hardness of Swedish products. The industry depended on charcoal for fuel and was seasonal (October through May) and small scale. In the second chapter, Hyde refutes the standard Thomas Ashton thesis that the use of coke in smelting was held back by the Darbys' refusal to reveal their process. Instead he contends that the capital cost of coke furnaces made the technique more costly. The Darbys only succeeded in making a profit because coke pig iron made superior, thin-walled castings, a process that was patented and closely guarded. A growing shortage of fuel threatened the industry after 1700. Only tariff protection and the high cost of transporting Swedish iron enabled the English ironmasters to maintain the charcoal iron industry to the middle of the century. In contrast G. Hammersley, in "The Charcoal Iron Industry and Its Fuel 1540–1750" (*EcHR* 26, 1973), contends that the industry did not destroy its fuel supply or suffer from unusual fuel problems. Rather, he states that ironmasters were pioneer students of arboriculture, attempting to preserve the woodlands to insure their future fuel supply.

The potteries were one of the earliest successes in the Industrial Revolution in England. Lorna Weatherill looks at the century from the era preceding the traditional period of expansion in her *Pottery Trade and North Staffordshire 1660–1760* (Manchester, 1971). Her aim is to determine the extent to which developments in this period presaged the more familiar and famous expansion personified by Wedgwood and Spode. Using probate inventories, tonnage books to determine the potteries' share of traffic on the rivers, commercial records of potteries, and archaeological evidence, she concludes that the growth was larger than has been assumed. The period 1715–1735 was particularly important for the introduction of new raw materials and innovations in the production of ware. The subsequent quarter century is characterized by increases in the size of the trade and in the sophistication of the commercial organization rather than by technological change.

No less than four accounts of London in the eighteenth century have appeared in the past decade. Dorothy Marshall's *Dr. Johnson's London* (New York, 1968) is the work of a senior scholar with a deep knowledge of the literature of her period. Treating the city in a variety of aspects, she does not fail to portray the execrable condition of many of its citizens. In addition to analyzing the life of the city, she also places it in the context of the country at large. Three more studies have the same basic design—a synthesis of existing studies by an experienced historian: George Rudé's *Hanoverian London 1714–1808* (Berkeley, 1971), Gordon Mingay's *Georgian London* (London, 1975), and G. R. Williams's *London in the Country: The Growth of Suburbia* (London, 1975). The most original and important work to appear on London is *Mid-Georgian London: A Topographical and Social Survey of Central and Western London about 1750* (London, 1964) by Hugh

Phillips. A mine of information about the appearance, business, society, and pastimes of London, it is filled with contemporary prints and drawings which enhance its usefulness and attractiveness. In contrast to these London studies, C. W. Chalkin treats *The Provincial Towns of Georgian England: A Study of the Building Process, 1740–1820* (Montreal, 1974). In this important work of original research, he has selected Birmingham, Manchester, and Nottingham to illustrate the rise of the new manufacturing centers; Hull, Liverpool, and Portsmouth as trading centers; and Bath as a special case. The nature of urban society, the investors, the developers, and the products of their labors and intentions all receive attention. This is a work of considerable technical mastery that contributes to our understanding of the evolution of the principal country towns over the course of the century.

The most striking new work in legal as well as social history to appear for the period is E. P. Thompson's *Whigs and Hunters: The Origin of the Black Act* (New York, 1975). The 1723 statute imposed the penalty of capital punishment for more than a score of offenses related to deer stealing, cattle maiming, and other crimes perpetrated in the forest. A legislative response to a series of outbreaks linked to conversion of forests to deer parks by newcomers, the key factor in its passage was, says Thompson, the Court connections of the newcomers. Government support for the act to protect property holders helped to strengthen Walpole and his allies in Parliament. Thompson has accomplished a major feat in retrieving fragmentary data from scattered archives to provide a coherent history of the act, the events that prompted its passage, and its impact. His study is marred and compromised by his imaginative extrapolations and his misuse and abuse of some of the evidence. His effort to transform the malefactors into social rebels against a tyrannical combination of government officials and landowners grossly distorts both his account and his conclusions. Withal, it is a fascinating excursion into a most obscure topic. Thompson joins other scholars in a related collection of essays entitled *Albion's Fatal Tree*, by Douglas Hay et al. (London, 1975). Also concerned with crime and the law, these essays range from smuggling and wrecking to Tyburn riots. The most important is Hay's on the importance of the criminal law for the support of the governing class. Pat Rogers, in "The Waltham Blacks and the Black Act" (*HJ* 17, 1974), attempts to show by previously unused evidence why the notorious Waltham Black Act of 1723, often cited as an example of extreme harshness, was necessary. He contends that the "Blacks" (actually two groups, one in Waltham and the other in Berkshire) were just local thieves or bullies, not a constitutional menace, but that they were highly visible and flamboyant and thus an embarrassment to the government, besides being a very real menace to local peace.

Crime is also the focus of J. M. Beattie's excellent article "The Pattern of Crime in England, 1660–1800" (*PP*, no. 62, 1974), which is based on court records from Surrey and Sussex. Beattie concludes that crimes against persons reached a peak in the 1720s and 1730s and declined thereafter, perhaps due to stricter governmental policy. He shows that crimes against property increased slightly from the Restoration to about 1760 and then declined. In rural Surrey and Sussex this seems related to poverty, while in urban Surrey especially noteworthy changes in the rate of crimes against property occurred during and just after the wars. *Crime in England 1550—1800*, edited by J. S. Cockburn (Cambridge, 1977), contains seven pieces which relate to the eighteenth century. J. H. Baker discusses criminal law procedure while John Beattie contends that judge and jury were more influenced by the character of the defendant than the crime when determining punishment. Peter Linebaugh, on "dying speeches," suggests that these products of the clergy assigned to the prisoners were often more reliable accounts of the deceased than historians have presumed. A description of Newgate is the topic of W. J. Sheean. P. B. Munsche has some interesting comments to make on the operation of the game laws, using Wiltshire as a case study. A useful annotated bibliography of secondary materials on crime and criminal justice is contributed by L. A. Knafla.

Social history has in recent years been increasingly marked by the demographic and statistical emphasis pioneered by the *Annales* school in France and taken up by the Cambridge Group led by Peter Laslett. Another model is surely the study of the structure of landed society in the seventeenth century inspired by the classic Tawney–Trevor-Roper–Stone debate. Lawrence Stone's massive *The Family, Sex, and Marriage in England 1500—1800* (New York, 1977) will be the point of departure for a generation of historians working in the early-modern period. He contrasts a "restricted patriarchal nuclear family," dominant in the seventeenth century, with the "closed domesticated nuclear family," the social norm of the eighteenth century. Just as Stone published his work, Randolph Turmbach completed his important study *The Rise of the Egalitarian Family*, which bears the subtitle *Aristocratic Kinship and Domestic Relations in Eighteenth-century England* (New York, 1978). He recognizes as the principal change "the increasing importance of domesticity" (p. 287). In the early Georgian period he discovers "the first generation in which romantic marriage became truly prestigious" (p. 291). The stronger attachment of husband and wife had increasingly beneficial effects upon the children and the extended family. A topical organization provides detailed analysis of the family, the relationship of its members, and the quality of family life. In "The New World of Children in Eighteenth-century England" (*PP*, no. 67, 1975), J. H. Plumb employs a variety of sources to illustrate the growing concern in this period for more humane treatment of children; the increased sharing of entertainment by parents and progeny; the rapid development of a market for toys, children's books, and other amusements that emphasized self-education and self-improvement; and especially the improvement of children's education in general. He points out that not all changes were for the better, for if children's lives were richer materially, their private lives were in many ways more restricted, particularly with regard to sexual matters.

David Thomas's statistical study "The Social Origins of Marriage Partners: The British Peerage in the Eighteenth and Nineteenth Centuries" (*Population Studies* 26, 1972) argues that the peerage had a stronger "ethnic of endogamy" than previously indicated by simple analysis of their marriages within and without the peerage, since the latter were usually to daughters of a broad "gentlemanly" class. Taken together, Christopher Clay's "Marriage, Inheritance and the Rise of Large Estates in England, 1660–1815" (*EcHR* 21, 1968) and B. A. Holderness's "The English Landmarket in the Eighteenth Century: The Case of Lincolnshire" (*EcHR* 27, 1974) suggest that we cannot apply equally to all parts of England H. J. Habakkuk's thesis that, from 1690 to 1750, land was generally consolidated in large estates by great magnates. Clay says the importance of marriage portions in extending the possessions of the landed class has been exaggerated and asserts instead that the extension was partly the result of a decline in the number of male heirs and an increase in indirect and female inheritance, which forced many lesser gentry to sell lands to large landholders. Holderness claims that the Habakkuk thesis simply does not apply for Lincolnshire, where the lesser gentry remained important in the land market and where numerous large estates were broken up. Two pertinent studies of individual families' landholding careers are H. C. F. Lansberry's "A Whig Inheritance" (*BIHR* 41, 1968), which deals with the Spencer inheritance from Sarah, duchess of Marlborough, and D. Rapp's "Social Mobility in the Eighteenth Century: The Whitbreads of Bedfordshire, 1720–1815" (*EcHR* 27, 1974), which describes the social and political rise of a merchant family who became landowners.

An intensive examination of the estate and financial concerns of the Yorkshire baronetage, with particular attention given to four families, is the focus of Peter Roebuck's *Yorkshire Baronets 1640–1760* (New York, 1980). Following the example of the many studies by mid-seventeenth-century specialists who examined the vicissitudes of the gentry, Roebuck provides a mass of useful data about landowning and land management without drawing any major conclusions. He does point to the impact of the individual and "the extent to which personal behaviour influenced dynastic fortunes" (p. 251). As the eighteenth century progresses, he notes an increasing employment of capital and a diversification of credit in contrast to a more conservative attitude toward agricultural practices.[5] The development of a single estate, that inherited by Thomas William Coke in 1776, is explored by R. A. C. Parker in *Coke of Norfolk: A Financial and Agricultural Study 1707–1842* (Oxford, 1975). Parker demonstrates that the model system of land management for which Coke is so renowned was essentially an inheritance from his immediate predecessors and not his own creation. In another study devoted to landownership and utilization in one locale, Alan Harris traces the pattern of changes by which *The Rural Landscape of the East Riding of Yorkshire 1700–1850* (London and New York, 1961) made the transition from a medieval to a modern landscape.

Another important revisionist work dealing with agriculture is Eric Kerridge's *The Agricultural Revolution* (London, 1967). In that work, he contends "that the agricultural revolution took place in England in the sixteenth and seventeenth centuries and not in the eighteenth and nineteenth" (p. 15). Although the book ranges over several centuries, it bears directly on the debate as to the importance of changes and improvements in agriculture introduced in the first half of the eighteenth century. Like J. D. Chambers and Gordon E. Mingay in *The Agricultural Revolution 1750–1880* (New York, 1966) and earlier works, he ascribes the major innovations to the seventeenth century, viewing the eighteenth century as a time of widespread adoption and refinement. Technological innovations are more a product of the nineteenth century. Two divergent views on agricultural economy are presented in A. H. John's "Agricultural Productivity and Economic Growth in England, 1700–1760" (*JEcH* 25, 1965) and M. W. Flinn's "Agricultural Productivity and Economic Growth in England, 1700–1760: A Comment" (*JEcH* 26, 1966). John argues that a post-Restoration rise in productivity plus a static population ended the rise in relative prices of farm products and led to a century of plenty with and increasing availability of food and raw materials. In the reply, Flinn contends that John exaggerates the extent and duration of low wheat prices, that the trend was erratic, and that actual reduction was insignificant over the long run.

Larry Neal, in "Deane and Cole on Industrialization and Population Change in the Eighteenth Century" (*EcHR* 24, 1971), challenges Deane and Cole's statistical technique for determining population increase in *British Economic Growth, 1688–1959* (Cambridge, 1962), saying they have overestimated natural increase and underestimated immigration. Cole acknowledges the criticism but for the most part defends the technique and resulting conclusions in a rejoinder to Neal's article (*EcHR* 24, 1971). A new approach is offered by P. E. Razzell in "Population Change in Eighteenth-century England: A Reinterpretation" (*EcHR* 18, 1965), where he argues that innoculation against smallpox accounts for the accelerated population growth of the mid-eighteenth century. Gordon Philpot, in "Enclosure and Population Growth in Eighteenth-century England" (*Explorations in Economic History* 12, 1975), says Razzell does not explain why mortality rose in the seventeenth century and why fertility declined and then rose at the midpoints of the seventeenth and eighteenth centuries. Philpot leans instead to T. McKeown and R. G. Brown's hypothesis of environmental improvement, which he links to enclosure. He observes that the breakdown in regulation of commons grazing rights resulting from the Civil War led to overstocking the commons and consequently to animal disease related to food shortage and overcrowding. Noting a correlation of animal disease epidemics with human disease, he argues that enclosure led to better regulation, in turn to a healthier animal population, and thus to a healthier human population. Another related study is "The Impact of the Epidemics of 1727–1730 in Southwest Worcestershire (*Medical History* 15, 1971), D. J. A. Johnston's examination of the catastrophic epidemic of preindustrial England, which he says was probably typhus or perhaps typhoid. The population increase of the late eighteenth and early nineteenth centuries has been linked to this by the "treble bulge" theory, which says that deaths led to early and fruitful marriages among the survivors, whose offspring grew up in a period of prosperity and married (earlier than usual) in the period 1755–1764, in turn giving birth to children who also grew up and married early in a period of prosperity. Johnston demonstrates that that was not the case in the southwest due to Worcestershire Catholic loyalties.

The evangelical revival of the eighteenth century has yet to receive the scholarly attention it requires. John Wesley and the Methodist movement have received treatment in some important though brief analyses. In 1971 Bernard Semmel published a translation of Élie Halévy's *The Birth of Methodism in England* (Chicago, 1971) with an introduction which places it in the context of Halévy's later writings and more recent literature. Halévy's essay, first published in 1906, explained the appearance of Methodism in terms of a convergence of a number of trends, events, and conditions rather than the inspiration of one or two men. A religious revival which extended back to the beginning of the century, the pioneering activities of several evangelical preachers, and domestic and foreign crises which provoked popular unrest are all critical to the Methodist movement. In the "Origins of the Evangelical Revival" (in G. V. Bennett and J. D. Walsh, eds., *Essays in Modern English Church History in Memory of Norman Sykes*, London, 1966), J. D. Walsh takes Halévy as a point of departure for his examination of several explanations for the revival: high church piety, a reaction against deism, and a renewal of Puritanism. He suggests that all had some influence, though he does not designate any one as dominant. Walsh returns to this theme in "Élie Halévy and the Birth of Methodism" in 1974 (*TRHS*, 5th ser., 25, 1975). Once again he restates and discusses the questions raised by Halévy without drawing any definitive conclusions. Unquestionably the new attention to Halévy's still-provocative essay is a salutary reminder that the phenomenon of Methodism cannot be explained simply by the person of John Wesley. English Catholics emerged from a persecuted condition in the late seventeenth century to one of grudging toleration in the eighteenth. With this toleration came the growth of congregations and a new vigor among the clergy, a development treated by John Bossy in *The English Catholic Community 1570–1850* (New York, 1976).

The study of the established church has received particular attention in its political dimension. The most important work is that by Gareth V. Bennett, *The Tory Crisis in Church and State 1681–1730* (Oxford, 1975). Bennett's book deals with several important issues. He uses the career of Atterbury to analyze the dilemma of the High Church party and the Tories in the post-Revolution period. Their dream was a return to the past "when Church and State had conjoined in a single authoritarian regime" (p. 22). Instead they had to fight a rearguard action and watch their power and monopoly of religious authority dissipate in a latitudinarian period. Betrayed in their trust in James II and spurned by William III, they made a last effort to maintain their position under Queen Anne. But their efforts were doomed by the triumph of the Whigs at the accession of George I. The forlorn dependence of the High Church leaders on the Pretender was the final tragedy. The church was reduced to being a patronage arm of the ministry; obedience and political regularity were alone rewarded. While Bennett focuses on the High Church party, the latitudinarians who triumphed after 1714 are the subject of Margaret C. Jacob's *The Newtonians and the English Revolution, 1689–1720* (Ithaca, N.Y., 1976). Although devoted largely to the period before 1714, it is an essential preliminary to understanding the alliance of Court Whigs and latitudinarian churchmen in the early Hanoverian period. The mechanical concept of the Newtonian universe appealed to moderate leaders in the late seventeenth and early eighteenth centuries because it proved a basis for a stable regime. The latitudinarian clergy who emerged as the leaders of the church after the Revolution, though moderates, were no more tolerant of the radicals and deists than they were of the high church clergy. They used the Boyle lectures to issue a warning against the dangers of freethinkers. Their limited, liberal outlook coincided nicely with that of the Whig oligarchs. An alliance was the result, and the partnership triumphed with the Hanoverian succession.

Approaching the subject of the "Church Whigs" from a different angle, T. F. J. Kendrick, in "Sir Robert Walpole, the Old Whigs and the Bishops, 1733–1736: A Study in Eighteenth-century Parliamentary Politics" (*HJ* 11, 1968), contends that Walpole controlled Parliament by conceding enough minor religious reforms to keep the support of the radical, antichurch "Old Whigs." He used his strength in the House of Lords to prevent passage of measures that would alienate the "Church Whigs" or that he could not afford to oppose in the Commons. Walpole's use of the Lords made the episcopate completely subservient to partisan politics.

J. H. Plumb has opened up a whole new area of study with his seminal lecture *The Commercialisation of Leisure in Eighteenth-century England* (Reading, 1973). He first emphasizes the importance of cheap books and newspapers and the development of the circulation library, another inducement to reading for the middle classes. Cheap printing and a large market led to titles catering to new interests:

cooking, music, gardening, and the emergence of specialized children's literature. For the commercialization of leisure, the advertisement and publicity made
possible by newspapers was critical. Sports, horticulture, and the expansion of
specialized trades, threatre, and opera are some of the manifestations. Holidays
were another eighteenth-century innovation and spawned the development of
towns dedicated entirely to leisure or retirement. Plumb continues this theme in
his introduction to the Yale Center for British Art catalog on *The Pursuit of Hap-
piness* (New Haven, Conn., 1977). In these two essays and in his article on children already discussed, Plumb has opened exciting and fascinating topics which
demand further examination and exploration. While Plumb stresses the entertainments of the middle classes, Robert W. Malcolmson, in *Popular Recreations
in English Society 1700–1750* (Cambridge, 1973), devotes his study to the leisure activities of the lower classes. Sports, fairs, and social events are the focus of
his attention. The traditional recreations he describes have a long, though obscure, history. They survived the onslaught of Puritanism in the seventeenth century and flourished in the first part of the eighteenth. The evidence for them is
sparse and fragmented, so that Malcolmson's reconstruction is the product of patient and diligent search for elusive material.

On the development of medicine, Peter Gibbons, in "The Medical Projectors,
1640–1720" (*Journal of the History of Medicine* 13, 1969), uses contemporary
pamphlets to illustrate the development of major, though not yet widely accepted,
ideas about medical care for the poor in this period (e.g., the importance of physical health to employment of the poor and the use of the sick poor to increase
medical knowledge in return for free treatment). Arthur Rook's "Medicine at
Cambridge, 1660–1760" (*Medical History* 13, 1969), in an attempt to rehabilitate Cambridge's reputation for this period, argues that Cambridge medical students could get acceptable and at times excellent medical training, though after
1730 considerable individual initiative was required since the medical school
shared the decline of both older universities.

Military and naval history appears to be undergoing a renaissance. One
can begin with A. P. C. Bruce's *An Annotated Bibliograpny of the British Army
1660–1914* (New York, 1975). This is a useful though hardly exhaustive compendium. Its chief deficiency is that it is limited to English-language titles so that
foreign conflicts in which Britain was engaged are provided with one-sided
coverage. *The British Army of the Eighteenth Century* by Colonel H. C. B. Rogers
(New York, 1977) is a conventional military history based upon standard printed
sources in which the superiority of British arms receives due praise. *The Art of
Warfare in the Age of Marlborough* (London, 1976) by David Chandler is a far
more sophisticated work. Covering the period from 1688 to 1745, it is a topical
study organized by branches: the horse, the foot, the artillery trains, and the engineering services. It provides the necessary organizational and logistical back-

ground for an understanding of the campaigns and functioning of the army, both British and continental. The first half of the eighteenth century forms the central section of J. R. Western's *The English Militia in the Eighteenth Century* (London, 1965). While attention and interest are usually centered on the professional army, Western devotes his attention to a much-neglected but nevertheless politically important military issue. For a century after the Interregnum, hostility toward a standing army made the militia the popular though ineffective alternative. Western discusses the unsuccessful attempts to reform it until the 1745 rising and the outbreak of war in 1756 provided the impetus to pass a militia act in 1757, a last effort to obviate the need for a large professional military force. Western compares the agitation that led to the militia act with the no-standing-army controversy following the Nine Years' War, though the parallels are not so close as he suggests. The increased opportunity for political power that a strengthened militia gave to the lord lieutenants was hardly a negligible factor in the debate.

The most detailed (and traditional) campaign history to appear in the past fifteen years is Lieutenant-general Sir Reginald Savory's *His Britannic Majesty's Army in Germany during the Seven Years' War* (Oxford, 1966). This is conventional tactics and strategy of the better sort devoted to a particularly unglamorous theater. The story is told with considerable detail and is carefully documented. The employment of the army for domestic purposes is treated at length by Tony Haytor in *The Army and the Crowd in Mid-Georgian England* (Totowa, N.J., 1978). It is to be expected that neither the public nor the government welcomed the use of troops to restore civil order. It is useful to know that the army did not like it either. Both officers and men were reluctant to be so employed, especially as they could face prosecution in the law courts for illegal action. The methods used, together with accounts of occasions where the troops were called in, are carefully described. Of related interest in Arthur N. Gilbert's article "Military and Civilian Justice in Eighteenth-century England: An Assessment" (*JBS* 17, 1978), in which he attempts a corrective to the traditional view that military justice was much harsher and more intolerant than civilian justice. In fact the military was quite often more lenient in punishing offenders than were the civil courts: "Until there is evidence that the poor, the illiterate, and the down-trodden fared better in civilian courts of eighteenth-century England, the condemnation of military justice is premature" (p. 65).

The navy has had its share of attention. The most important contribution is Daniel A. Baugh's *British Naval Administration in the Age of Walpole* (Princeton, N.J., 1965). His work is devoted to the management of the navy rather than its employment. He focuses on the fortunes of the navy in the war from 1739 to 1748 but includes a survey of its treatment in the period following the war of the Spanish succession (1702–1713). He finds that the navy did not suffer under Walpole but that this was a period of renovation and maintenance. The improved condition of the fleet, together with improvements in dockyards and overseas bases, resulted in a reasonable state of preparedness when war broke out in 1739. Conditions were not all they might be, and the strain of war coupled with inadequate training, preferment based on social position rather than merit, and corruption took their toll. Perhaps the most useful section is that on navy finance, a complex and technical subject. Elsewhere, he treats the subject with great lucidity and notes the impact of straightened finances and the critical role of public credit.[6] *Admiral Hawke* (Oxford, 1965) is the title and subject of Ruddock F. Mackay's biography of a hero of both wars in the mid-eighteenth century. Hawke's first great victory came at the mature age of forty-two in 1747 at the second battle of Cape Finisterre. As one of the first career officers to rise to flag rank on the basis of merit, he crowned his career as a commander with the decisive naval victory in the Seven Years' War when he defeated a French fleet a second time at the Battle of Quiberon Bay in 1759. Further honors awaited him when he was appointed first lord of the admirality in 1767 on the nomination of Chatham, a post he held until 1771 when ill health forced his resignation. The study does much to illuminate both mid-century naval strategy and command and the role of politics in naval management. It is based upon assiduous research and produces a rounded portrait of Hawke which is compelling and instructive.

David Aldridge, in "Admiral Sir John Norris, 1670 to 1749: His Birth and Early Service, His Marriage and Death" (*Mariner's Mirror* 51, 1965), uses new evidence to remove some of the obscurity surrounding portions of the career of Admiral Norris. Aldridge's "The Victualling of the British Naval Expeditions to the Baltic Sea between 1715 and 1727" (*Scandinavian Economic History Review* 12, 1964) describes the problems encountered in supplying royal naval vessels beyond the Sound of Copenhagen and concludes that, overall, the commissioners of victualling turned in a creditable performance. R. J. B. Knight, in "The Introduction of Copper Sheathing into the Royal Navy, 1779–1786" (*Mariner's Mirror* 59, 1973), uses this innovation to illustrate the strengths and weaknesses of the civil administration of the navy and to show how the British navy lagged behind the French because of unwillingness to try out theoretical improvements. In "The Admiralty and the Convoy System in the Seven Years' War" (*Mariner's Mirror* 57, 1971), R. P. Crowhurst describes the convoy system employed to protect British merchant shipping, a very necessary measure since merchant capital was an essential supplement to the land tax and excises in financing the war. He calls the system a complete success. David Syrett's "The Methodology of British Amphibious Operations during the Seven Years' and American Wars" (*Mariner's Mirror* 58, 1971) is an informative article in which the author argues that the British gained substantially through exploitation of naval power by amphibious operations in these two wars.

The study of the press and its impact is a time-honored topic, though its treatment has too often been subjective because of the dearth of evidence. The provincial press, in particular, has received little attention from scholars. Because it was established in the first half of the eighteenth century, this lacuna has been a glaring one; the appearance of two major scholarly studies is especially noteworthy. The first to appear was Lionel Cranfield's *The Development of the Provincial Newspaper 1700–1706* (Cambridge, 1962). It was followed closely by Roy Wile's admirable survey *Freshest Advices: Early Provincial Newspapers in England* (Columbus, Ohio, 1965). Both are excellent works of scholarship. Wiles's organizes his study topically, treating in turn content, format, finance, and advertising. Of special value is his Appendix C, a register of English provincial newspapers 1701–1760 which lists all known newspapers, their inclusive dates of appearance, and most important, locations of surviving copies. The influence of a London periodical on early English radicalism and the transmission of the seventeenth-century Country tradition to the later eighteenth-century scene is discussed by Marie Peters in "The 'Monitor' on the Constitution, 1755–1765: New Light on the Ideological Origins of English Radicalism" (*BIHR* 41, 1968).

Literary criticism is beyond the scope of this volume, but literary history does qualify where the link to those facets of the period that are covered is palpable and immediate. The denizens of the press and the society and mores from which they drew for their writings are the subject of *Grub Street: Studies in a Subculture* (London, 1972) by Pat Rogers, a work of interest to students of Augustan London of whatever specialization. The intrusion of politics into the world of drama is analyzed by John Loftus in *Politics of Drama in Augustan England* (Oxford, 1963). Loftus sees the stage as a useful mirror of domestic politics with potential interest for historians as well as literary scholars. The employment of the stage by the opposition to Walpole ultimately led to the licensing act of 1737, the terminal point of this study. For another example of opposition employment of the theater to stir up sentiment against Walpole and for war with Spain, see E. L. Avery and A. H. Scouten's "The Opposition to Sir Robert Walpole, 1737–1739" (*EHR* 86, 1971). The interaction of politics and the world of letters was never more important than in Augustan England. A topic of perennial interest to scholars in both fields, it is treated in William A. Speck's "Political Propaganda in Augustan England" (*EHR* 83, 1968) and at much greater length in *Les hommes de lettres et la politique en Angleterre de la Révolution de 1688 a la mort de George Ier* (Bordeaux, 1968) by Jean Beranger. Speck cites the shift in emphasis from religious and ideological concerns to social and economic ones about the time of the Hanoverian succession. He asserts that the use of satire later in the period he covers indicates that politics were taken less seriously than before. The unremitting torrent of political tracts from the time of the Popish Plot was to change the language of politics between the 1680s and 1740s. The international attention this topic has received is further illustrated by Hans-Joachim Müllenbrock, who also treats it in his *Whigs kontra Tories: Studien zum Einfluss der Politik auf die englische Literatur des frühen 18. Jahrhunderts* (Heidelberg, 1974). Studying selected literary works in the context of contemporary political ideas, he demonstrates once again the close political involvement of Augustan literature.

The study of contemporary publications is enhanced by David Foxon's monumental *English Verse 1701–1750: A Catalogue of Separately Printed Poems, with Notes on Contemporary Collections* (2 vols., Cambridge, 1975). Containing some ten thousand entries, this is a model bibliography and a mine of information about attributions, states, locations, and general bibliographical detail. This extraordinary work makes accessible to scholars a host of works that would otherwise be buried in obscurity, if not unknown. More limited in scope but fuller in detail is J. V. Guerinot's *Pamphlet Attacks on Alexander Pope 1711–1744: A Descriptive Bibliography* (New York, 1969). The study of eighteenth-century historical writing remains a neglected topic. With the notable exception of Edward Gibbon, historians active in the first half of the eighteenth century have received short shrift. One fascinating work has appeared that does bear upon the evolution of scientific history and learning in our period, Joseph M. Levine's *Dr. Woodward's Shield* (Berkeley, 1977). Dr. Woodward was an Augustan virtuoso, a physician by profession, a scientist and collector by preference. In tracing the history and controversy which centered on an Italian renaissance shield Woodward acquired and described as a Roman relic, Levine is able to suggest "the state of a whole group of kindred historical disciplines on the eve of their maturity: archaeology, chronology, numismatics, epigraphy, iconography, textual criticism, philology and antiquities" (p. 4). Another eighteenth-century virtuoso, John Hill, is surveyed by George S. Rousseau in his Clark Library Lecture "John Hill, Universal Genius *Manque*: Remarks on His Life and Times, with a Checklist of His Works" (in J. A. Leo LeMay and G. S. Rousseau, eds., *The Renaissance Man in the Eighteenth Century*, Los Angeles, 1978) as a preliminary to a forthcoming full-length treatment.

Art, like literature, was closely related to politics and must be studied for a fuller understanding of early Georgian society. One medium which became increasingly influential and popular for expressing opinions of customs and society and for espousing political views was the print. Herbert M. Atherton illustrates this application admirably in his *Political Prints in the Age of Hogarth* (Oxford, 1974). The celebrated artist William Hogarth, England's first great caricaturist and an eloquent commentator on contemporary mores, has been studied in depth by Ronald Paulson. The prints themselves are reproduced in all their splendor in Paulson's *Hogarth's Graphic Works* (New Haven, Conn., 1965). An extended commentary on the artist himself may be found in Paulson's *Hogarth: His Life*,

Art, and Times (2 vols., New Haven, Conn., 1971, abridged ed., 1974), a definitive study. Finally, Hogarth's prints together with contemporary literature, in particular the novel, are used as the primary materials from which Paulson reconstructs the culture of the lower and middle classes in the early Georgian period in his *Popular and Polite Art in the Age of Hogarth and Fielding* (Notre Dame, 1979). Paulson draws upon a wide range of printed material including *Joe Miller's Jests* and Hoyle's *Treatise on the Game of Whist* as a basis for his discussion. Another notable volume to appear is the eighteenth-century installment in the *Oxford History of English Art*. Volume 9, by Joseph Burke (Oxford, 1976) covers the period 1714–1800. Part 1 is devoted to "The Age of Burlington 1714–1753," Part 2 to "The Impact of the Rococo c. 1740–1760."

The country house, that unique British contribution to European society, was at once a home, a symbol of power, and the political center of the owner's county and electoral influence. It is the subject of an engrossing and fascinating book by Mark Girouard, *Life in the English Country House: A Social and Architectural History* (New Haven, Conn., 1978). Based on the Slade Lectures given at Oxford in 1975/1976, this is a distinguished contribution to the social as well as the cultural history of English society and has particular relevance for this period. The work is much enhanced by well-chosen, finely reproduced illustrations. One of the most important of the early Georgian architects, the designer of Houghton Hall, the seat of Sir Robert Walpole, was Colen Campbell. The first of the Georgian Palladians, his contributions have received expert evaluation in *The Architecture of Colen Campbell* (Cambridge, Mass., 1967) by Howard E. Stutchbury. An even more celebrated contemporary was Sir John Vanbrugh, the most flamboyant, if not the most celebrated, architect of the English baroque. In his *Vanbrugh* (London, 1977), Kerry Downes adds substantially to our store of knowledge both about his life and works. Downes's biography supersedes all previous studies in part because he draws upon previously unknown Vanbrugh manuscripts. The most important is his account book, which extends from 1715 to his death in 1726. Besides very detailed financial records of expenditures and receipts, Vanbrugh recorded all his journeys in the book and recorded payments for his architectural services. This valuable record is printed *in extenso*. Another appendix lists all known letters, adding to those published half a century ago by Webb. The work is richly illustrated, adding to both the pleasure and instruction to be gained from this handsome volume.[7]

Vanbrugh is a link to another work of architectural interest to appear in recent years, volume 5 of *The History of the King's Works* (London, 1976), which covers the period 1660–1782. This composite history is a formidable undertaking, and with the publication of this volume, only the predecessor entry is lacking to complete the series. Volume 5 is up to the distinguished level of those that have already appeared. Its authors include the general editor H. M. Colvin, J. Mordaunt Crook, John Newman, and Kerry Downes, the biographer of Vanbrugh. The dominant figure in this part is inevitably Sir Christopher Wren, who was surveyor-general for an incredible forty-nine years. Vanbrugh as comptroller was the unofficial head in Wren's last years. He confidently expected to be named Wren's successor upon the latter's dismisal in 1718. But the exigencies of politics dictated first William Benson and then otherwise, although Vanbrugh's protégé Colen Campbell did secure a minor place. The early Hanoverian period was not one noted for the erection of public buildings. The Treasury, the House Guards, and the conversion of Number 10 Downing Street may be the most familiar. But one does find a record of renovations and remodelings, such as those at Kensington Palace and the fitting out by William Kent of the Wren addition to Hampton Court Palace. Indeed it is the work of William Kent, protégé and successor to Vanbrugh, who provides the most interesting material in the volume, his designs for a new Palace of Whitehall and Houses of Parliament. His proposals were seriously considered in the 1730s; but the cost of the war in the 1740s suspended any implementation of the plans, and the need to reduce the debt outstanding after the war eventually caused the abandonment of the projects.

As these bibliographical essays are intended to focus attention on significant studies which contribute new knowledge or make the case for major revisions in previous interpretations, the titles included here are selective rather than comprehensive. A number of shorter pieces have been mentioned, in part to suggest the range and quantity of essays which have appeared. I should note that the periodical literature is particularly rich in local studies. The analysis of the social and economic structure of English society in its rural dimension continues to attract investigators. Many of the publications are of primary material, outside the scope of this volume. They do lay the foundation for further critical studies. Most heartening is the wide variety of really significant new studies which have appeared. Though one may feel that some areas, such as religion and the evangelical movement, have not received their full due, it is pleasing to recognize that the first half of the eighteenth century seems to be receiving something like its proper share of attention from scholars.

NOTES

1. See also John Cannon, "Polls Supplementary to the History of Parliament Volumes, 1715–1790," *BIHR* 47, 1974, which lists several elections that are not shown as contested in the History of Parliament or that are given without poll figures now available.
2. See also idem, "A General Theory of Party, Opposition and Government, 1688–1832," *HJ* 23, 1980, where he restates his conclusions about the period 1714–1760 and asserts, "Eighteenth-century government is being deeply misconceived by the preoccupation of modern scholarship with elections, poll books, the size of the electorate, and constituency politics"

(p. 298, n. 16). Cf. idem, "The Survival of Country Attitudes in the Eighteenth-century House of Commons," in J. S. Bromley and E. H. Kossmann, eds., *Britain and the Netherlands*, vol. 4, *Metropolis, Dominion, and Province: Papers Delivered to the Fourth Anglo-Dutch Historical Conference*, The Hague, 1971.

3. See also W. A. Speck, "Londoners at the Polls under Anne and George I," in *Guildhall Studies in London History*, vol. 1, 1975.

4. For a useful discussion of sources, both printed and manuscript, see Ragnhild Hatton's essay "In Search of an Elusive Ruler: Source Material for a Biography of George I as Elector and King," in Friedrich Engel-Jenosi, Grete Klingenstein, and Heinrich Lutz, eds., *Fürst, Burger, Mensch*, Vienna, 1975.

5. See also Peter Roebuck's essay "Post-restoration Landownership: The Impact of the Abolition of Wardship," *JBS* 18, 1978, in which he states that the effect of abolition was to stop "a relatively frequent and not insubstantial drain on the resources of landed families" (p. 85).

6. See also Daniel Baugh, ed., *Naval Administration 1715–1750*, Navy Records Society Publications, 120, London, 1977.

7. See also Sir Edward Lovett Pearce, *Architectural Drawings in the Library of Elton Hall*, Oxford, 1964.

Reinterpreting the Reign of George III

Robert A. Smith

The deluge of scholarly writing devoted to the reign of George III shows no sign of abating despite the publication of at least three thousand books and articles on the era during the past fifteen years. Everywhere our knowledge of events, individuals, groups, structures, and specific subjects has been broadened and deepened, but the pieces have not yet been reassembled into a comprehensive new understanding of the age.

The only interim attempts at comprehensive treatments of the reign since J. Steven Watson's excellent *The Reign of George III 1760–1815* (Oxford, 1960) are R. J. White's brief but sound and up-to-date *The Age of George III* (New York, 1968) and one "advanced textbook," John B. Owen's *The Eighteenth Century 1714–1815* (Totowa, N.J., 1975), which concentrates on political narrative and description. But there is at last an indispensable guide through the publications to 1975 for much of the literature old and new in Lucy M. Brown and Ian R. Christie's *Bibliography of British History 1789–1851* (Oxford, 1977). The compilers interpret their opening date generously enough to include much of the recent literature on the first half of George III's reign; the coverage for the second half is, with a few exceptions, almost definitive. The publication of this bibliography has been a major event in the recent historiography of this period. The way of the researcher has also been much eased by the publication of numerous specialized bibliographies and guides to subjects and sources, and especially by the printing or reprinting by photo offset, microfilm, or microcard of all sorts of catalogs, indexes, contemporary source material in print and manuscript, and many of the older monographs now out of print.

Important source material has also become increasingly available with the completion or near-completion of most of the great editions of letters and papers underway by the 1960s and the beginnings of others of equal magnitude. The magisterial Yale edition of *Horace Walpole's Correspondence* edited by Wilmarth S. Lewis and three generations of scholars in the "Walpole Factory" (New Haven, 1936–   ) is all but finished. This edition is essential for political, social, cultural, and intellectual history between the 1730s and the 1790s. Equally definitive editions of Walpole's much-maligned but indispensable political memoirs of the 1750s and 1760s are also underway. *The Correspondence of Edmund Burke*, edited by Thomas W. Copeland and nine other English, Irish, and American scholars since 1958 was completed with the publication of the tenth volume (Cambridge, 1978). This meticulous edition has contributed substantially to the continuing reassessment of later eighteenth-century politics as well as to the better understanding of one of the country's greatest minds. An equally definitive edition of Burke's works and speeches is just beginning under the general editorship of Paul Langford. The new *Collected Works of Jeremy Bentham* (1968–   ) has so far produced three volumes of his correspondence to 1788 and the texts of four of his more important treatises. Three volumes of Sheridan's letters, edited by Cecil Price, appeared in 1966 (Oxford). The *Works and Correspondence of David Ricardo* (Cambridge), edited by Pier Sraffa and Maurice H. Dobb, begun in 1951, was completed in 1975, while the Clarendon Press has been sponsoring a complete edition of the works and correspondence of Adam Smith by various hands (1976–   ).

The "scholarly" edition of the Yale–McGraw Hill edition of James Boswell's papers has progressed slowly, but the "reading" edition, containing most of the best material in that vast archive, is now almost complete. Boswell's journals and letters are a mine of information on the social and cultural history of England and Scotland. The social and political historian also neglects at his peril the impressive contemporary evidence and the extensive annotation in the numerous editions of the letters and works of literary and artistic figures. Among the more important recent ones, in addition to the Boswell papers, are the Yale edition of Samuel Johnson, edited by Herman W. Liebert et al. (New Haven, 1958–   ); the *Collected Letters of Coleridge*, edited by Earl L. Griggs (6 vols., Oxford, 1956–1971); his *Notebooks*, edited by Kathleen Coburn (London, 1957–   ); his *Collected Works*, edited by Kathleen Coburn et al. (Princeton, N.J., 1969–   ); Byron's letters and journals, edited by Leslie A. Marchand (London, 1973–1981); the reedition of Wordsworth's letters by Chester L. Shaver (Oxford, 1967–   ); *The Letters of David Garrick*, edited by David M. Little and G. H. Kaehl (3 vols., Cambridge, Mass., 1963); and the *Correspondence of John Constable*, edited by R. B. Beckett et al. (7 vols., Ipswich, Suffolk, 1962–1975).

Arthur Aspinall's editions of the *Later Correspondence of George III* (5 vols., Cambridge, 1962–1970) and *The Correspondence of George, Prince of Wales 1770–1812* (8 vols., London, 1963–1971) contain important material, although much of the royal and princely correspondence is trivial, and the unfortunate principle adopted of excluding most of George III's letters which had been printed elsewhere makes that collection less useful than it might have been. These editions have all contributed to the flood of secondary work in recent years, but this has been even more enriched and inspired by the immense quantities of un-published and often totally unexplored material that have become increasingly available through the steady transfer of family, estate, and business papers to pub-lic collections and county record offices.

What are the results of all this research? The relative distribution of publica-tions among the traditional categories of research has remained fairly steady since the 1940s; trends in interests and interpretation apparent by the mid-1960s have mostly continued undeflected to the edge of the 1980s. The most striking excep-tion is within social and economic history, where new interests, elevated almost to the status of autonomous subdisciplines, have developed particularly rapidly in the past fifteen years. Urban history, the history of technology, and historical de-mography particularly have expanded greatly, while social history has come to mean the study of basic social institutions and structures and the condition of the working classes and the poor, rather than miscellaneous information about the daily life and activities of the middle and upper classes. The social and economic historian has turned increasingly (and sometimes successfully) to new meth-odologies derived from the social sciences, especially to model building and quantification. These developments are yielding much new information and are raising more questions than they have yet begun to answer.

In contrast to these new directions, political history (often indistinguishable in this period from constitutional history) of a quite traditional sort has remained surprisingly popular and of high quality, stimulated by the revolution in inter-pretation and methods begun by Sir Lewis Namier in the 1930s and still continu-ing in its remoter effects. Administrative history, somewhat neglected during the first two postwar decades, has revived. Military and naval history continue to flourish; diplomatic and religious history, on the other hand, have been neglected by comparison to their earlier prominence in English historical writing. Cultural history is thriving, if often in a world too remote from political, social, and eco-nomic events. Books on the fine and decorative arts have multiplied, enriched by the remarkable advances in photographic reproduction since the war. The history of ideas has received rather more patchy attention; certain individuals and groups continue to be too much written about (Burke and the economists), while other subjects of fundamental importance for understanding the profound transition in values, outlook, assumptions, ideas, and taste between the late Augustan and early Victorian periods have been neglected. On the other hand, increasing research has been devoted to the history of late Georgian science and medicine, most of it still in the form of articles, very imperfectly incorporated into the general intel-lectual and cultural history of the age.

The ever-increasing concentration on economic, social, and technological change reflects the current overriding concern with these problems everywhere. The major ideological cleavage, as far as it has affected serious scholarship and the choice of subjects, lies increasingly not so much along the earlier lines of Marxist–non-Marxist interpretations as between the outlook and interests of an antiestablishment post-Marxian left and more orthodox historians of whatever specific political persuasion. The effect, particularly in the "new" social history, has been to widen our understanding of the more striking events of traditional history. The presentation is sometimes tendentious, occasionally slovenly, but infused with a degree of intellectual and moral commitment often lacking in the scholasticism of some of the studies on the high politics and econometrics of later Georgian England.

The most important development in the interpretation of late Georgian political and constitutional history has been the steady dilution of the Namierian orthodoxy that had become as uncritically accepted by the mid-1960s as the two-party scheme of "Whig" historiography had been before Sir Lewis demolished that myth in *The Structure of Politics at the Accession of George III* (London, 1929; 2d ed., slightly rev., 1957) and *England in the Age of the American Revolution* (London, 1930; 2d ed., very slightly rev., 1961). Namier's revolutionary interpretation extended far beyond the dismissal of a Whig–Tory dichotomy; he challenged directly or by implication nearly all accepted views of the character, contents, events, personalities, patterns, purposes, and significance of eighteenth-century politics. Political parties in a recognizably modern sense did not exist. Ideologies, professions of principle, proclamations of adherence to programs were so much rubbish, irrelevant to how men acted. What mattered was the structure of politics, that is, the electoral system, the numerous pyramids of influence and "interest," the backbenchers behind the facade of visible leaders and orators. These structures and the individuals who composed them were to be investigated in exhaustive detail, for the Namierian approach was a revolution in method as well as an interpretation.

Namier himself continued to elaborate his version of Georgian politics in lectures, articles, and reviews during the 1930s, 1940s, and 1950s (nearly all collected in *Crossroads of Power*, London, 1962); through the work of his students, assistants, and disciples; and even by the terror he inspired in most scholars outside his immediate circle in the fifteen years before his death in 1960. During the 1950s and early 1960s the Namierian approach and interpretation were extended beyond the politics and politicians of the 1750s and 1760s, rarely by Namier himself but frequently with his imprimatur. Three monographs, expressly intended as continuations of the narrative analysis begun in *England in the Age of the American Revolution*, anatomized three crucial periods in the first half of George III's reign: John Brooke's *The Chatham Administration 1766–1768* (London and New York, 1956); Ian R. Christie's *The End of North's Ministry 1780–1782* (London and New York, 1958); and Bernard Donoughue's *British Politics and the American Revolution: The Path to War 1773–1775* (London and

New York, 1964). Even before these saw print, the Namierian interpretation appeared to receive independent confirmation in Richard Pares's *King George III and the Politicians* (Oxford, 1953), which ranged over the whole reign and which was in fact free of the rigidity that came to characterize Namierian orthodoxy.

The capstone to this apparently successful historical revolution was the publication of the three volumes on the House of Commons between 1754 and 1790 begun by Namier and completed by John Brooke (London, 1964), containing not only biographical accounts of all members who sat during these years (an indispensable mine of information on much besides politics) and brief studies of each constituency, but a very long introduction by Brooke (published separately as *The House of Commons, 1754–1790*, Oxford, 1968). In this summation of the Namierian version of parliamentary politics in the later eighteenth century, there appeared, however, some indication of an impending modification of the Namierian interpretation: Brooke acknowledged, although he did not emphasize, the increasing importance of issues in politics from the mid-1760s; the increasing transformation of the factions into authentic political parties, especially among the Rockinghams; and the growing importance of public opinion outside Parliament. Other monographs tending to undermine parts of the new orthodoxy or emphasizing aspects of politics to which the Namierians had paid slight attention began to appear with increasing frequency. A number of studies, as thoroughly researched as Namier's own work, were published in the early 1960s: George Rudé's *Wilkes and Liberty* (Oxford, 1962); Ian R. Christie's *Wilkes, Wyvill and Reform* (London and New York, 1962); Eugene C. Black's *The Association* (Cambridge, Mass., 1963); and Archibald S. Foord's *His Majesty's Opposition, 1714–1830* (Oxford, 1964). In the past fifteen years much more new material has appeared in some seventy scholarly monographs, biographies, and articles. Most of the work, however, is too recent for the results to have been incorporated in general accounts of Georgian politics. The most extended attempt to present a portrait of the developing post-Namierian interpretation of the eighteenth century as a whole is Robert A. Smith's *Eighteenth-century English Politics: Patrons and Place Hunters* (New York, 1972), a long descriptive essay incorporating the results of most work through 1971.

George III himself has been portrayed in two excellent biographies, John Brooke's *King George III* (London, 1972) and Stanley Ayling's *George the Third* (New York, 1972); the former is the more impressive work of scholarship, based throughout on the Royal Archives at Windsor. Both concentrate on the king's personal life and character rather than on his political activity, and both present a sympathetic and convincing portrait of that once-much-maligned monarch. The king also appears as a much more consistently capable ruler and able politician than Namier, to say nothing of earlier historians, had depicted him. An important element in this reinterpretation has been the new understanding of George's supposed "insanity," which was most probably a recurrent metabolic disorder, porphyria, whose acute symptoms resemble advanced mania. This illness, the new view argues, could not have affected the king's judgment and behavior before the first violent attack in 1788/1789, and his contemporaries did not think him "mad" until then. Subsequently the king's fear of a recurrence indeed affected his and the politicians' behavior. The later attempt by historians to explain the first half of the reign in terms of incipient royal mental derangement is, however, no longer tenable. The new diagnosis was presented in two articles by Ida Macalpine and Richard Hunter in the *British Medical Journal* in 1966 and 1968, reprinted together with an important essay on the political implications by John Brooke in "Porphyria—A Royal Malady" (1968), and developed at much greater length in Macalpine and Hunter's *George III and the Mad-Business* (London, 1969), which also contains much information on Georgian psychiatry in general. (A somewhat different diagnosis but carrying the same implications was advanced in Charles P. Chenevix Trench's *The Royal Malady*, (London, 1964.) The career of the king's eldest son, interwoven with politics from the 1780s, is retold in a new two-volume biography, Christopher Hibbert's *George IV* (London, 1972–1973), the best treatment of its deplorable subject. George III's consort has also found a biographer, and a good one, in Olwen Hedley, who produced *Queen Charlotte* (London, 1975).

Other valuable books describe the institutional framework and the procedures of the central political forum, the House of Commons. The most important is Peter D. G. Thomas's *The House of Commons in the Eighteenth Century* (Oxford, 1971), a comprehensive summary of nearly everything that needs to be known. The appearance of Michael W. MacCahill's *Order and Equipoise: The Peerage and the House of Lords, 1783–1806* (London, 1978), the first book-length study of the upper House since Turberville, suggests that their lordships may at last be emerging from the obscurity to which both the Whigs and the Namierians consigned them. The only important study of the Cabinet is an essay on its development to 1790 in Ian R. Christie's *Myth and Reality*. Of the more comprehensive political studies, the most useful is John A. Cannon's *Parliamentary Reform, 1640–1832* (Cambridge, 1973). A more specialized study covering the entire eighteenth century is John R. Western's *The English Militia in the Eighteenth Century, 1660–1802* (London, 1965), which is more about politics than about the militia. Comprehensive, too, is Ian R. Christie's *Myth and Reality in Late-eighteenth-century British Politics and Other Papers* (London and Berkeley, 1970), which includes most of Christie's important articles published from the mid-1950s and adds several previously unpublished ones.

Major revision has begun with the first decade of the reign, once the Namierians' particular preserve. John Brewer's *Party, Ideology, and Popular Politics at the Accession of George III* (Cambridge, 1976) is the most important book about these years. Here the 1760s stand revealed as containing a permanent revival of issues as political focuses and a rapid development of political ideologies alternative to those of the governing classes. Against this background, the earlier treatments of 1760–1763 by Namier and of 1766–1768 by Brooke seem arid and incomplete. Paul Langford's *The First Rockingham Administration, 1765–1766* (London, 1973) is a more traditional study of a single administration, but the first to be devoted exclusively to this famous ministry. The principal issue in this administration, the repeal of the Stamp Act, which Langford discusses in terms of high politics, is explored in a wider context in Peter D. G. Thomas's *British Politics and the Stamp Act Crisis: The First Phase of the American Revolution 1763–1767* (Oxford, 1975).

For the subsequent decades, the Rockinghams and their successors, the Portland and Foxite Whigs, have been the subject of a remarkably extensive literature. This concentration has restored them to the political preeminence they enjoyed before Namier contemptuously demoted them to just another selfish faction. While the "Whigs" no longer appear as quite the noble band of Burke's rhetoric nor as the selfless defenders of British liberty of later Whig historians, nor even as having any exclusive claim to Whiggism, they have been convincingly reestablished as the most important organized parliamentary political group in Georgian politics and as the first recognizably modern party. Frank O'Gorman's *The Rise of Party in England: The Rockingham Whigs, 1760–82* (London, 1975) narrates their history in great if sometimes flawed detail, while Ross J. S. Hoffman's *The Marquis: A Study of Lord Rockingham, 1730–1782* (New York, 1973), the first biography of their leader, is as much a history of the party as it is a life of the marquis. John A. Cannon's *The Fox North Coalition: Crisis of the Constitution 1782–84* (London, 1969) describes the first two years of the group's life after Rockingham's death; if anything, Cannon overemphasizes the unquestionable importance of the crisis. Two other thorough studies continue the history of the group to its breakup in 1794 over the French Revolution: Leslie G. Mitchell's *Charles James Fox and the Disintegration of the Whig Party, 1782–1794* (London, 1971) and Frank O'Gorman's *The Whig Party and the French Revolution* (London, 1967). The party's (or at least Burke's) great cause of the later 1780s receives definitive treatment in Peter J. Marshall's *The Impeachment of Warren Hastings* (London, 1965), while the Regency Crisis of 1788/1789 is analyzed in another excellent monograph, John W. Derry's *The Regency Crisis and the Whigs, 1788–9* (Cambridge, 1963).

No one has attempted a political biography of Burke since Carl Cone's *Burke and the Nature of Politics* (2 vols, Lexington, Ky., 1957–1964), but a few of the too-numerous articles on this eminent man discuss aspects of his political career and are discussed below. Isaac Kramnick's psychobiography *The Rage of Edmund Burke* (New York, 1977) contains a few stimulating suggestions but a much greater proportion of nonsense based on serious factual errors and misunderstandings. Charles James Fox, on the other hand, has been the subject of two biographies, both much superior to the earlier ones. Loren D. Reid's *Charles James Fox: A Man for the People* (London, 1969) emphasizes the man and the orator; John W. Derry's *Charles James Fox* (London, 1972) is better on the politician and as a critical assessment. The substantial biography (again the first) of that great conservative Whig magnate the fourth earl Fitzwilliam—Ernest A. Smith's *Whig Principles and Party Politics: Earl Fitzwilliam and the Whig Party 1748–1833* (Manchester, 1975)—carries the party into the latter part of the reign. By contrast with the attention lavished on the Whigs between 1760 and 1794, however, they have been neglected as a group from the great rupture of 1794 until Waterloo. James J. Sack's *The Grenvillites, 1801–29: Party Politics and Factionalism in the Age of Pitt and Liverpool* (Urbana, Ill., 1979) helps fill part of the gap. Lloyd C. Saunders's *The Holland House Circle* (New York, 1969) also contains much on the Whigs during their years in the wilderness. Recent political treatment resumes in 1815 with Austin V. Mitchell's *The Whigs in Opposition 1815–1830* (Oxford, 1967), which carries the party beyond the period of this essay.

If the Rockinghams, Portlands, and Foxites have been examined to death, most of the other political groups in opposition have been ignored except for the Chathamites. The Great Commoner himself continues to attract biographies, two of substance, Stanley Ayling's *The Elder Pitt, Earl of Chatham* (London, 1976) and Peter D. Brown's *William Pitt, Earl of Chatham: the Great Commoner* (London, 1978). Brown's more general study, *The Chathamites* (London, 1967), is a group of biographical studies rather than a party history. The ministers, their followers, their politics, and their policies have fared much less well than the opposition, with a few outstanding exceptions. Recent literature devoted to this side of the political world has taken the form of biography or general studies of the English political background of the American Revolution. Lord North, of whom there was formerly no scholarly biography, is now the subject of two: Alan C. Valentine's *Lord North* (2 vols., Norman, Okla., 1967) and Peter D. G. Thomas's *Lord North* (London, 1976). Thomas's, although much more brief, is far superior as a critical but sympathetic assessment. The earlier years of the younger Pitt are exhaustively discussed in John Ehrman's *The Younger Pitt: The Years of Acclaim* (London, 1969). Three good biographies by John W. Derry (London, 1962), Derek Jarrett (London, 1974), and Robin Reilly (London, 1978) offer comprehensive assessments. One of the crucial events of Pitt's later years is fully discussed in Geoffrey C. Bolton's *The Passing of the Irish Act of Union: A Study in Parliamentary Politics* (Oxford, 1966).

Thorough scholarly biographies of two of Pitt's lackluster successors, Philip

Ziegler's *Addington* (London and New York, 1965) and Denis Gray's *Spencer Perceval: The Evangelical Prime Minister 1762−1812* (Manchester, 1963), between them reconsider most political events and crises during the early years of the nineteenth century. Addington's and Perceval's more colorful and dynamic colleagues Castlereagh and George Canning continue to attract biographies: on Castlereagh, Christopher J. Bartlett's *Castlereagh* (London, 1965); and John W. Derry's *Castlereagh* (London, 1976); and on Canning, books by Paul J. V. Rolo, *George Canning: Three Biographical Studies* (London, 1965); Wendy Hinde, *George Canning* (London and New York, 1973); and Peter Dixon, *Canning: Politician and Statesman* (London, 1976). All five are substantial and up to date, although it has not been easy to add to what was already known. The early postwar years of Liverpool's administration are thoroughly and sympathetically discussed in John E. Cookson's *Lord Liverpool's Administration: The Crucial Years, 1815− 1822* (Edinburgh, 1975); its economic policies are well investigated in Boyd Hilton's important *Corn, Cash, Commerce: The Economic Policies of the Tory Governments 1815−1830* (Oxford, 1977). Two men, never ministers, but with substantial political clout of quite different kinds, have received more attention than anyone but the two Pitts and the opposition Whigs, although for reasons partly extraneous to domestic politics: Robert Clive as the first great Indian proconsul and William Wilberforce as an abolitionist. Of the recent biographies of Clive, that by Richard Garrett (London, 1976) is perhaps the best.[1] Other good biographies of Clive are by Marck Bence-Jones (London, 1974), Nirad C. Chaudhuri (London, 1975), and James P. Lawford (London, 1976). The studies of Wilberforce by Robin Furneaux (London, 1974) and John Pollock (London, 1977) are both thorough and based on manuscripts.

The connections among domestic politics, the American crisis, the rise of the reform movement, and the growth of political radicalism continue to engage historians. The American crisis in its English political aspects is a recurrent theme in most of the recent monographs on domestic party politics between 1760 and 1783 and in the biographies of the leading politicians as well as a major theme in American historical writing. One of the more useful guides to the changing and conflicting views from the American perspective, assessed in an "imperial" context, is an essay by Ian R. Christie, "The Historian's Quest for the American Revolution," (in Anne Whiteman et al., eds., *Statesmen, Scholars and Merchants*, Oxford, 1973, 181−201). Christie's brief but comprehensive survey of the deteriorating situation in *Crisis of Empire: Great Britain and the American Colonies 1754−1783* (London, 1966) is an excellent introduction from the "standard" British view. The bicentenary of American independence provoked a flurry of publications on the subject from the British side, of which the most generally useful are the "debate" between Christie and Benjamin W. Labaree in *Empire or*

Independence 1760–1776: A British-American Dialogue on the Coming of the American Revolution (New York, 1976) and John W. Derry's *English Politics and the American Revolution* (London, 1976).

The growth of the domestic reform movement and the development of political radicalism, the most important political developments of the reign of George III, are closely interwoven with the American crisis and the loss of the colonies. The impact of the Revolution on the English reformers is the subject of Colin Bonwick's *English Radicals and the American Revolution* (Chapel Hill, N.C., 1977). Brewer's *Party, Ideology, and Politics* is a major contribution to the foundations of the reform movement and radicalism, but in general the growth of the agitation in the first three decades of the reign has been neglected recently. The first modern biography of the grand old man of the reform movement, John W. Osborne's *John Cartwright* (Cambridge, 1972), however, contains much on his prominent role in the earlier agitation as well as during the second half of the reign. Tony Hayter, in *The Army and the Crowd in Mid-Georgian England* (London, 1978), provides the first connected account of one of the government's responses to the more violent manifestations of the agitation through 1780; Hayter's study is as much concerned with the numerous popular disturbances that were purely economic in character as with those that were at least quasi-political.

Most of the recent literature concentrates on the French Revolutionary period and the early nineteenth century. Two general studies of the radicals and not-quite-so-radicals of the time are Carl B. Cone's *The English Jacobins: Reformers in Late Eighteenth-century England* (New York, 1968) and Albert Goodwin's *The Friends of Liberty: The English Democratic Movement in the Age of the French Revolution* (Cambridge, Mass., 1979), the most thorough study yet written. I. J. Prothero's *Artisans and Politics in Early Nineteenth-century London: John Gast and His Times* (Folkestone, 1978) ranges widely among the radicals, as do the earlier portions of Malcolm I. Thomis and Peter Holt's *Threats of Revolution in Britain, 1789–1848* (London and Hamden, Conn., 1977) and Edward Royle's *Radical Politics, 1790–1900: Religion and Unbelief* (Harlow, 1971). Many of the articles in the tedious debate over why the Whigs reformed Parliament in 1832 also look as far back as the reform agitation of the 1790s. Much information on developing working-class political consciousness and activity is scattered throughout Edward P. Thompson's *The Making of the English Working Class* (1963; 2d ed., Harmondsworth, 1968). The radical's radical, the ideologist of the movement, Tom Paine, has received several biographies, only one of much value, David F. Hawke's *Paine* (New York, 1974). Paine really deserves something better than the hagiographical or crudely Marxist treatment he usually receives. John W. Osborne's *William Cobbett: His Thought and His Times* (New Brunswick, N.J., 1966) and James Sambrooke's *William Cobbett* (London, 1973) are the most recent critical accounts of that major propagandist. At the very end of the reign, the debate over Peterloo has been reopened by Joyce Marlow in *The Peterloo Massacre* (London, 1969) and by Robert Walmsley in *Peterloo: The Case Reopened* (Manchester, 1969). Everywhere the more recent studies of political radicalism and reform merge with the numerous books and articles devoted to disturbances of all sorts in the late eighteenth and early nineteenth centuries which are more properly socioeconomic than political phenomena before 1820.

The revival in administrative history began shortly after the war with the appearance of scattered studies of parts of the administration. Such basic work as J. C. Sainty's lists, *Office-holders in Modern Britain* (London, 1972–   ) compiled since 1972 for most of the major departments, has been accomplished;[2] for the first time there exists a convenient source for discovering who was where and when below the Cabinet level and some indication of what he was supposed to be doing. Major departments have been investigated in some length. Much attention has naturally focused on the Treasury, which gave life to the whole, and to other aspects of financial administration. Henry Roseveare's *The Treasury: The Evolution of a British Institution* (New York, 1969) is especially full from the later seventeenth century, and his introduction to a collection of basic documents, *The Treasury 1660–1870: The Foundations of Control* (London and New York, 1973), is fundamental for understanding operations and changes in the Georgian period. The administration of the various resources of the Treasury has been studied extensively. Literature on the income tax is conveniently summarized in Basil E. V. Sabine's *A History of Income Tax* (London, 1966); Meade Emory's "The Early English Income Tax: A Heritage for the Contemporary" (*American Journal of Legal History* 9, 1965: 287–319) is also useful. Indispensable background material on the development of public credit can be found in Peter G. M. Dickson's *The Financial Revolution in England: A Study in the Development of Public Credit 1688–1756* (London and New York, 1967), the foundation of public finance in the next reign. The development of the public debt itself has been usefully summarized in Alice C. Carter's brief, lucid *The English Public Debt in the Eighteenth Century* (London, 1968). Two thorough studies investigate one major area of expenditure, supporting the army and navy: Bernard Pool's *Navy Board Contracts 1660–1832: Contract Administration under the Navy Board* (London and Hamden, Conn., 1966) and Norman Baker's *Government and Contractors: The British Treasury and War Supplies 1775–1783* (London, 1971). The younger Pitt's financial reforms (and the beginnings of his wider ranging administrative reforms) are also thoroughly described in Erhman's *The Younger Pitt*.

The rest of the central government has not yet received such vigorous scrutiny as the Treasury, but progress is apparent everywhere. The secretaries of state have recently been the subjects of Ronald R. Nelson's *The Home Office, 1782–1801* (Durham, N.C., 1969) and Charles R. Middleton's *The Administration of*

British Foreign Policy, 1782–1846 (Durham, N.C., 1977). David B. Horn's *The British Diplomatic Service, 1689–1789* (Oxford, 1961) supplies much information about the earlier direction of British foreign policy and the men who carried it out. The most important recent book on naval administration is Christopher Lloyd's *Mr. Barrow of the Admiralty: A Life of Sir John Barrow 1764–1848* (London, 1970), a biography of a great permanent administrator by a leading naval historian. Army administration, the most confused and obscure branch of the government, has not yet been assaulted directly, but it is mentioned in some of the recent general books dealing with the army and army reform mentioned below. The growing literature on the transformation of the old politicized bureaucracy into a nonpolitical civil service is summarized in the opening chapters of Henry W. Parris's *Constitutional Bureaucracy: The Development of British Central Administration since the Eighteenth Century* (London, 1969). The men who staffed some of the departments are discussed by Franklin B. Wickwire in *British Subministers and Colonial America 1763–1783* (Princeton, N.J., 1966) and in his comprehensive general article "King's Friends, Civil Servants, or Politicians?" (*AHR* 71, 1965–1966: 18–42).

Books and articles on diplomatic history proliferate, but the earlier work was so excellent that present scholarship has revised understanding less than in political and administrative history. The present state of interpretation is admirably summed up in Paul Langford's *The Eighteenth Century, 1688–1815* (London, 1976) and in the opening chapter of Paul M. Hayes's *The Nineteenth Century, 1814–80* (New York, 1975), which together provide a brief but comprehensive survey of the whole field of British international relations. Another excellent book covering much of the reign is David B. Horn's *Great Britain and Europe in the Eighteenth Century* (Oxford, 1967). The years between 1763 and the beginning of the American Revolution have been the scene of particularly vigorous activity. Michael Roberts's *Splendid Isolation 1763–1780* (Reading, 1970) is the best introduction. Nicholas Tracy, in a series of articles published between 1973 and 1975, has reexamined five incidents and areas of conflict in the international relations of the later 1760s and the 1770s,[3] while Michael Roberts and others have thoroughly explored Anglo-Baltic relations.[4] The diplomatic history of the American Revolution has been repeatedly retold without major changes in interpretation. The most interesting new material on relations with Europe between 1783 and the beginning of the French Revolution does not concern diplomacy directly, but cultural, intellectual, and financial relations as described in Derek Jarrett's *The Begetters of Revolution: England's Involvement with France, 1759–1789* (London, 1973), which is particularly enlightening on the ramifications of international finance in the 1770s and 1780s.

Of the numerous articles and monographs on the complex foreign relations of the French Revolutionary and Napoleonic periods, a few break new ground or make significant revisions. Howard V. Evans's "The Nootka Sound Controversy in Anglo-French Diplomacy—1790" (*JMH* 48, 1974: 609–640) is based on newly discovered manuscripts. Harvey Mitchell's *The Underground War against Revolutionary France: The Missions of William Wickham 1794–1800* (Oxford, 1965) and John W. Sherwig's *Guineas and Gunpowder: British Foreign Aid in the Wars with France, 1793–1815* (Cambridge, Mass., 1969) explore subjects formerly neglected. Other scattered studies chronicle British involvement elsewhere in the world, especially in the Near and Middle East, where Britain's interests were increasing. John Marlowe's *Perfidious Albion: The Origins of Anglo-French Rivalry in the Levant* (London, 1971), Matthew S. Anderson's *The Eastern Question 1774–1923: A Study in International Relations* (London, 1966), Sarah Searight's *The British in the Middle East* (London, 1969), and John B. Kelly's *Britain and the Persian Gulf 1795–1880* (Oxford, 1968) all complement each other. Articles by Edward Ingham fill in many details of British diplomacy in the Near and Middle East during the Napoleonic period.[5]

Military history, always popular, continues to flourish, although much of the work reexamines familiar themes and subjects, revising details rather than breaking really new ground. Of the general histories of the wars of the reign, the most important is Piers Mackesy's *The War for America, 1775–1783* (Cambridge, Mass., 1964), the best account yet written from the British perspective. No one has tackled all the constituent wars and operations of the French Revolutionary and Napoleonic periods, but the War of the Second Coalition is thoroughly discussed from different points of view in Mackesy's *Statesmen at War: The Strategy of Overthrow, 1798–1799* (London and New York, 1974) and Alexander B. Rodger's *The War of the Second Coalition, 1798–1801* (Oxford, 1964). The sideshow War of 1812 has also been exhaustively reinvestigated three times by H. L. Coles in *The War of 1812* (Chicago, 1965), J. Mark Hitson in *The Incredible War of 1812* (Toronto, 1965), and John K. Mahon in *The War of 1812* (Gainesville, Fla., 1972).

The army is comprehensively treated in Hugh C. B. Rogers's *The British Army of the Eighteenth Century* (New York, 1977), which summarizes much detailed work by many scholars on military organization and administration. Military developments in the reign are also considered in the context of several centuries of change in Corelli Barnett's provocative *Britain and Her Army 1509–1970: A Military, Political and Social Survey* (London, 1970) and in Frederick Myatt's *The Soldier's Trade: British Military Developments 1660–1914* (London, 1974). Military operations in the American Revolution, fully discussed by William B. Willcox in *Portrait of a General: Sir Henry Clinton in the War of Independence* (New York, 1964), have received less attention than those in the Peninsular War, but there has been useful work. John W. Shy, in *Toward Lexington* (Princeton, N.J., 1965), describes the British Army in North America before the war. Excellent biographical studies of previously neglected British commanders also expand our understanding, especially Ira D. Gruber's *The Howe Brothers and the American Revolution* (New York, 1972) and Franklin B. Wickwire and Mary Wickwire's *Cornwallis: The American Adventure* (Boston, 1970), continued for Cornwallis's later career in *Cornwallis: The Imperial Years* (Chapel Hill, N.C., 1980). The best of several recent biographies of Burgoyne is Gerald Howson's *Burgoyne of Saratoga* (New York, 1979).

Writing on the British Army in the French Revolutionary and Napoleonic periods understandably concentrates on the Peninsular War. Richard G. Glover's *Britain at Bay: Defence against Bonaparte 1803–14* (London, 1975), a collection of documents with a substantial introduction is, however, useful for military activities at home. Gordon C. Bond's *The Grand Expedition: The British Invasion of Holland in 1809* (Athens, Ga., 1979) is the first comprehensive study of that abortive adventure in more than a century. The history of the Peninsular War itself (and the subsequent history of England for forty-five years) is inextricably interwoven with the career of Arthur Wellesley, duke of Wellington. The best biography now is the near-definitive two-volume study by Elizabeth Pakenham, countess of Longford; the first volume, *Wellington: The Years of the Sword* (London, 1969), covers his life to 1815. Sir Arthur Bryant's *The Great Duke* (London, 1971) is another full-scale biography, and Michael Glover's *Wellington as Military Commander* (London, 1968) is an authoritative assessment. Roger Parkinson, in *The Peninsular War* (London, 1973), and Michael Glover, in *The Peninsular War, 1807–1814: A Concise Military History* (Newton Abbot, 1974), have written military histories of the war, while Glover, in *Wellington's Army in the Peninsular, 1805–14* (Newton Abbot, 1977), and Anthony Brett-James in *Life in Wellington's Army* (London, 1972), give accounts of life in Wellington's army. Wellington's colleagues in the expeditionary force, several of whom received up-to-date biographies in the 1950s and 1960s, have received only incidental attention recently, the exception being the Roger Parkinson *Moore of Corunna* (London, 1976), which does not, however, replace Carola Oman's biography of 1953, and the Richard L. Blanco *Wellington's Surgeon-General: Sir James McGriger* (Durham, N.C., 1974), which is also an important contribution to the development of military medicine.[6]

The Royal Navy in its greatest age continues to be more popular than the army. The most recent general history is the Oliver Warner work *The British Navy: A Concise History* (London, 1975), by one of the leading contemporary naval historians. More immediately concerned with the reign of George III are Geoffrey J. Marcus's *The Age of Nelson* (London, 1971), the second volume of his *A Naval History of England* and an excellent narrative of naval operations through 1815, and his *Heart of Oak: A Survey of British Seapower in the Georgian Era* (London, 1975). John Creswell, in *British Admirals of the Eighteenth Century: Tactics in*

Battle (London, 1972), covers all the wars of the century, as does Patrick Crow-hurst in *The Defence of British Trade, 1689–1815* (Folkestone, 1977), a study of defense against privateering, mostly in the Channel. C. Northcote Parkinson's *Britannia Rules: The Classic Age of Naval History, 1793–1815* (London, 1977) is the most recent general history of the naval side of the Revolutionary and Napoleonic wars. A dimmer view of the navy than that usually taken is Stanley H. Bonnett's *The Price of Admiralty: An Indictment of the Royal Navy, 1805–1966* (London, 1968), which is concerned with conditions of service rather than with performance in battle.

While naval history inevitably concentrates on the French Revolutionary and Napoleonic wars, the earlier part of the reign has not been neglected. Collections of documents with valuable introductions illuminate the concluding naval opera-tions of the Seven Years' War, the capture of Manila (Nicholas P. Cushner, ed., *Documents Illustrating the British Conquest of Manila, 1762–1763*, Camden So-ciety, 5th ser., 8, 1971), and the conquest of Havana (David Syrett, ed., *The Siege and Capture of Havana, 1762*, Navy Records Society, 1970). Rudolph F. Mackay, in *Admiral Hawke* (Oxford, 1965), and Peter Shankland, in *Byron of the Wager* (London, 1975), link the naval history of the Seven Years' War with that of the American Revolution. The naval side of the American crisis has re-ceived particular attention. The William B. Clarke, II, et al., editors, *Naval Documents of the American Revolution* (Washington, D.C., 1964–   ), which has now reached 1777 in seven volumes, is an essential, comprehensive collection of source material from British and American archives. Neal R. Stout's *The Royal Navy in America: A Study of the Enforcement of British Colonial Policy in the Era of the American Revolution* (Annapolis, Md., 1973) discusses the back-ground; David Syrett's *Shipping and the American War, 1775–83: A Study of British Transport Organization* (London, 1970) is concerned with the problems of supply. Operations and strategy are more directly discussed in Gruber's 1972 book on the Howe brothers and in David Spinney's *Rodney* (Annapolis, Md., 1969), the latest biography of the one real naval hero from the British point of view in that war.

All other periods in naval history, however, pale beside the events of 1793–1815. Professional and amateur historians alike continue to write about these years despite the vast library already in print. Nelson as usual dominates. Four of the recent books are more than the usual hagiographies or accounts of his sex life: David Walder's *Nelson: A Biography* (London, 1978); Oliver Warner's *Nelson* (Chicago, 1975), a brief life; Christopher Lloyd's *Nelson and Sea Power* (Lon-don, 1973); and Geoffrey M. Bennett's *Nelson the Commander* (New York, 1972), all studies by prominent naval historians. Of the scattered biographies of other naval leaders, the most important is Oliver Warner's *The Life and Letters of Vice-admiral Lord Collingwood* (London, 1968). Battles have fared rather better.

Oliver Warner's *Nelson's Battles* (Annapolis, Md., 1971) surveys all of them; Christopher Lloyd's *The Nile Campaign: Nelson and Napoleon in Egypt* (Newton Abbot, 1973) is an excellent account of that combined operation; Dudley Pope's *The Great Gamble* (London, 1972) is exhaustive on the Battle of Copenhagen; and the best recent study of Trafalgar is that by Geoffrey M. Bennett (London, 1977).

Miscellaneous problems of supply, naval equipment, life below decks, and the great mutiny of 1797 have all been studied. Joseph Malone, in *Pine Trees and Politics: The Naval Stores and Forest Policy in Colonial New England 1691−1775* (Seattle, 1965), discusses the problems of supply before the American Revolution. Numerous articles and books investigate the beginnings of dockyard reform, technical innovations, and improvements in navigation.[7] The perennial problems of recruitment are discussed in the introduction to John S. Bromley, editor's *The Manning of the Royal Navy: Selected Public Pamphlets 1693−1873* (Navy Records Society 119, 1976). Arthur N. Gilbert has even studied the problems of deviant sexual behavior in "Buggery and the Navy" (*Journal of Social History* 10, 1976−1977: 72−98). James Dugan's *The Great Mutiny* (London, 1966) is one of the best books yet written on the mutinies of 1797. Nowhere in any area of military history is there the least sign of any flagging productivity.

Not so in another once much-exploited field. The history of religion in the reign of George III is just beginning to emerge from the doldrums into which it drifted after the war. In the recent past at least a half-dozen substantial studies have investigated the interaction of religion, the churches, and society, considerably revising and expanding our understanding of the social implications and connections of the religious revival. The striking simularity of their themes is indicated by their titles: Richard A. Soloway, *Prelates and People: Ecclesiastical Social Thought in England, 1783−1832* (London, 1969); William R. Ward, *Religion and Society in England, 1790−1850* (London, 1972); Anthony Armstrong, *The Church of England, the Methodists and Society 1700−1850* (London, 1973); Alan D. Gilbert, *Religion and Society in Industrial England: Church, Chapel and Social Change, 1740−1914* (London, 1976); Edward R. Norman, *Church and Society in England 1770−1970* (Oxford, 1976); Robert Currie et al., *Churches and Churchgoers: Patterns of Church Growth in the British Isles since 1700* (Oxford, 1977); and a careful local study along the same lines, Arthur Warne's *Church and Society in Eighteenth-century Devon* (Newton Abbot, 1969). The rise of irreligion has attracted some attention, most notably in the earlier parts of Edward Royle's *Victorian Infidels: The Origins of the British Secularist Movement, 1791−1866* (Manchester, 1974); in the documents he has edited, *The Infidel Tradition from Paine to Bradlaugh* (London, 1976); and in its political connections, in his *Radical Politics, 1790−1900: Religion and Unbelief* (Harlow, 1971).

The debate over whether the evangelical revival pacified the lower orders continues unresolved. E. P. Thompson, in *The Making of the English Working Class* (1963; 2d ed., London, 1968) argues vigorously that they were neither as affected nor as pacified as Halévy assumed, but most other writers present a somewhat modified confirmation of Halévy's interpretation. The discussion can be followed from various and conflicting points of view in Bernard Semmel's excellent introduction to his translation of Halévy's famous articles on the genesis of Methodism, *The Birth of Methodism in England* (Chicago, 1971); in John Walsh's comprehensive "Élie Halévy and the Birth of Methodism" (*TRHS* 5th ser., 25, 1975: 1–20); and in numerous other articles on the theme.[8] The relation between religion and economic activity has attracted less attention than formerly. The most important discussion is in two articles by Charles M. Elliot which question incisively the usefulness of trying to find significant connections between religious views of all sorts, except possibly those of the Unitarians, and economic behavior: "The Ideology of Economic Growth: A Case Study" (in Eric L. Jones and Gordon E. Mingay, eds., *Land, Labour and Population in the Industrial Revolution*, London, 1967, 75–99) and "The Political Economy of English Dissent, 1780–1940" (in Ronald M. Hartwell, ed., *The Industrial Revolution*, Oxford, 1970, 144–166).

When one turns from general studies of the social role of religion and the churches, where there are signs of substantial renaissance, to the works more immediately concerned with the major subdivisions of religious life, the scene approaches that of a barren wilderness. Kenneth A. Thompson's *Bureaucracy and Church Reform: The Organizational Response of the Church of England to Social Change, 1800–1865* (Oxford, 1970), Geoffrey F. A. Best's *Temporal Pillars: Queen Anne's Bounty, the Ecclesiastical Commissioners and the Church of England* (Cambridge, 1964), and Norman Ravitch's *Sword and Mitre: Government and the Episcopate in France and England in the Age of Aristocracy* (The Hague, 1966) are solid on aspects of the established church. Add a few scattered articles and books on a few minor figures and small points, and one has a nearly complete account of all the work on the Church of England in the past fifteen years.

The Methodists have fared rather better than the Anglicans. Bernard Semmel's *The Methodist Revolution* (New York, 1973) is a major study of Methodist theology as intellectual history, stressing the "modernity" of Wesley's thought in contrast to that of the Calvinistic Methodists, and reaching conclusions similar to Halévy's about the historical role of Methodism and its influence in preventing revolution. The substantial essays in Rupert E. Davies and Ernest C. Rupp's *A History of the Methodist Church in Great Britain* (London, 1966) concentrate on the eighteenth century, while John C. Bowmer's *Pastor and People* (London, 1975) is a solid account of the so-called second period of Methodism. Stanley Ayling's *John Wesley* (London, 1979) is the best recent biography. The extensive specialized literature on all aspects of Methodism to 1970 is usefully summarized in Frederick A. Norwood's "Wesleyan and Methodist Historical Studies, 1960–70: A Bibliographical Article" (*Church History* 40, 1971: 82–99). Studies of other dissenters have languished; accounts of them in the reign of George III are usually incidental to larger themes and longer periods. The most important books are Michael R. Watt's *The Dissenters*, volume 1, *From the Reformation to the French Revolution* (Oxford, 1978), an ambitious attempt to discuss all varieties of dissent, and the C. G. Bolam et al. *The English Presbyterians* (London, 1968), the best recent treatment of that key group. Robert Carwardine's *Transatlantic Revivalism: Popular Evangelicalism in Britain and America, 1790–1865* (Westport, Conn., 1978) is a useful monography. The millenarians have been particularly thoroughly studied. J. F. C. Harrison's *The Second Coming: Popular Millenarianism, 1780–1850* (New Brunswick, N.J., 1979) is the most comprehensive survey.[9] At the other end of the religious spectrum, John Bossy's *The English Catholic Community, 1570–1850* (London, 1975) and Hugh Aveling's *The Handle and the Axe: The Catholic Recusants in England from the Reformation to Emancipation* (London, 1976) are outstanding accounts of the Roman Catholics; both challenge long-accepted platitudes. Nearly all the other studies of English religion concern minor points or specific congregations, but five articles by G. M. Ditchfield thoroughly reinvestigate the campaign for the repeal of the Test and Corporation Acts in 1787–1790.[10] Colin C. Bonwick's "English Dissenters and the American Revolution" (in Harry C. Allen and Roger Thompson, eds., *Contrast and Connection: Bicentennial Essays in Anglo-American History*, (London, 1976) is the most useful of many discussions of the subject. More study is essential on every topic connected with late Georgian religion.

Economic and social history and their multiplying subspecialties threaten to engulf all other subjects. The major areas of revision and renewed controversy have concerned the explanation of the causes of the rapid economic growth after 1750, with the influence of the presumed "triggers" and the relations among them repeatedly reexamined and rearranged; the social consequences of the changes for the lower classes, with a vigorous revival of the older and once virtually discredited "pessimistic" interpretation; and the part played in the changes and the effects of them on the "middling sort" and the established landed classes. Nearly everywhere there has been an increased emphasis on quantitative, statistical, and "econometric" approaches to economic development. The later method is often almost incomprehensible to the nonspecialist, and the sometimes-violent controversy it has occasioned when applied in specific instances suggests that it proves of limited use for understanding the Industrial Revolution. Two new versions of social histories have emerged, both influenced by methodologies adopted from the social sciences, quantitative approaches, and contemporary social and political concerns and ideologies. One of these new versions treats "social history" as primarily the history of the mass of the people, emphasizing popular and working-class movements and behavior, and has been written with more emotional and political commitment than dispassionate analysis. The other version is concerned with the study of basic social institutions such as the family, sex, and marriage; the changes in social structures and mores; and the study of groups and classes.

Valiant attempts have been made to keep on top of the burgeoning new material. The most useful one-volume general treatments are Eric Pawson's *The Early Industrial Revolution: Britain in the 18th Century* (New York, 1979), emphasizing the approach of the historical geographer; Phyllis Deane's *The First Industrial Revolution* (Cambridge, 1965; 2d ed., Cambridge, 1979), concerned with the years 1750–1850 and describing clearly the principal developments which produced the economic transformation; and the more extended account in Peter Mathias's *The First Industrial Nation: An Economic History of Britain 1700–1914* (London, 1969), the best one-volume description of the entire modern period. Eric J. Hobsbawm's *Industry and Empire: An Economic History of Britain since 1750* (London, 1968) is a stimulating, highly sophisticated Marxian interpretation, differing from Deane and Mathias on major points and far from convincing on all of them. Albert E. Musson's *The Growth of British Industry* (New York, 1978), one of the most recent general treatments, concentrates too much on strictly industrial development.

Studies of economic change in various counties and regions have continued to produce excellent results, especially in emphasizing the diversity of industrialization. Recent books have surveyed Essex, the Black Country, Merseyside, the Lake District, South Wales, Yorkshire, and Shropshire.[11] British economic development is related to that of Europe and the world most comprehensively in volumes 3 and 4 of the *Fontana Economic History of Europe*, edited by Carlo M. Cipolla (London, 1972–1976) and in volume 6 of the *Cambridge Economic History of Europe*, edited by Hrothgar J. Habakkuk and Michael Postan (Cambridge, 1965) and volume 7, edited by Peter Mathias and Michael Postan (Cambridge, 1978). Patrick K. O'Brien and Caglar Keyder's *Economic Growth in Britain and France, 1780–1914: Two Paths to the Twentieth Century* (London, 1978) is an important comparative study and the latest major contribution to the debate Why was England first? François Crouzet's "Angleterre et France au XVIIIe siècle: Essai d'analyse comparée de deux croissances économiques" (*Annales* 21, 1966: 254–291, trans. in Ronald M. Hartwell, ed., *The Causes of the Industrial Revolution in England*, London, 1967, 139–174) is another important discussion of the subject.

Volumes of the collected papers of Ronald M. Hartwell (*The Industrial Revolution and Economic Growth*, (London, 1971) and Eric J. Hobsbawm (*Labouring*

Men, London, 1964) present divergent views on many economic and social subjects. Peter Mathias's *The Transformation of England: Essays on the Economic and Social History of England in the Eighteenth Century* (London, 1979) reprints most of his important shorter pieces. Significant material on economic development from the standpoint of historical geography is included in Henry C. Darby, editor's *A New Historical Geography of England* (Cambridge, 1973) and Kenneth Warren's *The Geography of English Heavy Industry since 1800* (Oxford 1976).

Much of the recent literature has been concerned with the causes of the industrial revolution; each historian has his favorite "triggers."[12] Some of the most important contributions to these discussions as they existed before and during the mid-1960s are conveniently collected in Ronald M. Hartwell, editor's *The Causes of the Industrial Revolution in England*, which has a long introduction, very critical of the sufficiency of any of the explanations so far offered to explain what happened. Michael W. Flinn, in *The Origins of the Industrial Revolution* (London, 1966), provides one of the most sensible, balanced, and lucid discussions of the problems.

Government policy as an influence on economic development has been neglected. The only important book is Judith B. Williams's *British Commercial Policy and Trade Expansion 1750–1850* (Oxford, 1972), a comprehensive study. A few controversies over specific cases continue unresolved. The most important, because it influences explanations of the causes of the American Revolution, concerns the impact on the colonies of the tightened enforcement of the Navigation Acts after 1763.[13] Another debates the importance of smuggling, particularly of tea, and its influence in shaping the younger Pitt's commercial policies.[14] The economic effects of diplomacy are considered indirectly in much of the literature on these subjects as well as more directly in the studies of economic growth,[15] while the tacit encouragement of internal improvements through facilitating the passage of enclosure, turnpike, and canal acts is emphasized in work on these subjects. The growing literature on government finance concerns its administration rather than its economic impact, with two important exceptions, J. L. Anderson's "A Measure of the Effects of British Public Finance, 1793–1815" (*EcHR*, 2d ser., 27, 1974: 610–619) and Peter Mathias and Patrick K. O'Brien's "Taxation in Britain and France, 1715–1810: A Comparison of the Social and Economic Incidence of Taxes Collected for the Central Governments" (*Journal of European Economic History* 5, 1976: 610–650). The latter study emphasizes the increasing burden of taxation to fund the national debt.

While government influence on economic development was marginal, problems of capital formation and the development of credit and banking were central. With the exception of work on capital formation, however, not much new ground has been broken in the past fifteen years. Two books conveniently assemble much of the literature on capital formation: François Crouzet, editor's *Capi-*

tal Formation in the Industrial Revolution (London, 1972), which contains seven important essays and an excellent introduction; and J. P. P. Higgins and Sidney Pollard, editors' *Aspects of Capital Investment in Great Britain 1750–1850: A Preliminary Survey* (London, 1971), five papers presented at a conference. The entrepreneurs who used the capital and credit have been much discussed, and the study of entrepreneurship and management in the early stages of the Industrial Revolution has been transformed in the past fifteen years, following the paths pioneered by Sidney Pollard in *The Genesis of Modern Management: A Study of the Industrial Revolution in Great Britain* (London, 1965). John W. Gough's *The Rise of the Entrepreneur* (London, 1969), F. R. J. Jervis's *Bosses in British Business: Managers and Management from the Industrial Revolution to the Present Day* (London, 1974), Peter L. Payne's *British Entrepreneurship in the Nineteenth Century* (London, 1974), and C. Northcoate Parkinson's *The Rise of Big Business from the Eighteenth Century to the Present Day* (London, 1977), are surveys of the managerial revolution.

The impact of the so called transportation revolution—the building of canals, turnpikes, and river improvements in the age of George III—has been thoroughly reassessed, often in a more comprehensive economic framework than the earlier work. Two new major studies and an extensive revision of a third cover all parts of the subject. The most important is Harold J. Dyos and Derek H. Aldcroft's *British Transport: An Economic Survey from the Seventeenth Century to the Twentieth* (Leicester, 1969), which has an excellent critical bibliography; more recent is Philip S. Bagwell's *The Transportation Revolution from 1770* (London and New York, 1974) and the third (revised) edition of Theodore C. Barker and Christopher I. Savage's *An Economic History of Transport in Britain* (London, 1974). William Albert, in *The Turnpike Road System in England 1663–1840* (Cambridge, 1972) thoroughly surveyed the turnpikes, but Eric Pawson soon demonstrated that much more could be said in *Transport and Economy: The Turnpike Roads of Eighteenth-century Britain* (London, 1977). The development of regional and national carrying systems is also being increasingly discussed in regional studies, of which Laurence A. Williams's *Road Transport in Cumbria in the Nineteenth Century* (London, 1975) is a good example. Because the importance of the canals and river navigations for economic development has long been recognized, the work has revised their interpretation less than that on roads. Most studies concern individual canals, canal development in various regions of the country, or more occasionally, river navigation. Ellis C. R. Hadfield's *The Canal Age* (Newton Abbot, 1968), and the fifth edition of his *British Canals: An Illustrated History* (Newton Abbot, 1974), based on his series of regional studies (ten volumes of them published between 1955 and 1977), are the best general accounts. J. R. Ward's *The Finance of Canal Building in Eighteenth-century England* (Oxford, 1974) is an important monograph with implications for the study of the capital market and capital formation as well. The new version of Hugh Malet's standard biography (first published in 1961) of the duke of Bridgwater, *Bridgwater: The Canal Duke 1736–1803* (Manchester, 1978) is still the best work on that aristocratic entrepreneur.

Foreign trade, thoroughly investigated when it was believed to be the major impetus to economic transformation, has been relatively neglected recently. Some work has been done on the volume of trade, on individual ports, and on trade with Europe and the Levant.[16] Trade with the East is largely a history of the operations of the East India Company and its "servants" in the reign of George III. Important work on the company's involvement in domestic politics, its administration, and its activities in India was done in the 1940s and 1950s, but a good deal more has been written since, especially by Peter J. Marshall. Besides his study of the Hastings impeachment, which contains much on internal affairs in India, Marshall has edited a collection of documents, *Problems of Empire: Britain and India 1757–1813* (London, 1968), with a long and near-definitive introduction and, most recently, *East India Fortunes: The British in Bengal in the Eighteenth Century* (Oxford, 1976), a study of the economic foundations of these fortunes, trading activities within India, and to the east and west. Pamela Nightingale's *Trade and Empire in Western India 1784–1806* (Cambridge, 1970) is a thorough monograph. The staple of the eighteenth-century Asian trade, tea, has its own literature: the best recent discussion is Denys M. Forrest's *Tea for the British: The Social and Economic History of a Famous Trade* (London, 1973).

Work on trade with the Americas is equally divided between the North American and West Indian branches. Trade with the continental colonies is discussed in accounts of the causes of the American Revolution and is the subject of the debate over the impact of the Navigation Acts, but most recent work concerns limited topics. Thomas C. Barrow's *Trade and Empire: The British Customs Service in Colonial America 1660–1775* (Cambridge, Mass., 1967) is especially concerned with the years after 1760. More comprehensive is Thomas M. Divine's *The Tobacco Lords: A Study of the Tobacco Merchants of Glasgow and Their Trading Activities, c. 1740–1790* (Edinburgh, 1975), which describes a very complex operation with numerous effects on the economic development of Scotland. Trade with the West Indies meant primarily the slave and sugar trades and has been the subject of some outstanding books, notably by Richard Pares, in the 1940s and 1950s. Nothing of equal quality has appeared in the last fifteen years, although the literature on the slave trade has much to say about the economic relations between Britain and the West Indies. Two attempts have been made to draw up a balance sheet: Philip R. P. Coelho's "The Profitability of Imperialism: The British Experience in the West Indies 1768–1772 (*Explorations in Economic History* 10, 1972–1973) and Robert P. Thomas's "The Sugar Colonies of the Old Empire: Profit or Loss for Great Britain?" (*EcHR*, 2d ser., 21, 1968: 30–45), which concludes that they were a loss.

Louis M. Cullen has written a useful study on trade with Ireland in *Anglo-Irish Trade 1660–1800* (Manchester, 1968), but there is little else on that theme. Trade within England, although now considered more important than foreign trade in stimulating economic development, still awaits its comprehensive historian who will draw together the rapidly accumulating material on the subject in studies of individual trades and industries and provide a composite picture of the dramatic growth of the domestic market. Of the monographs, the most valuable are Thomas S. Willan's *An Eighteenth century Shopkeeper, Abraham Dent of Kirkby Stephen* (Manchester, 1970), a unique account of a successful small-scale provincial shopkeeper who also dabbled in brewing, hosiery merchanting, and dealing in bills of exchange; and Richard G. Wilson's *Gentlemen Merchants: The Merchant Community in Leeds, 1700–1830* (Manchester, 1971), which describes several generations of merchants in one town and the changes in their trade.

All major sectors of the domestic economy have been reinvestigated. Nowhere has there been more thoroughgoing reconstruction of older interpretations than in the history of later Georgian agriculture, which has been almost wholly rewritten since 1945. The effect of this recasting of English agrarian history has been to demolish the lingering notion of a spectacular "agricultural revolution" concentrated in the later eighteenth and early nineteenth centuries and to substitute a process of steady agrarian change, going well back into the seventeenth century, whose full effects were not felt until the 1850s. Nevertheless, most scholars working in the eighteenth century still believe that the tempo of change increased markedly about 1750 and that the continuing "revolution" after 1815 was of a different sort from that going on during the reign of George III. The presentation of this new agricultural history is especially associated with Jonathan D. Chambers and Gordon E. Mingay's *The Agricultural Revolution 1750–1880* (London and New York, 1966) and with Eric L. Jones in his important introduction to *Agriculture and Economic Growth in England 1650–1815* (London, 1967). Chambers and Mingay perhaps overstress the novelty of what occurred after 1750, while Jones looks backward to the origins. Together, they present a balanced analysis. Jones's volume also collects together some of the more important articles in which details of the new interpretation were being worked out in the 1950s and early 1960s. A similar collection of more recent essays, this time with a comprehensive introductory essay by Mingay, is *The Agricultural Revolution: Changes in Agriculture 1650–1880* (London, 1977). P. K. O'Brien's "Agriculture and the Industrial Revolution" (*EcHR*, 2d ser., 30, 1977: 166–181) is a useful review article on the current state of discussion. Jones's *Agriculture and the Industrial Revolution* (Oxford, 1974) assembles his important articles ranging over three centuries of developments. Walter E. Minchinton, editor's *Essays in Agrarian History* (2 vols., Newton Abbot, 1968) also reprints several important essays on the period.

A group of more specialized works contributes to the new agrarian history. The essays in Alan R. H. Baker and Robin A. Butlin, editors' *Studies of Field Systems in the British Isles* (Cambridge, 1973) summarize recent work on the subject to the breakup of the medieval patterns, which were by no means entirely gone by 1820. Eric J. Evans's *The Contentious Tithe: The Tithe Problem and English Agriculture 1750–1850* (London, 1976) is the first study of this central but usually ignored subject. Eric L. Jones's *Seasons and Prices: The Role of the Weather in English Agricultural History* (London, 1964) is a comprehensive chronological survey of the weather from 1728 to 1911. Sir Edward J. Russell's *A History of Agricultural Science in Great Britain, 1620–1954* (London, 1966) is a magisterial survey of the slow development of a truly scientific agriculture. Articles discuss the increasing employment of migrant, particularly Irish, labor; a few are concerned with agricultural prices; and another group investigates the special circumstances of the Napoleonic Wars.[17] Regional studies of "Wessex," Lincolnshire, Surrey, Hertfordshire, and Wales continue the tradition of crossfertilization between local and national studies. John G. Gazley's *The Life of Arthur Young 1741–1820* (Philadelphia, 1973) is an excellent biography of the leading propagandist for change, and Kenneth Hudson's *Patriotism with Profit: British Agricultural Societies in the Eighteenth and Nineteenth Centuries* (London, 1972) is a useful survey of these means of propagating the new agriculture.

The systematic investigation of individual great and medium-sized estates is supplying agrarian history with even more generally significant results than the work on geographical regions. A sample of such works include: John H. Bettey, *Rural Life in Wessex 1500–1900* (Bradford-on-Avon, 1977); David B. Grigg, *The Agricultural Revolution in South Lincolnshire* (Cambridge, 1966); D. W. Howell, *Land and People in Nineteenth-century Wales* (London, 1977); Barbara Kerr, *Bound to the Soil: A Social History of Dorset 1750–1918* (London, 1968); H. Lock, *Surrey in 1815* (Reading, 1974); and G. Longman, *A Corner of England's Garden: An Agarian History of S.W. Hertfordshire 1600–1850* (Bushey, Hertforshire, 1976). Robert A. C. Parker's *Coke of Norfolk: A Financial and Agricultural Study, 1707–1842* (Oxford, 1975), the most important estate work so far, definitively destroys the lingering myth of the younger Coke of Norfolk's having invented the agricultural innovations by demonstrating that nearly all the improvements for which Coke took, or was given, credit were in fact introduced and carried very far by his predecessor, the earl of Leicester, during the first half of the century. Other estate studies, most of them concentrating on the early nineteenth century, include books or articles on the Lumley-Saunderson estates in the north of England; the Leveson-Gower estates in the West Midlands; Lord William Bentinck's estate in Norfolk; the estates (at least the fortune) of the dukes of Devonshire; the Bramham estate in Yorkshire; and groups of estates in Essex, East Yorkshire, and Wales.[18] The investigation has spread, to Scotland, with Robert J. Adam, editor's *Papers on Sutherland Estate Management 1802–1816* (2 vols., Scottish History Society, 4th ser., 8–9, Edinburgh, 1972) and Ian G. Lindsay's *Inverrary and the Dukes of Argyll* (Edinburgh, 1973), a major study of the leading Scottish innovators, and to Ireland, where so many of the great English families were absentee owners, with an important article by David Large, "The Wealth of the Greater Irish Landowners, 1750–1815" (*IHS* 15, 1966–1967: 21–47), and a model estate study, William A. Maguire's *The Downshire Estates in Ireland, 1801–1845: The Management of Irish Landed Estates in the Early Nineteenth Century* (Oxford, 1972).

Closely connected with the history of the great estates is the question of the land market in the eighteenth century, a subject with wide ramifications for economic and social history. The classic interpretation, established by H. J. Habakkuk, suggested that the land market effectively dried up early in the century; subsequently there was only minimal fluidity through the effects of enclosure, which further enhanced the already existing large estates. Although evidence for a general revision is still spotty, current work indicates that such may not have been the case. The present state of the discussion is summed up in J. V. Beckett's "English Landownership in the Later Seventeenth and Eighteenth Centuries: The Debate and Its Problems" (*EcHR*, 2d ser., 30, 1977: 567–581).

The study of the great estates also merges with the controversies surrounding the history and effects of the enclosure movement, the aspect of agrarian change with which the landed class as a whole was most intimately involved. The old questions are still open. What were the causes, the speed, and the consequences of the revived movement? What were its effects on the redistribution of the land, the creation of a labor supply for the burgeoning industries and towns, on the men and women who remained in the countryside? The most important general studies, William E. Tate's *The English Village Community and the Enclosure Movement* (London, 1967), by a scholar who had previously published more than a dozen articles on enclosure, and Michael Turner's *English Parliamentary Enclosures* (Folkestone, 1980) minimize the disruptive effects and the callous injustice of the enclosures; so too does Gordon E. Mingay in his general studies and in essays of 1965 and 1968 on the subject.[19] Their interpretation continues to be sustained in most of the recent studies of individual enclosures.

Areas of growing rural distress and the accompanying disturbances have attracted much attention, particularly among the "new" social historians and others with their sights set more on the post-Napoleonic period than on the eighteenth century. Three general surveys of trouble are Asa Briggs's "Peasant Movements and Agrarian Problems in England and Wales from the End of the XVIIIth

Century up to Our Times" (*Cahiers internationaux de l'histoire économique et social* 6, 1977: 308–332); Eric J. Hobsbawm's "Les soulèvements de la campagne anglaise 1795–1850" (*Annales* 23, 1968: 9–30); and in greater detail, J. P. D. Dunbabin's *Rural Discontent in Nineteenth-century Britain* (London, 1974). Alfred J. Peacock's *Bread or Blood: A Study of the Agrarian Riots in East Anglia in 1816* (London, 1965) is a full-scale study of one set of disturbances. The literature on this subject merges with the extensive writing on all sorts of popular disturbances during the reign of George III and with that on the problems of poverty from the beginning of the wars.

Industry, in this ultimate of industrializing ages, continues to intrigue historians, but the reinvestigations of the major branches (textiles, iron and steel, and coal) and studies of some of lesser but expanding trades and industries reveal one very important change in emphasis. What is new is the elevation of technology into the most important single element in explaining the beginning and continuation of economic growth. The two major monuments to this approach appeared in 1969: David S. Landes's *The Unbound Prometheus: Technological Change and Industrial Development in Western Europe from 1750 to the Present* (London) and Albert E. Musson and Eric Robinson's *Science and Technology in the Industrial Revolution* (Manchester). Musson has continued to develop the argument in his long introduction to *Science, Technology and Economic Growth in the Eighteenth Century* (London, 1972), a collection of recent articles on the subject, and in his more general *The Growth of British Industry* (New York, 1978). The impact of the new emphasis and the related one of the relations between "pure" science and technology is already apparent in many of the recent general studies of technology as well as in most treatments of particular industries and in the numerous recent biographies of the inventors and the famous engineers. These include Brian Bracegirdle and Patricia H. Miles's *Thomas Telford* (Newton Abbot, 1973), K. Ellis's *Thomas Telford, Father of Civil Engineering* (London, 1974), Paul Clements's *Marc Isambaud Brunel* (Harlow, 1970), Ian McNeil's *Joseph Bramah: A Century of Invention, 1749–1851* (Newton Abbot, 1968), and Craig Mair's *A Star for Seamen: The Stevenson Family of Engineers* (London, 1978). Some of the more general works include Jennifer Tann's *The Development of the Factory* (London, 1970), lavishly illustrated with plans and elevations of all sorts of factories from the Boulton and Watt papers; K. T. Rowland's *Eighteenth-century Inventions* (Newton Abbot, 1974); William Steeds's *A History of Machine Tools, 1700– 1910* (Oxford, 1968); and Donald S. L. Cardwell's *From Watt to Clausius: The Rise of Thermodynamics in the Early Industrial Age* (Ithaca, N.Y., 1971).

One of the most important questions addressed in the new literature is the vexed one of the connection between "pure" science and technology in the early Industrial Revolution. Musson insists that it is intimate, but most of the evidence is still confined to the activities of the Lunar Society, the relations between James

Watt and Joseph Black, and a few developments in industrial chemistry. Robert E. Schofield's important *The Lunar Society of Birmingham: A Social History of Provincial Science and Industry in Eighteenth-century England (Oxford, 1963)* has been supplemented by a half-dozen articles on its activities in the *University of Birmingham Historical Journal* (11, 1967–1968), commemorating its bicentenary. Eric Robinson and Goulas McKie have edited the correspondence between Watt and Black in *Partners in Science* (Cambridge, Mass., 1970), and Donald S. L. Cardwell, in "Science and the Steam Engine, 1790–1825" (in Peter Mathias, ed., *Science and Society 1600–1800*, Cambridge, 1972, 81–96), emphasizes the role of science. For the negative, A. Rupert Hall, in "What Did the Industrial Revolution Owe to Science?" (in Neil McKendrick, ed., *Historical Perspectives*, 1974, 129–151), concludes, not much.

The diffusion of steam power, and even its importance, has been much discussed. Its successful harnessing by Watt and Boulton for more than pumping water out of mines, and the partners' creation of a model new industry for the manufacture and diffusion of steam engines, continue to receive nearly as much attention as ever, both as technological innovation and as entrepreneurial enterprise. The diffusion of steam power is the principal subject of Richard L. Hills's *Power in the Industrial Revolution* (Manchester, 1970), which covers other sources as well. G. N. von Tunzelmann, in *Steam Power and British Industrialization to 1860* (Oxford, 1978), however, questions whether the steam engine was nearly as important in industrial growth as is usually assumed.

Nowhere was the importance of technological innovation and diffusion greater than in the textile industry, and nowhere has the new technological emphasis in economic history been more thoroughly developed. Three comprehensive general histories are Stanley D. Chapman's *The Early Factory Masters: The Transition to the Factory System in the Midlands Textile Industry* (Newton Abbot, 1967), John Addy's *The Textile Revolution* (London, 1976), and Walter English's *The Textile Industry: An Account of the Early Inventions of Spinning, Knitting, and Weaving Machines* (Harlow, 1972). Cotton has received two general treatments— Stanley D. Chapman's *The Cotton Industry in the Industrial Revolution* (London, 1972), the more important, and Michael M. Edwards, *The Growth of the British Cotton Trade 1780–1815* (Manchester, 1967)—and two wide-ranging monographs: Seymour Shapiro's *Capital and the Cotton Industry in the Industrial Revolution* (Ithaca, N.Y., 1967) and Duncan Bythell's *The Handloom Weavers: A Study in the English Cotton Industry during the Industrial Revolution* (Cambridge, 1969). Wool has received one general treatment, John G. Jenkins, editor's *The Wool Textile Industry in Great Britain* (London, 1972), a collection of historical, technical, and regional treatments by many hands. Major regions of the industry—the West Riding, the West Country, the Southwest, Wales, and Scotland—have been the subject of books. These include D. T. Jenkins's *The West Riding Wool Textile*

Industry, *1770–1835: A Study of Fixed Capital Formation* (Edington, Wiltshire, 1975), Julia de Lacy Mann's *The Cloth Industry in the West of England from 1640 to 1880* (Oxford, 1971), Kenneth G. Ponting's *The Woolen Industry of South-west England: An Industrial, Economic and Technical Survey* (Bath, 1971), J. G. Jenkins's *The Welsh Woolen Industry* (Cardiff, 1969), and Clifford Gulvin's *The Tweed-makers: A History of the Scottish Fancy Woolen Industry, 1600–1914* (Newton Abbot, 1973).

Most of the great landed families had nothing to do with the growth of the textile industry, but several of them, including some of the richest and most influential, were intimately involved in the development of coal and iron and in the creation of heavy industry, and they grew richer year by year from their enterprise. Recent studies of these landed-industrial magnates include Trevor J. Raybould's *The Economic Emergence of the Black Country: A Study of the Dudley Estate* (Newton Abbot, 1973), Eric Richards's *The Leviathan of Wealth: The Sutherland Fortune in the Industrial Revolution* (London, 1973), and Graham Mee's *Aristocratic Enterprise: The Fitzwilliam Industrial Undertakings, 1795–1857* (Glasgow, 1975). Michael M. McCahill's "Peers, Patronage, and the Industrial Revolution, 1760–1800" (*JBS* 16, Fall, 1976: 84–107) is a brief but comprehensive consideration; and several of the essays in John T. Ward and Richard G. Wilson, editors' *Land and Industry: The Landed Estate and the Industrial Revolution* (Newton Abbot, 1971) are concerned with the same theme.

The classic study of coal mining by Thomas S. Ashton and Joseph Sykes (Manchester, 1929; 2d ed., 1964) has been by no means superseded. Of the three recent general surveys, Brian Lewis's *Coal Mining in the Eighteenth and Nineteenth Centuries* (Harlow, 1971) and Alan R. Griffin's *The British Coalmining Industry: Retrospect and Prospect* (Buxton, 1977) are principally concerned with later developments, and Griffin's *Coalmining* (Harlow, 1971) is mostly an essay in industrial archaeology. More useful is John R. Harris's "Skills, Coal, and British Industry in the Eighteenth Century" (*History* 61, 1976: 167–182), an important assessment. Studies of individual coal fields are more useful: F. Atkinson, *The Great Northern Coalfield, 1700–1900* (Durham, 1968); I. Leister, *The Sea-Coal Mine and the Durham Miners* (Durham, 1968); R. French, *Coals from Newcastle: The Story of the North-east Coal Trade in the Days of Sail* (Lavenham, 1973); A. R. Griffin, *Mining in the East Midlands 1550–1947* (London, 1971); and D. Anderson, *The Orrell Coalfield, Lancashire, 1740–1850* (Buxton, 1975). The history of iron has been much more thoroughly rewritten than that of coal, with heavy emphasis on technological innovation. Three general studies are Alan Birch's *The Economic History of the British Iron and Steel Industry 1784–1879: Essays in Industrial and Economic History with Special Reference to the Development of Technology* (London and New York,

1967); Walter K. V. Gale's *The British Iron and Steel Industry: A Technical History* (Newton Abbot, 1967); and most important, Charles K. Hyde's *Technological Change and the British Iron Industry 1700–1870* (Princeton, N.J., 1977). The most useful regional study is Barry Trinder, editor's *"The Most Extraordinary District in the World": Ironbridge and Coalbrookdale* (London, 1977). Steel, still a luxury good during the reign, is discussed by Cyril S. Smith in *Sources for the History of the Science of Steel 1532–1786* (Cambridge, Mass., 1968). For lead mining in the Pennines and northeast, Arthur Raistrick and Bernard Jenning's *A History of Lead-Mining in the Pennines* (London, 1965) is the definitive survey.

The literature on economic development between 1760 and 1820 so far described has been composed with surprisingly little reference to its impact on the men and women who participated in it. The themes are usually strictly economic or technological development, the operation of impersonal economic forces, or the construction and application of theoretical models. We certainly understand what happened, and to a degree why it happened, much better than we used to do. But the cost has been considerable: more and more an economic history with people left out. They have not, however, been forgotten. The literature on the social effects of economic change has been as extensive and frequently more contentious than that on the causes and course of the changes; and in much of it, the work of the economic historians has been as much ignored or misunderstood as it used to be. The "new" social historians (or as some of them call themselves, the "socialist historians") of the working classes in particular write in terms of a vigorous revival of the old "pessimistic" interpretation especially associated with the Hammonds, arguing that the effects of industrialization and the other changes were almost uniformly deleterious to most people until far into the nineteenth century.

An increasingly ill-tempered debate between Eric J. Hobsbawm for the reviving pessimists and Ronald M. Hartwell for the entrenched optimists over the standard of living during industrialization in the *Economic History Review* between 1957 and 1964 foreshadowed, indeed helped to provoke, the still-continuing controversy. The culmination of their exchanges, a "discussion" (*EcHR*, 2d ser., 16, 1963–1964: 119–146), only confirmed how irreconcilable their respective positions were. In so far as standards of living could be measured objectively, Hartwell seemed to have the better case, with Hobsbawm increasingly pressing arguments for the deteriorating "quality" of life and for Marxian rigidities of interpretation. Hobsbawm's position, however, simultaneously received powerful and independent support in Edward P. Thompson's *The Making of the English Working Class*, an impassioned portrait of an increasingly degraded and alienated working class, driven by its misery into a class consciousness and a self-conscious ideology that the lower classes had not previously possessed.

Thompson's interpretation combined neo-Marxian, or perhaps more accurately post-Marxian, assumptions with nondoctrinaire early-twentieth-century English socialist-liberal indignation at the Industrial Revolution.

The *Making of the English Working Class* now seems destined to be considered one of the classics of later twentieth-century English historical writing, but its reception at the time by the academic community was frosty. But whatever the historical establishment might think, in many cases quite correctly, of the precision and accuracy of Thompson's scholarship and the validity of many of his interpretations and his presuppositions, his powerful, sympathetic treatment of the working class struck fire in many younger scholars. At its most extreme, the approach he inspired now treats the working class as the only group that mattered in, or was affected by, industrialization; and it concentrates single-mindedly on the shortcomings of the age as the modern socialist intellectual, his eyes fixed on the future, conceives them to have been. While most of the recent work does not go quite this far, the drift everywhere is to overstress the growth of a quasi-revolutionary underground and an alienated, degraded working class as the most prominent features of late Georgian England.

The academic discussion of the standard of living has continued, much of it conveniently assembled in Arthur J. Taylor, editor's *The Standard of Living in the Industrial Revolution* (London, 1975), generally drifting toward a reaffirmation of a diluted optimism.[20] But consensus will never be possible; ultimately the historian's verdict depends not on objective measures but on subjective feelings and presuppositions, on whether one takes a short- or long-term view, and even on where one looks in England and in time for one's evidence. The "new" social historians are certainly not convinced that Thompson and Hobsbawm have gone too far. Their subsequent work has produced much new information on working-class conditions and culture, on popular movements and disturbances, and on poverty. Equally important, they have stimulated their critics and opponents to reexamine the evidence and to reconsider views that had become academic orthodoxy. Among the more general investigations of the working classes from the new point of view, John Foster's controversial *Class Struggle and the Industrial Revolution: Early Industrial Capitalism in Three English Towns* (London, 1975), a study of the quite different industrializing communities of Oldham, South Shields, and Northampton, is rigidly neo-Marxian. Malcolm I. Thomis's *Responses to Industrialization: The British Experience 1780–1850* (Newton Abbot, 1976) is the most important survey from the other side, arguing that the impact of industrialization was much less devastating than the new school thinks, that the benefits were very considerable for many of the lower classes, and that their response was far from unrelievedly hostile to the new order. Thomis's *The Town Labourer and the Industrial Revolution* (London, 1974), a thorough reconsideration of the Hammonds' famous book on the subject, is also highly critical of the new version of the supposed degradation of the laborers. Most of E. P. Thompson's recent work discusses aspects of working-class life outside the factory or workshop; while he continues to emphasize the growth of self-conscious class identity, the thrust of his articles is toward a description of lower-class culture.[21]

Popular protests have fared particularly well. George Rudé's continuing studies of mobs and riots, begun in the 1950s, have illuminated the composition of eighteenth-century mobs and underlined the changing character of popular protest in the period. His *Paris and London in the Eighteenth Century: Studies in Popular Protest* (London, 1971) collects his shorter studies, while *The Crowd in History 1730–1848* (New York, 1964) is an important comparative study of England and France. So too is Gwyn A. Williams's *Artisans and Sans culottes: Popular Movements in France and Britain during the French Revolution* (London, 1968). E. P. Thompson's "The Moral Economy of the Crowd in the Eighteenth Century" (*PP*, no. 50, 1971: 76–136) is an illuminating study of the surprisingly nonviolent disorder of the hunger rioters. Walter J. Shelton, in *English Hunger and Industrial Disorder: A Study of Social Conflict during the First Decade of George III's Reign* (Toronto, 1975), analyzes a very disturbed period; the essays collected in John Stevenson and Robert Quinault, editors' *Popular Protest and Public Order: Six Studies in British History, 1790–1820* (London, 1975) shed light on an even more tumultous period. David J. V. Jones's *Before Rebecca: Popular Protests in Wales 1793–1835* (London, 1973) discusses a long series of disturbances. John Stevenson's *Popular Disturbances in England, 1700–1870* (London, 1979) provides a longer perspective. Accounts of popular protest and lower-class alienation merge with studies of popular political radicalism and reform agitation as well as with the literature on more formal industrial relations and on strikes. Labor disputes on Tyneside during the reign have been thoroughly investigated; a few articles explore other examples of Georgian labor relations.[22] Malcolm I. Thomis's *The Luddites: Machine Breaking in Regency England* (Newton Abbot, 1970), essentially a reply to E. P. Thompson's extravagant praise of the movement, is the most important recent general study, supplemented by his edited collection of Home Office documents, *Luddism in Nottinghamshire* (Thoroton Society, Record Series 26, 1972).

The problems of poverty and poor relief have attracted as much attention as lower-class agitation, although much recent work has focused on the New Poor Law of 1834 and its immediate antecedents in the workings of the Old Poor Law in the 1820s. Norman J. Smith's brief *Poverty in England 1601–1936* (Newton Abbot, 1972) and Geoffrey W. Oxley's *Poor Relief in England and Wales 1601–1834* (Newton Abbot, 1974) provide a general perspective, as does a significant article by A. W. Coats, "The Relief of Poverty, Attitudes to Labor, and Economic Change in England, 1660–1782" (*International Review of Social History* 21, 1976: 95–115). Brian Inglis's *Poverty and the Industrial Revolution* (London, 1971), the most extensive consideration of the situation in the later eighteenth and early nineteenth centuries, condemns the men of the time in the too-usual manner of the "new" historians and is based almost wholly on printed sources, as are studies of changing ideas about poor relief by Raymond C. Cowherd (Athens, Ohio, 1977) and John R. Poynter (London, 1969).

Much had been written before 1965 on slavery, the slave trade, and the abolition movement, but more work has been published since than in the whole previous period. Some of it goes over familiar ground from similar points of view, but the best work is excellent indeed. All English problems and actions on the subject in the reign of George III are placed in the broadest perspective in two outstanding books by David B. Davis, *The Problem of Slavery in Western Culture* (Ithaca, N.Y., 1966) and, more immediately relevant, *The Problem of Slavery in the Age of Revolution 1770–1823* (Ithaca, N.Y., 1975). The condition of the blacks in Britain is investigated by James Walvin in *Black and White: The Negro and English Society 1555–1945* (London, 1973) and in his collection of documents, *The Black Presence: A Documentary History of the Negro in England, 1555–1860* (London, 1971) and also by Folarin O. Shyllon in *Black People in Britain 1555–1833* (Oxford, 1977). Those among them who were slaves are the subject of Shyllon's *Black Slaves in Britain* (Oxford, 1974), an impassioned but closely argued criticism of Lord Mansfield's decision in the Somerset Case (1772), previously believed to have outlawed slavery in Britain. Another important recent discussion of Mansfield's decision is William M. Wiecek's "Somerset: Lord Mansfield and the Legitimacy of Slavery in the Anglo-American World" (*University of Chicago Law Review* 42, 1974: 86–146). The British attitude toward the black, even when striving to free him, is the subject of Anthony J. Barker's *The African Link: British Attitudes to the Negro in the Era of the Atlantic Slave Trade 1550–1807* (Totowa, N.J., 1978) and of Charles H. Lyons's *To Wash an Aethiope White: British Ideas about Black African Educability, 1530–1960* (New York, 1975).

The outstanding account of the closely linked problems of the slave trade, the profitability of slavery in the West Indies, and the abolition movement in England is Roger Anstey's *The Atlantic Slave Trade and British Abolition 1760–1810* (London, 1975). Seymour Drescher's *Econside* (Pittsburgh, Pa., 1977), another major general account, is a vigorous restatement of the case of humanitarianism as the principal motive for abolition. The major work on the volume of the slave trade is Philip D. Curtin's *The Atlantic Slave Trade: A Census* (Madison, Wis., 1969). The value of the trade and the profitability of slavery are more difficult to discover than the numbers of slaves. Much discussion continues to center around the thesis of Eric Williams, advanced in 1941, that slavery was abolished only when and because it had ceased to be profitable, a view very severely criticized by Anstey, Stanley L. Engermann, and Howard Temperley in articles. The most recent attempts to measure profitability differ among themselves. The abolition movement, first of the trade and, when this was accomplished, of slavery itself, have most recently been the subject of Dale H. Parker's *The Abolition of the Slave Trade in England 1784–1807* (Hamden, Conn., 1970) and Edith M. Hurwitz's *Politics and the Public Conscience: Slave Emigration and the Abolition Movement in Britain* (New York, 1973).

Crime, often treated as the result of poverty provoked by economic change, and punishment, as the revenge of the established upon the unfortunate, have received attention of a very different sort from the older, anecdotal, romanticized treatment of highwaymen and the like. In part inspired by the superb study of the criminal law and its enforcement by Sir Leon Radzinowitz—*A History of the English Criminal Law and Its Administration from 1750* (4 vols., London, 1948–1968)—which has placed the study of the subject on new foundations, the recent work has also drawn on present-day interests in criminology, criminal justice, and penal reform. Much of the best work is collected in J. S. Cockburn, editor's *Crime in England 1550–1800* (London, 1977), which includes an excellent critical bibliography by L. A. Kafla on "Crime and Criminal Justice" (pp. 270–293), and in the Douglas Hay et al. *Albion's Fatal Tree: Crime and Society in Eighteenth-century England* (London, 1975). Other studies have approached crime through analyses of the records concerning the men and women transported to Australia, most of whom were "ordinary" criminals, not the political deportees of legend; the most comprehensive studies are by Lloyd L. Robson (Victoria and New York, 1965) and Alan G. L. Shaw (London, 1966). J. M. Beattie's "The Pattern of Crime in England, 1660–1800" (*PP*, no. 62, 1974: 47–95) and "The Criminality of Women in Eighteenth-century England" (*Journal of Social History* 8, 1975–1976: 80–116) are important essays.

Other books investigate prisons. The best is Michael Ignatieff's *A Just Measure of Pain: Penitentiaries in the Industrial Revolution 1750–1850* (New York, 1978). Prison reform has its own literature. J. R. S. Whiting's *Prison Reform in Gloucestershire 1776–1820: A Study of the Work of Sir George Onisiphorus Paul, Bart.* (London, 1975) is excellent on a leading practical reformer. Ursula R. Q. Henriques, in "The Rise and Decline of the Separate System of Prison Discipline" (*PP*, no. 54, 1972: 61–93), considers a central theme in the penal reform movement. Bentham's contribution is discussed in the general works on him cited below and in Barbee-Sue Rodman's "Bentham and the Paradox of Penal Reform" (*Journal of the History of Ideas* 29, 1968: 97–210). His Panopticon is discussed by L. J. Hume in *Historical Studies* (16, 1974: 36–54) and by Gertrude Himmelfarb in a most critical essay in her *Victorian Minds* (London, 1968, 32–81), where she argues that Bentham's scheme was not nearly as public minded, if eccentric, as is generally assumed.

Historical demography has been one of the most vigorously cultivated specialties in recent years, with much of the work concentrated on the reign of George III in an attempt to account for the dramatic change in the rate of growth that began about 1750 and was so closely connected with all the other economic and social developments of the period. Most of the scholars working on the subject appear to be approaching a consensus about the probable numbers of the British people in the eighteenth century and the general pattern of growth, but they still disagree among themselves about nearly everything else. We remain as far as ever from agreement about such fundamental questions as the causes of the population explosion and its impact on the economic transformation. The demographers are still debating whether it was a cause or a consequence of economic growth and whether the increase occurred because of a rising birth rate, a falling death rate, changes in fertility (either biological or induced by changing ages of marriage), improved nutrition, medical advances, all possible combinations of these factors, or none of them. Possibly the new and very complex approaches of family reconstitution and computer-based simulation studies may provide a solution, but so far they have only added to the confusion and uncertainty.

The methodology of modern historical demography, as well as indications of the state of conflicting interpretations in the mid-1960s, can be found in E. A. Wrigley, editor's *Introduction to English Historical Demography: From the Sixteenth to the Nineteenth Century* (London, 1966). Wrigley's subsequent *Nineteenth-century Society: Essays in the Use of Quantitative Methods for the Study of Social Data* (Cambridge, 1972) is important for methodology for all the newer sorts of historical sociology as well as for demography. Other important earlier studies on population, most of them written since the mid-1950s and ten of them directly concerned with eighteenth- and early-nineteenth-century England, are collected in D. V. Glass and D. E. C. Eversley, editors' *Population in History: Essays in Historical Demography* (London and Chicago, 1965). H. J. Habakkuk's *Population Growth and Economic Development since 1750* (Leicester, 1971) is an excellent worldwide survey, clear and comprehensive, which relates English patterns to those elsewhere. Michael W. Flinn's *British Population Growth 1700–1850* (London, 1970), a dispassionate general study, is the best brief discussion of all the probable causes for growth and the manner in which it took place. The pre-Malthusian eighteenth-century controversy over whether the population was declining or increasing and the resulting development of census-taking are thoroughly discussed in D. V. Glass's *Numbering the People: The Eighteenth-century Population Controversy and the Development of Census and Vital Statistics in Britain* (Farnborough, Hantshire, 1973). Thomas McKeown's *The Modern Rise of Population* (London, 1976) is an important study emphasizing improvements in nutrition and the control of infectious diseases. Much obviously remains to be done everywhere, but many more local studies, tedious as they are to compile and to study, seem to be the most promising approach to the solution of the many remaining problems.

The implications of family reconstitution and some of the other methodologies used by the historical demographers extend beyond the problems of population growth to become part of the underpinnings of another flourishing new approach to social history of a different sort from either the "new" history of the working classes or the descriptive and anecdotal "pots and pans" approach that used commonly to be written. This sort of "new" social history, really historical sociology, concentrates on the history of the family in all its ramifications, on social and professional groups as groups, and on the changing structure of society. It is heavily indebted to methodologies and concepts borrowed from sociology and social anthropology and is often quantitative and statistical in its foundations. At its best it has been presented without the disfiguring jargon and methodological rigidity of its relatives and has opened significant new vistas.

The manifesto for the new approach, Peter Laslett's *The World We Have Lost* (London, 1965), in its somewhat less strident second edition (London, 1971) is still a useful introduction to this "new" social history and to the old society being undermined during the reign of George III, even though Laslett still exaggerates the originality of the information now available and the usefulness of the new methodologies and though he overstates how completely the preindustrial world has been lost. Laslett's subsequent work in collaboration with other members of the Cambridge Group for the History of Population and Social Structure in *Household and Family in Past Time: Comparative Studies in the Size and Structure of the Domestic Group over the Last Three Centuries* (Cambridge, 1972) and in his own *Family Life and Illicit Love in Earlier Centuries* (Cambridge, 1977), largely a statistical study of the incidence of bastardy, is a substantial contribution to the history of the family and family life through the eighteenth century at all social levels. Perhaps the most important book yet published on the subject, however, is Lawrence Stone's *The Family, Sex and Marriage in England 1500–1800* (New York, 1977), nearly half of which is devoted to the eighteenth century. Much of Stone's material for the century is necessarily derivative, often repetitious, sometimes controversial, and some of his major illustrations for general themes are questionably representative; but the book as a whole is a most impressive recasting of our understanding of basic social institutions and structures in the process of fundamental transformation. Randolph Trumbach's *The Rise of the Egalitarian Family: Aristocratic Kinship and Domestic Relations in Eighteenth-century England* (New York, 1978) is more restricted in scope than Stone or the work of the Cambridge Group and, though written independently of them, continues their direction and is excellent on changing patterns of life among the upper classes.

The role of women in the late eighteenth century, with the exception of the fascination with Mary Wollstonecraft,[23] has not captured the attention that might have been expected, although their changing position is a very prominent theme in the new work on the family and marriage. The most important studies outside these books are two articles: Neil McKendrick's "Home Demand and Economic Growth: A New View of the Role of Women and Children in the Industrial Revolution" (in Neil McKendrick, ed., *Historical Perspectives*, London, 1974, 177–210), which argues that their increased consumption of goods at all social levels was both a cause and an effect of industrialization and had very important social consequences, and Eric Richards's "Women in the British Economy since About 1700: An Interpretation" (*History* 59, 1974: 337–357), a somewhat different view stressing those who produced rather than those who consumed. Most of the other essays and books, however, continue to concentrate on the Bluestockings, women authors and women in philanthropy, all familiar themes. With the exception of J. H. Plumb's "The New World of Children in the Eighteenth Century" (*PP*, no. 67, 1975: 64–95), children have received much the same merely descriptive treatment as ever, even in the two volumes of Ivy Pinchbeck and Margaret Hewitt, *Children in English Society* (London, 1968–1973).

Other studies influenced by the new historical sociology have concentrated on the changes brought about in working-class families by industrialization and urbanization, on the development of the professions and on social structure in general. The pioneering work on working-class families was Neil Smelser's study of Lancashire millworkers in 1959. Michael Anderson has carried the approach further in his *Family Structure in Nineteenth-century Lancashire* (Cambridge, 1971), a model study of Preston. Two suggestive articles are Hans Medick's "The Proto-industrial Family Economy: The Structural Function of Household and Family during the Transition from Peasant Society to Industrial Capitalism" (*Social History* 3, 1976: 291–315) and E. A. Wrigley's "The Process of Modernization and the Industrial Revolution in England" (*Journal of Interdisciplinary History* 3, 1972–1973: 225–259).

The "new" urban history so vigorously pursued in recent years, like most of the other major recent departures from old areas of study, has been strongly influenced by concern with twentieth-century urban problems, by the methodologies and assumptions of the social sciences, and by statistics and quantification. But again, as in the new social histories, the best work rises above its methodological underpinning to become description and narrative much richer than most of the old histories of towns and cities—and of counties, parishes, and villages, too, because the new approach has affected local history generally, not just that of urban communities. Harold J. Dyos, editor's *The Study of Urban History* (New York, 1968) is a useful introduction to the new concerns and methodologies. Comprehensive studies of eighteenth- and early-nineteenth-century urban England are G. E. Cherry's *Urban Change and Planning: A History of Urban Development since 1750* (Henley-on-Thames, 1972), Colin J. Bell and Rose Bell's *City Fathers: The Early History of Town Planning in Britain* (London, 1969), and C. W. Chalkin's *The Provincial Towns of Georgian England: A Study of the Building Process 1740–1820* (Montreal, 1974). I. A. Adams, in *The Making of Urban Scotland* (London, 1978), and R. A. Butlin, editor, in *The Development of the Irish Town* (London, 1977), survey of the other parts of Britain. Housing, especially for the working classes, is developing its own literature. Recent studies include Stanley D. Chapman, editor's *The History of Working-class Housing: A Symposium* (Newton Abbot, 1971), Enid Gauldie's *Cruel Habitations: A History of Working-class Housing, 1780–1918* (London, 1974), and M. A. Simpson and T. H. Lloyd, editors' *Middle-class Housing in Britain* (Newton, Abbot, 1977).

Much recent work takes the familiar form of histories of individual towns, sometimes less concerned with town planning and the "structures" of urban life and growth than the newest urban history, but all of them more concerned with these subjects and with the economic life of the towns and of the mass of their inhabitants than used to be common. London itself defies comprehensive treatment, although several outstanding books have appeared. The best are George Rudé's *Hanoverian London 1714–1808* (London, 1971), concentrating on the life and activity of the city outside the West End, and its companion volume in a new series of London histories, Francis H. W. Sheppard's *London 1808–1870: The Infernal Wen* (London, 1971). Donald J. Olsen's *Town Planning in London: The Eighteenth and Nineteenth Centuries* (New Haven, Conn., 1964), principally a study of the development of the Bedford and Foundling Hospital estates, is as much concerned with social history as it is with town planning. Olsen's *The Growth of Victorian London* (London, 1976) goes back to the end of the eighteenth century and is written in the same broad interpretative framework. Francis M. L. Thompson's *Hampstead: Building a Borough, 1650–1964* (London, 1975) is a model study covering every aspect of urban and social development.

Among the studies of the other larger towns, John Money's *Experience and Identity: Birmingham and the West Midlands 1760–1800* (Manchester, 1977) is one of the more interesting treatments in that it integrates the history of the town with its larger neighborhood. Wilfrid H. Thomson's *History of Manchester to 1852* (Altrincham, 1967) is the first modern general history of the cotton metropolis; P. M. Horsely's *Eighteenth-century Newcastle* (Newcastle, 1971) is the most recent study of the great coal center. Other books are Jack Simmons's *Leicester Past and Present* (2 vols., Newton Abbot, 1974), Malcolm I. Thomis's *Politics and Society in Nottingham, 1785–1835* (Newton Abbot, 1969), Alfred T. Patterson's *A History of Southampton, 1700–1914*, volume 1, *An Oligarchy in Decline 1700–1835* (Southampton, 1966), Sir Francis Hill's *Georgian Lincoln*

(Cambridge, 1966), Alan Armstrong's *Stability and Change in an English County Town: A Social Study of York 1801–51* (Cambridge, 1974), F. Mason's *Wolverhampton: The Town Commissioners, 1778–1848* (Wolverhampton, 1977), Roy Brook's *The Story of Huddersfield* (London, 1968), and H. Hughes's *Chronicles of Chester: The Two Hundred Years, 1775–1975* (London, 1975). The more recent volumes of the Victoria Histories of the Counties of England are also infused with the spirit and approach of the new urban and local history in their general chapters, although unhappily still confined to their older manorial framework everywhere else. Even these parts, however, now incorporate economic and social material in a manner unknown in the older volumes.

The history of education under George III is in a much less happy condition than most other branches of social history. The previous neglect, however, is slowly being reduced through more systematic attention to evidence about earlier elementary schools and by studies of the extent of literacy in the eighteenth century, but as yet the material is still scattered in articles. The most useful of these include Lawrence Stone's "Literacy and Education in England, 1640–1900" (*PP*, no. 42, 1969: 42–139), a survey of the probable extent of literacy over a long period; R. S. Schofield's "Dimensions of Illiteracy, 1750–1850" (*Explorations in Economic History*, 2d ser., 10, 1972–1973: 437–454); Michael Sanderson's "Literacy and Social Mobility in the Industrial Revolution in England" (*PP*, no. 56, 1972: 75–104); and a debate between Sanderson and Thomas W. Laqueur on the same subject (*PP*, no. 64, 1974: 96–112). Some substantial material on the private venture schools of all sorts is assembled in Laqueur's "Working-class Demand and the Growth of English Elementary Education, 1750–1850" (in Lawrence Stone, ed., *Schools and Society: Studies in the History of Education*, Baltimore, 1976, 192–205). Laqueur has also published an important book on the Sunday schools, *Religion and Respectability: Sunday Schools and Working-class Culture, 1780–1850* (New Haven, Conn., 1976). The only important book on secondary education in the past fifteen years is Richard S. Tompson's *Classics or Charity? The Dilemma of the Eighteenth-century Grammar School* (Manchester, 1971). Higher education has fared even worse, if possible. With the exception of three essays—Sheldon Rothblatt's "The Student Subculture and the Examination System in Early Nineteenth-century Oxbridge" and Arthur Engle's "The Emerging Concept of the Academic Profession at Oxford, 1800–1854" (both in Lawrence Stone, ed., *The University in Society*, vol. 1, *Oxford and Cambridge from the Fourteenth to the Early Nineteenth Centuries*, Princeton, N.J., 1974, 247–303, 305–352) and William J. Baker's "Beyond Port and Prejudice: Oxford's Renaissance Exemplified, 1808–1811" (*HLQ* 39, 1976: 133–149), a further illustration of the new day dawning at Oxford—there has been little of substance. Stone's long introductory study of changing enrollments from the sixteenth century to the present, also in *The University in Society* (pp. 3 – 110) does discuss the reasons for the decline in attendance and the changing structure of the student body during the reign of George III, but only in relation to larger themes.

Incidental evidence for the spread of literacy continues to be provided by the occasional studies of the growth of the popular press. Miscellaneous information on the growth of newspapers is contained in two recent collections of essays of varying quality: Donovan H. Bon, editor's *Newsletter to Newspapers: Eighteenth-century Journalism* (Morgantown, W. Va., 1978) and James Currier et al., editors' *Newspaper History: From the Seventeenth Century to the Present Day* (Beverley Hills, Calif., 1978). Lucyle Werkmeister's *A Newspaper History of England, 1792 – 1793* (Lincoln, Neb., 1967) is undigested, marred by excessive Foxite prejudice, and much less satisfactory than her *The London Daily Press 1772 – 1792* (Lincoln, Neb., 1963). More balanced are two essays by Ian R. Christie in his *Myth and Reality in Late-eighteenth-century British Politics and Other Papers:* "British Newspapers in the Later Georgian Age" (pp. 311 – 333) and "James Perry of the *Morning Chronicle* 1756 – 1821" (334 – 358). Potentially as valuable for the spread of reading and self-improvement as work on newspapers and periodicals are studies such as Paul Kaufman's brief "The Community Library: A Chapter in English Social History" (*Transactions of the American Philosophical Society*, n.s., 57, pt. 7, 1967) and Thomas Kelly's *Early Public Libraries: A History of Public Libraries in Great Britain to 1880* (London, 1966).

The life of the aristocracy, the landed classes, and the more prosperous middle classes, which once loomed so large in descriptions of English society in the reign of George III, has been neglected in recent years, with the exception of studies of their economic activities and a prominent place in the growing literature on the family. Two exceptions are Gordon E. Mingay's *The Gentry: The Rise and Fall of a Governing Class* (London and New York, 1976) and Mark Girouard's *Life in the English County House: A Social and Architectural History* (New Haven, Conn., 1978), neither confined to the eighteenth century. A strikingly different view from the usual financial success stories of the great families appears in Ray A. Kelch's *Newcastle: A Duke without Money* (Berkeley, 1974), a splendid case study of what extravagance, neglect, and mismanagement could do to the greatest estate and fortune if the possessor did not behave in the manner of the "improving" business-minded aristocrat. Aubrey N. Newman's *The Stanhopes of Chevening: A Family Biography* (London, 1969) is a model for how studies of the great families should be done; Lord David Cecil's *The Cecils of Hatfield House* (London, 1973) is a masterpiece of the genre, written from the inside with much on the family in the eighteenth century. By way of partial contrast with studies of the great landed families are two excellent books on prosperous upper-middle-class families, Sydney G. Checkland's *The Gladstones: A Family Biography, 1764–1850* (Cambridge, 1971) and Mary Hyde's *The Thrales of Streatham Park* (Cambridge, Mass., 1977).

Finally, numerous monographs on sports and recreation are also expanding our understanding: Roger Longrigg's *The English Squire and His Sport* (New York, 1977); three full-scale histories of fox hunting by Longrigg (London, 1975), Raymond Carr (London, 1976), and David C. Itzkowitz (Hassocks, 1977); R. Onslow's *The Heath and the Turf: A History of Newmarket* (London, 1971); W. Vamplew's *The Turf: A Social and Economic History* (London, 1976); John C. Reid's *Bucks and Bruisers: Pierce Egan and Regency England* (London, 1971); Rowland Bowen's *Cricket: A History of Its Growth and Development* (London, 1970); John Ford's *Prize-fighting: The Age of Regency Boximania* (Newton Abbot, 1971); and J. P. Jones's *Gambling Yesterday and Today: A Complete History* (Newton Abbot, 1973).

A few general studies of social subjects probe deeply and illuminate as well as describe the life of the times. Especially interesting are the essays by J. H. Plumb, Neil McKendrick, and John Brewer assembled in *The Birth of the Consumer Society: The Commercial Revolution of the Eighteenth Century* (London, 1979) discussing the commercialization of childhood, leisure, consumer spending, and politics in the later eighteenth century; taken together they suggest fundamental changes in the character of society taking place rapidly during the reign of George III. John Burnett's *A History of the Cost of Living* (Harmondsworth, 1969) is a good social history based on extensive research into the history of prices and styles of life. Burnett's *Plenty and Want: A Social History of Diet in England from 1815 to the Present Day* (London, 1966) and Derek Oddy and Derek Miller, editors' *The Making of the Modern British Diet* (London, 1976) are serious studies of changes in diet. Richard D. Altick's *The Shows of London* (Cambridge, Mass., 1978) is a fascinating account of all sorts of popular entertainments, exhibitions, and the like, mostly in the late eighteenth and early nineteenth centuries. Robert W. Malcolmson's *Popular Recreations in English Society 1700–1850* (Cambridge, 1973) and Hugh Cunningham's *Leisure in the Industrial Revolution, c. 1780–c. 1880* (New York, 1980) are serious studies in social history that discuss changes in recreation in relation to social and economic changes.

How far have all these strands of investigation into the lives of late Georgian Englishmen, all these new methods of analysis and new fields of study, been combined into a general recasting of the social history of the age? Not very far. The professed concern of so many of the "new" social historians for elucidating the human condition under the impact of industrialization has been as yet singularly unrewarding. The only good surveys are Harold Perkin's *The Origins of Modern English Society, 1730–1880* (London, 1969), an excellent study, and Vincent T. J. Arkell's *Britain Transformed: The Development of British Society since the Mid-eighteenth Century* (Harmondsworth, 1973). M. Dorothy George's *Hogarth to Cruickshank: Social Change in Graphic Satire* (London, 1967), is a splendid visual presentation of the age with an excellent commentary. Some of the general economic histories also contain extensive discussions of the social effects of economic change. Among the best of the older sorts of descriptive, anecdoctal histories are André Parreaux's *La societé anglaise de 1760 à 1810* (Paris, 1966, trans. Carola Cagreve as *Daily Life in England in the Reign of George III*, London, 1969); Elizabeth Burton Burton's *The Georgians at Home, 1714–1830* (London, 1967) by an indefatigable chronicler of "home life" through the ages; Roger Hunt's *English Life in the Eighteenth Century* (New York, 1970); and more restricted in scope, Donald A. Low's *That Sunny Dome: A Portrait of Regency Britain* (London 1977).

The artistic, cultural, and intellectual life of late Georgian England is too often a separate world from the rest of the age—chapters tacked onto accounts of what too many historians consider more central matters of life and governance. This unfortunate isolation of the arts is the inevitable result of the manner in which all subjects are now treated. The progressive fragmentation of knowledge through specialization makes many economic and political historians seem indifferent to, even ignorant of, the artistic and intellectual accomplishments of the age, while the art and literary historians appear ill-informed and unconcerned about the social, economic, and political foundations of the late eighteenth century. These mutual defects are a little less pronounced in some of the best work (and the best is very good indeed) on the fine arts—architecture, painting, sculpture—but they are very apparent in many of the recent books on the decorative arts. Studies of furniture design, china and porcelain, silver and pewter, and interior decoration continue to be directed too exclusively to the collector and connoisseur rather than being perceived as parts of a wider historical whole. Literary history is often anecdotal or concerned with unraveling the psyche of an author, while modern literary criticism is everywhere more concerned with the timeless features of the literary work than with the older approach to the work of art as a reflection of its age. The historian of ideas too often fails to achieve his aim of elucidating the essential intellectual character of the age. He concentrates instead on the major intellectual monuments rather than on the watered-down, muddled versions of fundamental ideas as they appear in widely held notions and assumptions; pursues byways rather than the mainstream of ideas; or devotes himself to currently fashionable but not very representative thinkers and themes. But these limitations have certainly not impeded the production of books and articles.

The recent history of the fine and decorative arts revolves around the "rediscovery" of neoclassicism. The major books on the "new" neoclassicism are David Irwin's *English Neoclassical Art: Studies in Inspiration and Taste* (London,

1966) with an important bibliography, Hugh Honour's *Neo-classicism* (Harmondsworth, 1968), James W. Johnson's *The Formation of English Neo-classical Thought* (Princeton, N.J., 1967), and Robert Rosenblum's *Transformations in Late Eighteenth-century Art* (Princeton, N.J., 1967).

Two books investigate the relations between the arts and literature, principally in terms of romanticism: Mario Praz's *Mnemosyne: The Parallel between Literature and the Visual Arts* (Princeton, N.J., 1970) and Peter Quennell's *Romantic England: Writing and Painting 1717–1851* (London, 1970). Edward G. Malins's *English Landscaping and Literature 1660–1840* (Oxford, 1966) is also concerned with the same theme. Another general book, primarily concerned with painting and caricature, is Ronald Paulson's *Emblem and Expression* (London, 1975), by a Hogarth and Rowlandson scholar who has been carried away by the symbolic elements in all the eighteenth-century arts.

The best brief introductions to the individual fine arts are still the relevant chapters in the latest editions of the volumes in the Pelican History of Art (Harmondsworth): Sir John Summerson's *Architecture in Britain, 1530–1830* (1953; 5th ed., 1969), Ellis K. Waterhouse's *Painting in Britain, 1530–1790* (1953; 4th ed., 1978), and Margaret D. Whinney's *Sculpture in Britain, 1530–1830* (1964). Joseph Burke's *English Art 1714–1800* (Oxford, 1976) is an important general treatment of all the fine arts, is the subsequent volume in the Oxford History of English Art by Thomas S. R. Boase, *English Art 1800–1870* (Oxford, 1959).

The completion in 1974 of Sir Nikolas Pevsner's *The Buildings of England* (Harmondsworth), begun in 1951, and new editions of many of the earlier volumes have provided an absolutely indispensable description of all important surviving buildings of the period. Joseph M. Crook's *The Greek Revival: Neoclassical Attitudes in British Architecture, 1790–1870* (London, 1972) and Dora Wiebenson's *Sources of Greek Revival Architecture* (London, 1969) follow the new interest in neoclassicism into architecture. Desmond Guinness and Julius T. Sadler, Jr.'s *The Palladian Style in England, Ireland and America* (New York, 1976) is the latest general treatment of that by-no-means-moribund style. Geoffrey W. Beard's *The Work of Robert Adam* (Edinburgh, 1968) is the most recent book on his architecture. John Harris's *Sir William Chambers, Knight of the Pole Star* (London, 1970) describes the life and work of a man who was influential in introducing the Chinese vogue in gardening. Dorothy Stroud has published major studies of Henry Holland (London, 1966) and George Dance (London, 1971). Terence Davis's *John Nash, the Prince Regent's Architect* (London, 1966) is the most recent biography. The most substantial recent work on Sir John Soane is Pierre Du Prey's *John Soane's Architectural Education 1753–80* (New York, 1977). Hermione Hobhouse, in *Thomas Cubbitt: Master Builder* (London, 1971), considers the work of a man whose "mass-produced" houses were already beginning to affect the appearance of London in the first two decades of the nine-teenth century. Landscape gardening merges with the history of architecture. The publication of *The Red Books of Humphry Repton* (4 vols., 1976) makes available the major source of late-eighteenth-century design. David Jarrett's *The English Landscape Garden* (London, 1978) is a general account, while Kenneth Woodbridge's *Landscape and Antiquity: Aspects of English Culture at Stourhead 1718 to 1838* (Oxford, 1970) discusses one of the most famous English gardens.

General surveys of painting include William Gaunt's *The Great Century of British Painting* (London, 1971), Jean-Jacques Mayoux's *English Painting from Hogarth to the Pre-Raphaelites* (New York, 1975), and David Piper, editor's *The Genius of British Painting* (New York, 1975). Sidney C. Hutchison's *The History of the Royal Academy* (London, 1968) is the most recent account of that famous institution. David Irwin and Francine Irwin's *Scottish Painters at Home and Abroad, 1700–1900* (London, 1975) is comprehensive. Some additional gossip about the art world will become available with the publication of the full version of the *Farrington Dairy, 1793–1821*, of which the first two volumes, edited by Kenneth Garlick and Angus MacIntyre, were published in New Haven, Con-necticut, in 1978, unfortunately unannotated.

Of the recent studies of special types of painting, the important books, most of them now the standard works on their subjects, include Luke Herrmann's *British Landscape Painting of the Eighteenth Century* (London, 1973), discussing both oils and watercolors; Martin Hardie's *Water-colour Painting in Britain* (Dudley Snel-grove et al., eds.), volume 1, *The Eighteenth Century* (New York, 1966), and volume 2 *The Romantic Period* (New York, 1967); Edward Croft-Murray's *Dec-orative Painting in England, 1537–1837*, volume 2, *The Eighteenth and Early Nineteenth Centuries* (London, 1971); Daphne Foskett's *A Dictionary of British Miniature Painters* (2 vols., New York, 1972); Mario Praz's *Conversation Pieces* (University Park, Pa., 1971), one of the most recent studies of this now-popular genre; and Stella A. Walker's *Sporting Art: England 1700–1900* (London, 1972). Two major studies discuss book illustration: Hanns Hammelmann and T. S. R. Boase's *Book Illustration in Eighteenth-century England* (New Haven, Conn., 1975) and Gordon N. Ray's *The Illustrator and the Book from 1790 to 1914* (New York, 1976). Herbert A. Atherton's *Political Prints in the Age of Hogarth* (Oxford, 1974) supplements but does not supersede M. Dorothy George's major study of political caricature in 1960.

Major work has been published on all the leading painters with the exception of Romney, Lawrence, and Robert Wilson, as well as on a number of lesser ones. Hogarth really belongs to the earlier Georgian period, but his influence con-tinued. Ronald Paulson's *Hogarth: His Life, Art and Times* (2 vols., New Haven, Conn., 1971) and *Hogarth's Graphic Works* (New Haven, Conn., 1965; rev. ed., 1970) are definitive. Ellis K. Waterhouse's *Reynolds* (New York, 1973),

by the author of the 1941 catalogue raisonée of Reynolds's work, is the best re-
cent study. John Hayes has studied Gainsborough thoroughly: *The Drawings of
Thomas Gainsborough* (2 vols., New Haven, Conn., 1971), *Gainsborough as
Printmaker* (New Haven, Conn., 1972), and *Gainsborough: Paintings and Draw-
ings* (London, 1975). Stubbs received two biographies in 1971 by Constance A.
Parker and Basil Taylor; Terrance Doherty's *The Anatomical Works of George
Stubbs* (Boston, 1975) supersedes all earlier editions and adds many new repro-
ductions. Roberts C. Alberts's *Benjamin West: A Biography* (Boston, 1978) is far
and away the best study; Jules D. Prown's biography of West's fellow American,
John Singleton Copley (2 vols., Cambridge, Mass., 1966) is definitive. Jack
Lindsay (London, 1966), Graham Reynolds (London, 1969), and Andrew Wil-
son (London, 1979) have written biographies of J. M. W. Turner; John Gage's
Colour in Turner: Poetry and Truth (New York, 1969) is a significant monograph.
More important still is the definitive catalogue raisonée of Turner's work by
Martin Buller and Evelyn Joll, *The Paintings of J. M. W. Turner* (New Haven,
Conn., 1977). Sir Geoffrey Keynes has continued his studies of Blake in *A Study
of the Illustrated Books of William Blake: Poet, Painter, Prophet* (London, 1965)
and in his *Blake Studies: Essays on His Life and Works* (Oxford, 1971); other recent work on Blake is in Morton D. Paley and Michael Phillips, editors' *William Blake: Essays in Honour of Sir Geoffrey Keynes* (Oxford, 1973). Two major
studies of Rowlandson are John Hayes's *Rowlandson: Watercolours and Drawings*
(London, 1972) and Ronald Paulson's *Rowlandson: A New Interpretation* (New
York, 1972). Gillray is the subject of a biography (London, 1965) and a volume
of reproductions (London, 1966) by Draper Hill, while Edwin B. Krumbaar
has published a catalogue raisonée and a brief life of Isaac Cruickshank (Philadelphia, 1966); a double number of the *Princeton University Library Chronicle*
(35, 1973–1974: 1–258) is devoted to a reevaluation of George Cruickshank.

Late Georgian sculpture has attracted less attention than architecture or paint-
ing. The only recent book, and an important one, is John F. Physick's *Designs for
English Sculpture* (London, 1969). N. B. Penny's "The Whig Cult of Fox in
Early Nineteenth-century Sculpture" (*PP*, no. 70, 1976: 94–105) is a model
art-historical essay linking ideas, politics, and art in a most illuminating manner.
Sarah Symons's "The Spirit of Despair: Patronage, Primitivism and the Art of
John Flaxman" (*Burlington Magazine* 117, 1975: 644–650) is one of the most
recent studies of that famous sculptor, while Michael J. McCarthy's "James
Jovell and the Sculptures at Stowe" (*ibid.* 115, 1973: 221–232) is typical of the
work on some of the less well-known ornamental sculptors.

The literature on the decorative arts has been, as usual, very extensive, often
definitive within the narrow confines of one art or the production of one artist or
factory, and almost always beautifully illustrated with examples of the work.
A few books are of somewhat more general scope. Geoffrey Beard's *Georgian*

Craftsmen and Their Work (London, 1966) is a scholarly study of the major decorators and craftsmen at work in the great houses of the century. Anthony Coleridge's *Chippendale Furniture* (London, 1968) is the best study of the subject, and Eileen Harris's *The Furniture of Robert Adam* (London, 1973) is the first serious study. Damie Stillman's *The Decorative Work of Robert Adam* (London, 1966) contributes important information. The new edition by Ralph Fastnedge (London, 1965) of Margaret Jourdain's *Regency Furniture, 1795–1830* is an outstanding guide to the furniture of the late Georgian period. The most useful material on porcelain, chinaware, and pottery is Robert J. Charleston, editor's *English Porcelain, 1745–1850* (London, 1965), with essays on all the major factories and full bibliographies by various experts, and Geoffrey A. Godden's *An Illustrated Encyclopaedia of British Pottery and Porcelain* (London, 1966), the latest in a series of definitive reference works he has compiled. D. Ash's *Dictionary of British Antique Silver* (New York, 1972) and John Hutchins and T. C. Barker's *A History of British Pewter* (London, 1974) are new standard works on their subjects; and Douglas Bennett's *Irish Georgian Silver* (London, 1972) and John Culme's *Nineteenth-century Silver* (London, 1977) are significant monographs. Of considerable interest is E. Delieb's *The Great Silver Manufactory: Matthew Boulton and the Birmingham Silversmiths 1760–1790* (London, 1971) on the development of "mass-produced" silver.

No one has undertaken a comprehensive study of later Georgian science nor of the related history of medicine, but much monographic work building toward these goals has been published. It is ever more clear that British accomplishments in both areas were very considerable and have probably been underestimated in most earlier works. The revised edition of Donald S. L. Cardwell's *The Organization of Science in England* (London, 1972) contains additional material on British science in general. Morris Berman has published a study of the Royal Institution founded in 1799 (Ithaca, N.Y., 1978), and Ian Inkster, a series of articles on the development of a scientific community in Sheffield, an interesting case study, and on the Askesian Society in London.[24] Edward Smith's biography of Sir Joseph Banks (New York, 1973), a significant naturalist, President of the Royal Society from 1778 to 1820, and czar of the sciences for most of the reign, does not really replace that by Hector Cameron. W. J. Sparrow (London, 1964) and Sandborn C. Brown (Cambridge, Mass., 1979) have written biographies of that famous scientific promoter Benjamin Thompson, Count Rumford; and Brown has also edited five volumes of his collected works (Cambridge, Mass., 1968–1970).

A few books range widely in various fields of science. Evan G. A. Taylor's *The Mathematical Practitioners of Hanoverian England, 1714–1840* (Cambridge, 1966) considers many figures. Philip C. Pitterbush's *Overtures to Biology: The Speculations of Eighteenth-century Naturalists* (New Haven, Conn., 1964), mostly concerned with Englishmen and with early experiments with electricity, has an extensive critical bibliography. Cook's voyages made an important contribution to natural history as well as to general intellectual history and the development of the arts. The editions of his journals by John C. Beaglehole (Cambridge, 1955–1967) and Beaglehole's biography (Stanford, Calif., 1974) are definitive. Roy A. Rauschenberg's *Daniel Carl Solander: Naturalist on the Endeavor* (Philadelphia, 1968) discusses one of the scientists who went with Cook and who was temporarily something of a rival to Banks, another passenger on that famous voyage. Other work on natural history has focused on Erasmus Darwin's speculations, the subject of numerous articles and of good modern editions by Desmond C. King-Hele of *The Essential Works of Erasmus Darwin* (London, 1968); the most recent biography is King-Hele's *Doctor of Revolution* (London, 1977). Margaret Deacon's *Scientists and the Sea, 1650–1900: A Study of Marine Science* (London and New York, 1971), Jane M. Oppenheimer's *Essays in the History of Embryology and Biology* (Cambridge, Mass., 1967), and Peter J. Bowler's *Fossils and Progress: Paleontology and the Idea of Progressive Evolution in the Nineteenth Century* (New York, 1976) include much material on England. The development of geology, so fundamental in undermining the received Mosaic chronology and in preparing the ground for the acceptance of progressive change through time, is surveyed to the early nineteenth century in Roy Porter's *The Making of Geology* (Cambridge, 1977) and in Sir Edward B. Bailey's *James Hutton: The Founder of Modern Geology* (Amsterdam and London, 1967), an excellent study of the most important figure in the story and the first "uniformitarian" geologist. The important British contributions to astronomy, especially in the work of William Herschel, his sister Caroline, and his son John, continue to be the subject of numerous articles and an occasional book, without much changing the older views.

Chemistry and physics, still imperfectly differentiated from each other as natural philosophy, underwent even more important developments during the reign of George III than did geology, natural history, and astronomy in the work of Priestley, Black, Dalton, Davy, and Henry Cavendish. Robert E. Schofield's *Mechanics and Materialism: British Natural Philosophy in an Age of Reason* (Princeton, N.J., 1970) is the outstanding general study. David P. Mellor's *The Evolution of the Atomic Theory* (Amsterdam, 1971) and Basil Schonland's *The Atomists 1805–1933* (Oxford, 1968) also discuss general developments. Major critical bibliographical studies of Davy and Dalton are June Z. Fullmer's *Sir Humphry Davy's Published Works* (Cambridge, Mass., 1969) and Albert L. Smyth's *John Dalton, 1766–1844: A Bibliography of Works by and about Him* (Manchester, 1966). The most recent biography of Davy is by Sir Harold B. Hartley, and there have been four of Dalton, including Donald S. L. Cardwell, editor's *John Dalton and the Progress of Science* (Manchester, 1968), Frank Greenaway's *John Dalton and the Atom* (London, 1966), Elizabeth C. Patterson's *John Dalton and*

the Atomic Theory (New York, 1970), and Arnold Thackray's John Dalton: Critical Assessments of His Life and Science (Cambridge, Mass., 1972). Priestley's scientific letters and works have been collected by Robert E. Schofield, editor, in A
Scientific Autobiography of Joseph Priestley, 1733–1804: Selected Scientific Correspondence (Cambridge, Mass., 1966).

   The history of medicine in the reign of George III is still primarily the history
of the advances in surgery pioneered by John and William Hunter and the more
controversial work on smallpox by Jenner, but it is becoming evident that the
epoch contained the birth of modern medicine in other areas as well. The important advances in military medicine, including surgery, nutrition, and primitive
immunology, have received much attention, with the developments related to civilian medicine, in Peter Mathias's "Swords and Plowshares: The Armed Forces,
Medicine, and Public Health in the Late Eighteenth Century" (in J. M. Winter, ed., War and Economic Development, Cambridge, 1978, 73–90). Peter H.
Niegyl, in "The English Bloodletting Revolution, or Modern Medicine before
1850" (Bulletin of the History of Medicine 51, 1977: 464–483), discusses a fundamental change in medical practice. E. M. Sigsworth, in "Gateways to Death?
Medicine, Hospitals, and Mortality, 1700–1850" (in Peter Mathias, ed., Science and Society 1600–1900, Cambridge, 1972, 97–110), considers the debated
role of hospitals in medical development. More general histories of medicine,
most of them not limited to England, include G. R. Williams's The Age of Agony:
The Art of Healing, ca. 1700–1800 (London, 1975), F. F. Cartwright's A Social History of Medicine (London and New York, 1977), Edwin Clarke, editor's
Modern Methods in the History of Medicine (London, 1971), G. M. Howe's
Man, Environment and Disease in Britain: A Medical Geography of Britain through
the Ages (Newton Abbot, 1972), Frederick N. L. Poynter, editor's The Evolution
of Pharmacy in Britain (London, 1961), and John Woodward's To Do the Sick No
Harm: A Study of the British Voluntary Hospital System to 1875 (London, 1974).
The agony is splendidly illustrated in Elizabeth Bennion's Antique Medical In-
struments (Berkeley, 1979). The doctors themselves are magisterially surveyed by
Sir George Clark in the second volume (from the late seventeenth century to
1858) of his and A. M. Cooke's A History of the Royal College of Physicians of
London (3 vols., Oxford, 1966–1972), and a lesser medical organization in
T. Hunt, editor's The Medical Society of London, 1773–1973 (London, 1973).
Noel Parry and José Parry, in The Rise of the Medical Profession: A Study in Collective Social Mobility (London, 1976), discuss the doctors from a different point
of view.

   The most recent biography of John Hunter is by Jessie Dobson (Edinburgh,
1969); and the most important study of Jenner, P. E. Razzell's Edward Jenner's
Cowpox Vaccine (Furle, 1977), is the most recent contribution to the controversy
over whether Jenner's vaccination did not in fact become, unrecognized, a rever-

sion to the earlier innoculation. Georgian psychiatry has been much investigated, partly as a result of the modern obsession with the subject and partly because of the famous case of George III. The development of the legal definition of insanity, a creation of the age, is exhaustively described in Nigel Walker's *Crime and Insanity in England*, volume 1, *The Historical Perspective* (Edinburgh, 1968). Other important general works are William L. Parry-Jones's *The Trade in Lunacy: A Study of Private Mad-houses in England in the Eighteenth and Nineteenth Centuries* (London, 1972), V. Skultans, editor's *Madness and Morals: Ideas on Insanity in the Nineteenth Century* (London, 1975), and Basil Clarke's *Mental Disorders in Earlier Britain* (Cardiff, 1975). The pieces are being assembled for a general reevaluation of Georgian medicine and of Georgian science as major facets of late-eighteenth-century cultural and intellectual life.

The wider intellectual and cultural life of the age is in a much less satisfactory condition. The great luminaries who command so much attention—Burke, Adam Smith, Ricardo, Bentham, James Mill, Hume, Gibbon, Dr. Johnson as a touchstone of the age for the literary scholars—were certainly typical of the age, but all of them transcend it in ways that make them imperfectly representative.

Some of the studies of Dr. Johnson's ideas, of Coleridge's often obscure philosophizing, and of the revolutionary aspects of the Romantics have contributed to a better understanding of the ideas and outlooks current in the late eighteenth and early nineteenth centuries. The conservative side of Romantic thought, which so often won out in the end, has been much less written about. Dr. Johnson, despite his reputation for undiluted Tory obscurantism of an early-eighteenth-century sort and despite the complex relations between his ideas and his peculiar personality, remained remarkably in touch with contemporary thought everywhere. Recent studies of his thought are Paul A. Alkon's *The Moral Discipline of the Mind* (Evanston, Ill., 1967), Chester Chapin's *The Religious Thought of Samuel Johnson* (Ann Arbor, Mich., 1968), Richard B. Schwartz's *Samuel Johnson and the New Science* (Madison, Wis., 1971), Thomas M. Curley's *Samuel Johnson and the Age of Travel* (Athens, Ga., 1976), and Donald J. Greene's *The Politics of Samuel Johnson* (New Haven, Conn., 1960). Greene's *The Age of Exuberance: Background to Eighteenth-century Literature* (New York, 1970) is an interesting survey of the intellectual background, as are two books by Ronald Harris, *Reason and Nature in the Eighteenth Century 1714–1780* (London, 1968) and *Romanticism and the Social Order, 1780–1830* (London, 1969). Most of the current energy of the Coleridge scholars is going into the new editions of his letters, works, and notebooks, but David P. Calleo's *Coleridge and the Idea of the Modern State* (New Haven, Conn., 1966) is a substantial study of his political thought, and J. Robert Barth's *Coleridge and Christian Doctrine* (Cambridge, Mass., 1969), a study of his religious thought. The politics of radical romanticism have been considered in J. L. Talmon's *Romanticism and Revolt* (London,

1967), Gary Kelly's *The English Jacobin Novel, 1780–1805* (Oxford, 1976), Gerald McNiece's *Shelley and the Revolutionary Idea* (Cambridge, Mass., 1969), Carl Woodring's *Politics in English Romantic Poetry* (Cambridge, Mass., 1970), and in much of the recent work on Blake.

The Burke industry continues unabated with its own journal, *Studies in Burke and His Time*, numerous articles elsewhere, and occasional books on his thought. The tone of the recent work is less polemical than in the heyday of the postwar Burke revival, but the work is often repititious and frequently inconsequential. Among the exceptions, besides Copeland et al.'s definitive *Correspondence of Edmund Burke*, are a few books and articles on his thought, but very little has been written recently on his life. Harvey C. Mansfield's *Statesmanship and Party Government: A Study of Burke and Bolingbroke* (Chicago, 1965) is often aridly political-scientific but is at times a penetrating analysis. Gerald W. Chapman's *Edmund Burke: The Practical Imagination* (Cambridge, Mass., 1967), Burleigh T. Wilkins's *The Problem of Burke's Political Philosophy* (Oxford, 1967), and Frank O'Gorman's *Edmund Burke: His Political Philosophy* (London, 1973) are all sound descriptions of his thought, emphasizing the unity of his ideas, but they by no means replace earlier studies. Michael Freeman's *Edmund Burke and the Critique of Political Radicalism* (Oxford, 1980) is the most recent analysis. The essays in Peter J. Stanlis, editor's *Edmund Burke, the Enlightenment and the Modern World* (Detroit, 1967) are concerned with the influence of Burke's life on his thought, as is the substantial introduction to Robert A. Smith, editor's *Edmund Burke on Revolution* (New York, 1971). How disappointing, though, that all the ink devoted to elucidating Burke in the past thirty-five years should have produced so little of permanent consequence beyond the edition of his letters and William B. Todd's definitive bibliography of his writings (London, 1964).

The development of the radical and reformist critique of existing ideas and institutions, which Burke so passionately opposed, has received as much attention as Burke himself. The subject is a leitmotif in the ever-burgeoning literature on political and popular radicalism, especially after 1789, and is a major theme in Ronald W. Harris's *Political Ideas, 1760–1792* (London, 1963), which is brief but comprehensive, and the closest approach to a general survey of late-eighteenth-century political thought. H. T. Dickinson's *Liberty and Property: Political Ideology in Eighteenth-century Britain* (New York, 1977) and several of John G. A. Pocock's essays collected in *Politics, Language, and Time: Essays on Political Thought and History* (London, 1977) also deal with themes common to (if glossed very differently by) Burke and the radicals, Whigs and Tories. Bernard Bailyn's masterly *The Ideological Origins of the American Revolution* (Cambridge, Mass., 1967) studies the earlier eighteenth-century radical Whig thought which nourished the later domestic radicals as well as the Americans.

H. Trevor Colbourne's *The Lamp of Experience: Whig History and the Intellectual Origins of the American Revolution* (Chapel Hill, N.C., 1965) is concerned with similar themes. Richard Price's version of the radical attack, so influential in the 1770s and again in 1789/1790 is the subject of major studies by Henri Laboucheix (Paris, 1970), D. O. Thomas, *The Honest Mind: The Thought and Work of Richard Price* (Oxford, 1977), and Bernard Peach in the long introduction and commentary to his edition of selections from Price's American pamphlets (Durham, N.C., 1979). Another leading radical theorist, James Burgh, has at last received a long-overdue appraisal in Carla H. Hay's *James Burgh: Spokesman for Reform in Hanoverian England* (Washington, D.C., 1979).

Still more radical critics of existing society, especially William Godwin and Robert Owen, have continued to attract much attention. The latest comprehensive study of Godwin is by Elton E. Smith and Esther Greenwell Smith (New York, 1965), while B. R. Pollin has published a "synoptic bibliography" of Godwin criticism (Toronto, 1967) and an edition of his uncollected writings (Gainesville, Fla., 1968). The most important work on Owen is contained in the three volumes of essays commemorating the bicentenary of his birth in 1971. These are Dame Margaret Cole, et al., editors' *Robert Owen: Industrialist, Reformer, Visionary* (London), Sidney Pollard and John Salt, editors', *Robert Owen: Prophet of the Poor* (London), and John Butt., editor's *Robert Owen, Prince of Cotton Spinners* (Newton Abbot). J. F. C. Harrison's *Robert Owen and the Owenites in Britain and America: The Quest for the New Moral World* (London, 1969) is the most recent full study.

Studies of economic ideas eclipse those on any other intellectual subject. The articles on Adam Smith alone are more numerous than those on Burke, and the work on his disciples and adapters is even more voluminous. A few works are comprehensive: William D. Grampp, *Economic Liberalism* (2 vols., New York, 1965); Robert V. Eagly, *The Structure of Classical Economic Theory* (Oxford, 1974); Denis P. O'Brien, *The Classical Economists* (Oxford, 1975); Phyllis Deane, *The Evolution of Economic Ideas* (Cambridge, 1978); H. D. Marshall, *The Great Economists: A History of Economic Thought* (New York, 1967); Marian Bowley, *Studies in the History of Economic Thought before 1870* (London, 1973); and Maurice H. Dobb, *Theories of the Value and Distribution since Adam Smith: Ideology and Economic Theory* (Cambridge, 1973), a Marxian analysis.

The major monument of the bicentenary of the *Wealth of Nations* is the definitive edition of Adam Smith's works and correspondence undertaken at Oxford, which so far includes a volume of letters edited by E. C. Mossner and I. S. Ross (Oxford, 1977), the *Wealth of Nations*, edited by R. H. Campbell and Andrew S. Skinner (Oxford, 1976), the *Theory of Moral Sentiments*, edited by D. D. Raphael and A. L. Macfie (Oxford, 1976), and *Lectures on Jurisprudence*, edited by Ronald L. Meek et al, (Oxford, 1978). These texts were accom-

panied by two thick volumes of essays ranging over all of Smith's work and beyond: Andrew S. Skinner and Thomas Wilson, editors' *Essays on Adam Smith*
(Oxford, 1975) and *The Market and the State: Essays in Honour of Adam Smith*
(Oxford, 1977).[25] Recent lives of Smith are by Horst C. Recktenwald (Munich,
1976), Ian S. Ross (Oxford, 1977), and E. G. West (New York, 1969). Jacob
Viner's *Guide to John Rae's Life of Adam Smith* (New York, 1965) also contains
much biographical information.

Work on the other classical economists is equally divided among Ricardo,
Malthus, and James Mill, with a few crumbs for lesser figures. Most of the work
on Malthus is an appendix to the debate over his ideas engendered by the neo-
Malthusianism of the 1950s and early 1960s. More recent are Jane S. Nicker-
son's *Homage to Malthus* (Folkestone, 1975) and William Peterson's *Malthus*
(Cambridge, Mass., 1979), which has an extensive bibliography. The most recent general study of Ricardo is by D. Weatherall (The Hague, 1976). Articles
by Frank W. Fetter, "The Rise and Decline of Ricardian Economics" (*History of
Political Economy* 1, 1969: 67–84), and John Hicks and Samuel Hollender,
"Mr. Ricardo and the Moderns" (*Journal of Economics* 91, 1977: 351–369), are
general appraisals; the rest of the recent work is concerned with specific points.
James Mill, that leading philosophic radical and political economist, plays a
prominent role in later Georgian intellectual history. Some of the most important
work, such as Joseph Hamburger's *James Mill and the Art of Revolution* (New
Haven, Conn., 1965), is primarily concerned with his career after 1820, but his
ideas were mostly formed well before then. Bruce Mazlish's *James and John
Stuart Mill: Father and Son in the Nineteenth Century* (New York, 1975) is an
essay in psychobiography. The essays in John M. Robson, editor's *James and John
Stuart Mill: Papers of the Centenary Conference* (Toronto, 1976) provide a convenient survey of recent studies, while Donald Winch, editor's *James Mill: Selected
Economic Writings* (Edinburgh, 1966) is a good collection of Mill's writing.
Wyndham H. Burston's *James Mill on Philosophy and Education* (London, 1973)
is a useful monograph.

Jeremy Bentham, perhaps the most seminal mind of the reign of George III,
has received remarkably little attention apart from the progress made on the new
edition of his works and correspondence. The best general book on him, despite
its shortcomings, is still Mary P. Mack's *Jeremy Bentham: An Odyssey of Ideas,
1748–1792* (London, 1962). C. W. Everett's *Jeremy Bentham* (London, 1966),
David J. Manning's *The Mind of Jeremy Bentham* (London, 1968), and James
Steintrager's *Bentham* (Ithaca, N.Y., 1977) are comprehensive but not wholly
satisfactory studies. Gertrude Himmelfarb's polemical essays on the Panopticon
in her *Victorian Minds* (New York, 1968, pp. 32–81) on "Bentham's Utopia:
The National Charity Company" (*JBS* 10, no. 1, 1970: 80–125), and especially
her "Bentham Scholarship and the Bentham 'Problem'" (*JMH* 41, 1969: 189–

206) are much more critical of his ideas, objectives, and influence than are most Bentham studies. John R. Dinwiddy's "Bentham's Transition to Political Radicalism, 1809–10" (*Journal of the History of Ideas* 36, 1975: 683–700) deals with an important change in his thought.

The most impressive intellectual movement in eighteenth-century Britain was the Scottish Enlightenment. The best general study is Anand C. Chitnis's *The Scotch Enlightenment: A Social History* (London, 1976). Besides the studies mentioned elsewhere of such luminaries as Robert Adam, Adam Smith, John Hunter, Joseph Black, and James Mill, Lord Kames has received biographies by William C. Lehmann (The Hague, 1971) and Ian S. Ross (Oxford, 1972). Emily L. Cloyd's *James Burnett, Lord Monboddo* (Oxford, 1972) is the latest book on this interesting speculator. The "conjectural historians," especially John Millar, have remained popular as forerunners of the social sciences. David Hume, perhaps the greatest Scotsman of them all, has received more attention than any other save Adam Smith. Most of Hume's work had been published before the accession of George III, but his ideas, especially on politics and economics, and his historical writings remained representative and influential throughout the century. One of the best recent studies of these sides of his work is Duncan Forbes's *Hume's Philosophical Politics* (Cambridge, 1975).

Other systematic philosophers, Scots or English, have been less written about, but Mark L. Clarke's *Paley, Evidences for the Man* (London, 1974) is a good account of a leading popularizer. Wilbur S. Howell's *Eighteenth-century British Logic and Rhetoric* (Princeton, N.J., 1971) is comprehensive. John Barker's *Strange Contrarities: Pascal in England during the Age of Reason* (Montreal, 1976) explores intellectual currents often overlooked.

Late Georgian scholarship, except for historical writing and the "discovery" of the East, has been little discussed since 1965. The books celebrating the quincentennial of the Oxford University Press, the first volume (extending to 1780) of a definitive history by Henry Carter (Oxford, 1975), and two more general accounts by N. Baker (Oxford, 1978) and Peter H. Sutcliffe (Oxford, 1978) all contain material on the propagation of learning in the period. Among the more recent monographs are Hans Aarsleff's *The Study of Language in England, 1780–1860* (Princeton, N.J., 1967); Richard M. Dorson's *The British Folklorists: A History* (London, 1968), with an extensive bibliography; and John D. Worthen's *The British Egyptologists, 1549–1906* (Norman, Okla., 1971). The development of oriental studies is well discussed in Peter J. Marshall's introduction to his *The British Discovery of Hinduism in the Eighteenth Century* (Cambridge, 1970), an edition of eight late-eighteenth century writings on this subject; in his excellent essay on Hastings as a scholar and patron in Anne Whiteman et al., editors' *Statesmen, Scholars and Merchants* (Oxford, 1973, 242–262); and in the literature on Sir William Jones, a leading pioneer, including a biography by Garland Cannon (New York and Bombay, 1964), who has also edited Jones's letters in two volumes (Oxford, 1970), and one by Sovmyendra N. Makenjee, *Sir William Jones: A Study in Eighteenth-century British Attitudes to India* (Cambridge, 1968). Another prominent intellectual is the subject of Warren Derry: *Dr. Parr: A Portrait of the Whig Dr. Johnson* (Oxford, 1966).

The development of archaeology and antiquarianism is discussed in some of the essays in Stuart Piggott's *Ruins in a Landscape* (Edinburgh, 1976). The British historians, especially Gibbon, remain popular, although there has been nothing written which compares with the essays in John B. Black's *The Art of History* (1926) nor that is of the more tedious thoroughness of Thomas P. Peardon's *The Transition in English Historical Writing 1760–1830* (1933). Hedva Ben-Israel's *English Historians on the French Revolution* (Cambridge, 1968) begins, however, with the contemporary observers and is a thorough study of this theme. Donald F. Shea's *The English Ranke: John Lingard* (New York, 1969) is a serviceable study of the leading Catholic historian who was one of the first Englishmen to be affected by the new critical, archival approaches pioneered by the German historians. The most useful introduction to the present state of Gibbon studies are the twenty essays in Glen Bowersock et al., editors' *Edward Gibbon and the Decline and Fall of the Roman Empire* (Cambridge, Mass., 1976), celebrating the bicentennial of the publication of the first volume. Sir Gaven de Beer's *Gibbon and His Work* (New York, 1968) is a study by one of the leading Gibbon scholars, and Joseph W. Swain's *Edward Gibbon, the Historian* (London, 1966) is another full study. Of the numerous articles, the most substantial is Dino T. Geanakoplos's "Edward Gibbon and Byzantine Ecclesiastical History" (*Church History* 35, 1966: 170–185), an appraisal, by a prominent Byzantine ecclesiastical historian, of a major theme in Gibbon's later volumes that most eighteenth-century scholars are ill-equipped to judge.

Where, then, is our present understanding of British history between 1760 and 1820? From one perspective, finally fragmented beyond repair after the activity of the past fifteen years. But perhaps the situation is not all bad. Most of the old formulations are shattered and as yet have not been convincingly replaced. But we do know much more about the events of late Georgian politics and about the speed and direction of underlying constitutional changes, about the changing administrative structure, about military and naval history and the composition of the military forces, especially about the economic and social developments in a more sophisticated complexity, and about the details of the cultural and intellectual achievements of the age. We can even understand a little better, if we try very diligently, the interrelations between all of these areas, even though we may not agree among ourselves what the connections were. But can we really hope for more than this when confronted by an age that contained fundamental changes everywhere, as the older order of Europe, and the world as it had existed from classical times, gave way to a new, with George III's Britain as its pioneer?

NOTES

1. Michael Edwardes, *Warren Hastings, King of the Nabobs* (London, 1976), is a good study of the other great proconsul.

2. The lists now include officials of the Admirality 1660–1870 (1975); Colonial Office 1794–1870 (1976); Foreign Office 1782–1870 (1979); Home Office 1782–1870 (1975); Board of Trade 1660–1870 (1974); Secretary of State 1660–1782 (1973); Treasury Officials 1660–1870 (1972); and Navy Board 1660–1832 (1978).

3. Tracy's articles are "The Administration of the Duke of Grafton and the French Invasion of Corsica," *Eighteenth-century Studies* 8, 1974: 169–182; "British Assessments of French and Spanish Naval Reconstruction, 1763–1768," *Mariner's Mirror* 61, 1975: 73–85; "The Falkland Islands Crisis of 1770: Use of Naval Force," *EHR* 90, 1975: 40–75; "The Gunboat Diplomacy of the Government of George Grenville, 1764–1765: The Honduras, Turk Island and Gambian Incidents," *HJ* 17, 1974: 711–731; and "Parry of a Threat to India, 1768–1774," *Mariner's Mirror* 59, 1973: 35–48.

4. Roberts's major study is *British Diplomacy and Swedish Party Politics, 1756–63*, Minneapolis, 1980. Other significant articles are "Great Britain, Denmark and Russia, 1763–1770," in Ragnhild Hatton and M. S. Anderson, eds., *Studies in Diplomatic History*, Harlow, 1970, 236–267; "Great Britain and the Swedish Revolution, 1772–73," *HJ* 7, 1964: 1–46; and "Macartney in Russia," *EHR*, suppl. 7, 1974. Other studies on Anglo-Baltic relations include Michael F. Metcalf, *Russia, England and Swedish Party Politics, 1762–1766*, Stockholm, 1977, and Heinz S. K. Kent, *War and Trade in Northern Seas: Anglo-Scandinavian Economic Relations in the Mid-eighteenth Century*, Cambridge, 1973.

5. Edward Ingham, "A Preview of the Great Game in Asia," *Middle Eastern Studies* 9, 1973: 1–14, 157–174, 296–314; ibid., 10, 1974: 15–35. Idem, "From Trade to Empire in the Near East," *Middle Eastern Studies* 14, 1978: 3–21, 182–204, 278– 306. Other articles by him on related subjects are in *HJ* 16, 1973: 509–533, and *Journal of Imperial and Commonwealth History* 3, 1974/5: 257–279.

6. Other useful work on aspects of military history include four studies of the Indian Army, a creation of the age: Philip Mason, *A Matter of Honour*, London, 1974, Roger A. Beaumont, *Sword of the Raj*, Indianapolis, 1977; James P. Lawford, *Britain's Army in India from Its Origins to the Conquest of Bengal*, London, 1978; and Raymond Callahan, *The East India Company and Army Reform, 1783–1798*, Cambridge, Mass., 1972. R. H. Thoumine, *Scientific Soldier: A Life of General Le Marchant 1766–1812*, London, 1968, is an interesting study of the pioneer of officer training. The blacker side of army life, little explored earlier, is investigated in John Prebble, *Mutiny: Highland Regiments in Revolt, 1743–1804*, London, 1975; several articles by Arthur N. Gilbert on military justice and courts martial in *Journal of the Society for Army Historical Research* 54, 1976: 38–47; *HJ* 19, 1976: 75–87; *JBS* 17 (2), 1978: 41–65; and *Albion* 8, 1976: 50–66; and Clive Emsley, "Political Disaffection and the British Army in 1792," *BIHR* 48, 1975: 230–245. Sylvia R. Frey, "The Common British Soldier in the Late Eighteenth Century: A Profile," *Societas* 5, 1975: 117–131, attempts a composite picture of the ranker, much less familiar than the common seaman.

7. Articles on dockyard reform, important in naval administration, include three by James M.

Hass in *JBS* 8 (2), 1969: 44–68; *HJ* 13, 1970: 191–215; and *Maritime History* 5, 1977: 99–115; and two by R. J. B. Knight in *Mariner's Mirror* 57, 1971: 175–192 and ibid. 61, 1975: 215–225. The Introduction of copper sheathing is discussed by Knight in *Mariner's Mirror* 59, 1973: 299–309 and by John R. Harris in *EcHR*, 2d ser., 19, 1966–1967: 550–568; and the improvements in block making are discussed in Keith R. Gilbert, *The Portsmouth Block-Making Machinery: A Pioneering Enterprise in Mass Production*, London, 1965. Useful books on improvements in navigation include Humphrey Quill, *John Harrison: The Man Who Found Longitude*, New York, 1966; Sir Archibald Day, *The Admirality Hydrographic Service, 1795–1919*, London, 1967; and Derek Howse and Michael Sanderson, *The Sea Chart*, Newton Abbot, 1973.

8. Other articles in this debate include John H. S. Kent, "Methodism and Revolution," *Methodist History* 12 (4), 1973–1974: 136–144; Elissa S. Itzkin, "The Halévy Thesis—A Working Hypothesis? English Revivalism—Antidote for Revolution and Radicalism, 1789–1815," *Church History* 44, 1975: 47–56; and case studies such as P. Stigant, "Wesleyan Methodism and Working-class Radicalism in the North 1792–1821," *Northern History* 6, 1971: 98–116; and John D. Walsh, "Methodism and the Mob in the Eighteenth Century," in G. J. Cuming and Derek Baker, eds., *Popular Belief and Practice*, Cambridge, 1972, 213–227.

9. Other studies of millenarianism include Ernest R. Sandeen, *The Roots of Fundamentalism: British and American Millenarianism 1800–1930*, Chicago, 1970; W. H. Oliver, *Prophets and Millennialists: The Uses of Biblical Prophecy in England from the 1790s to the 1840's*, Oxford, 1979; and from a rather different point of view, Clarke Garrett, *Respectable Folly: Millenarians and the French Revolution in France and England*, Baltimore, 1975.

10. Ditchfield's articles are "The Parliamentary Struggle over the Repeal of the Test and Corporation Acts, 1787–1790," *EHR* 89, 1974: 551–577; "Debates on the Test and Corporation Acts, 1787–90: The Evidence of the Division Lists," *BIHR* 50, 1977: 69–81; "The Campaign in Lancashire and Chesire for the Repeal of the Test and Corporation Acts, 1787–1790," *Transactions of the Historical Society of Lancashire and Chesire* 126, 1976: 109–138; "Dissent and Toleration: Lord Stanhope's Bill of 1789," *Journal of Ecclesiastical History* 29, 1978: 51–73; and "The Scottish Campaign against the Test Act—1790–1791," *HJ* 23, 1980: 37–61. Thomas W. Davis had edited the Minutes of the Committee for Repeal, 1786–1790 and 1827–1882 as vol. 14 of the *Publications of the London Record Society*, 1978. R. W. Davis, *Dissent in Politics, 1780–1830: The Political Life of William Smith, M.P.*, London, 1971, also has much on the subject.

11. The books on the various parts of England include A. F. J. Brown, *Essex at Work, 1700–1815*, Chelmsford, Essex, 1969; John Booker, *Essex and the Industrial Revolution*, Chelmsford, Essex, 1974; V. L. Davies and H. Hyde, *Dudley and the Black Country, 1760–1860*, Dudley, 1970; John R. Harris, ed., *Liverpool and Merseyside: Essays in the Economic and Social History of the Port and Its Hinterland*, London, 1969; Francis E. Hyde, *Liverpool and the Mersey: An Economic History of a Port*, Newton Abbot, 1971; J. D. Marshall and M. Davies-Shiel, *The Lake District at Work, Past and Present*, Newton Abbot, 1971; W. E. Minchinton, ed., *Industrial South Wales, 1750–1914: Essays in Welsh Economic History*, London, 1969; Sidney Pollard and C. Holmes, eds., *Essays in the Economic and Social History of South Yorkshire*, Barnsley, 1976; Arthur Raistrick, *Old Yorkshire Dales*, Newton Abbot, 1967; Frederick B. Singleton, *Industrial Revolution in Yorkshire*, Clapham, Yorkshire, 1970; and Barry S. Trinder, *The Industrial Revolution in Shropshire*, Chichester, 1973.

12. Two of the most persuasive arguments for the primacy of an ever-expanding home market are the essays David E. C. Eversley, "The Home Market and Economic Growth in England 1750–1800," in Eric L. Jones and Gordon E. Mingay, eds., *Land, Labour and Population in the Industrial Revolution*, London, 1967, 206–259, and Paul Bairoch, "Commerce interna-

tional et genèse de la révolution industrielle anglaise," *Annales* 28, 1973: 541–571. Eric Hobsbawm, however, continues to argue along traditional lines in *Industry and Empire* that the great expansion of foreign commerce provided the essential margin of demand to trigger sustained growth. The extensive rewriting of agrarian history continues to alter the role traditionally assigned to the "agricultural revolution" in promoting growth and provides strong support for arguments stressing the rapid growth of domestic demand.

13. The received view of the subject, developed primarily by Lawrence J. Harper around 1940, is that the economic impact of renewed enforcement was marginal and that the real importance was political, an interpretation sustained by an econometric article by Robert Thomas in *JEcH* 25, 1965: 615–638. This version was challenged through econometric models by Roger L. Ransom in *JEcH* 28, 1968: 427–435 and Peter D. McClelland in *American Economic Review* 59, 1969: 370–381, who argued that tightened enforcement placed an intolerable economic burden on the colonies. Some of the subsequent articles in the debate are Gary M. Walton, *EcHR*, 2d ser., 24, 1971: 533–542, and an inconclusive discussion among Frank J. A. Broeze, McClelland, Walton, and David J. Loschky, ibid., 26, 1973: 668–691.

14. The principal contributors to this debate have been Hoh-Cheung Mui and Lorna H. Mui, who began their case in specialized articles in 1961 and 1963, expanded and generalized it in *AHR* 74, 1968–1969: 44–73, and turned it into a comprehensive criticism of William A. Cole's 1958 interpretation of the economic importance of smuggling in *EcHR*, 2d ser., 28, 1975: 28–43, with a reply by Cole, ibid., 44–49.

15. Articles directly on the economic impact of the wars include François Crouzet, "Bilan de l'économie britannique pendant les guerres de la Révolution et de l'Empire," *Revue historique* 234, 1965: 71–110; Phyllis Deane, "War and Industrialization," in J. M. Winter, ed., *War and Economic Development*, Cambridge, 1975, 91–102; and Glenn Hueckel, "War and the British Economy, 1793–1815: A General Equilibrium Analysis," *Explorations in Economic History*, n.s. 10, 1972–1973: 365–396.

16. The most important contributions are J. J. McCusker, "The Current Value of English Exports, 1697 to 1800," *William and Mary Quarterly*, 3d ser., 28, 1971: 607–628; Jacob M. Price, "New Time Series for Scotland's and Britain's Trade with the Thirteen Colonies and States, 1740 to 1791," ibid., 32, 1975: 307–325; Patrick McGrath, *The Merchant Venturers of Bristol*, Bristol, 1975; idem, *Bristol in the Eighteenth Century*, Newton Abbot, 1972; Gordon Jackson, *Hull in the Eighteenth Century: A Study in Economic and Social History*, London, 1971; idem, *The Trade and Shipping of Eighteenth-century Hull*, York, 1975; Edward Gillett, *A History of Grimsby*, London, 1970; Gordon Jackson, *Grimsby and the Haven Company, 1796–1846*, Grimsby, Lincoln, 1971; and Harold E. S. Fisher, *Ports and Shipping in the Southwest*, Exeter, 1971; A. D. Francis, *The Wine Trade*, London, 1972; Harold E. S. Fisher, *The Portugal Trade: A Study of Anglo-Portuguese Commerce, 1700–1770*, London, 1971.

17. The most comprehensive discussion of migrant labor from the late eighteenth century is E. J. T. Collins, "Migrant Labour in British Agriculture in the Nineteenth Century," *EcHR*, 2d ser., 29, 1976: 38–59. For prices, where much remains to be done, C. W. J. Granger and C. M. Elliott, "A Fresh Look at Wheat Prices and Markets in the Eighteenth Century," ibid., 20, 1967: 257–265, is helpful. The most useful article on the war period is A. H. John, "Farming in Wartime, 1793–1815," in Eric L. Jones and Gordon E. Mingay, eds., *Land, Labour and Population in the Industrial Revolution*, 1967, 28–47. Two econometric articles on the same subject by Glenn Hueckel are in *Explorations in Economic History*, n.s. 13, 1975–1976: 331–345 and *EcHR*, 2d ser., 29, 1976: 401–414.

18. T. W. Beastall, *A North Country Estate: The Lumleys and Saundersons as Landowners 1600–1900*, London, 1975; Eric Richards, "'Leviathan of Wealth': West Midland Agriculture 1800–1850," *Agricultural History Review* 22, 1974: 97–117, on the Leveson-Gower estates;

David Cannadine, "The Landowner as Millionaire: The Finances of the Dukes of Devonshire, c. 1800–c. 1926," ibid. 25, 1977: 77–97; John Rosselli, "An Indian Governor in the Norfolk Marshland: Lord William Bentinck as Improver, 1809–27," ibid. 19, 1971: 42–64; John T. Ward, *East Yorkshire Landed Estates in the Nineteenth Century*, York, 1967; idem, "The Saving of a Yorkshire Estate: George Lane-Fox and the Bramham Estate," *Yorkshire Archaeological Journal* 42, 1967; Colin Shrimpton, *The Landed Society and the Farming Community of Essex in the Late Eighteenth and Early Nineteenth Centuries*, New York, 1977; and articles on Welsh estates by Richard J. Colyer, *Bulletin of the Board of Celtic Studies* 26, 1975: 200–217 and *Welsh Historical Review* 8, 1976–1977: 257–284.

19. Gordon E. Mingay's *Enclosure and the Small Farmer in the Age of the Industrial Revolution*, London, 1968, is a brief but lucid discussion of the problem. See also B. A. Holderness, "'Open' and 'Close' Parishes in England in the Eighteenth and Nineteenth Centuries," *Agricultural History Review* 20, 1972: 126–139, for an important difference between villages that accepted and those that refused newcomers, a distinction nearly as significant as enclosure for the life of the village. A furious econometric debate on the connections among enclosure, labor supply, and population growth can be followed in articles by Lawrence J. White, *Explorations in Economic History*, n.s. 6, 1968–1969: 175–186; John A. Tomaski, ibid., 8, 1970–1971: 223–227; Bennett D. Baack and Robert P. Thomas, *Journal of European Economic History* 3, 1974: 401–423; Gordon Philpot, *Explorations in Economic History* 12, 1975: 29–46; Michael Turner (with a reply by Philpot), ibid. 13, 1976: 463–471; and N. F. R. Crafts, ibid. 15, 1978: 172–183.

20. Recent general discussions of the debate, not in Taylor, include Duncan Bythell, "The History of the Poor," EHR 89, 1974: 365–377, and J. Elster, "Optimism and Pessimism in the Discussion of the Standard of Living during the Industrial Revolution," *Report of the Fourteenth International Congress of Historical Sciences*, New York, 1977.

21. E. P. Thompson's articles, not otherwise mentioned, include: "Patrician Society: Plebian Culture," *Journal of Social History* 7, 1974: 383–405; "'Rough Music': Le charivari anglais," *Annales* 27, 1972: 285–312; "Time, Work-discipline, and Industrial Capitalism," *PP*, no. 38, 1967: 56–97, reprinted in M. W. Flinn and T. C. Smout, eds., *Essays in Social History*, Oxford, 1968, 39–77; and "Eighteenth-century English Society: Class Struggle without Class?" *Social History* 3, 1968: 133–165.

22. The Tyneside articles are: Norman McCord and David E. Brewster, *International Review of Social History* 13, 1968: 366–383; D. J. Rowe, ibid. 13, 1968: 58–75; Norman McCord, *EHR*, 2d ser., 21, 1968: 127–143; idem, *Northern History* 2, 1967: 91–111. K. I. D. Master, "Masters and Men," *Library* 30, 1975–1976: 81–94, discusses labor relations in a London printing house; R. A. Morriss, "Labour Relations in the Royal Dockyards, 1801–1805," *Mariner's Mirror* 62, 1976: 337–346, the government and its employees. G. J. Barnsby, *The Working-class Movement in the Black Country*, Wolverhampton, 1977, is a useful regional study.

23. Mary Wollstonecraft has become an industry, with three recent biographies by Margaret George (Urbana, Ill., 1970), Eleanor Flexner (New York, 1972), and Claire Tomalin (London, 1974). Janet M. Todd appraises these lives in *Signs* 1, 1976: 721–734; she has also written a review article on the recent literature, "Mary Wollstonecraft: A Revival of Research and Comment," *British Studies Monitor* 7, 1977–1978: 3–23, and has compiled a bibliography of her writings and the secondary works (New York, 1976).

24. Inkster's articles included: "The Development of a Scientific Community in Sheffield, 1790–1850: A Network of People and Interests," *Transactions of the Hunter Archaelogical Society* 10, 1973: "Culture, Institutions, and Urbanity: The Itinerant Science Lecturer in Sheffield, 1790–1850," in Sidney Pollard and C. Holmes, eds., *Essays in the Social and Economic His-*

tory of South Yorkshire, Barnsley, 1976; and "Science and Society in the Metropolis: A Preliminary Examination of the Social and Institutional Context of the Askesian Society of London,
1796–1807," *Annals of Science* 34, 1977: 1–32.
25. These essays and some fifty other articles in journals are appraised in critical bibliographical
essays by Horst C. Recktenwald in the *Journal of Economic Literature* 16, 1978: 56–83; Larry
Venning in *Studies in Burke and His Time* 19, 1978: 61–71; Donald White in *Journal of the
History of Ideas* 37, 1976: 715–720; and E. G. West in *Scottish Journal of Economics* 45,
1978: 343–369.

In Search of a New Past
1820–1870

D. C. Moore

Occasionally, those who try to compose meaningful definitions of history resign themselves to the simple statement, history is what historians do. As definitions go, the statement is not very useful. But anything much less diffuse would scarcely be accurate. To some extent this has always been the case. Historians have always done many different things and done them in different ways. But recently the extent has grown immensely. Undoubtedly, in part, the reasons for this have to do with the flood of history Ph.D.s that crested some eight or ten years ago: each of them had to find a subject of his own to write on. But far more important than the flood are the reasons why the flood occurred. Of course there is no way of knowing precisely why each of those who decided to study history in the last few years did so. Presumably, however, what attracted some of them— apart from the increased number of academic jobs there were to fill—were the questions raised about the past by the increasing complexities of the present—or by the increasing awareness of these complexities, those raised about man and society by the discrepancies between the understandings which derive from conventional wisdom and those which derive from psychoanalysis and the various social sciences. What historians do is a function of the questions they ask. In the last few years the number and variety of these have increased greatly as the cultural consensus crumbled which, previously, kept them in check.

Not so long ago mid-nineteenth-century English history had particular appeal for those with a taste for peaceful progress. It still has such today. But for many historians today the notion of peaceful progress—of past and present somehow joined in mutual redemption—has become a bit anomalous. Many historians still find solace in the progress theme. For certain others the people and events of mid-nineteenth-century England have been and remain principally interesting for what they illustrate of a not-so-distant past: for those who qualify, items of extended memory which contribute to a heritage. But for some Englishmen and for many others as well, these people and events have become increasingly interesting for what they reveal of that process of radical and accelerating change which not only affected state and society but the very meaning of "history" itself. Previously, "history," as a rule, had been the means of chronicling the doings of great men. It became the means of linking a present to its past, of validating both past and present by stressing the continuities between them. But now, in significant fashion, one of the main functions of such linkages has lapsed. Not so long ago, for many people—perhaps for most—these linkages helped to sanctify present authority in whatever form it was manifest—cultural, social, economic, political. In the present circumstance, however, these linkages are rather less effective than they used to be. For some people far more than for others, and for some varieties of authority far more than for others, present authority can no longer obtain that sanctification from the past which these linkages once provided: for many people today, continuity with the past has ceased to be an excuse.

Historians are not the only ones who have experienced this circumstance. Nor have their reactions to it been any less diverse than the reactions of others. But in many cases their reactions have been more cerebral. And in some cases—in particular, perhaps, where the present circumstance prompted the interest in history—these reactions have directly affected their work. Many historians— and these range across the entire present political spectrum—have continued to do the same kinds of things their predecessors did before: they have continued to study the same kinds of institution, group, activity, or question in the light of the same kinds of concept and the same kinds of evidence. But others—again ranging across the entire present political spectrum—have begun to study things historians in the past scarcely ever studied. Also, in some cases—and whether the subjects of their investigations are traditional or nontraditional—their investigations themselves have been overlaid or prompted by epistemological and other considerations of a sort with which, previously, few historians troubled their minds.

The field as a whole is far more diversified than ever before. It is also more polarized both politically and at another and, possibly, more basic level between "humanists" and "social scientists." In some cases these polarizations coincide. In others they do not. But whichever the case, the "humanists," by and large, are concerned to acquire that understanding of the past which, ostensibly, contemporaries possessed. Many "social scientists" are concerned to acquire that understanding of the past which some of them claim contemporaries could not have possessed. In some cases, changes of view in the field have been the consequence of substantive work which provided new answers to old questions. But, principally, they have been the consequence of the posing of new questions. Many of these concern the assumptions on which, once-upon-a-time, explanations of behavior and the study of history were both so confidently based: that rationality and objectivity are meaningful concepts; that literary evidence provides a clear window on "reality"; and that historical change is mainly attributable to individual reason, intelligence, and consequent volition.

❧

Not so long ago the dominant theme in many works on mid-nineteenth-century English history concerned the efforts of men and women to bring an institutional structure up to date. These people were often described in glorious battle against tradition. Ostensibly, they had the advantage, armed, as they were, with Benthamite theory or some other form of "reason." At least they had the initiative. Today, a smaller proportion of historians conceive of these people in such heroic terms. The number has grown considerably of the others who see them less as the arbiters of their own fates, successfully modernizing the institutional frameworks of society and state, and more as persons agonized by changes in the world around them, trying as best they could to respond to the impact of forces which no one really controlled. Whatever the weapons they are now believed to have had, they have lost the initiative to population growth, urbanization, and industrialization. And in a way that involves an even greater distancing of the dynamic factors from individual volition and the literary sources in which such volition is ostensibly reported and explained, some historians are studying these phenomena from a comparative perspective. They are looking at what happened in England and Wales in the light of what happened in other industrializing countries at the time and in the light of what is happening in Third World countries today. They claim that this clarifies the crucial questions and puts them in proper perspective. But others contend that it only obscures the questions and distorts the perspective. However the question is answered, which it *really* does, the more substantive questions remain: In what ways were population growth, urbanization, and industrialization related to one another in England? In what ways were these phenomena discrete? Nor is there any real agreement about the precise consequences of these phenomena beyond the rather elementary points that all manner of things were bound to be different where the total population was growing rapidly and where the proportions of this population which resided in towns and the gross national product were growing even more rapidly.

For the period before 1838, when civil registration of vital information began, the population controversy is peculiarly intractable. Until then, there is simply no evidence on the basis of which really confident statements can be made about birth rates and death rates and the factors of fertility and mortality which affected them. The first census was taken in 1801, but its accuracy as well as the accuracy of the immediately succeeding censuses and the adequacy of the information they contain leave much to be desired.[1] There is general agreement that the parish registers which the Anglican clergy were supposed to keep, the main alternative source of information for the preregistration period, would have to be corrected before the statistical information they contain could be used with any confidence. But precisely what these corrections should be is another matter.[2] There is general agreement that population had been growing for many years before reliable statistical evidence becomes available. But speculation about whether growth was more the function of rising birth rates or of declining death rates and, whichever the case, what it signifies, is less constrained than it might be otherwise.

In the last few years, however, certain fairly well-established explanations of population growth have been seriously challenged. Mark Blaug and James Huzel have shown that the contemporary assumption according to which population growth was largely attributable to a rising birth rate, itself attributable to the Speenhamland system, or allowance system of poor relief, is probably wrong. This assumption, they claim, was a product of Malthusian fantasy which distorted the effects of the old poor law.[3] The more recent assumption that population growth was largely attributable to a declining death rate, itself attributable to developments in medicine and in the philanthropic attitudes which were responsible for the provision of hospitals has been challenged by the medical historian Thomas McKeown and his various collaborators. Basing their arguments upon the state of medical knowledge and the mortality rates for particular diseases at particular times, they claim that medicine and hospitals could not have begun to affect the general death rate until the 1930s, sanitary measures until the 1870s. Principally, they attribute the declining death rate and the consequent population growth in the previous period to improvements in diet which resulted from increasing food supplies.[4] Recently, those in the promedicine and prophilanthropy camps have been fighting back, stressing the importance of inoculations and, in general, trying to advance the date for which it might be reasonable to claim that medicine and hospitals as well as nutritional improvements affected the death rates.[5]

Whatever the ultimate resolution of this argument, there are various others, more fundamental, perhaps, concerning the relationships between population growth and economic growth. To some extent, these have to do with the determinants of those age-specific, class-specific, and regional-specific birth rates and death rates which, together, make up the aggregate rates. Many historians remain skeptical of E. A. Wrigley's evidence that, in the preregistration period, the mean age of first marriage of women went down and fertility went up.[6] Nor are they all convinced, as Phyllis Deane and W. A. Cole would like them to be, that in the regions where population growth was most rapid—by and large, the regions where economic growth was also most rapid—the rapidity of population growth is principally attributable to a high rate of natural increase.[7] Somewhat different are the questions concerning the decline of fertility. The evidence is indubitable. The decline was manifest among upper- and middle-class families, especially urban families, around the middle of the century and was reflected some twenty years later in the unmistakable beginnings of a decline in the national birth rate. Whether or not the concern to regulate family size was really new, a crucial change in the mode of regulation had occurred. Previously, family size was generally regulated—when it was regulated—by delay of marriage. But now it was increasingly regulated within marriage.[8] Sir John Habakkuk has tried to encompass these various phenomena, suggesting among other things, that at a certain stage of economic development population growth is stimulated by the weakening of old restraints and, at a subsequent stage, is inhibited by the development of those new restraints on which the modern small family is based.[9] The argument incorporates many variables. In particular, it applies to the towns whose rapid growth intimated a new civilization as well as new sets of problems.

Work in British urban history has burgeoned since the mid-1960s. Also, in many cases the attitudes reflected in this work are new, the expression, perhaps, of an increasing willingness to come to terms with urban society. The previous ambivalence, if not hostility, of many historians toward towns in general is suggested by the enduring belief, which has not really challenged until the 1950s, that the growth of urban populations in the late eighteenth and nineteenth centuries was principally attributable to a push from the countryside, which the enclosure movement ostensibly symbolized, rather than to any pull from the towns themselves.[10] A change of attitude was apparent in 1963 when Asa Briggs not only acknowledged the existence of "civic cultures" but discussed the differences among those of Manchester, Birmingham, Leeds, and Melbourne.[11] But the real change occurred when, as the late H. J. Dyos observed, various historians, responding to the somewhat earlier development of urban history in the United States, and to the development of urban sociology throughout the world, began trying to locate the general British experience, or the experience of particular towns, within the context of that general process of urbanization which constitutes such an important divide.[12] Certain historians began dealing with towns, not only as places in which disease, dirt, crime, and general turbulence were endemic and impersonal relationships ostensibly the order of the day, but as places to which increasing numbers of persons were drawn and in which a new society was being created. The forms of the argument are still somewhat rudimentary, but some obvious themes were suggested by several of the contributors in 1968, and to *The Victorian City*, which Dyos and Michael Wolff edited, and which was published in 1973. Others lie in the growing numbers of studies of professions and of urban adaptation.[13]

Whatever is ultimately done with Emile Durkheim's proposition that urban migrants, generally young, were "most impatient of all restraint and most eager for change" (p. 295),[14] an important aspect of urbanization has to do with the ways in which the increasing urban population was absorbed. Physical accommodation is basic: the development of urban space. The early involvements and noninvolvements of local government in conditioning the environments of Liverpool and Manchester have been studied by François Vigier.[15] Until well into the century, however, the role of formal local government was as small as its powers were contingent. E. P. Hennock has emphasized the important premises which continued to dominate the relations between central and local government until well past 1870: local government should be independent; its authority should really derive from the social authority or status of the men who participated in it.[16] The recognition of these premises has helped to condition the ways in which, increasingly, the so-called nineteenth-century revolution in government is being understood and the classical economists are being read.[17] Also, it has conditioned the terms in which urban development is being studied.

Because much urban and protourban land was owned by large landowners, private estate offices were the principal agencies of urban planning. These offices have become the starting points of a good deal of work since Dyos's pioneer study of Camberwell.[18] What these studies have described are the many factors and varieties of factor which both affected development and were affected by it. In an important series of books and articles, Donald Olsen has emphasized the increasing specialization of land use in London in particular and the increasing residential class segregation as landowners and builders indulged that peculiar English propensity to live in separate houses in ever-extending suburbs.[19] Developments in urban transport facilitated this segregation.[20] But its principal dynamics were the social considerations it expressed and reenforced: the wishes of prospective tenants and the strong preferences of many landowners that, whenever possible, their estates should be developed for the occupancy of members of the upper and middle classes. The role of landowners in affecting the conditions of urban development has become something of a platitude which confirms the importance of the institutions and modes of behavior associated with them.[21]

The building industry was extremely important as a focus of investment and a factor of economic growth.[22] But most builders were small speculators. Men like Thomas Cubitt were few.[23] In the 1840s there were important technological developments in the brick, tile, and glass industries which facilitated the solutions of certain general construction problems as well as those more specific matters of sanitation, space, and light which were coming to be regarded as problems.[24] In consequence, the question is all the more obdurate: Why, in so many cases, were these problems so difficult to solve?

Several historians have tried to determine for whom these problems were so difficult to solve. There is growing consensus that, from the 1840s on, those who could pay the price of unsubsidized housing were not badly housed.[25] But the question remains who these really were. At least indirectly this question explains the recent interest in Henry Mayhew and the identity of the people Mayhew and various other journalists described in a series of articles in *Morning Chronicle* in 1849–1852: Were they street people? Or were they some other category of poor?[26] Also, the identity question helps to define the context in which the general significance of charity is being reappraised.[27] As J. D. Marshall and John Tarn explain, privately subsidized housing existed in various towns to which a laboring population had to be attracted—by and large, company towns.[28] Also, from the 1860s there were a few charitable housing trusts in London, the Peabody Trust in particular. But in large measure these were designed to preserve the "respectable" working class from contamination by the others. In the context of this concern, the social work profession developed within the offices of the Charity Organization Society.[29] Whether the various boundaries social workers were concerned to protect had more to do with economic, social, or cultural factors, it now appears that many artisans could take care of themselves, that some of the "industrious poor" were cared for, but that no one cared in the same way for those who were not "respectable," those who were casually employed and who, as Gareth Steadman Jones has explained, could not afford to live far from the places where casual work was available—in London, as a rule, in the East End.[30] As Dyos has explained, migrants to the towns did not inhabit the slums. The majority of the London slum population was London-born and; in the 1840s, in a way that reveals the peculiar significance of the "respectability" problem, the word *slum*, newly coined to mean bad housing, was becoming synonymous with "rookeries," the retreats of the "criminal classes."[31]

Crime, like disease, was both more prevalent and more difficult to cope with in town than in countryside. Initially, police and boards of health were urban institutions. Towns were regarded by many people as a special case where such infringements upon liberty, however deplorable, were necessary because the traditional forms of social control were not effective and fresh air did not exist. And much as the question remains—what was the principal cause of the declining death rate?—so does the question remain, What was the principal cause of the apparently declining crime rate? What had been considered a peculiarly British experience is now recognized as far more general. But the question remains, Should it be attributed more to an expansion of labor demand and the increasing absorption of the "criminal classes" into legitimate activities? Or should it be attributed more to the increasing efficiency of the police? Whatever the answer to these questions, the police were, as R. D. Storch explains, an "all purpose lever of urban discipline."[32]

The realization that towns were the main arena of class is scarcely new. But in the last few years some historians have become dissatisfied with the explanations of this which, previously, most historians had found entirely cogent, that towns were the arenas of class because, increasingly, towns were the centers of industry. The questions are numerous and fundamental. They concern the nature of class and the effective dynamics of that social segregation which, in England and Wales in the nineteenth century, was associated with urbanization. They also concern the impact of industrialization upon the standards of living—however measured, of different classes—however defined, and the dynamics of the changing structures and functions of public, semipublic, and private institutions.

The point figures prominently in determining the context of the overall argument of Peter Mathias's recent study of industrialization in Britain: today, in many Third World countries, population growth soaks up whatever economic growth occurs, thus producing an absolute decline in working-class standards of living whether these be measured in terms of real wages or quality of life. In England and Wales in the nineteenth century, however, there was no such decline.[33] Thus has the oldest controversy in the field of nineteenth-century British history been somewhat redefined.

By and large, those who make this point emphasize the endemic poverty of the preindustrial condition and describe industrialization as the means by which a process of continuing economic growth was begun which, even if it has not solved the poverty problem, has greatly ameliorated it. But many others emphasize the emotional satisfactions of a nonbureaucratic society and describe the Industrial Revolution as the means by which a class society was created. Today, few historians in either group would take the position that, over the long term, industrialization has not had some beneficial effects upon working-class standards of living in Britain. But the former tend to emphasize the gains and to explain them largely in economic terms as a measure of the degree to which economic growth, achieved without positive governmental assistance, exceeded population growth. Many of the latter, while noting that industrialization made it possible to solve the poverty problem, deprecate the extent to which this problem has been solved and attribute whatever solution has been obtained to trade union activities or to riot and the threat of revolution.[34]

In broad terms, these arguments have been going on since the processes with which they are concerned began, but in the last few years new dimensions have been added. Aware of the difficulties of achieving growth in the Third World today, many economists have begun studying growth in Britain in the eighteenth and nineteenth centuries both to see how it happened and to sharpen their theories. Many historians disapprove of the influence these economists have come to exercise, whether because they object to the intrusion of self-conscious theory, or to the intrusion of that neoclassical theory which many of these economists profess, or because they deplore what, from their point of view, seems to be a tendency to abstract an economic from a social dimension.[35] But from another point of view, this tendency merely reveals the change of perspectives in economic history as literary evidence and unsystematic data give way to critical evaluation and systematic quantitative analysis[36]—in effect, as experience is transformed by analysis.

Of late, some economic historians have been busy assembling the data without which systematic quantitative analysis is impossible, in particular, data on capital formation and national product.[37] Until the 1850s and 1860s, the government itself did not collect such data. It is crucial in resolving questions which come from various sources about the relationships between industrialization and capital investment.

Other historians have dealt with specific industries. Several have been attracted to the textile industry, especially the cotton industry, whose development has often been regarded as prototypical. But according to D. C. Coleman, there are as many ways in which the textile industry differed from others as there are ways in which it was similar to them.[38] Furthermore, while some firms were successful, others were not.[39] It is a point which he and various others have emphasized while noting that national prosperity was the consequence of the prosperity of many individual firms.[40]

Several historians have been attracted by railways. Effectively nonexistent before the mid-1830s, by the 1850s they had displaced long-distance coaches and were putting serious pressure upon the canals.[41] A generation ago their role as agents of sustained and rational growth seemed assured for all time. Then the question was raised whether the rapid expansion of railways should not be explained more in terms of the pressures of surplus capital than in terms of rational economic decisions. For some historians, railways became a deus ex machina which, first by absorbing surplus capital, and then by prompting diversification from textiles into capital-goods production, enabled the British economy to survive the crisis of the early 1840s.[42] In an effort to determine the precise contribution of railways to the mid-nineteenth-century economy, the tools of quantitative analysis and the concepts of contrafactual or hypothetical history were used, producing the conclusion that the immediate economic importance of railways had been grossly exaggerated.[43] The method and conclusions are highly controversial.[44] There is less controversy about the new categories of problem which railways created. The scope of their operations required new forms of company organization.[45] Their relations with one another in the context of the national transportation system they comprised required some form of coordinating agency.[46] Nor could formal government remain aloof.[47] Their impact on cities is somewhat equivocal: apparently, they exacerbated urban congestion as much, or almost as much, as they relieved it.[48] But in the countryside they helped to solve the problems of underemployment;[49] and the nine hundred railway stations built across the kingdom had a significant impact upon the landscape, as did the lines, cuts, tunnels, bridges, and other civil engineering works which so impressed the Victorian imagination.[50]

The same interests in organization, the locus of responsiblity, and the rationality of decisions which are reflected in various railway histories are also reflected in several recent studies of the iron and steel industries.[51] But the principal expression of this interest is the pioneering book in which Sidney Pollard described the organizational and managerial innovations which certain firms in various industries adopted in the period before 1830.[52] Other historians have confirmed his points about the problems of transition which industrialization raised for entrepreneurs as well as for laborers.[53] In many cases, in the past industrialization was discussed as if the only problem it raised for the entrepreneur was where he should bank his money. Undoubtedly, some historians are now regarding the entrepreneur more sympathetically than was the practice a short time ago. But sympathy aside, many of them are now more willing to recognize the complexities of the total situation in which he and others found themselves. In consequence, more is being made of the entrepreneur's difficulties in adopting new attitudes toward risk and responsibility and in developing the accounting systems which reflected these attitudes. From the side of management as well as of labor, the problems of relationship and organization which factories tended to symbolize are being analyzed in new ways.

In many cases, the problems of entrepreneurial transition or transformation were obviously solved. But some historians, concerned to explain that deceleration of growth which looms large when compared with the experiences of certain other industrializing countries in the nineteenth century, have raised the question How successfully were they solved? By and large, whether dating the deceleration from mid-century or from twenty years later, they attribute it principally to social rather than to economic causes. According to David Landes, who dates it from the 1850s or 1860s, the sons of the English middle class were not being trained for the roles which industrial leadership increasingly required. Their education, reflecting the values of that landed elite with which many successful merchants and manufacturers wished to be assimilated, was not sufficiently scientific or technological.[54] Other historians, an increasing number of late, regard the deceleration of industrial growth as something quite normal in what has been called a "mature economy" and contend that the average response of English or British entrepreneurs to the challenges they faced was adequate or more than adequate.[55] Some doubt has been cast on the validity of the mid-Victorian "boom," the concept often applied to the period 1850–1873.[56] But recently, while emphasizing the degree to which, in 1850, Britain was still rural and preindustrial, A. E. Musson argued that the real Industrial Revolution did not occur until after mid-century, the period for which, as he puts it, some historians, asking the wrong questions, have been trying to explain a growing conservatism or stagnation.[57]

Landes's contention touches upon several related questions, among them the ways in which the existence of the landed elite either encouraged or discouraged economic growth and the ways in which this elite managed to retain its power into a period which, until fairly recently, was generally described as one of middle-class power. The argument that the landed elite, far from discouraging economic growth, did much to encourage it, is largely identified with David Spring. Many years ago Spring began describing the various cultural transformations of the landed elite which he associated with their ostensibly growing eagerness to get the largest profits from their estates "in the age of coal and iron." But he also noted the limits of this eagerness when it threatened other values, especially those having to do with family influence.[58] In the last few years, to determine, among other things, the components of this influence and the extent of the apparent tendency of landowners to withdraw from direct or indirect entrepreneurial roles as the century progressed—to exchange the entrepreneurial roles they or their agents performed in the past for rentier roles—various historians have been studying the economic histories of individual estates, especially those located in areas of major industrial or urban development.[59] Whether the apparent tendency of landowners to withdraw from entrepreneurial roles eroded their influence or strengthened it, and whether the continued assimilation of nouveaux riches into their ranks had any bearing at all upon the gross national product, their survival has been the subject of several recent studies.[60] But until W. D. Rubinstein began to exploit the available probate records, few historians realized the extent to which, until the last quarter of the century, the wealth of the larger "wealth-holders" consisted of land.[61]

The shifting basis of agricultural prosperity has been well documented. While the question has been raised whether there was a single "agricultural revolution" or several successive "revolutions," it is clear that prosperous farmers depended more and more upon upon meat, dairy products, and things other than wheat to pay their rents.[62] Whatever the economic effects of the corn laws and corn law repeal,[63] within the rural economy, the range of prosperity was scarcely smaller than it was in the economy as a whole. E. H. Hunt has emphasized the "under-developed" features of the southern and rural economy—low wages, low productivity, excess labor supply, and a low-wage philosophy among employers—and has distinguished these from the "developed" features of the northern and urban economy.[64] Essentially, this dual-economy concept derives from analyses of the Third World, but it is no less useful when applied to England and Wales in the mid-nineteenth century. In particular, it is conditioning the ways in which some historians are considering the standard-of-living question.

Until fairly recently, most historians who discussed this question strained after the widest possible generalizations. Although recognizing regional and occupational wage differences, they were generally intent on showing that industrialization was a "good thing" for the working class as a whole or a "bad thing" until its effects were mitigated by agitation or politics. All in all, they tended to allow that, in the period after the mid-1840s, things got better. Whatever the nonquantifiable evidence suggested, the quantifiable evidence of rising real wages seemed clear, at least for those who constituted the so-called aristocracy of labor.[65] Disagreements were focused upon the period before the mid-1840s; by and large they still are. But since the mid-1960s the straining for generalizations has been somewhat relaxed. Many historians have shifted their emphases toward the regional and occupational wage differences they previously tended to ignore. Also, they have emphasized the differences of life experience of the various cohorts who entered the labor market at times of rising or falling real wages and the importance of inflation and, even more, of deflation, in affecting real wages.[66] Presumably, these differences of experience conditioned the content of much of the literary evidence. Recently, too, accommodating the dual-economy concept, some of them have been stressing the size of the labor reserve in the low-wage economy in conditioning the wages paid in both. Those who define the problem in this way have various residual disagreements.[67] But they have far more in common with one another than they have with those other historians who are principally concerned with industrialization as a source of working-class consciousness. For the former, the standard-of-living question is largely an economic question affected by labor demand—and in particular, by labor demand in the industrial economy. For the latter, it is largely a social question, a measure of exploitation. At issue is the problem of class.

At the most fundamental level, perhaps, the class problem concerns the legitimacy of the social relationships associated with capitalism, industrial society, or modern urban society. But it also concerns the dynamics of that reform process, or of those reform processes, whose beginnings coincided with the emergence of this society, however defined, and which constitutes such an important part of its history. The question arises whether the reform process was really a single process. Whatever the answer to this question, the further question arises What was the relationship between this process, or set of processes, and the contemporary changes of social relationship?

Much of the recent discussion of these questions has stemmed from E. P. Thompson's *The Making of the English Working Class*.[68] Defining class as a measure of consciousness, Thompson contends that between 1780 and 1832, and mainly because of industrialization, most working people in England "came to feel an identity of interests between themselves and against their rulers and employers." In part, the importance of Thompson's book derives from the clarity with which he presents a two-class model of English industrial society, in part from the use he makes of this model to explain institutional change, in part from the example he provides of how to deal with men and women who were not members of those formally structured institutions on which historians have generally focused. Many historians share his interest in the relations among experience, consciousness, and action; some do so for humanistic reasons similar to his own. As he explains, one of his objects was "to rescue the poor stockinger, the Luddite cropper, the 'obsolete' hand-loom weaver, the 'utopian' artisan, and even the deluded follower of Joanna Southcote, from the enormous condescension of posterity" (p. 12). But others do so for other reasons entirely, some of them related to their interest in group cohesion and group motivation and the ways in which, from their point of view, such humanistic arguments distort the understanding of both. Nor are all historians convinced that working-class experiences were so uniform as to produce the sort of consciousness he describes either before 1832 or, indeed, at any other time before or since. Many are also unconvinced that the first Reform Act was a calculated measure of self-defense by an aristocracy and middle class prompted by the development of this consciousness to strengthen their own mutual alliances.

But Thompson is not alone. Focusing primarily upon Oldham, John Foster is mainly concerned to explain why the "revolutionary class consciousness" he finds manifest there in the 1830s and 1840s was lost—in effect, why the revolution Marx and Engels anticipated did not occur.[69] His answer lies in the very strength of the revolutionary consciousness itself: it prompted middle-class efforts to buy off the leaders, to split the working class by ameliorating the conditions of the so-called labor aristocracy. Attributing rather more importance to leadership and ideology than Thompson attributes to them, rather less to shared experience, he emphasizes the increasing social distance between the craftsmen and laborers. Ostensibly, this derived in part from the differential effects of Factory Acts upon different categories of worker and explains that break at mid-century between a period of class activism and a subsequent period of class collaboration or class quiescence. The argument touches on many questions concerning socialism, trade unionism, Chartism, radicalism in general, and the division of the century into periods.

Until recently there was general agreement about the identity and roles of Robert Owen and the Owenites: as native socialists they were important figures in the history of organized labor. But a new generation of social historians have described the Owenites as members of a communitarian movement important beyond the boundaries of the working class. J. F. C. Harrison, in particular, has minimized the importance of those few months in 1833/1834 when Owen found himself at the head of a large trade union and has emphasized the role of radical, paternalistic squires within the movement and the importance of the millenarian and sectarian elements within it which root it in a period of evangelical ascendency.[70] Others have complained that such views of Owen and Owenism trivialize the efforts to create an alternative culture which many working-class spokesmen have evoked.[71]

But a new generation of trade union historians, more concerned with industrial relations than with class, have been arguing that early-nineteenth-century trade unionism had less to do with socialism and class solidarity than with the efforts of different categories of worker to protect their sectional interests.[72] Recently, several historians who are more concerned with class than with industrial relations have implicitly subscribed to parts of the argument: they complain that the institutional development of trade unions in the nineteenth century was inimical to the real interests of the working class.[73] In effect, various of the propositions which, a generation or two ago, Sidney and Beatrice Webb, Mark Hovell, and G. D. H. Cole, in particular, combined into a strong interpretive framework are being challenged. For reasons partly empirical, partly political and theoretical, it is no longer so generally accepted that the social divisions implicit in the phrase "aristocracy of labor" were really new; that the so-called new-model unions associated with this aristocracy of labor were also new; that there really was a watershed at mid-century between a period of class-oriented unions and one of bourgeois unions; that trade unionism was a phenomenon of prosperity, political agitation a phenomenon of depression; and that violence was a measure of desperation.

As long as these propositions were accepted, there was general agreement not only that the depression of the late 1830s and early 1840s provided the principal dynamic of Chartism but also that the situation of the various domestic workers, the handloom weavers in particular, provided the principal dynamic of that physical-force Chartism which was clearly distinguishable from moral-force Chartism. The one was revolutionary. The other, associated with artisans and focused upon the franchise, was not. For some historians these propositions retain a good deal of their cogency.[74] For others less. The association between the handloom weavers and physical-force Chartism is no longer clear.[75] Nor is the boundary between moral- and physical-force Chartism. Biographical and local studies have revealed flows from one to the other and complex relations between Chartism and other movements.[76] Furthermore, the primacy of economic distress and the New Poor Law as background factors to the general problem of social unrest in the 1830s and 1840s has been challenged by arguments concerning the effects of change per se and, in particular, of pressures upon the internal structure of the working-class family.[77] There is general agreement about the importance of the trade cycle. Yet, while Dorothy Thompson insists that, for all intents and purposes, Chartism was a working-class movement, revolutionary in nature, which could not be accommodated within the sweep of radical liberalism,[78] others have found little coherence in the movement, thus little difficulty in recognizing the grounds of accommodation.[79]

Recently, the lack of coherence of radicalism has been illustrated in the biographies of various men from Cobbett, who died in 1835, and who is being recast as a radical reactionary, to George Howell, who became obsessed with respectability long before his death in 1906.[80] The Howell syndrome provides Trygve Tholfsen with a means of supplementing the traditional explanation of the collapse of early-nineteenth-century radicalism: not only did the working class adjust to a mature economy; it succumbed to the culture of "respectability."[81] But others contend that the image of working-class "respectability" is a myth created by various politicians in the 1860s to obscure what were, from their point of view, the unpleasant realities.[82] In part, the present state of these questions is the consequence of present political controversy; in part, of the growing concern about the limits of institutional history as traditionally practiced.

Some historians object on egalitarian grounds that the usual pictures traditional institutional history provides focus so largely upon the actions and attitudes of men, and of men who had power over "others" in state, church, trade union, or other comparable institution. Whether the "others" were really as impotent as the practice implies, they had to be "rescued" from the consequent "condescension." On more analytical grounds, other historians also object that such pictures often obscure important aspects of the very institutions and problems on which they focus: in particular, they tend to beg the questions of recruitment and of social identity, implying that the participation of the "others" was more spontaneous than it was conditioned.

The "people's history" which Raphael Samuel and the members of his History Workshop set out to write is largely expressive of egalitarian anti-institutionalism. The first of a projected twelve-volume series was concerned with village life in the middle of the nineteenth century. It described the enduring importance of various community components of this life, whether measured in terms of the communal elements of much rural work, or the continued observation of many local customs and rituals, or the widespread suspicion of outsiders. The second volume emphasized the differences between the lives of coal miners and other mineral workers and those of many factory workers. In the circumstances in which the miners lived and worked, close supervision by their employers was often impossible. In consequence, they frequently preserved or acquired considerable control over their own lives and patterns of work.[83] Eric Hobsbawm and George Rudé deal with somewhat more complex variables in *Captain Swing:* communities and the forces which impinged upon them.[84] They contend that the rick burnings of 1830 were entirely spontaneous, the results of local circumstances. They also claim that, in many cases, the rebelling farm workers had the sympathy of their neighbors, irrespective of status, in their efforts to resist the changes affecting their small worlds. But few in the government had the same sympathy. In both cases, rhythms, habits, and relationships are more strongly emphasized, formal institutions less strongly, than had been the practice before.

Similar changes are apparent in much recent work in women's history and family history. As a rule in the past, women and families were both regarded from the perspectives of a male-dominated world in which formal institutions were preeminently important. The focus in women's history was upon the efforts of a small minority of women, assisted by a still smaller minority of men, to remove the legal and political disadvantages of women. Similarly, in family history, the focus was upon the legal inequalities of men and women in matters of divorce, property, and so on. In effect, women were considered rather less in terms of their own roles and rather more in terms of their inability to perform other roles. They were regarded as a civil rights problem. This aspect of their case has not been forgotten. Indeed, one consequence of the women's liberation movement, to which so much of the recent interest in women's history should be attributed, has been an increased exploitation of the theme of the woman-as-victim.

Whether her victim status is used to symbolize the victim status of others in what Peter Cominos, referring to a somewhat later period, called a "respectable social system," or is treated as peculiarly her own, it has attracted considerable attention.[85] But another consequence of this movement has been an increased attention to women as participants rather than as victims. Whatever this may have cost in revolutionary élan, it has contributed much to the understanding of English society as a pluralistic universe which contained women's own different worlds as well as those their sons, husbands, and fathers inhabited and which they conditioned and helped to maintain. Undoubtedly, these tendencies have been strengthened by the recognition of the enhanced importance of family and family relationships in circumstances of increased geographical and, to some extent, social mobility. Michael Anderson emphasizes the point in his study of migration into Preston: in novel circumstances and circumstances of stress where other economic, social, and psychological supports and so on were not available, individual men and women depended rather more than they had before upon those which their families provided.[86]

Patricia Branca is more concerned to describe women's roles than to analyze changes of family structure. But in emphasizing the homemaking activities of Victorian middle-class women, she has, to some extent, done both.[87] Describing married women slightly higher in the middle-class range, Martha Vicinus emphasizes their roles in providing appropriate environments of respectability.[88] Leonore Davidoff's focus is higher still, upon those middle- and upper-class women who, from the 1820s, when "society" became too large to be policed as a kin group or set of kin groups, developed and administered the new rituals which guarded the access to the status levels they enjoyed.[89] Focusing upon the sizable numbers of unmarried or "surplus" women, Lee Holcombe tries to evaluate the role of the "women's movement" in helping them to create the various women's professions, those of nursing and teaching in particular, and concludes that the movement's role was small: the employment gains women enjoyed were mainly the product of larger economic causes.[90] To some extent, Pamela Horn's study of rural education confirms the message.[91] But domestic servants were far more numerous, and as Theresa McBride explains, it was for this reason that they were such an important factor in "modernizing" English society.[92] Branca, Judith Walkowitz, and others have developed further and rather complex aspects of the modernization theme while discussing women's roles in socializing their children and in responding to the Contagious Diseases Acts. Of a somewhat different nature was their frequent reluctance to exchange the attention of midwives for that of doctors.[93]

In educational history, similar departures from an institutional emphasis have been encouraged by the increasing tendency to regard education not only as a means of imparting information but also as a means of preparing children and adolescents for the roles of life in which they were expected to fill. Hence the increasing attention to the components of these expectations: education as part of an ongoing social system. This is new. Until fairly recently the principal themes in the history of popular education had to do with the increasing role of the state in the education system and with the reasons why this role did not increase more rapidly. The subject was treated as a branch of political, religious, and administrative history. D. W. Sylvester's sympathetic study of Robert Lowe and the educational policies of the early 1860s is one of the few recent works in this vein.[94] Most historians have moved to those other veins Richard Johnson helped to open when he suggested that, until at least 1870, most people involved in education in an official capacity were far more concerned with the unruliness of the population than they were with their ignorance.[95] In recent years some historians have emphasized the socialization or social-control aspects of education as seen "from above," others the instrumental aspects of it as seen by various members of the working classes, others the lack of working-class interest in education, and others still, that considerable interest which was manifest in the autonomous working-class Sunday schools and the culture of piety, thrift, and respectability they helped to create.[96] Some years ago, the proposition was popular that literacy must have declined in the early nineteenth century because factory workers could not have had the time or energy for such luxuries. Now it is recognized that the situation was far more complex than such a proposition allows.[97] Education meant different things to different people.

It has long been recognized that public schools catered to the social ambitions of an increasing number of parents, thus that these schools performed important functions in developing the values associated with these ambitions, those of state service in particular. In the mid-1960s Rupert Wilkinson added a new theme when he described the ways in which public school boys, isolated from their immediate families, developed enduring relationships among themselves.[98] The "muscular Christianity" theme which David Newsome emphasized figures prominently in the surveys by T. M. Bamford and, more recently, by J. R. de S. Honey, who has much to say about sin and social control, athleticism, the curricula of different schools, and school life and organization.[99] As Alicia Percival explains, the successful headmaster saw his school grow in size, wealth, and reputation, the latter dependent in no small way upon the establishment of close relations with particular Oxbridge colleges.[100]

There has been no survey of universities comparable in breadth to Bamford or Honey. In *Victorian Oxford*, W. R. Ward was mainly concerned with university organization and the formal development of studies.[101] Sheldon Rothblatt's discussion of Cambridge reflects broader concerns. In *The Revolution of the Dons*, he described the various influences which conspired to transform Cambridge into a "seminary of politicians" where undergraduates would receive a liberal education which would prepare them for service in church or state.[102] The theme is similar to that Melvin Richter developed in his study of the Oxford philosopher T. H. Green: the elaboration of an ethic of duty.[103] As Craig Jenks explains in his discussion of Green, such an ethic provided an effective defense against demands for institutional change.[104] The general relationship between the universities and society is somewhat differently conceived by Lawrence Stone, who, in his own contribution to *The University in Society*, suggests a correlation between the number of undergraduates at Oxford at any given date and the degree to which the channels between the University and the centers of society were open. As he points out, the enlargement of the University after 1860 coincided with the removal of religious tests.[105] Implicitly, Michael Sanderson describes a more complex set of social centers while explaining how the ethic of state service provided an effective means of preserving the anti-industrial orientations of Oxford and Cambridge, thus of preserving their isolation from those other movements in English society which found their expression in the new civic universities.[106]

The central importance of religion and religious themes in the nineteenth century has long been recognized, but in the last twenty years some historians have been considering these themes from a new perspective. They have shifted theirs focus away from law, politics, and doctrine, the activities of religious leaders and other intellectuals, and the relations between church and state. They have put more emphasis upon the relationships between religion and social environment and the networks which, radiating from the various churches and chapels, provided crucial mechanisms of social and political organization within the "respectable" world.

As in other parts of the field, however, much work is being done in the traditional veins. G. I. T. Machin's study of the Catholic question in the 1820s is mainly concerned with political maneuvers in Westminster.[107] The problems with which he deals in his study of the subsequent period down to 1868 are far more complex: the continuing challenge of the High Churchmen and Protestant Nonconformists to the existing Erastian Settlement and, manifesting the unyielding progress of religious liberty and the growing secularization of British life, the increasing assumption by the state of functions which, in some cases, had been performed previously within the general ambit of religion or the church.[108] Desmond Bowen has a different understanding of the story. He claims that the increasing functions of the state were really a measure of the church's success in implanting in the middle class "the old idea of *noblesse oblige* in the form of 'service' or 'duty'" (p. 380).[109] M. A. Crowther, on the other hand, describes a church which, weakened by the various doctrinal and other controversies the religious liberals intensified, was unable to retain its popular support or to cope with social problems.[110] Matters of belief are also Owen Chadwick's principal concern. The first volume of his magisterial two-volume study *The Victorian Church*, which deals rather more with Anglicans than with other denominations, ends in 1859, on the eve of *The Origin of the Species*. The second volume focuses upon the problems of belief which Darwin's work exacerbated. Different men tried to solve these problems in different ways. Chadwick attributes major responsibility for the subsequent decline in the numbers of educated men entering the clergy to the consequent confusion.[111]

But recently many historians have been considering religion and irreligion less as a matter of belief and more as a matter of social relations.[112] Studies of the Anglican clergy have focused upon them as members of social groups.[113] Studies of religious action have focused upon the varieties of network on which it depended and which it strengthened.[114] The complex relations between religion and class are the subject of James Obelkevich's study of Anglicans, Wesleyan Methodists, and Primitive Methodists in rural Lincolnshire.[115] Alan D. Gilbert is concerned with the question of why the rapid growth of Nonconformity came to such an abrupt halt around 1840 when many of the industrial villages in which it had been concentrated were absorbed into the expanding conurbations.[116] Whether the really crucial social divides were along the general lines of occupation and income or along those of respectability which religion tended to symbolize, the effort to use the law as an agent of cultural coercion in the 1850s was, as Brian Harrison explained, the cause of several riots.[117] The point illustrates an important political issue at the time, one on which the members of various denominations were significantly divided. It also illustrates certain limits of political action.

The recent changes in political history have been paticularly striking. Whether a further manifestation of the concern about the limits of traditional institutional history, or in response to Norman Gash's observation in *Politics in the Age of Peel*, that writers of national history should pay more attention to the provinces,[118] several historians have shifted their sights away from Westminster and Whitehall and the political leaders, intellectuals, and activists who were important on the London scene. But far more radical than such changes of venue are the efforts, whether focused on London or the provinces, to bring questions to bear upon the past analogous to those which various social scientists are bringing to bear upon the present.

Traditionally, politics provided the organizing framework of English history, the development of representative institutions toward an ultimate democracy its principal theme. And much as politics has often been regarded in rational terms as the implementation of ideas which intellectuals and other leaders articulated or, somewhat similarly, as a competition for power between a priori groups, so the development of these institutions has often been regarded as the realization of democratic theory. It is some years since some social scientists abandoned normative hypotheses and began studying the elements of present-day political systems in empirical terms. Far more recently did some historians follow their example while studying the political systems of the past and the changes which occurred within these systems. Occasionally, the conclusions reached by these procedures suggest the need for such radical revisions of the accepted pictures or stories as to greatly intensify the controversial nature of the procedures themselves. The audience for this work is still somewhat small. But for those who constitute this audience, the fact that much of the work has a quantitative base or is otherwise founded on impersonal evidence makes the conclusions that much more cogent. It is a point of controversy between them and many of the more humanistically oriented historians.

William O. Aydelotte is the doyen of the quantifiers in nineteenth-century English history. Much of his work has to do with the Parliament of 1841. Some of it has brought various arguments to a close. Using numerous division lists, he has shown, among other things, that there were clear ideological differences between the members of the Conservative and Liberal parties in this Parliament; that the claims which have been made on behalf of both, that they were responsible for social reform legislation, were misconceived (it was not a "party" question); that the Conservatives who split over the corn laws in 1846 had no previous parallel disagreements of remotely comparable importance on other issues; and that the relationships between MPs and their constituents were rather more complex than the usual understanding of elections suggests.[119]

By and large, the questions which parliamentary division lists have been used to answer are not new questions. What is new is the systematic exploitation of the information these lists contain. In some cases, the questions are new which pollbooks have been used to answer. The effective discovery of pollbooks, in which the voters' choices were reported, was stimulated, in part, by the work of Paul Lazarsfeld and his fellow sociologists.[120] But pollbooks made a kind of socio-political analysis possible for the mid-nineteenth century which is scarcely possible today, when voters have the secret ballot to hide behind. Not only could the question be anwered For whom did each voter vote? The further questions could also be raised: What conditioned their behavior? and How did the various reforms affect the balance of power in the state and the processes by which this balance was maintained or changed? Pollbooks reveal an intensely corporate or communal element in the behavior of many voters which has been used to challenge certain strongly held views about nineteenth-century individualism and the importance of issues as compared with loyalties in mid-nineteenth-century politics. Also, the groups which many voters constituted cannot be described in terms of occupation or class, and this has been used to challenge certain strongly held views about the relationships between politics and class.[121]

Somewhat more complex are the questions the pollbook evidence suggests concerning the dynamics of parliamentary reform and the role of reform in establishing an ultimate democracy.[122] All historians who use pollbooks are by no means agreed in their understanding of voter behavior. Even less are they agreed that the Reform Acts of 1832 and 1867/1868 were designed to control rather than to enhance the political effects of economic and social change. But these points aside, the historians whose primary focus is upon the behavior of their subjects, who regard other categories of evidence in the light of such behavior, tend to have far more in common with one another than they have with those other historians whose primary focus is upon the more traditional forms of literary evidence, who regard behavior in terms of the explanations which literary evidence often provides. A basic epistemological question has acquired a new importance because of the differences between the general conclusions to which they lead.

While the lines are fairly sharply drawn on such matters between some "humanists" and some "social scientists," many political historians do, however, go about their business relatively unaffected by the resultant controversies. Boyd Hilton's study of the economic policies of the Tory governments between 1815 and 1830 is traditional in scope, although he comes to the novel conclusion that the movement toward free trade was due neither to the pressures of a "rising bourgeoisie" nor to those of the classical economists but to the government's concern for the nation's food supply.[123] His argument has much in common with Susan Fairlie's argument about corn law repeal.[124] Austin Mitchell's study of the Whigs before 1830 illustrates their actual weakness and disorganization.[125] There have been several recent studies of the first Reform Act that place it in the context of that liberal movement in which the authors believe it belongs.[126] Several historians have described the general problems of the central party leaders in the two decades following the first Reform Act.[127] Claims made on behalf of Melbourne's intellectual stature have been belittled by Philip Ziegler.[128] John Russell's rashness and his exalted views of his family's importance have been emphasized by John Prest.[129] In such company, John Clive's Macaulay is very much the parvenu.[130] On the other side of the House, Norman Gash's Peel remains, in the second volume of his *Life*, a man of immense integrity.[131]

Several historians have dealt with the corn laws, emphasizing their importance to the general run of farmers,[132] or to certain politicians,[133] or to those inefficient agriculturists who, somewhat illogically, looked to the corn laws to protect them from their more efficient neighbors.[134] Implying a greater ministerial autonomy, Fairlie describes the corn laws as measures which had to be abandoned before an anticipated British dearth became real.[135] J. B. Conacher makes much of the ideological differences which, he claims, distinguished the Peelites from the Protectionists.[136] In *The Aberdeen Coalition*, he emphasized the common ground among Liberals, Radicals, and Peelites which would later make the Gladstonian Liberal Party a possibility.[137] W. D. Jones and Arvel B. Erickson tell a very different story of personal animosities stemming from the crucial corn law division which made it difficult for many Peelites to work in harmony with most Conservatives, thus ultimately driving them into alliance with the Liberals.[138]

Olive Anderson's interests in this period go beyond Parliament to the Crimea on the one hand, where the story was one of aristocratic incompetence and bravery, to the British provinces on the other where, ostensibly, the revelations about the Crimea had much to do with a resurgence of radicalism.[139] Paul W. Schroeder's interests are in the chancelleries of Europe, where, he contends, the concert of Europe broke down, largely because of the disdainful attitudes of the British, Clarendon in particular.[140] In a new biography by Jasper Ridley, Palmerston is portrayed as a paternalistic grandee.[141] In what some regard as the best recent biography of a nineteenth-century political leader, Robert Blake describes Disraeli's many complexities.[142] Gladstone, too, is being redone, the evidence from his newly available *Diaries* throwing much light on both his public and private activities, including those involving prostitutes which aroused so much titillating interest at the time.[143]

On a different note, emphasizing the degree to which "the mobilization of small blocs of dedicated voters" (p. 10) was facilitated by the small size of many constituencies, David Hamer describes the strategies of various reform associations or pressure groups.[144] Using both traditional and nontraditional procedures, John Vincent has tried to explain the development of that remarkably heterogenous party which acknowledged Gladstone's leadership.[145] Describing parliamentary leaders, intellectuals, local activists, and with the aid of pollbooks, the behavior of voters in certain boroughs, he has emphasized an important point, the degree to which political relationships overlapped other relationships.

But the questions remain to which, as yet, there are no agreed answers: Which relationships were the most fundamental? What affected them? How were they preserved? and Why did they change? T. J. Nossiter describes politics as a thing perceived. Assuming that there are really only three ways in which it can be perceived, in terms of "corruption," "influence," and "opinion," and assuming, further, that these are really distinct from one another, he traces the autonomous growth of "opinion" politics—from his point of view the only real politics—in the Northeast.[146] Focusing upon Buckinghamshire and applying somewhat similar assumptions, Richard Davis describes the increasing importance of "independent" opinions which neither corruption nor intimidation could control.[147] R. J. Olney's picture of Lincolnshire is both more descriptive and more complex.[148] Derek Fraser describes an integrated world of urban politics in which political forces "ran in a circle, launched from the minor institutions [of parish and township], transmitted through municipal government, expressed in a parliamentary election, forced into Parliament's view and bounced back again to the minor institution" (p. 280).[149] The dynamics derived from "conflict over the exercise of power in urban society." Real change, he contends, did not occur until after 1880. D. C. Moore has described mid-century politics less in terms of forward-looking programs than in terms of efforts to preserve the status of existing elites and the integrity of the various communities in which this status was recognized.[150]

There has been a good deal of recent disagreement about the second Reform Act which illustrates the differences among attitudes and methodologies. Royden Harrison describes the act as a fairly simple concession to the threat of revolution.[151] While insisting that the various provisions of the final Conservative measure were not fully understood at the time, F. B. Smith places it at the end of a long-term radical agitation which many MPs were concerned to settle.[152] Emphasizing how the final Conservative measure provided a wider extension of the franchise than the initial Liberal measure would have provided, Gertrude Himmelfarb describes the final measure as evidence of that confidence in the people which Tory democracy ostensibly symbolized.[153] Intensely skeptical of the role of ideology and of the degree to which nineteenth-century politicians were responsive to extraparliamentary pressures, Maurice Cowling places the final measure within the context of intraparliamentary rivalries.[154] Emphasizing conservative aspects of the second Reform Act similar to those he believes he found in the first, D. C. Moore describes the measure as an effort to preserve a political system in which power was more the consequence of social relationship than of bureaucratic role.[155]

Various of these descriptions of the political system as a whole and of the second Reform Act in particular emphasize the importance of those communities and networks of a nonbureaucratic society which have only really been noticed within the last ten or twenty years. This notice has not only affected the picture of politics. It has also affected certain aspects of the general story of nineteenth-century bureaucratic growth.

Traditionally, the story has contained a paradox. During the period when laissez-faire was supposed to have characterized government policy, the formal agencies of central and local government expanded rapidly in numbers, size, and power. Some years ago the late J. B. Brebner suggested a very simple way of resolving this paradox. It involved a reinterpretation of Jeremy Bentham. At the time Brebner wrote, the assumption was strong to which A. V. Dicey had given classical articulation: that government policies in the middle years of the nineteenth century reflected Bentham's influence. Brebner was happy to acknowledge this influence. But while Dicey's Bentham was an ardent individualist and spokesman of laissez-faire, Brebner's Bentham was "the archtype of British collectivism" (p. 61), whose *Constitutional Code* provided the plans which set Britain on the road toward the welfare state.[156] According to Oliver MacDonagh and, initially, to David Roberts, humanitarianism was a far more important dynamic than Benthamism in what MacDonagh called "the nineteenth century revolution in government."[157] Some historians, following in Brebner's footsteps, elaborated the general proposition that Bentham's influence, or the influence of the philosophic radicals—whether they got their ideas from Bentham, or from James Mill, or whomever—was mainly responsible for determining the reformist policies of the Liberal party in the years immediately after Bentham's death in 1832 and, more generally, the subsequent course of government growth.[158] Others belittled the degree to which the philosophic radicals comprised a coherent group.[159] Others, following in MacDonagh's footsteps, stressed the importance of that humanitarianism which, ostensibly, was aroused by the "intolerability" of urban and industrial conditions.[160] In effect, the question was joined whether the sources of the welfare state were more secular than religious, more Benthamite than humanitarian.[161]

In the last few years, at least for some historians, this question has been somewhat redefined. Not only has Aydelotte shown that, in the Parliament of 1841, neither the Radicals nor the Conservatives, as such, were responsible for welfare legislation, but studies of various departments of government have revealed differences in the patterns of departmental development which are scarcely compatible with the notion that there was a single process of government growth.[162] Even more important, perhaps, was the growing realization that the categories "individualist" and "collectivist" into which, for many years, nineteenth-century Englishmen had been divided, were inappropriate.

A generation ago Lionel Robbins made the point that many classical economists were not uncritical spokesmen of laissez-faire.[163] Recently, Warren T. Samuels carried the point further, emphasizing not only the importance the classical
economists attributed to informal social controls, but also the grounds of their
general ambivalence toward formal government: on the one hand, their assumption that any harmony of interests in society was created rather than natural; on
the other, their belief that formal government was usually corrupt, partisan, and
inefficient.[164] Some years ago the notion was growing that many classical economists were theoretical anarchists. Now, some of them are being recognized as
not unintelligent observers of a complex institutional world whose arguments,
greatly oversimplified in the retelling, had been read in the light of subsequent
controversies about the role of the bureaucratic state. In part, the difference illustrates the new anti-institutionalism. It reflects an increased interest in the many
relationships which, while serving to order the society in crucial ways, were neither matters of law nor, as a rule, subjects of contemporary analysis. In part, it
reflects a changing attitude toward contemporary rhetoric. As David Roberts suggested recently in a major departure from his earlier position, contemporary arguments about the functions of paternalism may have had more to do with the
defense mechanisms of a traditional society than with the development of the welfare state.[165]

Studies of poor-law policy and poor-law reform have been particularly ger-
mane to these questions. By illustrating the differences between theory and practice, they have raised the question whether these were a measure of the failure of
practice to accord with theory or an indication of the degree to which the functions of theory and practice were autonomous. J. D. Marshall has reiterated
Mark Blaug's conclusions, that the Speenhamland system of supplementing
wages out of poor rates had been abandoned in most parishes some years before
the poor law commissioners, for reasons of their own, reported its ostensible increase; also, that the system was not the unmitigated disaster it was purported to
be both then and later.[166] In the light of the growing realization that there were
major differences between the commissioners' report and the Poor Law Amendment Act,[167] questions arise about the traditionally assumed dynamics of reform
and the general problem of explanation. Recently, Raymond Cowherd repeated
the story of Malthusian and Benthamite propaganda culminating in centralizing
reform.[168] Distinguishing between propaganda and legislation and emphasizing
the importance of the questions the Poor Law Amendment Act left open for subsequent administrative negotiation, A. J. Brundage tells a very different story of
efforts to advise rather more than to centralize, and to advise as a means of preserving, not changing, the existing elites and the existing bases of social power.[169]

Some years ago the significance of the act seemed clear: it symbolized a middle-
class society replete with ostensibly Benthamite values, the society Dickens de-

scribed in *Hard Times* and *Oliver Twist*. Today, neither the nature of the act nor its significance is clear. N. C. Edsall describes the local resistance to the novelties the act introduced in the North.[170] Eric Midwinter describes the continuities of policy in Lancashire.[171] As Derek Fraser observed in his introduction to a recent collection of essays on the New Poor Law, "The New Poor Law is well known in image and theory. . . . The actual practice is less well known and is still in the process of exploration by historians."[172] His comment not only describes the present state of poor law studies, it goes on to describe the far larger arena in which questions have been raised about the roles of the theories and images which, once-upon-a-time, provided the outlines of the stories historians told. On the particular point of the poor laws and government growth, William C. Lubenow suggested a promising direction of further study when he observed that some of the conflicts and tensions generated by economic and social change in the early Victorian period were absorbed by the central government, some by local government, some publicly, some privately.[173] When certain government departments were established to help private individuals perform their "governmental" functions, the divisions between public and private become more a subject for further research and less a matter of a priori definition.

As the number of studies of John Stuart Mill suggest, he and his father are endlessly fascinating.[174] Cecil Woodham-Smith's new biography of Victoria somewhat reopens the question of Albert's influence in curtailing the monarch's political role.[175] Country houses and fox hunting are beginning to receive the attention they deserve.[176] In his survey of foreign policy, Kenneth Bourne focuses rather less upon diplomatic negotiations than had been usual and rather more upon the commercial factors in international relations.[177] In various case studies D. C. M. Platt illustrates the same tendency.[178] Eugene Rasor describes the changes which occurred in the treatment of sailors in the Royal Navy as routine discipline took the place of corporal punishment.[179] Allan Skelley tells a similar story about the army.[180] Hugh Cunningham stresses the importance of the fact that discipline among the volunteers depended far less upon military law than upon the social authority of individual officers.[181]

Many of these works illustrate changes of view in the field. More important, they illustrate the changing categories of problem on which some historians are working and the changing assumptions which inform their work.

Some years ago G. M. Young declared that "the function of the nineteenth century was to disengage the disinterested intelligence, to release it from the entanglements of party and sect—one might almost add, of sex—and to set it operating over the whole range of human life and circumstance" (p. 186).[182] Such assumptions, from the possible existence of a "disinterested intelligence" to the proposition that a century might have a "function," were not his alone. They were widely shared. They conditioned the content of "history." They provided the themes on which the authors of various surveys focused. Today, these assumptions are less widely shared. Furthermore, no substitute assumptions have emerged to take their place. This creates a difficult situation for the would-be author of a survey history. Not only have many "facts" been challenged; the frameworks of explanation which, once upon a time, served to organize these "facts" have also been challenged.

Traditionally, history was a game anyone could play because it was played in terms of those general cultural assumptions which, by and large, everyone within the culture shared. Most historians proclaimed this as a virtue. It was the guarantee of humanistic truth, a means of preserving the culture itself. Today, many historians have become skeptical of this truth and more concerned to analyze the culture than simply to preserve it. History is still a game which anyone can play, but some historians are adopting new rules which reflect their new concerns. Their games are very different from those the others play and increasingly different from those generally played in the past.

NOTES

1. M. Drake, "The Census, 1801–1891," in E. A. Wrigley, ed., *Nineteenth Century Society: Essays in the Use of Quantitative Methods for the Study of Social Data*, Cambridge, 1972, and P. M. Tillott, "Sources of Inaccuracy in the 1851 and 1861 Censuses," ibid.

2. According to J. T. Krause, "The Changing Adequacy of English Registration, 1690–1837," in D. V. Glass and D. E. C. Eversley, eds., *Population in History: Essays in Historical Demography*, London, 1965, different factors should be used for different periods to compensate, in particular, for the growing numbers of Non-Conformists and their changing relationships with the Anglican clergy. But according to P. E. Razzell, "An Interpretation of the Modern Rise of Population in Europe: A Critique," *Population Studies* 28, 1974, the errors were constant over time.

3. Mark Blaug, "The Myth of the Old Poor Law and the Making of the New," *JEcH* 23 1963; idem, "The Poor Law Report Reexamined," *JEcH* 24, 1964; J. Huzel, "Malthus, the Poor Law and Population in Early Nineteenth Century England," *EcHR*, 2d ser., 22, 1969. Questions concerning the poor laws themselves are discussed below.

4. The arguments in T. McKeown, R. G. Brown, and R. G. Record, "An Interpretation of the Modern Rise of Population in Europe," *Population Studies* 26, London, 1972, and in T. McKeown, *The Modern Rise of Population*, London, 1976, are, in part, criticisms of those in M. C. Buer, *Health, Wealth and Population in Eighteenth-century England*, London, 1926, and in G. T. Griffith, *Population Problems in the Age of Malthus*, London, 1926, which had been incorporated into many textbooks. As McKeown notes in "Fertility, Mortality and Causes of Death," *Population Studies*, 32, 1978, the evidence for improvements in nutrition in the late eighteenth and early nineteenth centuries is largely circumstantial. On this point see also J. Burnett, *Plenty and Want*, London, 1966; T. C. Barker, J. C. McKenzie, and J. Yudin,

eds., *Our Changing Fare*, London, 1966; and D. J. Oddy and D. S. Miller, eds., *The Making of the Modern English Diet*, London, 1976.

5. P. Razzell, "Population Change in Eighteenth-century England: A Re-interpretation," *EcHR*, 2d ser., 18, 1965; idem, "An Interpretation of the Modern Rise of Population in Europe: A Critique," *Population Studies* 28, 1974, which is a general criticism of McKeown's argument; E. M. Sigsworth, "Gateways to Death? Medicine, Hospitals and Mortality, 1700–1850," in P. Mathias, ed., *Science and Society*, Cambridge, 1972; M. Drake, *Population in Industrialization*, London, 1969; J. Woodward, *To Do the Sick No Harm: A Study of the British Voluntary Hospital System to 1875*, London, 1974; J. Woodward and D. Richards, eds., *Health Care and Popular Medicine in Nineteenth Century England*, New York, 1977.

6. E. A. Wrigley, "Family Limitation in Pre-industrial England," *EcHR*, 2d ser., 19, 1966. The question is further discussed in idem, *Population and History*, London, 1969.

7. P. Deane and W. A. Cole, *British Economic Growth, 1689–1959*, Cambridge, 1962. This question is discussed in M. W. Flinn, *British Population Growth 1700–1850*, London, 1970, which also provides a useful general survey.

8. J. Matras has tried to calculate the increased proportions of women born in different periods between 1831 and 1906 who practiced some form of birth control: "Social Categories of Family Formation: Data for British Female Cohorts Born 1831–1906," *Population Studies* 2, 1965. E. Shorter, "Female Emancipation, Birth Control and Fertility in European History," *AHR* 78, 1973; A. McLaren, "The Early Birth Control Movement: An Example of Medical Self-help," in Woodward and Richards, *Health Care and Popular Medicine*; and idem, *Birth Control in Ninteenth-century England*, London, 1978, discuss the question in more complex terms.

9. H. J. Habakkuk, *Population Growth and Economic Development since 1750*, Leicester, 1971. Other important recent discussions of these general problems are K. Helleiner, "The Population of Europe from the Black Death to the Eve of the Vital Revolution," *Cambridge Economic History of Europe* vol. 4, Cambridge, 1967, and N. Tranter, *Population since the Industrial Revolution: The Case of England and Wales*, London, 1973. R. Mitchison, *British Population Growth since 1860*, London, 1977, provides a useful general survey.

10. J. D. Chambers, "Enclosure and Labour Supply in the Industrial Revolution," *EcHR*, 2d ser., 5, 1953.

11. A. Briggs, *Victorian Cities*, London, 1963.

12. H. J. Dyos, Preface, to E. P. Hennock, *Fit and Proper Persons: Ideal and Reality in Nineteenth-century Urban Government*, London, 1973.

13. In particular, see F. M. Jones, "The Aesthetic of the Nineteenth Century Industrial Town," in H. J. Dyos, ed., *Studies in Urban History*, Leicester, 1968, and J. A. Banks, "The Contagion of Numbers," B. Harrison, "Pubs," J. Summerson, "London the Artifact," and M. R. Booth, "The Metropolis on Stage," all in H. J. Dyos and M. Wolff, eds., *The Victorian City: Images and Realities*, vol. 1, London, 1973. See also R. D. Altick, *The Shows of London: A Panoramic History of Exhibitions, 1600–1862*, Cambridge, Mass., 1978. W. Weber, *Music and the Middle Class: The Social Structure of Concert Life in London, Paris and Vienna*, London, 1975, discusses an increasingly important social arena. R. H. Kargon, *Science in Victorian Manchester: Enterprise and Expertise*, Baltimore, 1977, emphasizes the importance of the influence of Manchester upon science and vice versa. Towns as arenas of professional development are emphasized by G. Millerson, *The Qualifying Associations: A Study in Professionalization*, London, 1964; W. J. Reader, *Professional Men: The Rise of the Professional Classes in Nineteenth-century England*, London, 1966; H. Perkin, *The Origins of Modern English Society, 1780–1880*, London, 1969; and M. J. Peterson, *The Medical Profession in Mid-Victorian London*, Berkeley and Los Angeles, 1978. O. Anderson, "Did Suicide Increase with Industrialization in Vic-

torian England"? (*PP*, no. 86, 1980, suggests that the traditional association between industrialization, urbanization, and anomie has less to do with reality than with enduring bucolic
fantasies. L. H. Lees, *Exiles of Erin: Irish Migrants in Victorian London*, Ithaca, N.Y., 1979,
amplifies the argument in her "Patterns of Lower-Class Life: Irish Slum Communities in
Nineteenth-century London," in S. Thernstrom and R. Sennett, eds., *Nineteenth-century Cities: Essays in the New Urban History*, New Haven, Conn., 1969, concerning both the resilience
and the traditionalism of urban migrants, a point which M. Anderson emphasizes for Preston
in *Family Structure in Nineteenth-century Lancashire*, Cambridge, 1971. Whatever the meaning
of urbanization, D. Friedlander, "The Spread of Urbanization in England and Wales,
1851–1951," *Population Studies* 24 1970, attempts to measure its progress county by county.
See also D. Friedlander and R. J. Roshier, "A Study of Internal Migration in England and
Wales: Part I," *Population Studies* 19, 1966. R. Welch, *Migration Research and Migration in
Britain: A Selected Bibliography*, London, 1970, is more useful for the sociological than the
cultural aspects of urbanization.

14. E. Durkheim, *The Division of Labor in Society*, G. Simpson, trans., New York, 1966.

15. F. Vigier, *Change and Apathy: Liverpool and Manchester during the Industrial Revolution*, Lon-
    don, 1970.

16. Hennock, *Fit and Proper Persons*; idem, "Finance and Politics in Urban Local Government in
    England, 1835–1900," *HJ* 6, 1963.

17. These questions are discussed below.

18. H. J. Dyos, *Victorian Suburb: A Study of the Growth of Camberwell*, Leicester, 1961.

19. D. Olsen, *Town Planning in London in the Eighteenth and Nineteenth Centuries*, London, 1964;
    idem, "House upon House: Estate Development in London and Sheffield," in Dyos and Wolff,
    Victorian City; idem, "Victorian London: Specialization, Segregation and Privacy," *VS* 17,
    1974; idem, *The Growth of Victorian London*, London, 1976.

20. The theme is prominent in D. A. Reeder, "A Theatre of Suburbs: Some Patterns of Develop-
    ment in West London, 1801–1911," in Dyos, *Studies in Urban History*. See also T. C. Barker
    and M. Robbins, *A History of London Transport*, vol. 1, *The Nineteenth Century*, 1963, the
    standard work on nineteenth-century London transport; J. Simmons, "The Power of the Rail-
    way," in Dyos and Wolff, *Victorian City*; and H. J. Dyos and D. H. Aldcroft, *British Trans-
    port: An Economic History from the Seventeenth Century to the Twentieth* Leicester, 1969.

21. These points, which Dyos and Olsen made, have been developed by various others, among
    them F. M. L. Thompson, *Hampstead, Building a Borough 1650–1964*, London, 1974;
    D. Cannadine, "The Calthorpe Family and Birmingham, 1810–1910: A 'Conservative In-
    terest' Examined," *HJ* 18, 1975; idem, "The Landowner as Millionaire: The Finances of
    the Dukes of Devonshire, c. 1800–c. 1926," *Agricultural History Review* 25, 1975; idem,
    "Victorian Cities: How Different"? *Social History* 4, 1977; idem, "From 'Feudal' Lords to
    Figureheads," *Urban History Yearbook*, 1978; and especially, idem, *Lords and Landlords: The
    Aristocracy and the Towns 1774–1967*, Leicester, 1980.

22. J. P. Lewis, *Building Cycles and Britain's Growth*, London, 1965.

23. H. J. Dyos, "The Speculative Builders and Developers of Victorian London," *VS* 11, 1968;
    M. A. Simpson and T. H. Lloyd, eds., *Middle Class Housing in Britain*, Newton Abbot,
    1977; H. Hobhouse, *Thomas Cubitt: Master Builder*, London, 1971.

24. J. Burnett, *A Social History of Housing 1815–1970*, London, 1978.

25. See especially the contributions to S. D. Chapman, ed., *The History of Working Class Housing:
    A Symposium*, Newton Abbot, 1971, and to Simpson and Lloyd, *Middle Class Housing in
    Britain*.

26. According to E. P. Thompson, "The Political Education of Henry Mayhew," *VS* 11, 1967,
    they were the latter. See also E. Thompson and E. Yeo, *The Unknown Mayhew: Selections from*

the Morning Chronicle, 1849–1850, London, 1971. According to G. Himmelfarb, "May-hew's Poor: A Problem of Identity," *VS* 14, 1971, they were the former. See also idem, "The Culture of Poverty," in Dyos and Wolff, *Victorian City*, and A. Humphreys, *Travels into Poor Man's Country: The Work of Henry Mayhew*, Athens, Ga., 1977.

27. B. Harrison, "Philanthropy and the Victorians," *VS* 9, 1966, suggested the usefulness of a more extended definition than that used by D. Owen, *English Philanthropy, 1660–1960*, Cambridge, Mass., 1964.

28. J. D. Marshall, "Colonisation as a Factor in the Planting of Towns in North-west England," in Dyos, *Studies in Urban History*; J. N. Tarn, *Working-class Housing in Nineteenth-century Britain*, London, 1971; idem, *Five Per Cent Philanthropy: An Account of Housing in Urban Areas between 1840 and 1914*, London, 1974.

29. J. Fido, "The Charity Organisation Society and Social Casework in London, 1869–1900," in A. P. Donajgrodzki, ed., *Social Control in Nineteenth Century Britain*, London, 1977. See also A. S. Wohl, *The Eternal Slum: Housing and Social Policy in Victorian London*, London, 1977.

30. G. S. Jones, *Outcast London: A Study in the Relationship between Classes in Victorian Society*, Oxford, 1971.

31. H. J. Dyos, "The Slums of Victorian London," *VS* 11, 1967. Among other recent studies of housing is E. Gouldie, *Cruel Habitations: A History of Working Class Housing, 1780–1918*, London, 1974. Among other recent works in urban history are R. Newton, *Victorian Exeter, 1837–1914*, Leicester, 1968; F. Hill, *Victorian Lincoln*, London, 1975; and F. Sheppard, *London 1808–1870: The Infernal Wen*, London, 1971, which are somewhat traditionally focused upon politics, and A. Armstrong, *Stability and Change in an English Country Town: A Social Study of York, 1801–51*, London, 1974. S. Marcus, *Engels, Manchester and the Working Class*, London, 1974, is relatively untouched by the concerns of the "new" urban historians.

32. R. D. Storch, "The Policeman as Domestic Missionary: Urban Discipline and Popular Culture in Northern England, 1850–1880," *Journal of Social History* 9, 1976. See also idem, "The Plague of the Blue Locusts: Police Reform and Popular Resistance in Northern England, 1840–1857," *International Review of Social History* 20, 1975. The dynamics of urban property crime has become a matter of considerable controversy between those who take a more economic view of it and those who take a more social view. See, in particular, J. J. Tobias, *Crime and Industrial Society in the Nineteenth Century*, London, 1967; idem, *Nineteenth Century Crime: Prevention and Punishment*, London, 1972; and on the social side of the question, V. A. C. Gattrell and B. Hadden, "Criminal Statistics and Their Interpretation," in Wrigley, *Nineteenth Century Society*. Allan Silver, "The Demand for Order in Civil Society: A Review of Some Themes in the History of Urban Crime, Police and Riot," in D. J. Bordua, ed., *The Police: Six Sociological Essays*, New York, 1967, provides an important frame of reference for the discussion of the question whether crime and social unrest were more effectively controlled by mechanisms of social network or by those of an impersonal police. See also W. R. Miller, *Cops and Bobbies: Police Authority in New York and London, 1830–1870*, London, 1977; R. Quinault and J. Stevenson, eds., *Popular Protest and Public Order: Six Studies in British History, 1790–1920*, London, 1975; and with a wider geographical focus, T. R. Gurr, *Rogues, Rebels and Reformers: A Political History of Urban Crime and Conflict*, Beverly Hills, Calif., 1977. Other aspects of the general theme of crime are discussed in J. J. Tobias, *Prince of Foxes: The Life and Crimes of Ikey Solomon*, London, 1974, and M. May, "Innocence and Experience: The Evolution of the Concept of Juvenile Delinquency in the Mid-nineteenth Century," *VS* 17, 1973.

33. P. Mathias, *The First Industrial Nation: An Economic History of Britain 1700–1914*, London, 1969.

34. E.g., H. J. Habakkuk, *Population and Economic Growth since 1750*, Leicester, 1971, for the former position and B. Inglis, *Poverty and the Industrial Revolution*, London, 1971, for the latter.

35. E. J. Hobsbawm, "From Social History to the History of Society," *Daedalus* 100, 1971.

36. Mathias, *First Industrial Nation*.

37. P. M. Deane, "New Estimates of Gross National Wealth for the United Kingdom, 1830–1914," *Review of Incomes and Wealth* 14, 1968; idem, "The Role of Capital in the Industrial Revolution," *Explorations in Entrepreneurial History* 10, 1972–1973; J. P. P. Higgins and S. Pollard, with the assistance of J. E. Ginarlis, eds., *Aspects of Capital Investment in Great Britain, 1750–1850: A Preliminary Survey*, London, 1971; F. Crouzet, ed., *Capital Formation in the Industrial Revolution*, London, 1972; and C. H. Feinstein, "Capital Formation in Great Britain," *Cambridge Economic History of Europe* vol. 7, pt. 1, Cambridge, 1978.

38. D. C. Coleman, "Textile Growth," in N. B. Harte and K. G. Ponting, eds., *Textile History and Economic History*, Manchester, 1973.

39. Among recent studies of successful nineteenth-century textile firms are D. C. Coleman, *Courtaulds: An Economic and Social History*, vol. 1, *The Nineteenth Century, Silk and Crepe*, Oxford, 1970; F. A. Wells, *Hollins and Viyella: A Study in Business History*, Newton Abbot, 1968; D. A. Farnie, "John Rylands of Manchester," *BJRL* 56, 1973; and C. H. Lee, *A Cotton Enterprise, 1795–1840: A History of McConnel and Kennedy, Fine Cotton Spinners*, Manchester, 1972. Among recent studies of unsuccessful firms are R. Boyson, *The Ashworth Cotton Enterprise: The Rise and Fall of a Family Firm, 1818–1880*, Oxford, 1970; K. G. Ponting, *The Woolen Industry of South West England*, Newton Abbot, 1971; and J. de L. Mann, *The Cloth Industry of the West of England from 1640 to 1880*, Oxford, 1971.

40. Among other recent business histories are J. B. Addis, *The Crawshay Dynasty: A Study of Industrial Organization and Development*, Cardiff, 1967; R. A. Church, *Kendricks in Hardware: A Family Business, 1791–1966*, Newton Abbot, 1969; T. A. B. Corley, *Quaker Enterprise in Biscuits: Huntley and Palmers of Reading, 1822–1972*, London, 1972; A. E. Musson, *Enterprise in Soap and Chemicals, Joseph Crosfield and Sons Ltd, 1815–1965*, Manchester, 1965; A. Raistrick, *Dynasty of Ironfounders*, Newton Abbot, 1970; and C. Trebilcock, *The Vickers Brothers: Armaments and Enterprise, 1854–1914*, London, 1977. R. Burt, *John Taylor, Mining Enterpreneur and Engineer, 1779–1863*, Harrington, 1977, is an interesting industrial biography which illustrates the importance of religious networks in the industrial world. P. L. Payne, *British Entrepreneurship in the Nineteenth Century*, London, 1974, and idem, "Industrial Entrepreneurship and Management in Great Britain," *Cambridge Economic History of Europe*, vol. 7, pt. 1, Cambridge, 1978, provide valuable surveys.

41. W. Albert, *The Turnpike Road System in England, 1663–1840*, Cambridge, 1972, describes the challenge railways represented to the turnpike road system by 1840. J. Copeland, *Roads and Their Traffic 1750–1850*, London, 1968, is more anecdotal. L. A. Williams, *Road Transport in Cumbria in the Nineteenth Century*, London, 1975, carries an excellent local study past the time when railways had captured most of the long-distance traffic. But as F. M. L. Thompson indicates, horses continued to increase in number until motor cars displaced them: "Nineteenth-century horse sense," *EcHR*, 2d ser., 29, 1976. C. Hadfield, *The Canal Age*, London, 1968, is less useful than his *British Canals*, 2d ed., London, 1959. H. Perkin, *The Age of the Railway*, London, 1970, is an important study of changes in the modes of transportation and their impact upon society. F. C. Mather, *After the Canal Duke: A Study of the Industrial Estates Administered by the Trustees of the Third Duke of Bridgewater in the Age of Railway Building*, Oxford, 1970, focuses on the problem railways represented to an estate whose principal investments were in canals.

42. E. J. Hobsbawm, *Industry and Empire*, Pelican Economic History of Britain, Vol. 3, From 1750 to the Present Day, London, 1968; S. G. Checkland, *The Rise of Industrial Society in England*, London, 1964.

43. G. R. Hawke, *Railways and Economic Growth in England and Wales, 1840–1870*, Oxford, 1970.

44. See, especially, D. H. Aldcroft, "Railways and Economic Growth," *Journal of Transport History*, n.s., 1, 1972.

45. See, especially, T. J. Donaghy, *Liverpool and Manchester Railway Operations 1831–1845*, Newton Abbot, 1972, and T. R. Gourvish, *Mark Huish and the London and North Western Railway: A Study of Management*, Leicester, 1972.

46. P. S. Bagwell, *The Railway Clearing House in the British Economy, 1842–1922*, London, 1968.

47. H. Parris, *Government and the Railways in Nineteenth-century Britain*, London, 1965.

48. J. R. Kellett, *The Impact of Railways on Victorian Cities*, London, 1969.

49. D. Brooke, "Railway Navvies on the Pennines, 1841–71," *Journal of Transport History*, n.s., 3, 1975; T. Coleman, *The Railway Navvies*, London, 1965.

50. G. Biddle, *Victorian Stations*, Newton Abbot, 1973. An interesting collection of articles in railway history is M. C. Reed, ed., *Railways in the Victorian Economy: Studies in Finance and Economic Growth*, Newton Abbot, 1969. See also S. Broadbridge, *Studies in Railway Expansion and the Capital Market in England 1825–1873*, London, 1970, and P. W. Kingsford, *Victorian Railwaymen: The Emergence and Growth of Railway Labour 1830–1870*, London, 1970. P. S. Bagwell, *The Transport Revolution from 1770*, London, 1974, is a valuable general survey.

51. C. K. Hyde, *Technological Change and the British Iron and Steel Industry, 1700–1870*, Princeton, N.J., 1977, contends that rational economic decisions were responsible for the adoption and nonadoption of technological change. In abbreviated form the argument appeared in "The Adoption of the Hot Blast by the British Iron Industry: A Reinterpretation," *Explorations in Economic History* 10, 1973. See also K. Warren, *The British Iron and Steel Industry since 1840*, London, 1970, and A. Birch, *The Economic History of the British Iron and Steel Industry, 1784–1879*, London, 1967.

52. S. Pollard, *The Genesis of Modern Management: A Study of the Industrial Revolution in Great Britain*, London, 1965.

53. See, especially, D. Landes, "Technological Change and Industrial Development in Western Europe, 1750–1914," *Cambridge Economic History of Europe*, vol. 6, pt. 1, Cambridge, 1966, which was extended and separately published as *The Unbound Prometheus*, Cambridge, 1969, and E. P. Thompson, "Time, Work-discipline and Industrial Capitalism," *PP*, no. 38, 1967.

54. Landes, "Technological Change." The same points are made by M. Sanderson, *The Universities and British Industry, 1850–1970*, London, 1972; by M. Gillow, "Science, Technology and Education: England in 1870," *Oxford Review of Education* 4, 1978; by G. W. Roderick and M. D. Stephens, *Education and Industry in the Nineteenth Century*, London, 1978; by W. J. Reader, *Professional Men: The Rise of the Professional Classes in Nineteenth-century England*, London, 1966; and by idem, *Middle Classes*, London, 1972. H. J. Perkin, *The Origins of Modern English Society 1780–1880*, London, 1969, provides a much more positive view of the professional classes.

55. See, especially, D. N. McClosky, "Did Victorian Britain Fail"? *EcHR*, 2d ser., 23, 1970, and most of the papers in idem, ed., *Essays on a Mature Economy: Britain after 1840*, London, 1971.

56. R. A. Church, *The Great Victorian Boom, 1850–1873*, London, 1975.

57. A. E. Musson, *The Growth of British Industry*, London, 1978.

58. D. Spring, "The English Landed Estate in the Age of Coal and Iron: 1830–1880," *JEcH* 11,

1951; idem, "Aristocracy, Social Structure and Religion in the Early Victorian Period," *VS* 6, 1963; idem, *The English Landed Estate in the Nineteenth Century: Its Administration*, Baltimore, 1963; idem, "English Landlords and Nineteenth-century Industrialism," in J. T. Ward and R. G. Wilson, eds., *Land and Industry: The Landed Estate and the Industrial Revolution*, Newton Abbot, 1971; idem, Introduction to D. Spring, ed., *European Landed Elites in the Nineteenth Century*, Baltimore, 1977.

59. E. Richards, *The Leviathan of Wealth*, London, 1973; and idem, "The Industrial Face of a Great Estate: Trentham and Lilleshall, 1780–1860," *EcHR*, 2d ser., 27, 1974, places much emphasis upon the withdrawal of the aristocracy and gentry and describes their contribution to economic growth as less than it might have been. F. C. Mather, *After the Canal Duke*, is more equivocal. By and large the contributors to Ward and Wilson, *Land and Industry*, emphasize the scope of landlord contributions. M. J. Daunton, "Aristocrats and Traders: The Bute Docks, 1839–1914," *Journal of Transport History*, n s , 3, 1975, describes one of the roles of the Butes in Cardiff. D. Cannadine, "Aristocratic Indebtedness in the Nineteenth Century: The Case Re-opened," *EcHR*, 2d ser., 30, 1977, provides an overview of one aspect of the question as well as an excellent bibliography.

60. See, especially, Perkin, *Modern English Society*; D. C. Coleman, "Gentlemen and players," *EcHR*, 2d ser., 26, 1973; W. L. Arnstein, "The Survival of the Victorian Aristocracy," in F. C. Jaher, ed., *The Rich, the Well Born and the Powerful*, Urbana, Ill., 1973; G. E. Mingay, *The Gentry: The Rise and Fall of a Ruling Class*, London, 1976; and F. M. L. Thompson, "Britain," in D. Spring, ed., *European Landed Elites in the Nineteenth Century*, Baltimore, 1977.

61. W. D. Rubinstein, "Men of Property: Some Aspects of Occupation, Inheritance and Power among Top British Wealthholders," in P. Stanworth and A. Giddens, eds., *Elites and Power in British Society*, London, 1974; idem, "British Millionaires 1809–1949," *BIHR* 48, 1974; idem, "Wealth, Elites and the Class Structure of Modern England," *PP*, no. 76, 1977; idem, "The Victorian Middle Classes: Wealth, Occupation and Geography," *EcHR*, 2d ser., 30, 1977.

62. F. M. L. Thompson, "The Second Agricultural Revolution, 1815–1880," *EcHR*, 2d ser., 21, 1968, makes a case about the distinctness of the mid-nineteenth century which J. D. Chambers and G. Mingay, *The Agricultural Revolution, 1750–1850*, London, 1966, had not made. The extent to which technological change, drainage in particular, affected the clays is a point at issue among R. W. Sturgess, "The Agricultural Revolution on the English Clays," *Agricultural History Review* 14, 1966; E. J. T. Collins and E. L. Jones, "Sectoral Advance in English Agriculture, 1850–1880," *Agricultural History Review* 15, 1967, and A. D. Phillips, "Underdraining in the English Clay Lands, 1850–1870," *Agricultural History Review* 17, 1969. The implications of B. A. Holderness's evidence, that East Anglian landlords invested smaller proportions of their gross incomes in their estates in the mid-nineteenth century than they had invested earlier, are considerable: "Landlord's Capital Formation in East Anglia, 1750–1870," *EcHR*, 2d ser., 25, 1970. D. Taylor discusses the growth of the dairy industry and the factors which inhibited this growth: "The English Dairy Industry, 1860–1930: The Need for a Reassessment," *Agricultural History Review* 22, 1974; idem, "The English Dairy Industry, 1860–1930," *EcHR*, 2d ser., 29, 1976; idem, *The Changing Structure of the English Dairy Industry*, Reading, 1977. Although overtaken in certain respects by subsequent work, E. L. Jones, *The Development of English Agriculture 1815–1973*, London, 1968, provides a valuable survey.

63. In "The Nineteenth Century Corn Law Reconsidered," *EcHR*, 2d ser., 18, 1965, and "The Corn Laws and British Wheat Production 1829–1876," *EcHR*, 2d ser., 22, 1969, S. Fairlie reverses the tendency to argue that the corn laws and corn law repeal were more important

politically than economically and makes the novel suggestion that their repeal was prompted by the fear of an incipient dearth. Very different arguments are presented by W. O. Aydelotte, "The Country Gentlemen and the Repeal of the Corn Laws," *EHR* 82, 1967, and by D. C. Moore, "The Corn Laws and High Farming," *EcHR*, 2d ser., 18, 1965.

64. E. H. Hunt's argument in "Labour Productivity in English Agriculture, 1850–1914," *EcHR*, 2d ser., 20, 1967, was expanded in idem, *Regional Wage Variations in Britain, 1850–1914*, London, 1973. The relevance of the argument to the problems of the poor law is implied by A. Digby, "The Labour Market and the Continuity of Social Policy after 1834: The Case of the Eastern Counties," *EcHR*, 2d ser., 28, 1975.

65. Increasingly important of late are the questions whether the differentiation between different categories of workers which provides the logic of the phrase "aristocracy of labor" was greater in the mid-nineteenth century than it had been earlier, whether the possible bourgeoisation of this sector of the working class or classes was responsible for the ostensible reduction in social tension around the middle of the century, and if so, to what this process should be attributed. Among those who emphasize the importance of the ostensibly increasing differentiation are Perkin, *Modern English Society*; T. Tholfsen, *Working-class Radicalism in Mid-Victorian England*, London, 1977; idem, "The Intellectual Origins of Mid-Victorian Stability," *Political Science Quarterly* 86, 1971; and E. J. Hobsbawm, whose classical statement is included in his *Labouring Men*, London, 1964. Revisionist arguments are provided by A. E. Musson, "Class Struggle and the Labour Aristocracy, 1830–60," *Social History* 3, 1976; idem, British Trade Unions, 1800–1875, London, 1972; idem, *Trade Union and Social History*, London, 1974; R. G. Kirby and A. E. Musson, *The Voice of the People: John Doherty, 1798–1854: Trade Unionist, Radical and Factory Reformer*, Manchester, 1975; and H. Pelling, *A History of British Trade Unionism*, London, 1963. G. Crossick, "The Labour Aristocracy and Its Values: A Study of Mid-Victorian Kentish London," *VS* 19, 1976, is an important recent discussion of the question. So, too, is R. J. Morris, *Class and Class Consciousness in the Industrial Revolution*, London, 1979.

66. R. S. Neale, "The Standard of Living, 1780–1844: A Regional and Class Study," *EcHR*, 2d ser., 19, 1966; J. E. Williams, "The British Standard of Living, 1750–1850," ibid.; J. Burnett, *A History of the Cost of Living*, London, 1969; M. W. Flinn, "Trends in Real Wages, 1750–1850," *EcHR*, 2d ser., 27, 1974.

67. These differences are discussed in S. Pollard, "Labour in Great Britain," *Cambridge Economic History of Europe*, vol. 7, pt. 1, Cambridge, 1978.

68. E. P. Thompson, *The Making of the English Working Class*, London, 1963. Thompson's book has generated a good deal of controversy, much of which is discussed in Morris, *Class and Class Consciousness*.

69. J. Foster, *Class Struggle and the Industrial Revolution: Early Industrial Capitalism in Three English Towns*, London, 1974, contains a fuller statement of the argument made in idem, "Nineteenth-century Towns: A Class Dimension," in Dyos, ed., *Studies in Urban History*.

70. J. F. C. Harrison, *Quest for a New Moral World: Robert Owen and the Owenites in Britain and America*, London, 1969; idem, "A New View of Mr Owen," in S. Pollard and J. Salt, eds., *Robert Owen: Prophet of the Poor*, London, 1971.

71. E. Yeo, "Robert Owen and Radical Culture," in Pollard and Salt, *Robert Owen*. Those elements in Owen and Owenism which Harrison emphasized are either ignored or less strongly emphasized in R. G. Garnett, *Cooperation of the Owenite Socialist Communities in Britain*, Manchester, 1972, and by most of the contributors to J. Butt, ed., *Robert Owen: Aspects of His Life and Work*, Newton Abbot, 1971.

72. Pelling, *British Trade Unionism*; Musson, *British Trade Unions, 1800–1875*; idem, *Trade Union and Social History*; Kirby and Musson, *Voice of the People*.

73. K. Burgess, *The Origins of British Industrial Relations: The Nineteenth-century Experience*, London, 1975; D. Kynaston, *King Labour: The British Working Class, 1850–1914*, London, 1976; D. Douglas, "The Durham Pitman," and "Pit Talk in County Durham," in R. Samuel, ed., *Miners, Quarrymen and Saltworkers*, London, 1977.

74. *Inter alia*, I. Prothero, "Chartism in London," *PP*, no. 44, 1969; idem, "London Chartism and the Trades," *EcHR*, 2d ser., 24, 1971; H. Weisser, *British Working Class Movements and Europe, 1815–48*, Manchester, 1975; and D. Goodway in *Society for the Study of Labour History*, Bulletin 20, London, 1970.

75. D. Bythell, *The Hand-loom Weavers: A Study in the English Cotton Industry during the Industrial Revolution*, Cambridge, 1969.

76. These are emphasized in B. Harrison and P. Hollis, "Chartism, Liberalism and the Life of Robert Lowery," *EHR* 82, 1967; D. J. Rowe, "The People's Charter," *PP*, no. 36, 1967; idem, "The Failure of London Chartism," *IIJ* 11, 1968; R. S. Neale, "Class and Class-consciousness in Early Nineteenth-century England: Three Classes or Five?" *VS* 12, 1968; and A. Plummer, *Bronterre: A Political Biography of Bronterre O'Brien 1804–1864*, London, 1971. The media by which proletarian class theory was disseminated beyond the limits of the proletariat is the subject of J. Weiner, *The War of the Unstamped*, London, 1969, and P. Hollis, *The Pauper Press*, London, 1970. D. J. V. Jones, *Before Rebecca: Popular Protests in Wales, 1793–1835*, London, 1973, tends to attribute violence to exploitation. D. W. Howell, *Land and People in Nineteenth Century Wales*, London, 1978, provides more complex explanations.

77. N. Smelser, *Social Change in the Industrial Revolution: An Application of Theory to the British Cotton Industry*, London, 1959, and idem, "Sociological History: The Industrial Revolution and the British Working-class Family," *Journal of Social History* 1, 1967, are important applications of the theory of structural differentiation. After many years during which Smelser's arguments were generally described as "controversial" and left at that, they are beginning to attract critical attention. See M. M. Edwards and R. Lloyd Jones, "N J Smelser and the Cotton Factory Family: A Reassessment," in Harte and Ponting, *Textile History and Economic History*, and M. Anderson, "Sociological History and the Working-class Family: Smelser Revisited," *Social History* 3, 1976.

78. D. Thompson, *The Early Chartists*, London, 1971.

79. F. C. Mather, *Chartism*, rev. ed., London, 1972, provides a useful short survey pending the time a satisfactory new synthesis is available. J. T. Ward, *Chartism*, London, 1973, is a more recent work reflecting both a more traditional and a more unsympathetic approach. A. M. Hadfield, *The Chartist Land Company*, Newton Abbot, 1970, is the first full-length study of the land plan.

80. J. W. Osborne, *William Cobbett: His Thought and His Times*, New Brunswick, N.J., 1966; F. M. Leventhal, *Respectable Radical: George Howell and Victorian Working Class Politics*, London, 1971; F. B. Smith, *Radical Artisan: William James Linton, 1812–97*, Manchester, 1973; and L. E. Grugel, *George Jacob Holyoake: A Study in the Evolution of a Victorian Radical*, Philadelphia, 1975.

81. T. Tholfsen, *Working-class Radicalism in Mid-Victorian England*, London, 1977.

82. C. G. Hanson, "Craft Unions, Welfare Benefits, and the Case for Trade Union Law Reform, 1867–75," *EcHR*, 2d ser., 28, 1975. P. Thane provides a dissenting view in "Craft Unions, Welfare Benefits, and the Case for Trade Union Law Reform, 1867–75: A Comment," ibid., 29, 1976. In one sense, the problem concerns the overlapping functions of trade unions and friendly societies. P. H. J. H. Gosden, *Self Help*, London, 1973, is a comprehensive but essentially institutional study of friendly societies. B. Supple, "Legislation and Virtue: An Essay on Working-class Self-help and the State in the Early Nineteenth Century," in N. McKendrick, ed., *Historical Perspectives: Studies in English Thought and Society*, London, 1974, is less in-

stitutional. See Pelling, *British Trade Unionism*; Musson, *British Trade Unions, 1800–1875*; idem, *Trade Union and Social History*; Kirby and Musson, *Voice of the People*; and W. H. Fraser, *Trade Unions and Society: The Struggle for Acceptance 1850–1880*, London, 1974, which makes a strong case for the growing respectability of trade unions in middle-class eyes.

83. R. Samuel, ed., *Village Life and Labour*, London, 1975, and idem, ed., *Miners, Quarrymen and Saltworkers*, London, 1977.

84. E. J. Hobsbawm and G. Rudé, *Captain Swing*, London, 1969. See also J. Marlow, *The Tolpuddle Martyrs*, London, 1971, a study of those who suffered most for their participation in the rural revolt and, more generally, J. P. D. Dunbabin, *Rural Unrest in Nineteenth Century England*, London, 1974.

85. P. T. Cominos, "Late-Victorian Sexual Respectability and the Social System," *International Review of Social History* 8, 1963. Similar in general argument are S. Marcus, *The Other Victorians: A Study of Sexuality and Pornography in Mid-nineteenth Century England*, London, 1966, and F. Harrison, *The Dark Angel: Aspects of Victorian Sexuality*, New York, 1977. B. Harrison, "Underneath the Victorians," *VS* 10, 1967, and F. B. Smith, "Sexuality in Britain, 1800–1900: Some Suggested Revisions," in M. Vicinus, ed., *A Widening Sphere: Changing Roles of Victorian Women*, Bloomington, Ind., 1977, are pleas for greater conceptual sophistication.

86. M. Anderson, *Family Structure in Nineteenth Century Lancashire*, Cambridge, 1971. See also idem, "The Study of Family Structure," in Wrigley, *Nineteenth Century Society*. Family structure, the woman's role within the family, and affective relationships within the family are among the newer themes which have attracted their share of controversy. See, in particular, E. Shorter, *The Making of the Modern Family*, New York, 1975, where the small nuclear family is described as a triumph of sentiment and privacy and, as a criticism of this, J. W. Scott and L. A. Tilly, "Women's Work and the Family in Nineteenth-century Europe," *Comparative Studies in Society and History* 17, 1975. See also T. K. Rabb and R. I. Rotberg, eds., *The Family in History*, New York, 1974, and A. S. Wohl, ed., *The Victorian Family: Structures and Stresses*, London, 1978. I. Pinchbeck and M. Hewitt, *Children in English Society*, vol. 2, *From the Eighteenth Century to the Children Act, 1948*, London, 1973, is largely concerned with the child-as-victim who was rescued by Dr. Bernardo and the law.

87. P. Branca, "Image and Reality: The Myth of the Idle Victorian Woman," in M. S. Hartman and L. Banner, eds., *Clio's Consciousness Raised: New Perspectives on the History of Women*, New York, 1974, and idem, *Silent Sisterhood: Middle Class Women in the Victorian Home*, London, 1975.

88. M. Vicinus, "Introduction: The Perfect Victorian Lady," in M. Vicinus, ed., *Suffer and Be Still: Women in the Victorian Age*, Bloomington, Ind., 1972, and idem, Introduction, in M. Vicinus, ed., *A Widening Sphere: Changing Roles of Victorian Women*, Bloomington, Ind., 1977.

89. L. Davidoff, *The Best Circles: Women and Society in Victorian England*, London, 1973.

90. L. Holcombe, *Victorian Ladies at Work: Middle Class Working Women in England and Wales, 1850–1914*, Newton Abbot, 1973.

91. P. Horn, *Education in Rural England 1800–1914*, London, 1978.

92. T. McBride, *The Domestic Revolution: The Modernization of Household Service in England and France 1820–1920*, London, 1976. See also P. Horn, *The Rise and Fall of the Victorian Servant*, London, 1975, and, with a more specific focus, J. Franklin, "Troops of Servants: Labour and Planning in the Country House 1840–1914," *VS* 19, 1975.

93. Branca, *Silent Sisterhood*; J. L'Esperance, "Doctors and Women in Nineteenth Century Society: Sexuality and Role," in Woodward and Richards, *Health Care and Popular Medicine*;

J. E. Donnison, *Midwives and Medical Men*, London, 1977. N. McKendrick, "Home Demand and Economic Growth: A New View of the Role of Women and Children in the Industrial Revolution," in McKendrick, *Historical Perspectives*, brings the analysis of middle-class women's roles to bear on the problems of economic growth. J. R. Walkowitz, *Prostitution and Victorian Society: Women, Class and the State*, Cambridge, 1980, considers the complex ways in which class, class cultures, pressure groups, and the state affected the roles of many working-class women. S. B. Kanner's bibliographies in Vicinus, *Suffer and Be Still*, and idem, *A Widening Sphere*, are invaluable for further work in women's history.

94. D. Sylvester, *Robert Lowe and Education*, London, 1975.

95. R. Johnson, "Educational Policy and Social Control in Early Victorian England," *PP*, no. 49, 1970. See also idem, "Educating the Educators: 'Experts' and the State 1833–9," in A. P. Donajgrodski, ed., *Social Control in Nineteenth Century Britain*, London, 1977.

96. D. Wardle, *The Rise of the Schooled Society: The History of Formal Schooling in England*, London, 1974, reflects the influence of the de-schooling controversy. P. McCann, ed., *Popular Education and Socialization in the Nineteenth Century*, London, 1977, is an important collection of articles most of which are concerned with specific local situations. P. Silver and H. Silver, *The Education of the Poor: The History of a National School 1824–1914*, London, 1974, concerns a school in Lambeth. P. Horn, *Education in Rural England 1800–1914*, London, 1978, describes the teachers and the taught and the impact of the state upon both, principally in Devon. J. Hurt, *Education in Evolution: Church, State, Society and Popular Education*, London, 1971, and J. Roach, *Public Examinations in England*, London, 1971, are more institutional in focus. T. W. Laqueur, *Religion and Respectability: Sunday Schools and Working-class Culture, 1780–1850*, London, 1976, emphasizes the role of autonomous working-class Sunday schools in popular education.

97. See, in particular, E. G. West, "Literacy and the Industrial Revolution," *EcHR*, 2d ser., 31, 1978; idem, *Education and the Industrial Revolution*, London, 1975; and L. Stone, "Literacy and Education in England, 1640–1900," *PP*, no. 42, 1969.

98. R. Wilkinson, *The Prefects: British Leadership and the Public School Tradition*, London, 1964.

99. D. Newsome, *Godliness and Good Learning*, London, 1961; T. M. Bamford, *The Rise of the Public Schools*, London, 1967; J. R. de S. Honey, *Tom Brown's Universe: The Development of the Victorian Public School*, London, 1977. These themes are also developed in the various essays included in B. Simon and I. Bradley, eds., *The Victorian Public School: Studies in the Development of an Educational Institution*, Dublin, 1975.

100. A. C. Percival, *Very Superior Men: Some Early Public School Headmasters and Their Achievements*, London, 1973. See also idem, *The Origins of the Headmasters' Conference*, London, 1969.

101. W. R. Ward, *Victorian Oxford*, London, 1965.

102. S. Rothblatt, *The Revolution of the Dons: Cambridge and Society in Victorian England*, London, 1968. See also idem, *Tradition and Change in English Liberal Education: An Essay in History and Culture*, London, 1976, and idem, "The Student Sub-culture and the Examination System in Early Nineteenth Century Oxford," in L. Stone, ed., *The University in Society*, vol. 1 *Oxford and Cambridge from the Fourteenth to the Early Nineteenth Century*, Princeton, N.J., 1977. See also A. Engel, "Emerging Concepts of the Academic Profession at Oxford, 1800–1854," ibid.; J. Sparrow, *Mark Pattison and the Idea of a University*, London, 1967; and E. B. W. Bill, *University Reform in the Nineteenth Century: A Study of Henry Halford Vaughan, 1811–1885*, London, 1973. Dealing more with the product than the producers are C. Kent, *Brains and Numbers: Elitism, Comtism and Democracy*, London, 1978, and C. Harvie, *The Lights of Liberalism and the Challenge of Democracy, 1860–86*, London, 1976.

103. M. Richter, *The Politics of Conscience*, London, 1964.

104. C. Jenks, "T. H. Green, the Oxford Philosophy of Duty and the English Middle Class," *British Journal of Sociology 28, 1977*.

105. L. Stone, "The Size and Composition of the Oxford Student Body 1580–1910," in Stone, *University in Society*.

106. M. Sanderson, *Universities and British Industry*. Part of the background of the development of the civic universities is described by R. H. Kargon, *Science in Victorian Manchester: Enterprise and Expertise*, Baltimore, 1977.

107. G. I. T. Machin, *The Catholic Question in English Politics, 1820–1830*, Oxford, 1964.

108. Ibid., *Politics and the Churches in Great Britain 1832–1868*, Oxford, 1977. Among other recent works which focus upon the relationship between politics and religion are G. F. A. Best, *Temporal Pillars: Queen Anne's Bounty, the Ecclesiastical Commissioners and the Church of England*, Cambridge, 1964; R. W. Davis, *Dissent in Politics, 1780–1830: The Political Life of William Smith, M.P.*, London, 1971; and E. J. Evans, *The Contentious Tithe: The Tithe Problem and English Agriculture*, London, 1976.

109. D. Bowen, *The Idea of the Victorian Church: The Role of the Church of England in State and Society, 1833–1889*, Montreal, 1968.

110. M. A. Crowther, *Church Embattled: Religious Controversy in Mid-Victorian England*, Newton Abbot, 1970. Among other recent works which discuss religion principally as a matter of belief or thought are B. M. G. Reardon, *From Coleridge to Gore: A Century of Religious Thought in Britain*, London, 1971, and with a somewhat narrower concern, G. Rowell, *Hell and the Victorians*, London, 1974. The Oxford movement retains its appeal as evidenced in two recent biographies, P. Brendon, *Hurrell Froude and the Oxford Movement*, London, 1974, and B. W. Martin, *John Keble: Priest, Professor and Poet*, London, 1977.

111. O. Chadwick, *The Victorian Church*, 2 vols., London, 1966–1970. In the last few years there has been a good deal of work on Darwin and his impact. H. E. Gruber, *Darwin on Man: A Psychological Study of Scientific Creativity*, London, 1974, is the work of a psychologist interested in the processes by which Darwin reached his conclusions. R. M. Young, "The Impact of Darwin on Conventional Thought," in A. Symondson, ed., *The Victorian Crisis of Faith*, London, 1970, describes Darwin as part of "a larger movement of naturalistic approaches to the earth, life and man" and emphasizes the efforts both to discourage this movement and to accommodate it within the existing theological framework. On these points, see also D. L. Hull, *Darwin and His Critics: The Reception of Darwin's Theory of Evolution by the Scientific Community*, London, 1973, an anthology of contemporary scientific reviews of *Origin of the Species* and *Descent of Man*.

112. The general contention that Victorian England was "religious" has been challenged by J. Kent, "The Victorian Resistance: Comments on Religious Life and Culture, 1840–80," *VS* 12, 1968, who distinguishes between a "religious England which was fixed in anti-modernist positions" and another England which was not. With a different focus, F. B. Smith, "The Atheist Mission," in R. Robson, ed., *Ideas and Institutions of Victorian Britain*, London, 1967, describes the weakness of organized irreligion. See also E. Royle, *Victorian Infidels: The Origins of the British Secularist Movement 1791–1866*, Manchester, 1974, and S. Budd, *Varieties of Unbelief: Atheists and Agnostics in English Society, 1850–1960*, London, 1977.

113. B. Heeney, *A Different Kind of Gentleman: Parish Clergy as Professional Men in Early and Mid-Victorian England*, Hamden, Conn., 1976; R. Soloway, *Prelates and People: Ecclesiastical Social Thought in England, 1783–1852*, Toronto, 1969; and G. Kitson Clark, *Churchmen and the Condition of England 1832–1885*, London, 1973.

114. C. Binfield, *So Down to Prayers: Studies in English Nonconformity 1780–1920*, London, 1977, is a collective biography with a focus upon Congregationalists. The network theme is also

prominent in idem, *George Williams and the Y.M.C.A.*, London, 1973. See also E. A. Isichei, *The Victorian Quakers*, London, 1970. The importance of religious networks as mechanisms of political recruitment has been stressed by various historians, among them J. R. Vincent, *The Formation of the Liberal Party 1857–1868*, London, 1966.

115. J. Obelkevich, *Religion and Rural Society: South Lindsey 1825–1875*, London, 1976. See also W. R. Ward, *Religion and Society in England*, 1790–1850, London, 1972, and E. R. Norman, *Church and Society in England, 1770–1970*, London, 1976.

116. A. D. Gilbert, *Religion and Society in Industrial England: Church, Chapel and Social Change*, *1740–1914*, London, 1976. Among other recent works in religious history are P. Backstrom, *Christian Socialism and Cooperation in Victorian England*, London, 1975, and J. D. Holmes, *More Roman than Rome: English Catholicism in the Nineteenth Century*, London, 1978, which is more anecdoctal than analytical.

117. B. Harrison, "The Sunday Trading Riots of 1855," *HJ* 8, 1965. See also idem, "Religion and Recreation in Nineteenth Century England," *PP*, no. 38, 1967; idem, *Drink and the Victorians*, London, 1971; and on many of the same questions, R. W. Malcolmson, *Popular Recreations in English Society, 1700–1850*, London, 1973.

118. N. Gash, *Politics in the Age of Peel*, London, 1953, rev. ed., 1977, exercises a continuing influence toward the study of local politics as part of a national political system and, indeed, toward the study of politics as a system.

119. W. O. Aydelotte, "Parties and Issues in Early Victorian England," *JBS* 5, 1966; idem, "The Conservative and Radical Interpretations of Early Victorian Social Legislation," *VS* 11, 1967; idem, "The Disintegration of the Conservative Party in the 1840s: A Study of Political Attitudes," in W. O. Aydelotte, A. G. Bogue, and R. W. Fogel, eds., *The Dimensions of Quantitative Research in History*, Princeton, N.J., 1972; idem, "Constituency Influence on the British House of Commons, 1841–1847," in W. O. Aydelotte, ed., *The History of Parliamentary Behavior*, Princeton, N.J., 1977. J. R. Bylsma, "Party Structure in the 1852–1857 House of Commons: A Scalogram Analysis," *Journal of Interdisciplinary History* 7, 1977, has begun the application of Aydelotte's principal technique to other parliaments than that on which Aydelotte focused.

120. P. E. Lazarsfeld, B. Berelson, and H. Gaudet, *The People's Choice*, New York, 1944, was the seminal work in modern election studies.

121. Among recent studies of pollbooks and works in which pollbooks and related concepts have been systematically used are J. Vincent, *Pollbooks: How Victorians Voted*, London, 1967; idem, *The Formation of the Liberal Party 1857–1868*, London, 1966; D. C. Moore, "Social Structure, Political Structure and Public Opinion in Mid-Victorian England," in Robson, *Ideas and Institutions*; T. J. Nossiter, "Voting Behaviour 1832–1872," *Political Studies* 18, 1970; idem, "Aspects of Electoral Behaviour in English Constituencies, 1832–1868," in E. Allardt and S. Rokkan, eds., *Mass Politics: Studies in Political Sociology*, London, 1970; P. Joyce, "The Factory Politics of Lancashire in the Latter Nineteenth Century," *HJ* 18, 1975; and J. C. Mitchell and J. Cornford, "The Political Demography of Cambridge, 1832–1868," *Albion* 9, 1977. While pollbooks are not available for London constituencies for the period with which he is concerned, the themes pollbooks suggest are prominent in M. Baer, "Social Structure, Voting Behavior and Political Change in Victorian London," ibid.

122. See, in particular, D. C. Moore, "Concession or Cure: The Sociological Premises of the First Reform Act," *HJ* 9, 1966; idem, *The Politics of Deference*, Hassocks, 1976; and for criticisms of Moore's arguments, E. P. Hennock, "The Sociological Premises of the First Reform Act: A Critical Note," *VS* 14, 1971; R. W. Davis, "The Whigs and the Idea of Electoral Deference," *Durham Historical Journal*, n.s., 36, 1974; and idem, "Deference and Aristocracy in the Time of the Great Reform Act," *AHR* 82, 1976.

123. B. Hilton, *Cash, Corn, Commerce: The Economic Policies of the Tory Governments 1815–1830*, Oxford, 1977.

124. Fairlie, "Corn Law Reconsidered"; idem, "Corn Laws and British Wheat Production."

125. A Mitchell, *The Whigs in Opposition, 1815–1830*, Oxford, 1967.

126. M. Brock, *The Great Reform Act*, London, 1973, and J. Cannon, *Parliamentary Reform 1640–1832*, Cambridge, 1973.

127. G. B. A. M. Finlayson, *England in the Eighteen Thirties: Decade of Reform*, London, 1969; A. Llewellyn, *The Decade of Reform: The 1830s*, Newton Abbot, 1972; N. Gash, *Reaction and Reconstruction in English Politics 1832–1852*, Oxford, 1965; T. L. Crosbie, *Sir Robert Peel's Administration 1841–46*, Newton Abbot, 1970. See also R. Blake, *The Conservative Party from Peel to Churchill*, London, 1970, and R. Stewart, *The Foundations of the Conservative Party 1830–1867*, London, 1978.

128. P. Ziegler, *Melbourne: A Biography of William Lamb, 2nd Viscount Melbourne*, London, 1976.

129. J. Prest, *Lord John Russell*, London, 1972.

130. J. Clive, *Macaulay: The Shaping of the Historian*, London, 1973. J. Hamburger, *Macaulay and the Whig Tradition*, London, 1976, provides a variant picture of a man whose main concern was the preservation of social peace.

131. N. Gash, *Sir Robert Peel: The Life of Sir Robert Peel after 1830*, London, 1972.

132. T. L. Crosbie, *English Farmers and the Politics of Protection, 1815–52*, Hassocks, 1977.

133. R. Stewart, *The Politics of Protection*, Cambridge, 1971.

134. D. C. Moore, "The Corn Laws and High Farming," *EcHR*, 2d ser., 18, 1965.

135. Fairlie, "Corn Law Reconsidered"; idem, "Corn Laws and British Wheat Production."

136. J. B. Conacher, *The Peelites and the Party System, 1846–52*, Newton Abbot, 1972.

137. Ibid., *The Aberdeen Coalition, 1852–1855: A Study in Mid-nineteenth Century Party Politics*, Cambridge, 1968.

138. W. D. Jones and A. B. Erickson, *The Peelites 1846–1857*, Columbus, Ohio, 1972.

139. O. Anderson, *A Liberal State at War: English Politics and Economics during the Crimean War*, London, 1967.

140. P. W. Schroeder, *Austria, Great Britain, and the Crimean War*, London, 1972.

141. J. Ridley, *Lord Palmerston*, London, 1970.

142. R. Blake, *Disraeli*, London, 1968.

143. S. G. Checkland, *The Gladstones: A Family Biography, 1764–1851*, Cambridge, 1971, focuses upon the antecedents, ending with the death of William Ewart Gladstone's father. E. J. Feuchtwanger, *Gladstone*, London, 1975, focuses upon the prime minister's political life. With the publication of *The Gladstone Diaries*, Oxford, 1968–   , a vast increase of information on his personal as well as political life has become available, which the initial editor, M. R. D. Foot, and the subsequent editor, H. C. G. Matthew, have discussed in their introductions.

144. D. A. Hamer, *The Politics of Electoral Pressure: A Study in the History of Victorian Reform Agitation*, Hassocks, 1977.

145. J. Vincent, *The Formation of the Liberal Party 1857–1868*, London, 1966.

146. T. J. Nossiter, *Influence, Opinion and Political Idioms in Reformed England: Case Studies from the North-east 1832–1874*, Hassocks, 1975.

147. R. W. Davis, *Political Change and Continuity, 1760–1885: A Buckinghamshire Study*, London, 1972.

148. R. J. Olney, *Lincolnshire Politics 1832–1885*, London, 1973.

149. D. Fraser, *Urban Politics in Victorian England: The Structure of Politics in Victorian Cities*, Leicester, 1976.

150. D. C. Moore, *The Politics of Deference*, Hassocks, 1976.

151. R. Harrison, "The Tenth April of Spencer Walpole: The Problem of Revolution in Relation to Reform, 1865–67," in idem, *Before the Socialists: Studies in Labour and Politics 1861–1881*, London, 1965.

152. F. B. Smith, *The Making of the Second Reform Bill*, Cambridge, 1966.

153. G. Himmelfarb, "The Politics of Democracy: The English Reform Act of 1867," in idem, *Victorian Minds*, New York, 1968.

154. M. Cowling, "Disraeli, Derby and Fusion, October 1865 to July 1866," *HJ* 8, 1965; idem, *1867: Disraeli, Gladstone and Revolution*, Cambridge, 1967, which *inter alia*, provides a lengthy criticism of Harrison, "Tenth April of Spencer Walpole."

155. Moore, *Politics of Deference*, chap. 9.

156. A. V. Dicey's Bentham was described in his *Lectures on the Relation between Law and Public Opinion in England during the Nineteenth Century*, London, 1905, Brebner's in his *"Laissez-faire* and State Intervention in Nineteenth-century Britain," *JEcH* 8, 1948. Brebner's argument was an early response to work being done on the Bentham Papers at University College, London. This work tends to substantiate his criticisms of Dicey, but some of it suggests that Bentham was far more complex than he allowed. In the last few years these more complex aspects of Bentham have been emphasized by, among others, D. Lyons, *In the Interest of the Governed*, Oxford, 1973, and the contributors to B. Parekh, ed., *Jeremy Bentham, Ten Critical Essays*, London, 1974, in particular, J. H. Burns, "Bentham's Critique of Political Fallacies." Dicey is the subject of a recent biography, R. A. Cosgrove, *The Rule of Law: Albert Venn Dicey, Victorian Jurist*, Chapel Hill, N.C., 1980.

157. O. MacDonagh, *Early Victorian Government 1830–1870*, London, 1977, is an extended and slightly modified version of idem, "The Nineteenth Century Revolution in Government: A Reappraisal," *HJ* 1, 1958. D. Roberts, *Victorian Origins of the British Welfare State*, New Haven, Conn., 1960, contains an argument similar to MacDonagh's which has been significantly altered in *Paternalism in Early Victorian England*, New Brunswick, N. J., 1979.

158. S. E. Finer, "The Transmission of Benthamite Ideas 1820–1850," in G. Sutherland, ed., *Studies in the Growth of Nineteenth-century Government*, London, 1972, emphasizes the importance of the Benthamite role. J. Hart, "Nineteenth-century Social Reform: A Tory Interpretation of History," *PP*, no. 31, 1965, made a somewhat stronger case.

159. In particular, W. Thomas, "The Philosophic Radicals," in P. Hollis, ed., *Pressure from Without in Early Victorian England*, London, 1974.

160. E.g., J. Roach, *Social Reform in England 1780–1880*, London, 1978.

161. G. Himmelfarb, "Bentham Scholarship and the Bentham 'Problem,'" *JMH* 41, 1969, surveyed the state of affairs at that time.

162. The point was made by G. Sutherland in her Introduction to idem, *Growth of Nineteenth-century Government*. In "Recent Trends in Administrative History," *VS* 13, 1970, she emphasized the continuity of political patronage in government service as well as the growing efficiency of this service and the importance of the point Hennock (*Fit and Proper Persons*; idem, "Urban Local Government") had made about the independence of local government and the concern to preserve the status of the men who participated in it. See also H. Roseveare, *The Treasury, 1660–1870*, London, 1969; M. Wright, *Treasury Control of the Civil Service, 1854–74*, Oxford, 1969; H. Parris, *Constitutional Bureaucracy*, London, 1969; and R. Jones, *The Nineteenth Century Foreign Office: An Administrative History*, London, 1971.

163. L. Robbins, *The Theory of Economic Policy in Classical Political Economy*, London, 1953.

164. W. T. Samuels, *The Classical Theory of Economic Policy*, Cleveland, Ohio, 1966. See also A. W. Coats, Introduction, in A. W. Coats, ed., *The Classical Economists and Economic Policy*, London, 1971.

165. D. Roberts, *Paternalism in Early Victorian England*, New Brunswick, N.J., 1979.

166. J. D. Marshall, *The Old Poor Law 1795–1834*, London, 1968. M. J. Cullen, *The Statistical Movement in Early Victorian Britain: The Foundations of Empirical Social Research*, Hassocks, 1975, has interesting things to say about the attitudes of those who gathered "facts" in this period.

167. M. E. Rose, "The Allowance System under the New Poor Law," *EcHR*, 2d ser., 19, 1966, did much to enhance this realization.

168. R. G. Cowherd, *Political Economists and the English Poor Laws*, Athens, Ohio, 1977. In the same general tradition, but more comprehensive in its coverage, is J. R. Poynter, *Society and Pauperism: Ideas on Poor Relief, 1795–1834*, London, 1969.

169. A. J. Brundage, *The Making of the New Poor Law*, New Brunswick, N.J., 1978, is an expansion and development of the arguments in idem, "The Landed Interest and the New Poor Law: A Reappraisal of the Revolution in Government," *EHR* 87, 1972, and idem, "The English Poor Law of 1834 and the Cohesion of Agricultural Society," *Agricultural History* 48, 1974.

170. N. C. Edsall, *The Anti–Poor Law Movement, 1834–1844*, Manchester, 1971.

171. E. C. Midwinter, *Social Administration in Lancashire, 1830–1860: Poor Law, Public Health and Police*, Manchester, 1969.

172. D. Fraser, Introduction to D. Fraser, ed., *The New Poor Law in the Nineteenth Century*, London, 1976. In various respects D. Fraser, *The Evolution of the British Welfare State: A History of Social Policy since the Industrial Revolution*, London, 1973, has been overtaken by subsequent work and by the concern to avoid both the altruistic and the programmatic fallacy.

173. W. C. Lubenow, *The Politics of Government Growth*, Newton Abbot, 1971.

174. Conservative strains in John Stuart Mill have been stressed by G. Himmelfarb, *On Liberty and Liberalism: The Case of John Stuart Mill*, New York, 1974; E. August, *John Stuart Mill: A Mind at Large*, New York, 1975; and R. J. Halliday, *John Stuart Mill*, London, 1976. More traditionally liberal pictures are provided by most of the contributors to J. M. Robson and M. Laine, eds., *James and John Stuart Mill: Papers of the Centenary Conference*, Toronto, 1976. D. F. Thompson, *John Stuart Mill and Representative Government*, Princeton, N.J., 1976, tries to recruit Mill to the normative side of the present-day controversy between the normative and empirical theorists of democracy. B. Mazlish, *James and John Stuart Mill: Father and Son in the Nineteenth Century*, London, 1975, is an effort to exploit the abundant materials which the Mills provide for a psychohistorical study with predictably controversial results.

175. C. Woodham-Smith, *Queen Victoria*, vol. 1, London, 1972, describes her life until the death of Albert and repeats the argument most recently associated with F. Eyck, *The Prince Consort: A Political Biography*, London, 1959, that the development of the theory and practice of apolitical or constitutional monarchy in the nineteenth century was largely the consequence of Albert's influence upon Victoria both during his life and after his death. The argument is discounted in what is generally regarded as the finest biography of the Queen, E. P. Longford, *Victoria R. I.*, London, 1964, and in F. Hardie, *The Political Influence of the British Monarchy, 1868–1952*, London, 1970. Continuing interest in certain traditional humanistic themes is reflected in the publication of Victoria's correspondence with her eldest daughter, edited by R. Fulford, *Dearest Child: Letters between Queen Victoria and the Princess Royal, 1858–1861*, London, 1964; *Dearest Mama: Letters between Queen Victoria and the Crown Princess of Prussia, 1861–1864*, London, 1968; and *Your Dear Letter: Private Correspondence of Queen Victoria and the Crown Princess of Prussia, 1865–1871*, London, 1971; and in the biography of her lady of the bedchamber in the 1840s and early 1850s, V. Surtees, *Charlotte Canning: Lady in Waiting to Queen Victoria and Wife of the First Viceroy of India 1817–1861*, London, 1975. J. L. Lant, *Insubstantial Pageant: Ceremony and Confusion at Queen Victoria's Court*, New York, 1979, reflects a newer interest in the growing concern for efficient pageantry

and the consequent shift of focus from the feelings of elite participants to those of nonelite observers.

176. M. Girouard, *The Victorian Country House*, Oxford, 1971, and D. C. Itzkowitz, *Peculiar Privilege: A Social History of Foxhunting, 1753–1885*, Hassocks, 1977.

177. K. Bourne, *The Foreign Policy of Victorian England, 1830–1902*, Oxford, 1970.

178. D. C. M. Platt, *Finance, Trade and Politics in British Foreign Policy, 1815–1914*, Oxford, 1968. See also idem, *The Cinderella Service: British Consuls since 1825*, London, 1971, and C. H. D. Howard, *Britain and the 'Casus Belli' 1822–1902*, London, 1974.

179. E. L. Rasor, *Reform in the Royal Navy: A Social History of the Lower Deck, 1850–1880*, Hamden, Conn., 1976. See also A. N. Gilgert, "Buggery in the British Navy, 1700–1861," *Journal of Social History* 10, 1976.

180. A. R. Skelley, *The Victorian Army at Home: The Recruitment and Conditions of the British Regular, 1859–1899*, London, 1977. See also G. Harries-Jenkins, *The Army in Victorian Society*, London, 1977.

181. H. Cunningham, *The Volunteer Force: A Social and Political History, 1859–1908*, London, 1975.

182. G. M. Young, *Victorian England: Portrait of an Age*, London, 1936.

British History
1870–1914

Peter Stansky

H. J. Hanham has edited and compiled a *Bibliography of British History 1870–1914* (Oxford, 1976), consisting of 10,829 entries, and many of them contain comments and further bibliographical listings. His magisterial bibliography goes a long way toward making it unnecessary for me to attempt to provide any such systematic coverage. His compilation is there, available for all to use, and so are two columns in the Conference on British Studies series: Josef L. Altholz's *Victorian England 1837–1901* (Cambridge, 1970) and Alfred Havighurst's *Modern Britain 1901–1970* (Cambridge, 1976), both highly useful as well. So I have been able to construe my task as gathering together some commentaries on a number of books that I regard as particularly significant. Far more briefly, I annotate some further books at the conclusion of this essay.

Before proceeding I should mention some obvious points. Journals provide a means to discover new developments in shorter compass, and it is helpful to keep abreast of relevant articles that appear in *Past and Present, Victorian Studies, English Historical Review, Historical Journal*, and so forth. Particularly valuable is the annual bibliography published in the June issue of *Victorian Studies*, which treats both history and literature. Also useful is the relevant section in the American Historical Association's *Recently Published Articles*. G. R. Elton is now editing a series of valuable annual bibliographies, having started out with a single catch-up volume on publications on British history, *Modern Historians on British History, 1485–1945: A Critical Bibliography* (Atlantic Highlands, N.J., 1970); the successor volumes are the *Annual Bibliography of British and Irish History*.

In the area of women's history, one is told much by the splendid bibliographical work of S. Barbara Kanner, in her essays contained in Martha Vicinus, editor's *Suffer and Be Still* (Bloomington, Ind., 1972) and *A Widening Sphere* (Bloomington, Ind., 1977). Both these volumes also include excellent essays on aspects of women's history in the nineteenth century. S. Barbara Kanner has edited *The Women of England from Anglo-Saxon Times to the Present* (Hamden,

Conn., 1979), which has essays by Sheila Ryan Johansson on demography and Patricia Otto Klaus on the novel, which deal, in part, with the period 1870–1914.

Let me consider first biography or studies in which biographical considerations are relevant. I am particularly conscious of this, having just published a brief biography, *Gladstone: A Progress in Politics* (Boston, 1979), which attempts to consider his life through paying attention to his major speeches. This is in the Library of World Biography series, edited by J. H. Plumb, and there are in the series as well incisive studies of *Disraeli* (Boston, 1976) by Richard W. Davis and of *Rhodes* (Boston, 1974) by John E. Flint. Robert Blake's splendid *Disraeli* (New York, 1966) appeared in the year of the publication of *Changing Views* and was not recorded in it. As Hanham remarks in his bibliography, the Blake biography "is a better book but does not entirely replace Monypenny and Buckle" (p. 187), whose biography, *The Life of Benjamin Disraeli* (London), was in six volumes published in 1910–1920. There has also been a more traditional life of Gladstone than my own by E. J. Feuchtwanger, *Gladstone* (New York, 1975), a volume in the series British Political Biography.

Publications on Gladstone have been numerous down to our own day, most notably *The Gladstone Diaries* (Oxford, 1968–   ), the ongoing publication of his diary, which has only now reached the year 1868 in six thick volumes edited by M. R. D. Foot and H. C. G. Matthew. A biography which made full use of the original documents available would have to be on the mammoth scale of the continuing life of Winston Churchill. Such books are essential for historians; at the same time, one needs a comparatively brief life which either emphasizes one particular aspect of the career or, as Feuchtwanger does, surveys the entire life using the full range of available secondary material and some primary sources. A sympathetically critical picture emerges: Gladstone's weakness in handling other people, his obsessions, are here, as well as his extraordinary ability to make a popular appeal. It seems to be a characteristic of great men that they devote themselves to whatever they are doing with an almost demonic energy. When the cause is right, as in the case of the Bulgarian atrocities and home rule in Ireland, such men are deeply admirable and powerful. But they can appear ludicrous and pathetic when they devote themselves in the same way to causes not worthy of such single-minded dedication, for example, the Maynooth grant at the beginning of his career and naval spending at the end. Feuchtwanger presents personality, politics, and the general story of nineteenth-century England with excellent balance. His emphasis on both the dedication and disdain of Gladstone's personality is very well done, although perhaps he somewhat overemphasizes the latter.

Michael Barker has made an important contribution to the history of the Liberal party in the late nineteenth century in *Gladstone and Radicalism: The Reconstruction of Liberal Policy in Britain 1885–1894* (New York, 1975). His book reaffirms the adage of W. S. Gilbert, "Things are seldom what they seem," so pertinent to historians, and when put to use, the chief justification of any detailed study. By looking at events with care and a disregard for received opinion, one may well achieve a picture more varied and interesting, and perhaps closer to the truth, than the standardized versions fading through the decades. For some years now, the conception of an inflexible Gladstone has been undergoing modification, and Barker's study, continuing the task, is less an innovation than a reinforcement of what is coming to be the more accepted view of Gladstone. This conception gives Gladstone a consistency and an amplitude of approach that he at times did his best to conceal through the complexity of his rhetoric and the complications of his personality. Perhaps, after all, it is characteristic of the greatest of politicians that contradictory generalizations can be made and be true of them, as Barker remarks of Gladstone: "There were no bounds to his ingenuity, and no knowing the measures which he might eventually adopt" (p. 13). The old view, accordingly, need not be consigned utterly to the scrap heap, but held in reserve as a kind of corrective against an excess of revisionism.

The old view had it that Gladstone was committed to home rule for Ireland virtually to the exclusion of any other political concerns, but Barker demonstrates that, however strong the commitment, Gladstone did not allow the Irish cause to eliminate radical moves in other directions. We have not come so far yet as to have a Gladstone who was a socialist, or even very much of a radical; nor can there be any question that he was profoundly skeptical of some of the trends, in particular toward social legislation, within his own party. But his extraordinary strength sprang from the fact that, despite appearances to the contrary, he was not doctrinaire and was quite willing, even anxious, to use the Irish cause as an umbrella for other Liberal causes.

His justified moral indignation, as in his denunciation to the National Liberal Federation in 1887 of what he deemed to be illegal police action in Ireland, helped keep the party together: "I say that the law was broken by the agents of the law, and that it is idle to speak to the Irish people about obeying the law, if the very Government that so speaks . . . has agents which break the law by advisedly and violently breaking the order of public meetings, and who are sustained in that illegal action" (pp. 80–81). What is demonstrated here is that the removal of the more opportunistic radicalism of Chamberlain, and of almost all the Whigs, made the party better able to adapt a flexible radicalism, which made certain issues, most notably the question of an eight-hour day, every ticklish. Although there were still enough old-fashioned Liberals within the party—either by doctrine, such as John Morley, or by interest, as in the case of some of the rich businessmen who remained—the party was able to go forward, in a fairly united way, making proposals to improve the conditions of the working classes, and moving more and more toward an active social policy.

Undoubtedly, though, because of Gladstone's interest in Ireland, domestic causes were not as publicly emphasized as they might have been, but it was often those colleagues who were not enthusiastic about home rule who tended unjustly to blame the Irish cause for preventing action at home. But the policy of concentration on Ireland would almost inevitably have worked brilliantly for the success and strengthening of the Liberal party, and it was the right policy, on almost every ground, for the party to pursue from 1886 to 1890. It was undone not by Gladstone's megalomania but by the fall of Charles Parnell. The Newcastle program of 1891, which was used when convenient by the party's leaders, even though they had doubts about it, was an attempt to cope with a future without a united Irish party by putting greater emphasis on other issues. Despite these reversals, as Barker refreshingly points out, the Liberal government of 1892–1895 had great accomplishments to its credit, particularly in the area of administrative changes, which involved, in large part, working conditions. Under Gladstone's inspiration, the ground was prepared for the great Liberal ministry to come a decade later.

The picture that emerges from this study is not as neat as its title would suggest. There is a very good sense of the interplay between the party leadership and interests within the party. But "reconstruction" implies that a clear Liberal policy emerged by 1894. Rather, the effect was one of strength through diversity, which meant that Liberal policy tended to be somewhat incoherent and even contradictory. The leadership attempted to balance conflicting interests, perhaps most cleverly in the area of education, where, on the whole, they were moderately successful in not fatally offending the contrary positions held by the Irish and the Nonconformists. While justly praising Gladstone, Barker fails to give sufficient emphasis to the inevitable sense of limitation and, indeed, almost oppression that his dominance of his party for so many years imposed upon his heirs, some of whom were getting on in years themselves.

Gladstone dominates this book—as he dominated the party—as a man who was able to sympathize with and support radical causes. More than is suspected, vision and practicality marked the Liberal party in its final Gladstonian epoch and made a lasting contribution to British society, as well as shaping the subsequent history of the party itself. It will be very surprising if the last volumes of Gladstone's *Diaries*, when they are published, present a different picture. The first six volumes of the *Diaries* have shown us the complexity and tension of his personality. Barker's study is lower-keyed and perhaps does not sufficiently emphasize the negative aspects of his leadership. But it is useful to have this intelligent discussion of an important decade of Liberal history, when the party was still, essentially, Mr. Gladstone's.

The decline of the Liberal party (and the rise of the Labour party) as found in the pioneering work of Philip Poirier, *The Advent of the British Labour Party 1880–1900* (New York, 1958), and Henry Pelling, *The Origins of the Labour*

Party 1880–1900 (New York, 1954), have been issues of continuing concern, and the post-Gladstonian history of the Liberals has been well discussed in H. C. G. Matthew's *The Liberal Imperialists: The Ideas and Politics of a Post-Gladstonian Elite* (New York, 1973) and H. V. Emy's *Liberals, Radicals and Social Politics 1892–1914* (New York, 1973). It is clearly untrue that historians are only interested in the successful, as the growing body of work on the Liberal party demonstrates. The party can be studied from many angles, most particularly at its time of great achievement, potential, and danger: the period before the First World War. These two books are important contributions to that investigation.

In a sense, Matthew's study is the more traditional, concentrating on a considerable part of the more "advanced" leadership of the party as it attempted to adjust to a political world in which Gladstone was no longer the great father figure whom one could adore, or rail against. Matthew has written a very skillful and perceptive book, using a wide range of private papers. He is endowed with a keen sense of the fascinating, and frequently irritating, personalities of the Liberal Imperialist leadership and of the degree to which they shared the preoccupations of their own time. As he remarks about Rosebery, he "used his rhetoric to popularize imperialism and national efficiency—the slogans of the *fin de siècle* Britain of which he was so typical an ornament" (p. 11). Matthew is fully aware of the extent to which Rosebery, as well as Asquith, Haldane, and Sir Edward Grey, used these ideas as ways in which to revive their party, but also to enhance their position in it. Their frequently awkward attempts to balance those two aims help explain their somewhat inconclusive nature as politicians. One of the many virtues of the book is that it does not limit itself to just the most prominent of the Liberal Imperialists but includes others, mostly members of Parliament, who were attempting to work out policies which would not only be "efficient" but contain ideological appeal. In effect, it was an effort to combine the businesslike traditions of Liberalism with the emotional appeal of an updated view of the empire.

A sense of confusion about Britain's position in the world and what should be the role of her political leaders within the country itself pervaded this group; and a continual problem in writing about them has been to integrate their intrigues with their ideas. Matthew neatly, if perhaps somewhat overschematically and arbitrarily, solves the dilemma—simply dividing his book into two sections: "Babies in Intrigue" and "Ideas and Policies." On the whole, his solution works. Perhaps the elite's greatest weakness was that they *did* operate on two levels and were not able to transform—as politicians should—their concern with their own careers into their more elevated purposes. They lacked the assured conviction, even if falsely so, of many of their elders that personal and British progress were closely united. In this, Grey and Asquith, to a degree, shared with Rosebery a fin de siècle lack of commitment which provides one explanation for their crumbling before that more twentieth century figure: David Lloyd George. They had been attempting to work out a form of imperialism, a sort of "higher patriotism" that would free their party from the taint of "Little Englandism" which the Tories had managed to put upon the Liberals and which was designed to convey the impression that the Tories were the true national and patriotic party. In fact, the Liberal Imperialists were juggling too many balls at once: not only Liberalism and Whiggism, patriotism and social welfare—but their own sense of their elite position. The events of the First World War truncated what might have been the expected development within the Liberal party, as the generation discussed by Matthew made way—in the sense of those who would set the pace for the future—for those less important figures (or to put it another way, for those who never had a full opportunity to realize themselves) who figure in H. V. Emy's superb study.

It was within the Liberal party that a belief in a combination of state action—forms of collectivism—*and* individualism, characteristics of contemporary Britain, took their modern shape. It is one of the established generalizations that the new Liberals of the period before the First World War attempted to modernize their party, but heretofore it has proved extremely difficult to discuss in a unified way their ideas and their activities within a context of general parliamentary and political life. There is a much more "modern" feeling about the men and actions Emy treats than in the case of the "post-Gladstonians"—perhaps, as Virginia Woolf said, human character did change in the early twentieth century. Emy has an extraordinarily firm grasp of the many elements of the political picture: the various theoreticians and politicians, the numerous committees both inside and out of Parliament, those multifarious organized pressure groups, the problems in the constituencies. He demonstrates how, through the endless complications of political life, the Liberal party was working out a tenable position which would cope with the growing intensity of class politics. The growth of the Labour party was a goad and an irritation. There was some awareness that Labour's was a potentially mortal challenge and that the Liberal need—which also represented genuine feeling—was to work out policies which would appeal to Labour and yet would not lose Liberal voters to any significant degree. The war prevented the position of the social radicals from being put to the test: if the general election of 1915 had taken place, it might have marked a considerable victory for their policies, particularly if Liberal constituency organizations could have been revitalized to appeal to potential Labour voters.

Emy is excellent in discussing the role of those businessmen who remained in the party, such as the "model employers"—Sir John Brunner, Alfred Mond, W. H. Lever, W. Pearson—and the extent to which they and others could, with exceptions, disregard their more immediate interests in the service of social politics. But it was a paradoxical and transitional situation which could not last. Most of these men were committed, in Churchill's phrase, to spreading "a net over the abyss," but ultimately the Liberal party would need to recruit many more politicians, not to mention voters, from the abyss itself. During this period, the differentiation between those who believed in social politics within the Liberal party and most of the supporters of the Labour party was not very noticeable. Potentially the period might have represented—indeed to an extent did represent—a triumph of British empiricism. There was a considerable group on the left of the Liberal party, and on the right of the Labour movement—practically the entire trade union movement to begin with—who did not think in terms of concocting a new economic system but who were not afraid of state action and who were willing to modify the system of capitalism so drastically that it might in fact (if nobody was so rude as to point it out!) have been considered a very mild form of socialism. As Emy writes: "The choice confronting the trade unions paralleled the dilemma of the Social Radicals—how to achieve the broadest enactment of a minimum throughout society without offending against the economic dictates governing society's progress. . . . The demand for social minima—for safety, in health, education and housing, and at work, the demand for minimum levels of income, the creation of social safety-nets —became the overriding goal, a goal which private producers saw as economically unjustifiable, and which socialism treated as a palliative" (p. 248). Emy has provided a discussion of events within the Liberal party and their implications for the politics of the period which is complete within itself yet is also highly suggestive of areas which might repay further investigations—particularly those various groups and organizations mentioned in his study. He has managed, as Matthew has also, to enrich one's understanding of the period and the Liberals' role within it.

Despite the present floodtide of social history, the study of politics is still very strong, and indeed it has been enriched by the new approaches which tend to emphasize the interplay of personalities and the need to approach politics in a not purely political way but with an awareness of how many factors other than the obvious may be in play. Certain works suggest both the richness and the limitations of new approaches, such as the work of Andrew Jones, *The Politics of Reform 1884* (Cambridge, 1972), and D. A. Hamer, *Liberal Politics in the Age of Gladstone and Rosebery* (Oxford, 1972).

These are two intriguing political studies, very different in method, that together bring fresh insights and material to bear on the Liberal party and its problems. Andrew Jones analyzes minutely an event and the politics surrounding it— the third Reform Act of 1884, rather the Cinderella of reform acts—that D. A. Hamer treats very briefly in his narrative of Liberal politics from 1867 to 1906. Both authors, understandably, are somewhat overassertive in the claims they make for their valuable studies, and although neither would say anything so distinctly "illiberal" as that he has discovered the one proper way to study political history, there is some feeling that each believes he has chosen an approach to late-nineteenth-century politics much richer than that of others.

Andrew Jones's tone is at times needlessly defensive. Why bother to refute the charge that "between the archive and the monograph there lies only a simple manipulation of cards" (p. 231)? Again, why disparge those who choose not to do as he does and investigate the subject of reform through high politics? In a single paragraph he manages to be first disparaging, and then defensive: "The conclusion emerges from discouraging experience that the return is marginal for involvement in pamphlet literature, newspapers and most especially provincial newspapers, for such a study. . . . The narrowness which others detect in concentration upon Hawarden, Hatfield and Highbury is, it is contended, more apparent than real" (p. 11). The allusiveness in the latter sentence, invoking Gladstone, Salisbury and Chamberlain by their country houses, suggests that Jones is writing for those who are already familiar with the rough outlines of his story. Yet he realizes that they, too, may well get lost in his detail, and he attempts to help the reader by providing a chronology, a Cabinet list, and a "Portrait Gallery" (more simply called "Biographical Notes" in Hamer's work). Even so, it is almost impossible to maintain the narrative line—the coming about of further franchise reform, combined with redistribution of seats, the burden of the story—with all its encumberances of detail, fascinating as they are.

It is the game of politics that we have here, in a way in its most obvious and yet most private and relatively unstudied area: the mechanism of Parliament and the dealings between the political leaderships that assist the system to move forward. Jones makes clear the intermeshing of issues; day-to-day parliamentary and private meetings made it inevitable that Irish, Egyptian, and reform questions would intertwine. The ideological divisions of issues and individuals which historians tend to impose while looking back misleadingly simplify. There is some slight attention to popular agitation here: the 1,277 public meetings in the summer of 1884 on behalf of the bill. But one suspects that Jones shares Salisbury's opinion in his characterization of these meetings as an attempt to legislate "by picnic." The real action for Jones is in Parliament itself and in such meetings as that of the Redistribution Committee—even there, as Sir Charles Dilke claimed, "the majority . . . did not know what they were doing nor why they were doing it" (p. 187). Redistribution was truly settled by Salisbury, Gladstone, and Dilke. Jones is undoubtedly correct in his conclusion that the act was not, unlike the two previous acts, a major crisis, although it was a major question. It is not clear, however, that he has told us why. There are likely to be more general considerations of personalities and principles which might answer that question. But the detailed working of the politics of leadership, based on an exhaustive use of private papers, is here very well presented, and the reader is entwined in its texture.

Hamer's study is much broader in scope, much more narrative history, based upon a wide range of primary and secondary sources. Among the former, he makes excellent use of Sir Edward Hamilton's diary. Hamer has drawn a convincing pattern for Liberal party history from 1867 to 1906, with the conflicting thrusts of sectionalism and various causes—or to use the more derisive term, fads—of Liberalism, in contrast to the search for the one question to hold the sections together and make them loyal to the party, be it a reform bill, home rule, antagonism to the House of Lords, or free trade.

It is very helpful to see the great issues —more particularly home rule—in this light. Gladstone did believe in the principle of home rule (there is a danger of losing sight of this in a pragmatic discussion of strategy), but he also thought he could use it as a cementing force for the party and as a way of keeping the initiative from Chamberlain. Rosebery, too, in his own style, practiced a form of Gladstonian politics in the 1890s in an attempt to unify the party with himself as leader, and he continued to do so even after he had resigned.

Hamer gives an excellent picture of the Liberal party fighting within itself and on various fronts to avoid being identified as a vehicle of particular causes and factions while attempting to maintain the loyalty of the Celtic, Temperance, and Nonconformist groups. At the same time, it was willing to cooperate, perhaps in a somewhat patronizing way, with the growing Labour movement in order not to be pushed to the right and become exclusively a middle- and upper-class party, increasingly hard put to differentiate itself from the Tories.

Hamer is acute on the role of Sir Henry Campbell-Bannerman and Herbert Gladstone in maintaining an identity for the Liberals. They were assisted by the Tories, who provided an issue in their attack on free trade, and who also obliged by indulging in sectionalisms of their own, diffusing their own effectiveness. But when the Liberals did come into power in 1905, Hamer argues that they were not prepared to face the challenges of the new century, still content to cite a particular issue as the obstruction "on the line" (railway imagery was common in the political rhetoric of the time), and continuing their negative stratagem of waiting for the other side to make mistakes.

But again, as in Jones's study, there does not seem to be quite a sufficient allowance made for either personality or principles in the actual working of politics. Hamer has presented the middle ground of party life where mechanisms and ideas meet. One is not completely convinced, however, that it is here that the virtual disappearance of the Liberal party can be explained. If the party had survived, the very same political characteristics used to account for its failures might well have suggested the intelligent pragmatism and imagination of the Liberal leadership; indeed, one could argue that through the events described by Hamer the party managed, despite its seeming disappearance, to shape the dominant political mood of twentieth-century Britain. The eventual infusion of Liberal ideas and personalities into both Labour and Conservative parties helped prevent them from being purely class parties. It also made them heirs to the strengths and disabilities of sectionalism.

There is the apotheosis of politics in and of itself in J. R. Vincent and A. B. Cooke's *The Governing Passion: Cabinet Government and Party Politics in Britain 1886–1889* (New York, 1974). It is one of the most important, and irritating, books on nineteenth-century politics to be written in many years. The authors have brought to their study decided hypotheses and theories on the nature of politics and the writing of history. The result, not surprisingly—and, one suspects, not undeliberately—is unusual in its procedure, odd in its proportions, and arguable in its conclusions. The first third of the book, entitled "Commentary," is a provocative, tendentious, clever, exhilarating, and frequently convincing essay. The remaining two-thirds, entitled "Diary" and the inspiration for the preceding "Commentary," is a voluminously, wearisomely detailed chronicle—wholly free of analysis, interpretation, or editorial emphases—of events at the highest level of politics from 1 January 1885 to 5 August 1886.

Before this work appeared, we had believed, in our innocence, that the period was dominated by the crisis over Irish home rule, Gladstone's decision to commit himself to that policy, and the subsequent breakup of his party, marked by the departure of that incongruous pair Lord Hartington and Joseph Chamberlain and their followers. Traditional explanations, which appeared to hinge on the passion of Hartington and Chamberlain for the preservation of the union and on Gladstone's passion for "justice" for Ireland, have never been completely convincing; and twentieth-century cynicism about politics and politicians has been highly useful in searching for other motives, revealing Gladstone as a far more calculating politician than had been believed before, without necessarily decreasing his stature. Vincent and Cooke have carried this approach to its logical extreme. In the process they have produced a much more plausible account of what happened in those twenty months than has existed before.

It is a hermetic view of politics and politicians, according to which, leaders may perhaps have reacted to what they read in the newspapers but apparently not at all to what the rank and file of their own parties, from the secondary leaders on down to the lowliest voters, felt and did. Presuming that the major concern of each of the leaders of the two great parties was to preserve his own power—Gladstone against Chamberlain and Hartington within the Liberal party, Salisbury against Randolph Churchill within the Tory party—Vincent and Cooke present a very powerful case. They depict the moderation of the dissidents, forced by the great master politicians into positions far more extreme than they intended, with the result that Gladstone preserved his own position and that of the traditional Liberal party to a far greater extent than has been realized; and Salisbury's strategy was equally successful, as his years as prime minister were to demonstrate.

The authors' argument is circular in its development. The basic premise is that only politics at the very highest level counts; therefore, research is done by locating all relevant papers at that level and then using them to prove the premise. Private papers of politicians will support the contention of the importance of politicians. I would certainly agree that high-level politics is extremely important and would not agree with those who maintain that only local politics, or indeed events outside politics, really matter. One might even argue that what happens at the highest level is of the greatest importance; but it is going too far to say that it is the only arena that matters and it is only the major politicians who count. Admittedly, Vincent and Cooke were thorough in tracking down minor politicians, but they feel they do not really add to the story. As they put it in one of their quasi-Wildean remarks: "There are no interesting papers, except at the top, because there was nothing of much interest, except at the top, to put on paper" (p. 160).

Paradoxically, the authors would seem also to support those who are dismissive of high politics. Political leaders, as they are presented here, are concerned only with power and position and have nothing to do with principles and what is actually happening in the country. They are participating in a word game, fascinating, but ultimately trivial, unconnected with reality: "Governing is the use of words, chiefly in speech, and chiefly to colleagues, in private surroundings, in groups of two or three" (p. 62).

The first third of the book argues brilliantly and tightly for this view of politics. But the argument, although extensively footnoted, consists to a fair degree of assertions, indeed with some repetition and an excessive amount of knowing allusiveness; some perceptions which have the power one associates with G. M. Young; and others which simply fall flat. The authors rise to verbal heights in the conclusion of the first part with such remarks as "Englishmen want their history to be agreeable. By this they mean that problems should have solutions and that liberals should be in power" (p. 162) and "Concealment is the totalitarianism of the non-coercive society."

After the glitter of the "Commentary" comes the dull reality of the "Diary" upon which Vincent and Cooke have based their conclusions. But having argued hard for their own view of events, they now seem to abdicate, or absent themselves, from the remainder of the book with a statement that suggests that this is simply what they happen to believe and they can quite sympathize if others reach different conclusions: "Since what is believed about the roles of people like Gladstone, Churchill, Salisbury, and Parnell in 1886 will be determined by prejudice as much as by anything else, the assembly of much of the relevant evidence in the following chronicle without seeking to relate it directly to our conclusions and prejudices, may be of help to all parties" (pp. 167–168).

Of course the material that follows reinforces their own views to the extent that it exclusively deals with Cabinet meetings and other gatherings at country homes and dinner tables of leading politicians. Naturally, too, it supports their contention that Ireland was not all that important, as the Cabinets had to discuss other issues, frequently foreign and imperial; but the amount of time and trouble devoted to an issue does not necessarily indicate its position in the hierarchy of importance.

The authors' hope that "the assembly of much of the relevant evidence . . . may be of help" is overly modest. The extensive chroncile they have assembled will prove an invaluable guide to events and documents of the period. In this respect, certainly, they have done the profession a considerable service. But they have done themselves, as historians who might have grappled more fully with their own arguments, a disservice by choosing not to unite their bifurcated text. Perhaps some of the brilliance and conciseness of the "Commentary" would have been lost had they done so, but its arbitrariness and self-indulgence would probably have vanished as well. A more traditional book—that is, one that unified chronicle and commentary, each reinforcing the other—might have argued its case more persuasively, and the "Diary" would not have been so often tedious. Without any sort of intervention from the "absent" authors, the triviality of much of high-level political rhetoric and table talk is reflected here with an exhausting fidelity.

Vincent, and also Andrew Jones, are associated with a school of historians centered on Peterhouse, Cambridge, which tends to emphasize high politics. A somewhat more comprehensive tradition is associated with Trinity College, Cambridge, where from his rooms in the great gatehouse the late George Kitson Clark wielded great influence, placing an emphasis on seeing Victorian politics in a wide context. His influential *The Making of Victorian England* (Cambridge, Mass. and London) was published in 1962 and his *An Expanding Society: Britain 1830–1900* (Cambridge, 1967) five years later. Brief but wide-ranging, the latter covers the heart of politics and society in nineteenth-century England. It is not surprising, then, that some of the material should be familiar, in contrast to the new disclosures and finds one would look for in a tightly constructed monograph on some particular aspect of the period. The chapters provide the sort of imaginative and often profound insights that we expect from Kitson Clark, along with exciting calls for new investigations into the working of Victorian society.

He was a historian who would not accept received opinions, but viewed every field afresh, and his students—as is testified to in the *Festschrift* in his honor edited by Robert Robson (*Ideas and Institutions of Victorian Britain*, London, 1967) and in their own volumes—have pursued his insights and substantiatcd them by their investigations. At the same time, this book and its predecessor are evidence that he "held the ring." That is, he offered some sort of comprehensive overview of Victorian society, while his students' views of it, necessarily, have been more microscopic as they have set out to challenge generalizations in special areas within the whole. The trail has led into the suburbs, into party offices, into officials' offices, and the finds have not been insignificant. But as always with the microscopic view, there is some danger of exaggerating the trivial, of seeing more than is in fact there; and to my mind, it is when the investigations of his students cast light on traditional political concerns, as in R. T. Shannon's *Gladstone and the Bulgarian Agitation 1876* (London, 1963), that they are at their best.

In his flight from misleading generalizations, as well as in his very proper suspicion of them, Kitson Clark has perhaps gone too far. His eighth chapter, "The Modern State," three times as long as any of the others and approximately a third of the book, is in effect a defense of himself and his school, a response to the attack launched by Jennifer Hart in *Past and Present* (Nineteenth Century Social Reform," 31, 1965) which is generously cited in the bibliography for the chapter. Right in calling into question the emphasis placed upon the great intellectual figures of the nineteenth century as determining the events of the century as they occurred, he was also right to believe that it is not among abstractions that all answers are to be found. He found his own answers in the mid-nineteenth century when the course of social policy as it was practiced, not thought about, shaped modern England. But generalizations and theories have their value to historians as well as particularities, and it is excessive for Kitson Clark to have remarked about the use of such a term as the *period of laissez-faire* or the *period of collectivism*: "Worst of all, it tends to divert men's attention towards theory and away from the most powerful factor involved, the impact of particular circumstance" (p. 163). Ideas are excessively demoted, and to some degree history is reduced to inevitable events which determined the behavior of those who made decisions and took actions in the nineteenth century: "What they thought affected what they did, but a preponderant factor in any decision they had to make was always the need to find a practical solution to the immediate problem which necessity, or their sense of humanity, presented to them: and that need might easily override preconceived principles" (p. 163). And at the very end of the book, he wrote: "But men's intentions had to conform, not to what was recommended by theory, but to what was demanded by fact, and they were not masters of the future" (pp. 182–183). In fact Kitson Clark is himself within the great Tory tradition of anti-ideology; working within that tradition he and his students have produced some of the most important work to be done on the nineteenth century in recent years.

Although G. M. Young's *Portrait of an Age: Victorian England* (Oxford, 1977) was first published in 1934, and then it covered only the period up to

1865, the version of it published in 1936 went up to 1901. It was an important work in shaping historian's views of the entire nineteenth century. It is also an appropriate memorial to both men that Kitson Clark's last work should be an annotated version of Young's seminal essay. The original in eighty-nine pages summed up the period in a manner at once brilliant, allusive, epigrammatic, and informed. Within a short compass and using a wealth of material from contemporary historical and literary sources, Young traced first the triumph of the critical cast of mind of utilitarianism and evangelicalism to its apogee in the 1850s and then the decline of that achievement. But this is hardly to suggest the richness of detail contained in so brief a space; the topics illuminated range from the role of Benthamism to the significance of the Boer War.

In this edition there are 206 pages of annotations to the text, the vast majority of them written by George Kitson Clark. There is an exhilarating appropriateness about the entire endeavor. For in this present work, two past masters of Victorian England meet on the printed page. They have come together for a dialogue that is essential reading for anyone interested in nineteenth-century England. Here present are mostly complementary but at times conflicting approaches to the English past, written by men who have done so much to shape the way we see the Victorian period.

Portrait of an Age is a masterly essay which should be well thumbed by the beginner (who will be stimulated and confused) and by all students of the period until they abandon their studies. Young's essay reveals both the strengths and weaknesses of the English "amateur" tradition—an extraordinary range of knowledge, which from time to time collapses into knowingness. Almost any sentence in the book is intriguing, and whether one agrees with it or not, it could provide the text—and has, I suspect, frequently done so—for a thesis or a monograph. In that sense, too, the work repays rereadings, for sentences passed over on one reading have a way of standing out on the next.

If *Portrait of an Age* is a continuing and rewarding challenge to how one thinks about the nineteenth century, it is also a tease—to see how many of the references and the quotations, mostly in English but a few in Greek and Latin, one can recognize. It is this task of recognition and elucidation that Kitson Clark set himself. It began as a game, then as a lure to bring new readers to what he regarded as a seminal essay. Kitson Clark was in the next generation of historians of Victorian England, more professional and systematic, a teacher of generations of undergraduates and research students at Cambridge, whereas Young, a retired civil servant, maintained a connection with All Souls, Oxford. Quite a few of the allusions—mostly quotations—eluded even Kitson Clark, his assistants, and consulted experts, but the great majority were run to ground. And it turned out that *Portrait* is full of errors! Dates are off by a year or two, quotations are wrongly given, and material alluded to by Young and investigated by Kitson Clark fails to bear out Young's interpretations. Along the way, Kitson Clark has provided much fascinating information and, in the manner of the brilliant supervisor that he was, he also provided the direction and the beginning bibliography with which the student can explore Young's insights. Kitson Clark's annotations enrich our enjoyment of one of the most remarkable historical essays of our century; they have the added virtue of enriching our understanding of England in the nineteenth century.

Another striking development in the studies of this period—indeed in almost all historical periods—has been an impressive enrichment through the use of other disciplines, a belief that all aspects of a society can inform, particularly if approached in a systematic and analytical way. For historians, there has always been information available on the world of art and architecture, but too frequently it has been used in an antiquarian way, with little regard for what its broader significance might be. One example of the new use of such material is in the various publications of Mark Girouard, and here I would like to pay particular attention to *Sweetness and Light: The "Queen Anne" Movement, 1860–1900* (Oxford, 1977). Girouard is a major architectural historian, and only occasionally is he too technical for the lay reader. Keeping a firm sense of the social context of his subject, he has managed, I believe, a tour de force and has revised the picture of the second half of the nineteenth century.

It is a commonplace that most transformations start earlier than is generally believed (counterbalanced by the other commonplace that older tendencies last longer than one suspects), and Girouard shows how early in the century Victorian heaviness began to give way to something different, lighter, jollier, and less serious. He takes his title from Matthew Arnold, whose *Culture and Anarchy* (1869) urged the middle classes to move toward the Hellenic virtues of "sweetness" (beauty) and "light" (intellectual curiosity) in contrast to the Hebraic values of drive which had given them the wherewithal to move on to "finer" things. Architecturally, there was the parallel of the strength and massiveness of the Gothic revival, and in general the architecture of power and religiosity was most appropriate for Britain in the first half of the nineteenth century. It became less in keeping as Britain became, so to speak, more reflective about her position while she was still rich and powerful. With great verve, Girouard gives the Queen Anne movement its place in intellectual history. This is no mean feat, as the movement was rather eclectic. It was only rather marginally connected with the period of Queen Anne herself, perhaps mostly through sharing with the earlier period an affection for brick.

As usual, William Morris is a pivotal figure. Certainly he was heavily influenced by the Gothic revival and Ruskin, for he was an "aesthetic Goth," yet his firm, founded in 1861, helped lead the way to a lighter and less massive style, particularly in its great popularization of the light, rush-seated "Sussex" chair.

(At the same time, it also made extremely popular another traditional Sussex chair, known as the Morris chair, which was quite heavy and more in keeping with the massiveness of the earlier part of the century.) But Girouard is surely right that the main thrust of the firm was against mid-Victorian heaviness and toughness. The Queen Anne style picked up bits from the seventeenth and eighteenth centuries, used lots of brick and contrasting elements of symmetry, and created delightful and pretty buildings, mostly for the middle class. As Girouard points out, the style "went public" in the early 1870s with Norman Shaw's business buildings; the New Zealand Chambers in the city, designed in 1871; and the Red House, a home designed in the same year by J. J. Stevenson. The style was antiheroic, friendly, and unaggressive, adapted to a society beginning to have doubts about itself, but not to such an extent that it was unwilling to enjoy its prosperity. " 'Queen Anne' succeeded not because it was sensible but because it was pretty, and because by the 1870s it exactly suited the mood of the public."

The style also had a more public dimension; Girouard discusses its dominance in the design of the new Board Schools in London, which were made necessary by the passing of W. E. Forster's Education Act of 1870. Also, in a brilliant section, he makes clear the sort of approach the style represented by contrasting the heavier architecture favored by the more severe and earnest purposes of Girton, the first women's college at Cambridge, to the more light-handed approach of Newnham, with its Queen Anne buildings designed by Basil Champneys. Girouard uses a wide range of examples to demonstrate his point, including gardens and the children's literature of Walter Crane, Kate Greenaway, and Randolph Caldecott. Perhaps the need for illustration goes on a little too long: the sections on Queen Anne by the sea, in shops, in pubs, and in America, while enjoyable, do not seem to me to be necessary.

As William Morris is an important figure in the world of design, art, and architecture, so too he is obviously a political figure, and the reissue of E. P. Thompson's mammoth study *William Morris, Romantic to Revolutionary* (New York, 1977) is significant in dealing with all aspects of Morris, but particularly his politics. Two impressive figures, William Morris as subject and E. P. Thompson as author, are conjoined in this immense biographical-historical-critical study, and both of them have gained in interest since the first edition of the book was published in England twenty-two years ago. In 1955 Morris's once-great reputation was no longer what it was. He seemed to be receding into the haze of the nineteenth century as yet another eminent Victorian too remote to be relevant to our own concerns—no matter that Nikolaus Pevsner, as late as 1936, had placed him among *The Pioneers of the Modern Movement from William Morris to Walter Gropius* (London). As for Edward Thompson, he was an obscure young historian at the start of his career, writing from a Marxian point of view, no special advantage in 1955. Unpopular politics aside, the conjunction of unknown

author and unfashionable subject would have been sufficient to explain why the
book was virtually ignored by the literary establishment and dropped, as Thompson remarks in this second edition, "into an academic silence."

But times and circumstances change. We are in the midst now of what promises to be an enduring Morris revival; and the book that was ignored in 1955 has
meanwhile become something of an underground classic—almost impossible to
locate in secondhand bookstores, pored over in liberaries, required reading for
anyone interested in Morris and, increasingly, for anyone interested in one of the
most important of contemporary British historians.

Since the publication in 1963 of Thompson's masterpiece, *The Making of the
English Working Class* (London), his reputation has been growing, and it was further enhanced with *Whigs and Hunters* (New York, 1975), a study of the Black
Act against poachers of 1723. His interests, as is often the case with historians,
have been moving back in time, but the centerpiece of his accomplishments is
still the study of the working class coming to consciousness of itself as a class at
the end of the eighteenth century and the beginning of the nineteenth. Whatever
faults one may find in his work, he has the distinguishing characteristic of a great
historian: he has transformed the nature of the past so that it will never look the
same again; and whoever works in the area of his concerns in the future must
come to terms with what Thompson has written.

So too with his study of William Morris. Morris is so protean a figure, so
varied in his ambitions, talents, and achievements, so unflagging in his energies,
that he is difficult to encompass. A force in the Victorian age, yes; but also an
innovator, an influence, a revolutionary, a precursor of the age of the modern in
art and politics. As much as anyone of his time, he was a latter-day version of the
Renaissance man—a compliment he would not have valued, given his hatred of
the Renaissance with its emphasis upon individual genius. And yet, how else to
describe a man who tried his hand, often with remarkable success, at such an
astonishing variety of endeavors?

He was a prolific poet (his greatest fame in his lifetime—and he might have
succeeded Tennyson as poet laureate had he not been a socialist); a translator of the
Icelandic sagas; the author of several prose romances. As the founder of Morris
& Co., that firm of decorators whose influence continues to be felt up to this very
day, he took part in all its operations, from the manufacture and design of fabrics
to wallpapers to furniture to stained glass. He threw himself energetically into
politics and the protection of ancient buildings and, as the founder of the Kelmscott Press, into the revival of printing as a fine art.

What Morris was unprepared to recognize was that his was truly the exceptional case, and this would have been apparent to any discerning observer: it
seems to have been something one felt even at a first meeting. The young Henry
James, for example, who was taken to meet him in 1869 at his house (and shop)

in Queen's Square, Bloomsbury, was impressed "most agreeable" and afterward wrote to his sister Alice in Cambridge, "He's an extraordinary example, in short, of a delicate sensitive genius and taste, served by a perfectly healthy body and temper."

The problem confronting any biographer or student of Morris in all his variety is to find some unifying principle, some cohering line throughout his life, or—to call upon Henry James for a phrase once again—"the figure in the carpet." Thompson's answer, and he argues for it most persuasively, is in Morris's politics: his progression from romantic to revolutionary, beginning under the influence of Keats and ending under the influence of Marx. Earlier writers, most notably R. Page Arnot, have pointed out that the political Morris was essential and must not be submerged in folds of Morris chintz. The arts and crafts tradition, to which Morris contributed so much, is vitally important in the English past, and present; but it cannot be allowed to take him out of politics, any more than Pevsner's placing him among the forerunners of modernism, or the enthusiasts of fine printing who celebrate the achievements of the Kelmscott Press.

It has taken quite a while for the view of the political Morris to establish itself, and it is continually in danger of being vitiated by those who quite legitimately are more interested in the literary or the artistic Morris. Four years after the publication of the first edition of Thompson's study in London—and two years before it was belatedly published in America—a contributor to the catalog of an important Morris show at Brown University allowed himself to suggest that Morris's "outmoded socialism" was of no interest and irrelevant to a consideration of his major achievements. Not so: one may disagree with Morris's politics; I do not see how, for reading Thompson, one can deny their importance to him, in his own life, and hence, since he never attempted the separation of the two, in his work.

For some years now, one has heard rumors that Thompson was dissatisfied with the first edition of the study, that he thought it too militant and was at work on a much milder version. With the second edition in hand, it is pleasant to discover that the rumors had no substance. Thompson is one of these rare former Communists who, although they have left the party, have not felt called upon to renounce the idealistic motives that led them into it and who have not felt it necessary to abandon their Marxist beliefs. This is fundamentally the same book that was published twenty-two years ago, with some of the more extravagant, hortatory, and conjectural sentences excised.

The picture of Morris that emerges here shows him to be more independent of Marx than may have been the case in the first edition—a parallel thinker, as it were, though less systematic, great in his own English pragmatic fashion, in his way indeed an English Marx. A postscript has been added—primarily to review the major literature on Morris over the past twenty years—in which Thompson reveals both his own independence and that of his subject in maintaining that Morris must be seen neither as a doctrinaire Marxist nor as a jolly, nonideological Englishman who happened to subscribe to a few Marxist ideas as a kind of window dressing.

But Thompson's greatest contribution, I believe is to uncover the figure in the carpet. Even many of those who have recognized Morris's importance as a socialist have been content to show him as a fragmented personality, writing a poem one day, designing a tapestry the next, and preaching socialism the day after that, with no relation between. Thompson presents a much more integrated and much more powerful conception. In this respect, I fear that his subtitle ("Romantic to Revolutionary") may do a disservice, being more euphonious than precise. Of course there was a progression in Morris's life, but what is striking is to learn how early he was "in revolt"—a posture he would maintain to the end—having committed himself to "Holy Warfare against the age" when he was still an undergraduate at Oxford.

The age in which Morris lived (rather like our own) was notable for its shoddiness ("Shoddy is king!"), its hypocrisy, its selfishness, its ugliness, its vulgarity and divisiveness. It was the age of the first rank flowering of industrialism, against which in their respective ways Dickens, Ruskin, and Carlyle would wage war also. In the beginning, to be "in revolt," for Morris, was to seek out a private romantic escape—in poetry, in love, and in a not especially happy marriage to the exotically beautiful Jane Burden, whose face stares out from so many pre-Raphaelite portraits; and then, moving toward a wider vision of what life might be, in the creation of beautiful things at Morris & Co. But poetry, marriage, even the firm, did not answer to the needs of his vision: a better life, not only for himself and for those who could afford the productions of Morris & Co., but for all men and women. Politics, radical politics, running counter to the drives and aspirations of Victorian England, was the logical answer for the middle-aging genius who was still, and would always be, "in revolt."

Approximately two-thirds of Thompson's study is devoted to Morris's political career: a brilliant recreation of left-wing politics in the late nineteenth century. Ironically, it might seem that of all his protean activities, politics was the least rewarding to Morris. In the short run there was a record of failure and disappointment. He broke with the Social Democratic Federation, two years after having joined it in 1883, because it was too concerned with parliamentary politics. He broke with his own creation, the Socialist League, because it was taken over by anarchists. In the end he was left with only his own local organization, the Hammersmith Socialist Society, meeting in his London house.

Even in the long run his political career might be judged a failure: all of these organizations were to be ancestors of the present-day Labour party and the welfare state—the world of "demi-semi-socialism" where commercialism and statism and the values of the middle class still prevail. But the impulse to be "in revolt" continued to inspire Morris—as it had, in a sense, from the beginning—and informed whatever he would do, virtually to the day of his too-early death in 1896, at the age of 62.

In his politics, as Thompson remarks, "the long romantic breach between aspiration and action was healed." If his vision of a transformed society, creating not equality of opportunity but a society of equals, has yet to be realized, it is not an ignoble one. "We have to make up our minds about William Morris," Thompson writes in his postscript. His book is indispensable to the task, now and in the future.

Thompson has been a dominating and exciting figure on all periods of British history; ironically, he has replaced Sir Lewis Namier as a shaper of historians' approaches, this being a period more historically concerned with how people live rather than with the working of political power. Despite their obvious differences, Namier and Thompson have both the characteristic of great historians in wishing to discover what may be the reality behind events.

Thompson has had a great influence upon working-class history. The thrust in that field, or so it seems to me, is to attempt to move away from the institutional, as in Standish Meacham's *A Life Apart: The English Working Class 1890–1914* (Cambridge, Mass., 1977), in which the English working class is examined with care and consideration. It is, on the whole, a static study, except toward the end, when the great sense of disorder before 1914 conveys some sense that a revolution might have been impending and that it was prevented by the advent of war. The book reveals an extensive command of the literature that deals with the period; it also makes much use of the oral history collected by Thea Vigne and Paul Thompson, available at the University of Essex. Oral history is yet another source, adding variety, immediacy, and depth to what is already available; but it does not appear to alter the picture of the period that we would have had in any case.

What sort of picture emerges in a comparatively brief book which is broken down into such chapters as "House, Neighborhood and Kin," "Women at Home," "Working Wives and Mothers," "Husbands and Fathers," "Children"? It tends to be a picture of the working class on the defensive. Except in the chapter on husband and fathers, Meacham tends to ignore the more traditional picture of working-class history—the dynamics of the labor movement itself—in favor of an attempt to catch the laborer at home, so to speak. Putting an emphasis on the worker's domesticity, he leaves an impression of the isolation of the working-class family, although they might be closer to their kin, particularly their mothers, than to their contemporaries.

There is a heavy emphasis on respectability, of "keeping oneself to oneself," for it is the more respectable poor who are depicted here, who attempted cleanliness and order against the most formidable odds. As Meachan remarks, "life in a late Victorian working-class slum too often meant death." The struggle is heroic, yet the picture that emerges is rather fatalistic. The degree of class consciousness seems rather low and certainly not of a sort that will provide the energy for political change. These workers seem to have little interest in taking over the state. In fact they quite rightly regard it with profound suspicion as an agency which, through education, wishes to diminish their control of their children and their potential as wage earners.

The last chapter, "A View of Life," is insightful on the threats and inconvenience represented by the growing state bureaucracy: "The state—its police and its inspectors, its directives and its circulars—threatened the working class in a way the middle class never fully understood. The state was part of 'them,' an alien imposition which workers and their families had tried their best to fend off or ignore." It is a sad picture which emerges, and if it is hard to accept that the working class were quite as beaten down as Meacham pictures them, his is a fine depiction of the texture of their lives.

Meacham has also complemented this study with an essay in Roy Flukinger, Larry Schaaf, and Standish Meacham's *Paul Martin, Victorian Photographer* (Austin, Tex., 1977). There, he demonstrates how much the extensive work he has done for *A Life Apart* has taught him. He takes the photographs Martin made in the 1890s and creates convincing biographies of a working-class wife, two costermongers, an alleged cabinetmaker in the park with his daughter, and a young girl on Hampstead Heath on a bank holiday and on Yarmouth sands. As Meacham remarks at the conclusion of his essay, "Men, women, and children are on the move, confronting not just each other but the world—the place where historians must encounter them, if they hope to understand them."

This essay subscribes to the convention of the crucial importance of 1914, the date of the outbreak of the First World War. We all know that many of the events of the post–First World War world were shaped before; yet the quality of British life does change after 1914, as Paul Fussell has brilliantly argued in *The Great War and Modern Memory* (New York, 1975). Thus it may be appropriate to conclude by discussing three books on the period just before the war: Barbara Tuchman's *The Proud Tower: A Portrait of the World before the War, 1890–1914* (New York, 1966), A. M. Gollin's *Balfour's Burden: Arthur Balfour and Imperial Preference* (London, 1965), and Geoffrey Marcus's *Before the Lamps Went Out: Britain's Golden Age, Christmas 1913–August 1914* (Boston, 1965). The Victorian age did not end with the death of the monarch nor even with the death of her eldest son, but with the outbreak of the First World War. In her foreword, Tuchman writes, "The Great War of 1914–18 lies like a band of scorched earth dividing that time from ours. . . . it created a physical as well as psychological gulf between two epochs" (p. xiii). Her book is "an attempt to discover the quality of the world from which the Great War came." Other historians, who locate the origins and first stirrings of the modern epoch in the period 1890–1910, will call into question the "scorched earth" theory. But while Tuchman acknowledges the "new tensions and accumulated energies" that began to be felt before 1914 and that, at least by implication, had something to do with the post-1918 world, the cumulative effect of her mosaic is to establish a qualitative difference. Her final judgment of the period is that "its inhabitants lived, as compared to a later time, with more self-reliance, more confidence, more hope; greater magnificence, extravagance, and elegance; more careless ease, more gaiety, more pleasure in each other's company and conversation, more injustice and hypocrisy, more misery and want, more sentiment including false sentiment, less sufferance of mediocrity, more dignity in work, more delight in nature, more zest" (p. 463). In spite of the intrusion of hypocrisy, misery, want, and injustice, this catalog makes a splendid, even a glamorous, effect. But is it true?

Is it true, for example, about Arthur Balfour, who dominates the English chapters in Tuchman's book, and who is the central figure in Alfred Gollin's study? Balfour certainly had, to a high degree, many of the qualities listed in Tuchman's catalog, and they were qualities he shared with many of the politicians of the period—the air of unquestioned authority, "the unbought grace of life" (Burke's phrase)—which made them so formidable and effective but which, once challenged, proved in many cases to be as evanescent as the emperor's new clothes. What makes Balfour particular fascinating is that the qualities appeared in him in so attenuated a form (or style) that it is hard to realize that he had the strength to be an effective political leader. He surprised his comtemporaries by his ruthlessness in Ireland. His policy on the question of protection and his policy on the House of Lords were not, as it would appear, policies of weakness but rather of concealed strength, designed to allow the Tories to ride out the storm of protest both issues had aroused. As it happened, neither policy succeeded, but what one had not realized about the protection crisis before reading Gollin, who makes use of fine primary material, is how close Balfour came to success. He was playing the game with excruciating precision; he was attempting the most delicate operation in order to force the free traders out of his Cabinet without losing the duke of Devonshire. In the end he was outfoxed by that phlegmatic politician, who had "the unbought grace of life" in the largest possible quantities and would not go along with Balfour's game. It is surprising that Balfour did not take into account how important loyalty would be to Devonshire. That "rock" might take longer to allow himself to move than his colleagues, but his very reluctance to do so would make his eventual move even more devastating to the Tory party, and to Balfour as its leader.

How is one to account for Balfour's eagerness to remain in office? To begin, there is little question that he enjoyed the exercise of power, whatever his loung-

ing manner in the House of Commons and in conversation. Also, with not uncommon Tory arrogance, he felt that the "interests" of the country demanded
Tory rule. As he wrote to Devonshire—in a letter quoted in Gollin—"Our business is to prevent our decisions reaching a point which may convert them into a
national disaster, and may deprive the greatest interests of the country of the
guardianship by which since 1886 they have been protected" (p. 104). But perhaps Balfour was too devious for his own good. His attempt to rid himself of the
troublesome Joe Chamberlain and also of the free traders backfired and left him
weaker than before. In his own acceptance of tariff retaliation, he was really
closer to Chamberlain than to the free traders, but perhaps Balfour did not mind
getting rid of someone so "vulgar" as Chamberlain. (Joe's son Austen, brought
into the Cabinet as his father's representative, was more suitable: he had been to a
public school, and he had *not* become a manufacturer.)

A politician's motives and activities, when examined as meticulously as Gollin
has done, come to seem somewhat timeless; one looks in vain for those special
qualities that Tuchman seem to associate with the age. Perhaps it might be argued
that the Edwardian grandees had a belief in their indispensableness to a degree
unknown before or since, as if all the elements of Victorian self-satisfaction, but
not Victorian doubt, had crystallized in a profound conviction of one's own importance. In Balfour's case, doubt was restricted to philosophy: he expressed the
hesitations in his life in his thinking about God, not in his political actions. Both
Gollin and Tuchman suggest that in 1903 Balfour felt that he must stay in office
because he feared the Liberals would not be willing to prepare England for war,
either in terms of her diplomatic relations or her military arrangements. One can
question Balfour's effectiveness, if not his sincerity, in this regard. It seems fair
to assume that the Liberals would have refurbished the military machine. Neither
Campbell-Bannerman, nor Grey, nor Haldane, nor Churchill were unconcerned
about Britain's military needs and would very likely have taken considerable steps
to satisfy them, even if Balfour had not committed them to such a course. After
all, less than a decade earlier, Gladstone had been forced out of office by his colleagues on the question of naval preparedness, and this had not been merely a
political stratagem. Balfour did not anticipate that his delicate maneuvering
would lead to the electoral catastrophe that ensued. He hoped to be master of his
own Cabinet in 1903. But even if he should be defeated then, and in 1906, he
could not lose his "unbought grace of life"—and the House of Lords.

Geoffrey Marcus is a good deal less ambitious than Tuchman, but he goes
much further than she in providing documentation for the style of life, the sense
of innocence which could not survive World War I. *Before the Lamps Went Out* is
a somewhat curious book, as it seems to draw upon childhood memories of Sussex
as well as on more usual historical sources. This is an unassuming book that manages, in a variety of ways, to tell the reader much about England at the end of the

prewar epoch. Marcus covers a considerable amount of English life, from the countryside to the North, and without neglecting London or the politics of that terminal year. (As a naval historian, it is not surprising that he should dwell on those aspects of the year that have to do with the navy, on everything from naval reviews to the craze for sailor suits for children.) He reminds us how much of the style of English life was still rural and how easy it was for even the Londoner to get away from the city, either on his own or in the organized jollities of the cockneys on Derby Day or on August Bank Holiday on Hampstead Heath. At moments, his evocations of rural life verge on the sentimental; his political discussion bogs down in "glorious nights, unforgettable memories"—but lapses of this sort are rare, and he has a firm grip on the realities, as opposed to the myths, of the period. He recognizes the importance of the Irish problem, which the international situation did not dispel until very shortly before the outbreak of the war—or indeed until John Redmond's response to the king's speech—and he illuminates the arrogant style of the politicians of the period in his descriptions of the debates over Ireland and the "mutiny" at the Curragh. The circumstances were such that even Balfour lost his customary sangfroid—perhaps a sign, a foreshadowing, of the old order on its way out—and for the first time a former prime minister spoke in Hyde Park.

The double standard of different rules for the rulers and the ruled became much more obvious in the year before the war than it had been in the past, and hence more offensive: a source of potential danger. Churchill was aware of its implications in international terms as well, and his concern is evident in the extraordinarily frank memorandum he prepared for the Cabinet, and which, Marcus informs us, he printed in a revised version in *The World Crisis:* "We are not a young people with an innocent record and a scanty inheritance. We have engrossed to ourselves, in times when other powerful nations were paralysed by barbarism or internal war, an altogether disproportionate share of the wealth and traffic of the world. We have got all we want in territory, and our claim to be left in the unmolested enjoyment of vast and splendid possessions, mainly acquired by violence, largely maintained by force, often seems less reasonable to others than to us." But there were few who could see as dispassionately as this, and to most Tories it was perfectly reasonable that Ulster should arm to defend her rights, and perfectly unreasonable that Southern Ireland should do the same; it was perfectly reasonable that officers might refuse to attack Ulster, and perfectly unreasonable that ordinary soldiers might refuse to fire upon workers. No wonder that E. M. Forster's "only connect" of *Howards End* was such an appropriate idea (and epigraph) for an Edwardian novel. The need for exactly this sort of connection was powerfully argued in Parliament by Churchill himself and by the Lib-Lab MP John Ward; but the reactions from the Tories, frequently led by Balfour's cousin Lord Hugh Cecil, were "telegrams and anger," the screams and yells of the abyss. The ruling classes in England had justified themselves in the past by managing to convince the country that they represented its true and total interest, that they were larger than themselves. They may still have had that larger-than-life quality that Tuchman finds in them, but the period in which they could claim without second thought to speak for the country was running out. The two Englands had existed long before Disraeli called attention to them, but the antagonisms between them, in various forms, appeared to be reaching a climax in 1914. The coming of the war accelerated, but it did not inaugurate, the end of an epoch that was already moribund.

Yet it is tempting to accept the "scorched earth" theory when one considers how ordinarily life went on, through the Irish crisis, even through the growing international crisis, almost to the last day of peace. There were the noisy pleasures of August Bank Holiday for the people; Churchill was with his children on the sands of Cromer; Grey was fishing at Itchen Abbas. Balfour looked down from his eminence, and when he heard that Churchill had ordered the fleet to its war station, he found himself "looking at all the people in the street going along happily, and saying to myself that I knew that war was coming upon them" (p. 209). The country folk were probably much more concerned with the harvest than with the war; and in London the crowd was surging happily up and down Whitehall. One bobby, a veteran of the Boer War, remarked of the crowd to Edgar Wallace, "They're making a terrible fuss about a terrible thing, sir," but more and more people, in government and out, were coming to feel that it was time for the war to start.

Marcus, through his juxtaposition of the familiar political and military story with unfamiliar details of ordinary life at various levels in England, does manage to suggest that there was a style, somewhat hard to define, assured yet innocent, powerful yet considerate, a style that characterized the period, a style that, as such things as the Irish crisis and the handling of the suffragettes demonstrated, was beginning to dwindle into a kind of aristocratic form without force.

The war brought with it a new style, something closer to the people, more democratic, less mannerly, which failed to take into deferential account "the unbought grace of life." The war was not of the people's making, except in the important sense that a people receive the government they deserve (or are willing to put up with); but they did, as A. J. P. Taylor has argued, save their government and their country. There is much to be said for Lloyd George's war leadership, but it was full of defects, and the same was true of the leadership of the military. If it had not been for the immense contribution in lives, in effort, in money put out by the English people, Germany might well have won the war. Class was not eliminated in England as a result of the war, but class lines were weakened, and there was a new mingling of society which allowed England to become more democratic after 1918. "War socialism," necessary in order to wage war more effectively, brought along with it a dramatic change in habits and styles of life. If it took some time for the English people to get used to the idea of war and to abandon their attitude of "business as usual," they did eventually rise to the occasion, and they proved themselves able to save a society in which they had played a subordinate part. But the people did not perform so magnificent a service without exacting something in exchange. Thereafter the traditional governing classes would no longer be able to claim their birthright. Admittedly the new style had made itself felt in the Tory party before the war in the person of the blunt Bonar Law, but even he did not have to woo the public as his successors would need to do. Neither Stanley Baldwin nor Neville Chamberlain could assume, as Balfour had done, that he could have grace without works.

I have merely attempted to suggest here in an extremely selective way a few recent approaches to the period 1870–1914. Since 1966 when *Changing Views* was published, more has been discovered about the period; events, people, trends have been looked at thoroughly and imaginatively. No doubt the next bibliographical discussion fifteen or twenty years on will draw a similar conclusion about the years to come. The fascinating endlessness of the quest has its moments of depression, but more frequently it provides excitement and new glimpses of the changing panorama of the past.

❧

I add here a list of books on the period published since 1965 which seem to me to be significant. These titles emerged from discussions I have had with James Bailey and Kirk Willis, and I have provided their comments on particular books.

First let mention titles that deal primarily with politics: Bentley B. Gilbert's *The Evolution of National Insurance* (London, 1966) is a superb and richly detailed analysis of the Liberal social welfare legislation passed after 1906 together with a discussion of the forces which shaped the resultant welfare system. Henry M. Pelling's *The Social Geography of British Elections, 1885–1910* (New York, 1967) is a pioneering study of the local base of national politics in the period that successfully fills in many of the gaps in the official record. Paul Thompson's *Socialists, Liberals and Labour* (London, 1967) is an important combination of social and political history that adds a significant local dimension to the study of the emergence of the Labour political interest in the late nineteenth century. Peter F. Clarke's *Lancashire and the New Liberalism* (Cambridge, 1971) is a significant and original interpretation of the decline of the Liberal party and the rise of Labour and is based on a richly detailed regional study. An original and revealing survey of the elections of 1910, Neal Blewett's *The Peers, the Parties and the People* (Toronto, 1972) enriches our understanding of the national mood in that critical year. Using quantitative techniques for the first time in studying late

Victorian politics, T. W. Heyck, in *The Dimensions of British Radicalism* (Urbana, 1974), clearly demonstrates why the radicals in the Liberal party did not follow Chamberlain in 1886.

Some titles that deal more with problems of society: Richard Price's *An Imperial War and the British Working Class* (Toronto, 1972) convincingly demonstrates the lack of support for imperial policies among the working class. A brilliant study of the problems of casual labor and working-class housing in late Victorian London, Gareth Stedman Jones's *Outcast London* (Oxford, 1971) reveals new perspectives on middle-class attitudes to social reform in the period. Standish Meacham's *A Life Apart* (Cambridge, Mass., 1977) is a major reinterpretation of the late Victorian working class, emphasizing its defensive qualities. Richard Price's *Masters, Unions and Men* (Cambridge, 1980) is a ground-breaking study of the connections between work and the system of industrial relations in Britain as it developed before the First World War.

Some books on the economy: Derek Aldcroft, editor's *The Development of British Industry and Foreign Competition* (Toronto, 1968) is a reassessment of Britain's economic performance in several industrial sectors by many of the most important economic historians practicing in the field today. Donald McCloskey's *Economic Maturity and Entrepreneurial Decline* (Cambridge, Mass., 1973) is a major, if controversial, reinterpretation of the decline of the British economy in the late nineteenth century, using the steel and iron industries as an example. A pamphlet by S. B. Saul, *The Myth of the Great Depression* (London, 1969), has managed to force a reassessment of the traditional interpretation of the late Victorian economy. Two business studies are Donald Coleman's *Courtaulds* (2 vols., Oxford, 1969), an important analysis of one of Britain's major twentieth-century textile firms from its beginnings, a major contribution to business history, and W. J. Reader's *Imperial Chemical Industries*, volume 1, *The Forerunners, 1870–1924* (London, 1970), also a major contribution to business history and to our understanding of a crucial sector of the British economy during the "second industrial revolution." Sidney Pollard and Paul Robertson's *The British Shipbuilding Industry, 1870–1914* (Cambridge, Mass., 1979) is a major study of the development of the British shipbuilding industry in the age of its greatest growth and importance. It includes a significant contribution to the debate over the decline of the economy in this period, as well as to the discussion of work and labor relations before the war.

Some books on intellectual history during the period: Stefan Collini's *Liberalism and Sociology: L. T. Hobhouse and Political Argument in England 1880–1914* (Cambridge, 1979) rescues Hobhouse from the sociologists and restores his reputation as an influential thinker. The subtitle is exactly right: Collini discusses the development of Hobhouse's thought and places it squarely in the midst of late-nineteenth- and early-twentieth-century social and political argument. Collini's treatment is analytical and closely argued, although at times the writing is too cute. Michael Freeden's *The New Liberalism* (Oxford, 1978) is an impressively analytical and intelligently critical study of late-nineteenth- and early-twentieth-century Liberal thought. Perhaps the most refreshing thing about the book is that it is not the usual collective biography. Freeden argues that the New Liberal theoreticians were successful in modernizing Liberalism and that by the summer of 1914 they had formulated an intelligent, coherent, and compassionate new social ideology. David Marquand's *Ramsay MacDonald* (London, 1977) is probably the finest political biography of any twentieth-century politician. It is intelligent and sympathetic (rather uncommon for treatments of MacDonald), though Marquand does not shy from passing rather harsh judgment on Macdonald. Richard Wollheim's *F. H. Bradley* (Harmondsworth, 1969) presents the leading nineteenth-century neo-Hegelian philosopher. After Russell, Moore, and the logical positivists had finished with him, his reputation was in ruins. Wollheim offers an elegantly written and masterfully argued presentation of Bradley's arguments. David Thatcher's *Nietzsche in England* (Toronto, 1970), a much neglected work, is more ambitious than the title suggests. It deals with the reception of other foreign and avant-garde writers in England—Ibsen, for instance. Thatcher describes and explains the remarkable receptivity to these works on the part of many English men and women.

Some Recent Writings on Twentieth-century Britain

Henry R. Winkler

When *Changing Views on British History* was published in 1966, most of the public archives for the study of twentieth-century issues were still inaccessible. The Public Record Act of 1958 had of course eliminated some of the inconsistency with which even the fifty-year rule was administered by individual guardians of public records, but it required an intense lobbying campaign by a group of senior historians to lower the closed period from fifty years to thirty. The Public Record Act of 1967 has now laid open a sizable body of basic source material for more than half the years since 1914. Other depositories have followed the Public Record Office in opening their materials more liberally to scholars. Aside from the "instant histories" of writers whom Donald Watt has called the professional cream-skimmers, rushing to meet publishers' deadlines by exposing the new materials released each New Year's Day,[1] substantial alteration of many of the tentative judgments of a short while ago has characterized the scholarship of the last decade.

Whatever may be the revisions in interpretation, a few persistent general themes provide the frame of reference within which much of that scholarship finds its place. The crucial effects of the two world wars, the inexorable decline of Britain's international position, and the long-term erosion of her economic power have continued in one way or another to invite the attention of a large number of commentators. Within these broad categories, contemporary experience has clearly encouraged increased study of certain discrete and obvious developments. Not only politicians, but historians and sociologists, have addressed questions—for example, about whether the welfare state has actually increased equality in British society—raised by the implementation of the concept of universal social security. Similarly, they have sought to explicate the development of other relatively current phenomena by searching for their roots in the recent past. In the political arena, changes in the character and procedures of the major parties, the patterns of electoral politics, and the increased absorption of government with economic functions have all continued to be widely investigated. So too has the puzzling collapse of the Liberal party after the First World War, while the Labour party has ceased to be a subject for the quizzical wonder of a few idiosyncratic scholars—many of them Americans—and has become the subject of a virtual avalanche of new books and articles.

Good general accounts of the entire period are still relatively scarce. The new edition of Alfred E. Havighurst's popular survey is called *Britain in Transition: The Twentieth Century*.[2] It is still the best single-volume elementary text, despite the appearance of T. O. Lloyd's *Empire to Welfare State*.[3] This latter volume, one of the Short Oxford History of the Modern World series, suffers no less from the fact that its depiction of the period after 1945 is essentially an extended chronicle than from its almost total neglect of foreign policy questions before the late 1930s. By contrast, W. N. Medlicott's balanced contribution to Longman's History of England in Ten Volumes will better serve those who already have some acquaintance with the period. His *Contemporary England, 1914–1964* assesses "the impact of an almost continuous series of external crises on the domestic outlook, economy, and national policy" of the country. Not content to cry havoc over the decline of British power, Medlicott, although he has no illusions about British problems and British failures, also points out the achievements of the period. His observations on the democratization of politics, the creation of the welfare state, and the acceptance of an uneven but basic social revolution, and on the end of rural isolation with the revolution in mass communication media, are more persuasive than his emphasis upon the continued centrality of Britain's international position. Nevertheless, Medlicott is at his best in discussing foreign policy between the wars, to which he devotes perhaps a disproportionate share of his book. Altogether, however, *Contemporary England* belongs with A. J. P. Taylor's *English History, 1914–1945* as the standard general account for much of the twentieth century.[4]

Three other works of a general character merit brief mention. *The British Revolution, 1880–1939* (New York, 1977) by the practiced biographer Robert Rhodes James is essentially a political history, but its main strength is in the character sketches and evaluations of the politicians who dominated the scene from the latter decades of the nineteenth century until the outbreak of World War II. Arthur Marwick, on the other hand, is concerned less with the men at the top than with how ordinary people lived. He writes that this book is "about the social effects of modern war," but *Britain in the Century of Total War: War, Peace and Social Change, 1900–1967* (Boston, 1968) is actually a social history of Great Britain in the present century. It is especially effective in conveying the spirit of "business as usual" that prevailed during so much of the First World War and in describing the mood for change and the consequent welfare state engendered by the second. A third general study is the work of a group of Nuffield scholars, entitled *Trends in British Society since 1900: Changing Social Structure of Britain*.

It is a collection of data and essays on a variety of subjects—the labor force, schools, crime, social mobility, immigration, urbanization, higher education, and local government, among others. Historians will find many of the data suggestive and various of the perceptions useful in their own explorations of related subjects.[5]

On the issue of social structure there is an excellent article by B. A. Waites. "The Effect of the First World War on Class and Status in England, 1910–20" concludes that, in those years, English society changed from a complex hierarchy in which stratification by status overlay the basic three-tier class structure, to a simpler form.[6] The distinctions which had graded Edwardian manual workers as much as they had the middle class became rather less distinct, the basic social classes rather more so. The result, among other things, was a polarization that fostered greater industrial conflict in the years ahead. By way of contrast, *The Fragmentary Class Structure*, by K. Roberts, F. G. Cook, S. C. Clark, and Elizabeth Semenoff of the University of Liverpool, presents evidence to question the thesis that the working class is gradually becoming "embourgeoised" and equally challenges the notion that there is a serious revolutionary potential within the blue collar ranks, even though the gulf between the working and middle classes remains real and substantial. As for the middle class, like the working class, it is becoming increasingly "fragmented." Indeed, while in the past the working class was the main threat to middle-class cohesion, it may now be the management of conflict between the various sections of the middle class that poses the most challenging political task of the future.[7]

It is not surprising that numerous aspects of the First World War continue to invite analysis. The war was the great divide in twentieth-century history, and its study has been facilitated by the thirty-year rule. There is no evidence that Sir Llewelyn Woodward used the recently opened materials in his general work on Great Britain and the war,[8] but his survey dissects the mistakes of British leaders, no less than French and German, with devastating effect. Woodward's account of the mobilization of British resources for war, while it makes clear the British talent for improvisation, implicitly confirms the view that even the crunch of war only modified to a degree customary ways of doing business.

For some time, Lord Beaverbrook's trilogy dealing with the rise, the heyday, and the decline of David Lloyd George's governments has been a major source for much of the high-level—or perhaps the word is low-level—politics of the wartime leaders.[9] Now we have studies by Stephen Koss and Cameron Hazlehurst to raise serious questions about the accuracy of Beaverbrook's account of intrigue in the halls of power. Koss, first in an article in the *Journal of Modern History*,[10] then in *Lord Haldane: Scapegoat for Liberalism*,[11] has argued that the last Liberal government was destroyed in May 1915, by a conspiracy, spearheaded by Winston Churchill, to force the dismissal of Lord Kitchener and Sir

Edward Grey. Ironically, Kitchener and Grey survived, but Haldane, for a variety of reasons including his opposition to conscription and the suspicion aroused by his Berlin mission of 1912, was dispensable. Koss's book goes far beyond a mere assessment of the events of May, but it is his interpretation of the crisis that is the focus of his analysis. He is persuasive in indicating why Haldane was the chief victim of the governmental reorganization; his evidence for the conspiracy may be a bit more shaky. Hazlehurst, whose *Politicians at War, July 1914 to May 1915* is a detailed account of high politics in the first nine months of the war,[12] has planned it as the first volume of a trilogy covering the period up to the elevation of Lloyd George to the prime ministership. Somewhat pedantically rejecting the conspiracy theory with virtually no qualification, he nevertheless manages to be convincing, although there remain reasons for questioning Churchill's discretion and good sense. Perhaps more important, Hazlehurst goes on to make the case that Lloyd George was a loyal colleague of Asquith in the wartime Liberal government. It may be that he accepts Lloyd George too readily at his own valuation, but it is refreshing to find what the Welsh firebrand actually did, rather than what he is presumed to have been, becoming increasingly the focus of scholarly attention. Both Koss and Hazlehurst can profitably be supplemented by Barry McGill's *Journal of Modern History* article, which uses the Elibank papers effectively in picturing the dilemmas faced by Asquith that hastened the destruction of the Liberal party.[13]

The literature on the objectives of the war effort the politicians sought to direct is extensive, but a few important special studies can be singled out. Although V. H. Rothwell unnecessarily minimizes the role of unofficial pressure groups, his analysis of British official thinking on war aims and peace negotiations is thorough and revealing.[14] Most important is his demonstration of how much the British leaders underestimated the collapse of Germany in the last weeks of the war. They hurried along the armistice negotiations, even though it might have better served Britain's future interests to have been a little less anxious. By way of contrast, S. J. Kernek, in a dull but useful study of the Lloyd George government's reactions to Woodrow Wilson, concludes that British interests were preserved without substantive concessions, whether to Wilson's peace initiatives early in the war or his war aims in its latter stages.[15] That Britain and the United States did indeed remain substantially together was in part at least the work of Sir William Wiseman, the secret agent whose relationship with Colonel Edward House served both countries well. In *British-American Relations, 1917–1918*, W. B. Fowler uses the Wiseman Papers at Yale University well in outlining the story of that partnership.[16] On still another front, Wm. Roger Louis shows how men like Lord Curzon, J. C. Smuts, Sir W. Harcourt, and Lord Milner were determined to wrest away direct control of Germany's possessions—and that they succeeded, whatever the fiction of the mandates system.[17] Finally, George W. Egerton has gone far beyond a work I wrote some quarter of a century ago and has written the definitive study of official British policy—limited, cautious, suspicious of internationalist concepts—toward the proposed League of Nations.[18]

Some of the radical League of Nations advocates were root-and-branch pacifists; some were active supporters of peace by negotiation. Keith Robbins has attempted to study the diverse strands of the wartime peace movement by dealing with such groups as the No-Conscription Fellowship and the Union of Democratic Control as well as with key individuals like Bertrand Russell.[19] The result is somewhat uneven, perhaps because Robbins has little sympathy for, and consequently an inadequate understanding of, such war resisters as Russell. Because of its ambitious sweep, his work is worth some study, but much remains to be done on the peace movement in World War I. Rather more satisfactory, perhaps because its subject is more sharply defined, is Marvin Swarz's study of the Union of Democratic Control, that group of Liberals and Labourites who agitated during World War I for parliamentary control of foreign policy, an end to secret diplomacy, a postwar international organization, and particularly a negotiated peace.[20] To round out the picture, there is a monograph by John Rae that describes the struggle that took place between the government and conscientious objectors to the war.[21] Rae makes clear how far from the forefront of government thinking the issue of conscientious objection really was. At the same time, he offers insights into the government's point of view that will help to balance earlier accounts that were more sympathetic to the objectors, particularly those who resisted on religious grounds.[22] Those who did were a small minority of clergy as of laymen. The vast majority of clergy became tub-thumping supporters of the all-out effort as they reacted to the issues of the conflict. That unsurprising conclusion is developed by Albert Marrin, whose *The Last Crusade* goes substantially beyond the attitudes of the Church of England that is the major denomination he has examined.[23]

Pacifists and conscientious objectors were a small minority during the war years. What was the war like for the vast majority of participants who served, suffered, searched for words to capture their experience, too often died before they had somehow come to grips with the horrors of modern war? There is no latter-day *Testament of Youth* encapsulating the experiences of a generation, but Paul Fussell's *The Great War and Modern Memory* shows us how much the images produced by trench warfare on the western front have conditioned our interpretations of the First World War and helped shape our twentieth-century perceptions of war in general.[24] Writers and ordinary soldiers alike, disillusioned by the realities of mud and blood and death, transmuted their earlier idealism and naiveté into the irony and skepticism that have become the dominant literary means by which the war has been remembered. The shock of recognition that Fussell's sensitive reading elicits does not conceal the originality and brilliance of this unique contribution.

"The Government promised a land fit for Heroes to live in; you had to be a Hero to live in it." That remark sums up the customary implication that postwar planning during the First World War was either a charade indulged in by cynical politicians or an experiment virtually preordained for failure.[25] The implication is no longer tenable. Paul B. Johnson's extremely important monograph on reconstruction dissects the administrative faults of the successive authorities set up to plan postwar reconstruction, describes the development of institutions such as the ineffective Reconstruction Committee, and assesses the performance of Christopher Addison's new Ministry of Reconstruction.[26] Making clear the excessive optimism of those who looked to the Whitley Councils as the models for future social change, he also indicates that real achievements, such as the creation of the Ministry of Health, came out of the planning process. That the armistice caught the planners by surprise and that subsequent retrenchment spelled the end for most reconstruction plans is not permitted to conceal Johnson's view that substantial planning efforts were made and that the reasons for the failure of social reform after 1919 were very complex. Considerable light may be thrown upon that failure, if only indirectly, by a pair of books that deal with related topics. Susan Armitage's *The Politics of Decontrol in Industry* revises, among other subjects, the standard view of Lloyd George's conflict with the miners after 1919;[27] and *The Cost of War, 1914–1919* by Robert E. Bunselmeyer, while it has nothing to do with social change, demonstrates how the appeal of reparation and indemnity became the panacea that supplanted almost all other programs that bore upon the productivity upon which reconstruction depended.[28]

David Lloyd George led his country to victory in the First World War. More than any other person, he inaugurated the welfare state. He handled more successfully than anyone before or since the centuries-old feud between Ireland and Great Britain. And he spent the last quarter century of his life out of office when patently lesser men held the seals of office. Despite his supposed deviousness and his unpredictability, the evidence from the booming "Lloyd George industry" makes it easier to share A. J. P. Taylor's puzzlement over the mistrust Lloyd George engendered if not to agree with him that Lloyd George was the greatest ruler of England since Oliver Cromwell.[29] Much of the new literature deals with the Welsh wizard's early career, but there are numerous contributions for the period after 1914 as well. Peter Rowland's 872-page biography is the most comprehensive to appear since the massive effort of Frank Owen.[30,31] Like Owen's work, it is a useful chronicle of Lloyd George's activities, but there is little thoughtful analysis, nor is there sufficient attention paid to the broad political world within which Lloyd George operated. Less comprehensive, but also less satisfied with conventional interpretations, is a series of twelve essays, edited by A. J. P. Taylor, dealing with various aspects of Lloyd George's career.[32] Based on seminars organized by Taylor at which users of the Beaverbrook Library discussed their work in progress, the essays range from studies of Lloyd George's approach to foreign policy before 1914 to his search for a compromise peace in the Second World War.

Taylor has brought two additional volumes to publication. The first, the diary of Frances Stevenson, Lloyd George's long-time confidential secretary and mistress and finally second wife, is particularly valuable for parts of Lloyd George's premiership during the war and after.[33] His charm, his ability to manipulate people, and more important, his tenacity when he had made up his mind, all come through in these observations of an intelligent and perceptive woman. The collection of their letters, published as *My Darling Pussy*, dramatically verifies the sincerity of Lloyd George's love for Frances, his abiding attachment to his wife, and his concern that his private life not jeopardize his public position.[34]

Even more than A. J. P. Taylor, Kenneth O. Morgan has advanced the study of Lloyd George's career. His edition of *Lloyd George Family Letters*, *1885–1936* is less valuable than the Stevenson materials in illuminating his later public life, but it gives us real insight into the Welsh radicalism that informed so much of Lloyd George's general outlook.[35] Morgan has also written a brief biography[36] and, in *The Age of Lloyd George*,[37] an account of recent research on the decline of the Liberals that includes documents which illustrate Lloyd George's part in that decline; but his most important contribution is to be found in *Consensus and Disunity: The Lloyd George Coalition, 1918–1922*.[38] This well-balanced assessment weighs the virtues and the faults of Lloyd George's much-maligned postwar coalition. The "hard-faced" profiteers of 1919 are a political myth; the coalition government introduced a number of imaginative social reforms; Lloyd George, whatever his mistake in backing Greece against Turkey, endeavored almost single-handedly to achieve a European settlement; and the Irish Treaty was of course a great triumph. Altogether, Morgan concludes, the coalition registered no inconsiderable achievement in the face of unprecedented difficulties. For the later years of Lloyd George's sojourn in the political wilderness, the diary of his principal private secretary, A. J. Sylvester, provides some interesting personal detail to a story reasonably well known.[39]

A few specialized monographs should be mentioned briefly. The second volume of Michael Fry's *Lloyd George and Foreign Policy* is likely to be more valuable than the first, which comes down only to 1916.[40] Before 1916, indeed, he had little interest in foreign policy, the Mansion House speech to the contrary notwithstanding. It might have been interesting if Chris Wrigley had also promised a second volume; well-researched though it is, his *David Lloyd George and the British Labour Movement: Peace and War* confirms previous assessments of the wartime prime minister's alienation of the leaders of the working class and his dissipation of potential future support.[41] *Lloyd George's Secretariat* by John Turner concludes that the Garden Suburb, the prime minister's private secretariat of five close advisers, promoted administrative efficiencies in certain key areas and gave a greater coherence to central government in a time of all-out-war.[42] Michael Kinnear attempts to see the events of 1922 as they were viewed by contemporaries, concluding that it was by no means certain that the coalition be broken up and Lloyd George and the Liberals dismissed.[43] His analysis of the 1922 general election at the constituency level has been challenged by R. McKibbin,[44] but his doubts about the extent of Conservative premeditation before the Carlton Club meeting and the inevitability of the political crisis will stimulate, I suspect, further investigation in this tangled jungle. Finally, there is John Campbell's *Lloyd George: The Goat in the Wilderness, 1922–1931*,[45] which confirms the view that Lloyd George's reputation for untrustworthiness was greatly exaggerated and suggests that the slander was deliberately encouraged by his enemies. Campbell is particularly informative in elaborating the Keynesian "New Deal" proposed by the Liberal party in 1929, the election which was the real beginning of the end of the Welsh politician.

Along with Lloyd George, Winston Churchill was the most important political leader of the twentieth century; and like Lloyd George, he has attracted almost numberless investigators. Even before his death, the hyperbolic myths that surrounded him had begun to be challenged. The process has continued unabated, with the result that we already have a more balanced, and in some ways a more sympathetic, picture, as Churchill is seen in the complex reality of his controversial career. By far the most formidable account of that career is still in progress. Martin Gilbert's continuation of the expansive biography started by Randolph Churchill has already required five volumes, to say nothing of the companion volumes of documents.[46] The result is an extremely valuable record, strong on administrative and military history, less satisfactory on the intricacies of politics, but monumental in arraying the documentary sources. With a few exceptions, Churchill the man seldom shines through, but these tightly packed pages may well become the Moneypenny and Buckle of the twentieth century.

Henry Pelling's *Churchill*, a balanced one-volume work that seems not to have attracted the notice it deserves, is the best brief account of Churchill's career.[47] In addition, several other general assessments are of considerable value. Robert Rhodes James has not been one of Churchill's greatest admirers, as the subtitle of his *Churchill: A Study in Failure, 1900–1939* makes clear.[48] He argues that if Churchill's story had ended in 1938 or even 1939, we should be in the presence of a great personal tragedy, a remarkable failure rather like his father, Lord Randolph Churchill's. The argument is sound but perhaps irrelevant, for Churchill will be remembered for 1940, not for 1938. Composite appreciations of recently deceased statesmen are seldom too probing in character, but several recent collections are exceptions. *Churchill: A Profile* contains one interesting perception after another, whether in the sensible introduction by Peter Stansky or A. G. Gardiner on Churchill at fifty or Isaiah Berlin on Churchill in 1940 or Arno J. Mayer on the power politician and counterrevolutionary.[49] Equally discriminating is a collection by A. J. P. Taylor and others in which B. H. Liddell Hart, for example, concludes that, as a miliary strategist in the First World War, Churchill received more blame than he deserved while in the Second World War the value of his contribution has been overrated.[50] Even more iconoclastic is *Churchill in Power*, a collection of comments about Churchill made during the war.[51] It attempts to debunk not Churchill but the Churchill legend, emphasizing his remarkable communion with the British people in 1940 and reaching a mixed verdict about his subsequent performance.

The account by Lord Moran, Churchill's physician, which portrays him as a worn-out man during most of his last twenty-five years, has been widely circulated.[52] A group of six men, among them Sir Ian Jacob and Lord Bridges, who worked closely with Churchill, have published a volume that takes sharp issue with that conclusion.[53] They agree that after 1953 Churchill struggled against a growing weight of age and physical infirmity, but their more positive picture helps to temper the sensationalism of Moran's criticism.

Other monographs deal with particular aspects of Churchill's career. Nothing in English begins to match a German-language study of Churchill's anti-Bolshevik stance during the Russian civil war. Churchill's reputation as a crusader was well deserved, Alex P. Schmid finds; allied intervention owed much to his urging and to his ability to convince the Lloyd George coalition of the need to smash the Bolsheviks.[54] For the same period, Donald Graeme Boadle has carefully studied Churchill's attitudes toward Germany. His stimulating monograph explains how closely related were Churchill's aim to restore the European balance of power and his virtually hysterical hatred for the Bolshevism he regarded as the inevitable destroyer of a renewed Franco-Russian alliance.[55]

Finally, there are the materials that deal directly with Churchill's performance as a war leader. "Winston Is Back: Churchill at the Admiralty, 1939–1940" has subsequently appeared as chapter 4 in Arthur Marder's authoritative collection of essays entitled *From the Dardanelles to Oran*.[56,57] Marder concludes that Churchill's influence on the navy and the war at sea was, in the main, extremely beneficial. For the period when he took over the supreme command, however, Stephen Roskill emphasizes the mistakes and the wasteful expenditure of efforts caused by Churchill's erratic and idiosyncratic interference in strategic decisions. The price paid for his dynamic leadership, Roskill avers, was far from negligible.[58]

Materials on Churchill's more general wartime leadership are less satisfactory. Ronald Lewin and Patrick Cosgrave tend to be simplistically panegyrical, although Lewin understands the doubts that have been raised about Churchill's amateur generalship.[59,60] Maxwell Phillip Schoenfeld, too, writes uncritically of the conduct of military and administrative matters in which Churchill interested himself,[61] while by contrast, R. W. Thompson bitterly condemns Churchill's strategy in the first three years of the war.[62] None of these efforts can compare with those of Marder and Roskill on the naval side, but they have some value until more penetrating evaluations appear.

Perhaps this is the place to note some of the biographies and a few of the memoirs that have poured endlessly from the presses. On the Conservative side, the most important single publication is the huge attempt by Keith Middlemas and John Barnes to stake out Stanley Baldwin's claim to greatness.[63] They do not succeed, nor can they conceal Baldwin's failures of will and shortcomings of judgment; but the biography is an excellent picture of Baldwin the man, ruminative, fitfully energetic, a decent human being best suited for service in quiet times. Their account of the abdication crisis shows Baldwin at his best and is the high point of a densely packed 1,149 pages. Essentially the same delineation appears in Kenneth Young's much shorter biography, which somehow better manages to sugggest the complexity of this unusual statesman.[64]

No major biography of another Tory prime minister has appeared in recent years. The distinguished journalist Anthony Sampson has written an intriguing short profile of Harold Macmillan which emphasizes the discrepancy between the exciting young radical Tory of prewar days and the stuffy postwar leader, unable in the end to grapple with Britain's real problems.[65] Sampson exaggerates Macmillan's failures and neglects his real contribution in pulling Britain together after Suez. The differences between rhetoric and performance during Macmillan's prime ministership remain unexplained. His own almost-interminable memoirs offer no satisfying clues to the puzzle. They are required reading, but they reveal more about his charm and civilization than about the whys and wherefores of the policies he pursued.[66] One of those who differed with the young Macmillan before the Second World War was Sir Samuel Hoare. J. A. Cross's *Sir Samuel Hoare: A Political Biography* is the one first-rate look at a secondary Conservative figure published in the last decade.[67] Although overly generous to Hoare, it is especially valuable on the Hoare-Laval pact, but Cross has used the Templewood papers and other archives effectively in elucidating Hoare's role in politics from the destruction of the Lloyd George coalition to the evolution of the policy of appeasement.[68] Finally, there is A. J. P. Taylor's *Beaverbrook*, overly hagiographical, but bringing to live a fascinating and almost unclassifiable second-rank politician and first-rank man of affairs.[69]

Stephen Koss appears to have made virtually a monopoly of Liberal figures in public life. In addition to the study of Haldane already noted, he has written informative biographies of Sir John Brunner, best known for his work with the National Liberal Federation;[70] A. G. Gardiner, the editor of the *Daily News*;[71] and H. H. Asquith.[72] Of these, the biography of Asquith is by far the most valuable. Koss has ransacked much new material to find a middle ground between the panegyrics of earlier writers and the detractions of recent analysts. He comes down hard on Asquith for his complacency and lack of imagination after 1915, but he effectively demonstrates Asquith's political skills in the prewar years and his not-inconsiderable contributions to the New Liberalism.

Only two other recent biographies of Liberal figures warrant comment. Alfred F. Havighurst's modest study of H. W. Massingham, which deals particularly with that Liberal journalist's ideas, illustrates the radicalism that supported the New Liberalism before the First World War, became increasingly disillusioned thereafter, and more than occasionally found its way into the Labour party.[73] Peter Clarke's *Liberals and Social Democrats* brilliantly evokes the views and intellectual problems of four Liberal intellectuals, Graham Wallas, J. L. Hammond, J. A. Hobson, and L. T. Hobhouse.[74] Like Massingham, several of them shakily moved toward Labour in their later years, but all four were committed to an essentially Liberal tradition. Clarke's work will be literally indispensable, not merely for its keen appreciations of four fascinating men, but because their dilemmas and values also reflected those of many of their contemporaries.

David Marquand's long-awaited *Ramsay MacDonald* is one of the best political biographies of the twentieth century.[75] Written with sensitivity and grace, it rescues the first Labour prime minister from the legends that savaged his reputation while he lived and colored the assessment of his career after his death. The notion that he was a second-rate figure will have to be revised. Sympathetically but critically, Marquand brings to life a complicated Lib-Lab politician, hardly understanding the socialism he professes, yet clearly overshadowing his more pedestrian colleagues. It is probable that Marquand exaggerates the accomplishments of MacDonald, just as he denigrates the evident contributions of an Arthur Henderson; but his big book is filled with the evidence for the former's unique contribution to the growth of the labour movement and the success of the Labour party. For decades, the ascendancy of MacDonald has been something of a puzzle to students of British political history. It is the great virtue of Marquand's biography that it helps appreciably in providing a solution to the puzzle.

Two contemporaries of MacDonald were among the great teachers of the labour movement. In *R. H. Tawney and His Time: Socialism as Fellowship*, Ross Terrill illuminates the attractiveness of this pragmatic socialist through a study of Tawney's thought.[76] Less effectively but still usefully, L. P. Carpenter has authored an intellectual biography of G. D. H. Cole[77] shortly after the publication of a life by Cole's widow[78] that highlights Cole's pedagogical influence upon an almost-countless collection of students from the undergraduates and graduates in university halls to the adults he reached through the workers' education movement.

One of the great struggles in the Labour party after the Second World War was between Aneurin Bevan and Herbert Morrison over the issue of socialism. Both men have recently been the subjects of very good, but very different, biographies. Michael Foot's passionate account of Bevan's career is particularly informative about the establishment of the National Health Service, while its explanation of his differences with his colleagues over disarmament is less satisfactory. This work is uncomfortably hagiographical, but its case for Bevan's various positions needs to be understood.[79] *Herbert Morrison: Portrait of a Politician* is a genuine tour de force. Morrison destroyed most of his papers in 1960, and Bernard Donoughue and G. W. Jones painstakingly reconstructed his career from fragments that remained, the public record, the papers of other participants, and the recollections of those who had known Morrison.[80] The result is a well-balanced evaluation that makes clear, as the authors note, Morrison's contributions in local government, in Parliament, in the Cabinet, in the development of public corporations, and of course in the growth of the Labour party. One other study of a leading Labour politician, *Hugh Gaitskell*, by Philip Williams is particularly valuable for its analysis of recent Labour party politics.[81] Although Labour's "lost leader" remains a somewhat shadowy figure at the end of this long biography, the issues that divided the Labour party in the postwar years are coolly and effectively outlined in this major work.

Ranging across all three major parties is a collection of essays edited by John P. Mackintosh, *British Prime Ministers in the Twentieth Century*.[82] Volume 1, which is entitled *Balfour to Chamberlain*, is particularly helpful on Asquith, Lloyd George, and Neville Chamberlain. Cameron Hazelhurst's balanced inquiry into Asquith's leadership concludes that he did indeed overcome many crises but points out that some were of his own making. Even today, after sixty years, the verdict on Asquith appears still to be out. Kenneth Morgan rightly emphasizes the tension between Lloyd George's instinctive populism and his urge for power. For years, he performed an impressive feat of equilibrium, but at last, Morgan puts it, the greatest show on earth came to an end. Alan Beattie makes the best possible case for Neville Chamberlain as a strong and effective prime minister. If he fails to be fully convincing, he has written the most challenging in a generally effective collection of studies on leadership in twentieth-century politics. Volume 2, *Churchill to Callaghan*, is rather less satisfactory. As in the first volume, there are three essays that merit comment. Paul Addison conveys a sense of the charisma that Churchill exercised over his associates; Robert Dowse rather overemphasizes the ruthlessness but captures the efficiency of Clement Attlee; and Robert Blake makes Anthony Eden somehow a sympathetic figure as he twists his way through the tragedy of the Suez episode. But generally, this volume does not come up to the standard set by several of the essays in volume 1.

To round out this gallery of politicians, there is the ubiquitous Maurice Hankey. Secretary before the First World War to the Committee of Imperial Defence; secretary during the war to the War Council, the Dardanelles Committee, the War Committee, and the War Cabinet; secretary between the two world wars to the Cabinet and the Committee of Imperial Defence; and clerk to the Privy Council, he was involved in almost everything that mattered politically, whether at home or abroad. More secrets passed through his hands than those of any other British statesman, but Captain Stephen Roskill, in writing his three-volume *Hankey, Man of Secrets*, has been limited by the unavailability of Hankey's most confidential files from exploring some of the more interesting intelligence aspects of his work.[83] At any rate, this huge account of an astonishing career shows Hankey at his best and his worst. On issues of defense, for example, he was sound and often far-seeing. As a politician, he was a disaster. He bitterly opposed the entry of Labour into the government during the First World War and, as a Cabinet minister from 1939 to 1941, failed utterly to understand Churchill's hold on the British people during the Second. Nevertheless, during his quarter of a century behind the scenes, he was perhaps the most nearly indispensable man to inhabit the corridors of Whitehall.

Finally, there is the perceptive and balanced biography of *Edward VIII* by Frances Donaldson.[84] Analyzing his career as prince of Wales, king, and duke of Windsor, she emphasizes the period of crisis and personal calamity. Edward emerges as a stubborn, vain, and essentially small man, shielded until it was too late by advisers who did not dare to warn him of the consequences of his actions. What is most striking in her portrayal is that his judgment was almost invariably flawed and that, both before and after his abdication, he was so clearly out of touch with British public opinion.

Nothing has been published recently to compete with Charles Mowat's *Britain between the Wars, 1918–1940*,[85] but an excellent social and economic history by Sean Glynn and John Oxborrow uses current scholarship effectively in covering economic growth and living standards, overseas trade, industrial development, economic policy, unemployment, labor, population, housing, and social policy.[86] They conclude that significant unemployment was accompanied by fairly rapid economic growth and tend to give relatively good marks to the orthodox Treasury approach to the mid-period crisis as opposed to a Keynesianism that was only half-formulated by 1931. In *The Politics of Reappraisal, 1918–1939*, some ten scholars deal varyingly with issues of adaptation.[87] "Reappraisal" is perhaps an artificial tie to bind together some disparate essays, but on balance this volume calls attention to elements of change that had attracted little analysis until recently. In somewhat similar fashion, a *Festschrift* for A. J. P. Taylor contains three valu-

able essays in which Stephen Koss investigates the last stages of the Asquith–
Lloyd George rivalry; John Stevenson contrasts the myths of the 1930s with the
realities; and Donald Watt weighs various contributions to the history of
appeasement.[88]

Watt makes clear his impatience with many of the critics of the appeasement
policy. An impressive measure of literature now centers about the issue, but it
must be seen in the context of foreign policy in the whole interwar period. The
best general survey is *The Troubled Giant: Britain among the Great Powers,
1918–1939* by F. S. Northedge.[89] It is a tale of decline and self-delusion, as
British leaders in all parties assumed that economic questions rather than political
issues were the major determinants of international relations, that they could be
compromised on some business principle of the rational bargain, and that Britain
somehow needed to pursue policies suited to her supposed status as a wealthy,
contented power. Narrower in its scope is *Great Britain and International Security, 1920–1926* by Anne Orde.[90] It is a careful account of British government
policy on international security from the end of the Paris Peace Conference until
the post-Locarno years, when the world appeared to be more secure than at any
time since before the outbreak of war. Orde concludes that while Locarno was not
"the worst of both worlds," it was not enough. Britain's defense policy was un-
suited to her position; the British people were allowed to nurture their illusions of
peace; and in the end, at a considerable cost, they had to use force to uphold what
remained of the territorial settlement in eastern Europe.

A handful of valuable specialized studies have appeared, two of them continuations of earlier well-received works. Ian Nish continues his study of Anglo-
Japanese relations for the years 1908 to 1923.[91] His two volumes, based on both
Britain and Japanese records, revise the earlier accounts of many points. Sir Edward Grey's Far Eastern policy in particular is made more creditable, and Japanese motives are much more clearly described. This is likely to be the standard
English monograph for some time to come. So too is Richard Ullman's penetrating analysis of Anglo-Soviet relations between 1917 and 1921, the concluding
volume of which deals with the de facto recognition of the Soviet regime and the
trade agreement of March 1921.[92] Ullman lays bare the decision making of
the Lloyd George government and concludes, like other recent scholars, that the
Welshman, whatever his deficiencies, was "the best of his contemporaries." The
judgment is all the more compelling because it is the result of one of our most
impressive current studies of foreign affairs. In *Britain and the Bolshevik Revolution: A Study in the Politics of Diplomacy, 1920–1924*, Stephen White has written
an effective sequel to Ullman's three volumes.[93] White makes clear that fear of
war, not sympathy for Bolshevism, motivated the Councils of Action in 1920;
minimizes the influence of direct action (and in so doing further erodes the legend of the Jolly George); and illuminates how conservative businessmen, what-

ever their domestic social and economic views, were eager to reach out to Russia on business grounds. For still another part of the world, Michael Fry outlines the coalition-period debate between the amateurs like Phillip Kerr who wanted closer relations with the United States and the professionals who looked upon her with suspicion.[94] Not till the Second World War, as he notes in his conclusion, was effective if limited Anglo-American cooperation to become real.

The opening of the archives has resulted in a torrent of solid monographs that are making the 1930s a rival for the years before 1914 in their extent of scholarly attention. One general work by Wm. Roger Louis briefly surveys the debate on Far Eastern policy in the Foreign Office between the wars.[95] Thoughtful and compact, it is a useful introduction to the dilemmas of British diplomacy which, among other things, gives short shrift to the myth that Henry L. Stimson was prevented from pursuing a more forceful line toward Japan after 1931 by British resistance. The outstanding specialized work is Christopher Thorne's *The Limits of Foreign Policy*, a marvelous analysis not only of the diplomacy of the Manchurian crisis of 1931–1933 but of the ideological and domestic frameworks within which it had to operate.[96] Thorne destroys the illusions that dominated consideration of the subject for so long. Without accepting a high risk of extensive costs, he concludes, there was little the United States, Britain, and France could do to make the Japanese surrender over Manchuria. For the period between 1933 and 1937, Ann Trotter's *Britain and East Asia, 1933–1937* is valuable if somewhat tedious.[97] Trotter highlights the British problem: how to safeguard British interests in China, appease Japan, and simultaneously avoid alienating China or the United States. The dilemma could never be solved. Two other works deal with the Far East after 1937. Bradford A. Lee concludes that the Chamberlain government scarcely considered a policy of appeasing Japan, partly because many policymakers continued to assume that Britain was a greater Asiatic power than Japan.[98] His findings need to be supplemented by Peter Lowe's *Great Britain and the Origins of the Pacific War*, which is subtitled *A Study of British Policy in East Asia, 1937–1941*.[99] Lowe confirms the mistaken belief of British —and American—officials that Japan could be relatively easily contained. Churchill especially opposed concessions, Lowe makes clear, and although he does not draw the conclusion himself, his evidence for Churchill's share of responsibility for the disasters of 1941 is considerably more than suggestive.

The Cabinet and Foreign Office papers dealing with East Asia have been much better exploited than have the materials on the Abyssinian crisis. Frank Hardie's monograph of that name is useful in outlining Conservative opinion about the League of Nations, but it adds little to what is known of British policy in the crisis.[100] More valuable is *British Public Opinion and the Abyssinian War, 1935–6*, in which Daniel Waley makes clear that, while public opinion had some considerable impact upon the official statements of politicians, it had little real influence

on the decisions they made during the Abyssinian conflict.[101] Even more important, Lawrence R. Pratt explores the consequences and the implications of the
Italo-League crisis for Britain's long-term strategic and diplomatic situation, particularly in the east Mediterranean, and offers a convincing analysis of British
Mediterranean strategy as it evolved down to 1939.[102]

    While there appears to be little prospect of consensus in interpreting the policy
of appeasement after 1937, it is no longer possible to share Donald Watt's ill-
concealed contempt for what he regards as the naiveté of Neville Chamberlain's
critics.[103] For one thing, a number of valuable memoirs now help us obtain a
vivid inside look at the Chamberlain Cabinet and its policymaking. Lord Harvey's
Diplomatic Diaries, 1937–40 provides ample materials to confirm the scorn of
Neville Chamberlain or Nevile Henderson by the worst critics of each.[104] *The
Diaries of Sir Alexander Cadogan, 1938–1945*, edited by David Dilks, tend to
confirm the narrowness, the stubbornness, and ultimately the inadequacy of the
men who led Great Britain on the eve of war.[105] For another, recent studies based
upon the newly available archival material on the whole tend to strengthen the
case of Chamberlain's critics rather than that of his defenders, although they also
reveal how little room for maneuver Great Britain actually enjoyed.

    For the period of Chamberlain's ascendancy in foreign policy, the most signifi-
cant—and most frustrating—recent monograph is Maurice Cowling's *The Impact of Hitler*.[106] Turgid, convoluted, indeed abominably written, it argues essentially that there was a strong and respectable conservative case against British
interference in Eastern Europe. Cowling's impressive command over a vast
range of private papers and official materials suggests an authoritativeness that is
flawed by the narrowness of his point of view. His argument that Viscount Hali-
fax, out of party loyalty, served as the instrument of Chamberlain's downfall is
unconvincing, and his elucidation of Churchill's motives for opposing Chamberlain borders on caricature. Altogether he overemphasizes political maneuvering and minimizes other considerations in assessing the policies pursued by the
prewar Conservative government. Like Cowling, Keith Robbins is a revisionist,
but his tone is less strident and his sympathetic account of British policy more
moderate. *Munich 1938* was published before some of the archival material was
available for study, but Robbins uses private papers and published documents
effectively in this thoughtful summary.[107] Munich was the necessary purgatory,
he concludes, through which Englishmen had to pass before the nation could
emerge united in 1939. Quite on the other side and even more important is
Munich: The Price of Peace by Telford Taylor, an effective study of both German
and British policy.[108] Speculating on whether Britain and France would have been
in a better position to win a war against Germany in 1938 than they were a year
later, Taylor suggests that they were comparatively stronger in the earlier year. So

determined was Chamberlain to have peace that he blinded himself to any realistic evaluation of the balance of military potential. The notion that Chamberlain
fought for peace while preparing for war is demolished by Taylor's review of his
role in British rearmament both as chancellor of the Exchequer and as prime
minister.

Beyond the works of Cowling, Robbins, and Taylor, there are only a couple of
other monographs that need to be singled out of the flood of materials on the
diplomacy of the prewar years. One is Neville Thompson's study of Conservative
opposition to appeasement in the 1930s.[109] His major contribution is to show that
antiappeasement developed late in the decade and that few of its proponents were
either consistent or firm in their position. The second valuable monograph is Simon Newman's study of the British guarantee to Poland in 1939.[110] Newman follows several previous scholars in seeing the guarantee as the logical conclusion to
the policy followed by the national government since Hitler's accession to power.
By 1939 the Inner Cabinent decided that appeasement had failed and that Britain
could not permit Hitler another bloodless victory. In so doing, it relied almost not
at all on the conflicting advice offered by officials at the Foreign Office, to whom, as
Donald Lammers has shown, the guarantees to Rumania and Poland must have
come as a stunning surprise.[111] The March guarantee was intended either to hu-
miliate Hitler or to force him into war.

One other aspect of the foreign policy of the 1930s was, of course, the defense
situation. In *The Continental Commitment*, his Ford Lectures for 1971, Michael
Howard ranges far beyond the prewar years; but for that period he shows how the
determination not to fight Italy, Germany, and Japan simultaneously was a major
element in the search for appeasement by both Stanley Baldwin and Neville
Chamberlain.[112] Emphasizing that successive chancellors of the Exchequer, including Winston Churchill, had argued against the doctrine that Britain could
afford three first-rank armed services, Howard outlines the strategic dilemmas
which fostered the hesitations of the interwar period. But could Britain maintain
a policy of "limited liability" toward the Continent, as Chamberlain in particular
believed? The chiefs of staff, Peter Dennis shows, did not agree. His *Decision by
Default: Peacetime Conscription and British Defence* is considerably broader than
its title suggests.[113] Its effect is to indict Chamberlain for allowing his policy of
appeasement to transform the strategic situation in Europe. As if to corroborate
Dennis, Robert Paul Shay, Jr., concludes, in *British Reararmament in the Thirties: Politics and Profits*, that the national government chose to run risks in the
defense sector rather than the financial.[114] Basically, he demonstrates that Treasury control of defense expenditure was maintained until the events of March
1939 forced the acceptance of the primacy of military requirements in Britain's
rearmament. What emerges on balance from further exploration of defense issues

is, among other things, abundant evidence of official deference to vested economic interests. The adverse judgements of Baldwin and Chamberlain that have
been so widely challenged by revisionist historians are inevitably reinforced.

As for the opposition, there has always been a considerable amount of
political—and scholarly—controversy over the purposes and the effect of Labour's foreign policy positions. John Naylor's sensible study of Labour's international policy in the 1930s shows convincingly that the party's international stance
tended to be reasonably temperate and responsible. Coming into existence as the
Labour party reached maturity and faced the realities of office holding, it was
frequently more nearly liberal than it was socialist in character.[115] In interesting
contrast, but not as convincing as Naylor, Michael G. Gordon maintains that
there was indeed a socialist foreign policy, based on the four principles of interna-
tionalism, international working-class solidarity, antimilitarism, and anticapital-
ism. He concludes that the doctrinaire outlook of those who opposed the policies
of Labour's leaders on ideological grounds resulted in a stalemate that curbed
Labour's freedom of action.[116]

Still another specialized area of investigation has been opened up by the availability of new documentation in the Public Record Office. Three important new
works on southeast Europe deal mainly with the Second World War, although
John S. Koliopoulos's *Greece and the British Connection, 1935–1941*, as the title
indicates, begins with the restoration of King George II and terminates with the
German occupation of Greece in 1941.[117] Dispassionately and fairly, Koliopoulos
assays the background of Anglo-Greek wartime collaboration and explains the
fragility of their alliance in the face of German strength. Elizabeth Barker, in her
study *British Policy in South-east Europe in the Second World War*, shows, first,
how efforts to bolster the resistance of the southeast European governments to
Nazi enticements were inhibited by a lack of resources as well as the fear of
provoking Hitler and, second, how policy was subsequently limited by the dominant power of the Soviet Union in the area.[118] Considerable color and individual
insights are provided in a disparate collection of articles based on papers
presented at a conference at the University of London in 1973. *British Policy towards Wartime Resistance in Yugoslavia and Greece*, edited by Phyllis Auty and
Richard Clogg, gathers together the perceptions of people like F. W. D. Deakin
and C. M. Woodhouse, most of whom were participants in the events they
describe.[119]

In the Middle East, the trouble spot was Palestine. Michael J. Cohen, in *Palestine: Retreat from the Mandate. The Making of British Policy: 1936–45*, shows
how the British government turned more and more to appeasement of the
Arabs.[120] Once the Arab states became involved in the Palestine issue from 1937,
there was little doubt that British policy in the area would be one acceptable to
them. After the war began, he shows, the strategic nuisance value of the Arab

states far outweighed any advantages the Zionists could hope to offer. During the war, only Churchill and a few who shared his views seriously challenged the Foreign Office's pro-Arab doctrine on Palestine. Among much else, Martin Gilbert reveals how that doctrine was accompanied by a singular insensitivity to the growing horror of the anti-Jewish policies of Nazi Germany. In *Exile and Return: The Struggle for a Jewish Homeland*, he documents the hard line taken by the British Cabinet toward the Jewish refugees even as word of large-scale massacres reached England.[121] The policy of barring immigration to Palestine worked well. By May 1944 even the 1939 White Paper quota of seventy-five thousand had not been filled. On the other hand, even in the 1930s, the policy toward acceptance of refugees in Britain itself was reluctant but somewhat different. Guided by the conviction that Britain was not a country of immigration and that its large population and substantial unemployment precluded any but a carefully restricted reception of refugees, the British, to be sure, sought elsewhere than at home or in Palestine for areas of mass settlement for Jews. Eventually even the relatively small flood of refugees from Nazi-occupied Europe became difficult for refugee organizations to absorb. The government, A. J. Sherman concludes in what is likely to be the authoritative study of the subject, was tragically limited in what it could do.[122] Compared with other countries, such as the United States or France, Britain emerges as comparatively compassionate, even generous.

The same cannot be claimed for British policy after the war broke out. In *Britain and the Jews of Europe, 1939–1945*, Bernard Wasserstein argues that British bureaucrats and politicians did pitifully little to rescue even a handful of Jews from Hitler's Final Solution.[123] In part, they could not imagine what it might be like to be hunted to death; in part, they refused to save the few because they feared a flood of refugees. Churchill had the Jewish question close to his heart, Wasserstein concludes, but he was misled by the officials and thwarted in every way, so that the British government became an accessory to genocide. Saving a few Jews was regarded as a distracting side issue, not to be allowed to interfere with getting on with the war.

Were the interwar years the decades of catastrophe, as they have often been labeled? Such was the "master myth" of two literary generations, writes George Watson, from D. H. Lawrence's *Rainbow* in 1915 to the Marxist apocalyptics of W. H. Auden in the 1930s.[124] For the older generation of the 1920s, catastrophe had already happened, and the West, "as impotent as Clifford Chatterley," might as well be dead already. For the youthful optimists and utopians of that decade, catastrophe was a revolutionary faith, and the collapse of the old meant the triumph of the new. Perhaps, but other literary critics have found it wise to be less categorical in describing what writers wrote and what they did. The Spanish Civil War, above all else in these decades, exerted a crucial emotional appeal on writers, artists, and intellectuals, many of whom believed that "cowardice had been elevated to national foreign policy" in the 1930s. Some went to Spain; others in England or America fought their battles at home. The Left has romanticized their words and actions as "the zenith of political idealism in the first half of the twentieth century"; less enthusiastic critics talk of "despair" and "disillusion" as the products of the fall of the Spanish Republic. But for many—not for a George Orwell shattered by the brutalities of party-line Communism in Spain nor, on the other side, a William Lewis aiding the Franco cause by satirizing the literary supporters of his enemies—Spain was the *Last Great Cause* described by Stanley Weintraub.[125] He emphasizes the element of innocence and self-deception that was the hallmark of the supposed illusions of the 1930s. George Watson, in the work already cited, ranges far wider than Spain and bitterly denies the innocence of the literary intellectuals. He contends that, between 1930 and 1939, poets and novelists were attracted to the most violent system on earth because they knew it was that. Soviet dictatorship, he insists, looked to them a highly disciplined system that could and should conquer the world. Accepting purges and exterminations, British intellectuals under the age of fifty knowingly supported what may well have been the greatest act of mass murder in European history.[126]

More convincing, Samuel Hynes shows us in *The Auden Generation* that the decade was not monolithically of a piece, that Auden, Spender, Day Lewis, and Orwell had, by the end of the period, moved in quiet different directions, however the myths of the 1930s might have it.[127] But whatever his judgment of their political sophistication—he writes as a critic whose grasp of literature is stronger than his mastery of politics—he makes clear how much of the literature was suffused with the sense of the futility of contemporary history. "What a decade!" Hynes quotes Orwell as writing in 1940. "A riot of appalling folly that suddenly becomes a nightmare, a scenic railway ending in a torture-chamber" (p. 393). But also, as he points out, it was a decade that produced poems by Auden and Spender and MacNiece and Empson; novels by Isherwood and Greene and Warner; Orwell's *The Road to Wigan Pier* and *Homage to Catalonia*; Isherwood's *Journey to a War*; Empson's *Some Versions of Pastoral*; and Christopher Caudwell's *Illusion and Reality*. One's assessment depends on one's angle of vision.

As for Orwell himself, Bernard Crick, in *George Orwell: A Life*, goes far beyond Peter Stansky and William Abrahams in giving us detail after detail.[128] Yet somehow their Orwell (in Stansky's *The Unknown Orwell* and Abraham's *Orwell: The Transformation*) stands out more clearly—despite their somewhat precious play on the differences between "Eric Blair" and "George Orwell"—than Crick seems able to make his.

Finally, because the major spy scandal which erupted in the postwar period had its origins in the 1930s, this is perhaps the place to refer to Andrew Boyle's *The Climate of Treason: Five Who Spied for Russia*.[129] This popular account is marked by the author's appallingly naive and oversimplified view of the world in which his middle-class traitors lived. Nevertheless, for the reader who takes Boyle's "background" material with several grains of salt, his dissection of the motives, if not of the sordid achievement, of Kim Philby, Guy Burgess, and Donald Maclean (to say nothing of the hints that led to the exposure of Anthony Blunt, curator of the queen's art collection) is required reading for anyone who attempts to understand the prewar decade.

The "official" diplomatic history of World War II was written by Sir Llewelyn Woodward between 1942 and 1950, originally for official reference only.[130] Its four volumes have the value of his experience, thoroughness, and integrity, but inevitably they present a Foreign Office view of the issues discussed. They will be most helpful as guides to what policy was and why, least serviceable in placing that policy within the framework of a world from which the Foreign Office sometimes seemed curiously remote. Definitely not "official" history is Christopher Thorne's *Allies of a Kind*, an account of the United States, Britain, and the war against Japan between 1941 and 1945.[131] Like his *The Limits of Foreign Policy*, this long monograph is detailed, penetrating, and persuasive. Thorne emphasizes, on the American side, suspicion of the British and an assumption of conflicting interests; on the British, a belief in mutual interests and a hope for close collaboration. Central, too, to the British dilemma was the rapidly increasing difference in power between Washington and London. Despite Thorne's evident antipathy for Winston Churchill's political opinions, he shows Churchill as much the larger man than Franklin Roosevelt, however tragic may have been his unrealistic clinging to dreams of empire.

For the period after 1945, there are two solid and thoughtful general surveys. Joseph Frankel's *British Foreign Policy*, 1945–1973, a publication of the Royal Institute of International Affairs, goes substantially beyond a mere recounting of events.[132] It treats Britain's postwar foreign policy as the latest phase of a long-drawn-out process of adjustment to a position of gradually decreasing power which, by and large, consisted of the withdrawal from exposed positions around the world and of the acceptance of interdependence with Western Europe. Frankel examines his material in the light of a series of hypotheses about the interaction of foreign policy and domestic politics and about the impact of the international environment that are consistently stimulating and provoking. Finally, there is F. S. Northedge's *Descent from Power: British Foreign Policy*, 1945–1973, a sequel to *The Troubled Giant*.[133] Inevitably, the central theme, just as it is essentially Frankel's, is decline from the summit of power Britain briefly occupied in 1945 among the major states in Western Europe. Reconstructing the successive situations in international affairs which confronted British governments since 1945, he analyzes the grounds on which they decided each issue. As all the documents become accessible, it is probable that details of this account will have to be revised, but it seems unlikely that its principal thrust will be significantly changed.

Turning to domestic aspects of the interwar period, one must immediately come to grips, on the political side, with Maurice Cowling's extremely detailed study of *The Impact of Labour, 1920–1924*.[134] Cowling insists that after Labour's victory in the Spen Valley by-election of January 1920, resistance to socialism became the central fact in political calculation. His themes are the attempts to organize an effective alternative to Lloyd George other than Labour, the failure of those attempts to keep Labour permanently out of office, and the success of Stanley Baldwin's Conservatives in emerging as the dominant force in a two-party system. As in his other work, Cowling concentrates almost exclusively on political tactics and dismisses politicians' public statements as rhetoric having little relationship to their real aims. Whatever the substantial questions raised by his worm's eye view of politics, his monograph is a genuinely major treatment of an important crossroad in modern British politics.

While unemployment and the economic depression are the central focus of Robert Skidelsky's study of the Labour government of 1929–1931, it too is essentially about politics.[135] Skidelsky portrays a government pressed from within and without by those who wanted change but unable to make the connection between socialism on the one hand and economic reality and parliamentary democracy on the other. There was no practical socialist economic policy, no theory of how to use Parliament for furthering socialist aims. Almost certainly Skidelsky understates the differences among the parties, overdraws the inexperience and naiveté of Labour ministers, and gives insufficient weight to the minority status of the Labour government. Despite these faults, *Politicians and the Slump* helps make clear why most socialist leaders found themselves on the side of the status quo, whatever their position on the issues of economic policy that divided their party.

Two other works concentrate upon electoral politics. Chris Cook draws some rather broad conclusions from a study of electoral change at the constituency level between 1922 and 1929.[136] The decline of the Liberals, he concludes, came about, not as a result of the war and the split between Asquith and Lloyd George, but rather, from fundamental and long-term characteristics in the structure, social composition, and outlook of the party in the major industrialized and mining areas. An essentially middle-class party was unable to accommodate working-class candidates or to formulate a relevant radical industrial policy. By that reading, the tendencies were already present before 1914, and the advent of universal manhood suffrage in 1918 only accentuated them. Cook's monograph may usefully be augmented by a collection of essays, of which he is one of the editors, on by-elections in British politics.[137] Some of its authors are particularly effective in destroying myths, such as that the Newport by-election of 1922 caused the fall of Lloyd George's coalition; but the main value of these essays is in the confirmation they provide to most of the conventional interpretations of voting behavior in the years since 1918.

Allusion to electoral politics leads naturally to a consideration of political parties in the twentieth century. For understandable reasons (a new phenomenon perhaps required more explanation), the Labour party has attracted the bulk of scholarly attention, but neither the Conservative nor the Liberal nor even the Communist party has been neglected. Longman's multiauthored history of the Conservative party promises to be a valuable addition to the several individual histories that already exist. For the twentieth century, the volume on the "age of Balfour and Baldwin" is already in print.[138] John Ramsden makes good use of the monographic literature in outlining the issues faced by the Conservatives between 1902 and 1940 and in delineating the significant changes undergone by the party during that period. More analytical is Andrew Gamble's *The Conservative Nation*, a study of the way in which leading Conservatives perceived and adjusted to political reality.[139] He emphasizes the constraints imposed upon political practice by the necessary involvement of politicians in both politics and government. The historical achievement of the Conservative party, he notes, was to find sufficient support in the political nation after 1867 to make it the normal party of government, identifying itself firmly with the traditional institutions of the state system—the monarchy, the aristocracy, the established church, the army, the law, the old universities —while first the Liberals were identified more with the institutions of capitalism and the nonconformist churches and later the Labour party made a relatively narrow appeal to trade unionists, working-class communities, and small groups of intellectuals. To those traditional institutions, the Conservative party added, as it moved into the twentieth century, the institutions of industrial property and private capital. Within the framework, it accepted the "welfare consensus" that began to emerge just before the First World War and came to maturity after 1945. But he suggests that welfare consensus, within which interest-group bargaining has taken place, has begun to break down, with unpredictable consequences for future political alignments.

Somewhat similar themes, even though they are not directly addressed to the Conservative party alone, are to be found in a stimulating sociological analysis of tradtionalism, conservatism, and political culture.[140] Bob Jessup of Downing College, Cambridge, develops contemporary definitions of the twin elements of civility and deference that "best fit" the political culture of a stable democracy. Deference he sees as an expression of commitment to a dominant order which takes forms more or less conducive to support of the Conservative party; civility ensures the moderation of political demands and participation whatever party is supported. But, it goes without saying, commitment to these dominant values is not equally distributed throughout society.

Both Gamble and Jessup emphasize the conflicting currents within the Conservative party and make clear how far from a monolithic, ideological party it is. Those differences are the main thread of Nigel Harris's revealing study of the tensions between competition and corporatism within the Conservative party. Focusing on the period after World War II, he concludes that the Conservative party survived not despite, but because, of its lack of principle and refusal to espouse any coherent political philosophy.[141]

The decline and, to a lesser extent, the possible revival of the Liberal party has continued to absorb historians and political scientists alike. What were the reasons for the disastrous performance of the party at the polls after the First World War? Do the modest electoral gains of recent years suggest a possible realignment of parties? Can the Liberals reap advantage from the problems of identity and policy faced by both Conservative and Labour parties? Roy Douglas, himself committed to the maintenance of an independent Liberal party, is convinced that Liberal failure rested upon errors of strategy and tactics, beginning with the crucial Liberal-Labour pact of 1903 and continuing thereafter on issue after issue. What failed, he insists, "was not Liberalism, but Liberals." His *History of the Liberal Party, 1895–1970* has been well received, but it fails to cope with the major social and economic changes that were transforming the context of politics within which traditional Liberalism had flourished.[142] Chris Cook has also written a brief history of the party,[143] less didactic, beholden to Douglas and to Trevor Wilson for many insights,[144] and particularly convenient for the facts and figures which help explain the Liberals' electoral fate in recent times.

Much more interesting on the question of decline is *The Liberal Mind, 1914–1929* by Michael Bentley.[145] Bentley was a student of Maurice Cowling, and his monograph is as concerned with "high politics"—the hallmark of the contemporary Cambridge school of modern history—as are the works of Cowling or Andras Jones or A. B. Cooke and John Vincent. Diligently burrowing in the private papers and almost haughtily dismissing most public pronouncements, he seeks insight into Liberal doctrine as it was created "in parallel with, or even in the train of" ongoing parliamentary activity. His method throws substantial light on the emergence of two divergent outlooks even before the issues of coalition and constriction laid bare the split in the Liberal leadership. Asquith and his followers came to adopt a "passive" point of view, emphasizing "faith" and "principles." The outlook of Lloyd George, on the other hand, was flexible, expedient, empirical-minded. Lloyd George and his followers were never able to exorcize the quasi-religious attitudes of the Asquithians; the latter in turn were unable to cope with Lloyd George. Bentley is more convincing in his depiction of the Asquithian mentality than he is in demonstrating that it was the cause of Liberal decline, but he has the one great virtue that he has avoided much of the opaqueness that suffuses the prose of his mentor.

To round out the picture, political scientist Arthur Cyr raises questions not only about decline but about the persistent presence of the Liberal party as something more than a quaint survival of the past in a well-functioning two-party system of government.[146] Building on Samuel Beer's now-classic *British Politics in the Collectivist Age*,[147] Cyr takes its analysis a bit further. He sees the Liberal party as reflecting a dimension of individualism versus collectivism which the "class-based conflict" of the two major parties obscures, and he makes effective use of the theme in discussing the party's heritage, the policies it has emphasized in recent years, its internal structure, its voting base, and the reasons why its activists get involved in it. In view of so much recent work on the diminution of ideological politics among Conservatives and Labourites alike, his assumptions about the Liberal party as quintessentially the vehicle for the expression of certain humanitarian and individualistic values need to be challenged. But the historian has much to learn from the questions Cyr forces him to confront.

The conflict between the attempt to improve capitalism and the endeavor to replace it are central to an understanding of the twentieth-century Labour party. It is a major merit of David Howell's *British Social Democracy: A Study in Development and Decay* that he faces that issue squarely.[148] His informed history of the party since 1931, with an extensive look back to 1900, describes what he calls the birth, achievement, and destruction of social democracy. After the 1945–1950 "heroic age," the party stumbled from expedient to expedient. Like Ralph Miliband, Howell views social democracy as the child of parliamentarianism, a concern for making a national rather than a sectional appeal, trade union defensiveness, Fabianism, and the absence of any effective left-wing theory. This account will persuade the Left and be dismissed by social democrats, but whatever the bias of its political viewpoint, it effectively documents the complex pressures that have operated on the Labour party. Ringing changes on the same theme from a Marxist standpoint outside and to the left of the Labour party, David Coates insists that Labour governments systematically failed to live up to the promises of the party in opposition.[149] Whatever the rhetoric, Labour party politics did not—and cannot—culminate in the creation of a genuinely socialist society. Indeed, he sees the Labour party and its claims as the major handicap to the creation of the kind of party and the kind of labor movement the struggle for socialism requires. In similar vein, Barry Hindness suggests, on the basis of some interesting sociological evidence, that the Labour party has been undergoing a process of deradicalization and of increasing control by the middle class.[150] That argument is challenged by Tom Forester, whose case is that the party's relationship to the working class has not changed significantly over the years and that the place of socialist ideology in the Labour party has not appreciably lessened.[151] Finally, there is a more specialized study of *Labour and the Left in the 1930s* by Ben Pimlott, who writes that, during the 1930s, the Labour Left was consistently wrong on tactics and contends that, had it been politically skillful, it might have made an important contribution to the effectiveness of Labour.[152] Pimlott agrees that Ramsay MacDonald believed that the split in Labour's ranks in 1931 would be only temporary, but notes how the permanence of the split had its influence on the disaffiliation of the Independent Labour party and the formation of the Socialist League. But the latter failed to take advantage of constituency party discontent, so that unity campaigns and popular fronts bowed to the rigidities of the majority leadership. Pimlott is sound on the poor showing of the Left in the formation of domestic policy, but he underestimates how the Left's agitation against fascism gradually deepened the Labour party's understanding of the international crisis.

Even earlier, the Left's view of the Soviet Union clashed sharply with the suspicions of most Labour party leaders. Stephen Graubard's *British Labour and the Russian Revolution* has now been superseded by an Italian work which draws much more heavily upon Labour party archives, upon numerous collections of private papers, and upon the newly available Foreign Office records.[153] It needs to be supplemented by a first-rate journalistic detective story that makes clear that the notorious Zinoviev letter was, as most historians suspected, a fraud;[154] by a thoroughly researched sequel to 1924 which explores the precarious relations between Great Britain and the Soviet Union after the Labour government succumbed to panic over that forgery;[155] and by a detailed exploration of how the Soviet Union tried—and failed, despite the ineptness of a few British trade union leaders—to make contact with the European labor movement by first establishing a special relationship with the British Trades Union Congress.[156]

It is a considerable leap from the 1920s to the 1950s and 1960s, but so much has recently been written from the standpoint of the Left that it is almost a relief to call attention to a fine study dealing with the social democratic mainstream of Labour politics. In *The Gaitskellites*, Stephen Haseler develops the thesis that Labour was rescued from the threat of extremism after 1951 by the very forces that brought it into existence, the trade unions.[157] The trade union Right, he suggests, needed an intellectual justification for its stand against the Left. The followers of Hugh Gaitskell provided it and in so doing reasserted majority, moderate opinion.

To get back to the earlier period, *The Evolution of the Labour Party, 1910–1924* by Ross McKibbin, which turns arguments like those of Howell and Hindness on their heads and from a wholly different viewpoint confirms the indictment made by Coates, is the best account of Labour's rise to office that has yet been written.[158] The growth of the Labour party and the slow attrition of the Liberal party, McKibbin argues, both came from an acutely developed working-class consciousness. The First World War accelerated the attainment of that awareness, with the result that Labour achieved significant gains at the expense of the Liberals, who could make no particular claims on the loyalties of any class. The Labour movement itself and service to the movement became substitutes for any firmly held ideology. The criticism that the Labour party has not served well the cause of socialism or the socialist vision of the true interests of the working class is beside the point. The Labour party was never designed to do so. Confirmation of McKibbin's contention is to be found in a work on education and politics by Rodney Barker.[159] Surveying the period from 1900 to 1951, he fails to find a distinctly socialist statement of objectives. From the beginning, educational policy reflected Labour's Liberal inheritance. There were occasional challenges, but as Barker puts it, the Labour party's "vision was limited by the existing order, in education as in other fields of policy. It sought to distribute the benefits of that order, not to change it."

Two publications, although they are not historical monographs, merit special attention. Norman Mackenzie has now completed his editing of the letters on Beatrice and Sidney Webb in three massive volumes.[160] The third deals with the period discussed in this survey, but all are necessary to understand this remarkable couple. The picture that emerges is of a vital and emotional pair, deeply in love with one another, a far cry from the dry bureaucrats whose caricature was first fixed in 1910 in H. G. Wells's *The New Machiavelli*. The cast of political figures who parade across Beatrice Webb's diaries are here, with all the accuracy and all the distortions of Sidney's and Beatrice's peculiar vision. Equally important are the diaries of Richard Crossman, which made such a commotion when Labour ministers attempted to prevent or delay their publication.[161] The first volume appeared when Crossman was still alive; the remaining two were published posthumously. They will be of significant value to students of Cabinet government, not because they reveal any state secrets—there are few juicy revelations here—but because they give a fascinating inside glimpse of how a government actually operates. The domination of civil servants over government ministers, the overwork of most ministers, the inadequate sense of priorities, these are themes that appear again and again in all three volumes. The picture is not flattering to Crossman's Labour colleagues, but a similar diary by an equally percipient insider would doubtless do the same for any group to hold the reins of power.

Not only the civil servants but the House of Lords posed problems for Labour in office. *The House of Lords and the Labour Government, 1964–1970* by Janet P. Morgan,[162] who helped Crossman edit his diaries, is, in a way, a sequel to P. A. Bromhead's useful *The House of Lords and Contemporary Britain*, which took the story down to 1957.[163] Morgan develops the complex account perceptively from the breakdown of the Interparty Conference created "to reduce the present powers of the House of Lords and to eliminate its present hereditary basis" to the failure of Labour's own Parliament Bill with its two tiers of membership. Altogether, her evidence reveals the skill and restraint with which the leaders of the Lords made their case, a good clue, as more than one observer has commented, to the survival of the institution itself.

What about the fringe parties, the Communists and the Fascists? The standard general history of the British Communist party still remains the work of Henry Pelling, first published in 1958 and reissued in 1975 with an introduction that discusses recent monographs on the subject. While Pelling is on safe ground in emphasizing the controlling role of the Soviet Union over the Communist party of Great Britain, he almost certainly overstates the "non-English" character of its membership.[164] Various observers have attempted to explain the limited appeal of Marxism in Britain as compared with its spread among the European working class and intelligentsia. In *A Proletarian Science: Marxism in Britain 1917–1933*, Stuart MacIntyre deplores the influence of middle-class intellectuals on Marxism and concludes that its failure in Britain resulted from its isolation from the working class.[165] It could be argued that such dissemination of Marxist ideas as there was among the working class came in the first instance from the work of the intellectuals whose role MacIntyre deplores, but in any event, the issue is intriguing but hardly of mainstream importance. For the period after 1945, a German work by Paul-Wolfgang Herrman may be profitably consulted.[166] Herrmann has some peculiar notions about the "reformism" of the Soviet Union, but his is a serious study of a movement whose ineptitude and political irrelevance is the major lesson that emerges from its history.

On fascism, Robert Benewick's *Political Violence and Public Order* is by far the most satisfactory work.[167] Describing how a movement which attempted to use political violence in an organized and systematic fashion failed to emerge as a political force, Benewick shows, nevertheless, the considerable effect it had on public order and public policy. He also makes clear that, trite though the finding may be, the fascist political style, "with its emphasis on revolution or counter-revolution, rather than continuity and evolution, and its search for order through political violence" was alien to British political traditions, at least in the interwar years. The British Union of Fascists (BUF) was largely the institutional shadow of Oswald Mosley, who has now stimulated a gifted scholar to write an important and thoroughly wrong-headed biography. Robert Skidelsky has rightly been fascinated by the imagination and energy of Mosley as a young Labour politician in the late 1920s and early 1930s. But he has allowed his determination to be fair to Mosley to obscure the ugliness of Mosley's anti-Semitism and to cloud his judgment about the viciousness of the BUF during the marches through London's East End. *Osward Mosley* tries to make its subject a bigger man than he was.[168] It fails.

Mosleyism grew in part at least out of the failures of the second Labour government. The governmental crisis of 1931 was Labour's traumatic political experience of the interwar years. It was paralleled on the industrial side by the General Strike of 1926. The fiftieth anniversary of the strike in 1976 produced a rash of new publications, made all the more useful by the fact that considerably more documentation was available as a result of the thirty-year rule. The Cabinet Papers have been used more fully than in previous accounts by both Patrick Renshaw and G. A. Phillips.[169] Of the two, Phillips's work, if somewhat colorless, is by far the most authoritative. Large-scale strikes in Britain, he contends, unlike those in France, rarely had a political purpose. The General Strike was a product of the growth of trade unionism, almost an interval in the development of institutionalized and peaceful industrial relations. His conclusion that the Trade Union Congress (TUC) General Council was propelled toward peace by its conviction from the outset that the strike was bound to weaken and die has been challenged by Alastair Reid and Steven Tolliday, who have argued that even Phillips's evidence shows conclusively that the main reason for calling off the strike was that the movement was getting too strong and threatening to evade the General Council's control.[170] They also complain that Renshaw and Phillips emphasize the diplomacy of the strike while neglecting the relationship between Labour militancy and the deep-seated interwar crisis of the economy. Some left-wing writers have emphasized the economic crisis, but much of their writing, even when the work of professional historians, has been less concerned with reconstructing the historical record than either with identifying "revolutionary situations" or with justifying the role of the Communist party in the strike.[171]

One of the criticisms leveled by Reid and Tolliday at most recent accounts is that they are "London-based," failing to give attention to the various local manifestations of the strike. One exception, which they cite but insist is about an unusual area, is Anthony Mason's study of *The General Strike in North East.*[172] Margaret Morris, too, in an unpretentious Penguin history of the strike, has looked at the experience and the actions of the strikers at the local level. By and large, her work, like that of Renshaw and Phillips, corroborates the findings of previous accounts.[173] Curiously, so too do the caveats of Reid and Tolliday. Despite their insistence that labour militancy has been underestimated by the "academic" historians, they conclude that the potential of the General Strike was explosive, though almost certainly not revolutionary. The significance of its defeat was that it ended the possibility of concerted political action by the working class to resolve the postwar crisis in its own interests, and as a result, the Labour party was able to channel the political discontents of the working class into parliamentary forms.

The relationship of the trade unions to the Labour party in this century has spawned a polemical literature that has somewhat obscured the increasing sophistication of scholarly contributions in this area. In 1954, a Conservative member of Parliament called his colleagues who received money from outside sources "kept men." About a third to 40 percent of the Labour members of twentieth-century Parliaments have been such kept men. William D. Muller's fine monograph on trade union–sponsored MPs informs us that sponsorship was once used as an honorable form of retirement for unwanted officials but is not so used any longer.[174] Sponsored MPs, he shows, participate fully in debates directly affecting their unions; on the other matters they speak less than other MPs, hold fewer positions in governments or shadow cabinets, even ask fewer parliamentary questions. Generally, they have been more loyal to the leadership in internal party battles than the rest of the parliamentary rank and file, but on the other hand the trade unions have usually bypassed them in dealing with governments. The unions influenced Labour party policy more through their bloc votes at the annual conference and through their representatives on the party's Executive Committee than through their sponsored MPs.

The men and women who were active in trade councils were neither the mass of the working class nor the leaders of individual unions, the TUC, or the Labour party. They were the "active soldiers and non-commissioned officers" of the trade union army. Alan Clinton's work on the councils describes how the local bodies changed from being important constituents in a movement that still relied on local initiative into humble instruments of a professional trade union leadership whose relations with employers and the state had become firmly fixed at the top.[175] He does not carry his story beyond 1940, but it seems appropriate to conclude, on his evidence, that the main lines of the trade councils' activities had been established by that time and that structurally very little has changed since the peak of their power and influence in the mid-1920s.

Focusing on the bargaining that is central to the trade union purpose, Gerald Dorfman examines the behavior of the TUC toward government's efforts after 1945 to deal with Britain's economic problems through more direct intervention in the economy.[176] As he points out, although government needed the TUC's advice and cooperation, the TUC had only limited power to speak with authority for its member unions. Since there were some 170 of them, consensus was often impossible, especially on the issue of wages. As both major parties became committed to full employment policies, the traditional loyalties of the unions to the Labour party were strained. The satisfaction of specific trade union interests largely determined whether there would be "collaboration or conflict" with a Labour government. While Dorfman's prediction that the TUC was unlikely to cooperate with either party on an incomes policy has proved incorrect, his analysis of relations in the two decades after the war makes clear the essential tentativeness of any arrangements that are made.

Antiunion hysteria has grown steadily in recent years. Despite the fact that the unions have lost on issue after issue—since 1974 alone, for example, over the European Economic Community, import controls, cuts in public expenditure— the myth somehow persists of unions dictating their will to the rest of the population. Its essential unreality is laid bare by Robert Taylor, whose *The Fifth Estate: Britain's Unions in the Seventies* describes factually and sensibly the present state of the Britain trade union movement.[177] Not surprisingly, although critical of some of the unions on a number of issues, he concludes that "the fantasy world of brutish union bosses dictating what we read or where we work belongs to fiction writers in Fleet Street."

The development of the techniques of collective bargaining at the national and the industrial levels is thoroughly traced by Rodger Charles.[178] He assesses the joint attempts made by trade unionists and employers to improve that system through such instruments as the Industrial Council from 1911 to 1913, the Whitley approach from 1916 through 1939, the National Industrial Conference from 1916 to 1921, and the Conference on Industrial Reorganization and Industrial Relations in 1928 and 1929. His identification of all these efforts, not just the Whitley Councils which have hitherto been the focus of attention, as having a common theme, the establishment by the parties concerned of norms to govern their collective bargaining relationship, broadens our perception of the nature of employee–employer relations in Britain. For the period after 1945, Kevin Hawkins shows that industrial relations have changed substantially as a result of developments in the technological, market, and political environment.[179] Thus, for example, the increasingly greater role played by government in dealing with inflation inevitably has modified traditional employer–employee relations; and of course the arrival of full employment after the war transformed profoundly the expectations of ordinary working-class people, not only in terms of their economic standard of living, but in the form of insistence upon the right to be consulted by managements about decisions likely to affect their working lives.

If trade union power can paralyze an economy, so too can control over critical management functions. But just as sectional fragmentation has characterized the behavior of British unions, fragmentation, Stephen Blank informs us, has conditioned the activities of the British Federation of Industries (FBI).[180] More often than not, that large and representative body was incapable of speaking with one voice to government on matters of real importance. Differences which led to the formation of the National Union of Manufacturers and the British Employers' Confederation and were not reconciled until 1965 when the three rivals were amalgamated into the Confederation of British Industry (CBI), together with fundamental disagreements over issues such as protection versus free trade, had the result that the FBI was never a very effective pressure group. Instead, with the parallel growth of a government bureaucracy, there developed "interpenetration" of private and public organizations, leading to an extensive sharing of authority. The CBI, in this new environment, has been substantially more influential than its predecessor, but it is too early to evaluate the effect of what Blank sees as an equally important fact, that it will become a major channel through which governments can mobilize cooperation and consent of industry on behalf of public policy.

Much of the interesting recent work on Britain's economic history has dealt with limited periods and specialized topics. Whatever the views of "catastrophists" to whom I have already alluded, Derek W. Aldcroft in particular, sometimes with H. W. Richardson, has examined various aspects of the interwar period and has challenged the view that its years were depressed and wasted as far as economic growth is concerned. Admitting that over a million people were out of work in the 1920s and 1930s, Aldcroft makes two major points: first, seen in terms of past achievement, Britain's growth indexes showed remarkable improvement; and second, the economy as a whole was much more dynamic than is often imagined.[181] This view is confirmed, though somewhat less insistently, by J. A. Dowie, whose quantitative studies confirm the reality of significant growth, particularly in the manufacturing and distribution sectors of the economy.[182]

The influence of monetary policy on the economy has been a central theme for the years after 1919. The return to the gold standard in 1925 and its subsequent abandonment in the 1930s has intrigued a number of scholars. Whatever the verdict of the economists, students of the history of the era will be interested in D. E. Moggridge's explorations of the expertise—or its absence—with which the governors of the Bank of England approached the decisions that had to be made.[183] Perhaps he exaggerates somewhat, but his evidence tends to support his contention that the bank depended much more on qualitative judgments by men who passed through Montagu Norman's office than on any analysis of basic trends. His perceptions are confirmed in the massive three-volume study of the Bank of England by R. A. Sayers.[184] Essentially a history of the bank as seen by bank officials, it makes clear that statistics and monetary theory were not a major part of the intellectual baggage of the bank's leaders. Sayers's impressive work is particularly absorbing in describing Norman, secretive, superior, mesmerizing politicians and market operators to approve what he and his confidants recommended. Keynes and a few others were unconvinced of Norman's wisdom, but they were in a minority. In a slightly different way, Sidney Pollard has commented on the astonishing survival of a central banking institution, enjoying full powers to affect in vital ways the economic health of society independent of government, yet itself representing a narrow sector of the economy and responsible to no one else.[185] On the government side, Susan Howson examines *Domestic Monetary Management in Britain, 1919–38*.[186] She concludes that monetary policy plus debt management helped keep the economy in the doldrums after the return to the gold standard and that in the 1930s, after gold had been abandoned, the Treasury's cheap money policy did indeed fulfill its intended purpose. It served to initiate the housing boom and hence general recovery.

Histories of business firms have continued to range from evident potboilers ground out to order to serious studies of industrial firms that are valuable contributions to economic history. An example of the latter, though it is a commissioned work, is W. J. Reader's history of Imperial Chemical Industries.[187] One of the largest concerns in Western Europe, national in its outlook despite its international character, ICI attempted to monopolize the "imperial" market while avoiding competition with suppliers and customers at home. It made serious investment mistakes before 1939, yet after the war accommodated somewhat to new conditions, even if not aggressively and imaginatively enough. The independence of Reader's scholarship appears to have been in no way cramped by the nature of his support. His assessment seems balanced, and it is certainly lively and absorbing.

More broadly, Leslie Hannah, even though limiting his scope to manufacturing concerns, tells the story of the development of the corporate economy after the First World War.[188] He shows how more and more business was absorbed by fewer giant companies, particularly through mergers, as in the chemical and automobile industries. Concentration of manufacturing by 1930, he believes, contributed much to the rise of productivity, but he is not willing to draw up a balance sheet for or against the corporate economy.

Most of the economic studies mentioned have the advantage of some measure of perspective. For the period after the Second World War, however, and especially from the 1950s to the present, what has recently been written belongs too often in the realm of contemporary commentary or debate to be very valuable in capturing the historical past. One such area of debate centers about the performance of the industries nationalized after 1945. There is already a huge literature on nationalization, but one or two recent publications must be mentioned. Most important is *British Nationalisation, 1945–1973* by R. Kelf-Cohen,[189] author of several earlier studies of the British experience with nationalization.[190] Alluding to the postwar concern that the executive branch of government has been growing at the expense of the legislative, he tries to show that the nationalized industries have been a prime factor in driving the government to take more and more power to control the national economy. In fact, he concludes, the achievements of some of the industries, notably gas and electricity, have been very great. But others, especially those which are labor intensive such as coal, railways, and postal services, have found it very difficult to adjust to the needs of the last quarter of the twentieth century. Some of the same findings, weighted a bit more in favor of the nationalized industries, emerge from Richard Pryke's revealing assessment of public enterprise in practice.[191] Thoroughly airing the pros and cons of public ownership, he finally judges that the nationalized industries have in fact earned their profits by what on balance have been superior means, in terms of the national welfare, to those employed by private industry.

The expansion of the social services and the implementation of the concept of universal social security are as central to the history of twentieth-century Britain as are the two world wars. Beginning with the New Liberalism after 1906 (some would argue much earlier), there is a clear line of development to the legislation sponsored by the Labour government between 1945 and 1951 and to the acceptance of the welfare revolution among all major groups in British society. The work of Richard B. Titmuss, published mainly in the 1950s and 1960s, is the greatest single corpus of insights into countless aspects of the British system of social security. A bit more recently, Bentley B. Gilbert's *The Evolution of National Insurance in Great Britain* has become the standard work on the origins of the welfare state in Edwardian England.[192] He has since further strengthened his position as the most knowledgeable American scholar working in the field of twentieth-century social policy. *British Social Policy, 1914–1939* is not precisely the second volume of Gilbert's earlier work, but it is a follow-up study dealing with the search for a new "political consensus" on social policy.[193] As early as 1921, British leaders accepted the workers' insistence on the right to work or maintenance, and by 1939 they had arrived at an understanding, whether publicly articulated or not, that a national minimum standard of living had to be guaranteed to all citizens.

Most accounts of the development of the welfare state pay scant attention to the contributions of the Labour party before 1945. Arthur Marwick, however, argues that Labour had thought hard about issues of social security for a long time. As a result, he maintains, its share in influencing the making of welfare policy was, even prior to 1945, a substantial one.[194] How the social service state came into existence has been further and succinctly described by Kathleen Woodruffe, who develops three points in an important article in the *Journal of Social History*.[195] First, she defines what is meant by the phrase "welfare state." She then summarizes the evolution of state control that prepared the way, even before the "origins" of 1906 to 1914, for the social policies of a later period. She comments too on the criticisms from the Left and Right that have been made both of individual features of the social legislation and its administration and of its general assumptions and goals.

The complexity of welfare issues may perhaps be illustrated by two very different publications. A. F. Young, in *Social Services in British Industry*, attempts a consideration of those services which are associated with working people and which deal specifically with the problems found in industry.[196] She studies the agencies affecting the young, the disabled, or those changing their jobs, then turns to those services operating within the industries themselves, and finally addresses such questions as the financial arrangements for income maintenance during periods of unemployment. Making no firm judgment on the merits of one or another approach to the administration of social security, she nevertheless displays the arguments that have been marshaled to support various points of view.

Growth and Welfare: A New Policy for Britain by John Mills raises a central issue that underlies the differences of opinion on the scope of social services in Great Britain.[197] Analyzing the policy conflict between the claims of economic growth and those of social welfare, he insists that measures to ensure optimum growth must take precedence over any other consideration. Mills is probably too harsh in his assessment of Britain's economic performance after 1945, as Roy Harrod points out in an introduction to this book, but his conclusion is one that has been shared by a wide range of economists, historians, and other social observers.

The postwar ventures into greatly expanded social security and the nationalization of selected industries were foreshadowed in the reformation of British politics during the Second World War. Participation by Labour's leaders in Churchill's coalition and the very social and administrative pattern of the war effort ensured that the influence of the Left and the Center would be maximized. Paul Addison finds the signposts to the undertakings of 1945 to 1951 in the wartime egalitarianism and community feeling that become to a large extent the pervasive ideals of social life. Although the zeal for social reconstruction faded with the "affluence" of the 1950s, he holds, the new consensus at the top which had been forged between 1940 and 1945 remained. The thesis is perhaps pushed somewhat beyond the data, but Addison's fresh perceptions and new materials make his work a very suggestive monograph.[198] No discussion of the welfare state would be complete without a discussion of the contribution of Sir William Beveridge. José Harris, in *William Beveridge: A Biography*, makes clear that the picture of Beveridge as the "champion of new forms of collective altruism" is significantly oversimplified.[199] This impressive study considers the underlying assumptions of Beveridge's philosophy, assesses his role in the process of government growth and administrative rationalization, and evaluates his influence on the history of social policy. Above all, it makes clear how important Beveridge considered the contribution of the professional bureaucrat, whatever his view of any individual administrator. The work concentrates on these particulars of Beveridge's public career and places him in the long line of social reformers who helped mold the institutions of Britain over the last several centuries. Yet, in the end, the reader is left with a rounded and judicious picture of a complex, often imaginative, and equally often contradictory social thinker, whose precise contribution is likely to be debated for years to come.

Popular accounts of the war on the home front abound, but apart from specialized studies such as Addison's few break any new ground. Angus Calder's *The People's War*, which dramatically assesses domestic responses to the many pressures of wartime, is an exception.[200] Like *The Road to War*, Calder's book suffers from a disputable thesis, in his case that the wartime move toward social democracy was purposely thwarted by vested interests, but it serves effectively to remind us that not all Britons were heroes, not all generous in wartime, not even all subject to equal rations of suffering. However one-sided it may be, it is a thought-provoking evocation of Britain's "finest hour."

Part of that finest hour was captured in the broadcasts of a Tommy Handley or Vera Lynn or J. B. Priestley over the British Broadcasting Corporation. The third volume of Asa Briggs's authoritative *History of Broadcasting* discusses the complex tensions engendered at Broadcasting House in wartime—described by George Orwell as "something half way between a girls' school and a lunatic asylum"—as the BBC played its role in developing an information policy at home and a propaganda policy abroad.[201] Within the BBC at the beginning of the war, there was an inadequate appreciation of credible news as an important wartime requirement, but Briggs makes clear how improvisation, luck, and a measure of trial and error led to effective use of the broadcast medium at home. After a similarly hesitant start, the BBC's modest accomplishment was to bolster the propaganda effort by presenting credible news broadcasts to at least some portion of English-speaking listeners on the continent. How effective the war of words really was, either at home or abroad, is difficult to judge, but Briggs has given us the best single description of wartime information policy in Britain. It makes an important contribution to his monumental history of the BBC.

Naval policy both during and before the Second World War has been better explained by independent scholars than have the conduct and planning of operations on land and in the air. Incidentally, because such exaggerated claims have been made about the contribution made by the intelligence center at Bletchley Park to victory in the war, it is good to have Peter Calvocoressi's knowledgeable (at Bletchley Park he headed a section dealing with Luftwaffe messages) account of the breakup of the German "Enigma" code and the swift distribution of secret intelligence to military and political leaders alike. In *Top Secret Ultra* he makes it clear that Ultra did indeed play a significant role in a number of the key decisions made first by Winston Churchill and then by Dwight Eisenhower.[202] For the army, the official histories and various memoirs are still the most useful groups of publications, although we have recently had several informative biographies of army leaders and an occasional superior history of a particular campaign.[203,204] On the Royal Air Force, the most revealing work is Robert Wright's rehabilitation of Chief Marshall Lord Dowding, who emerges out of the rather unpalatable struggle between fighter-plane and bomber theorists, not perhaps as *The Man Who Won the Battle of Britain*, but at least as one of the organizers of victory whose fall owed more to intraservice intrigue than to any balanced assessment of his contributions.[205]

On the naval side, the two major scholarly works deal with the period before the Second World War. Arthur J. Marder has now completed his wide-ranging account of the Royal Navy in the "Fisher era."[206] Coolly and clearly, he guides his readers through one difficult question after another. In volume 4, which deals with 1917, he is particularly skillful in laying bare the dilemmas and the strategic outlooks of those who had to deal with the submarine peril. In volume 5, he deals with such matters as the success of the convoy system, the problems of cooperating with the U.S. Navy, and the surrender of the German fleet and its disposition. However outspoken Marder is on the deficiencies of the British navy, he points out that, in any event, the navy had indeed contributed its own overwhelming victory to the war in which Britain triumphed.

For the immediately succeeding period, Stephen Roskill's *Navy Policy between the Wars* is likely long to remain the standard treatment.[207] It is more than a study of naval history or strategy; it is also important for the light it throws on the diplomacy of the interwar period. Its first volume, published in 1968, was in a way "official" history, making full use of official materials as permitted under the rules of the 1958 Public Records Act. The second volume was delayed until 1976 while Roskill completed his biography of Maurice Hankey, and thus it benefited from the passage of the thirty-year rule.

Finally, for the postwar period, C. J. Bartlett has overcome the obvious paucity of available sources to complete a most useful assessment of British defense policy after 1945.[208] Essentially bipartisan, that policy, despite such dramatic incidents as Aneurin Bevan's attack on Clement Attlee over the defense issue, was dictated by military and economic factors substantially beyond the control of British politicians. Shrinking resources and escalating costs exacerbated uncertainties about military technology and resulted in a steady reduction of commitments overseas. Step by step, Britain's obligations had to be tailored to her contemporary capacity. The same story, with special emphasis on Britain's nuclear strategy, is told by R. N. Rosecrance, who makes clear the nature of the debate on the relative merits of the nuclear emphasis and conventional strength in the 1950s and 1960s.[209] In the end, Rosecrance raises a query that is implicit in much of the writing on military policy after 1945. Is it possible that the abandonment of extra-European responsibilities may lead Britain to a new exercise of leadership in Europe and thus to greater security and influence with fewer resources?

Since the Second World War, questions of defense policy, along with nationalization, economic growth or stagnation, and social security, were the significant themes in British history. Starting in 1958, when racial disturbances erupted in Notting Hill in West London, one other current became increasingly disquieting. In a Britain quick to be smugly superior about American handling of the race issue, an influx of immigrants from the West Indies, East Africa, and Asia posed problems not easily solved. Demagogues like Enoch Powell played on the prejudices of a group resentful of the "foreigners"—whether they were British subjects mattered little—who competed for jobs and housing and were in any case "different." Eventually, legislation was adopted, ironically by a Labour gov-

ernment, severely restricting the entry of immigrants even from the Commonwealth. The subject has produced a flourishing polemical literature, but it has
also called forth sober analysis of a spectrum of economic, political, and sociological questions bearing on the recent immigration and the white attitudes
and beliefs it evoked.

Ceri Peach, to illustrate, in a thorough study of West Indian migration, argues
that, while conditions in the West Indies encouraged migration, it was the demand for a "replacement population" at the lower end of the occupational and
residential ladder that determined the movement to Britain.[210] Migration rose
and fell in accordance with the demand for labor, and the geographical distribution of West Indians, Indians, and Pakistani, she contends, shows that the
colored population was acting as a replacement for white population in areas of
usually deteriorating housing. The shortage of labor made the migrants economically acceptable; the shortage of housing made them socially undesirable. The
dilemma created the tensions of the last two decades and continues to exacerbate
them. Much the same kind of assessment is made by Sheila Patterson, whose
solid study *Immigration and Race Relations in Britain, 1960–1967* takes up, in
turn, the government's immigration policies, the major spheres of association of
colored and whites, voluntary associations concerned with immigrant and race
relations, and such related topics as health, crime and its enforcement, as well as
extremist, racist, and fringe organizations such as the National Front.[211] As in the
case of Peach, she gives pride of place to housing and employment as the focal
points of race relations since the 1950s. Even more valuable is a "report" on race
relations published for the Institute of Race Relations in 1969 after seven years of
work. E. J. B. Rose and his collaborators range over a formidable territory in
describing, first, the background of racial tensions and the dynamics of migration
and, second, the major issues and the policies and practices that fed the fires of
white–colored tensions. Like other observers, they stress the dichotomy between
the economic gains and the social stress experienced by the immigrants and by the
society into which they came.[212] How difficult the problem is can be gleaned in a
study of the Campaign against Racial Discrimination (CARD) which flourished
briefly in the 1960s and collapsed as a functioning organization after the Commonwealth Immigration Act of 1968 took away with one hand what the Race Relations Act of 1965 had provided with another. Long, bitter, and divisive arguments among its leaders ensured, insists Benjamin W. Heineman, Jr., that in
CARD "powerlessness perpetuated itself through faction."[213]

It will have been apparent from what has gone before that the historical scholarship on the period after 1945 is still scattered, tentative, heavily contemporary
in its orientation. There are exceptions, and many areas of study have little use for
official papers; but in many other cases the standard works will have to wait until
the opening of the archives permits their authors to study the relevant documen-

tary materials. Meanwhile, there are a few general histories that serve to put those later years into perspective. The best of them is C. J. Bartlett's *A History of Postwar Britain, 1945–1974*, which treats the Labour governments with an even-handedness often missing in other accounts.[214] Bartlett concentrates his attention on the retreat from empire, the nation's economic and social problems, and the fluctuating fortunes of the two major political parties. He also pays more than lip service to an investigation of the role of scientists and engineers in postwar Britain. The British, he sums up, accomplished a good deal between 1945 and 1974. National wealth and per capita income were roughly doubled; unemployment was held usually below 2.6 percent; achievements in welfare, health, and education were impressive; the nationalized gas and electricity industries outperformed the private sector in the mid-1960s. There was, however, no such record of success in coal or the railways or the nationalized steel industry; and equally disappointing, other states, in much the same environment, did better than Britain both in economic growth and in the provision of social services. Nevertheless, Britain had made the transition from the weakest of the major powers to the rank of the medium states, even though her consolidation of that new position was not achieved.

Like Bartlett, Peter Calvocoressi is sober but not excessively pessimistic about the problems Britain has faced since the war.[215] Emphasizing domestic affairs more than in much of his previous work, he is struck, like most observers, by the conflict between dreams of retaining world power and aspirations for social justice for all. Eventually, the ambition to play a world role was abandoned, but the demand for a reasonably equitable society placed a heavy burden on an economy that did not expand sufficiently for Britain easily to pay the bill. Calvocoressi's contingent optimism is a refreshing—and persuasive—outlook at a time when so many Americans have written Britain off as hopelessly in decline. Similarly indisposed to wallow in pessimism, Mary Proudfoot writes of the years between 1951 and 1970 as those in which Britain was an "affluent society."[216] Her study of British government and politics is a useful summary of events which places particular emphasis on the way in which Labour and Conservative parties became more alike during the 1950s and 1960s.

That similarity does not trouble Michael Stewart, who sees the period between 1964 and 1976 as "twelve wasted years."[217] Living standards increased by only a fifth compared with a rise of more than a third between 1951 and 1964. All other major criteria of economic policy—unemployment, the rate of inflation, the balance of payments position—testified that the situation was far worse in 1976 than in 1964. Of course various worldwide forces played their role, but successive governments, Labour and Conservative, pursued no coherent economic strategy, failing to establish a workable long-term incomes policy and failing likewise to achieve a high and stable rate of industrial investment. Above all, he argues, lack of continuity in economic policy from government to government was a political luxury Britain could no longer afford.

How, then, can one sum up the twentiety-century history of Great Britain? Is it an account of the fall from nineteenth-century grace, punctuated by the horrors and accomplishments of two great wars, but inexorably pointing to further weakness, recurrent crisis, and the imperative need for drastic surgery? Or is it the story of a civilized people making a sensible adjustment to the "postindustrial" environment, concerned as much with the quality of life as with the quantity of goods, pointing the way toward a workable future? Each view contains elements of validity, yet each is essentially a caricature. For the years before the Second World War, in any case, there has been sufficient time and adequate documentation to enable scholars to explode many of the conventional myths. The availability of new archival materials has made possible significant changes in interpretations current when the predecessor of this essay was published in 1966. The hungry 1920s and 1930s, for example, turn out to be a period of economic growth; appeasement becomes much more than the stubbornness or wisdom of Neville Chamberlain and his associates; David Lloyd George somehow grows in stature despite each new revelation of his personality and character. After 1945, the record is one of contemporary commentary, useful in giving us a sense of the period but handicapped in many areas by the paucity of data, often colored by current concerns and contemporary values, still highly tentative. Already it is being rewritten and while we cannot predict the new interpretations that will emerge from access to new materials and the perspective of time, we can be confident that the 1950s and 1960s and 1970s will look as different from present impressions as the war years and the 1920s and 1930s have appeared from the vantage point of the last decade of historical scholarship.

NOTES

1. Donald Watt, "The Historiography of Appeasement," in Alan Sked and Chris Cook, eds., *Crisis and Controversy: Essays in Honour of A. J. P. Taylor*, London and Basingbroke, 1976, 120–121.

2. Alfred F. Havighurst, *Britain in Transition: The Twentieth Century*, Chicago, 1979.

3. T. O. Lloyd, *Empire to Welfare State: English History, 1906–1967*, New York, 1970.

4. W. N. Medlicott, *Contemporary England, 1914–1964*, New York, 1967; A. J. P. Taylor, *English History, 1914–1945*, London, 1965.

5. Robert Rhodes James, *The British Revolution, 1880–1939*, New York, 1977; Arthur Marwick, *Britain in the Century of Total War: War, Peace and Social Change, 1900–1967*, Boston, 1968; A. H. Halsey, ed., *Trends in British Society since 1900: A Guide to the Changing Social Structure of Britain*, New York, 1972. Halsey's work should be used in conjunction with John H. Goldthorpe (in collaboration with Catriona Llewellyn and Clive Payne), *Social Mobility and Class Structure in Modern Britain*, Oxford, 1980. This volume presents the findings

of Nuffield College's Social Mobility Research Group, based upon a national sample carried out in 1972, which provide an approach, if not many answers, to the question of the openness of British society. It is indispensable if only for its demonstration of the complexity of dealing with issues of class and social mobility in that society.

6. B. A. Waites, "The Effects of the First World War on Class and Status in England, 1910–20," *Journal of Contemporary History* 11, 1976: 27–48.

7. K. Roberts, F. G. Cook, S. C. Clark, and Elizabeth Semenoff, *The Fragmentary Class Structure*, Atlantic Highlands, N.J., 1978. I have found two other works useful in understanding issues of social structure, mobility, affluence and inequality, planning, etc.,: Judith Ryder and Harold Silver, *Modern English Society*, London, 1970, and Trevor Noble, *Modern Britain: Structure and Change*, London, 1975.

8. Llewelyn Woodward, *Great Britain and the War of 1914–1918*, London, 1967.

9. Lord Beaverbrook, *Politicians and the War, 1914–1916* 2 vols., London, 1928–1932; idem *Men and Power, 1917–1918*, London, 1956; idem, *The Decline and Fall of Lloyd George*, London, 1963.

10. Stephen Koss, "The Destruction of Britain's Last Liberal Government," *JMH* 40, 1968: 257–277.

11. Ibid., *Lord Haldane: Scapegoat of Liberalism*, New York and London, 1969.

12. Cameron Hazlehurst, *Politicians at War, July 1914 to May 1915*, London, 1971.

13. Barry McGill, "Asquith's Predicament, 1914–1918," *JMH* 39, 1967: 283–303.

14. V. H. Rothwell, *British War Aims and Peace Diplomacy, 1914–1918*, Oxford, 1971.

15. S. J. Kernek, *Distractions of Peace during War: The Lloyd George Government's Reactions to Woodrow Wilson December 1916–November 1918*, Transactions of the American Philosophical Society, n.s., 65, Philadelphia, 1975.

16. W. B. Fowler, *British-American Relations, 1917–1918*, Princeton and London, 1969.

17. Wm. Roger Louis, *Great Britain and Germany's Lost Colonies, 1914–1919*, New York, 1967.

18. George W. Egerton, *Great Britain and the Creation of the League of Nations: Strategy, Politics, and International Organization, 1914–1919*, Chapel Hill, 1978. See also idem, "The Lloyd George Government and the Creation of the League of Nations," *AHR* 79, 1974: 419–444. Peter Raffo tends to agree with me rather than Egerton on the British contribution; see his "The Anglo-American Preliminary Negotiations for a League of Nations," *Journal of Contemporary History* 9, 1974: 153–176. My views are in *The League of Nations Movement in Great Britain, 1914–1919*, New Brunswick, N.J., 1952; rep., Metuchen, N.J., 1967.

19. Keith Robbins, *The Abolition of War: The "Peace Movement" in Britain, 1914–1919*, Cardiff, 1976.

20. Marvin Swarz, *The Union of Democratic Control in British Politics during the First World War*, Oxford, 1971.

21. John Rae, *Conscience and Politics*, London, 1970.

22. See, for example, David Boulton, *Objection Overruled*, London, 1967. The jingoistic intolerance of a frightened and bellicose public, to which government policy reacted, is well captured in Thomas C. Kennedy, "Public Opinion and the Conscientious Objector, 1915–1919," *JBS* 12, 1973: 105–119.

23. Albert Marrin, *The Last Crusade: The Church of England in the First World War*, Durham, N.C., 1974.

24. Paul Fussell, *The Great War and Modern Memory*, New York and London, 1975.

25. I have cheerfully appropriated the remark from a review by Stephen E. Koss, AHR 75, 1969: 126–127.

26. Paul B. Johnson, *Land Fit for Heroes: The Planning of British Reconstruction, 1914–1919*, Chicago, 1968.

368   HENRY R. WINKLER

27. Susan Armitage, *The Politics of Decontrol in Industry: Britain and the United States*, London, 1969.
28. Robert E. Bunselmeyer, *The Cost of War, 1914–1919: The British Economic War Aims and the Origins of Reparation*, Hamden, Conn., 1975.
29. Taylor's comments are in the introduction to Kenneth O. Morgan, *Lloyd George*, London, 1974, 7–8. Also worth consulting is Morgan's stimulating article "Lloyd George's Premiership: A Study in 'Prime Ministerial Government,'" *HJ* 1970, 13, 130–157.
30. Peter Rowland, *David Lloyd George: A Biography*, New York, 1976.
31. Frank Owen, *Tempestuous Journey: Lloyd George, His Life and Times*, New York, 1955.
32. A. J. P. Taylor, ed., *Lloyd George: Twelve Essays*, New York, 1971.
33. Ibid., ed., *Lloyd George: A Diary by Frances Stevenson*, London, 1971.
34. A. J. P. Taylor, ed., *My Darling Pussy: The Letters of Lloyd George and Frances Stevenson, 1913–1941*, London, 1975.
35. Kenneth O. Morgan, ed., *Lloyd George Family Letters, 1885–1936*, Cardiff and London, 1973.
36. Ibid., *Lloyd George*.
37. Ibid., *The Age of Lloyd George*, Historical Problems: Studies and Documents, no. 12, New York, 1971.
38. Ibid., *Consensus and Disunity: The Lloyd George Coalition, 1918–1922*, London, 1979.
39. Colin Cross, ed., *Life with Lloyd George: The Diary of A. J. Sylvester, 1931–45*, New York, 1975.
40. Michael Fry, *Lloyd George and Foreign Policy*, vol. 1, *The Education of a Statesman: 1890–1916*, Montreal, 1977.
41. Chris Wrigley, *David Lloyd George and the British Labour Movement: Peace and War*, New York, 1976.
42. John Turner, *Lloyd George's Secretariat*, Cambridge, 1979.
43. Michael Kinnear, *The Fall of Lloyd George: The Political Crisis of 1922*, London, 1973.
44. In a review in the *EH Review* 90, 1975: 229–230. The crisis, within the broader context of Conservative party attitudes toward coalition, is studied by David Close, "Conservatives and Coalition after the First World War," *JMH* 45, 1973: 240–260.
45. John Campbell, *Lloyd George: The Goat in the Wilderness, 1922–1931*, London, 1977.
46. The volumes by Martin Gilbert are: 3, *The Challenge of War, 1914–1916*, Boston, 1971; 4, *The Stricken World, 1916–1922*, Boston, 1975; 5, *The Prophet of Truth, 1922–1939*, Boston, 1977; plus of course the accompanying volumes of documents.
47. Henry Pelling, *Churchill*, London, 1974.
48. Robert Rhodes James, *Churchill: A Study in Failure, 1900–1939*, London, 1970.
49. Peter Stansky, ed., *Churchill: A Profile*, New York, 1973.
50. A. J. P. Taylor et al., *Churchill Revisited: A Critical Assessment*, New York, 1969.
51. Brian Gardner, *Churchill in Power As Seen by His Contemporaries*, Boston, 1970.
52. *Churchill Taken from the Diaries of Lord Moran: The Struggle for Survival, 1940–1965*, Boston, 1966.
53. Lord Normanbrooke, et al., *Action This Day: Working with Churchill Memoirs*, ed. Sir John Wheeler Bennett, New York, 1969.
54. Alex P. Schmid, *Churchills Privater Krieg: Intervention und Konterrevolution im Russischen Bürgerkreig, November 1918–März 1920*, Zurich, 1974.
55. Donald Graeme Boadle, *Winston Churchill and the German Question in British Foreign Policy, 1918–1922*, The Hague, 1973.
56. Arthur Marder, "Winston Is Back: Churchill at the Admiralty, 1939–1940," *EHR*, suppl. 5, 1972.

57. Arthur Marder, *From the Dardanelles to Oran: Studies of the Royal Navy in War and Peace, 1915–1940*, London, 1974.
58. Stephen Roskill, *Churchill and the Admirals*, London, 1977.
59. Ronald Lewin, *Churchill as Warlord*, London, 1974.
60. Patrick Cosgrove, *Churchill at War*: vol. 1, *Alone, 1939–40*, London, 1974.
61. Maxwell Phillip Schoenfeld, *The War Ministry of Winston Churchill*, Ames, Iowa, 1972.
62. R. W. Thompson, *Generalissimo Churchill*, New York, 1973.
63. Keith Middlemas and John Barnes, *Baldwin: A Biography*, London, 1969. Barbara C. Malament's review article, "Baldwin Re-restored?" *JMH* 44, 1972: 87–96, is a critical evaluation of Middlemas and Barnes which sensibly concludes that their defense of Baldwin is open to serious question.
64. Kenneth Young, *Stanley Baldwin*, London, 1976.
65. Anthony Sampson, *Macmillan: A Study in Ambiguity*, London, 1967.
66. Harold Macmillan, *Winds of Change, 1914–1939*, London and New York, 1966; idem, *The Blast of War, 1939–1945*, London, 1967, New York, 1968; idem *Tides of Fortune, 1945–1955*, London, 1969; idem, *Riding the Storm, 1956–1959*, London, 1971; idem, *Pointing the Way, 1959–1961*, London, 1972; idem, *At the End of the Day, 1961–1963*, London, 1973.
67. J. A. Cross, *Sir Samuel Hoare: A Political Biography*, London, 1977.
68. Cross's account of the Hoare-Laval agreement needs to be supplemented by James C. Robertson, "The Hoare-Laval Plan," *Journal of Contemporary History* 10, 1975: 433–464, which mixes sympathy for Hoare with a realistic assessment of his role in misleading Parliament and public about the conduct of British foreign policy.
69. A. J. P. Taylor, *Beaverbook*, London, 1972.
70. Stephen Koss, *Sir John Brunner: Radical Plutocrat: 1842–1919*, Cambridge, 1970.
71. Ibid., *Fleet Street Radical: A. G. Gardiner*, New Haven, Conn., 1973.
72. Ibid., *Asquith*, British Political Biography, New York, 1976
73. Alfred F. Havighurst, *Radical Journalist: H. W. Massingham, 1860–1924*, New York, 1974.
74. Peter Clarke, *Liberals and Social Democrats*, London, 1978.
75. David Marquand, *Ramsay MacDonald*, London, 1977.
76. Ross Terrill, *R. H. Tawney and His Time: Socialism as Fellowship*, Cambridge, Mass., 1975. A useful footnote to Terrill's work is J. A. Hall, "The Roles and Influence of Political Intellectuals," *British Journal of Sociology* 28, 1977: 351–362, which explores the implications of the involvement of reforming intellectuals in labour movements. Also useful is Gertrude Himmelfarb's evaluation of the radical dualism of means and ends, science and morals in the thought and action of Sidney and Beatrice Webb; see "The Intellectual in Politics: The Case of the Webbs," *Journal of Contemporary History* 3, 1971: 3–11.
77. L. P. Carpenter, *G. D. H. Cole: An Intellectual Biography*, New York, 1973.
78. Margaret Cole, *The Life of G. D. H. Cole*, London, 1971.
79. Michael Foot, *Aneurin Bevan: A Biography*, vol. 2, *1945–1960*, New York, 1974. The first volume was published in 1963. Foot's study now needs to be supplemented by Mark Jenkins's study of the "Bevanite" movement, *Bevanism: Labour's High Tide*, Nottingham, 1980, which insists that Bevanism existed independently of Bevan and shows that it was not simply a spontaneous movement of eager idealists.
80. Bernard Donoughue and G. W. Jones, *Herbert Morrison: Portrait of a Politician*, London, 1973.
81. Philip Williams, *Hugh Gaitskell*, London, 1979.
82. John P. Mackintosh, ed., *British Prime Ministers in the Twentieth Century*, 2 vols., London, 1977–1978.
83. Stephen Roskill, *Hankey, Man of Secrets*, London, 1970–1974.

84. Frances Donaldson, *Edward VIII*, London, 1974.

85. Charles Mowat, *Britain between The Wars, 1918–1940*, Chicago, 1955.

86. Sean Glynn and John Oxborrow, *Interwar Britain: A Social and Economic History*, New York, 1976.

87. Gillian Peele and Chris Cook, eds., *The Politics of Reappraisal, 1918–1939*, London, 1975.

88. Alan Sked and Chris Cook, eds., *Crisis and Controversy: Essays in Honour of A. J. P. Taylor*, London, 1976.

89. F. S. Northedge, *The Troubled Giant: Britain among the Great Powers, 1918–1939*, New York, 1966.

90. Anne Orde, *Great Britain and International Security, 1920–1926*, London, 1978.

91. Ian Nish, *Alliance in Decline: A Study in Anglo-Japanese Relations, 1908–1923*, London, 1972.

92. Richard Ullman, *Anglo-Soviet Relations, 1917–1921*, vol. 3, *The Anglo-Soviet Accord*, Princeton, 1972. M. V. Glenny is much more critical of Lloyd George in "The Anglo-Soviet Trade Agreement, March 1921," *Journal of Contemporary History* 2, 1970: 63–82.

93. Stephen White, *Britain and the Bolshevik Revolution: A Study in the Politics Diplomacy, 1920–1924*, London, 1979.

94. Michael Fry, *Illusions of Security: North Atlantic Diplomacy, 1918–22*, Toronto, 1972.

95. Wm. Roger Lewis, *British Strategy in the Far East, 1919–1939*, Oxford, 1971.

96. Christopher Thorne, *The Limits of Foreign Policy*, London, 1973. Three other articles by Thorne help round out the picture: "The Shanghai Crisis of 1932: The Basis of British Policy," *AHR* 75, 1970; "Viscount Cecil, the Government and the Far Eastern Crisis of 1931," *HJ* 14, 1971: 805–826; "The Quest for Arms Embargoes: Failure in 1933," *Journal of Contemporary History* 4, 1970: 129–149.

97. Ann Trotter, *Britain and East Asia, 1933–1937*, New York, 1975.

98. Bradford A. Lee, *Britain and the Sino-Japanese War, 1937–1939: A Study in the Dilemmas of British Decline*, Stanford, 1973.

99. Peter Lowe, *Great Britain and the Origins of the Pacific War: A Study of British Policy in East Asia, 1937–1941*, New York, 1977.

100. Frank Hardie, *The Abyssinian Crisis*, London, 1974.

101. Daniel Waley, *British Public Opinion and the Abyssinian War*, London, 1975.

102. Lawrence R. Pratt, *East of Malta, West of Suez: Britain's Mediterranean Crisis, 1936–1939*, Cambridge, 1975.

103. See Watt, "Historiography of Appeasement." A useful survey of the more recent literature is in William R. Rock, "British Appeasement (1930's): A Need for Revision?" *South Atlantic Quarterly* 78, 1979: 290–301.

104. Lord Harvey, *Diplomatic Diaries, 1937–40*, London, 1970.

105. David Dilks, ed., *The Diaries of Sir Alexander Cadogan, 1938–1945*, London, 1971.

106. Maurice Cowling, *The Impact of Hitler: British Politics and British Policy, 1933–40*, Cambridge, 1975.

107. Keith Robbins, *Munich 1938*, London, 1968.

108. Telford Taylor, *Munich: The Price of Peace*, New York, 1979.

109. Neville Thompson, *The Anti-Appeasers: Conservative Opposition to Appeasement in the 1930s*, New York, 1971. A very recent article by Roy Douglas emphasizes how ambivalent was the opposition to Chamberlain's policy even when it led to resignation from his government; see "Chamberlain and Eden, 1937–38," *Journal of Contemporary History* 13, 1978: 97–116.

110. Simon Newman, *March 1939: The British Guarantee to Poland. A Study in the Continuity of British Foreign Policy*, Oxford, 1976.

111. Donald Lammers, "From Whitehall after Munich: The Foreign Office and the Future Course of British Policy," *HJ* 16, 1973: 831–856.

112. Michael Howard, *The Continental Commitment*, London, 1972.

113. Peter Dennis, *Decision by Default: Peacetime Conscription and British Defence*, London, 1972.

114. Robert Paul Shay, Jr., *British Rearmament in the Thirties: Politics and Profits*, Princeton, 1977.

115. John Naylor, *Labour's International Policy: The Labour Party in the 1930s*, Boston, 1969.

116. Michael G. Gordon, *Conflict and Consensus in Labour's Foreign Policy, 1914–1965*, Stanford, Calif., 1969.

117. John S. Koliopoulos, *Greece and the British Connection, 1935–1941*, London, 1977.

118. Elisabeth Barker, *British Policy in South-east Europe in the Second World War*, New York, 1976.

119. Phyllis Auty and Richard Clogg, eds., *British Policy towards Wartime Resistance in Yugoslavia and Greece*, New York, 1975.

120. Michael J. Cohen, *Palestine: Retreat from the Mandate. The Making of British Policy: 1936–45*, London, 1978.

121. Martin Gilbert, *Exile and Return: The Struggle for a Jewish Homeland*, Philadelphia, 1978. See also idem, "British Strategy and the Palestine Question 1936–39," *Journal of Contemporary History* 7, 1972: 157–183; idem, "Appeasement in the Middle East: The British White Paper on Palestine, May 1939," II. The Testing of a Policy, 1942–1945," *HJ* 19, 1976: 727–758.

122. A. J. Sherman, *Island Refuge: Britain and Refugees from the Third Reich, 1933–1939*, Berkeley, 1973. See also the doctoral dissertation of Joshua Berton Stein, *Britain and the Jews of Europe, 1933–1939*, University Microfilms, Ann Arbor, 1972.

123. Bernard Wasserstein, *Britain and the Jews of Europe, 1939–1945*, New York, 1979.

124. George Watson, *Politics and Literature in Modern Britain*, Totowa, N.J., 1977.

125. Stanley Weintraub, *The Last Great Cause: The Intellectuals and the Spanish Civil War*, New York, 1968.

126. Watson, *Politics and Literature*.

127. Samuel Hynes, *The Auden Generation: Literature and Politics in England in the 1930s*, New York, 1976.

128. Bernard Crick, *George Orwell: A Life*, London, 1980; Peter Stansky, *The Unknown Orwell*, London, 1972; William Abrahams, *Orwell: The Transformation*, New York, 1980.

129. Andrew Boyle, *The Climate of Treason: Five Who Spied for Russia*, London, 1979.

130. Llewelyn Woodward, *British Foreign Policy in the Second World War*, 4 vols., London, 1970–1975.

131. Christopher Thorne, *Allies of a Kind*, London, 1978.

132. Joseph Frankel, *British Foreign Policy, 1945–1973*, London, 1975.

133. F. S. Northedge, *Descent from Power: British Foreign Policy, 1945–1973*, London, 1974.

134. Maurice Cowling, *The Impact of Labour, 1920–1924*, Cambridge, 1971. Some of the articles in Kenneth D. Brown, ed., *Essays in Anti-labour History: Responses to the Rise of Labour in Britain*, London, 1974, deal with the Liberal party's reaction to the rise of the Labour party; others discuss a variety of less well-known antisocialist individuals and groups. Both sets of essays give some insight into the broader universe of attitudes within which Cowling's politicians at the top played their roles. See also Patrick Renshaw, "Anti-labour Politics in Britain, 1918–1927," *Journal of Contemporary History* 12, 1977: 693–705.

135. Robert Skidelsky, *Politicians and the Slump: The Labour Government of 1929–1931*, London, 1967.

136. Chris Cook, *The Age of Alignment: Electoral Politics in Britain, 1922–1929*, London, 1975.

137. Chris Cook and John Ramsden, eds., *By-elections in British Politics*, London, 1973.

138. John Ramsden, *The Age of Balfour and Baldwin, 1902–1940*, London, 1978.

139. Andrew Gamble, *The Conservative Nation*, London, 1974.

140. Robert Jessup, *Traditionalism, Conservatism and British Political Culture*, London, 1974.

141. Nigel Harris, *Competition and the Corporate Society: British Conservatives, the State, and Indus-*

try, *1945–1964*, London, 1972. I made the same argument about the Labour party in 1967 as the main theme of my Taft Lectures at the University of Cincinnati; see my "The British Labour Party in the Contemporary World," in Han-Kyo Kim, ed., *Essays on Modern Politics and History Written in Honor of Harold M. Vinacke*, Athens, Ohio, 1969, where I conclude that "the very heterogeneity of the Labour Party, its ability to encompass such disparate views, seems an element of strength, not weakness."

142. Roy Douglas, *History of the Liberal Party, 1895–1970*, London, 1971.
143. Chris Cook, *A Short History of the Liberal Party, 1900–1976*, London, 1976.
144. Trevor Wilson, *The Downfall of the Liberal Party, 1914–1935*, London, 1966.
145. Michael Bentley, *The Liberal Mind, 1914–1929*, New York, 1977.
146. Arthur Cyr, *Liberal Party Politics in Britain*, London, 1977.
147. Samuel Beer, *British Politics in the Collectivist Age*, New York, 1965.
148. David Howell, *British Social Democracy: A Study in Development and Decay*, London, 1976.
149. David Coates, *The Labour Party and the Struggle for Socialism*, Cambridge, 1975.
150. Barry Hindness, *The Decline of Working-class Politics*, London, 1971.
151. Thomas Forester, *The Labour Party and the Working Class*, London, 1976. Forester needs to be tempered, too, by reference to Asa Briggs and John Saville, eds., *Essays in Labour History*, *1918–1939*, Hamden, Conn., 1977, where a major theme is the gulf of misunderstanding that separated the official Labour and trade union leadership from its mass base.
152. Ben Pimlott, *Labour and the Left in the 1930s*, Cambridge, 1977.
153. Adele Massardo Maiello, *Laburismo e Russia Sovietica, 1917–1924*, Milan, 1974.
154. Lewis Chester, Stephen Fay, and Hugo Young, *The Zinoiev Letter*, Philadelphia, 1968.
155. Gabriel Gorodetsky, *The Precarious Truce*, Cambridge, 1977.
156. Daniel F. Calhoun, *The United Front: The TUC and the Russians, 1923–1928*, Cambridge, 1976.
157. Stephen Haseler, *The Gaitskellites: Revisionism in the British Labour Party, 1951–64*, London, 1969.
158. Ross McKibbin, *The Evolution of the Labour Party, 1910–1924*, New York, 1974.
159. Rodney Barker, *Education and Politics, 1900–1951: A Study of the Labour Party*, New York, 1972.
160. Norman Mackenzie, ed., *The Letters of Sidney and Beatrice Webb*: vol. 1, *Apprenticeships 1873–1892*; vol. 2, *Partnership 1892–1912*; vol. 3, *Pilgrimage 1912–1947*; Cambridge, 1978.
161. Richard Crossman, *The Diaries of a Cabinet Minister:* vol. 1, *Minister of Housing, 1964–66*, London, 1975; vol. 2, *Lord President of the Council and Leader of the House of Commons 1966–68*, London, 1976; vol. 3, *Secretary of State for Social Services, 1968–70*, London, 1977. Crossman's *The Backbench Diaries*, ed. Janet Morgan, were published in London, 1981.
162. Janet P. Morgan, *The House of Lords and the Labour Government, 1964–1970*, New York, 1975.
163. P. A. Bromhead, *The House of Lords and Contemporary Britain*, London, 1958.
164. Henry Pelling, *The British Communist Party: A Historical Profile*, London, 1975. See, on Soviet control, Walter Kendall, *The Revolutionary Movement in Britain 1900–1921: The Origins of British Communism*, London, 1969, and on the composition of the Communist party membership, Leslie J. MacFarlane, *The British Communist Party: Its Origin and Development until 1929*, London, 1966. The official history of the Communist party is James Klugman, *History of the Communist Party in Great Britain*: vol. 1, *Formation and Early Years, 1919–1925*, New York, 1968; vol. 2, *The General Strike*, New York, 1969.
165. Stuart MacIntyre, *A Proletarian Science: Marxism in Britain, 1917–1933*, London, 1980.
166. Paul-Wolfgang Herrman, *Die Communist Party of Great Britain: Untersuchungen zur geschicht-*

lichen Entwicklung, Organisation, Ideologie und Politik der CPGB von 1920–1970, Meisenheim am Glan, 1976.

167. Robert Benewick, *Political Violence and Public Order: A Study of British Fascism*, London, 1969.

168. Robert Skidelsky, *Oswald Mosley*, London, 1975.

169. Patrick Renshaw, *The General Strike*, London, 1975; G. A. Phillips, *The General Strike: The Politics of Industrial Conflict*, London, 1976.

170. Alastair Reid and Steven Tolliday, "The General Strike, 1926," *HJ* 20, 1977: 1001–1012.

171. See, for example, most of the essays in Jeffrey Skelley, ed., *The General Strike, 1926*, London, 1976.

172. Anthony Mason, *The General Strike in the North East*, Hull, 1970.

173. Margaret Morris, *The General Strike*, Harmondsworth, 1976.

174. William D. Muller, *The 'Kept Men'? The First Century of Trade Union Representation in the British House of Commons, 1874–1975*, Atlantic Highlands, N.J., 1977.

175. Alan Clinton, *The Trade Union Rank and File: Trade Councils in Britain, 1900–40*, Manchester, 1977.

176. Gerald Dorfman, *Wage Politics in Britain, 1945–1967: Government vs. the TUC*, Ames, Iowa, 1973.

177. Robert Taylor, *The Fifth Estate: Britain's Unions in Seventies*, London, 1978.

178. Rodger Charles, *The Development of Industrial Relations in Britain 1911–1939: Studies in the Evolution of Collective Bargaining at National and Industrial Level*, London, 1972.

179. Kevin Hawkins, *British Industrial Relations, 1945–1975*, London, 1976.

180. Stephen Blank, *Industry and Government in Britain: The Federation of British Industries in Politics, 1945–65*, Farnborough, 1973.

181. H. W. Richardson and D. W. Aldcroft, *Building the British Economy between the Wars*, London, 1968; Derek W. Aldcroft, "Economic Growth in Britain in the Inter-war Years: A Reassessment," *EcHR* 20, 1967: 311–326; idem, *The Inter-war Economy: Britain, 1919–1939*, New York, 1970. Aldcroft has also collaborated with Neil K. Buxton to edit *British Industry between the Wars: Instability and Industrial Development, 1919–1939*, London, 1980, which explores a variety of manufacturing problems between the wars. See also *The Slump: Society and Politics during the Depression*, London, 1978, by John Stevenson and Chris Cook, which coolly and judiciously explodes some of the myths about the 1930s. They too conclude that, for those in work, the decade was one of rising living standards and new levels of consumption upon which a considerable degree of economic growth was based. Most people in Britain were better off in 1939 than they had been a decade before.

182. J. A. Dowie, "Growth in the Inter-war Period: Some More Arithmetic," *EcHR* 21, 1968: 93–112.

183. D. E. Moggridge, *The Return to Gold, 1925: The Formulation of Economic Policy and Its Critics*, Cambridge, 1969; idem, *British Monetary Policy, 1924–1931: The Norman Conquest of $4.86*, Cambridge, 1972.

184. R. A. Sayers, *The Bank of England, 1891–1944*, 3 vols., New York, 1976.

185. In the introduction to Sidney Pollard, ed., *The Gold Standard and Employment Policies between the Wars*, London, 1970.

186. Susan Howson, Domestic Monetary Management in Britain 1919–38, Cambridge, 1975.

187. W. J. Reader, *Imperial Chemical Industries: A History*: vol. 1, *The Forerunners, 1870–1926*, London, 1970; vol. 2, *1926–1952*, London, 1975. Another substantial contribution in this area is David Fieldhouse, *Unilever Overseas: The Anatomy of a Multi-national*, Stanford, 1978.

188. Leslie Hannah, *The Rise of the Corporate Economy: The British Experience*, Baltimore, 1976. See also idem, "Managerial Innovation and the Rise of the Large-scale Company in Interwar

Britain," *EcHR* 27, 1974: 252–270, which shows how various managerial developments were both an inspiration and a response to the wave of mergers that characterized the 1920s and 1930s.

189. R. Kelf-Cohen, *British Nationalisation, 1945–1973*, London, 1973.

190. The other recent such study by R. Kelf-Cohen is *Twenty Years of Nationalisation: The British Experience*, London, 1969.

191. Richard Pryke, *Public Enterprise in Practice: The British Experience of Nationalization over Two Decades*, London, 1971.

192. Bentley B. Gilbert, *The Evolution of National Insurance in Great Britain: The Origins of the Welfare State*, London, 1966.

193. Ibid., *British Social Policy, 1914–1939*, Ithaca, 1970.

194. Arthur Marwick, "The Labour Party and the Welfare State in Britain, 1900–1948," *AHR* 73, 1967: 380–403.

195. Kathleen Woodruffe, "The Making of the Welfare State in England: A Summary of Its Origin and Development," *Journal of Social History* 1, 1968: 303–324. William Beveridge's influence on welfare policy is effectively outlined by José Harris, whose *William Beveridge: A Biography*, Oxford, 1972, and New York, 1977, is likely to be the authoritative account for a long time to come.

196. A. F. Young, *Social Services in British Industry*, London, 1968.

197. John Mills, *Growth and Welfare: A New Policy for Britain*, London, 1972.

198. Paul Addison, *The Road to 1945*, London, 1975.

199. Harris, *William Beveridge*.

200. Angus Calder, *The People's War: Britain—1939–1945*, New York, 1969.

201. Asa Briggs, *The History of Broadcasting in the United Kingdom*, vol. 3, *The War of Words*, London, 1970.

202. Peter Calvocoressi, *Top Secret Ultra*, London, 1980.

203. Nigel Nicolson, *Alex: The Life of Field Marshall Earl Alexander of Tunis*, New York, 1973; Alan Chalfont, *Montgomery of Alamein*, New York, 1976.

204. Stanley L. Falk, *Seventy Days to Singapore*, New York, 1975, is such a superior campaign history.

205. Robert Wright, *The Man Who Won the Battle of Britain*, New York, 1969.

206. Arthur J. Marder, *From the Dreadnought to Scapa Flow: The Royal Navy in the Fisher Era, 1904–1919:* vol. 4, *1917: Year of Crisis*, London, 1969; vol. 5, *Victory and Aftermath, 1918–19*, London, 1970.

207. Stephen Raskill, *Naval Policy between the Wars:* vol. 1, *The Period of Anglo-American Antagonism, 1919–1929*, London, 1968; vol. 2, *The Period of Reluctant Rearmament, 1930–1939*, London, 1976.

208. C. J. Bartlett, *The Long Retreat: A Short History of British Defence Policy, 1945–70*, London, 1972.

209. R. N. Rosecrance, *Defence of the Realm: British Strategy in the Nuclear Epoch*, New York, 1968. See also Andrew J. Pierre, *Nuclear Politics: The British Experience with an Independent Strategic Force, 1939–1970*, New York, 1972, which makes clear the reasons—above all the need to have some influence over the United States—that Britain persisted with a strategy "appropriate to a great power when she had ceased to be one."

210. Ceri Peach, *West Indian Migration to Britain: A Social Geography*, London, 1968.

211. Sheila Patterson, *Immigration and Race Relations in Britain, 1960–1967*, London, 1969.

212. E. J. Rose in association with Nicholas Deakin and Mark Abrams, Valerie Jackson, Maurice Peston, A. H. Vanags, Brian Cohen, Julia Gaitskell, Paul Ward, *Colour and Citizenship: A Report on British Race Relations*, London, 1969. Some valuable recent confirmation of many of

their perceptions may be found in a series of essays by a number of professional anthropologists. See James L. Watson, ed., *Between Two Cultures: Migrants and Minorities in Britain*, London, 1977.

213. Benjamin W. Heineman, *The Politics of the Powerless: A Study of the Campaign against Racial Discrimination*, London, 1972.

214. C. J. Bartlett, *A History of Postwar Britain, 1945–1974*, London, 1977.

215. Peter Calvocoressi, *The British Experience, 1945–75*, New York, 1978.

216. Mary Proudfoot, *British Government and Politics, 1951–1970: A Study of an Affluent Society*, London, 1974.

217. Michael Stewart, *The Jekyll and Hyde Years: Politics and Economics since 1964*, London, 1977.

Scottish History since 1966

Maurice Lee, Jr.

"It's our oil!"—and everyone, including, conspicuously, the politicians in Westminster, is very much aware of the existence of Scotland these days, far more so than at the time of the writing of the article on Scottish history for the earlier *Changing Views*.[1] The shrugs and pitying looks which used to greet the statement that one was interested in Scottish history, and actually did research in it, have vanished; if it is not yet exactly modish to be a historian of Scotland, it is, at least, respectable. And since 1966 there has been an enormous increase in the amount of excellent work in virtually all fields of Scottish history, including a number of very valuable reference works.[2] This increase is not beholden to the growth of Scottish nationalist feeling or the political power of the Scottish National Party (SNP), though those phenomena have helped Scottish historians to find both publishers and readers.

The most important single publication to appear in the past decade is the four-volume *Edinburgh History of Scotland*, under the general editorship of Gordon Donaldson, who wrote one of the volumes.[3] They are all, in their differing ways, excellent; all have some weaknesses which do not much detract from their usefulness. A. A. M. Duncan picks his way with admirable caution through the minefield of prefeudal history and interrupts his narrative at the death of William the Lion in 1214 to supply a series of brilliant and original topical chapters on high-medieval Scotland. The material on social and economic history is especially good. Ranald Nicholson's chapters on the fourteenth century are extremely interesting. He thinks much less well of Robert Bruce than does Bruce's biographer G. W. S. Barrow, and he does not accept Barrow's assessment of the place of the community of the realm in Bruce's achievements. He reiterates the interpretation of the aggressive policy of Edward III prior to his involvement in France (spelled out in an earlier monograph) and also repeats in most persuasive fashion his favorable assessment of David II, which he and Bruce Webster made simultaneously in articles published in 1966 and which have effectively reversed the previously unfavorable view of that king.[4] When he gets to the fifteenth century, Nicholson supplies us with a long political narrative which is rather traditional, save for the persuasive interpretation of James II as the aggressor against the swollen power of the house of Douglas. The two volumes on modern Scotland are only about half the length of the medieval volumes and therefore far more compressed. Professor Donaldson supplies an interesting and very unflattering view of James V (and, in passing, of Queen Elizabeth); the central section of his work, an analytical account of the reign of James VI, is masterful. William Ferguson also is at his best on the period of his specialty, the eighteenth century, which occupies over half of his book; his analysis of the nonpolitical aspects of the period is especially fine. These four volumes will stand as the standard, large-scale account of Scottish history for the next generation at least.

It is not customary to discuss general surveys in an article of this kind, but since no good brief ones existed before, mention should be made of Rosalind Mitchison's *A History of Scotland*, an extremely skillful narrative which reflects the author's interest in social and economic affairs, and Gordon Donaldson's *Scotland: The Shaping of a Nation*, a topic survey which stresses political and constitutional development. Both these books reflect their authors' skepticism regarding certain aspects of the current nationalist movement. Donaldson has also done *The Scots Overseas*, a general overview of emigration from Scotland, its causes and consequences, the best chapters of which are those dealing with the years before 1800. Finally, there is T. C. Smout's *A History of the Scottish People 1560–1830*, a really remarkable synthesis which gets away from what Professor Duncan likes to call "king-history" and which is especially good on demography and in its emphasis on the social impact of the Reformation—Smout's starting date is no accident.[5]

The explosion of interest in Scottish history has not spread to historiography. There has been little more than a handful of articles, the most significant of which are two by T. I. Rae, on George MacKenzie and Thomas Innes, and on Drummond of Hawthornden.[6] The badly needed large-scale history of Scottish historical writing awaits its author.

In medieval history perhaps the most interesting volume to appear in the past decade, apart from those in the *Edinburgh History*, is G. W. S. Barrow's *The Kingdom of the Scots*. This is a collection of essays, all but one of which had appeared elsewhere; the new one, on shires and thanes in prefeudal Scotland, makes a strong case for a linkage between the two in the tenth and eleventh centuries. Throughout these articles Barrow is concerned to show that Scottish institutional development was similar to that of other western European states, that royal initiative was crucial, and that the development of such institutions as the justiciar should not be denigrated as "inferior" to that of the Angevins merely because it was different: the form the office took in Scotland was appropriate to the Scottish structure. Professor Barrow has also contributed *The Acts of William I* to the Regesta Regum Scottorum series; his introduction supplies the best account we have of the political career of William the Lion, a man of dogged energy and, frequently enough, woeful political judgment, and a detailed analysis of the work-ings and personnel of his administraion.[7] This volume is an excellent example of the fruitfulness of the continued work on governmental records which has been the central development in medieval Scottish history in the past decade. Professor Duncan, for example, is the editor of the volume on the acts of Robert Bruce for the Regesta series; his work on that record prompted a valuable review article of Professor Barrow's biography which takes a far less favorable view of Bruce's behavior before 1306 than does Barrow, and two pieces on the Declaration of Arbroath which regard it less as an expression of community spirit than as a tacti-cal step in Bruce's search for allies against Edward II,[8] as well as a careful factual account of the Scottish Parliament to 1331.[9] As for Professor Barrow, he does not seem to be ordering any sackcloth from his tailor; he has recently restated his view of the importance of Lothian to Bruce's cause, as opposed to Nicholson's interpretation in the *Edinburgh History*. He has also provided a cogent analysis of the steadily increasing English severity in the wake of their conquests in Scot-land, from the comparatively lenient behavior of Edward I in 1296 to the large-scale confiscations and repeated devastation inflicted by Edward III in the 1330s, a severity caused by the growing English conviction that the Scots were incorrigi-ble.[10] The controversies which have swirled around the reigns of the two Bruces are apt to continue for some time.[11]

In later medieval history the most interesting recent work is Jennifer Brown's *Scottish Society in the Fifteenth Century*, a frankly revisionist attempt to combat the traditional view that the period is one of decline, characterized by conflict be-tween the crown and the magnates. The title is misleading; the book deals with far more than social structure and social history. It concentrates on the first three Jameses and takes the line that the prevalent gloomy picture is owing chiefly to uncritical acceptance of biased sixteenth-century chroniclers like Pitscottie, espe-cially in connection with James III. Like most revisionist arguments, this one is occasionally pushed too far, but many of the chapters are uncommonly interest-ing, especially those by N. A. T. Macdougall on the sources, Brown on the exer-cise of power, S. G. E. Lythe on the economy, and I. B. Cowan on the church. An article worth reading in connection with Brown's chapter is A. Grant's "The Development of the Scottish Peerage," in which he argues persuasively that the "lords of parliament" as a distinctive layer of the peerage emerged in the 1440s, during the minority of James II, not, as had previously been thought, in conse-quence of the statute of 1428.[12]

The religious history of the fifteenth century has been the subject of two un-usually interesting articles.[13] David McRoberts argues that the character of Scot-tish nationalism changed in the fifteenth century, from the negative anti-English feeling of the fourteenth century to one of positive pride in Scotland, and that churchmen had a major part in creating this new feeling. The interest in the cult of Scottish saints considerably increased, for example; and starting with James III, the kings began to make pilgrimages to their shrines. Yet, as both McRoberts and Leslie MacFarlane point out, James III did not welcome the elevation of the see of St. Andrews to an archbishopric because it looked to be a move which would make it easier for the papacy to interfere in Scottish ecclesiastical politics. MacFarlane's analysis of the primacy leads him to the conclusion that the office was purely political, did the church no good, and brought about no reform and further, that the archbishops, except for David Beaton, never even got control over the hierarchy. In addition to these two articles there have been a number of studies of individual dioceses,[14] and an interesting introduction by Ian Cowan to a collection of Scottish supplications to Rome which shows that the crown and lay patrons effectively controlled appointments to church office as early as the reign of James I and that the Indult of 1487 simply recognized a fait accompli.[15]

The financial practices of James III, who was lazy and greedy, and James IV, who was hard working and extravagant, especially in connection with feudal casualties, have been the subject of two ground-breaking articles.[16] Both kings, especially James IV, whose life-style became especially costly after his marriage in 1503, did as Henry VII did and squeezed all they could out of their positions as feudal superiors. One of Athol Murray's series of pioneering studies of the administrative history of the central government, his account of the development of the office of comptroller from its beginnings to the death of James III, belongs in this period. Murray's skill at piecing together coherent accounts from records which are sometimes very fragmentary is remarkable; it is to be hoped that he will continue this work and eventually collect his articles in a single volume.[17] One other piece of administrative history should be mentioned here, T. I. Rae's *The Administration of the Scottish Frontier 1513–1603*, a careful account, first of the administrative machinery itself, and then of how it functioned during the ninety years in question. This is a first-class piece of work which shows what can be done by mining record sources.[18] Denys Hay, "England, Scotland, and Europe: The Problem of the Frontier," is a brilliant sketch of the nature of the border. A different sort of book on border history is George McD. Fraser's *The Steel Bonnets*.[19] Fraser is best known as the editor of the memoirs of Harry Flashman, whose behavior was rather like that of some of the types of ruffian Fraser describes in a lively piece of popular history.

That venerable industry, the production of biographies of Mary Queen of Scots, has flourished mightily in the past decade and, against all the odds, has produced two fine pieces of work. It is hardly necessary to say anything at this late date about Antonia Fraser's celebrated biography, save that it is long, exculpatory, underestimates, as Mary did, the importance of Protestantism as an ideology, and has a really splendid account of Mary's upbringing in France. The best available

assessment of Mary's career is that of the dean of Scottish historians of the sixteenth century, Gordon Donaldson, who is not overly sympathetic but argues that
Mary had more support at the time of her overthrow than had previously been
supposed. Professor Donaldson has also provided the first full-length account of
Mary's so-called trial at the hands of the English government in 1569, written
with his usual impeccable scholarship, in which he takes the line that both Mary
and her accusers had unclean hands in the matter of Darnley's death and that
Elizabeth's solution was altogether political. One of the results of Mary's deposition and trial was a wave of propaganda literature on both sides which has been
analyzed by a literary scholar, J. E. Phillips. Marcus Merriman has provided a
detailed study of the Scottish collaborators with England, mostly border lairds,
during England's "rough wooing" of Mary in the 1540s. The queen's celebrated
antagonist John Knox has also found two biographers. Jasper Ridley has some
interesting ideas but displays a shaky command of the sources. Stanford Reid's
account is lively and readable but has nothing much new to say.[20]

The political history of the reign of James VI has not attracted much attention
of late, save for an amicable dispute between this writer and Jennifer (Brown)
Wormald over James's attitude toward the aristocracy and their place in government, and for a reassessment by the former of James's methods of government
after his departure for England.[21] There has been one significant contribution to
Jacobean intellectual history, Arthur Williamson's *Scottish National Consciousness
in the Reign of James VI*, more of a series of essays than a book, dealing with the
reactions of Scottish intellectuals, mostly clerics, lawyers, and humanists, to the
two great events of the later sixteenth century, the coming of Protestantism and
the prospective (and actual) union of the crowns.[22]

But the reign of Charles I and the Civil War is a different story. Here the
outstanding work is that of David Stevenson, who has written the first full-scale
account of Scotland and the Civil War, in two volumes which take the story from
1637 to 1651.[23] In these volumes Stevenson has been more concerned to work out
the details of the story than to provide large amounts of analysis; his intepretive
summary chapters are clear, cautious, and unstartling. His basic position is that
politics rather than religion was at the root of the matter; at the end of the first
volume, the analogy that he draws for Scotland is with Catalonia rather than the
Netherlands. Stevenson has also written a number of noteworthy articles which
pull together, and add to, some of the material in the two books; especially good is
the series which describes the emergence of the radical party in the kirk, its strategy and tactics, and the impact it had on society.[24] Throughout, Stevenson stresses
the conservative nature of the Scottish revolution. It was an aristocratic affair, and
the upper class retained its grip without too much difficulty until after the defeat
of the king—a point on which he differs with Ian Cowan, who argues that the
nobility had to struggle hard to keep control.[25] It was not until very late in the

day, with the split between the radical clerical leadership and the aristocracy over the Engagement, that the radicals began to interest themselves in the plight of the poor. Even the intervention in England was defensive in nature, to protect the gains already won by preventing any possibility of a royalist victory. By contrast, Lawrence Kaplan, echoing the view expressed in S. A. Burrell's well-known article, is inclined to assign far more weight to the Scots' religious vision; they intervened in England because they wished to impose their version of God's church upon England.[26] There have been biographies of some of the outstanding figures of this period, including several of Montrose; that of E. J. Cowan is interesting because Cowan is more concerned with Montrose's political ideas, in which he finds more consistency than perhaps is there, than with his battles.[27] The politics of the decade of English military rule have been the subject of two articles on protectorate parliaments, one of which tends to challenge, the other to support, the standard view that those who sat for Scottish seats, whether Scotsmen or Englishmen, served the English interest.[28] Finally, F. D. Dow's *Cromwellian Scotland* is a very detailed administrative history of this decade, told from the occupiers' point of view.[29]

One book on a post–Civil War figure deserves mention, Rosalind Marshall's *The Days of Duchess Anne*, a study of the career and life-style of the duchess of Hamilton, based on an unrivaled knowledge of the Hamilton archives. The emphasis of the study is on how the duchess spent her money, ran her house, and raised her children; but inevitably there is a good deal about politics as well. Otherwise, the political history of the Restoration period continues to suffer from neglect; apart from Rosalind Mitchison's perceptive though generalized essay in G. Menzies, editor's *The Scottish Nation* and an informative but narrowly focused article on the parliamentary session of 1673, nothing of consequence has appeared.[30]

One of the major effects of the upsurge of nationalist sentiment in Scotland in the past decade has been a great deal of writing about the union of 1707, its causes and its consequences. The first casualty of this reappraisal is the traditional Whiggish view that the union was inevitable, necessary, and in some sense "right." Broadly speaking, there are now two camps. One is composed of the nationalists; their leader, William Ferguson, has continued his attack, first made in an article published in 1964, on the determinist school of historians of the union, which, he argues, almost nobody wanted and which was the result of a lot of corruption and shoddy political maneuvering.[31] The argument is impressive but is marred by Ferguson's rather unnecessary assaults on those who do not agree with him and, more seriously, by his failure to give sufficient weight to those factors working in favor of union, such as dislike of Catholicism. P. W. J. Riley, having written a detailed administrative study of the consequences of the union, has turned his attention to its origins; he shares Ferguson's view that shabby political maneuvering is the true explanation of the union.[32] The Scottish legislation of 1703, which has usually been regarded as reflecting aggrieved nationalist feeling, was, in Riley's view, the product of internecine warfare among the Scottish factions themselves. The real key to the passage of the treaty, Riley argues, lay in London, not Edinburgh: once the various English factions agreed that union was desirable and necessary, a Scottish majority could be constructed for it—an argument which hinges upon an even less flattering view of Scottish politicians than Ferguson's. The English factions came to this agreement because they saw that the Scottish Parliament, with its conflicting, magnate-led factions, had becomes unmanageable; the union was devised to bring Scottish politicians back under control, and it did.

The principal target of Ferguson's attack is T. C. Smout, whose views are most succinctly expressed in his article "The Road to Union."[33] That road, Smout argues, was paved with economic considerations—not only expectations, but also contemplation of the catastrophic consequences of separation, since Scotland was now dependent on the English market for its major exports. Smout finds the bribery argument unpersuasive, both because it is hard to prove that anyone's vote was changed by a bribe and because England accepted Scottish amendments in the final stages of the treaty-making process, which would have been unnecessary with a bought majority. Most other recent writers on the union, such as David Daiches,[34] tend to follow Smout's line of argument; but the end of this particular controversy is nowhere in sight.

Difference of opinion over the union has helped to stimulate interest in the eighteenth century. There has been a flood of writing on this period in the past decade, especially on various aspects of the Scottish Enlightenment. Pride of place should go to the fine collection of essays edited by N. T. Phillipson and Rosalind Mitchison, *Scotland's Age of Improvement*.[35] The emphasis of these essays, which deal with the growth of political stability, with various aspects of the role of the gentry, and with intellectual history, is on Scotland and the wider world; there is nothing here about the Jacobites. Parenthetically, it might be noted that the Bonnie Prince Charlie industry has fallen on evil days. There has been some of the usual nonsense, a competent if unoriginal biography, and one pioneering piece of work, John Gibson's *Ships of the '45*, which discusses the naval activity of both sides and shows that the French contribution was more substantial than has usually been supposed.[36] It was in his laudatory foreword to this book that the late Sir James Fergusson made his celebrated remark that "for many years now it has been my conviction that any further publication of narratives about the '45 as well as of biographies of Mary Queen of Scots and Robert Burns ought to be banned by statute under heavy penalities." Adding Montrose, and with the exceptions herein noted, Amen.

Since the road to union was paved with economic expectations, the economic consequences have been carefully canvassed of late. The traditional view that the union, by extending to Scotland the privileges of the Navigation Act, was ultimately responsible for her undoubted prosperity in the later eighteenth century, has come under challenge. In the view of R. H. Campbell, the union did not provide an automatic means of economic development; it was at best "a necessary but not a sufficient cause of economic growth."[37] To Bruce Lenman, who subscribes to Ferguson's view of the union, it was not even that; it was economic growth which made the union tolerable.[38] On the other hand, studies of two individual industries which benefited greatly from colonial markets suggest that the revisionists may have pushed their gloomy thesis a bit too far.[39]

The social roots of the Enlightenment have been the principal concern of Nicholas Phillipson, who accepts Professor Smout's interpretation and in fact declares that the Scottish elite deliberately provoked the crisis over the union in order to solve an otherwise insoluble economic problem. Having won their victory, they then had to learn to live with their success and also to preserve their identity and prevent the Jacobites from monopolizing nationalist sentiment. This they did by founding societies for economic improvement and by the capture, and to some degree the remoulding, of those institutions left to Scotland after the union: the bar, the church, and the university system.[40] J. R. R. Christie is not convinced that this interpretation explains the emergence of so many eminent scientists in this period; he emphasizes the key role of the Edinburgh medical school and its faculty in linking up the elite and the intellectuals and also the successful attempt to interest the upper classes in science by pointing out the military benefits of mathematics and turning chemistry into a "liberal art" to attract gentlemen.[41] Two of the remarkable polymaths of this age have received biographies: Lord Monboddo, a judge who wrote books on the origin of language and on ancient metaphysics, and Lord Kames, also a judge, who wrote on almost everything—law, history, aesthetics, education, farming, even physics.[42] Principal Robertson has been shown to have had feet made at least partly of clay: he obtained his post, and the appointment as historiographer royal for Scotland at a considerable advance over his clerical salary, by promising his patron, Lord Bute, to write a history of England more Christian than David Hume's, and then not doing it.[43]

Writing on post–eighteenth-century political history, apart from some work on nineteenth-century parties and electoral politics,[44] has, not surprisingly, centered on nationalism. The major work is the full-scale account by H. J. Hanham, *Scottish Nationalism*, which is especially good on the nineteenth and twentieth centuries and is judicious and well balanced, perhaps because Hanham is neither English nor Scots, but a New Zealander by origin who spent some years on the faculty of the University of Edinburgh.[45] A much more controversial book, because of its different balance, is Christopher Harvie's *Scotland and Nationalism*, a survey which begins in 1707 but half of which deals with the period since 1945.[46] Harvie concentrates on the elites, whom he divides into "red" Scots who fully accepted the union because it gave them a broader field in which to operate, and the "black" Scots, the people who dominated rural and small-town Scotland and who wanted nothing so much as to be left alone to maintain their sway. The heyday of the "red" Scots ran from the later eighteenth century to perhaps the 1860s; then, very gradually, inspired in part by the Irish example, in part by those economic troubles which made the "greater Scotland" of the empire a less attractive surrogate than it once had been, there began the agitation for home rule, which suffered a great many vicissitudes and has reached its peak in the past decade. Harvie's account raises as many questions as it answers, and its New Left bias is not always helpful, but it is extraordinarily stimulating. Finally, there is J. G. Kellas's *Modern Scotland: The Nation since 1870*, a careful description of those institutions peculiar to Scotland and an assessment of the extent to which each contributed to the maintenance of Scottish identity.[47]

There are serious difficulties in writing distinctively Scottish political or general history for the century and a half which extends from the end of the Dundas era to the rise of the SNP; it tends to become the history of North Britain. In economic and social history, however, the story is altogether different. Here the majority of the work lies in the postunion period, and a great deal has been done, mostly of a traditional kind; as one economic historian wrote in 1976, the methodological innovations of the "new economic history" have made little progress in Scotland.[48] In addition to Lenman's general economic history already cited, a comprehensive if somewhat diffuse brief survey of Scottish industrial history by R. H. Campbell,[49] and a variety of sources published by the Scottish History Society, there have been a number of studies of particular branches of economic activity. Some of them are pioneering, like M. L. Anderson's enormous and not always systematic study of Scottish forestry and the careful, scholarly work on the coal industry by Baron Duckham and on fishing by Malcolm Gray. Others replace earlier works, like S. G. Checkland's excellent history of Scottish banking, a book which is not merely an institutional analysis but which also deals with the contributions of banking to the fluctuations in the economy.[50] Still others will, perhaps, provide the materials for larger synthetic studies, like the recent work on various aspects of the textile industry.[51] There have also been two significant pieces of regional history, Bruce Lenman's study of the eastcoast ports in the period from 1800 to the outbreak of the Second World War and Anthony Slaven's work on the west of Scotland since 1750, a book which is the first of a projected series of regional socioeconomic histories.[52] It is in fact mostly about economic development and is especially good on the cotton industry; Slaven rather neglects the social consequences of this development, save for some discussion of urbanization. The book raises the question of the soundness of the regional approach; it is difficult to discuss industrialization in the west without reference to the rest of Scotland.

In the preunion period there are a few articles worth mention: J. B. Dow's ground-breaking work on Scottish trade with Sweden in the sixteenth century, culled from a doctoral dissertation left unfinished by the author's tragic early death,[53] and a revision article on the economy under James VI by T. M. Devine and S. G. E. Lythe, which for the most part reinforces rather than revises the conclusions in Lythe's well-known monograph but points to work that needs doing on Anglo-Scottish trade, which was certainly larger than had been thought.[54] Professor Lythe has also been the recipient of a most interesting *Festschrift* in which Devine's contribution—the only one, curiously, from Lythe's own period, the sixteenth and seventeenth centuries—argues that Scottish trade during the period of the Cromwellian union did recover from the dislocations of the 1640s and that the reasons for the unpopularity of that union must be sought elsewhere.[55] In the modern period, one area which received a good deal of attention in this *Festschrift* is the comparatively new field of business history, which has also seen the publication of a collection of essays edited by P. L. Payne and some studies of individual firms and industries, of the working class, and of Scottish investment in the United States.[56] Two works deserve special mention. Alexander Wilson's *The Chartist Movement in Scotland* relates Chartism very skillfully to its social milieu and points out that because the Chartists were diverted by the explosive religious situation which led to the Disruption and because they became so deeply involved in the repeal of the corn laws, they identified Tories and landowners as the enemy and so never focused their attention on the ills of industrialism.[57] R. Q. Gray's *The Labour Aristocracy in Victorian Edinburgh* bears out this analysis; the unionists he studies overwhelmingly adopted the ethic of Samuel Smiles.[58]

A second major area of interest has been the economic development of Glasgow. T. C. Smout has expertly analyzed "The Glasgow Merchant Community in the Seventeenth Century."[59] T. M. Devine has concentrated on the rise and especially the fall of the tobacco trade in a major book and two significant articles.[60] Devine follows Jacob Price in stressing the importance of the French market to the Scots before the American Revolution; the abrupt elimination of their source of supply was less damaging to the tobacco lords than was previously thought, Devine argues, both because they had a substantial stock on hand owing to the sluggish continental market after 1773 and because they had already begun to diversify their investments, going into industries which were about to expand with the coming of the Industrial Revolution. Devine's conclusion is that the American Revolution was not, as previously supposed, a watershed in Scottish economic history. There is also a brief and thoughtful study of the social and economic pattern of life in Glasgow in the last century by S. G. Checkland, *The*

Upas Tree: Glasgow, 1875–1975, a book which speaks not only to the history of Glasgow but to that of all large industrial cities.[61]

The Industrial Revolution has been the subject of three articles of considerable interest, Wray Vamplew's careful account of the impact of the railroads; T. C. Smout's discussion of the crucial importance of the landowners in the encouragement of economic, particularly rural industrial, development, especially in the middle years of the eighteenth century; and R. H. Campbell's revisionist piece on the revolution as a whole.[62] Campbell points out that Henry Hamilton's classic account of the Industrial Revolution in Scotland dealt with the Scottish aspects of those developments which were common to Britain as a whole rather than with uniquely Scottish problems, which, Campbell argues, should receive more consideration.

Among the desiderata on Campbell's list is more study of agricultural development, particularly on the local level; and some work of this sort is beginning to appear. Especially interesting is R. A. Dodgshon's study of two border counties, which leads him to the conclusion that the origins of the effort to improve Scottish agriculture must be pushed back considerably, perhaps as far as the later seventeenth century.[63] This conclusion is reinforced in Ian Whyte's important *Agriculture and Society in Seventeenth Century Scotland*, an immensely scholarly full-scale assault on the accepted theory of Scottish agricultural development.[64] This theory holds that the centuries-long period of agricultural stagnation ended only in the eighteenth century, thanks in part to the union of 1707 and in larger part to the efforts of a handful of far-sighted improving landlords. This picture, Whyte argues, was painted by the improvers themselves and has been uncritically accepted by subsequent historians who have not taken the trouble to examine the manuscript sources. Like many other revisionists, Whyte pushes his theory too far, but he has conclusively shown that, after 1660, virtually all those conditions the eighteenth-century improvers applauded themselves for introducing could be found in the lowlands in some places, and some in many places.

The increasing availability of the estate papers of the great landowning families has helped to fuel the growing interest in rural history.[65] The most spectacular example is the amount of work which has emerged on the vast Sutherland estate and the Highland clearances. R. J. Adam has edited the papers and provided a long interpretive introduction, and Eric Richards has mined them for his assessment of various aspects of the problem.[66] The Sutherland case is especially interesting, not only because of the huge size of the estate, but because the countess of Sutherland and her husband, the enormously rich marquis of Stafford, had the money to carry out their projects, which were characterized by paternalistic benevolence, no consultation with the people who were cleared, and in the end, economic disaster. Richards believes that a good deal of forethought went into the planning; Adam's view is that it was rather more haphazard. They agree that the intention was not to depopulate the estate but simply to move the tenants from the areas designed for sheep runs to coastal settlements, where they would be retrained to other, more productive employment. These ventures failed, however, and the people either emigrated or became crofters.

Richards and Adam have approached the economic and social history of the Highlands from the point of view of the landowners and their agents. A. J. Youngson approaches it from that of the bureaucrats.[67] The prospect of depopulation worried them as well as some of the landowners; Youngson gives an admirable account of the theories on which they operated and a melancholy one of their failures. An altogether different point of view informs the absorbing work of James Hunter on the crofting community.[68] Hunter, writing from the point of view of the crofters themselves, documents the long, dismal story of exploitation which began, in his view, with the conversion of the clan chiefs into estate managers in the later eighteenth century. The crofters were slow to react to their wretched treatment; when they did, their first gesture was to join the Free Church, whose ministers sympathized with them as against the landlord and his appointee, the incumbent of the established benefice. Finally, in the 1880s, came violence, inspired partly by the Irish example, partly by the landlords' conversion of sheep runs into deer parks with the collapse of the wool market in the 1870s. Since the passage of the Crofters Act of 1886, there has been improvement—Hunter feels that the agitation of the 1880s produced more substantial results than does H. J. Hanham[69]—but not all that much; and Hunter is not optimistic that the discovery of oil will rehabilitate the Highlands. The comparison he sees is with the disastrous aftermath of the kelp boom in the 1820s, with the oil companies behaving, when the oil runs out, as selfishly as the landlords did then.

Finally, one general survey deserves mention, Alexander Fenton's *Scottish Country Life*, a work which, although brief, provides a detailed and readable account of the practical activities of Scottish farmers, in all their variety, from the beginning down to the present century.[70] The book's topical organization makes for some repetition, and Fenton is more concerned with the actual physical processes of farming than with the society of his rural communities; but his grasp of agricultural technology is unequaled, and he is not afraid to draw general conclusions from his material.

In social history the most important works to appear in recent years are Professor Smout's survey, already mentioned, and a pioneering work on demography, Michael Flinn, editor's *Scottish Population History from the 17th Century to the 1930s*, a cooperative venture whose contributors include Smout and Rosalind Mitchison.[71] This is the first comprehensive study of the subject; it is aimed at those interested in both demography and social history and is designed to provide a general framework for more specialized studies. The techniques of quantification are used whenever possible, but the authors are scrupulously careful not to try to extract more from their sources than they contain. There have also been a number of surveys of institutions, especially educational institutions, of very good quality; of these, J. Durkan and J. Kirk's *The University of Glasgow 1451– 1577* is a really outstanding piece of detailed, painstaking scholarship, and D. B. Horn's *A Short History of the University of Edinburgh* is a fine brief overview. Special mention must also be made of D. E. R. Watt's *A Biographical Dictionary of Scottish Graduates to* A.D. *1410*, a series of long biographical notices of these men, who were all graduates of non-Scottish universities; St. Andrews was not founded until 1412. Watt's work is a mine of information for intellectual and cultural history, as well as an enormously useful work of reference.[72]

Of the large number of articles which social history is generating these days, a handful are outstanding. Margaret Sanderson's careful analyses of the feuars and tenants of kirklands has shown that, contrary to the prevailing view, about half the feuars were small men, below the rank of laird, and probably sitting tenants, who may well have accepted feus under pressure from clerical landlords who felt insecure by the sixteenth century and wanted a quick profit. Ecclesiastical tenants, she concludes, were not so badly off as has been supposed; leases were longer in the sixteenth century than they had been before, and they frequently remained in the same family.[73] Christina Larner's splendid study of James VI and witchcraft suggests that James picked up his ideas about witchcraft during his visit to Denmark, which explains both the timing of the first great batch of Scottish trials and the fact that the accusations followed the continental rather than the English pattern. She also indicates that James was becoming uneasy about the genuineness of such accusations before 1603, not after he reached the supposedly more rational atmosphere of England.[74] Gordon Donaldson has given us a masterful survey in "The Legal Profession in Scottish Society in the Sixteenth and Seventeenth Centuries";[75] Rosalind Mitchison has provided a careful and informative discussion of "The Making of the Old Scottish Poor Law";[76] and Geoffrey Best has supplied an impressionistic account of the special character of the city in Victorian Scotland, concentrating on Glasgow, which he calls the Chicago of Victorian Britain.[77]

One special category of books should be mentioned, those dealing with the history of art and architecture. The Royal Commission on the Ancient and Historical Monuments of Scotland has continued to turn out its fascinating and important series of volumes, on Peeblesshire, Argyll, volumes 1 (Kintyre) and 2 (Lorn); and Lanarkshire, volume 1.[78] M. P. Apted's *The Painted Ceilings of Scotland 1550–1650* is a picture book of extraordinary interest. D. Irwin and F. Irwin's *Scottish Painters at Home and Abroad 1700–1900* is an excellent, detailed piece of art history which sets these painters and their work in the general context of European art of their times and assesses that work accordingly.[79] J. G. Dunbar's *The Historic Architecture of Scotland* has provided a first-class survey from the Middle Ages to the early nineteenth century, with a lot of original material, especially on lairds' houses, and concentrating on types rather than individual examples. Much can be done with individual examples, properly chosen, of course, as I. G. Lindsay and M. Cosh show in their *Inveraray and the Dukes of Argyll*, an account of the building of the castle and the town which goes beyond the erection of buildings to discuss the dukes' encouragement of agricultural improvements and local industries. J. M. Macaulay's *The Gothic Revival, 1745–1845* deals with the northern counties of England as well as Scotland and pulls together a lot of useful information. Finally, there is A. J. Youngson's enormously interesting *The Making of Classical Edinburgh 1750–1840*, which is something more than a piece of architectural history, although it certainly deals with the building of buildings and the aesthetics of town planning in its discussion of the creation of the New Town, which is the central theme of the book.[80]

Apart from the biographies of Knox already mentioned, most of the significant work done on religious history in the period between the Reformation and the Civil War has taken the form of articles. There are some exceptions. J. K. Cameron, in *The First Book of Discipline*, has provided a scholarly edition of the printed text of 1621, which differs in various minor ways from that supplied in Knox's *History*, along with an introduction which is a detailed account of the origins and content of the book.[81] Duncan Shaw's *The General Assemblies of the Church of Scotland, 1560–1600* provides a series of topical essays on various aspects of the assembly's functions which pull together a lot of useful material. W. R. Foster's *The Church before the Covenants: The Church of Scotland, 1596–1638* is the first full-length account of the church under the bishops. It is institutional history with no discussion of theology; its topical organization renders it a bit static, and Foster minimizes the amount of opposition which James's and especially Charles's religious policy generated. But it is a ground-breaking book and is especially good on the subject of clerical incomes. It should be read in connection with Walter Makey's *The Church of the Covenant, 1637–1651*, for his analysis of the social origins of the clergy, the level of their incomes, and so on adds to and confirms Foster's work.[82] To a far greater extent than David Stevenson, whose work has already been discussed, Makey sees the church as independent of lay influence and the revolutionary period as marking the beginning of the end of feudal Scotland. His argument is not altogether convincing, but his book is uncommonly interesting.

As for the Reformation itself, two articles by Margaret Sanderson and Ian Cowan, taken together, give a rather different view of the relative strength of Protestantism and Catholicism than is generally accepted.[83] Cowan argues that Protestantism was limited to very few areas, was not significant before the late

1550s and succeeded for political rather than religious reasons, with the lairds the key to its success. Sanderson contends that although it was not strong enough to challenge the Protestant establishment, there was a good deal of Catholic opinion and practice, even in the burghs, in the later sixteenth century and that many Protestant ministers were not cut in the mold of Knox and were quite tolerant of the ancient faith. The impression these articles leave is confirmed by Michael Lynch's analysis, "The Two Edinburgh Town Councils of 1559–60."[84] Lynch concludes that, even at the height of the Wars of the Congregation, the people who counted in Edinburgh were more concerned about their economic interests than anything else. The *Festschrift* for the Reverend Hugh Watt contains a number of interesting articles on this period, among them the editor's on John Willock, T. A. Kerr's on John Craig, and Ian Cowan's on the Five Articles of Perth.[85] This writer has argued that James VI considered alternative methods of controlling the church before settling on diocesan episcopacy; David Stevenson has provided the first detailed study of depositions of ministers during the Civil War period, which were more numerous than previously thought; and Gordon Donaldson has speculated that the religious conservatism of the northeast was owing to the area's lack of contact with England, and he has pointed out that schism was what he calls a late-blooming and feeble plant in Scotland until after 1687, save in the 1650s, when the penalties for nonconformity were removed.[86] Professor Donaldson has also provided an admirable summary of his many years of work on the subject of "The Scottish Church, 1567–1625."[87]

Ian Cowan has taken a new look at *The Scottish Covenanters 1660–1688*, a restrained narrative account, nonpartisan save for an overcritical view of Bishop Leighton (who has, perhaps, previously received more than his share of praise). Cowan argues that, by contrast with their predecessors in the 1640s, the Covenanters' chief significance after 1660 lies in the defensive nature of their struggle against what they regarded as the wrong-headed and impious Erastianism of Charles II's government, rather than in any effort to make converts outside of Scotland. He has also provided an overview of the whole movement, with comments on the work of other historians, in a revision article.[88] For the period after the establishment of Presbyterianism, the major work has been the two volumes of A. L. Drummond and James Bulloch which carry the story from 1688 to 1874, with emphasis on the nineteenth century and particularly on the Disruption, which they blame on the indifference of the government and the impossibility of changing the way the church operated to accommodate the changing times, in connection with the patronage question.[89] To Drummond and Bulloch, the Disruption was more than a schism in the church; it was a traumatic experience for Scotland which in effect put an end to Scotland's national history, since it destroyed the last Scottish national institution that counted for something. One need not subscribe to this view in order to admire these volumes, which are urbane, witty, and thoughtful and explode a few cherished myths. Scottish clergy in the nineteenth century were not especially well educated, the authors say, nor was the Bible all that familiar to the average householder. G. I. T. Machin argues that it was not indifference but politics which determined the attitudes of successive British governments to the Disruption;[90] for electoral reasons, neither party had any wish to support Chalmers and his friends, and both underestimated the size of his following. Finally, a very interesting study by A. A. MacLaren of the eldership of the Free Church in Aberdeen has a lot of useful material in it and employs the kind of interdisciplinary approach rarely found in works on Scottish history.[91]

MacLaren's book, Flinn's work on demography, and a collection of essays MacLaren has recently edited, *Social Class in Scotland, Past and Present*, the gem in which is T. C. Smout's piece on nineteenth-century sexual behavior, suggest that Scottish studies are about to move in the interdisciplinary direction which has become fashionable of late.[92] As this article has attempted to show, much of the enormous amount of useful work in Scottish history in the past decade has been gap-filling: the careful study of problems which simply had not received proper scholarly attention before. This has been absolutely essential; there is much more of it to do, and it should be done first, because there is no point in attempting the "new" economic and social history until the political and institutional framework is firmly in place. Too often the popularizers still hold the field, and the best of them, like John Prebble, can be seductively dangerous when they wax polemical, as Prebble does in *Mutiny: Highland Regiments in Revolt, 1743–1804*, which argues indirectly that the old Highland society and culture were being deliberately destroyed by outside forces, a thesis he never explicitly tests or proves, and in *Glencoe*, which, Prebble argues, was an act of genocide.[93] But the romantics no longer have the field all to themselves. A number of academic scholars are turning their hands to popular history; an outstanding example is Gordon Donaldson's *Scottish Kings*, which, after some preliminary discussion of the evolution of the monarchy and the nature of kingship, provides a series of penetrating sketches of the six Jameses and Mary.[94] We need more books of this kind, to bring the results of scholarly research to the general public, whose appetite both inside and outside Scotland recent political events have whetted. The flood tide is now with us; we will neglect it at our peril.

NOTES

1. No attempt has been made in this article to deal with Scottish history before the eleventh century, since this writer is not competent to evaluate the literature dealing with that period. Also omitted are all works on English history which discuss Scotland. A few books and articles published before 1966 are noted, either because they came to hand too late for inclusion in *Chang-*

ing Views or in order to provide a more complete listing of contributions to an argument, as, e.g., those in note 32 below.

2. The most notable are P. McNeill and R. G. Nicholson, eds., *An Historical Atlas of Scotland c.400–c. 1600*, Conference of Scottish Medievalists, St. Andrews, 1975; *The Early Maps of Scotland to 1850*, published by the Royal Scottish Geographical Society, 3d ed., vol. 1, with a *History of Scottish Maps* by D. G. Moir, Edinburgh, 1973, a completely revised version of the work first published in 1934; H. G. Aldis, *A List of Books Printed in Scotland before 1700*, Edinburgh, 1971, a reprint of the 1904 edition with additions; W. F. H. Nicolaisen, *Scottish Place-Names: Their Study and Significance*, London, 1976; D. E. R. Watt, *Fasti Ecclesiae Scoticanae Medii Aevi ad annum 1638*, 2d draft, Edinburgh, 1969; I. B. Cowan, *The Parishes of Medieval Scotland*, Scottish Record Society, Edinburgh, 1967; I. B. Cowan and D. E. Easson, *Medieval Religious Houses, Scotland*, 2d ed., London, 1976. A new edition of *The Statistical Account of Scotland, 1791–1799*, East Ardsley, 1979–   , under the general editorship of D. J. Withrington and I. R. Grant, is under way; two volumes have appeared. B. Webster, *Scotland from the Eleventh Century to 1603*, Ithaca, N.Y., 1975, is a useful essay on the sources.

3. A. A. M. Duncan, *Scotland: The Making of the Kingdom*, Edinburgh, 1975; R. G. Nicholson, *Scotland: The Later Middle Ages*, Edinburgh, 1974; G. Donaldson, *Scotland: James V– James VII*, Edinburgh, 1965; W. Ferguson, *Scotland: 1689 to the Present*, Edinburgh, 1968; all with useful annotated bibliographies.

4. R. G. Nicholson, *Edward III and the Scots*, Oxford, 1965; idem, "David II, the Historians, and the Chroniclers," *SHR* 55, 1966; B. Webster, "David II and the Government of Fourteenth-century Scotland," *TRHS*, 5th ser., 16, 1966.

5. R. Mitchison, *A History of Scotland*, London, 1970; G. Donaldson, *Scotland: The Shaping of a Nation*, Newton Abbot, 1974; idem, *The Scots Overseas*, London, 1966; T. C. Smout, *A History of the Scottish People 1560–1830*, London, 1969.

6. T. I. Rae, in R. F. Brissenden, ed., *Studies in the Eighteenth Century*, vol. 2, Canberra, 1973, and *SHR* 54, 1975, respectively. See also idem, "The Political Attitudes of William Drummond of Hawthornden," in G. W. S. Barrow, ed., *The Scottish Tradition: Essays in Honour of Ronald Gordon Cant*, Edinburgh, 1974. Other historiographical articles include A. M. Starkey on Robert Wodrow, *Church History* 43, 1974; J. Anderson on William Forbes Skene, *SHR* 46, 1967; M. Lee, Jr., on John Knox, *SHR* 45, 1966; idem, on Archbishop Spottiswoode, *JBS* 13, 1973–1974.

7. G. W. S. Barrow, *The Kingdom of the Scots*, London, 1973; idem, *The Acts of William I*, Edinburgh, 1971.

8. A. A. M. Duncan, "The Community of the Realm of Scotland and Robert Bruce," *SHR* 45, 1966; idem, "The Making of the Declaration of Arbroath," in D. A. Bullough and R. L. Storey, eds., *The Study of Medieval Records*, Oxford, 1971; idem, *The Nation of Scots and the Declaration of Arbroath (1320)*, Historical Association pamphlet, London, 1970. See also G. G. Simpson, "The Declaration of Arbroath Revitalised," *SHR* 56, 1977.

9. A. A. M. Duncan, "The Early Parliaments of Scotland," *SHR* 45, 1966. Another outstanding example of historical editing is E. L. G. Stones and G. G. Simpson, eds., *Edward I and the Throne of Scotland, 1290–1296: An Edition of the Record Sources for the Great Cause*, New York, 1978, with a long introduction which discusses all the major questions to which these records give rise.

10. G. W. S. Barrow, "Lothian in the First War of Independence, 1296–1328," *SHR* 55, 1976; idem, "The Aftermath of War: Scotland and England in the Late Thirteenth and Early Fourteenth Centuries," *TRHS*, 5th ser., 28, 1978.

11. See, e.g., R. Frame, "The Bruces in Ireland, 1315–18," *IHS* 19, 1974, which argues that a

conquest of the island was seriously intended as a way of making the balance between England and Scotland more equal. For David Bruce, see Nicholson, "David II," and Webster, "David II."

12. J. Brown, ed., *Scottish Society in the Fifteenth Century*, New York, 1977; A. Grant, "The Development of the Scottish Peerage," *SHR* 57, 1978.

13. D. McRoberts, "The Scottish Church and Nationalism in the Fifteenth Century," *Innes Review* 19, 1968; L. MacFarlane, "The Primacy of the Scottish Church, 1472–1521," ibid. 20, 1969.

14. M. Ash, "The Diocese of St. Andrews under Its Norman Bishops," *SHR* 55, 1976; N. F. Shead, "The Administration of the Diocese of Glasgow in the Twelfth and Thirteenth Centuries," *SHR* 55, 1976; I. B. Cowan, "The Medieval Church in the Diocese of Aberdeen," *Northern Scotland* 1, 1973; C. H. Haws, "The Diocese of Aberdeen and the Reformation," *Innes Review* 22, 1971; idem, "The Diocese of St. Andrews at the Reformation," *R(ecords of the) S(cottish) C(hurch) H(istory) S(ociety)* 18, 1973.

15. A. I. Dunlop and I. B. Cowan, eds., *Calendar of Scottish Supplications to Rome 1428–1432*, Scottish History Society, Edinburgh, 1970.

16. R. G. Nicholson, "Feudal Developments in Late Medieval Scotland," *Juridical Review*, n.s., 18, 1973; C. Madden, "Royal Treatment of Feudal Casualties in Late Medieval Scotland," *SHR* 55, 1976.

17. A. L. Murray, "The Comptroller, 1425–1488," *SHR* 52, 1973; idem, "The Scottish Treasury, 1667–1708," *SHR* 45, 1966; idem, "Notes on the Treasury Administration," in C. T. McInnes, ed., *Accounts of the Lord High Treasurer of Scotland*, vol. 12, *1566–1574*, Edinburgh, 1970. His article "The Lord Clerk Register" is contained in a special number of *SHR* 53, 1974, commemorating the bicentenary of the Register House. The other contributors are A. A. Tait on the building; M. D. Young on the office of deputy clerk register; John Imrie, the present keeper, on the modern Record Office; and Gordon Donaldson on the vicissitudes of the records during World War II. Together they form a valuable study of archive administration.

18. T. I. Rae, *The Administration of the Scottish Frontier 1513–1603*, Edinburgh, 1966.

19. D. Hay, "England Scotland, and Europe: The Problems of the Frontier," *TRHS*, 5th ser., 25, 1975; G. McD. Fraser, *The Steel Bonnets*, London, 1971.

20. A. Fraser, *Mary Queen of Scots*, London, 1969; G. Donaldson, *Mary Queen of Scots*, London, 1974; idem, *The First Trial of Mary Queen of Scots*, London, 1969; J. E. Phillips, *Images of a Queen: Mary Stuart in Sixteenth Century Literature*, Berkeley, 1964; M. H. Merriman, "The Assured Scots," *SHR* 47, 1968; J. Ridley, *John Knox*, Oxford, 1968; W. S. Reid, *Trumpeter of God*, New York, 1974. See also Donaldson's perceptive "Queen Mary and Her Scottish Contemporaries," *Scotia* 3, 1979. This number of *Scotia* is entirely given over to various aspects of Mary's life and times.

21. J. Brown, "Scottish Politics, 1567–1625," in A. G. R. Smith, ed., *The Reign of James VI and I*, New York, 1973; M. Lee, Jr., "James VI and the Aristocracy," *Scotia* 1, 1977; J. Wormald, "James VI: New Men for Old?" ibid 2, 1978; M. Lee, Jr., "James VI's Government of Scotland after 1603," *SHR* 55, 1976.

22. A. Williamson, *Scottish National Consciousness in the Reign of James VI*, Edinburgh, 1979.

23. D. Stevenson, *The Scottish Revolution, 1637–1644*, Newton Abbot, 1973; idem, *Revolution and Counter-revolution in Scotland, 1644–1651*, London, 1977.

24. D. Stevenson, "Conventicles in the Kirk, 1619–37: The Emergence of a Radical Party," *RSCHS* 18, 1973; idem, "The Radical Party in the Kirk, 1637–45," *Journal of Ecclesiastical History* 25, 1974; idem, "The General Assembly and the Commission of the Kirk," *RSCHS* 19, 1977; idem, "Church and Society under the Covenanters, 1637–51," *Scotia* 1, 1977. See

also idem, "The Financing of the Cause of the Covenents, 1638–51," *SHR* 51, 1972; idem, "The King's Scottish Revenues and the Covenanters, 1625–1651," *HJ* 17, 1974; and idem, "The Covenanters and the Court of Session, 1637–1650," *Juridical Review*, n.s., 17, 1972.

25. I. B. Cowan, "Church and Society in Post-reformation Scotland," *RSCHS* 17, 1972.

26. L. Kaplan, *Politics and Religion during the English Revolution: The Scots and the Long Parliament, 1643–1645*, New York, 1976. See also idem, "Steps to War: The Scots and Parliament, 1642–1643," *JBS* 9, 1969–1970, and idem, "English Civil War Politics and the Religious Settlement," *Church History* 41, 1972. S. A. Burrell, "The Apocalyptic Vision of the Early Covenanters," *SHR* 43, 1964. On the related subject of the Scots and the Committee of Both Kingdoms, see L. Mulligan, "The Scottish Alliance and the Committee of Both Kingdoms, 1644–46," *Historical Studies* 14, 1970, and idem, "Peace Negotiations, Politics, and the Committee of Both Kingdoms, 1944–46," *HJ* 12, 1969.

27. E. J. Cowan, *Montrose: For Covenant and King*, London, 1977. For the battles, there are R. Williams, *Montrose, Cavalier in Mourning*, London, 1975, and M. Hastings, *Montrose, The King's Champion*, London, 1977.

28. P. J. Pinckney, "The Scottish Representation in the Cromwellian Parliament of 1656," *SHR* 46, 1967; J. A. Casada, "The Scottish Representatives in Richard Cromwell's Parliament," *SHR* 51, 1972.

29. F. D. Dow, *Cromwellian Scotland*, Edinburgh, 1979.

30. R. Marshall, *The Days of Duchess Anne*, London, 1973; G. Menzies, ed., *The Scottish Nation*, London, 1972; J. Patrick, "The Origins of the Opposition to Lauderdale in the Scottish Parliament of 1673," *SHR* 53, 1974.

31. W. Ferguson, *Scotland's Relations with England: A Survey to 1707*, Edinburgh, 1977; idem, "The Making of the Treaty of Union of 1707," *SHR* 43, 1964.

32. P. W. J. Riley, *The English Ministers and Scotland, 1707–1727*, London, 1964; idem, "The Formation of the Scottish Ministry of 1703," *SHR* 44, 1965; idem, "The Scottish Parliament of 1703," *SHR* 47, 1968; idem, "The Union of 1707 as an Episode in English Politics," *EHR* 84, 1969; idem, "The Structure of Scottish Politics and the Union of 1707," in T. I. Rae, ed., *The Union of 1707: Its Impact on Scotland*, Glasgow, 1974; idem, *King William and the Scottish Politicians*, Edinburgh, 1979; idem, *The Union of England and Scotland*, Manchester, 1979.

33. T. C. Smout, "The Road to Union," in G. Holmes, ed., *Britain after the Glorious Revolution*, London, 1969. See also Smout's contribution to Menzies, *Scottish Nation*, and idem, "The Anglo-Scottish Union of 1707: The Economic Background," *EcHR*, 2d ser., 16, 1964.

34. D. Daiches, *Scotland and the Union*, 1977. There is a summary of the literature in M. Lee, Jr., "The Anglo-Scottish Union of 1707: The Debate Renewed," *British Studies Monitor* 9, 1979.

35. N. T. Phillipson and R. Mitchison, *Scotland's Age of Improvement*, Edinburgh, 1970.

36. D. Daiches, *Charles Edward Stuart*, London, 1973; J. Gibson, *Ships of the '45*, London, 1967.

37. R. H. Campbell, "The Anglo-Scottish Union of 1707: The Economic Consequences," *EcHR*, 2d ser., 16, 1964; idem, "The Union and Economic Growth," in Rae, *Union of 1707*. The quotation is from the former article, p. 477.

38. B. Lenman, *An Economic History of Modern Scotland, 1660–1976*, Hamden, 1977. This is a very good narrative survey which incorporates recent findings.

39. C. Gulvin, "The Union and the Scottish Woollen Industry, 1707–1760," *SHR* 50, 1971; A. J. Durie, "The Market for Scottish Linen, 1730–1775," *SHR* 52, 1973.

40. The two key articles are N. T. Phillipson, "Towards a Definition of the Scottish Enlightenment," in P. Fritz and D. Williams, eds., *City and Society in the Eighteenth Century*, Toronto, 1973, and idem, "Culture and Society in the 18th Century Province: The Case of Edinburgh

and the Scottish Enlightenment," in L. Stone, ed., *The University in Society*, vol. 2, Princeton, N.J., 1974. See also idem, "Nationalism and Ideology," in J. N. Wolfe, ed., *Government and Nationalism in Scotland*, Edinburgh, 1969, and idem, "Lawyers, Landowners, and the Civic Leadership of Post-union Scotland," *Juridical Review*, n.s., 21, 1976. Other works worth mention which by-and-large support Phillipson's thesis are A. C. Chitnis, *The Scottish Enlightenment*, London, 1976; D. D. McElroy, *Scotland's Age of Improvement*, Pullman, Wash., 1969; and R. L. Emerson, "The Social Composition of Enlightened Scotland: The Select Society of Edinburgh," *Studies in Voltaire and the Eighteenth Century* 114, 1973.

41. J. R. R. Christie, "The Origins and Development of the Scottish Scientific Community, 1680–1760," *History of Science* 12, 1974.

42. E. L. Cloyd, *James Burnett, Lord Monboddo*, Oxford, 1972; W. C. Lehmann, *Henry Home, Lord Kames, and the Scottish Enlightenment*, The Hague, 1971; I. S. Ross, *Lord Kames and the Scotland of His Day*, Oxford, 1972.

43. J. L. McKelvey, "William Robertson and Lord Bute," *Studies in Scottish Literature* 6, 1968–1969; J. J. Cater, "The Making of Principal Robertson," *SHR* 49, 1970.

44. E.g., articles by J. G. Kellas and D. W. Urwin in *SHR* 44, 1965; A. B. Cooke in *SHR* 49, 1970; and J. E. McCaffrey and W. H. Fraser in *SHR* 50, 1971. See also W. Ferguson, "The Reform Act (Scotland) of 1832: Intention and Effect," *SHR* 45, 1966, and the introduction by J. I. Brash to *Scottish Electoral Politics 1832–1854*, Scottish History Society, Edinburgh, 1974. There are also two good political biographies, K. O. Morgan, *Keir Hardie, Radical and Socialist*, 1975, and C. Tennant, *The Radical Laird*, Kineton, 1970, a study of George Kinloch, an improving landlord who became a leader in the movement for parliamentary reform.

45. H. J. Hanham, *Scottish Nationalism*, London, 1969; idem, "The Development of the Scottish Office," in Wolfe, *Government and Nationalism in Scotland*.

46. C. Harvie, *Scotland and Nationalism*, London, 1977.

47. J. G. Kellas, *Modern Scotland: The Nation since 1870*, London, 1968; see also the excellent brief introductory survey by G. Donaldson et al., "Scottish Devolution: The Historical Background," in Wolfe, *Government and Nationalism in Scotland*.

48. R. H. Campbell, in *Scottish Journal of Political Economy* 23, 1976: 183.

49. Ibid., in his introduction to *Scottish Industrial History: A Miscellany*, Scottish History Society, Edinburgh, 1978.

50. M. L. Anderson, *A History of Scottish Forestry*, 2 vols., London, 1967; B. F. Duckham, *A History of the Scottish Coal Industry*, vol. 1, *1700–1815*, Newton Abbot, 1970; M. Gray, *The Fishing Industries of Scotland, 1790–1914: A Study in Regional Adaptation*, New York, 1978; S. G. Checkland, *Scottish Banking: A History, 1695–1973*, London, 1975.

51. C. Gulvin, *The Tweedmakers: A History of the Scottish Fancy Woollen Industry 1600–1964*, Newton Abbot, 1973; E. Gauldie, ed., *The Dundee Textile Industry 1790–1885*, Scottish History Society, Edinburgh, 1969; B. Lenman, S. G. E. Lythe, and E. Gauldie, *Dundee and Its Textile Industry 1850–1914*, Dundee, 1969.

52. B. Lenman, *From Esk to Tweed*, Glasgow, 1975; A. Slaven, *The Development of the West of Scotland 1750–1960*, 1975.

53. J. B. Dow, "Scottish Trade with Sweden, 1512–1580, 1580–1622," *SHR* 48, 1969.

54. T. M. Devine and S. G. E. Lythe, "The Economy of Scotland under James VI: A Revision Article," *SHR* 50, 1971. Lythe summarizes his views in his chapter on the Scottish economy in Smith, *Reign of James VI and I*.

55. J. Butt and J. T. Ward, eds., *Scottish Themes: Essays in Honour of Professor S. G. E. Lythe*, Edinburgh, 1976.

56. P. L. Payne, ed., *Studies in Scottish Business History*, 1967; W. Vamplew, *Salveson of Leith*,

Edinburgh, 1975; M. S. Moss and J. R. Hume, *Workshop of the British Empire: Engineering and Shipbuilding in the West of Scotland*, 1977; I. Donnachie, *A History of the Brewing Industry in Scotland*, Edinburgh, 1979; A. Tuckett, *The Scottish Carter*, 1967; J. E. Handley, *The Navvy in Scotland*, Cork, 1970; K. J. Logue, *Popular Disturbances in Scotland, 1780–1815*, Edinburgh, 1979; W. T. Jackson, *The Enterprising Scot: Investors in the American West after 1873*, Edinburgh, 1968; W. G. Kerr, *Scottish Capital on the American Credit Frontier*, Austin, 1976.

57. A. Wilson, *The Chartist Movement in Scotland*, Manchester, 1970.

58. R. Q. Gray, *The Labour Aristocracy in Victorian Edinburgh*, Oxford, 1976. For evidence that the ethic was deliberately inculcated, see A. Tyrrell, "Political Economy, Whiggism, and the Education of Working-class Adults in Scotland, 1817–40," *SHR* 48, 1969.

59. T. C. Smout, "The Glasgow Merchant Community in the Seventeenth Century, *SHR* 47, 1968.

60. T. M. Devine, *The Tobacco Lords: A Study of the Tobacco Merchants of Glasgow and Their Trading Activities c. 1740–1790*, Edinburgh, 1975; idem, "Glasgow Merchants and the Collapse of the Tobacco Trade, 1775–1783," *SHR* 52, 1973; idem, "The Colonial Trades and Industrial Investment in Scotland, c. 1700–1815," *EcHR*, 2d ser., 29, 1976. See also his more general analysis, "An Eighteenth-century Business Elite: Glasgow–West India Merchants, c. 1750–1815," *SHR* 57, 1978.

61. S. G. Checkland, *The Upas Tree: Glasgow, 1875–1975*, Glasgow, 1977.

62. W. Vamplew, "Railways and the Transformation of the Scottish Economy," *EcHR*, 2d ser., 24, 1971; T. C. Smout, "Scottish Landowners and Industrial Growth, 1650–1850," *Scottish Journal of Political Economy* 11, 1964; R. H. Campbell, "The Industrial Revolution," *SHR* 46, 1967.

63. R. A. Dodgshon, "Farming in Roxburghshire and Berwickshire on the Eve of Improvement," *SHR* 54, 1975. Also of interest are R. Mitchison, "The Movement of Scottish Corn Prices in the Seventeenth and Eighteenth Centuries," *EcHR*, 2d ser., 18, 1965; V. Morgan, "Agricultural Wage Rates in Late Eighteenth-century Scotland," ibid. 24, 1971; and T. M. Devine, "Social Stability and Agrarian Change in the Eastern Lowlands of Scotland, 1810–1840," *Social History* 3, 1978.

64. I. Whyte, *Agriculture and Society in Seventeenth Century Scotland*, Edinburgh, 1979.

65. I owe this suggestion to Professor Gordon Donaldson.

66. R. J. Adam, *Sutherland Estate Management, 1802–1816*, 2 vols., Scottish History Society, Edinburgh, 1972; E. Richards, *The Leviathan of Wealth: The Sutherland Fortune in the Industrial Revolution*, London, 1973; idem, "The Prospect of Economic Growth in Sutherland at the Time of the Clearances, 1809 to 1813," *SHR* 49, 1970; idem, "Structural Change in a Regional Economy: Sutherland and the Industrial Revolution, 1780–1830," *EcHR*, 2d ser., 26, 1973.

67. A. J. Youngson, *After the Forty-five: The Economic Impact on the Scottish Highlands*, Edinburgh, 1973.

68. J. Hunter, *The Making of the Crofting Community*, Edinburgh, 1976; idem, "The Emergence of the Crofting Community: The Religious Contribution, 1798–1843," *Scottish Studies* 18, 1974; idem, "The Politics of Highland Land Reform, 1873–1895," *SHR* 53, 1974; idem, "The Gaelic Connection: The Highlands, Ireland, and Nationalism, 1873–1922," *SHR* 54, 1975.

69. H. J. Hanham, "The Problem of Highland Discontent, 1880–1885," *TRHS*, 5th ser., 19, 1969; see also E. Richards, "Patterns of Highland Discontent, 1790–1860," in J. Stevenson and R. Quinault, eds., *Popular Protest and Public Order, 1780–1920*, 1974, for an account of the ineffective riots which took place in the Highlands before those of the 1880s, and

J. W. Mason, "The Duke of Argyll and the Land Question in Late Nineteenth-century Britain," *VS* 21, 1977–1978, for the reaction of an unreconstructed Benthamite spokesman of the landed classes to the latter riots and the ensuing land legislation for both Ireland and Scotland.

70. A. Fenton, *Scottish Country Life*, Edinburgh, 1976.

71. Michael Flinn, ed., *Scottish Population History from the 17th Century to the 1930s*, Cambridge, 1977.

72. J. Durkan and J. Kirk, *The University of Glasgow 1451–1577* (Glasgow, 1977); D. B. Horn, *A Short History of the University of Edinburgh*, Edinburgh, 1967; D. E. R. Watt, *A Biographical Dictionary of Scottish Graduates to A.D. 1410*, Oxford, 1977. Other surveys worth noting are J. Scotland, *The History of Scottish Education*, 2 vols. London, 1970; M. Cruikshank, *A History of the Training of Teachers in Scotland*, London, 1970; W. S. Craig, *History of the Royal College of Physicians of Edinburgh*, Oxford, 1976; H. P. Tait, *A Doctor and Two Policemen: The History of the Edinburgh Health Department 1862–1974*, Edinburgh, 1974; A. R. B. Haldane, *Three Centuries of Scottish Posts: A Historical Survey to 1836*, Edinburgh, 1971; and idem, *The Glorious Privilege: The History of "The Scotsman,"* Edinburgh, 1967, written by seven members of the staff.

73. M. Sanderson, "Some Aspects of the Church in Scottish Society in the Era of the Reformation," *RSCHS* 17, 1972; idem, "The Feuars of Kirklands," *SHR* 52, 1973; idem, "Kirkmen and Their Tenants in the Era of the Reformation," *RSCHS* 18, 1973. See also idem, "Manse and Glebe in the Sixteenth Century," *RSCHS* 19, 1977, which deals with the efforts of the new church after 1560 to extricate manses and glebes, or their equivalent, from the grip of the feuars.

74. C. Larner, "James VI and I and Witchcraft," in Smith, *Reign of James VI and I*. Larner has also edited *A Source Book of Scottish Witchcraft*, a full listing of cases with references to the sources, available from the Department of Sociology of the University of Glasgow.

75. G. Donaldson, "The Legal Profession in Scottish Society in the Sixteenth and Seventeenth Centuries," *Juridical Review*, n.s., 21, 1976.

76. R. Mitchison, "The Making of the Old Scottish Poor Law," *PP*, no. 63, 1974; See also her subsequent exchange with R. A. Cage, *PP*, no. 69, 1975.

77. G. Best, "The Scottish Victorian City," *VS* 11, 1968. A perceptive piece on the problem of urban growth in this period is F. McKichan, "A Burgh's Response to the Problems of Urban Growth: Stirling, 1780–1880," *SHR* 57, 1978.

78. The Royal Commission on the Ancient and Historical Monuments of Scotland, Peeblesshire (H.M.S.O., 1967), Argyll (H.M.S.O., 1971, 1974), and Lanarkshire (H.M.S.O., 1978).

79. M. P. Apted, *The Painted Ceilings of Scotland 1550–1650*, Edinburgh, 1966; D. Irwin and F. Irwin, *Scottish Painters at Home and Abroad 1700–1900*, London, 1975.

80. J. G. Dunbar, *The Historic Architecture of Scotland*, London, 1966; I. G. Lindsay and M. Cosh, *Inveraray and the Dukes of Argyll*, Edinburgh, 1973; J. M. Macaulay, *The Gothic Revival, 1745–1845*, Glasgow, 1975; A. J. Youngson, *The Making of Classical Edinburgh 1750–1840*, Edinburgh, 1966.

81. J. K. Cameron, *The First Book of Discipline*, Edinburgh, 1972.

82. D. Shaw, *The General Assemblies of the Church of Scotland, 1560–1600*, Edinburgh, 1964; W. R. Foster, *The Church before the Covenants: The Church of Scotland, 1596–1638*, Edinburgh, 1975; W. Makey, *The Church of the Covenant, 1637–1651*, Edinburgh, 1979.

83. M. Sanderson, "Catholic Recusancy in Scotland in the Sixteenth Century," *Innes Review* 21, 1970; I. B. Cowan, *Regional Aspects of the Scottish Reformation*, Historical Association pamphlet, 1978.

84. M. Lynch, "The Two Edinburgh Town Councils of 1559–60," *SHR* 54, 1975.

85. D. Shaw, ed., *Reformation and Revolution*, Edinburgh, 1967.

86. M. Lee, Jr., "James VI and the Revival of Episcopacy in Scotland, 1596–1600," *Church History* 43, 1974; D. Stevenson, "Deposition of Ministers in the Church of Scotland under the Covenanters," ibid. 44, 1975; G. Donaldson, "Scotland's Conservative North in the Sixteenth and Seventeenth Centuries," *TRHS*, 5th ser., 16, 1966; idem, "The Emergence of Schism in Seventeenth Century Scotland," in D. Baker, ed., *Studies in Church History*, vol. 9, 1972.

87. G. Donaldson, "The Scottish Church, 1567–1625," in Smith, *Reign of James VI and I.*

88. I. Cowan, *The Scottish Covenanters 1660–1688*, London, 1976; idem, "The Covenanters: A Revision Article," *SHR* 47, 1968; see also idem, "Worship and Dissent in Restoration Scotland," *Scotia* 2, 1978.

89. A. L. Drummond, *The Scottish Church, 1688–1843*, Edinburgh, 1973; J. Bullock, *The Church in Victorian Scotland, 1843–1874*, Edinburgh, 1975.

90. G. I. T. Machin, "The Disruption and British Politics, 1834–43," *SHR* 51, 1972.

91. A. A. MacLaren, *Religion and Social Class: The Disruption Years in Aberdeen*, 1974; see also idem, "Presbyterianism and the Working Class in a Mid-ninteenth Century City," *SHR* 46, 1967.

92. A. A. MacLaren, ed., *Social Class in Scotland, Past and Present*, Edinburgh, 1977.

93. J. Prebble, *Mutiny: Highland Regiments in Revolt, 1743–1804*, London, 1975; idem, *Glencoe*, London, 1966.

94. G. Donaldson, *Scottish Kings*, London, 1967.

Ireland since 1500

L. P. Curtis, Jr.

The writing of Irish history since 1966 has been marked by a widening and deepening of channels already being dug before that date.[1] If political history still dominates the historical economy, and if presentist concerns arising out of the troubles in Northern Ireland rumble just below the surface of much of the literature, there are distinct signs of greater depth and maturity in most fields of Irish historical endeavor. The slow but steady shift away from the partisanship of previous generations dates from the historical revolution of the latter 1930s which embodied a more analytical and far better documented historiography, the chief function of which was to explain, not assign blame for, the past.[2] Two of the leaders of that "new departure" in Irish historical consciousness and the co-founders of *Irish Historical Studies* in 1937/1938, T. W. Moody and R. Dudley Edwards, have recently retired from their chairs of modern history at Trinity College and University College, Dublin, respectively; but both are still actively engaged in promoting the study of Irish history through their own scholarship as well as that of their many students. The gathering momentum of research activity which these two men have done so much to accelerate may be gauged by the increase in the number of theses now in progress in Irish universities—from 60 in 1966 to 165 in 1977.[3]

Much of the recent writing on historical subjects reflects a continuing quest for the origins and nature of Ireland's transformation from quasi-colony to independent (and divided) nation-state. Historians who are fond of the harder (but still soft) social sciences prefer to lump these long-term trends together into a concept called "modernization" or "national development," whereas more empirical historians who shun macromodels choose to particularize and isolate for study specific changes or processes over a limited span of years. Whatever their objects of inquiry, most Irish historians working since the mid-1960s have eschewed those shrill asides about British imperial oppression or exploitation which were the hallmark of an earlier generation of nationalist historiography. Even scholars with strong feelings about partition and the presence of British troops on (northern) Irish soil have come to recognize that professional history involves the obligation to find, test, and make use of the primary source materials of the past in such a way as to preserve the integrity and the logic of that evidence.

BIBLIOGRAPHY

Because bibliographies are the *fons et origo* of so much historical work, some of the more important guides to the Irish past deserve mention here. The prodigious energy and skill of the late Richard J. Hayes, former director of the National Library of Ireland, resulted in two monumental productions which are essential points of departure for virtually all Irish historians: *Manuscript Sources for the History of Irish Civilisation* and *Sources for the History of Civilisation: Articles in Irish Periodicals.*[4] Among the many virtues of these guides are the topical and name indexes and the wide range of archives as well as periodicals canvassed by the editor.

The most useful bibliography of historical writing since the 1930s originally appeared in *Irish Historical Studies* in 1967/1968 and 1970. These seven essays survey the best work done in Irish history over this thirty-five year period; they were edited by T. W. Moody and brought out as *Irish Historiography, 1936–1970.*[5] Moody ends this anthology with a summary essay which discusses the variety of Irish historical writing and then introduces that major undertaking, positively Actonian in its scope, *A New History of Ireland* (hereafter, *NHI*). Organized and written under the auspices of the Royal Irish Academy, this "large-scale, broadly-based, cooperative history of Ireland" will run eventually to nine volumes. The historical implications and parameters of this project are discussed below. Suffice to say here that the *NHI* also involves bibliographical work of prime importance. J. G. Simms's fine bibliography in volume 3, *Early Modern Ireland, 1534–1691* (hereafter, *NHI* 3) augurs well for the bibliographical prospects of this venture.[6] Several other guides to Irish history deserve mention: Helen F. Mulvey has surveyed Irish history insofar as it relates to the British Commonwealth,[7] and Edith M. Johnston has produced a useful pamphlet, *Irish History: A Select Bibliography.*[8] Another welcome contribution from the *NHI*'s ancillary publications is a scholarly edition of Giraldus Cambrensis's *Expugnatio Hibernica: The Conquest of Ireland.*[9] Military history has profited from the late Gerard A. Hayes-McCoy's "Twenty-five Years of Irish Military History" in the *Irish Sword*; and modern political historians may find some helpful archival information in Chris Cook, *Sources in British Political History, 1900–1951.*[10] Since all bibliographies become dated, it is necessary to keep a close watch on the annual list of publications in the September issue of *IHS*.

In recent years various works of reference, including biographical and statistical material, have eased the burdens of Irish historians. Among the most useful of these are two of the ancillary volumes of the *NHI: Irish Historical Statistics: Population*, *1821–1971* and *Parliamentary Election Results in Ireland*, *1801–1922*.[11] Volume 8 of the *NHI* will contain a chronology of Irish history along with maps and other reference material, and volume 9 will be "general Bibliography, illustrations, and other reference matter." An Irish equivalent of the *Abstract of British Historical Statistics* remains a desideratum, but the ancillary publications of the *NHI* seem to be moving in that direction.

In *An Atlas of Irish History*, Ruth Dudley Edwards has provided a curious mixture of maps and historical commentary organized in a rather arbitrary manner.[12] Biographical material may be found in Henry Boylan, *A Dictionary of Irish Biography*, which ranges from St. Patrick to Eamon De Valera. Students of "the quality" may profit from the fifth edition of *Burke's Irish Family Records*, the "narrative pedigrees" of Irish landed families, most of whom fall today into the category of landless Anglo-Irish gentry.[13] This volume contains the genealogical particulars of some 514 families which belonged neither to the peerage nor the baronetage. No more than 20 percent of these families could claim descent from Irish or Celtic forebears.

HISTORIOGRAPHY

General histories of Ireland run the gamut from bland, factual textbooks to subjective works or highly interpretive essays. Single-author texts have the advantage of providing a reasonably coherent view of the past, in contrast to the serial or multivolume history which contains as many different styles and emphases as there are authors. Admittedly, the prospect of writing the "total history" of Ireland—or any other country for that matter—presents a challenge sufficiently daunting to deter all but the hardiest historian. J. C. Beckett, the author of that impressive text *The Making of Modern Ireland*, *1603–1923*, has drawn an important distinction between the history of the land and that of the people; and he has emphasized the cultural consequences of the uneasy relationship between colonizers and colonized in Ireland since the early seventeenth century.[14] Political myths have exercised almost as powerful a pull on Irishmen as has the hunger for land, and T. W. Moody's lecture "Irish History and Irish Mythology" expose to daylight some of the pervasive myths about political conflict and loyalty which have dedeviled the past as well as the "living present" in Ireland.[15]

The production of anthologies containing essays on aspects of Irish history for a general audience has steadily increased since the 1960s, and among the best of these are the Thomas Davis Lecture series, which have introduced the work of prominent historians in Ireland to countless friends of Irish history. Most of these Radio Telefís Éireann (RTE) broadcasts have been revised for publication in book form. For those making their first foray into Ireland's past, the best field guide remains *The Course of Irish History*, edited by T. W. Moody and F. X. Martin, which contains twenty-one essays covering the centuries from prehistoric times to 1966.[16] This anthology serves as a reminder of what can be done through scholarly popularization and choice illustrations to educate a citizenry about its past.

The teaching of Irish history has been greatly helped in recent years by the appearance of a serial history under the general editorship of James Lydon and Margaret MacCurtain. Called *The Gill History of Ireland*, this series begins with the pre-Viking period and ends with the early 1970s.[17] The eleven short volumes vary considerably in perspective and quality. Fortunately, the few dull or unilluminating texts are outnumbered by the bright, bold, or thoughtful contributions. For the modern era, two volumes deserve special mention: Gearóid Ó Tuathaigh's *Ireland before the Famine, 1798–1848* strikes a judicious balance between specialist and generalist history; and Joseph Lee's *The Modernisation of Irish Society, 1848–1918* is both original and idiosyncratic. Lee uses the keyword *modernisation* in a way that smacks more of politicization than "the growth of equality of opportunity." The book fairly bristles with provocative arguments, some of which might just be taken too literally by the uninitiated.[18]

By all odds, the most ambitious venture in Irish historiography in the last several decades has been *A New History of Ireland*. Although the indefinite article "A" should be replaced by "The," and although only one volume of this enterprise has appeared so far, it is fair to say that these volumes will become the standard interpretation of the Irish past against which revisionist-minded historians will react for years to come.[19] The editors have envisioned this collaborative work as "not a series of isolated volumes but a harvesting of the best contemporary scholarship available for each period up to the end of 1974."[20] Conceived in 1962 and launched as a funded project in 1968, the *NHI* will place Irish historiography on a firmer footing no matter how dated some of the individual contributions may become. For T. W. Moody, the chief architect and master builder of the *NHI*, this project represents a lifetime of objectifying Irish history and encouraging the kind of scholarly cooperation that transcends personalities, politics, and generations. The first volume to appear, *Early Modern Ireland* has lived up to expectations. The narrative contributions of Aidan Clarke, G. A. Hayes-McCoy, Patrick J. Corish, and J. G. Simms go far to explain the political and social disruptions of this period. Here is that rarity in historical writing, a work that can be read with profit and pleasure by both educated laymen and professional historians.[21]

There has been no dearth of "imaginative" essays about the Irish Question. Apart from several short texts on Irish history,[22] there is a lively, eclectic discussion of Anglo-Irish misunderstandings in Patrick O'Farrell's *Ireland's English*

Question, Anglo-Irish Relations, 1534–1970.[23] In this work, O'Farrell rightly stresses the powerful Catholic presence in Irish nationalism, as both clerical and episcopal forces joined the mass protest against British rule and Irish landlordism. In a remarkably magisterial survey, *Ireland since the Famine*, F. S. L. Lyons has combined a flowing narrative with fine detail to produce the best one-volume history of Irish politics and society for the 120-year period in question.[24] This work has some of that Leckyan quality of gravitas which will preserve it from carping criticism for years to come. For the general reader who likes a readable text broken up by pleasing illustrations, there is L. M. Cullen's *Life in Ireland*, which provides glimpses of Irish social and economic conditions, especially since the conquests of the Tudor-Stuart period.[25]

POLITICAL HISTORY

The nature of the English conquest and administration of the country, the growth of a national identity, and the causes of rebellion against British authority are themes that continue to inspire a great deal of historical activity. Most of the work in the political category focuses on particular epochs or events, but several volumes transcend these limits and traverse centuries. In Brian Farrell, editor's *The Irish Parliamentary Tradition*, a group of historians discusses the nature and function of representative institutions since Gaelic times.[26] A long and detailed narrative of the Irish struggle for independence appears in Robert Kee's *The Green Flag*, the bulk of which deals with the years 1865–1923.[27] Based on extensive research in newspapers as well as in secondary sources, Kee's book supersedes Dorothy Macardle's impassioned and triumphal study, *The Irish Republic.*[28] Owen Dudley Edwards has written a long and thoughtful essay—almost a small book—on the mythic and historical roots of Irish national aspirations, which contains some moving passages about the meaning of being Irish and Catholic in a British Protestant, imperial context.[29]

As for monographic studies, the history of Tudor Ireland has been dominated by two closely related themes: the nature of the Reformation and the expansion of the English state in Ireland. The intimate connections between church and state make it unwise to separate religious and secular policies in this age. R. Dudley Edwards has compiled a straight and narrow narrative of Anglo-Irish relations in the sixteenth century.[30] Brendan Bradshaw has produced a very different book on Henrician (and Thomas Cromwellian) strategies in Ireland: *The Dissolution of the Religious Orders in Ireland under Henry VIII* deals incisively with church–state relations in both England and Ireland and explores the condition of the Irish monastic orders.[31] Tudor efforts to pacify Ireland and make it a land fit for profitable colonization are ably analyzed by Nicholas P. Canny in *The Elizabethan Conquest of Ireland: A Pattern Established.* Canny contends that Lord Deputy Sir Henry Sidney's vigorous administration in the 1560s and 1570s represented a new departure in Anglo-Irish relations.[32] English attitudes toward the Irish and the kind of enforced acculturation some Englishmen wished to impose upon the "inferior" inhabitants of Ireland are considered by Canny in a suggestive article.[33] Here his argument complements and extends that offered by David Beers Quinn in his important short study, *The Elizabethans and the Irish.*[34] One reason why the Tudor state fell so far short of its goal of consolidating the conquest of Ireland had to do with the inadequacy of its information gathering and storage system. J. H. Andrews confronts this interesting subject and points up how little most English settlers knew about the Irish terrain and climate.[35]

John J. Silke has written an informed account of the doomed Spanish invasion of Munster in 1601/1602,[36] and Canny has shed some new light on Ulster under the aegis of Hugh O'Neill as well as the events leading up to the famous flight of the earls.[37] The attempts of the English government to tighten control over Ireland in the reign of James I are treated in Victor Treadwell's article on the Irish customs.[38] In *The Old English in Ireland, 1625–1642*, Aidan Clarke studied the declining fortunes of the Anglo-Norman elite during the reign of Charles I.[39] This book affords many insights into the conflicting loyalties and interests which culminated in the rebellion of 1641/1642. Besides his sterling contribution to *NHI 3*, Clarke has also delved into the organization and politics of the Irish military establishment in the latter 1620s.[40]

The Cromwellian era in Ireland has elicited several important studies. Using a computerized "profile" of English investors in Irish land, Karl S. Bottigheimer has analyzed the economic and social bases of the mid-seventeenth-century plantation.[41] Robert C. Simington has used the books of survey and distribution to produce a meticulous record of those Irishmen who acquired land in Connacht after being driven off their properties to the east.[42] T. C. Barnard's *Cromwellian Ireland: English Government and Reform in Ireland, 1649–1660* is a significant contribution to the study of English policy during the interregnum.[43] Barnard argues that, far from being repressive, Henry Cromwell tried hard to improve the quality and the efficiency of the Irish administration. Despite the loss of so much documentation in the great fire at the Four Courts (1922), Barnard has pieced together an impressive account of Cromwell's efforts to impose the "benefits" of direct rule on the country.[44]

Irish history during the Restoration has not been as well served as the Cromwellian regime, but J. G. Simms surveys the years 1660–1685 in a learned manner in chapter 17 of *NHI 3*.[45] In *Jacobite Ireland, 1685–91*, Simms effectively covers the political and military history of these critical years.[46] Irish politics and Anglo-Irish relations after the Williamite conquest are carefully considered in Francis G. James's *Ireland in the Empire, 1688–1770*.[47] James deals with a period slighted by Lecky and other political historians for whom eighteenth-century Irish history really meant Grattan, the Patriots, the Volunteers, and legislative independence.[48] More recently, James has done some work on the Irish peerage and the Irish House of Lords in the same era.[49] In a recent article J. C. D. Clark has questioned James's emphasis on the Irish initiative in Anglo-Irish relations, arguing that English ministers wielded effective control over the course of Irish politics.[50]

R. B. McDowell, author of the still valuable *Irish Public Opinion, 1750–1800*, has reviewed Ireland's position within the empire;[51] and J. C. Beckett has examined the constitutional relations between Ireland and England.[52] Together these essays form a useful background for Maurice R. O'Connell's *Irish Politics and Social Conflict in the Age of the American Revolution*.[53] O'Connell deals deftly with the turbulent political scene in these years and examines government responses to popular unrest and the Volunteer movement.[54] In *John Foster: The Politics of the Anglo-Irish Ascendancy*, A. P. W. Malcolmson has used a biographical mode to illuminate both domestic politics and political relations with England before and after the union.[55] In this monograph and in various articles, Malcolmson has shed much light on the workings of patronage and influence in eighteenth-century Leinster and Ulster.[56] Political historians will find useful information in Peter Jupp's book on elections in Ireland and Britain from the 1780s to the 1830s.[57]

There is need of more analytical work on politics in the latter half of the eighteenth century—above and beyond what Edith M. Johnston accomplished in her neo-Namierite study *Great Britain and Ireland, 1760–1800*.[58] Admittedly, R. B. McDowell's latest book, *Ireland in the Age of Imperialism and Revolution 1760–1801* goes a long way to fill the gaps in our knowledge of this period.[59] This long and broad book represents empirical history in its purest form. It may lack a historiographical dimension and could use a central thesis or line of argument; but it draws life from a formidable array of primary sources—manuscript as well as printed. Returning to the terrain he traversed many years ago in *Irish Public Opinion, 1750–1800*, McDowell ranges far and wide across the social, political, and cultural landscape, and his grasp of English politics shows to advantage in the sections on Anglo-Irish relations. Half of this hefty volume (the text runs to 704 pages) is devoted to the 1790s; and the chapters on the agitation for Catholic relief, the ideas and activities of the United Irishmen, and the insurrection of 1798 are particularly valuable. This marathon work notwithstanding, we still could use scholarly studies of the Volunteer movement and the Society of United Irishmen. Both Henry Grattan and Wolfe Tone deserve full-length biographical portraits.[60] Thomas Pakenham merits praise for his eminently readable account of the rising of 1798, *The Year of Liberty*, which derives much of its vitality from a host of manuscript sources.[61] The author's fondness for dramatic description make the battle scenes in this book echo with the sounds of swords and pikes clashing and muskets and cannon firing. This is epic history informed by wide research and designed for an audience much larger than the readership of *Irish Historical Studies.*[62]

Surveys of Irish politics and Anglo-Irish relations since the Act of Union have proliferated of late. Among the most useful of these introductions to the Irish Question are Oliver MacDonagh's *Ireland: The Union and Its Aftermath*; Patrick O'Farrell's *England and Ireland since 1800*; and Lawrence J. McCaffrey's *The Irish Question, 1800–1922.*[63] In one way or another, all these "texts" deal with themes that emerge in Nicholas Mansergh's standard work on Ireland's place within the British imperial matrix.[64] Some rather superficial views of Irish secret societies and underground groups may be found in a volume of Thomas Davis Lectures edited by T. Desmond Williams.[65] These short studies of the Whiteboys, United Irishmen, Ribbonmen, Fenians, and other associations point up the need for deeper research into these clandestine groups.

G. C. Bolton discusses the origins and implications of the Act of Union in his painstaking monograph, *The Passing of the Irish Act of Union: A Study in Parliamentary Politics.*[66] Hereward Senior has diligently traced the evolution of Protestant property-defense groups in county Armagh and elsewhere into the powerful counterrevolutionary and anti-Catholic force known as the Orange Order.[67] Given the paucity of internal records and the political sensitivities of the present membership, the complex history of Orangeism up to the present day has still to be written.[68] For the period 1812–1847, much of the extant work deals with either the administration of justice (coercion acts, police, and agrarian unrest) and famine relief or with O'Connellite politics. Norman Gash reveals some of the atrocious features of agrarian crime during Peel's chief secretaryship (1812–1818) in his near-definitive biography of Peel;[69] and Galen Broeker has explained the difficulties faced by authorities in Dublin Castle in trying to apprehend and punish the perpetrators of such crimes.[70]

The most helpful guide through the maze of Dublin Castle's twenty-two departments (as of 1801) is R. B. McDowell's *The Irish Administration, 1801–1914.*[71] Even though the author skirts the perimeter of the MacDonagh-Parris debate over the origins of government growth, this study is essential reading for all those concerned about the British presence in Ireland during the union. In the realm of O'Connellite studies, Maurice R. O'Connell has provided scholars with a great stimulus in the form of eight volumes of the Liberator's *Correspondence.*[72] Containing some thirty-five hundred letters from Daniel O'Connell's private letters, this labor of editorial devotion and skill reveals much about O'Connell, his family, and his friends and foes from 1792 to his death in 1847. It is to be hoped that these letters will form the nucleus of a full-length biographical portrait of O'Connell.[73] Maurice O'Connell has also discussed his namesake's Irishness, indebtedness, and aversion to religious discrimination as well as political violence in several thoughtful essays.[74] Lawrence McCaffrey has chronicled O'Connell's political moves and motives in 1843, when the repeal campaign peaked and the leader refused to run the risk of an Irish "Peterloo" at Clontarf.[75] Jacqueline R. Hill has investigated the political attitudes of Dublin's middle-class Repealers;[76] and Patrick O'Donoghue has written three detailed articles about the tithing system and the spreading resistance to payment of tithes in the early 1830s.[77]

In marked contrast to the continuing neglect of Young Ireland during the last two decades, historians have shown an appetite for Fenian activities and attitudes.[78] Among the more valuable biographies of prominent Fenians are Desmond Ryan's *The Fenian Chief: A Biography of James Stephens* and Marcus Bourke's *John O'Leary: A Study in Irish Separatism*.[79] Leon Ó Broin's *Fenian Fever: An Anglo-American Dilemma* considers the revolutionary movement on both sides of the Atlantic.[80] Two short anthologies contain several perceptive essays about Fenian attitudes and achievements.[81] But the riches of the Fenian papers in the State Paper Office in Dublin and the full potential of the subject have yet to be exploited.[82] The doyen of Irish underground studies, Leon Ó Broin, has also published a general history of the Irish Republican Brotherhood in which the Fenians play their part and the political legacy of Fenianism receives recognition.[83]

The politics of Irish land legislation have earned their rightful place in both British and Irish historiography. A good example of the Cambridge school of "high politics" is E. D. Steele's *Irish Land and British Politics: Tenant Right and Nationality, 1865–1870*.[84] In this important book, Steele reconstructs the making of William Gladstone's first Irish Land Act of 1870 and explains the compromises of ideology and interest within the Liberal party which made possible that landmark measure. Despite oversimplications of tenant right, agrarian crime, and nationalist sentiment in Ireland, this microscopic analysis of the Irish policymaking process at Westminster possesses value. Steele has also written something of an apologia concerning Gladstone's mission to pacify Ireland, arguing that the Grand Old Man's Irish concerns sprang from a mixture of conservatism, liberal Anglicanism, and a profound belief not only in the power of prayer but in his own ability to shape public opinion.[85] In an unusual article with a comparative dimension, Clive Dewey has argued that historicist thinking about tenant right and other supposedly Celtic customs strongly influenced Liberal land reform in both Ireland and Scotland.[86]

The task of analyzing Irish elections has been greatly eased by Brian M. Walker's data-laden article on the electorate and also by the volume he compiled and edited for the *NHI*. Both works contain vital information about the changing franchise and electorate as well as parliamentary divisions and Irish MPs at Westminster.[87] K. T. Hoppen has carried forward and extended the work of

John H. Whyte on electoral behavior in the nineteenth century, documenting numerous instances of landlord pressure on the tenantry in order to ensure the victory of their own candidates.[88] Students of twentieth-century politics and elections will find much utility in Cornelius J. O'Leary's new book *Irish Elections, 1918–1977.*[89]

Since 1966 the historiography of the land war (1879–1882 and thereafter) has undergone something of a revolution. Analytical studies based on fuller documentation (especially newspapers and police reports) and using more sophisticated quantitative techniques have begun to replace the traditional narrative accounts of John E. Pomfret and Norman D. Palmer.[90] The authors of these newer works have tried to explain political phenomena in essentially social terms or have concentrated on the political implications of social and economic change. In pursuit of conclusions for their premises, they have ventured well beyond the frontiers of political history and have given much thought to structural changes in Irish rural society.

A good example of the new genre of land-war studies may be found in James Donnelly's book on nineteenth-century Cork, almost one-third of which is devoted to "the two phases" of this climactic agitation against landlordism.[91] Moving back and forth across the borders of county Cork, Donnelly's two long chapters illuminate many facets of the land war at both the local and national level. Among other, younger historians who have combined micro and macro analytical approaches to this subject is Samuel Clark, the historical sociologist, who published a pioneering article in 1971 entitled "The Social Composition of the Land League."[92] In this essay, Clark uses the occupational status of persons arrested under the coercion act of 1881 to show the relatively high involvement of "townsmen" in the rural agitation. As Clark sees it, the Land League owed much of its success to shopkeepers, small businessmen, and publicans in the towns, men who had some vested interests in the fortunes of Irish agriculture and also possessed the political skills necessary to launch and sustain a coalition of this magnitude. In his recent book *The Social Origins of the Irish Land War*, Clark pursues this line of argument, delving into the causes and consequences of the political mobilization of large and small farmers and their allies in the towns.[93] The ultimate aim of this "challenging collectivity" was to undo the English conquest of Ireland and return the land to the people—Gaelic and Catholic. Invoking the models of collective behavior used in *l'atelier Tilly*, Clark uses an impressive array of data and statistical procedures to explain why the tenants and their urban allies chose certain forms of protest—legal and illegal—in their quest for radical agrarian reform. Although this book goes far to clarify some of the basic changes in post-famine rural society, the author's central thesis about the Land League's successful integration of rural and urban communities in Catholic–nationalist Ireland tends to obscure (if not deny) the existence of powerful tensions and conflicts within "the challenging collectivity."

The historiographical challenge inherent in Clark's book has been taken up by Paul Bew, whose *Land and the National Question in Ireland 1858–82* contends that the Land League was no more unified a collectivity than the peasantry from which it sprang.[94] Working within a fundamentally Marxian tradition, Bew insists that the conflict between small farmers in the west and large farmers or graziers in the south and east shaped the course of the land war. Much of this book is concerned with the "class struggle" between the near-subsistence farmers of Connaught and the prosperous farmers of Munster and Leinster, and there are moments when one wonders whether or not this conflict was more important than that between tenants and landlords. The extent to which large and small farmers constituted mutually antagonistic "classes" and the nature of the "hegemony" established by the "bourgeois" graziers over the small farmers are questions in need of more answers than Bew provides. But leaving these more conceptual problems aside, this book significantly advances our understanding of the ideological and strategic disputes within the league, and it rightly stresses the offensive (as distinct from defensive) nature of the league's operations. Rich in detail and forceful in argument, Bew's book captures the dynamic interplay between the forces of agrarianism and nationalism in this era.

Another line of inquiry into "the challenging collectivity" has been opened up by William L. Feingold's investigation of the bid by nationalist farmers to wrest control of the Boards of Guardians from the landlords and their clients after 1878.[95] Feingold sees this electoral assault on a traditional bastion of landlordism —local poor law administration—as a major step toward representative self-government. His maps of the results of Board of Guardian elections reveal sweeping gains by the tenantry during the early 1880s in most of Munster, western Connaught, and northern Leinster. But the landlords did manage to control poor law patronage in at least half the unions, and they dominated the influential grand juries in most parts of the country until the passing of the Local Government Act in 1898.

Apart from the perennial appeal of the land war, the principal attraction of this phase of Irish history remains Parnell. The lure of this improbable leader of a Catholic, democratic, and antilandlord movement has increased rather than diminished over the past decade, owing in large part to the central paradox of the man and the career, not to mention the romantic and tragic elements in his personal life. At long last there is a biography that comes close to capturing both the man and the myth: F. S. L. Lyons's *Charles Stewart Parnell*.[96] The dearth of Parnell papers makes it unlikely that this study will be superseded for decades to come. Lyons's fluent pages may give some informed readers a sense of déjà

connu, but this biography has the merit of placing Parnell's personality and career firmly within a framework of Irish and British political history, and the author's judgments continually inspire confidence. Parnell, of course, has long been
ripe for psychoanalytical treatment, and Joseph Woods's preliminary diagnosis of
the patient as "a depressive type" tormented by self-destructive impulses and deluded by fantasies of omnipotence deserves wider circulation and fuller discussion by both the doubters and believers in post mortem analysis.[97]

An unusual experiment in "contextual biography," which complements and
reinforces Lyons's biography, is R. F. Foster's *Charles Stewart Parnell: The
Man and His Family*.[98] Foster examines the social and economic ambience of the
Parnells—the landed elite of county Wicklow—and scrutinizes the roots and
branches of the family, including Delia, the "eccentric" American mother; and
Fanny and Anna, the two most "political" and therefore rebellious (or vice versa)
daughters. Foster stops short of dealing with Parnell's career after 1875, but he
has much to say about the emotional and financial instability of the whole family
and sheds light on Parnell's frantic efforts to make his estate pay, through mining
and timber ventures, which yielded no profit. Despite Parnell's talents, the sands
(or stones) of Avondale did not turn into gold. Parnell's "state trial" in 1887–
1880, arising out of the *Times's* spurious charges of complicity in Irish "political crimes," has been covered in two judicious articles by T. W. Moody and
F. S. L. Lyons.[99] Michael Hurst has drawn an impressionistic sketch of Parnell, which emphasizes the latter's "emotional self-indulgence" and "lack of
self-restraint."[100]

In another long and masterly biography, *John Dillon*, the prolific Lyons has
traversed the career of that influential politician who served the cause of home
rule so single-mindedly during the "reigns" of Parnell and Redmond.[101] Based
on the Dillon family papers, this biography not only enlarges Dillon's stature
but reveals the complexities of the man and the political situation in which he had
to function. Dillon's former comrade-in-arms and subsequent foe William
O'Brien has been treated to a lucid biography by Joseph V. O'Brien, who explains why his protagonist was so often isolated or far removed from the mainstream of Irish nationalism after the 1890s.[102] This spate of biographies of the
leading home rulers makes the absence of a new portrait of John Redmond all the
more regrettable.

Historians continue to explore the alternating currents of British policy in Ireland and the ways in which Irish affairs affected and were affected in turn by
Westminster politics. Several new studies focus on ministerial efforts to enlist the
Pope (and also the Irish Catholic hierarchy) on the side of unionism, or of "law
and order," in Ireland.[103] The ambivalent response of the Gladstonian ministry to
Parnellism in the 1880s has also received some attention.[104] A rather different
angle on the Parnellite party may be found in Alan O'Day's book *The English Face*

of Irish Nationalism.[105] After considering the social origins, occupations, and affiliations of the Irish nationalist MPs in the Parliament of 1880–1885, O'Day embarks on a detailed tour of their individual and collective involvement in British politics and society. Although this book has its revisionist moments, these are neither so long nor so original as the author would have his readers believe, and it is important to bear in mind that this is a portrait of the face rather than the body of the Irish parliamentary party and that that face was more often than not Janus-like, presenting different features to different constituents or audiences. A rather different, indeed dangerous, face to Irish nationalism may be found in Tom Corfe's book *The Phoenix Park Murders: Conflict, Compromise and Tragedy in Ireland, 1879–1882.* Leon Ó Broin's *The Prime Informer: A Suppressed Scandal* tells the intriguing story of William Henry Joyce, the resourceful police detective who helped Dublin Castle wage its war against Fenians and other Irish agitators at home and abroad.[106] K. R. M. Short penetrates the underworld of Irish-American dynamiters and their pursuers—the Irish Special Branch, Scotland Yard's Criminal Investigation Division, and assorted spies—in his detailed study of the bombing campaign in England during the 1880s, *The Dynamite War, Irish-American Bombers in Victorian Britain.*[107]

Given the separatist tendencies long at work in the north-eastern part of Ireland, there may be some excuse for placing studies of Ulster unionism or Protestant loyalism in a separate category. Several important works on the roots of northern Irish unionism have appeared in recent years. The most radical and sociological of these is undoubtedly Peter Gibbon's *The Origins of Ulster Unionism.*[108] This slender volume contains more controversial matter than most books three times as long. The concepts and the terminology of an eclectic sociology underlie this analysis of occupation, ethnicity, ideology, and socioeconomic class in the province. Dismissing all previous writing on the subject as "speculative," the author has tried to reconstruct the social and economic structure of nineteenth-century Ulster in neo-Marxian terms. Although hardly free from speculation, Gibbon's thesis about the hegemonic activities of Belfast's Protestant businessmen will, it is hoped, give rise to an informed discussion rather than an ideological shindy.

Another noteworthy attempt to locate the taproot of Protestant loyalism in the north comes from David W. Miller, who argues in his article "Presbyterianism and 'Modernization' in Ulster" that evangelical Protestantism met the emotional or spiritual needs of an artisanal class (mostly weavers) who were undergoing the painful process of "modernization."[109] Miller's new monograph on the historical origins of northern unionism, *Queen's Rebels: Ulster Loyalism in Historical Perspective,* is an interesting mixture of past and present politics, personal insights, and several more doses of modernization theory.[110] The result deserves the attention of all students of modern Irish (not just Ulster) politics, whether or not they subscribe to Ernest Gellner's ideas about the relationship of nationalism to modernization.

The study of Irish unionism has made much progress since the 1960s. In his two-volume work *Irish Unionism*, Patrick Buckland has diligently explored the archives and newspapers of Belfast and Dublin.[111] His survey of unionism, north and south of the border, moves rather ponderously at times across the political landscape. If they lack a social as well as economic context, these volumes remain essential reading for students of the antinationalist movement. The efforts of Liberal and Conservative unionists to woo moderate nationalists or home rulers before World War I have been examined by several historians.[112] A. T. Q. Stewart has narrated the dramatic story of how the leaders of northern unionism mobilized their followers into the Ulster Volunteer Force (UVF) between 1912 and 1914.[113]

Students of Ireland's place in the transatlantic triangle represented by Washington, London, and Dublin should consult Alan J. Ward's concise book *Ireland and Anglo-American Relations, 1899–1921*.[114] Ward outlines the ways in which the Irish question and Irish-American politicians left their mark on American politics and diplomacy. This book concentrates on the wartime years, when the Irish-American lobby thwarted attempts to improve Anglo-American relations.[115]

Irish history since 1914 continues to be shaped by the climactic events of Easter week 1916. The elaborate celebrations of the fiftieth anniversary of the rebellion served to stimulate the 1916 industry. Commemorative brochures and stamps as well as compilations of historical essays and reminiscences almost flooded the market. F. X. Martin, who is both a medievalist and an expert on 1916, has written several long and useful commentaries on the recent literature concerning the rebellion, and these should be consulted before venturing into so crowded a field.[116] Among the best accounts of the political and military aspects of the Rising are the contributions of the late Maureen Wall and G. A. Hayes-McCoy to the official commemorative volume.[117] In a lively and authoritative work, Leon Ó Broin has viewed the Rising from the windows of Dublin Castle, and his picture of the government's myopia and bungling adds an important dimension to this subject.[118] George Dangerfield has produced an eloquent account of the origins and aftermath of Easter 1916 in *The Damnable Question: A Study in Anglo-Irish Relations*.[119] This work contains compassionate portraits of the "rebel" leaders and traces Lloyd George's tortuous steps toward a negotiated settlement after 1916. The book is uneven in both coverage and documentation, but the author's fondness for the epic mode and his urbane style make it eminently readable.

Patrick Lynch has reflected on the social and ideological premises of the Easter Rising and discusses the reasons why socialism failed to appeal to the Irish people in the 1920s.[120] In a profound and sobering essay, full of lessons for our own times, the late Father Francis Shaw has drawn attention to the destructive mythology of violence and hatred engendered by the Rising.[121]

The biographers have been busy with the principals of 1916. Ruth Dudley Edwards has written a sympathetic but not uncritical study of Patrick Pearse;[122] Richard P. Davis has helped to revive interest in Arthur Griffin (who did not, of course, participate in the Rising);[123] and Samuel Levenson as well as Owen Dudley Edwards have paid homage to James Connolly.[124] Constance, Countess de Markievicz, whose life made mockery of Yeats's lament that "romantic Ireland was dead and gone," has been the subject of two impressive and affectionate biographies.[125] Roger Casement, the haunted humanitarian and violator of British social and political codes of behavior, has also had the benefit of two fluent biographies, which seek the sources of his martyrdom.[126] The "official" biography of De Valera suffers from the inherent drawbacks of that genre but contains interesting material from "Dev's" personal papers.[127] From the English version of the original Irish edition of the biography, De Valera emerges as a politician of far greater moderation than even his mildest critics would allow.

The turbulent years 1916–1924, when constitutionalism fell victim to the long-pent-up forces of anger and frustration, have been reviewed in countless book and articles. The fifteen essays in T. Desmond Williams, editor's *The Irish Struggle, 1916–1926* cover aspects of the Rising, the Anglo-Irish war, and the civil war years.[128] David Savage has examined in detail both Liberal and Lloyd Georgian efforts to curb Irish extremists and deal with the moderate nationalists.[129] R. B. McDowell's lucid look on the Irish Convention of 1917–1918 provides an introduction to D. G. Boyce's valuable study of the ambivalent response of the British government and public to the guerilla war and the official reprisals of the military in Ireland.[130,131] Charles Townshend has exposed the ineptness of British Cabinet policy and military strategy in *The British Campaign in Ireland, 1919–1921*. This tightly argued work points up the absence of a coherent Irish policy at Westminster and the tragic consequences of employing military forces untrained for guerilla warfare in an operation marred by inadequate supplies and tactics.[132]

The triangular negotiations between political (and paramilitary) leaders in Dublin, Belfast, and London which culminated in the treaty of 1921 have received much notice. Besides the more general discussion found in Lyons, Kee, and Dangerfield, there are biographies of several of the participants: Margery Forester's life of Michael Collins and Andrew Boyle's book on Erskine Childers.[133,134] These are admiring portraits of two talented men who fought hard for Irish freedom and then fought each other, only to be killed by the violent forces they had helped to unleash after 1916. F. S. L. Lyons has followed the course of the Dail debates in 1921 over the treaty,[135] and several historians have studied different sections of the tangled skein of convictions and interests which made the partition of Ireland virtually unavoidable.[136]

Freedom fighters and underground armies rarely create or leave behind much documentation, and students of the Irish Republican Army must perforce depend on uncorroborated memoirs, diaries, and anecdotes as well as newspapers for their material. T. P. Coogan's *The IRA* is a chatty piece of informed journalism which suffers from numerous misspellings. But the author has gathered some revealing information about IRA operations.[137] By contrast J. Bowyer Bell, in *The Secret Army: A History of the I.R.A.*, *1916–70*, provides a deeper foundation, although he too relies on interviews with veterans and "actors" who are not exactly *hors de combat*.[138]

Only recently has the history of Irish labor and working-class politics begun to emerge as a separate and almost equal field. Emmet Larkin's study *James Larkin* was something of a landmark in this respect, and since then Connolly's writings have been "rediscovered" by a newer generation of admirers.[139] Patrick Berresford Ellis has produced a pastiche of political history, drawing on Connolly's perceptions, in *A History of the Irish Working Class*.[140] Undoubtedly the most rigorous work in this field since J. D. Clarkson's classic text *Labour and Nationalism in Ireland* is Arthur Mitchell's *Labour in Irish Politics*, *1890–1930*.[141] This study ranges far and wide across the embattled zones of Irish trade unionism and socialism, and Mitchell delves deeply into the sources of conflict within Liberty Hall and among socialists of varying hues.[142]

Of all the recent writing on Irish politics since the fall of Parnell, perhaps the most challenging and heuristic comes from several social (and political) geographers who have tried to measure and map the various elements of Irish nationalism. Here the title of pioneer goes to the German scholar Erhard Rumpf, who set out in the 1950s to identify the ingredients of Irish political allegiance since 1921. His doctoral dissertation has now been translated from the German, revised, and given a firmer historical framework with the help of A. C. Hepburn. The result of this collaboration is an impressive book: *Nationalism and Socialism in Twentieth-century Ireland*.[143] Rumpf used a number of variables to account for voter support of Sinn Fein, Labour, and the other major parties after the civil war had ended. Avoiding the statistical procedures of the cliometricians (rank correlation coefficients, multiple regression etc.), he relied instead on visual comparisons of frequency and intensity distributions of a wide range of political behavior, using a series of county-based maps to record these differences. However rough and ready some of the hypotheses and data in this study, there is no doubt that political historians have much to learn from the questions and answers posed by Rumpf.

In the wake of Rumpf's inquiry but making its own waves comes David Fitz-patrick's work on the social and political dimensions of modern Irish nationalism. His book *Politics and Irish Life, 1913–21* is a fresh and exhaustive treatment of county Clare during the revolutionary era.[144] Fitzpatrick has made impressive use of manuscript, newspaper, and official or government sources, supplemented by interviews with those who knew the Clare scene well in those turbulent years. Students of both the "old" and the "new" politics, especially those interested in the interplay of social and political change after the Easter Rising, will have to read this work and address its arguments. In a subsequent essay of remarkable scope and statistical bravado, entitled "The Geography of Irish Nationalism, 1910–1921," Fitzpatrick has extended and improved upon the variables of po-litical participation used by Rumpf.[145] This article concentrates on three "major manifestations" of Irish nationalism: "violence, voting, and participation in na-tionalist organizations." Both statistical and qualitative evidence moves him to conclude that nationalism was distinctly rural in character, being most deeply rooted in the poorer and overcrowded parishes of Munster and Connacht. Ques-tions remain about the relative significance of ideology, social class, status, and leadership in fomenting the various expressions of nationalism, but Fitzpatrick's statistical work does help to penetrate some of the "self-deceptions" so widespread in both Irish society and historiography.[146]

The history of Ireland since 1921 has been surveyed in several series of Thomas Davis Lectures, which supplement and complement Lyons's informative chapters in *Ireland since the Famine*.[147] A scholarly history of the civil war has yet to be written, but Calton Younger's popular narrative, *Ireland's Civil War* out-lines the basic divisions and ugly incidents of those years. Given the centrality of the civil war in modern Irish political life, it is revealing of lingering sensitivities that so little serious work has been done on that brutal conflict.[148] In *Ireland since the Rising*, T. P. Coogan skims the surface of politics and society up to the mid 1960s.[149] Two heavyweight studies of politics and finance have appeared of late: Basil Chubb's *The Government and Politics of Ireland*, which explains how government actually works in the twenty-six counties, and Ronan Fanning's *The Irish Department of Finance, 1922–58*, which analyzes in depth state financial policies and interests.[150]

In *The Restless Dominion*, D. W. Harkness has placed Ireland within an impe-rial context, arguing that the Free State left an indelible impression on the evolv-ing Commonwealth of Nations.[151] Nicholas Mansergh discusses the constitutional implications of Ireland's dominion status in *The Commonwealth Experience*.[152] As for domestic politics, Maurice Manning's *The Blueshirts* tells the story of that drab brigade and disposes of some of the myths concerning Ireland's brush with protofascism.[153] The vexatious question of Irish neutrality in World War II and

Allied efforts to alter that position are considered in two recent books which devote much space to the Washington-Dublin connection.[154]

The far more vexatious question of Northern Ireland has given rise to a host of
books, articles, and "position papers," not to mention all the reporting of death
and destruction in the mass media. A useful bibliography of the origins and
nature of the conflict since the establishment of the so-called Orange State is
Richard Deutsch's *Northern Ireland, 1921–1974: A Select Bibliography*. Owen
Dudley Edwards's *The Sins of Our Fathers: Roots of Conflict in Northern Ireland*
and Conor Cruise O'Brien's *States of Ireland* contain profoundly personal as well
as historical passages which afford insights into the fierce tribal loyalties and
animosities which have sustained that strife.[155] In their hybrid book *Belfast,
Approach to Crisis: A Study of Belfast Politics, 1613–1970*, Ian Budge and Cornelius O'Leary have anatomized municipal politics and political attitudes.[156]
T. W. Moody's historical précis of the Northern Irish imbroglio, *The Ulster
Question, 1603–1973*, provides a sharp contrast to Liam de Paor's indictment of
the imperial policies ("divide and rule") of the English ruling class in *Divided
Ulster*.[157]

The most perceptive analysis of the political dimensions of the conflict in
Northern Ireland comes from the political scientist Richard Rose, whose *Governing without Consensus: An Irish Perspective* is based on wide reading and a revealing (if now outdated) survey of public opinion (1,291 persons scattered through
the six counties). With skill and sympathy, Rose discusses the political and religious forces which have polarized the two communities in the north.[158] Another
work of quality by a social scientist, who also raises the level of discussion above
the din of partisan pronouncements, is *Prejudice and Tolerance in Ulster*.[159] The
author, Rosemary Harris, has written a sensitive account of "interreligious" as
well as intersocial relations in a small Ulster "town," near the border with Eire.
Based on field observations made between 1952 and 1965, this study deals with
the parameters of the Protestant-Catholic dichotomy and shows how distinctions
of class and status as well as sect affected the lives and outlook of the local people.
Harris's English (and Protestant) background may help to explain why this book
sheds so much light on Protestant *mentalités* in "Ballybeg."

Since studies of the roots and branches of Ulster's deadly Upas tree will continue to flow from the commercial as well as university presses, it is hoped that
their authors will emulate the analytical rigor and sympathetic detachment of
scholars like Rose and Harris, whose writings are refreshingly free from not only
social scientific jargon but also from judgmental passages which identify the
saints and the sinners, the victims and the villains, in terms which allow of no
compromise, not to mention surrender.

CHURCH HISTORY

The study of Irish *religious* history, which includes theology, canon law, and matters of faith and morals, has taken second place to *ecclesiastical* history—the study of church organization and functions with particular emphasis on the ways church leaders used their power and influence to protect the vital interests of their respective churches. Despite the myriad connections between the churches and Irish society, state, and nation, church history deserves a category of its own. The ambitious Gill series, *A History of Irish Catholicism*, published intermittently in fasicle form under the general editorship of Monsignor Patrick J. Corish, makes a useful, if rather disjointed, introduction to this central subject.[160] Emmet Larkin's projected multivolume history of the Catholic Church in Ireland since the late eighteenth century represents a more monographic as well as "mosaic" approach to ecclesiastical history and will presumably emphasize the politics, broadly construed, of the Irish hierarchy.[161] The disproportionate amount of documentation available for the student of the Irish episcopacy means, of course, that far more is known about diocesan than parochial politics, and the daily routine of parish priests or canons lies in deep shadow.

A valuable guide to recent writing on the Catholic Church is John J. Silke's extended commentary in *Studia Hibernica*.[162] Relatively little work has been done on the church during the penal-law period, and only with the advent of the nineteenth century does the subject come alive with contributions and controversies.

In the first of three bold and ground-breaking articles, Emmet Larkin has estimated the increase in the wealth of the Catholic populace.[163] Although the economic argumentation depends rather heavily on conjecture, this essay raises important questions about the church's income and expenses and also about their impact on the Irish economy. In his second essay, "The Devotional Revolution in Ireland, 1850–75," Larkin gives credit to Paul, Cardinal Cullen for transforming Irish Catholics from nonchurchgoers and sinners to devout worshippers.[164] The absence of hard data about church attendance in the 1840s and the 1860s does not strengthen this hypothesis, but Larkin's suggestion that Cullen was the chief architect of an Irish *Catholic* identity, ripe for politicization by a leader of Parnell's stature, does carry some conviction. In the last and most problematical essay in this "historical trilogy," "Church, State, and Nation in Modern Ireland," Larkin contends that the strong tenant-farmers, or those who farmed more than thirty acres, constituted "the nation-forming class" in Ireland.[165] According to Larkin, Parnell used this class to transform the Land League into a de facto state, precursor of the modern Irish state. The Catholic clergy along with some of the bishops, so the argument goes, accepted the legitimacy of the Parnellite state and thereby forged a working alliance of nation, state, and church. These assertions would carry more force if such terms as *nation* and *state* were clearly defined and if there were more evidence about the class basis of Irish nationalism.

David W. Miller deals with Catholic Church attendance in prefamine Ireland in a stimulating article which relies on a sample from an official survey in 1834 and which suggests that more people went to mass in urban areas where English was widely spoken than in rural, Gaelic-speaking districts.[166] Oliver MacDonagh considers O'Connell's efforts to convert the hierarchy to his political objectives,[167] and E. R. Norman uses the Maynooth grant dispute of 1845 to probe the strength of popular Protestantism at Westminster.[168]

In his book *The Catholic Church and Ireland in the Age of Rebellion, 1859– 1873*, Norman examined the conflict between Cullenism and Gladstonianism. This erudite and densely documented work contains many forceful arguments about the nature of ecclesiastical politics in this era. Most historians would agree that the presiding genius of Irish Catholicism at mid-century was Paul Cullen, but they tend to disagree about the quality of that genius. In particular they dispute his role in advancing or retarding the progress of nationalism. E. D. Steele, an apostle of Cullenism, has argued that Cullen was the true champion of "O'Connellite nationalism" in the 1850s and 1860s.[169] By contrast, R. Dudley Edwards, F. S. L. Lyons, and others have argued that Cullen tried to keep the priests out of politics because of his worries about the spiritual health of the church and his fears of secularism.[170] An essential source for the study of these and óther issues is Father Peadar MacSuibhne's edition of Cullen's correspondence.[171] What the cardinal needs is a full-scale biography written by someone who is neither too pious nor too impious in the presence of Cullen's achievements and legend.

In the first three volumes of his serial history of the Catholic church in Ireland, Emmet Larkin shows how the hierarchy came to terms with the nationalist movement, the British state, and the Holy See. Larkin has combed the archives of Ireland, England, and the Vatican in order to reconstruct the high politics of church and state during the nineteenth century. These volumes deal at length with the hierarchy's position on the land question, home rule, education, church patronage, clericalism, the Plan of Campaign, and Parnell's fall from moral as well as political grace. Heavily laden with excerpts from the documents, Larkin's narrative is designed as a "mosaic" which aspires to greater historical "reality" through direct quotation. The assumption here is that the protagonists (and antagonists) should be allowed to tell their own story by means of their voluminous letters. Students of ecclesiastical politics and Parnellism will find these volumes essential reading. But some readers may wonder whether "the many varied and colored bits and pieces of evidence" add up to an effective overall design, and others may yearn for a more interpretive or structured approach.[172]

By way of contrast, there is an abundance of interpretation and argument in David W. Miller's *Church, State and Nation in Ireland, 1898–1921*.[173] Adopting the essentials of Larkin's triangular model of the Irish polity, Miller carefully traces the efforts of the Irish hierarchy to control education and influence the quality of life in an independent Ireland.[174] As for ecclesiastical politics in the twentieth century, there is no better guide than John H. Whyte's *Church and State in Modern Ireland, 1923–1970*, which deals judiciously with the hierarchy's various campaigns to establish the spiritually correct codes for the new state in an age of increasing secularism.[175]

Compared with the Protestant dissenting sects (or chapels), including northern Presbyterianism, the episcopal Church of Ireland has received more than its share of scholarly attention. The rise and fall of the established church in Ireland remains a subject of fascination to historians both within and outside the comfortable confines of Anglicanism. Donald H. Akenson's *The Church of Ireland* contains a number of useful chapters on the structure and functions—though not the theology—of the church during the nineteenth century.[176] Some informative essays about the church's trials and tribulations since disestablishment may be found in Michael Hurley, editor's *Irish Anglicanism, 1869–1969*; and R. B. McDowell has written a concise, affectionate history of the church covering the same century.[177]

Desmond Bowen's *The Protestant Crusade in Ireland, 1800–70* is the only major study of the vital evangelical awakening which spread far beyond the pale of Irish Anglicanism.[178] This book contains important chapters on the "Protestant mind," sectarian strife, and the anti-Catholic missions of Exeter Hall in Ireland. Bowen's earlier work on "souperism" deals with Protestant missionary activity during the famine and disposes of the still popular myth concerning the allegedly high price paid by the Catholic peasantry for a bowl of soup cooked in Protestant kitchens.[179] The disestablishment of the Church of Ireland has received a good deal of scholarly attention,[180] but what Irish Anglican history needs is more work on the church's role in Irish society and its contribution to maintaining the ascendancy before and after the union.

ECONOMIC HISTORY

Over the last decade, Irish economic history has advanced from infancy to adolescence, and signs of adulthood are beginning to appear in various sectors. That such rapid growth has taken place may be attributed in part to the stimulus provided by the late Kenneth H. Connell and also to the work of the prolific as well as versatile Louis M. Cullen. This field has also been nourished by the paradigms of economic history displayed in the (English) *Economic History Review* and by the powerful groundswell known in some quarters as the "new social history." The founding in 1970 of the Economic and Social History Society of Ireland has provided institutional support for a host of individual and collective enterprises. As L. A. Clarkson rightly observes in his succinct survey "The Writing of Irish Economic and Social History since 1968," the huge increase in the quantity of published work has no equivalency in terms of quality: "Much recent economic history in the work of general historians, economists, archivists, folklorists, antiquarians, and enthusiastic amateurs."[181] Nevertheless, there is no need to despair. Enough good work—professional and imaginative—has been done since the late 1960s to convince even English economic historians that the field in Ireland has entered into the stage of "self-sustaining growth" (to use the obvious cliché). The journal of the new society, *Irish Economic and Social History*, launched in 1974, has been growing steadily in both size and significance, and it serves as an effective bridge across not only disciplines but political or geographical divisions.

L. M. Cullen has written the ony respectable, modern textbook on Irish economic development, a survey that combines wide reading and tight compression.[182] It is regrettable, however, that there is no comprehensive and annotated text on the subject for seasoned readers. Writing against the traditional historicism of Froude and Lecky, Cullen makes a strong case for the autonomy of economic forces in Irish history and presses his revisionist views of both economic and demographic change. Parts of this survey rest on the solid foundation of his *Anglo-Irish Trade*, *1660–1800*, which covers economic activity in town and country and shows how Irish exports to England rose dramatically after the early eighteenth century.[183]

Eileen McCracken's study of forests and the uses of timber sheds light on a vital natural resource;[184] and W. H. Crawford shrewdly explains the changing nature of tenant right under the leasing system at work in eighteenth-century Ulster.[185] Agricultural improvements in Leinster during the later years of that century are charted by the historical geographer F. H. A. Aalen.[186] David Large's ambitious attempt to estimate the wealth of the greater Irish landowners in the age of Grattan has yet to be supplanted, although the subject requires a much larger sample of estates.[187] The process of urbanization and the quality of urbanism in the Irish hinterland have been sorely neglected by historians. L. A. Clarkson's occupational analysis of Armagh in 1770 makes a promising start in this direction, but few Irish towns possess the kind of private census which made this study possible.[188] L. M. Cullen's indefatigable researches have taken him from smuggling to flour milling during the eighteenth century;[189] and he has also helped to expose the flaws in Lynch and Vaizey's once-fashionable model of the dual economy in Ireland.[190]

Irish economic history in the nineteenth century has been much enhanced by the appearance of three notable books, each of which involves the land in one way or another. Barbara L. Solow's *The Land Question and the Irish Economy*, *1870–*

1903 deals a number of blows at long-standing beliefs about the inequities of landlordism. There are neither villains nor heroes in this cool, analytical study of agricultural yields, prices, rents, and landlord–tenant relations. Only a bold and risk-taking historian would have argued that the tenantry were actually "under-exploited" by their landlords on the basis of such slender reeds of evidence. Solow's dependence on the often-partisan testimony of witnesses summoned before the Royal Commissions on Irish land and her avoidance of estate papers tend to weaken the argument in places, but the vigor and incisiveness of her arguments make this book a major work of revisionism.[191]

The second book, W. A. Maguire's *The Downshire Estates in Ireland, 1801– 1845*, is an empirical, microanalytical study of the wealthiest estate in the country. Meticulously and deftly, Maguire explains how this great estate operated and compares its problems with those of other estates in Ireland. His chapters on estate finances, land agents, and landlord–tenant relations make this a work of prime importance.[192] The third book, James Donnelly's *The Land and the People of Nineteenth Century Cork: The Rural Economy and the Land Question*, is laden with important questions and answers. Relying on a rich variety of archival, newspaper, and parliamentary sources, Donnelly has produced a fascinating account of the economy and society of County Cork in a manner faintly reminiscent of the *Annales* school. His interest in political as well as social conflict may be judged from the amount of space (roughly one-third) devoted to the land war in Cork from 1878 to 1892. Even some Cork-born historians may question his assertion that the county was (or is) "a microcosm of the entire country"; but such overstatement may be excused by the sheer merit of the work.[193]

Students of Irish agriculture and the land question should consult an eccentric but original book which belongs in some respects more to the twentieth than to the nineteenth century: R. D. Crotty's *Irish Agricultural Production: Its Volume and Structure*.[194] Crotty's arguments about the nature of the postfamine adjustment need more testing against the regional or local realities, but they cannot be altogether ignored. Padraig G. Lane has explored the fate of insolvent estates and the working of the Incumbered Estates Court in Connacht;[195] and Cormac Ó Gráda has speculated about the modest investments of Irish landlords in permanent improvements to their estates during the third quarter of the century.[196] The extent of landlord wealth and indebtedness, and the reasons for both, stand in need of far more research.[197]

Two of the mainstays of the Irish economy in the nineteenth century—butter and drink—have received some attention of late. Donnelly has revealed the workings and profits of the Cork butter market,[198] and Joseph Lee, in an article aimed at Lynch and Vaizey's study of the Guinness brewery and their "dual-economy" thesis, has some perceptive comments to offer about the brewing industry, the circulation of money, and economic development.[199] The important subject of railway capitalization and construction stands in need of sustained and scholarly investigation. In the meantime, economic historians must rely on only one significant article in this field—Joseph Lee's "The Provision of Capital for Early Irish Railways, 1830–53."[200] For the general reader there are several new books on railways and other modes of transportation in Ireland.[201]

The growth and performance of retail markets in the nineteenth century have long been neglected, and Líam Kennedy's articles on this subject afford many insights into the workings of rural credit, profit, traders, and cooperative societies. Kennedy makes good use of government reports on the rural economy and has an impressive grasp of the competitive forces at work in the marketplace. His work points up the need for a comprehensive account of the retail and wholesale trades in Ireland, including discussion of purchasing power and credit as well as the conflicts between gombeenism and the cooperative movement.[202] Besides Kennedy's essay on the interplay of priests, traders, and cooperators, there is Patrick Bolger's new book, *The Irish Co-operative Movement*, which delves into subjects of interest to all students of Irish agriculture.[203]

The industrialization of Ulster during the nineteenth century has been receiving more attention of late, and some of the results fall somewhere between the categories of regional and national economic history. W. H. Crawford's unrivaled knowledge of the local terrain and the archives has enabled him to explain the dynamic relationship of agriculture and industry in south Ulster in the late eighteenth and early nineteenth century.[204] H. D. Gribbon has followed the course of water or hydraulic power in Ulster from the waterwheel to the turbine engine;[205] and W. E. Coe has written a useful history of engineering in the north.[206]

Economic trends since 1921 have been surveyed for the twenty-six counties by James Meenan, whose book *The Irish Economy Since 1922* is the standard work.[207] Meenan discusses government policy toward finance, taxation, population, and emigration along with a host of other economic topics. Maurice Moynihan has chronicled state banking and fiscal policies in his *Currency and Central Banking in Ireland, 1922–1960*, which complements in several respects Ronan Fanning's book on the Department of Finance.[208]

In the related field of historical demography, no book has appeared equal in scope or imagination to Kenneth Connell's *The Population of Ireland, 1750–1845*.[209] The heated debate provoked by Connell's thesis about early marriage and higher fertility continues to sputter in one form or another. L. M. Cullen has raised a dissenting voice by estimating the population of Ireland in 1600 as close to 1.4 million, which is far removed from the conventional estimate of a half million.[210] For the eighteenth century Michael Drake has tried to gauge the disastrous effects of the famine and resultant diseases in 1740–1741;[211] and Joseph

Lee has stressed the importance of regional and class variations in fertility differentials during the prefamine era.[212]

L. M. Cullen has heightened the controversy over Irish fertility rates by arguing that the potato did not dominate the diet of the poorest class of rural laborers (cottiers) until the turn of the nineteenth century.[213] The potato could not, therefore, have played the prominent role in the population increase that Connell and others alleged. For the postfamine period, two demographers, Brendan M. Walsh and Cormac Ó Gráda, have carried forward the pioneering work of S. H. Cousens on regional variations in population behavior. Walsh has shown how prefamine patterns in the western counties persisted well into the 1870s, having found a positive correlation between nuptiality, marital fertility, and inheritance of land.[214] To this regional model, Ó Gráda has added the variable of seasonal migration of laborers from the poorer districts of Connacht and Munster, a pattern which lasted into the 1890s.[215] Edward E. McKenna uses multivariate regression analysis to modify Walsh's argument about the arranged "match" and the relationship of inheritance to marriage patterns.[216] But the much firmer data available to researchers in the postfamine period leave less room for the controversies that have enlivened discussion of prefamine population trends.

SOCIAL HISTORY

Compared with economic and demographic history, Irish social history is still in the latency stage. Here and there a few signs of maturation may be discerned, but for too long the study of Irish social structure and behavior has lain in the shadow of politics. The paradigms of social history now current in English, European, and American universities seem to have made little impact on Irish historical studies. Only a few scholars have come close to using computers or quantitative methods, and some of these are still primarily concerned with political, not social, phenomena. Historians who intend to work in this still-fallow field will need to acquaint themselves with not only sociological concepts but cliometric procedures.

To date, only a few studies provide insights into Irish social structure and behavior since the sixteenth century. David Quinn's *The Elizabethans and the Irish*, for example, depicts English images of the Irish rather than the Irish realities, and it is a rare reality that is not distorted in the imaging process. Quinn and K. W. Nicholls have collaborated on a perceptive panorama of Ireland in 1534 for the *NHI*, and their chapter makes some of the most interesting reading in that volume.[217] Donald Jackson's short monograph *Intermarriage in Ireland, 1550–1650* literally charts the extent and effects of miscegenation between prominent colonizers and colonized.[218] M. Perceval-Maxwell concentrates on the Scottish roots of those migrants who moved into Ulster during the reign of James I.[219] Some of the stark contrasts between northeast and far west in the early seventeenth century may be found in Robert J. Hunter's article on town planning and building in south Ulster and in Jean M. Graham's survey of conditions in Connacht.[220,221]

Apart from L. M. Cullen's fleeting allusions to social conditions in his introductory work, *Life in Ireland*, little new light has been shed on urban and rural society during the eighteenth century. That vital subject "the origins of modern Irish society" still awaits its Harold Perkin, and in the meantime we must continue to cull the footnotes of Lecky's *History of Ireland* and savor the old-fashioned virtues of Constantia Maxwell's *Country and Town in Ireland under the Georges* for clues about the way rich and poor lived and died.[222] Several local historians have given us glimpses of social realities,[223] but only James Donnelly's searching inquiries into the Whiteboy movement of the early 1760s and the Rightboy agitation of the latter 1780s begin to open up the necessary vistas. Coming from an empirical or un-Marxist tradition, Donnelly's studies are like flares which penetrate the pitch darkness and illuminate the social and economic conflicts in those counties where the agents of popular justice rose up against arbitrary exactions, high prices, and other "offenses against the people."

With the advent of the nineteenth century, Irish social history begins to show signs of greater vitality and precision, owing in large part to the existence of better documentation. In a valuable work of both reference and interpretation, *The Irish: Emigration, Marriage, and Fertility*, Robert E. Kennedy blurs the thin line between historical sociology, demography, and social history.[224] Kennedy provides a number of tables in order to document the social and economic forces underlying the massive movement of people from rural to urban areas. Then there are two important essays by the late Kenneth Connell on social codes, religious imperatives, and sexual morality: "Illegitimacy before the Famine" and "Catholicism and Marriage in the Century after the Famine." Both essays reveal a probing and provocative mind at work, and Connell's strong opinions about such topics as clerical repression of youthful sexuality in the Catholic hinterland will hopefully stimulate further research by social historians.[225]

Irish historians often avoid definitions of the term *peasant*, in large part because it is a pejorative as well as a highly convenient epithet. Some well-informed reflections about the quality of life in the countryside may be found in a collection of essays about the Irish peasantry written in honor of the late Martin J. Waters, whose own study of the social composition of the Irish Ireland movement stands out in this anthology.[226] (Parenthetically, Michael Anderson's quantitative study of family structure in Lancashire makes some passing comparisons with rural

Ireland, but there is no equivalent of Anderson's book for nineteenth-century Ireland.)[227] James W. Hurst has made effective use of agrarian crime statistics for the mid-nineteenth century and concludes that social unrest in "disturbed Tipperary" was no greater than in other parts of the country.[228] Pamela L. R. Horn alludes to the hard lives of agricultural laborers during the 1870s;[229] and Donnelly's book on county Cork contains many rich veins of social history. Louis Hyman has written the only modern chronicle of Irish Jewry, which includes a fascinating chapter on Leopold Bloom's ancestry.[230] Dublin awaits an urban historian capable of surpassing the standard (but hardly definitive) book by Maurice Craig, *Dublin, 1660–1860*.[231] In a suggestive article, F. O. C. Meenan has used the changing occupancy of Dublin's Georgian squares to illustrate social mobility within the professions, especially law and medicine.[232]

The history of Irish immigrants in Britain has prospered of late. Ironically, more significant work has been done on the Irish working-classes in London than in Dublin or any other Irish city. Lynn Lees' articles on the social and economic conditions of the Irish in London shed much light on spatial relations and occupations in the metropolis and yield dividends denied to noncomputerized historians.[233]

In the related field of anthropology, there has been considerable activity in recent years. Studies of what is considered to be "traditional" Irish or Gaelic society can be helpful to historians, provided they are prepared to sift the evidence and filter the premises and conclusions of the anthropological participant-observers. Most of the fieldwork done since the 1930s has been more or less synchronic and derives in one way or another from the classic work of Conrad Arensberg and Solon Kimball on west Clare in the early 1930s.[234] In recent years a more pessimistic and radical kind of anthropology has emanated from students of the Gaeltacht. Instead of the rather romantic functionalism of the Arensberg-Kimball school, which celebrated the close ties of kinship, friendship, and cooperation in these Irish-speaking communities, some of the younger workers in these western regions have adopted a critical stance that partakes of Marx, Durkheim, and Lévi-Strauss, with a dash here and there of Spengler and Althusser. Although there are significant disagreements within this cluster of radical anthropologists, most would subscribe to the view that capitalism (or the British imperial, variant of that system) has caused the ruin, decay, or demoralization of the old Gaelic world. Hugh Brody, for example, argues that the inhabitants of "Inishkillane" have lost their sense of communal purpose and self-worth since the 1930s, and, he attributes this anomie to the advent of the "new entrepreneurs" or gombeenmen, who have replaced the traditional community values and affections with the impersonal profit motive.[235] But another critic of capitalist society, Peter Gibbon, finds fault with both Brody's work and the "trail of mystification" laid down by

Arensberg and Kimball in the 1930s. Convinced that the postfamine economy was characterized by "the steadily increasing hegemony of commodity economy," he accuses the two American anthropologists of having indulged in "an extremely one-sided ethnography" and then pronounces Brody guilty of illogicality by rejecting their blatant functionalism while accepting all their assumptions about the harmony and unity of the peasant community in west Clare during the 1930s. Although these "radical" studies of decline and despair—including mental illness—in the Gaeltacht purport to be more "scientific" than the now-dated work of Arensberg and Kimball, the political burden of their messages makes them almost as vulnerable to the charge of subjectivism or presentism as the work of the more liberal, less critical anthropologists of the earlier generation.[236]

CULTURAL HISTORY

Under the rubric of cultural activities may be subsumed a wide range of historical writing concerning language, literature, architecture, and education. The changing forms and fortunes of the Irish language are discussed in twelve essays aimed at an informed audience in Brian Ó Cuív, editor's *A View of the Irish Language*.[237] W. B. Stanford has written a richly allusive book, *Ireland and the Classical Tradition*, which reveals how Ireland has been both "beneficiary and benefactor" of constantly changing classical influences.[238] Moving from humanistic to scientific matters, there is K. Theodore Hoppen's cogent study *The Common Scientist of the Seventeenth Century*, which considers the methods used by members of Dublin's Philosophical Society to observe and explain a wide range of natural phenomena.[239]

In a long and rather personal essay, *The Anglo-Irish Tradition*, J. C. Beckett has distilled a lifetime of reading and thinking about the cultural (and political) achievements of the ascendancy. Although in some respects an apologia for the values of Ireland's governing class in the eighteenth century, this work is also much more than that. Preferring the term *tradition* to *culture*, Beckett stresses the Irish elements within the thought and writings of such Anglo-Irish paragons as Swift, Goldsmith, Burke, Shaw, and Yeats. For Beckett, the chief characteristics of the Anglo-Irish were ambivalence and arrogance or the pride that so often accompanies domination. These qualities made them insensitive to and fearful of the forces of Catholic nationalism, which were destined to overwhelm Anglo-Ireland after the 1870s. The irony was, of course, that some of the most influential promoters of the other great "tradition" in Ireland—Gaelic Irish—were themselves Anglo-Irishmen. In an epilogue redolent with the spirit of Grattan, Beckett expresses his hope that "the Anglo-Irish, though now stripped of political influence and dwindling . . . towards a painless extinction . . . may even yet be able to make a healing contribution to the tormented politics of their country" (p. 152).[240]

In general, the conflicts and connections between the various cultures and subcultures in Ireland have not been studied systematically or in the spirit of detachment. But there are some exceptions as well as signs of better things to come. In the published version of the Ford Lectures delivered at Oxford in 1978, *Culture and Anarchy in Ireland, 1890–1939*,[241] F. S. L. Lyons has amplified and extended the theme of cultural conflict which he addressed so fluently in chapter 5, part 2, of *Ireland since the Famine*. The Provost of Trinity deals here with the clash of not two, but four, "cultures" in Ireland—Gaelic, English, Anglo-Irish, and Ulster Presbyterian—and argues that this cultural diversity has been a powerful agent of "anarchy," causing an untold amount of political dissension and social tension in the country. Through the six chapters of this book there runs the basso ostinato of Yeats's own ambivalence about "the battle of two civilisations"—Irish and Anglo-Irish—and the effect of that battle upon his poetry as well as his politics. Lyons's reflections on the cultural conflicts of post-Parnellite Ireland will stimulate much thought. It is to be hoped they will also serve as a point of departure for scholars seeking to discover whether the culture (or "tradition") called Anglo-Irish was more English than Irish or vice versa.

L. M. Cullen has had the courage to question one of the shibboleths of nationalist historiography by denying the claim of Daniel Corkery's hallowed work *The Hidden Ireland* to represent the social and political realities of eighteenth-century Munster.[242] Using both external evidence and some of the poems cited in that book, Cullen argues that Corkery's own nationalist ardor moved him to impose on his Munster poets a political consciousness that was simply not present in their work. The growth of the Irish press has suffered from almost studious neglect. Robert Munter's *The History of the Irish Newspaper, 1685–1760* stands almost alone in this important field.[243] The history of Irish architecture, on the other hand, continues to flourish, owing in part to the sterling efforts of the Irish Georgian Society to prevent the destruction of the ascendancy's architectural legacy. Among those who have contributed generously to the historical record of Ireland's historic buildings are Desmond Guinness; Maurice Craig, the Knight of Glin; Edward McParland; and Mark Bence-Jones.[244] In *Burke's Guide to Country Houses*, volume 1, *Ireland*, Bence-Jones has provided an invaluable as well as elegant reference work for big-house buffs as well as social and architectural historians.[245]

For operatic and musical tastes in eighteenth-century Dublin, T. J. Walsh's *Opera in Dublin, 1705–1797: The Social Scene* should be read; and for the theater in both Dublin and the provinces, there is Michael Ó hAodha's *Theatre in Ireland*.[246] The history of philosophy and political thought in eighteenth-century Ireland has attracted scant attention since the 1960s. There is no comprehensive study of how the Enlightenment affected Ireland, and the Irish political economists have been virtually ignored. Conor Cruise O'Brien has written a powerful introduction to the *Reflections on the Revolution* which explains how Burke's membership in a denigrated minority (Catholic and Irish) colored his politics and his loyalties.[247]

As might be expected, Irish novels and novelists have not been neglected, but most of the work in this sector lacks a sharp cutting edge in terms of historical understanding. Marilyn Butler has done an impressive literary biography of Maria Edgeworth.[248] James F. Carens is the general editor of a long series of short studies of Irish writers published by Bucknell University Press. Malcolm Brown's *The Politics of Irish Literature: From Thomas Davis to W. B. Yeats* should appeal to students of literature who like their history adulterated or softened by impressionism.[249] Peter Costello concentrates on the literary legacy of Parnell's fall and the Rising in his book *The Heart Grown Brutal*.[250] In a published lecture, Oliver MacDonagh has reflected on the historical value of certain nineteenth-century Irish novels.[251] The dynamic partnership of Somerville and Ross has received a painstaking as well as sympathetic scrutiny from the French scholar Guy Fehlmann.[252]

The authors of several classic works of Irish history have not gone unnoticed. Donal McCartney contends that Froude wrote his *History of the English in Ireland* to protest both Catholic nationalism in Ireland and Gladstonian Liberalism.[253] Anne Wyatt concludes that the Irish historical writings of both Froude and Lecky represented conservative reactions to Parnellism and the land war despite their apparent differences in style and substance.[254] L. P. Curtis, Jr., in his introduction to an abridgment of Lecky's *History of Ireland*, has emphasized the ambivalence of the author's Anglo-Irish intellect.[255] Among the leading literati of early-twentieth-century Ireland who have been well-served by biographers in the last decade are J. P. Mahaffy, Eoin MacNeill, Alice Stopford Green, Douglas Hyde, and AE, not to mention the man in New York who knew them all, John Quinn.[256]

In a different category of "cultural history" may be found the study of prejudice, image making, and stereotyping, with reference to English attitudes toward the Irish over the centuries of conquest and colonization. Here readers may begin with Patrick O'Farrell's early chapters in *Ireland's English Question* and then move on to two sequential interpretations of English images of the Irish. In *Anglo-Saxons and Celts* and *Apes and Angels*, L. P. Curtis, Jr. focuses on English ethnic prejudices against Irishmen and attributes the popularity of the image of the wild, brutish, even bestial (or simian) Irish Celt to the convergence of social and psychological pressures in Victorian England. Stimulated by the realities of Fenian rebellion in the 1860s and agrarian agitation in the 1880s, these prejudices took the form of a strident ethnocentrism, labeled Anglo-Saxonism, which drew much of its strength from pseudo-scientific theories of race.[257] Neither racial nor religious prejudices alone provide a sufficient explanation of the failures of British policy in Ireland, but taken together these negative attitudes toward Celtic and Catholic Irishmen account for that great gulf of distrust and suspicion into which so many reforms and good intentions disappeared over the years.

The history of Irish education has been dominated by the work of Donald Harman Akenson, whose three books on the role of the state as well as individual reformers in primary schooling since the 1830s are not only authoritative but readable.[258] One of Akenson's principal concerns is the relentless quest of organized religion in Ireland to make education a more sectarian than intellectual experience for the majority of the population. Norman Atkinson has produced a useful outline of Irish educational systems since Celtic times,[259] and J. M. Goldstrom offers some insights into the ideological content of children's readers in Irish schools during the nineteenth century.[260]

CONCLUSION

Irish historiography since 1966 has made a number of advances, and here and there the term *breakthrough* is fully justified. But in some important respects the movement has been sideways, and in others, there has been no motion to record. Among the more sorely neglected subjects are the history of women, the family, popular culture, urban growth, social mobility, nonpolitical crime, sexual behavior, gombeenism, and agricultural credit. Little work has been done on agricultural laborers, artisans, and paupers; and even the much-publicized Fenians await their definitive monograph. Hardly anything of substance has been written about priests and parsons, civil servants, shopkeepers, middlemen, and lawyers. In other words, the history or lives of more ordinary and politically obscure people remains uncharted, while the well-documented careers of the elites in church, nation, and states stand out in bold print. There are, of course, a few exceptions: by combing newspapers and local archives and by quantifying social or demographic data, a handful of social historians has started to open up some of this unknown territory. But it will take years, possibly decades, before the *menu peuple* of Ireland receive the historical attention they deserve.

To ensure its continuing vitality, Irish historiography may need the kind of controversy in which English historians have long been engaged (or embroiled) over the origins and nature of the seventeenth-century Civil War, or rebellion. It should not be hard to find a comparable cause célèbre in Irish history, where rebellions and revolutions—depending on the ways historians define these terms— may be found in every century since Tudor times. Such a running controversy might well drive scholars deeper into the archives (and therefore further away from "commercial texts" on the Irish Question) and might spur them to use more imagination and sounder methods to explain why "the course of Irish history" took this and not that turning at some particular point. Even with all its diversity and cross-currents, Irish historiography is still too close to the kind of comfortable consensus that discourages innovation. With some notable exceptions, Irish historians have tended to cultivate already well-tilled or overfertilized soil, and the yield per acre has not been commensurate with the expenditure of capital and labor. The concentration of so much historical talent and energy on such standard topics as, say, O'Connellite politics, Parnell and his party, church–state relations in the latter nineteenth century, and the Easter Rising has given us many useful studies, but it has also deprived other, less accessible, and equally important sectors of Ireland's past of much-needed attention.

Now that the weighty volumes of the *NHI* are slowly emerging from the Clarendon Press, this compendium of the country's collective or academic historical wisdom is bound to take on an aura of "higher authority." It may prove hard for all but doctrinaire Marxists and impetuous youth (or a combination of the two) to challenge the Royal Irish Academy's history; and the trouble with so much of this dissenting history is that the fragile evidence is usually bent or crushed beneath the weight of ironclad models of human behavior—all in the name of social-scientific precision. Historians can and do perpetuate their own myths, and the irony is that they do so in the process of "demythologizing" the past. To avoid this fate, Irish historians will have to take the time and thought necessary to define their terms, exhaust the sources, and then make the connections between political, social, economic, and other forms of behavior. Whatever paths they choose to pursue in the future, they should bear in mind that no national historiography can be called healthy unless or until the forces of informed revisionism are constantly at work.[261]

NOTES

Special thanks are due to Professor Mulvey for her valuable counsel in the preparation of this essay.

1. For a discerning review of work done in the years 1940–1965, see Helen F. Mulvey, "Modern Irish History since 1940: A Bibliographical Survey (1600–1922)," *Historian* 27, 1965: 516–559, reprinted in E. C. Furber, ed., *Changing Views in British History*, Cambridge, Mass., 1966.
2. F. S. L. Lyons pays tribute to this "quiet revolution" in Irish historiography in *Ireland since the Famine*, London, 1971, 680–681.
3. These figures represent estimates of all theses in progress for higher degrees (Ph.D., M.A., and M. Litt.) in Irish universities, culled from the January issues of *IHS* 1966 and 1977.
4. Richard J. Hayes, ed., *Manuscript Sources for the History of Irish Civilisation*, 11 vols.,

Boston, 1966; idem, ed., *Sources for the History of Civilisation: Articles in Irish Periodicals*, 9 vols., Boston, 1970.

5. T. W. Moody, *Irish Historiography, 1936–1970*, Dublin, 1971. The contributions of Francis John Byrne, A. J. Otway-Ruthven, R. Dudley Edwards, David B. Quinn, J. G. Simms, Sir Herbert Butterfield, and Helen F. Mulvey all appeared under the heading "Thirty Years' Work in Irish History," in *IHS* 15(60), 1967; 16(61), 1968; 17(65), 1970; and 17(66), 1970.

6. J. G. Simms, *Early Modern Ireland, 1534–1691*, *NHI* 3, Oxford, 1976. One of several important spin-offs from the *NHI* will be a comprehensive bibliography compiled by Helen F. Mulvey and P. W. A. Asplin.

7. Helen F. Mulvey, "Ireland's Commonwealth Years, 1922–1949," in Robin W. Winks, ed., *The Historiography of the British Empire-Commonwealth*, Durham, N.C., 1966, 326–343.

8. Edith M. Johnston, *Irish History: A Select Bibliography*, London, 1969. Johnston revised this bibliographical essay for the Historical Association in 1972, but there are gaps or omissions.

9. Giraldus Cambrensis, *Expugnatio Hibernica: The Conquest of Ireland*, ed. and trans. A. B. Scott and F. X. Martin, Dublin, 1978. For the medieval period, there is P. W. A. Asplin's ancillary volume of the *NHI*, *Medieval Ireland, c. 1170–1496: A Bibliography of Secondary Works*, Dublin, 1971.

10. Gerald A. Hayes-McCoy, "Twenty-five Years of Irish Military History," *Irish Sword* 12(47), 1975: 90–97; Chris Cook, *Sources in British Political History, 1900–1951*, London, 1975, and New York, 1977, app. 1, "Archives in Ireland," 1:293–305.

11. W. E. Vaughan and A. J. Fitzpatrick, eds., *Irish Historical Statistics: Population, 1821–1971*, *NHI*, Dublin, 1978; Brian Walker, ed., *Parliamentary Election Results in Ireland, 1801–1922*, *NHI*, Dublin, 1978.

12. Ruth Dudley Edwards, *An Atlas of Irish History*, London, 1973. For a critique of the maps in this atlas, see J H Andrews's review in *IHS* 19, 1974: 96–97 The organization of the contents by topic means that chronology is led astray: map 21, for example, "Ireland and the Second World War," is followed by map 22, "Ireland before the Normans."

13. Henry Boylan, *A Dictionary of Irish Biography*, New York, 1978; *Burke's Irish Family Records*, 5th ed., London, 1976. Several informative essays about these remnants of the Irish Ascendancy may be found in a thin companion volume compiled by Hugh Montgomery-Massingberd, *Burke's Introduction to Irish Ancestry*, London, 1976.

14. J. C. Beckett, *The Making of Modern Ireland, 1603–1923*, London and New York, 1966; idem, "The Study of Irish History: An Inaugural Lecture." This lecture was originally delivered at Queen's University, Belfast in 1963 and is reprinted in Beckett's collection of essays, *Confrontations Studies in Irish History*, London and Totowa, N.J., 1972, 11–25.

15. T. W. Moody, "Irish History and Irish Mythology," *Hermathena* 124, Summer 1978: 7–24. For some other reflections on the perils of Irish historiography, see F. S. L. Lyons, "The Dilemma of the Irish Contemporary Historian," ibid. 115, 1973: 45–56.

16. T. W. Moody and F. X. Martin, eds., *The Course of Irish History*, Cork, 1967.

17. The enterprising publisher of this series is Gill and Macmillan of Dublin. The volumes concerned with the centuries covered in this essay are: Margaret MacCurtain, *Tudor and Stuart Ireland*, Dublin, 1972; Edith M. Johnston, *Ireland in the Eighteenth Century*, Dublin, 1974; and John A. Murphy, *Ireland in the Twentieth Century*, Dublin, 1975.

18. Gearóid Ó Tuathaigh, *Ireland before the Famine, 1798–1848*, Dublin, 1972, and Joseph Lee, *The Modernisation of Irish Society, 1848–1918*, Dublin, 1973. James Donnelly has written a review of Lee's book which manages to be both critical and supportive; see *IHS* 20, 1976: 206–212.

19. This reviewer has seen the contributions to vol. 6 in typescript, but short of having read all the

forthcoming volumes in manuscript, there is bound to be an element of conjecture in this prediction.

20. *NHI* 3, Oxford, 1976, 1978, Preface, v. For the "history" of the *New History*, see T. W. Moody, "A New History of Ireland," *IHS* 16, 1969: 241–257.

21. *Early Modern Ireland, 1534–1691*, *NHI* 3, Oxford, 1976. In his thoughtful review of this volume, Nicholas P. Canny has stressed the need for firmer social and demographic foundations to support the political history of this period: "Early Modern Ireland: An Appraisal Appraised," *Irish Economic and Social History* (hereafter, *IESH*) 4, 1977: 56–65. The other volumes in the *NHI* are: 1, *Prehistoric and Early Medieval Ireland*; 2, *Medieval Ireland, 1169–1534*; 4, *Eighteenth-century Ireland, 1691–1800*; 5, *Ireland under the Union*, pt. 1, *1801–70*); 6, *Ireland under the Union*, pt. 2, (*1870–1921*); and 7, *Ireland since 1921*. The remaining volumes are scheduled for publication between 1982 and 1984.

22. See, for example, Giovanni Costigan, *A History of Modern Ireland*, New York, 1969; Edward R. Norman, *A History of Modern Ireland*, London, 1971, and Coral Gables, Fla., 1971; and R. Dudley Edwards, *A New History of Ireland*, Dublin and London, 1972. Despite the strange coincidence of title, Edwards's text (which lacks footnotes and bibliography) should not be confused with the Royal Irish Academy's *NHI*.

23. Patrick O'Farrell, *Ireland's English Question, Anglo-Irish Relations 1534–1970*, London, 1972.

24. F. S. L. Lyons, *Ireland since the Famine*, London, 1971. Roughly 41 percent of Lyons's text deals with the period 1850–1914; 20 percent is devoted to the origins of the Rising and the struggle for independence; and 39 percent covers the decades since 1923. A paperback edition of this book (Fontana, Collins) appeared in 1973 and a second impression in 1974.

25. L. M. Cullen, *Life in Ireland*, London, 1969.

26. Brian Farrell, ed., *The Irish Parliamentary Tradition*, Dublin and New York, 1973. Sixteen of the essays in this volume were first broadcast as the Thomas Davis Lectures for 1972.

27. Robert Kee, *The Green Flag*, London and New York, 1972.

28. Dorothy Macardle, *The Irish Republic*, London, 1937.

29. See Owen Dudley Edwards et al., *Celtic Nationalism*, London, 1968, 5–209. Students of Irish military history should consult G. A. Hayes-McCoy, *Irish Battles*, London, 1969, wherein the author discusses fourteen famous battles fought on Irish soil from Clontarf (1014) to Arklow (1798).

30. R. Dudley Edwards, *Ireland in the Age of the Tudors: The Destruction of Hiberno-Norman Civilisation*, London, 1977.

31. Brendan Bradshaw, *The Dissolution of the Religious Orders in Ireland under Henry VIII*, Cambridge, 1974. See Karl S. Bottigheimer's review of Bradshaw's book: "The Reformation in Ireland Revisited," *JBS* 15, 1976: 140–149. Relevant articles by Bradshaw include: "The Opposition to the Ecclesiastical Legislation in the Irish Reformation Parliament," *IHS* 16, 1969: 285–303, and "Sword, Word and Strategy in the Reformation in Ireland," *HJ* 21, 1978: 475–502. See also R. Dudley Edwards, "The Irish Reformation Parliament of Henry VIII, 1536–7," *Historical Studies* 6, 1968: 59–80.

32. Nicholas P. Canny, *The Elizabethan Conquest of Ireland*, London and New York, 1976. See Brendan Bradshaw's penetrating review essay about Canny's book in *Studies* 65, 1977: 38–49.

33. Nicholas P. Canny, "The Ideology of English Colonization: From Ireland to America," *William and Mary Quarterly* 30, 1973: 575–598.

34. David Beers Quinn, *The Elizabethans and the Irish*, London and Ithaca, N.Y., 1966.

35. J. H. Andrews, "Geography and Government in Elizabethan Ireland," in Nicholas Stephens and Robin E. Glasscock, eds., *Irish Geographical Studies in Honour of E. Estyn Evans*, Belfast, 1970, 178–191.

36. John J. Silke, *Kinsale: The Spanish Intervention in Ireland at the End of the Elizabethan Wars*, Liverpool, 1970.

37. Nicholas P. Canny, "Hugh O'Neill, Earl of Tyrone, and the Changing Face of Gaelic Ulster," *Studia Hibernica (SH)*, no. 10, 1970: 7–35; idem, "The Flight of the Earls, 1607," *IHS* 17, 1971: 380–399.

38. Victor Treadwell, "The Establishment of the Farm of the Irish Customs, 1603–13," *EHR* 93, 1978: 580–602.

39. Aidan Clarke, *The Old English in Ireland, 1625–1642*, London, 1966.

40. Ibid., "The Army and Politics in Ireland, 1625–30," *SH* 4, 1964: 28–53. See also Clarke's contribution to the historical debate, "Ireland and the General Crisis," *PP*, no. 48, 1970: 79–99. For the effects of Strafford's policies toward the Ulster Scots in 1638–1640, see M. Perceval-Maxwell, "Strafford, the Ulster-Scots and the Covenanters," *IHS* 18, 1973: 524–551.

41. Karl S. Bottigheimer, *English Money and Irish Land: The 'Adventurers' in the Cromwellian Settlement of Ireland*, Oxford, 1971; see J. G. Simms's review in *IHS* 18, 1972; 262–264. Bottigheimer's "preliminary" article with the same title as his book appeared in *JBS* 7, 1967: 12–27.

42. Robert C. Simington, *The Transplantation to Connacht, 1654–58*, Shannon, 1970. A popular account of English oppression in Ireland during the 1650s may be found in Peter Berresford Ellis, *Hell or Connaught! The Cromwellian Colonisation of Ireland, 1652–1660*, London and New York, 1975.

43. T. C. Barnard, *Cromwellian Ireland*, London, 1975.

44. Barnard discusses the issue of legislative independence during the Convention Parliament of 1659 in "Planters and Policies in Cromwellian Ireland," *PP*, no. 61, 1973: 31–69.

45. J. G. Simms, "The Restoration, 1660–85," *NHI* 3: 420–453. See also Karl Bottigheimer's article on the political and social consequences of Cromwellian confiscation of land: "The Restoration Land Settlement in Ireland: A Structural View," *IHS* 18, 1972: 1–21.

46. J. G. Simms, *Jacobite Ireland, 1685–1691*, London, 1969.

47. Francis G. James, *Ireland in the Empire, 1688–1770*, Cambridge, Mass., 1973.

48. W. E. H. Lecky's *History of Ireland in the Eighteenth Century*, 5 vols., London, 1892, devoted only 13 percent of its 2,503 pages to the years 1700–1760, whereas the period 1760–1800 took up 75 percent of that monumental work.

49. Francis G. James, "The Active Irish Peers in the Early Eighteenth Century," *JBS* 18, 1979: 52–69. For the attempts of Irish commercial interests to wring concessions from Westminster, see idem, "The Irish Lobby in the Early Eighteenth Century," *EHR* 81, 1966: 543–557.

50. J. C. D. Clark, "Whig Tactics and Parliamentary Precedent: The English Management of Irish Politics, 1754–1756," *HJ* 21, 1978: 275–301.

51. R. B. McDowell, *Irish Public Opinion, 1750–1800*, London, 1944, rep. 1975; idem, "Ireland in the 18th Century British Empire," *Historical Studies* 9, 1974: 49–63.

52. J. C. Beckett, "Anglo-Irish Constitutional Relations in the Later Eighteenth Century," *IHS* 14, 1964: reprinted in *Confrontations: Studies in Irish History*, Totowa, N.J., 1973, 123–141.

53. Maurice R. O'Connell, *Irish Politics and Social Conflict in the Age of the American Revolution*, London and Philadelphia, 1965.

54. This book was reprinted in 1976 by the Greenwood Press. For a critique of O'Connell's handling of "social conflict" in the context of Irish class structure, see L. M. Cullen's review in *IHS* 15, 1967: 488–491.

55. A. P. W. Malcolmson, *John Foster: The Politics of the Anglo-Irish Ascendancy*, London, 1978.

56. See also ibid., "John Foster and the Speakership of the Irish House of Commons," *Proceedings of the Royal Irish Academy* 72, 1972: 271–303; idem, "Election Politics in the Borough of

Antrim, 1750–1800," *IHS* 17, 1970: 32–57; and idem, "The Newtown Act of 1748: Revision and Reconstruction," *IHS* 18, 1973: 313–344.

57. Peter Jupp, *British and Irish Elections, 1784–1831*, Newton Abbot, 1973; see also idem, "County Down Elections, 1783–1831," *IHS* 18, 1972; 177–206. John Cannon surveys Irish representation and the franchise in *Parliamentary Reform, 1640–1832*, Cambridge, 1973, 98–107, 114–115.

58. Edith M. Johnston, *Great Britain and Ireland, 1760–1800*, Edinburgh, 1963. For an overview of parliamentary politics in this era, see J. L. McCracken's pamphlet for the Dublin Historical Association, *The Irish Parliament in the Eighteenth Century*, Dundalk, 1971. Anglo-Irish politics in the latter eighteenth century are treated in Paul Kelly, "British and Irish Politics in 1785," *EHR* 90, 1975: 536–563, and in R. B. McDowell, "The Fitzwilliam Episode," *IHS* 15, 1966: 115–130. McDowell's new book, *Ireland in the Age of Imperialism and Revolution*, also deals with Lord Fitzwilliam's vice-royalty.

59. R. B. McDowell, *Ireland in the Age of Imperialism and Revolution, 1760–1801*, Oxford, 1979.

60. The revised edition of Frank MacDermot's standard biography, *Theobald Wolfe Tone*, Tralee, 1968, first published in 1939, is helpful but no substitute for the comprehensive biography Tone deserves.

61. Thomas Pakenham, *The Year of Liberty*, London, 1969.

62. For a useful local perspective, see Peadar Mac Suibhne, *'98 in Carlow*, Carlow, 1974.

63. Oliver MacDonagh, *Ireland: The Union and Its Aftermath*, London, 1977 (a rev. ed. of his *Ireland*, Englewood Cliffs, N.J., 1968); Patrick O'Farrell, *England and Ireland since 1800*, London, 1975; Lawrence J. McCaffrey, *The Irish Question, 1800–1922*, Lexington, Ky., 1968.

64. Nicholas Mansergh, *The Irish Question, 1840–1921*, new and rev. ed., London, 1965. Originally published in 1940 under the title, *Ireland in the Age of Reform and Revolution*, this work has now entered its third edition in 1975.

65. T. Desmond Williams, ed., *Secret Societies in Ireland*, Dublin and New York, 1973. See, especially, Maureen Wall's chapter on the Whiteboys, pp. 13–25, and Joseph Lee's on the Ribbonmen, pp. 26–35. M. R. Beames has challenged Lee's view that most agrarian crime of the Ribbon variety stemmed from conflicts between farmers and laborers, arguing instead that landlord efforts to "rationalize" their estates triggered a number of assassinations; see Beames, "Rural Conflict in Pre-famine Ireland: Peasant Assassinations in Tipperary, 1837–1837," *PP*, no. 81, 1978: 75–91. By far the most detailed work on agrarian agitations comes from James S. Donnelly, whose two recent essays are models of empirical research: "The Whiteboy Movement, 1761–5," *IHS* 21, 1978: 20–54, and "The Rightboy Movement, 1785–8," *SH*, nos. 17 and 18, 1977–1978: 120–202. Donnelly is working on a two-volume study of agrarian unrest dealing with the organization, motivation, composition, and activities of secret societies in rural areas in the period, 1760–1845.

66. G. C. Bolton, *The Passing of the Irish Act of Union: A Study in Parliamentary Politics*, London, 1966.

67. Hereward Senior, *Orangeism in Ireland and Great Britain, 1795–1836*, London and Toronto, 1966.

68. For an official and appreciative history of the movement, see the Revs. M. W. Dewar, John Brown, and S. E. Long, *Orangeism: A New Historical Appreciation*, Belfast, 1967.

69. Norman Gash, *Mr. Secretary Peel*, London, 1961, 96–236. Gash deals with agrarian crime and police activity in Ireland at pp. 138–191 and Daniel O'Connell's campaign for Catholic emancipation at pp. 508–598. For the Irish problems facing Peel in the 1840s, see vol. 2, *Sir Robert Peel* London and New York, 1976, 393–428 and 526–561. For a sidelight on Peel's

first sojourn in Ireland, see Robert Shipkey, "Problems of Irish Patronage during the Chief Secretaryship of Robert Peel, 1812–18," *HJ* 10, 1967: 41–56.

70. Galen Broeker, *Rural Disorder and Police Reform in Ireland, 1812–36*, London and Toronto, 1970. Other features of police organization and activity are discussed by Tadhg Ó Ceallaigh, "Peel and Police Reform in Ireland, 1814–18," *SH*, no. 6 1966: 25–48, and Stanley Palmer, "The Irish Police Experiment: The Beginning of Modern Police in the British Isles, 1785–1795," *Social Science Quarterly* 5, 1975: 410–424.

71. R. B. McDowell, *The Irish Administration, 1801–1914*, London, 1964.

72. Maurice R. O'Connell, ed., *The Correspondence of Daniel O'Connell*, vols. 1–2, Shannon, 1972, and vols. 3–8, Dublin, 1974–1979. Helen Mulvey has written a discerning foreword about the marital felicity of Daniel and Mary, which appears in 1:xix–xxx. The editor transcribed a total of almost four thousand letters, and some of the letters published have been pruned of petty details.

73. Raymond Moley's *Daniel O'Connell, Nationalism without Violence*, New York, 1974, does not answer this description, but admirers of O'Connell will appreciate this eulogy.

74. See the following essays by Maurice O'Connell: "Daniel O'Connell and the Irish Eighteenth Century," *Studies in Eighteenth-century Culture* 5, 1976: 475–495; "Daniel O'Connell: Income, Expenditure and Despair," *IHS* 17, 1970: 200–220; "Daniel O'Connell and Religious Freedom," *Thought*, June, 1975; and "O'Connell, Young Ireland, and Violence," ibid., 52, 1977: 381–406.

75. Lawrence McCaffrey, *Daniel O'Connell and the Repeal Year*, Kentucky, 1966.

76. Jacqueline R. Hill, "Nationalism and the Catholic Church in the 1840s," *IHS* 19, 1975: 371–395; see also F. A. D'Arcy, "The Artisans of Dublin and Daniel O'Connell, 1830–47: An Unquiet Liaison," *IHS* 17, 1970: 221–243; and Douglas C. Riach, "Daniel O'Connell and American Anti-slavery," *IHS* 20, 1976: 3–25.

77. Patrick O'Donoghue's three articles on opposition to the payment of tithes in 1830–1838 are: "Causes of the Opposition to Tithes 1830–38," *SH*, no. 5, 1965: 7–28; "Opposition to Tithe Payments in 1830–31," *SH*, no. 6, 1966: 69–98; and "Opposition to Tithe Payment in 1832–33," *SH*, no. 12, 1972: 77–108.

78. With the exception of Leon Ó Broin's brief biography of Charles Gavan Duffy, Dublin, 1967, little of note has been written on Young Ireland since the mid-1960s.

79. Desmond Ryan, *The Fenian Chief: A Biography of James Stephens*, Dublin, 1967; and Marcus Bourke, *John O'Leary: A Study in Irish Separatism*, Tralee, 1967.

80. Leon Ó Broin, *Fenian Fever: An Anglo-American Dilemma*, London and New York, 1971.

81. T. W. Moody, ed., *The Fenian Movement*, Cork, 1968, contains eight essays which were first broadcast as the Thomas Davis Lectures for 1967 (being revisions of a series originally delivered in 1959). Maurice R. Harmon, ed., *Fenians and Fenianism: Centenary Essays*, Dublin, 1968, comprises seven essays first published in *University Review*, Winter, 1967.

82. See Brendán MacGiolla Choille, "Fenian Documents in the State Paper Office," *IHS* 16, 1969: 258–284. Two useful, select bibliographies of the Fenian movement are Patricia F. Guptill, "A Popular Bibliography of the Fenian Movement," *Eire-Ireland (EI)* 4(2), 1969: 18–25, and James W. Hurst, "The Fenians: A Bibliography," *EI* 4(4), 1969: 90–106.

83. Leon Ó Broin, *Revolutionary Underground: The Story of the Irish Republican Brotherhood, 1858–1924*, Dublin, 1976. The reactions of the Catholic hierarchy to Fenianism receive close attention in E. R. Norman, *The Catholic Church and Ireland in the Age of Rebellion, NIH*, Cambridge and Ithaca, N.Y., 1965; see also Tomas Ó Fiaich, "The Clergy and Fenianism, 1860–70," *Irish Ecclesiastical Record* 109, 1968: 81–103.

84. E. D. Steele, *Irish Land and British Politics: Tenant Right and Nationality, 1865–1870*, London, 1974.

85. Ibid., "Gladstone and Ireland," *IHS* 17, 1970: 58–88. For a contrary view of Gladstone's motives in opting for home rule, see A. B. Cooke and John Vincent, *The Governing Passion, Cabinet Government and Party Politics in Britain, 1885–86*, London and New York, 1974, esp. 48–56.

86. Clive Dewey, "Celtic Agrarian Legislation and the Celtic Revival: Historicist Implications of Gladstone's Irish and Scottish Land Acts, 1870–1886," *PP*, no. 64, 1974: 30–70.

87. Brian M. Walker, "The Irish Electorate, 1868–1915," *IHS* 18, 1973: 359–406; idem, *Parliamentary Election Results*.

88. K. T. Hoppen, "Landlords, Society, and Electoral Politics in Mid-nineteenth-century Ireland," *PP*, no. 75, 1977: 62–93; see also P. J. Jupp, "Irish Parliamentary Elections and the Influence of the Catholic Vote, 1801–20," *HJ* 10, 1967: 183–196.

89. Cornelius J. O'Leary, *Irish Elections, 1918–1977: Parties, Voters, and Proportional Representation*, Dublin, 1979.

90. John E. Pomfret, *The Struggle for Land in Ireland, 1800–1923*, Princeton, N.J., 1930; Norman D. Palmer, *The Irish Land League Crisis*, New Haven, Conn., 1940.

91. James Donnelly, *The Land and the People of Nineteenth-century Cork, the Rural Economy and the Land Question*, London and Boston, 1975, 251–376.

92. Samuel Clark, "The Social Composition of the Land League," *IHS* 17, 1971: 447–469. Clark expounds on his thesis about the role of urban men (shopkeepers, publicans, etc.) in organizing the tenantry for rebellion in an article addressed more to social scientists than to Irish historians: "The Political Mobilization of Irish Farmers," *Canadian Review of Sociology and Anthropology* 22, 1975: 483–499. David Fitzpatrick takes issue with this part of Clark's argument in his essay "The Geography of Irish Nationalism, 1910–21," *PP*, no. 78, 1978: 113–144.

93. Samuel Clark, *The Social Origins of the Irish Land War*, Princeton, N.J., 1979.

94. Paul Bew, *Land and the National Question in Ireland 1858–82*, Dublin and New York, 1978.

95. William L. Feingold, "The Tenants' Movement to Capture the Irish Poor Law Boards, 1877–1886," *Albion* 7, 1975: 216–231. This article is based on Feingold's unpublished dissertation "The Irish Boards of Poor Law Guardians, 1872–86: A Revolution in Local Government," University of Chicago, 1974.

96. F. S. L. Lyons, *Charles Stewart Parnell*, London, 1977.

97. Joseph Woods, "Towards a Psychoanalytical Interpretation of Charles Stewart Parnell," *Bulletin of the Menninger Clinic* 42, 1978: 463–492. Woods describes Parnell as a depressive personality type caught up in a vicious cycle of rage, guilt, self-destruction, and depression. In order to compensate for an early traumatic loss, the precise nature of which remains a mystery, Parnell, according to Woods, was driven by "insatiable demands for greatness." For both the initiates and the nonbelievers in psychoanalytical "reconstructions," this essay raises profound questions too demanding to be dealt with here.

98. R. F. Foster, *Charles Stewart Parnell: The Man and His Family*, Sussex, 1976.

99. T. W. Moody, "*The Times* versus Parnell and Co., 1887–90," *Historical Studies* 6, 1968: 147–182; F. S. L. Lyons, "'Parnellism and Crime,' 1887–90," *TRHS* 24, 1974: 123–140. Among other essays by Lyons on Parnell, see "The Political Ideas of Parnell," *HJ* 16, 1973: 749–775; "Charles Stewart Parnell" and "The Irish Parliamentary Party," two chapters in Farrell, ed., *Irish Parliamentary Tradition*, 181–207. For the incident which led to Parnell's being rusticated from Cambridge and his decision not to return to the university, see Ged Martin, "Parnell at Cambridge: The Education of an Irish Nationalist," *IHS* 19, 1974: 72–82.

100. Michael Hurst's short study, *Parnell and Irish Nationalism*, London, 1968, deserves mention here largely because it triggered one of the most devastating reviews ever to appear in *IHS*; see Conor Cruise O'Brien, Review, *IHS* 16, 1968: 230–236.

101. F. S. L. Lyons, *John Dillon: A Biography*, London, 1968. Lyons has amplified Dillon's role in the struggle against landlordism in "John Dillon and the Plan of Campaign," *IHS* 14, 1965: 313–347. For some of Dillon's thoughts on the political situation after his defeat in the election of 1918, see Virginia E. Glandon, "John Dillon's Reflections on Irish and General Politics, 1919–1921," *EI* 9(3), 1974: 21–43. Michael Tierney has written a flattering review of Lyons's biography, "John Dillon and the Home Rule Movement," *Studies* 58, 1969: 63–73.

102. Joseph V. O'Brien, *William O'Brien and the Course of Irish Politics, 1881–1918*, Berkeley and Los Angeles and London, 1976.

103. See, for example, C. J. Woods, "Ireland and Anglo-Papal Relations, 1880–85," *IHS* 18, 1972: 29–60. Emmet Larkin, *The Roman Catholic Church and the Creation of the Modern Irish State, 1878–1886*, Dublin and Philadelphia, 1975; idem, *The Roman Catholic Church in Ireland and the Plan of Campaign, 1886–1888*, Cork, 1978; idem, *The Roman Catholic Church in Ireland and the Fall of Parnell, 1888–1891*, Chapel Hill, N.C., 1979.

104. Richard Hawkins, "Gladstone, Forster, and the Release of Parnell, 1882–8," *IHS* 16, 1969: 417–445; J. Enoch Powell, "Kilmainham—the Treaty that Never Was," *HJ* 21, 1978: 948–959.

105. Alan O'Day, *The English Face of Irish Nationalism: Parnellite Involvement in British Politics, 1880–86*, Dublin and Toronto, 1977. That involvement would be the more remarkable, needless to say, if it were not for the centuries of Anglicization which lay behind those activities. A number of English historians have considered the impact of Irish politicians and affairs on the political scene at Westminster: D. A. Hamer, *Liberal Politics in the Age of Gladstone and Rosebery*, Oxford, 1972; Michael Barker, *Gladstone and Radicalism*, New York, 1975; Thomas W. Heyck, *The Dimensions of British Radicalism: The Case of Ireland, 1874–95*, Urbana and Chicago, 1974; and Cooke and Vincent, *Governing Passion*. Cooke and Vincent have edited the Irish sections of Herbert Gladstone's journal, "Herbert Gladstone, Forster and Ireland, 1881–2," *IHS* 17, 1971: 521–548, and *IHS* 18, 1972: 74–89; they have also published extracts from Sir Hugh Holmes's memoir concerning the 1880s, "Ireland and Party Politics, 1885–7: An Unpublished Conservative Memoir," *IHS* 16, 1968–1969: 154–172, 321–338, and 446–471.

106. Tom Corfe, *The Phoenix Park Murders*, London, 1968; Leon Ó Broín, *The Prime Informer: A Suppressed Scandal*, London, 1971.

107. K. R. M. Short, *The Dynamite War*, Atlantic Highlands, N.J., 1979.

108. Peter Gibbon, *The Origins of Ulster Unionism: The Formation of Popular Protestant Politics and Ideology in Nineteenth Century Ireland*, Manchester, 1975. For a constructive review of Gibbon's book (although the trees tend to obscure the woods), see Sybil Gribbon, "The Social Origins of Ulster Unionism," *IESH* 4, 1977: 66–72.

109. David W. Miller, "Presbyterianism and 'Modernization' in Ulster," *PP*, no. 80, 1978: 66–90. Miller's sociological model seems rather top-heavy in places even though he has counted weavers and power looms and has tried to identify the chiliastic preachers who brought spiritual relief to those undergoing the strains of industrialization.

110. Ibid., *Queen's Rebels: Ulster Loyalism in Historical Perspective*, Dublin and New York, 1978.

111. Patrick Buckland, *Irish Unionism*, vol. 1, *The Anglo-Irish and the New Ireland, 1885–1922*, Dublin and New York, 1972. Only around 10 percent of this volume deals with the years 1885–1914, whereas the author devotes some 48 percent to the period 1916–1919. Buckland's periodization of Irish unionism into "eight phases" and the sharp distinction he draws between northern and southern unionism before 1921 do not always carry conviction. The second volume is entitled *Ulster Unionism and the Origins of Northern Ireland, 1886–1922*, Dublin and New York, 1973. See also idem, "The Southern Irish Unionists, the Irish Question, and British Politics, 1906–14," *IHS* 15, 1967: 228–255, and his edition of selected docu-

440   L. P. CURTIS, JR.

ments from the Public Record Office of Northern Ireland, *Irish Unionism, 1885–1923: A
Documentary History*, Belfast, 1973.

112. Catherine B. Shannon, "The Ulster Liberal Unionists and Local Government Reform,
1885–98," *IHS* 18, 1973: 407–423; Ronan Fanning, "The Unionist Party and Ireland,
1906–10," *IHS* 15, 1966: 147–171; Ian d'Alton, "Southern Irish Unionism: A Study of
Cork Unionists, 1884–1914," *TRHS* 23, 1973: 71–88; idem, "Cork Unionism: Its Role in
Parliamentary and Local Elections, 1885–1914," *SH*, no. 15, 1975: 143–161; A. C. Hepburn, "The Irish Council Bill and the Fall of Sir Antony MacDonnell," *IHS* 17, 1971:
470–498.

113. A. T. Q. Stewart, *The Ulster Crisis*, London, 1967. The author carries the story of the UVFs
bid for power up to 1916, when the Covenant was "sealed in the blood" of the Somme and
other great battles on the Western Front.

114. Alan J. Ward, *Ireland and Anglo-American Relations, 1899–1921*, London and Toronto,
1969.

115. Ward deals with other aspects of American involvement in the Irish Question in "Fre-
wen's Anglo-American Campaign for Federalism, 1910–21," *IHS* 15, 1967: 256–275, and
"America and the Irish Problem, 1899–1921," *IHS* 16, 1968: 64–90.

116. F. X. Martin, "1916—Myth, Fact, and Mystery," *SH*, no. 7, 1967: 7–126; idem, "The
1916 Rising: A *Coup d'Etat* or a 'Bloody Protest'?" *SH*, no. 8, 1968: 106–137. See also
Martin's edited volume (comprising the Thomas Davis Lectures broadcast over RTE in
1966), *Leaders and Men of the Easter Rising: Dublin, 1916*, London and Ithaca, N.Y., 1967.

117. Maureen Wall, "The Background of the Rising . . . ," and idem, "The Plans and the Counter-
mand: The Country and Dublin," in Kevin B. Nowlan, ed., *The Making of 1916: Studies in the
History of the Rising*, Dublin, 1969, 157–251; G. A. Hayes-McCoy, "A Military History of the
1916 Rising," ibid., 255–338. Other interesting essays on the rebellion may be found in Owen
Dudley Edwards and Fergus Pyle, eds., *1916: The Easter Rising*, London, 1968. See also the
narrative sections on 1916 in Lyons, *Ireland since the Famine* and Kee, *Green Flag*.

118. Leon Ó Broin, *Dublin Castle and the 1916 Rising*, Dublin, 1966.

119. George Dangerfield, *The Damnable Question*, Boston and Toronto, 1969.

120. Patrick Lynch, "The Social Revolution That Never Was," in T. Desmond Williams, ed., *The
Irish Struggle*, London, 1966, 41–54.

121. Francis Shaw, "The Canon of Irish History: A Challenge," *Studies* 61, 1972: 113–153.

122. Ruth Dudley Edwards, *Patrick Pearse: The Triumph of Failure*, London, 1977.

123. Richard P. Davis, *Arthur Griffith and Non-violent Sinn Fein*, Dublin, 1974; see also Sean Ó
Luing, "Arthur Griffith 1871–1922: Thoughts on a Centenary," *Studies* 60, 1971: 127–138.

124. Samuel Levenson, *James Connolly: A Biography*, London, 1973; Owen Dudley Edwards, *The
Mind of an Activist: James Connolly*, Dublin, 1971; see also Owen Dudley Edwards and Bernard Ransome, eds., *James Connolly 1868–1916: Selected Political Writings*, London, 1973.
See also J. W. Boyle, "Connolly, the Citizen Army and the Rising," in Nowlan, *Making of
1916*, 51–68.

125. Anne Marreco, *The Rebel Countess: The Life and Times of Constance Markievicz*, Philadelphia
and New York, 1967; Jacqueline Van Voris, *Constance de Markievicz in the Cause of Ireland*,
Amherst, 1967.

126. Brian Inglis, *Roger Casement*, London, 1973; B. L. Reid, *The Lives of Roger Casement*, New
Haven, Conn., and London, 1976. Both authors accept the authenticity of the "Black Diaries"
and refrain from pop psychologizing about Casement's private life. Inglis devotes only four
pages to Casement's origins and youth, concentrating on the "good works" in the Congo and
Putamayo as well as the commitment to Irish republicanism. Reid's long and searching study

treats Casement as an archetypal figure, epitomizing all the contradictions and tensions of the modern world.

127. Earl of Longford and Thomas P. O'Neill, *Eamon de Valera*, London, 1970, and Boston, 1971. The original Irish version of this biography—Tomás Ó Néill and Pádraig Ó Fiannachta, *De Valera*, Dublin, 1968—is almost twice as long as the English edition. Donal McCartney compares the two versions in a review in *IHS* 17, 1970: 283.

128. T. Desmond Williams, ed., *The Irish Struggle, 1916–1926*, London, 1966.

129. David Savage, "The Attempted Home Rule Settlement of 1916," *EI* 2, 1967: 132–145; idem, "'The Parnell of Wales Has Become the Chamberlain of Wales': Lloyd George and the Irish Question," *JBS* 12, 1972: 86–108.

130. R. B. McDowell, *The Irish Convention, 1917–18*, London and Toronto, 1970.

131. D. G. Boyce, *Englishmen and Irish Troubles: British Public Opinion and the Making of Irish Policy, 1918–22*, London and Cambridge, Mass., 1972. For the travail of H. E. Duke, who inherited Augustine Birrell's tattered mantle as chief secretary, see D. G. Boyce and Cameron Hazlehurst, "The Unknown Chief Secretary: H. E. Duke and Ireland, 1916–18," *IHS* 20, 1977: 286–311.

132. Charles Townshend, *The British Campaign in Ireland, 1919–1921*, London, 1975. Many of the official documents concerning the British military campaign in Ireland are restricted under the one hundred year rule, so the full story of army activities in 1919–1921 will not be known until the next century. An important source for Cabinet policy in these years is the diary of Lloyd George's confidant (and assistant cabinet secretary) Thomas Jones: *Whitehall Diary*, vol. 3, *Ireland, 1918–1925*, ed. Keith Middlemas, London, 1971.

133. Margery Forester, *Michael Collins: The Lost Leader*, London, 1971.

134. Andrew Boyle, *The Riddle of Erskine Childers*, London, 1977.

135. F. S. L. Lyons, "From War to Civil War in Ireland: Three Essays on the Treaty Debate," in Farrell, *Irish Parliamentary Tradition*, 221–256. Calton Younger has sketched the personalities and politics of Griffith, Collins, Craig, and De Valera in *A State of Disunion*, London, 1972.

136. For sidelights on the discussions culminating in the treaty and partition, see Boyce, *Englishmen and Irish Troubles*; and idem, "British Conservative Opinion, the Ulster Question, and the Partition of Ireland, 1912–21," *IHS* 17, 1970: 89–112; Joseph M. Curran, "Lloyd George and the Irish Settlement, 1921–22," *EI* 7(2), 1971: 14–46; John D. Fair, "The Anglo-Irish Treaty of 1921: Unionist Aspects of the Peace," *JBS* 12, 1972: 132–149; and Nicholas Mansergh, "The Government of Ireland Act, 1920: Its Origins and Purposes . . . ," *Historical Studies* 9, 1974: 19–48.

137. T. P. Coogan, *The IRA*, London, 1970.

138. J. Bowyer Bell, *The Secret Army*, London, 1970, and New York, 1971. Ó Broin alludes to the IRA in *Revolutionary Underground*, and John A. Murphy has produced an essay "The New IRA, 1925–62," in T. Desmond Williams, ed., *Secret Societies in Ireland*, Dublin and New York, 1973, 150–165.

139. Emmet Larkin, *James Larkin*, Cambridge, Mass., 1965.

140. Patrick Berresford Ellis, *A History of the Irish Working Class*, London, 1972.

141. J. D. Clarkson, *Labour and Nationalism in Ireland*, New York, 1925; Arthur Mitchell, *Labour in Irish Politics, 1890–1930*, Dublin, 1974.

142. See also Arthur Mitchell's article on that pivotal figure in the Irish labour movement, "William O'Brien, 1881–1968, and the Irish Labour Movement," *Studies* 60, 1971: 311–331. Edward MacLysaght has edited O'Brien's reminiscences, *William O'Brien, Forth the Banners Go*, Dublin, 1969.

143. Erhard Rumpf and A. C. Hepburn, *Nationalism and Socialism in Twentieth-century Ireland*, London and New York, 1977.

144. David Fitzpatrick, *Politics and Irish Life, 1913–21: Provincial Experience of War and Revolution*, Dublin, 1977. Fitzpatrick lays emphasis on the social functions of political participation in the Irish countryside as a means of breaking down "the barrier of boredom." He finds a high positive correlation between militant nationalist activity and districts in the west (especially Munster) where most holdings were valued at less than fifteen pounds.

145. Ibid., "The Geography of Irish Nationalism, 1910–1921," *PP*, no. 78, 1978: 113–44.

146. For some revealing studies of Sinn Féin before and after the treaty of 1921, see Michael Laffan, "The Unification of Sinn Féin in 1917," *IHS* 17, 1971: 340–352; Peter Pyne, "The Third Sinn Féin Party, 1923–6," *Economic and Social Review*, 1, 1969–1970: 29–50, 229–258; and also the *Capuchin Annual* 37, 1970; the entire issue being devoted to Sinn Féin and the struggle for independence. Rumpf and Hepburn also discuss the origins and nature of Sinn Féin's appeal in *Nationalism and Socialism*, chaps. 1–3.

147. Three volumes of Davis Lectures cover the period in question: Williams, *Irish Struggle, 1916–26*; Francis MacManus, ed., *The Years of the Great Test, 1926–1939*, Dublin, 1967; and Kevin B. Nowlan and T. Desmond Williams, eds., *Ireland in the War Years and After, 1939–51*, Dublin, 1969.

148. Calton Younger, *Ireland's Civil War*, London, 1968. Some facets of the civil war are exposed in Michael Hayes, "Dáil Eireann and the Irish Civil War," *Studies* 58, 1969: 2–23, and John O'Beirne-Ranelagh, "The I.R.B. from the Treaty to 1924," *IHS* 20, 1976: 26–39.

149. T. P. Coogan, *Ireland since the Rising*, London and New York, 1966.

150. Basil Chubb, *The Government and Politics of Ireland*, London and Stanford, 1970; Ronan Fanning, *The Irish Department of Finance, 1922–58*, Dublin, 1978. In *Censorship: The Irish Experience*, Dublin, 1968, Michael Adams deals dispassionately with a sensitive topic.

151. D. W. Harkness, *The Restless Dominion: The Irish Free State and the British Commonwealth of Nations, 1921–31*, London and Dublin, 1969.

152. Nicholas Mansergh, *The Commonwealth Experience*, London, 1969.

153. Maurice Manning, *The Blueshirts*, Dublin, 1970; see also David Thornley's short essay, "The Blueshirts," in MacManus, *Years of the Great Test*, 42–54.

154. Joseph T. Carroll, *Ireland in the War Years, 1939–1945*, Newton Abbot, 1975; T. Ryle Dwyer, *Irish Neutrality and the USA, 1939–47*, Dublin and Totowa, N.J., 1977.

155. Richard Deutsch, *Northern Ireland, 1921–1974: A Select Bibliography*, New York, 1975; Owen Dudley Edwards, *The Sins of Our Fathers: Roots of Conflict in Northern Ireland*, Dublin and London, 1970; Conor Cruise O'Brien, *States of Ireland*, London and New York, 1972.

156. Ian Budge and Cornelius O'Leary, *Belfast, Approach to Crisis*, London, 1973. Rather like the city itself, this book is deeply divided—along disciplinary and thematic lines—between a historical analysis of Belfast politics since the seventeenth century (O'Leary) and a psephological cum public opinion survey (Budge) carried out in 1966. Historians should find the first five chapters far more useful than the last eight. Andrew Boyd has chronicled the bitter and bloody realities of sectarian strife in a popular book, *Holy War in Belfast*, Tralee, 1969.

157. T. W. Moody, *The Ulster Question, 1603–1973*, Dublin and Cork, 1974; Liam de Paor, *Divided Ulster*, Harmondsworth, 1970. John F. Harbinson has written a convenient survey of northern unionism, *The Ulster Unionist Party, 1882–1973: Its Development and Organization*, Belfast, 1974.

158. Richard Rose, *Governing without Consensus: An Irish Perspective*, London and Boston, 1971. Rose's book has received much deserving praise; it has also been criticized for slighting the (fundamental) social and economic bases of the conflict in Northern Ireland. See, for example, Paul Bew's review in *IHS* 20, 1977: 366–368. Rose has written a topical sequel to this major

work—*Northern Ireland: A Time of Choice*, Washington, D.C., 1976. Designed primarily for novices who wish to peer into the dark tunnel of Northern Irish politics (at the end of which there is still no light), this study provides somes fleeting illumination. The last two chapters deal with the issues, parties, and personalities involved in the election of the Northern Irish Constitutional Convention in 1975.

159. Rosemary Harris, *Prejudice and Tolerance in Ulster: A Study of Neighbours and "Strangers" in a Border Community*, Manchester and Totowa, N.J., 1972. Harris's work as an empirical social anthropologist has yielded many significant insights. Those in need of an informed survey of the political (and institutional) bases of the troubles in the north should consult John Darby, *Conflict in Northern Ireland: The Development of a Polarised Community*, Dublin and New York, 1976, which also contains a helpful bibliography of writings on the conflict between 1969 and 1975.

160. The distinguished contributors to this series include Father Aubrey Gwynn, Father Benignus Millet, Geoffroy Hand, John H. Whyte, and the editor. Volumes 3–5 cover the seventeenth, eighteenth, and nineteenth centuries. Whyte and Corish have contributed two illuminating essays or chapters on the political problems of the church from 1850 to 1878: *A History of Irish Catholicism*, Dublin and Melbourne, 1967, 3(2): 1–39, and 5(3): 1–59.

161. According to the latest projections, Larkin's monumental study will run to ten volumes, of which three have now appeared.

162. John J. Silke, "The Roman Catholic Church in Ireland, 1800–1922: A Survey of Recent Historiography," *SH*, no. 15, 1975: 61–104.

163. Emmet Larkin, "Economic Growth, Capital Investment, and the Roman Catholic Church in Nineteenth-century Ireland," *AHR* 72, 1967: 852–884.

164. Ibid., "The Devotional Revolution in Ireland, 1850–75," *AHR* 77, 1972: 625–652.

165. Ibid., "Church, State, and Nation in Modern Ireland," *AHR* 80, 1975: 1244–1276.

166. David W. Miller, "Irish Catholicism and the Great Famine," *Journal of Social History* 9, 1975: 81–98. Miller argues here that the devotional revolution represented a popular response to the pressures of modernization.

167. Oliver MacDonagh, "The Politicization of the Irish Catholic Bishops, 1800–1850," *HJ* 18, 1975: 37–53.

168. E. R. Norman, "The Maynooth Question of 1845," *IHS* 15, 1967: 407–437. Kevin Nowlan explores clerical and O'Connellite tactics in "The Catholic Clergy and Irish Politics in the Eighteen Thirties and Forties," *Historical Studies* 9, 1974: 119–135.

169. E. D. Steele, "Cardinal Cullen and Irish Nationality," *IHS* 19, 1975: 239–260.

170. For references to the arguments of these historians about Cullenism, see ibid., 239–240.

171. Peadar MacSuibhne, ed., *Paul Cullen and His Contemporaries, with Their Letters from 1820 to 1902*, 5 vols., Naas, 1961–1977.

172. Larkin, *Modern Irish State*; idem, *Plan of Campaign*; idem, *Fall of Parnell*. A discerning review of Larkin's first volume by his former student, David Miller, may be found in *IHS* 20, 1976: 212–216. For another view of the church's position on the Parnell–O'Shea scandal, see Dom Mark Tierney, "Dr. Croke, the Irish Bishops, and the Parnell Crisis . . . 1890–91," *Collectanea Hibernica* 11, 1968: 111–148.

173. David W. Miller, *Church, State and Nation in Ireland, 1898–1921*, Pittsburgh, 1973.

174. See also Miller's summary article, "The Roman Catholic Church in Ireland: 1898–1918," *EI* 3(3), 1968: 75–91.

175. John H. Whyte, *Church and State in Modern Ireland, 1923–1970*, 2d ed., Dublin, 1980. Whyte devotes two chapters to Noel Browne's celebrated clash with the hierarchy and its allies over the Mother and Child scheme of 1951.

176. Donald H. Akenson, *The Church of Ireland: Ecclesiastical Reform and Revolution, 1800–1885*,

New Haven, Conn., and London, 1971; see also Desmond Bowen's review of Akenson's book in *IHS* 18, 1972: 268–271.

177. Michael Hurley, ed., *Irish Anglicanism, 1869–1969*, Dublin, 1970; R. B. McDowell, *The Church of Ireland, 1869–1969*, Boston, 1975.

178. Desmond Bowen, *The Protestant Crusade in Ireland, 1800–70*, Dublin and Montreal, 1978.

179. Ibid., *Souperism: Myth or Reality? A Study of Catholics and Protestants during the Great Famine*, Cork, 1970.

180. Hugh Shearman, *How the Church of Ireland Was Disestablished*, Dublin, 1970; Tadhg Ó Ceallaigh, "Disestablishment and Church Education," *SH*, no. 10, 1970: 36–69; Philip M. H. Bell, *Disestablishment in Ireland and Wales*, 1969.

181. L. A. Clarkson's critical bibliography appears in the *EcHR* 33, 1980: 100–111. Many of Clarkson's observations are addressed to work done in Irish social history and represent the increasing difficulty in drawing clear or useful distinctions between economic and social history.

182. L. M. Cullen, *An Economic History of Ireland since 1660*, London, 1972. For some essays of a survey nature, designed for a wider audience, see the Thomas Davis Lecture series, edited by ibid., *The Formation of the Irish Economy*, Cork, 1969.

183. Ibid., *Anglo-Irish Trade, 1660–1800*, Manchester, 1968. Several significant essays dealing with Irish economic activity (including one by W. E. Vaughan on landlord-tenant relations, 1850–1878) may be found in L. M. Cullen and T. C. Smout, eds., *Comparative Aspects of Scottish and Irish Economic and Social History, 1600–1900*, Edinburgh, 1977. For insights into the seventeenth-century cattle trade, see Donald Woodward, "The Anglo-Irish Livestock Trade of the Seventeenth Century," *IHS* 18, 1973: 489–523, and Carolyn Edie, *The Irish Cattle Bills: A Study in Restoration Politics*, Philadelphia, 1970.

184. Eileen McCracken, *The Irish Woods since Tudor Times, Distribution and Exploitation*, Newton Abbot, 1971.

185. W. H. Crawford, "Landlord–Tenant Relations in Ulster, 1609–1820," *IESH* 2, 1975: 5–21.

186. F. H. A. Aalen, "The Origin of Enclosures in Eastern Ireland," in N. Stephens and R. G. Glasscock, eds., *Irish Geographical Studies in Honour of E. E. Evans*, Belfast, 1970, 209–223.

187. David Large, "The Wealth of the Greater Irish Landowners, 1750–1815," *IHS* 15, 1966: 21–47.

188. L. A. Clarkson, "An Anatomy of an Irish Town: The Economy of Armagh, 1770," *IESH* 5, 1978: 27–45.

189. L. M. Cullen, "The Smuggling Trade in Ireland in the Eighteenth Century," *Proceedings of the Royal Irish Academy* 67, 1969: 299–317; idem, "Eighteenth-century Flour Milling in Ireland," *IESH* 4, 1977: 5–25.

190. Ibid., "Problems in the Interpretation and Revision of Eighteenth-century Irish Economic History," *TRHS* 17, 1967: 1–22. For other critiques of the simplistic dichotomy between the maritime-monetary and the subsistence economies posited in P. Lynch and J. Vaizey, *Guinness's Brewery in the Irish Economy, 1759–1876*, Cambridge, 1960, see Joseph Lee, "The Dual Economy in Ireland, 1800–50," *Historical Studies* 8, 1971: 191–201, and James H. Johnson, "The Two 'Irelands' at the Beginning of the Nineteenth Century," in Stephens and Glasscock, *Irish Geographical Studies*, 224–243, Belfast, 1970.

191. Barbara L. Solow, *The Land Question and the Irish Economy, 1870–1903*, Cambridge, Mass., 1971. For two perceptive reviews of Solow's book, see James S. Donnelly's critique in *SH*, no. 13, 1973; 185–190, and W. E. Vaughan's assessment in *IHS* 19, 1974: 222–223.

192. W. A. Maguire, *The Downshire Estates in Ireland, 1801–1845*, Oxford, 1972. For documents relating to this estate, see idem, *Letters of a Great Irish Landlord: A Selection from the*

Estate Correspondence of the Third Marquess of Downshire, 1807–45, Belfast, 1974. Maguire has also chronicled the financial collapse of a great estate through the reckless expenditure of a prodigal son and heir in "The 1822 Settlement of the Donegall Estates," *IESH* 3, 1976: 17–32. Some insights into the structure and operations of an early-nineteenth-century estate may be found in William Greig, *General Report on the Gosford Estates in County Armagh, 1821*, ed. F. M. L. Thompson and D. Tierney, Belfast, 1976.

193. James Donnelly, *The Land and the People of Nineteenth Century Cork*, London and Boston, 1975. Three helpful reviews of Donnelly's book are: Joseph Lee, Times Literary Supplement, Oct. 17, 1975; John B. O'Brien, "The Land and the People of Nineteenth Century Cork," *Journal of the Cork Historical and Archaeological Society*, 80, 1975: 95–101; and W. A. Maguire, *Agricultural History Review* 25, 1977, pt. 2, 151–152.

194. R. D. Crotty, *Irish Agricultural Production: Its Volume and Structure*, Cork, 1966. The historical sections of Crotty's book are original, provocative, and in places, misleading. As Joseph Lee points out in a review essay, Crotty goes too far in down-playing the famine as a watershed in Irish demographic and social history; he incorrectly assumes that the poorer farmers and laborers of the 1830s evolved into the "rural bourgeoisie" of the 1860s and after; and he exaggerates the extent of the swing from tillage to pasturage between 1815 and 1845: Lee, "Irish Agriculture," *Agricultural History Review* 17, 1969, pt. 1, 64–76. Much of Crotty's book concerns the stagnation of Irish agriculture during the twentieth century, and to cure this ailment Crotty prescribes the raising of minimum farm size by the state, making more effective use of land, improving the price mechanism governing land use, and introducing a land tax.

195. Padraig G. Lane, "The General Impact of the Encumbered Estates Act of 1849 on Counties Galway and Mayo," *Journal of Galway Archaeological and Historical Society* 33, 1972–1973: 44–74; idem, "The Management of Estates by Financial Corporations in Ireland after the Famine," *SH*, no. 14, 1974: 67–89.

196. Cormac Ó Gráda, "The Investment Behaviour of Irish Landlords, 1850–75: Some Preliminary Findings," *Agricultural History Review* 23, 1975: 139–155.

197. One new entry in this field of landlord studies is L. P. Curtis, Jr., "Incumbered Wealth: Landed Indebtedness in Post-famine Ireland," *AHR* 95 1980: 332–367.

198. James Donnelly, "Cork Market: Its Role in the Nineteenth Century Irish Butter Trade," *SH*, no. 11, 1971: 130–163; see also Donnelly's semirevisionist article "The Irish Agricultural Depression of 1859–64," *IESH* 3, 1976: 33–54.

199. Joseph Lee, "Money and Beer in Ireland, 1790–1875," *EcHR* 19, 1966: 183–190; see also idem, "Dual Economy in Ireland." For the spirit trade, see E. B. McGuire, *Irish Whiskey: A History of Distilling, the Spirit Trade and Excise Controls in Ireland*, Dublin and New York, 1973.

200. Joseph Lee, "The Provision of Capital for Early Irish Railways, 1830–53," *IHS*, 16, 1968: 33–63. Students of railway history should take note of Joseph Leckey's unpublished thesis "The Organization and Capital Structure of the Irish North Western Railway," Queen's University, Belfast, 1974. A popular introduction to the subject may be found in Henry C. Casserley, *Outline of Irish Railway History*, Newton Abbot, 1974.

201. Patrick Flanagan, *Transport in Ireland 1880–1910*, Dublin, 1969; Kevin B. Nowlan, ed., *Travel and Transport in Ireland*, Dublin, 1973.

202. Líam Kennedy, "Retail Markets in Rural Ireland at the End of the Nineteenth Century," *IESH* 5, 1978: 46–63; idem, "Traders in the Irish Rural Economy, 1880–1914," *EcHR* 32, 1979: 201–210.

203. Ibid., "The Early Response of the Irish Catholic Clergy to the Co-operative Movement," *IHS* 21, 1978: 55–74; Patrick Bolger, *The Irish Co-operative Movement*, Dublin, 1977.

204. W. H. Crawford, "Ulster Landowners and the Linen Industry," in J. T. Ward and R. G. Wil-

son, eds., *Land and Industry*, Newton Abbot, 1971, 117–144; idem, "Economy and Society in South Ulster in the Eighteenth Century," *Clogher Record*, 1975: 241–258.

205. H. D. Gribbon, *The History of Water Power in Ulster*, Newton Abbot, 1969.

206. W. E. Coe, *The Engineering Industry of the North of Ireland*, Newton Abbot, 1969.

207. James Meenan, *The Irish Economy since 1922*, Liverpool, 1970.

208. Maurice Moynihan, *Currency and Central Banking in Ireland, 1922–1960*, Dublin, 1975.

209. Kenneth Connell, *The Population of Ireland, 1750–1845*, Oxford, 1950.

210. L. M. Cullen, "Population Trends in Seventeenth-century Ireland," *Economic and Social Review* 6, 1975: 149–165; see also his chapter in *NHI* 3, "Economic Trends, 1660–91," 388–389.

211. Michael Drake, "The Irish Demographic Crisis of 1740–41," *Historical Studies* 6, 1968: 101–124.

212. Joseph Lee, "Marriage and Population in Pre-famine Ireland," *EcHR* 21, 1968: 283–295. In his response to Lee's article, G. S. L. Tucker supports Connell's thesis by relying on the fertility ratios found in the (statistically defective) Census of 1841: "Irish Fertility Ratios before the Famine," *EcHR* 23, 1970: 267–284.

213. L. M. Cullen, "Irish History without the Potato," *PP*, no. 40, 1968: 72–83. Although hampered by a dearth of statistical evidence, Cullen's argument that the spread of the potato monoculture was a response to, and not a cause of, population growth cannot be dismissed out of hand. For two different perspectives, see P. M. Austin Bourke, "The Use of the Potato Crop in Pre-famine Ireland," *Journal of Statistical and Social Inquiry Society of Ireland* 21, 1968: 72–96, and F. J. Carney, "Pre-famine Irish Population: The Evidence from the Trinity College Estates," *IESH* 2, 1975: 35–45.

214. Brendan M. Walsh, "Marriage Rates and Population Pressure: Ireland, 1871 and 1911," *EcHR* 23, 1970: 148–162.

215. Cormac Ó Gráda, "Seasonal Migration and Post-famine Adjustment in the West of Ireland," *SH*, no. 13, 1973: 48–76.

216. Edward E. McKenna, "Age, Region, and Marriage in Post-famine Ireland: An Empirical Examination," *EcHR* 31, 1978: 238–256.

217. David Quinn, *The Elizabethans and the Irish*; David Quinn and K. W. Nicholls, "Ireland in 1534," *NHI* 3: 1–38. Aspects of Irish society in c. 1600 and c. 1685 are discussed in passing by R. A. Butlin and J. H. Andrews, respectively, in ibid., 142–167 and 454–477.

218. Donald Jackson, *Intermarriage in Ireland, 1550–1650*, Montreal, 1970.

219. M. Perceval-Maxwell, *The Scottish Migration to Ulster in the Reign of James I*, London, 1973.

220. Robert J. Hunter, "Towns in the Ulster Plantation," *SH*, no. 11, 1971: 40–79.

221. Jean M. Graham, "Rural Society in Connacht, 1600–1640," in Stephens and Glasscock, *Irish Geographical Studies*, 192–208.

222. Constantia Maxwell, *Country and Town in Ireland under the Georges*, London, 1940, and Dundalk, 1949.

223. See, for example, Dom Mark Tierney, *Murroe and Boher: The History of an Irish Country Parish*, Dublin, 1966, and Jeremiah Sheehan, *South Westmeath, Farm and Folk*, Dublin, 1978. For some primary source materials, carefully selected and edited, see W. H. Crawford and B. Trainor, eds., *Aspects of Irish Social History, 1750–1800*, Belfast, 1969.

224. Robert E. Kennedy, *The Irish: Emmigration, Marriage, and Fertility*, Berkeley and London, 1973.

225. Kenneth Connell, *Irish Peasant Society: Four Historical Essays*, Oxford, 1968.

226. Daniel J. Casey and Robert E. Rhodes, eds., *Views of the Irish Peasantry, 1900–1916*, Hamden, Conn., 1977. This volume contains a useful bibliography of Irish peasant culture compiled by John C. Messenger.

227. Michael Anderson, *Family Structure in Nineteenth-century Lancashire*, Cambridge, 1971, chap. 7.

228. James W. Hurst, "Disturbed Tipperary: 1831–1860," *EI* 9(3), 1974: 44–59. For an interesting explanation of the motives underlying some of the agrarian crime in Tipperary in 1837–1847, see Beames, "Rural Conflict in Pre-famine Ireland."

229. Pamela L. R. Horn, "The National Agricultural Labourers' Union in Ireland, 1873–9," *IHS* 17, 1971: 340–352. Timothy P. O'Neill discusses rural poverty in "Clare and Irish Poverty, 1815–1851," *SH*, no. 14, 1974: 7–27, and idem, "The Catholic Church and Relief of the Poor, 1815–45," *Archivium Hibernicum* 31, 1973: 132–145.

230. Louis Hyman, *The Jews of Ireland from Earliest Times to the Year 1910*, Shannon, 1972.

231. Maurice Craig, *Dublin, 1660–1860*, Dublin and London, 1952.

232. F. O. C. Meenan, "The Georgian Squares of Dublin and the Professions," *Studies* 58, 1969: 405–414.

233. Lynn Lees, "Patterns of Lower-class Life: Irish Slum Communities in Nineteenth Century London," in S. Thernstrom and R. Sennett, eds., *Nineteenth-century Cities: Essays in the New Urban History*, New Haven, 1969, 359–85; idem, "Mid-Victorian Migration and the Irish Family Economy," *VS* 20, 1976: 25–43; see also Kevin O'Connor, *The Irish in Britain*, London, 1972. Sheridan Gilley examines the "cure" of Irish souls in London's Irish districts in three articles in *Recusant History* 10 1969: 123–145; ibid., 1970: 210–230; and ibid. 11, 1971: 21–45. Gilley deals with the efforts of English missionaries, both Protestant evangelicals and Roman Catholics, to provide both spiritual and material assistance to the poor Irish of London during the mid-nineteenth century.

234. Conrad Arensberg and Solon Kimball, *Family and Community in Ireland*, Cambridge, Mass., 1940, rep., Gloucester, Mass., 1961. See also Conrad Arensberg's popular account of his researches in and around Luogh, County Clare, between 1931 and 1934: *The Irish Countryman*, New York, 1937; rep., Gloucester, Mass., 1959.

235. Hugh Brody, *Inishkillane, Change and Decline in the West of Ireland*, 1973; see, especially, pp. 1–17 and 184–209.

236. Peter Gibbon, "Arensberg and Kimball Revisited," *Economy and Society* 2, 1973: 479–498. Another example of a "radical" revisionist approach comes from the fieldwork done by Nancy Scheper-Hughes on the Dingle peninsula in Kerry. She blames the high incidence of schizophrenia among older males (most of these being bachelors) on the traumatic effects of mature capitalism or "agribusiness" in these western regions; see her article "Inheritance of the Meek: Land, Labor and Love in Rural Ireland," *Marxist Perspectives* 5, Spring 1979: 46–76. Scheper-Hughes's new book, *Saints, Scholars and Schizophrenics*, Berkeley, 1979, was not available for discussion in this essay. By comparison with these studies, John C. Messenger's study of an Aran island, *Inis Beag, Isle of Ireland*, New York, 1969, seems only mildly revisionist in spite of his discovery of pronounced oedipal conflicts among the males of Inisheer. For another "island study," steeped in genealogical lore and linkage, see Robin Fox, *The Tory Islanders: A People of the Celtic Fringe*, Cambridge and New York, 1978. F. H. Aalen and Hugh Brody collaborated on a study of decline that contains a number of interesting historical as well as ethnographic features: *Gola: The Life and Last Days of an Island Community*, Cork, 1969. P. Gibbon and C. Curtin have made an impressive foray into family history by quantifying a sample of households taken from the Census of 1911; see their article, "The Stem Family in Ireland," *Comparative Studies in Society and History* 20, 1978: 429–453.

237. Brian Ó Cuív, ed., *A View of the Irish Language*, Dublin, 1969.

238. W. B. Stanford, *Ireland and the Classical Tradition*, Dublin, 1976.

239. K. Theodore Hoppen, *The Common Scientist of the Seventeenth Century: A Study of the Dublin Philosophical Society, 1683–1708*, Charlottesville, Va., 1970. Hoppen's book has been criti-

cized by T. C. Barnard, who challenges the contention that Ireland lacked an environment conducive to scientific inquiry before the early 1680s. Barnard takes as his case in point the intellectual activities of Samuel Hartlib and his friends: "The Hartlib Circle and the Origins of the Dublin Philosophical Society," *IHS* 19, 1974: 56–71. Hoppen has sprung to his own defense in a rejoinder in *IHS* 20, 1976: 40–48.

240. J. C. Beckett, *The Anglo-Irish Tradition*, London, 1976. Beckett's description of this essay as "a work of reflection rather than of research" helps to explain the interweaving of historical insights and a distinct note of nostalgia for the loss of Ireland's "high civilization." That nostalgia may account in part for Brendan Bradshaw's bristling review of *The Anglo-Irish Tradition* in *Studies*, 66, 1977: 240–244, in which he dwells on "the self-confident arrogance" of that Protestant elite. But R. F. Foster has some kinder things to say in *IHS* 20, 1977: 354–358. For a different view of the Anglo-Irish elite in the early twentieth century, see L. P. Curtis, Jr., "The Anglo-Irish Predicament," *Twentieth Century Studies* 4, 1970: 37–63.

241. F. S. L. Lyons, *Culture and Anarchy in Ireland, 1890–1939*, Oxford, 1979.

242. Daniel Corkery, *The Hidden Ireland: A Study of Gaelic Munster in the Eighteenth Century*, 1924, often reprinted as well as praised; L. M. Cullen, "The Hidden Ireland: Reassessment of a Concept," *SH*, no. 9, 1969: 7–47. To appreciate this article fully, the reader should "have the Irish." Despite Cullen's critique, veneration of Corkery's approach and interpretation will last as long as there are people who insist on finding the roots of modern Irish nationalism in the Irish poets of eighteenth-century Munster. For two glowing tributes to Corkery's qualities as an Irish nationalist and literary historian, see the essays by Lawrence McCaffrey and Emmet Larkin in *EI* 8(1), 1973: 35–51.

243. Robert Munter, *The History of the Irish Newspaper, 1685–1760*, Cambridge, 1967.

244. See, for example, Maurice J. Craig, *Classic Irish Houses of the Middle Size*, London, 1976, and New York, 1977; Edward McParland, "The Wide Streets Commissioners . . . ," *Irish Georgian Society* 15, 1972: 1–32.

245. Mark Bence-Jones, *Burke's Guide to Country Houses*, vol. 7, *Ireland*, London, 1978.

246. T. J. Walsh, *Opera in Dublin, 1705–1797: The Social Scene*, Dublin, 1973; Michael Ó hAodha, *Theatre in Ireland*, Oxford, 1974.

247. Edmund Burke, *Reflections on the Revolution in France*, Harmondsworth, Pelican Classics, 1968, 9–81. This edition has been reprinted in 1969, 1973, and 1976. Other recent work on Burke includes Gerald W. Chapman, *Edmund Burke: The Practical Imagination*, Cambridge, Mass., 1967, and Isaac Kramnick, *The Rage of Edmund Burke: Portrait of an Ambivalent Conservative*, New York, 1977. At long last, that great tribute to the genius of Burke and the cause of transatlantic scholarly collaboration, *The Correspondence of Edmund Burke*, has been completed. Volumes 6 through 10 (the *Index*) have been published between 1967 and 1978, by Cambridge University Press and University of Chicago Press.

248. Marilyn Butler, *Maria Edgeworth: A Literary Biography*, Oxford, 1972; see also Christina Colvin's edition of Maria Edgeworth's *Letters from England, 1813–1844*, Oxford, 1971, and Michael Hurst, *Maria Edgeworth and the Public Scene: Intellect, Fine Feeling and Landlordism in the Age of Reform*, London, 1969.

249. Malcolm Brown, *The Politics of Irish Literature: From Thomas Davis to W. B. Yeats*, Seattle, 1972.

250. Peter Costello, *The Heart Grown Brutal: The Irish Revolution in Literature from Parnell to the Death of Yeats, 1891–1939*, Dublin and Totowa, N.J., 1977.

251. Oliver MacDonagh, *The Nineteenth-century Novel and Irish Social History: Some Aspects*, Dublin, 1971. This O'Donnell Lecture was delivered at the University of Cork, 21 April 1970.

252. Guy Fehlmann, *Somerville et Ross: Témoins de l'Irlande d'hier*, Caen, 1970. Students of Anglo-

Irish literature should consult Maurice Harmon's valuable guide *Select Bibliography for the Study of Anglo-Irish Literature and Its Backgrounds*, Dublin, 1977.

253. Donal McCartney, "James Anthony Froude and Ireland: A Historiographical Controversy of the Nineteenth Century," *Historical Studies* 8, 1971: 171–190.

254. Anne Wyatt, "Froude, Lecky and 'the Humblest Irishman,'" *IHS* 19, 1975: 261–285.

255. W. E. H. Lecky, *A History of Ireland in the Eighteenth Century*, abridged and with an introduction by L. P. Curtis, Jr., Chicago and London, 1972.

256. In order of appearance these biographical studies are: W. B. Stanford and R. B. McDowell, *Mahaffy: A Biography of an Anglo-Irishman*, London, 1971; F. X. Martin and F. J. Byrne, eds., *The Scholar Revolutionary: Eoin MacNeill, 1867–1945, and the Making of the New Ireland*, Shannon, 1973; R. B. McDowell, *Alice Stopford Green: A Passionate Historian*, Dublin, 1967; Dominic Daly, *The Young Douglas Hyde: The Dawn of the Irish Revolution and Renaissance*, Dublin and Totowa, N.J., 1974; Henry Summerfield, *That Myriad-minded Man: A Biography of George William Russell, 'AE,' 1867–1935*, London and Totowa, N.J., 1976; B. L. Reid, *The Man from New York: John Quinn and His Friends*, New York, 1968. For admirers of Yeats there is Samuel Levenson's new biography, *Maud Gonne*, New York, 1976.

257. L. P. Curtis, Jr., *Anglo-Saxons and Celts: A Study of Anti-Irish Prejudice in Victorian England*, Bridgeport, Conn., 1968; idem, *Apes and Angels: The Irishman in Victorian Caricature*, Washington, D.C., and Newton Abbot, 1971. Students of image making who prefer a political science model based on Festinger's concept of cognitive dissonance should consult Richard N. Lebow, *White Britain and Black Ireland*, Philadelphia, 1976.

258. Donald Harman Akenson, *The Irish Education Experiment: The National System of Education in the Nineteenth Century*, London and Toronto, 1970; idem, *Education and Enmity: The Control of Schooling in Northern Ireland, 1920–50*, Newton Abbot and New York, 1973; idem, *A Mirror to Kathleen's Face: Education in Independent Ireland, 1922–1960*, Montreal and London, 1975.

259. Norman Atkinson, *Irish Education: A History of Educational Institutions*, Dublin, 1969.

260. J. M. Goldstrom, "Richard Whately and Political Economy in School Books, 1833–80," *IHS* 15, 1966: 131–146; idem, *The Social Content of Education, 1808–1870: A Study of the Working-class Reader in England and Ireland*, Shannon, 1972. For a study of a noted Irish philanthropist and educational reformer, see Mary McNeill, *Vere Foster, 1819–1900: An Irish Benefactor*, Newton Abbot, 1971.

261. Among the books which appeared too late for inclusion in this essay are: T. W. Moody, ed., *Nationality and the Pursuit of National Independence*, Belfast, 1978; F. S. L. Lyons and R. A. J. Hawkins, eds., *Ireland under the Union: Varieties of Tension. Essays in Honour of T. W. Moody*, Oxford and New York, 1979; and Hilary Robinson, *Somerville and Ross: A Critical Appreciation*, Dublin and New York, 1980.

Problem Child of British History: The British Empire-Commonwealth

Robin W. Winks

Few aspects of British history as traditionally conceived have grown so rapidly in sheer bulk of literature, or suffered so many changes in interpretation, including changes thrust upon the field from outside and arising from nonscholarly issues, as the history of the British Empire and of the Commonwealth that is customarily said to have grown from it. Once little more than an adjunct to constitutional, economic, or diplomatic history, the study of imperialism and of empires has both grown and fragmented to the point that no one person, or even body of persons, can grasp the totality of the literature as once defined. No publisher's catalog is without two or three titles which may be construed as contributions to imperial studies, and while other empires are under ever more intensive investigation, the British empire remains—as it was in its time—the largest and most demanding. While controversy swirls about the figure of Cromwell or of Lloyd George, while questions such as how and when a working class was "made" or precisely how the English country house was a reflection of social values resonate with special significance for the present, such debates tend to be contained within the confines of a discrete body of literature, while argument over empire has long been since hemorrhaged into a number of other arguments. The student of empire must look to the history of art; to literature, economics, and political theory; and assuredly to anthropology to remain in touch with the field; and his reach will always exceed his grasp.

One sign of the rapidity of change is that not one of the half dozen titles in British imperial history that would today be considered most significant in shaping the field as it now exists was mentioned by the essay which, published in 1966, may be considered the predecessor to the present survey. Another sign of the value-laden shifts in the field is that the famous call by Vincent Harlow, at the 1960 International Committee of Historical Sciences in Stockholm, to abandon use of the word *imperialism* entirely as no longer useful (which was little heeded though much quoted) is seldom heard today. The call, by this writer, in a different essay in 1966, for new works of syntheses has been met in abundance; and yet we are not really closer to the answer to such basic questions as: Did colonies pay? What was the prime engine behind the imperialist thrust? Did the empire oil the wheels of the Industrial Revolution? What is the balance sheet on empire?[1]

Taking 1966 as a base date, a number of clear trends, most so forceful as to be labeled "changes," are now apparent. Nine of these stand out. Some contribute to the "historiographical revision" which David K. Fieldhouse charted in his significant essay with that subtitle in 1961;[2] others follow after and, depending upon one's vantage point, run contrary to it. Each is worth a comment even at the risk of excluding other, less immediately obvious trends. Taken collectively, they represent an additional change which may be the most significant of all.

Perhaps the most notable trend is that toward embedding the history of the British Empire, and of the Commonwealth (which, to many scholars, appears to be viewed as a species of decolonization), into the comparative history of imperialism. Comparative history has enjoyed something of a vogue in the United States, as American scholars have sought to break away from the "exceptionalist" interpretations which had taken American historiography out of the Western mainstream, and it was inevitable that students of American imperialism would seek to compare their insights with those of British and continental scholars.[3] In fact, few did so successfully, and the literature on American imperialism is, on the whole, marked by a clear ignorance of what European scholars had written of their own imperialisms. Nonetheless, some American and many British, African, and Asian scholars began to ask whether the British Empire was unique, or representative, and if either, unique when set against what or representative when measured against which? While much that passed for comparative history proved, upon examination, to consist of several parallel case studies of annexation, or economic exploitation, or overseas settlement, some was genuinely comparative in that it hinted at a different methodology and at conclusions that would not have been reached in another context.

The most explicitly comparative history was David K. Fieldhouse's *The Colonial Empires: A Comparative Survey from the Eighteenth Century* (London) which appeared in our (somewhat fictitious) watershed year 1966. Not only did he survey the "imperial museum" of lands once colored red on world maps, but Fieldhouse commented on all imperialisms, including Russian and American. Inevitably some sections were superficial (perhaps the American particularly so), but the conclusion, that each empire was the product of an expanding metropolitan center, that each produced a unique elite bureaucracy with a differing professional ethos, and that broadly viewed, all imperialisms were markedly similar, was well argued. He did not go on to say, but might well have on his own evidence, that the essence of imperialism lay in the impact of expanding high-technology societies on those with lesser technologies.

The effect of Fieldhouse's work, together with that of others with similar conclusions, most notably Raymond F. Betts's *Europe Overseas: Phases of Imperialism* (New York, 1968), Rudolf von Albertini's *Europäische Kolonialherrschaft, 1880–1940* (Zurich, 1976),[4] and Donald C. Gordon's more focused examination of power as a discretely identifiable factor in intercultural relations, *The Moment of Power: Britain's Imperial Epoch* (Englewood Cliffs, N.J., 1970), was to bring the metropolitan center back on stage. In the late 1950s and early 1960s, imperial history, and especially British imperial historiography, had been driven toward the periphery in an appropriate revulsion against the London-centric views of the earlier constitutional historians who wrote books under variants of such titles as *From Colony to Nationhood*, historians who subtly purveyed a Whiggish bias that history was essentially about the rise of the nation state and that British imperial history was about the gift of independence, and thus nationhood, to a variety of peoples. But Ottawa-, Cape Town-, or Lagos-centric history did not prove sufficient in itself to an understanding of empire, and Fieldhouse's work represented a clear tendency toward movement back to the centers. Indeed, because of his emphasis on the nature of colonial bureaucracies, he may have overcorrected the wayward vessel; for while movement from the periphery to the center was a second obvious trend, the better scholarship might be described as multicentric, a logical impossibility all too indicative of the state of the field.

For comparative history to be effective, the units of comparison must be genuinely comparable. Reasonable men may differ on definitions, but few would think that scholarly work was much forwarded by comparing the British and the Roman empires (a favorite game of the British themselves in the heyday of empire), for example, since the technologies, international environments, and economies were so different. Even Sir Ronald Syme's influential comparison of *Colonial Élites* (London, 1958) had limited itself to Rome, Spain, and the English American colonies. But the search for that which might be usefully compared led to a substantial growth in studies of slavery in all of its aspects, and no scholar of the British Empire could afford to ignore this bursting, and controversial, literature, since it also was a bridge to other controversies within the field.

The study of slavery within the British Empire has always been three studies: of the slave trade, of variants within slave systems in specific colonies, and of the movement to abolish first the trade and then slavery itself. All three subjects were invitations to comparisons with, in particular, the history of the United States. The classic statement by Eric Williams, in *Capitalism and Slavery* (Chapel Hill, N.C., 1944), had prepared the ground, and Williams's rise to the prime minis-

terial position in Trinidad had assured continued visibility for his view. Too simply put, Williams argued that the abolitionists had been pushing on an open
door, that the planting class of absentee landlords in Britain were aware that the
slave-based sugar economy of the West Indies already was in irremediable decline, and that the abolitionists had been given credit for a victory on the high
road which was actually a capitulation on the low. Further, Williams suggested
(and in this his work fell parallel to that of several nationalist historians from
India), the Industrial Revolution had been financed from the profits of the slave
trade, and of the sugar islands—that is, without slavery there would have been no
British preeminence industrially or imperially. The most direct reply to Williams's argument came from two British scholars, Howard Temperley in *British
Antislavery, 1833–1870* (London, 1972) and, more resoundingly, Roger Anstey
in *The Atlantic Slave Trade and British Abolition, 1760–1810* (London, 1975).
For their respective time periods, Temperley and Anstey showed that aboli-
tionism in Britain was a genuine, not hypocritical, religious movement which
made skillful use of those elements in the British community which thought in
economic or political terms first. Anstey challenged the views that the trade was
profitable or that it was central to the Industrial Revolution, and he pointed up a
number of deficiencies in Williams's work.

Of course the argument would not rest there, and as it was elaborated by a
number of scholars, it became increasingly apparent that the history of slavery
shared, in many ways, the problems of intellectual rather than institutional history. While a growing number of historians chose to examine slavery as one species of the genus forced labor rather than as a distinct condition, drawing heavily
on the earlier work of two Dutch scholars, H. J. Nieboer in *Slavery as an Industrial System* (The Hague, 1910) and Willemina Kloosterboer in *Involuntary Labour since the Abolition of Slavery* (Amsterdam, 1960; first published in Dutch in
1954), others saw slavery as an aspect of intellectual history. Increasingly, publications shifted the questions from how slave systems worked to inquiries concerning the profitability of slavery, the nature of competing sources of labor supply, the problems of economies which required productive capacity over that
supply, and studies of societies (chiefly in Africa) which were not slaveowning,
and why.[5] The effect of such studies was to raise again the division between
Marxist and non-Marxist interpretations of history and to reveal even more
clearly that questions about profitability and about alternative labor systems were,
at base, questions in intellectual history, since prevailing opinions of what constituted sufficient profit, just price, or available options were embedded in value
systems. Thus slave studies both promoted and more clearly revealed two major
changes in imperial history, to which I return shortly.

Other works on slavery which were central to British imperial history included
David Brion Davis's *The Problem of Slavery in Western Culture* (Ithaca, N.Y.,

1966), which systematically compared Britain, the British colonies, and Latin America, and Davis's *The Problem of Slavery in the Age of Revolution, 1770– 1823* (Ithaca, N.Y., 1975), which between them were the most important contribution to the subject in several decades. Philip D. Curtin's *The Atlantic Slave Trade: A Census* (Madison, Wis., 1969) brought sophisticated calculations to bear on the question of how many, to the conclusion that the total trade was somewhat smaller than polemicists had argued. But Curtin's statistics were soon questioned in a spate of articles, and attention also shifted toward the slave trade of East Africa, especially after the publication of R. W. Beachey's work of that title (London, 1976), and toward slavery in Muslim lands, so that Curtin (and Anstey) were felt to have unraveled only part of the story. To their work one must add Suzanne Miers's *Britain and the Ending of the Slave Trade* (London, 1975); Leslie Bethell's *The Abolition of the Brazilian Slave Trade* (London, 1970), which showed Britain at work within a culture not annexed; and Edmund S. Morgan's *American Slavery, American Freedom: The Ordeal of Colonial Virginia* (New York, 1975), which demonstrated how closely the need for a dependable labor supply was related, in an open-space–open-resource environment, to the rising rhetoric of political freedom for settlers. These books, together with one that added an unusual comparative dimension—Albert Wirz's *Vom Sklavenhandel zum Kolonialen Handel* (Zurich, 1972), which closely probed Germany's enforced labor practices in Kamerun to 1914—and two that attempted general syntheses (Michael Craton's *Sinews of Empire: A Short History of British Slavery*, Garden City, 1974, and C. Duncan Rice's *The Rise and Fall of Black Slavery*, New York, 1975—defined the shape of the field as it related to the British Empire.

For the most part, the British West Indies continued to be approached through the lens of slavery or of labor systems. Many books were glosses or attacks on Lowell J. Ragatz's classic work *The Fall of the Planter Class in the British Caribbean, 1763–1833*, originally published in 1928 and reissued in 1963 (New York). The most significant were Richard S. Dunn's *Sugar and Slaves: The Rise of the Planter Class in the English West Indies, 1624–1713* (Chapel Hill, N.C., 1972), which brilliantly filled a major gap in the literature; Elsa V. Goveia's *Slave Society in the British Leeward Islands at the End of the Eighteenth Century* (New Haven, Conn., 1965); Alan H. Adamson's *Sugar without Slaves: The Political Economy of British Guiana, 1838–1904* (New Haven, Conn., 1972); Michael Craton's *Searching for the Invisible Man: Slaves and Plantation Life in Jamaica* (Cambridge, Mass., 1978), which centered on a single sugar plantation, Worthy Park; Douglas Hall's *Free Jamaica, 1838–1865: An Economic History* (New Haven, Conn., 1959), which examined the ways in which Jamaica adjusted to modern wage-labor problems; Donald Wood's *Trinidad in Transition: The Years after Slavery* (New York, 1968); and Geoffrey Dutton's *The Hero as Murderer: The Life of Edward John Eyre, Australian Explorer and Governor of*

Jamaica, 1815–1901 (Sydney, 1967). Perhaps most sophisticated of all in methodology was Jerome S. Handler's close study of *The Unappropriated People: Freedmen in the Slave Society of Barbados* (Baltimore, 1974).

Over the long run, however, the most discussed book is likely to be Seymour Drescher's complex analysis of *Econocide*, subtitled *British Slavery in the Era of Abolition* (Pittsburgh, 1977). Drescher moved even more forcefully in the direction taken by the late Roger Anstey in showing that abolition took place contrary to the best interests of the planters. For the first time a statistical base has been provided by which Eric Williams's broad assumptions might be tested; further, Drescher had the wit to use the economic indicators in the way they were viewed during the period, so that we know what the planters believed to be true. His conclusion is that "economic interests cannot account for either the timing, the occurrence, or the maintenance of the abolition of the slave trade between 1787 and 1820." The trade was thriving yet abolished—a conclusion that speaks directly from the rising body of non-Marxist scholarship and to the infrastructure of imperialism, that is, racism.

Slavery is, of course, only one small aspect of British imperial studies. But these books revealed more clearly than did any other cluster of literature the major trends in the field. This is true not only for those trends already remarked upon—the move toward comparative studies, the concern for the intellectual dimensions of the problems under investigation, and the search for non-Marxist explanations for phenomena abandoned for a time to Marxist argumentation—but also for trends not yet noted—the rise of substantial American contributions to the field, so that one no longer automatically assumes London or Oxford as the first place of publication; the obvious impact of current political and social controversies on the choice of subjects for scholarly examination; and the need to incorporate the findings and sometimes the methodologies of anthropology, since much of the evidence is not open to the historian's traditional methods of approach.

Indeed, today it is possible to maintain that British imperial history is essentially an aspect of world intellectual history, for one clear change is toward studies of perception, of the making of stereotypes, and of how those stereotypes, once made, were reinforced by a number of elements in society, including the public schools, the romantic fiction of empire, the needs of explorers to exaggerate the exotic worlds they found, the imperative for missionaries to justify their activities, and the rise of "scientific racism."[6] Again, most studies in these areas examined European imperialisms as a whole, though (also again) the British Empire was at their core.

The move to intellectual history presented at once a strength and a weakness for imperial studies. On the one hand, the realization that such questions as profitability were, at base, matters of prevailing conventional wisdoms, was liberating to the body of scholarship, for it was not necessary to fight over the same old Marxist—anti-Marxist ground. The rise of a non-Marxist school of thought, which felt no obligation to examine empires within the constraints of Marxist theory, was both effect and further cause. At the same time, some authors used the self-evident fact that intellectual history is less amenable to documentation to engage in flights of fancy, or to duck hard questions on the dubious ground either that there were no answers or that all answers were relative. Whether slavery paid or not, slaves suffered.

Intellectual history is notoriously difficult to define, and perhaps its dimensions, within British imperial studies, are best indicated by an indicative census. Five works have been especially influential. That which works at the highest level of generalization is Henri Baudet's *Paradise on Earth: Some Thoughts on European Images of Non-European Man* (New Haven, Conn., 1965), translated from the Dutch by Elizabeth Wentholt. Seldom cited, one discovers this lovely little book lurking in the hedgerows of much scholarship-by-nonattribution. Pushing in the same direction more blatantly, two other volumes, Frantz Fanon's *The Wretched of the Earth* (first published in Paris in 1961), with the imprimatur of Jean-Paul Sartre, and O. Mannoni's *Prospero and Caliban: The Psychology of Colonization* (first published in Paris in 1950 and in English in 1956), were standard fare for generations of undergraduates. These books, one fundamentally about Algeria and the other about Madagascar, attracted large publics in British as well as continental universities. Their great service was to draw attention to the psychological-intellectual problems of understanding the colonial experience from within. Their disservice was to enhance two counterprevailing stereotypes: if read carelessly, they could be taken as saying that all Europeans were imperialists and all nonwhites were victims, thus adding in subtle ways to the notion that indigenous societies had few dynamics of their own other than the dynamics of response and counterresponse, as though the history of "native peoples" could not stand alone. Read with care, both books showed that the Western power was also victimized by the process of colonialism, but such a message still left the reader with the conclusion that imperial history was a receptacle for grievance collecting and that the ill powerfully outweighed the good (perhaps a valid judgment, but not one examined in the body of literature that arose from the Fanon-Mannoni line of argument).

Against the work of these three continentally based authors, there also arose a body of literature that, in tone and temper, found the British Empire, in particular, more easily open to honorable defense than any other empire. Not so much a defense of empire, as a wry examination of the nostalgia with which we now view an ordered world, James Morris's trilogy, begun with *Pax Britannica: The Climax of Empire* (London, 1968), was rich in anecdote and insight, chiefly about the British. With *Heaven's Command: An Imperial Progress* (London, 1973) and

Farewell the Trumpets: An Imperial Retreat (London, 1978), Morris's impressionistic evocation was widely popular. Coming at a time when many younger British scholars appeared to be writing of their imperial history from a sense of shame—and collective shame may prove to be no better tool for analysis than assumptions of collective guilt or collective pride—Morris's expansive and beautifully written series of set pieces was, like Fanon and Mannoni, a necessary corrective. Morris was primarily interested in how the British saw their empire at the time, and since most saw it with "mingled sensations of admiration, dislike, amusement, pity, pride, envy and astonishment," his complex work was one model for how best to write intellectual history. That one could hear the faint strains of "Men of Harlech" in the background as one read did not invalidate the obvious historical truth, that one writes history in terms of what people believed to be true at the time rather than in terms of the truths another generation's experiences thrust upon those participants.

Between these poles in intellectual history fall other titles of major importance. Two were essentially studies of perception and how perceptions were formed and manipulated, and both gave rise to many imitators: Philip D. Curtin's *The Image of Africa: British Ideas and Action, 1780–1850* (Madison, Wis., 1964), and Norman Daniel's *Islam, Europe and Empire* (Edinburgh, 1966). Every chapter of Curtin's inquiry produced a dozen extenders—one sign of the rapid growth in African history, and the organization and opening of African archives—while few of Daniel's did so—another sign of the paucity of scholarship in the West on Islam in general. A key chapter for Curtin was his analysis of how West Africa came to be viewed as the "white man's grave," and his excursion into the history of medicine was followed by a number of studies, most notably Gordon Harrison's fine *Mosquitos, Malaria and Man: A History of the Hostilities since 1880* (New York, 1978). Bernard Smith, in *European Vision and the South Pacific, 1768–1850* (London, 1960), had brought imperial studies together with the history of art, and C. A. Burland, in *The Exotic White Man* (London, 1969), turned the coin over to show how non-European societies perceived Europeans. Following upon these books there have appeared, or are in preparation, various studies of artists and architects who built, either in the mind or on the ground, imperial visions. Studies of Sir George Goldie, the romantic limner of the Maori; of Sir Edwin Landseer, he of the Stag at Bay; or of imperial architects such as Sir Edward Lutyens and Sir Herbert Baker, and of the layout of Jamaican slave plantations in relation to the needs of slavery in all its dimensions, promise to enrich our understanding of the British Empire.

Another approach to intellectual history is through collective biography. While several proconsuls of empire have received new biographical treatment (including Joseph Chamberlain's), the happiest development is the essay-length inquiry into figures—some major but increasingly those who are significant simply for being typical of a class, occupation, or geographically related point of view—who illumine new facets of "the vision of empire." A. P. Thornton, long one of the most productive students of British imperialism, perhaps did his best service for the cause in a work ostensibly about Britian itself, *The Habit of Authority: Paternalism in British History* (London, 1966), a contribution to the debate over deference which, to imperial historians, has seemed oddly sterile when the imperial dimension (which Thornton controls) has been lacking. Bernard Semmel's provocative essays in *Imperialism and Social Reform: English Social-Imperial Thought, 1895–1914* (Cambridge, Mass., 1960) may be said to have launched the subgenre (or to have taken William Hazlitt's *Spirit of the Age* into the realm of scholarship) with fascinating essays on Chamberlain, Benjamin Kidd, Karl Pearson, William Cunningham and Sir William Ashley, and Sir Halford John Mackinder, among others. (One still awaits full scale biographies of all.) More superficially, yet with much insight, Richard Faber, in *The Vision and the Need: Late Victorian Imperialist Aims* (London, 1966), reexamined Rosebery, Sir Charles Dilke, J. A. Froude, Sir J. R. Seeley, and others, while Christine Bolt, in *Victorian Attitudes to Race* (London, 1971), looked to Jamaica and India through the eyes of individual commentators. Richard Ned Lebow, in *White Britain and Black Ireland: The Influence of Stereotypes on Colonial Policy* (Philadelphia, 1976), intelligently if woodenly built a case for how the British convinced themselves that "good government" would not arise from Irish politics or culture. This subject was confronted more centrally by J. M. Lee in a striking work, *Colonial Development and Good Government: A Study of the Ideas Expressed by the British Official Classes in Planning Decolonization, 1939–1964* (Oxford, 1967).[7]

Literature and intellectual history obviously bisect, and especially so when one seeks to understand how generations at home came to receive their conventional wisdom about their empire abroad. Two approaches have dominated to date: the one, straightforward examinations of how "serious" authors (novelists, poets, and popular scholars) have dealt with non-Western cultures and the impact of the West upon them, and the other, quasi-anthropological inquiries—much influenced by the French scholar Philippe Ariès through his *Centuries of Childhood* (London, 1962), and contributions to the *Annales* school—into how romantic children's fiction of empire gave rise to attitudes that would be supportive of imperial expansion. The most direct, and therefore helpful, of the former is Martin Green's *Dreams of Adventure, Deeds of Empire* (New York, 1979), which examined "modern empire, caste, and adventure" through the prism of Defoe, Scott, Kipling, and Conrad, with a cranky brilliance. Less daring and more in tune with undergraduate needs is Jonah Raskin's *The Mythology of Imperialism* (New York, 1971), which chose Joyce Cary, E. M. Forster, D. H. Lawrence, and the inevitable Kipling and Conrad, to ask how the realities of empire shaped their art. Again, these kinds of inquiries may be said to have been launched by a single book, in this case Alan Sandison's *The Wheel of Empire: A Study of the Imperial Idea in Some Late Nineteenth and Early Twentieth-century Fiction* (London, 1967), which added Rider Haggard and John Buchan to the inevitable two. Perhaps the most sensible is Molly M. Mahood's *The Colonial Encounter: A Reading of Six Novels* (London, 1977), which added Chinua Achebe, R. K. Narayan, Graham Greene, and V. S. Naipaul to Conrad and Forster. To such synthetic studies as these one must add the spate of new studies of Rudyard Kipling, of which Angus Wilson's *The Strange Ride of Rudyard Kipling* (London, 1977) is surely the most interesting, and of lesser figures such as R. M. Ballantyne, viewed somewhat superficially by Eric Quayle in *Ballantyne the Brave: A Victorian Writer and His Family* (London, 1967).[8] Other studies include examinations of Australia, Burma, and South Africa, and three books which point the way toward the assimilation of the Asian subcontinent into imperial intellectual history: Allen J. Greenberger's *The British Image of India* (London, 1969), *Delusions and Discoveries: Studies on India in the British Imagination, 1880–1930* (London, 1972) by Benita Parry, and D. C. R. A. Goonetilleke's *Developing Countries in British Fiction* (London, 1977). Finally, there is Edward W. Said's vigorous attack on *Orientalism* (New York, 1978), which is about how the West (but especially France) sought to invent an East that it could control.

The anthropological thrust into British imperial history is obvious, and most clearly it takes place in the context of African or Asian studies (and to a lesser extent, Pacific Island studies), where Western scholars cannot gain access to the indigenous story without the use of oral tradition. A subbody of literature on the problems of research in Africa, in particular, has developed; and many studies of Fulani, Hausa, or Nandi responses to British rule are clearly more nearly anthropology than history.[9] Many historians of Africa, though writing about the interaction between indigenous cultures and the British, insist that they are African and not imperial historians, and unless one is simply to allow a person to nominate labels for himself, this distinction is perhaps made most manifest and rendered most valid in terms of the way in which anthropology is used in shaping the study. But anthropologists themselves have been supporters of imperialism, and at the moment the work of self-conscious anthropologists appears mired down in a series of accusatory statements about the role anthropology has played, with or without intent, in increasing dependency relationships. The most direct statement may be found in Jean Copan's *Anthropologie et impérialisme* (Paris, 1975), a series of extracts relating to the debate. The work of Claude Lévi-Strauss has been most influential, both in literature and anthropology, and his work on the structure of myth has been used, often in inappropriate ways, by those who seek to understand images as transmitted through oral tradition, literature, or even photography. Edmund Leach, in *Lévi-Strauss* (London, 1970), has provided one means of access to the debate, as do the burgeoning studies of structuralism. As yet, however, the real meaning of this impact within British imperial history is unclear, and we must await, among others, the forthcoming work of John Cell on anthropologists, Lord Hailey, and colonialism. In the meantime, imperial historians will be well served by two books, Brian V. Street's *The Savage in Literature: Representations of 'Primitive' Society in English Fiction, 1858–1920* (London, 1975) and Emmanuel Terray's *Marxism and 'Primitive' Societies: Two Studies*, originally published in Paris in 1969 and in New York in English in 1972. (Ronald L. Meek, *Social Science and the Ignoble Savage*, Cambridge, 1976 is, unhappily, far less good.) The anthropological impact may also be seen in Joseph Rykwert's *On Adam's House in Paradise* (New York, 1972), which is a close study of the idea of the primitive hut in architectural history and which brings us full circle back to Baudet, who concludes that the study of empire is "an inextricably interwoven complex of myth and reality" which operates at two levels, "the level of real and imagined rememberance."[10]

Perhaps imperial history has moved too far onto the soft ground of images, perception, speculation, and mythology. Certainly there is a counterbalancing trend, as yet less strong, back toward asking what it was that one clerk said to another clerk. This phrase, by which G..M. Young categorized but did not damn diplomatic history, if stripped of its pejorative undertones, correctly describes a still-important body of literature. What colonial officers thought and did in London remains important to any understanding of empire. Examinations of "the official mind of imperialism" tend to arrive at conclusions contrary to Marxist orthodoxy, so that such studies in fact demark two trends: the one back toward the center, and even more significantly, toward the official records as supplemented by the private papers of important actors in the drama, and the other toward a non-Marxist set of interpretations. The latter, clearly, does not seek to be anti-Marxist; rather the debates now admits of Marxist interpretations where relevant (that is, where questions concerning the mode of production and distribution are at the heart of a given problem) and will admit of non-Marxist views where they appear to offer a more reasonable explanation of perceived phenomena.

These two trends, overlapping but not coterminous, are best represented by two different studies, one an instant classic, the other destined to be. It is instructive to note that the first of these—*Africa and the Victorians*, by Ronald Robinson and John Gallagher, with Alice Denny (London, 1961), which in England bore the subtitle *The Official Mind of Imperialism* and in the United States *The Climax of Imperialism in the Dark Continent*—was not mentioned by Philip Curtin when he reviewed the historiography of the British Empire and Commonwealth for the predecessor to this volume in 1966 but was discussed by John Clive in his essay on British history from 1870 to 1914. At that time, this was the right judgment, for Robinson and Gallagher, as their names came to be linked, were saying at least as much about the imperial setting in Britain as in Africa. Yet over time, their seminal work—so much discussed as to be the most influential contribution to British imperial history in the last two decades—came to be seen as fundamental to an understanding of European expansion.

Robinson and Gallagher added to their work, as first expressed in their influential article "The Imperialism of Free Trade" (London, 1953), through their book; an extension of its argument in a chapter in the *New Cambridge Modern History* in 1962; some intervening articles, defenses and ripostes; and most recently (1978) by Robinson writing alone of "European Imperialism and Indigenous Reactions in British West Africa, 1880–1914."[11] Their names joined those of Frederick Jackson Turner, Charles Beard, R. H. Tawney, Arnold Toynbee, André Gunder Frank, and G. M. Trevelyan in having offered up a "thesis" which is now presumed to be summarized upon the invoking of their names.

This thesis may, setting aside some ornamentation upon it, be summarized as follows. The new imperialism of the 1870s marked no significant break with the past, as usually argued, but showed marked continuity with that which went before. Free trade, rather than formal annexation, helped promote an informal empire which was as tenacious as any created by troops and treaties. The essential dynamic which drew European powers, often reluctantly, into formal empire arose from within the dynamics of African and Asian societies, so that one cannot expect to understand imperialism without a close study of those societies as well. Imperialism worked best and most subtly through a matrix of collaborators which developed in reference to local, indigenous needs and on the basis of traditional, and later of newly emergent, local elites. White settler societies, such as South Africa, constituted prefabricated collaborator groups, while interaction with indigenous societies required a readiness to shift support from one group to another as the need arose. The British were pulled into maintenance of Mediterranean and Persian Gulf colonies and acquisition of much of East Africa in order to protect a conventionally defined lifeline to India. Their empire was, in the end, and despite sincerely held humanitarian rhetoric, essentially negative and conservative.

This view is obviously laden with value judgments and is open to numerous angles of attack, many of which are summarized in a convenient small book, *Imperialism: The Robinson and Gallagher Controversy*, edited by Wm. Roger Louis (New York, 1976). While placing much weight on economic matters, Robinson and Gallagher's use of the collaborator matrix shifted much responsibility for the European presence in Africa or Asia to active, even eager, collaborators and *compradors* who welcomed British technology, political leadership, communications systems, trading partnerships, protection, or simple intervention as a counterweight to a locally prevailing power that might, by the British presence operating on a political Heisenbergian principle, be displaced by another local group. Such an argument displeased those who wished to see all Africans and Asians as simple victims, though it pleased those who argued that they were complex victims. The argument went badly against orthodox Marxism of the more simple-minded variety but could in fact be reconciled to the more sophisticated Marxism of a new crop of scholars as well as to the emerging body of Latin American scholarship customarily referred to as dependency theory. Further, the argument made it possible to wed an interest in informal empire (the British in Argentina, for example) with formal empire (the British in Yorubaland) and showed that one could not divide the two types of empire into discrete areas of inquiry.

Paradoxically, Robinson and Gallagher were both conservative and radical in their influence. Conservative, in that one implication of their emphasis on the collaborator was to focus attention once more upon the staples by which the British sought to integrate a colonial economy and its people with their own: issues of transportation, education, sanitation, and "good government." It was also conservative in that it revived the waning school that equated strategic motivations with economic, political, and intellectual-racist motivations to empire, for their work appeared to give strategic considerations a position of their own in official thinking, whereas the scholarship of the 1950s had been suggesting that strategic motivations were a subset of economic motivations, since an area is of strategic importance only in relation to a defined goal, usually economic in base content. But the work, in its demand that one study indigenous societies as well, in the ease with which it could be used to support cynical interpretations of allegedly high motives, and in the manner in which it arrived at an essentially negative balance sheet, was welcomed by the more perceptive anti-imperialist scholars. Hence, Robinson and Gallagher were read, or ought to have been read, by all and especially by those studying "the power of the weak."

That Robinson and Gallagher are only now being discovered by the dependency theorists, and the latter only now by imperial historians, suggests the unhappy conclusion, however, that the field remained fragmented and that it continued to be important to many scholars whether their segment of former empire was colored the conventional red—as distinct from blue, orange, or green—on the maps of the world. Language barriers contributed to this isolation for some time, since the best of the dependency theorists was initially available only in Spanish,[12] but the old Whig barriers were the more resolute in their defense of isolated examinations of individual empires.

At first glance, the overlapping trend may appear Whiggish, though it is distinctly not so upon closer examination. Here the representative book is John Manning Ward's *Colonial Self government: The British Experience, 1759–1856* (London, 1976), which brings us firmly back to the old questions now much maligned in that phrase "from colony to nationhood," but in a new manner.

Ward's thesis is that the Whig interpretation of colonial history has always been out of touch with reality, since the empire builders did not hold the views later historians argued they held. The notion of responsible government, which the older generation of historians maintained came out of a knowledgeable rethinking of the problem of colonial self-government, in part as a result of the American Revolution, was in fact a theoretical construction after the developments had taken place. When Lord Durham went to Canada, he had no theory in mind; what he found convinced him that the Canadians were bent upon running (and possibly ruining) the colony for themselves, and he concluded that since Britain could not prevent them from doing so, some rubric must be found to give Britain the appearance of having devolved power rather than having had it once again wrestled away. The principle he applied to Canada, and which he said he was bringing in from Britain—that a ministry must be able to hold a parliamentary majority on major issues or resign—was not even established in Britain itself, must less within the thinking of anyone at Westminster who, with authority, concerned himself about the colonies. Still, Durham carried the day with his assertion of an unproven principle for the Canadians. In this sense, Canada was far less the Mother Dominion, Durham more the contriver of a means by which the empire might be held together. Later generations of historians turned what had been an ad hoc solution to a specific problem into a program of evolutionary constitutionalism and made Durham the opportunist into Durham the statesman.

Ward's work, which adds to his previous examinations of colonial policy, stands with earlier volumes by Vincent Harlow, C. A. Bodelsen, Helen Taft Manning, and W. P. Morrell, on a short shelf of indispensable literature. His argument had been heralded in a short, and perhaps too consciously revisionist, book, *The Durham Report and British Policy* by Ged Martin (London, 1972). Ward was strong on Canada and the West Indies, in particular. W. P. Morrell, in *British Colonial Policy in the Mid-Victorian Age* (London, 1969), which was a sequel to his *British Colonial Policy in the Age of Peel and Russell* (London, first published in 1930 and reissued in 1966), focused on South Africa and New Zealand, as well as the West Indies, as seen from the Colonial Office. The office itself has received less direct attention than one might suppose, for since D. M. Young's *The Colonial Office in the Early Nineteenth Century* (London, 1961) and Robert Heussler's *Yesterday's Rulers: The Making of the British Colonial Service* (Syracuse, 1963), there has been relatively little extension of the inquiry. Still, Brian L. Blakeley, in *The Colonial Office, 1868–1892* (Durham, N.C., 1972), was especially informative on the relationship with the Treasury, as was the wider net flung by John W. Cell in *British Colonial Administration in the Mid-nineteenth Century: The Policy-making Process* (New Haven, Conn., 1970). The new *Journal of Imperial and Commonwealth History*, began in 1972, contains many articles on the office and the making of policy, as does the older *Journal of*

Commonwealth and Comparative Politics, begun in 1962.[13] But we await the major synthesis.

The view from the center is not, of course, truly centric, for one quickly learns that there is the Treasury view and the Foreign Office view and the Admiralty view. These various centers, shifting in significance as they vie for power, have been the focus of several studies which do not, taken collectively, yet provide the needed synthesis. W. David McIntyre was particularly wide ranging in his *The Imperial Frontier in the Tropics, 1865–75* (London, 1967), which looked to colonial policy in West Africa, Malaya, and the South Pacific, while Robert V. Kubicek preferred to focus on a single exemplar of the colonial bureaucracy in *The Administration of Imperialism: Joseph Chamberlain at the Colonial Office* (Durham, N.C., 1969). Of many studies of the relationship to the Foreign Office, by far the most significant was Wm. Roger Louis's *Imperialism at Bay* (London, 1978), which showed how the United States brought pressures to bear to shape the nature and to speed the timing of the decolonization of the British Empire during World War II. Louis showed that Churchill thought Franklin Roosevelt's rhetoric concerning trusteeship was a guise for American expansion at the cost of the British, and he revealed how ill-informed American planners were about the nature of empire. Donald C. Gordon, on the other hand, in *The Dominion Partnership in Imperial Defense, 1870–1914* (Baltimore, 1965), showed how a growing nationalism in the Dominions also contributed to the ultimate fragmentation of the empire, all efforts at a common military and naval policy notwithstanding. To Gordon, one must add three books that are concerned with Canada largely, though not exclusively, their titles to the contrary: Richard A. Preston's *Canada and "Imperial Defense"* (Durham, N.C., 1967), which showed how the Commonwealth's defense organization developed from Confederation to Versailles; Carl Berger's *The Sense of Power: Studies in the Ideas of Canadian Imperialism, 1867–1914* (Toronto, 1970), which showed how one Dominion sought a voice in imperial and foreign policy; and Norman Penlington's *Canada and Imperialism 1896–1899* (Toronto, 1965), which showed how imperial unity was based in important measure on anti-Americanism. The obverse side, though for an earlier period, was discussed in D. B. Swinfen's *Imperial Control of Colonial Legislation, 1813–1865* (Oxford, 1970).

The center does not end with the bureaucracy, of course, and studies have continued to appear on how imperial questions reverberated in British politics. Robert Rhodes James, in *The British Revolution, 1880–1939* (New York, 1977), was astute on the Boer War, as was Stephen Koss in *The Pro-Boers: The Anatomy of an Antiwar Movement* (Chicago, 1973). Richard Price, in *An Imperial War and the British Working Class* (London, 1972), showed that the working class was not so jingoistic in the Boer War as heretofore thought; while Bernard Porter, in *Critics of Empire* (London, 1968), examined the entire body of radical thought about

British colonialism in Africa from that war to 1914. While leaning too heavily on
J. A. Hobson and E. D. Morel, Porter's work is an acute analysis of what lay
behind the notion of "indirect rule." Porter also took on the dogma of "capitalist
imperialism," though less acutely than Hugh Stretton in a book too little known,
The Political Sciences (London, 1969), which contains one of the most interesting
statements on what caused imperialism now available.

Stretton's answer is not primarily an economic one, but economic questions
remain fundamental to an understanding of any empire. Quite possibly the most
exciting book on this subject does not appear to be about the British Empire at all:
A. G. Hopkins's *An Economic History of West Africa* (London, 1973). Hopkins's
book is organized around the concept of the market, which normally is taken to
have three dimensions (volume and value of goods and services transacted, geographical variations in exchange activity, number and social status of the parties
engaged in exchange) that were, in fact, developed to analyze Western capitalist
systems. Seeking a balance between the conventional view at the end of World
War II—that Europe made African economic growth possible by injecting European technology and substituting a market for a subsistence economy—and the
Marxist view that precapitalist economies were static until replaced by exploita-
tive capitalism, and also refuting the romantic notion argued by some African
nationalist historians that precolonial West Africa was expansive and healthy
prior to its disruption by Europeans, Hopkins intelligently blended the views in
a complex interaction of internal and external forces, achieving for economic history a position akin to that taken by Robinson and Gallagher in political history.

Also of substantial importance is a set of three works which are best read to-
gether. Two, indeed, speak to each other directly: Bernard Semmel's *The Rise of
Free Trade Imperialism: Classical Political Economy, the Empire of Free Trade, and
Imperialism 1750–1850* (London, 1970) and Judith Blow Williams's *British
Commercial Policy and Trade Expansion 1750–1850* (London, 1972). Earlier,
E. J. Hobsbawm, in *Industry and Empire: An Economic History of Britain since
1750* (London, 1968), had argued that the economic booster to Britain's great
financial and industrial growth came from the expansion of overseas trade, and
here Semmel showed how economic theory was reformulated to make free trade
imperialism possible, while Williams examined the actual methods of commercial expansion. D. C. M. Platt, in turn, made Latin America and British trade
his special preserve, most particularly in a book of that title (London, 1972), but
also in *Finance, Trade, and Politics: British Foreign Policy, 1815–1914* (London,
1968) and *Business Imperialism, 1840–1930: An Inquiry Based on British Experience in Latin America* (London, 1978). These, together with Platt's *The Cinderella Service: British Consuls since 1825* (London, 1971), have substantially altered our views of informal empire and, though clearly non-Marxist (rather than

anti-, pro-, or neo-, among the choices available), also challenge that other bulwark of non-Marxist argumentation, Robinson and Gallagher.

Even Hobsbawm did not achieve the synthesis he sought, and it still eludes us. But one may move toward such a synthesis if one adds to the above investigations into trade equal degrees of awareness of three other forms of export: capital, technology, and people. The first is stalked, although not trapped, in seven essays brought together by A. R. Hall in *The Export of Capital from Britain, 1870– 1914* (London, 1968), to which one must add two succinct summary volumes, *British Overseas Investment in the Nineteenth Century* (London, 1975) by P. L. Cottrell and *British Entrepreneurship in the Nineteenth Century* (London, 1974) by P. L. Payne. The export of technology remains surprisingly unexamined within the British Empire, although three general works are rich in insights. The best by far is David S. Landes's *The Unbound Prometheus: Technological Change and Industrial Development in Western Europe from 1750 to the Present* (London, 1969), which is about change. Two books that attempted to examine the impact itself are William Woodruff's well-titled *Impact of Western Man: A Study of Europe's Role in the World Economy, 1750–1960* (London, 1967) and Kurt Mendelssohn's more tendentious, though valuable, *The Secret of Western Domination* (London, 1976), which is, more precisely, about science. As for immigrants and the wealth they represent, there is a large body of literature, most of it in fact social history, from which four hard-headed economic studies stand out: H. J. M. Johnston's *British Emigration Policy, 1815–1830: "Shovelling out Paupers"* (London, 1972); Ian M. Drummond's *Imperial Economic Policy, 1917–1939* (Toronto, 1974), a title which masks a study of empire settlement programs, as well as the Ottawa Agreements; and two books on the greatest swarming of the empire, the movement of South Asians to labor-intensive areas, by Hugh Tinker: *A New System of Slavery: The Export of Indian Labour Overseas, 1830–1920* (London, 1974) and *Separate and Unequal: India and the Indians in the British Commonwealth, 1920–1950* (London, 1976).

Here, then, are the dominant trends, the "changing views" in British imperial history since 1966. The mode of asking questions is increasingly comparative and often more productive because of that. The ability to avoid the pro- and anti-Marxist mudbath is more marked, by scholars who think of themselves as simply non-Marxist. The intensity of political controversy, while not abated in the arena, is less among academics, in the sense that, while no one (or very few) would, with Lord Rosebery, declare themselves proud to be called an imperialist, relatively few assume that to label an act or a policy imperialist is automatically to assign to it wholly negative values. Dependency theory, as developed to explain nonannexed areas of the world, is now being felt in annexed areas, in the sense that models developed to explain the relationship between the interior and the

coast of Brazil, or "satellization" in Mexico, may now be applied to the relationship between Lagos and the interior of Nigeria or to the nature of the New Zealand economy (though this tendency is still so slight as to be but a bridge of crys-
tal between two still-distinct historiographies). History is increasingly informed
by the insights and methods of anthropology, just as anthropology is driven
asunder by ideologically related debates with which historians struggled a generation and two ago. Substantially more explicit intellectual history of empire is
being written, and much apparently economic or political history is implicitly
intellectual or social history in fact. It is once again respectable to study empire
from the metropolitan centers. Once again what one clerk said to another clerk is
important, although in a vastly altered context. And the field is in no sense dominated by British-based or London-published books any longer, with Canadians,
Americans, and Australians, as well as scholars from the continent of Europe
and, as I show later, from Africa and Asia, contributing significantly to the field.

These developments, somewhat arbitrarily stated, represent a further, or
tenth, development when read collectively: there are now not one (the imperial)
or two (the imperial and the anti-imperial) historiographies. There are several
historiographies, overlapping, each unavoidable, yet distinct. Multiarchival research has led to multifocal vision. Syntheses therefore still elude us. But the field
is the richer for its several historiographies which break along both the traditional
geographical or national planes—that is, certain books on Canada, or Malaysia,
or Kenya, while about a single nation, are essential to the broader field of British
imperial history—and along less traditional planes determined by problems
rather than boundaries. The two may meet, as they do brilliantly in Geoffrey
Blainey's controversial study of how *The Tyranny of Distance* (Melbourne, 1966)
shaped Australia intellectually and economically, dealing with a problem which
may be generalized to the empire but which is assessed within a single historiography; or the planes may bisect only for the reader (as in G. C. Bolton's
equally fine work, *A Fine Country to Starve In*, Perth, 1973, whose examination
of "the anatomy of hardship" may be generalized to other frontier experiences,
though not by the author himself, who resolutely and properly restricts himself to
Western Australia in the Depression) who is able to bring to a book a broader set
of questions than those posed within it.

Still, one may not conclude a survey of the significant new literature in British
imperial history simply by declaring that the field now lets a thousand flowers
bloom. A number of important books do not fit comfortably into the outlines of
change as suggested here, and they require recognition precisely for that reason.
The field remains more intractable than any artificial coherence we may force
upon it.

The least intractable, in a sense, are studies in decolonization which ask a simply stated though complex question—How does one divest oneself of a colony?—and efforts at synthesis undertaken from a single point of view, which are not, therefore, truly syntheses at all so much as briefing papers.[14] In the former category fall both formal studies of decolonization and a variety of sometimes polemical books on the "fall of the British Empire." Of these, the most magisterial is Rudolf von Albertini's massive *Decolonisation: The Administration and Future of the Colonies, 1919–1960*, translated by Francisca Garvie, first published in German in 1966 and subsequently in English (Garden City, N.Y., 1971). The book is consciously comparative, and it shows, not surprisingly, that the methods used by the colonial powers to rid themselves of colonies arose from their differing notions of what a nation was. Also comparative in intent was a special number of the *Journal of Contemporary History* devoted to "Colonialism and Decolonization" (4, 1969). Brian Crozier has written, from a conservative point of view, *The Rebels: A Study of Post-war Insurrections* (London, 1960), a book overlooked at the time of publication but brought into a certain vogue during the decade, and *The Morning After: A Study of Independence* (London, 1963). His views were tempered by W. P. Kirkman in *Unscrambling an Empire: A Critique of British Colonial Policy, 1956–1966* (London, 1966). Best of all was David Goldsworthy's careful examination of *Colonial Issues in British Politics, 1945–1961: From "Colonial Development" to "Wind of Change"* (London, 1971).

Still, the studies were few in number, partially because the official records, under the twenty-five–year rule, were not yet available to scholars until nearer the end of the survey period. As recently as 1958, after all, Sir Hilary Blood had written in a Conservative party pamphlet that, with the possible exception of Jamaica, none of the British Caribbean possessions could expect to become independent. In the parliamentary debate on small territories, in 1959, most members appeared to agree that independence was unthinkable for Malta, Guyana, or the Gambia; and it was generally accepted that the possibility of Sierra Leone obtaining independence, perhaps in the early 1960s, raised profound problems, since one could scarcely equate the leader of Sierra Leone (then Sir Milton Margai) with the leader of Australia (then Robert Menzies). Yet Sierra Leone was independent in 1961, Trinidad and Tobago in 1962, Malta in 1964, and the Gambia in 1965. If the British were so ill prepared for such rapid divestiture of power, neither archivists nor historians could be blamed for having been caught flat-footed.

Rather, the study of the decline of the empire was left largely to those who wrote impressionistically, usually, from Britain. Of these, Max Beloff was perhaps the most acute, and his *Imperial Sunset*, volume 1, *Britain's Liberal Empire*,

1897–1921 (London, 1969), which set the stage, unhappily has not been followed by a second volume. Richard Symonds provided a study in the development of the government services in the new states (the subtitle to his *The British and Their Successors*, London, 1966), and Colin Cross, in *The Fall of the British Empire* (London, 1968) showed how the journey was downhill all the way from 1918. Less satisfactory, though intelligent and well written, is George Woodcock's combative *Who Killed the British Empire? An Inquest* (London, 1974). In a rather special category come two studies of how Britain sought to use the principle of federalism to achieve decolonization: Thomas M. Franck, editor's *Why Federations Fail* (New York, 1968), which examined the failed federations of East Africa, Central Africa, the West Indies, and Malaysia; and R. L. Watts's *New Federations: Experiments in the Commonwealth* (London, 1966).

As for the general syntheses, those tended to be for use in classrooms, which meant that they were largely descriptive and, for the most part, consciously at the middle-of-the-road on the more controversial issues. Some were specifically on the British Empire while others were on European expansion overseas, largely in the traditional mold, with Britain taking *The Lion's Share*—the title of the best of the short histories, by Bernard Porter, which carried the subtitle *A Short History of British Imperialism, 1850–1970* (London, 1975). Porter's work happily broke from the older traditions, however, in being about the manifestations of British power rather than about the transfer of the Westminster model of Parliament to the old White Dominions, so that Canada and Australia played small roles, West Africa and India correspondingly larger roles, within it. C. C. Eldridge, in *Victorian Imperialism* (London, 1978) was more consciously didactic, with specific sections devoted to the leading controversies, that is, the meaning of Durham's report, the rise of free trade imperialism, theories of capitalist imperialism, or the implications of responsible government. Both books tended to show that imperialism was an attempt to stave off British decline rather than a sign of British greatness. Two other survey histories, while not so pessimistic, also lacked the surge of pride one detected in the older works of such scholars as Paul Knaplund, A. L. Burt, C. E. Carrington, and Eric Walker: Robert A. Huttenback's *The British Imperial Experience* (New York, 1966) focused on a limited number of incidents and individuals, while Geoffrey Bolton's *Britain's Legacy Overseas* (London, 1973) sought to show how lines of communication, movement of peoples, and common preoccupations with questions of defense, were as powerful in binding former colonies to Britain as the oft-studied legal and constitutional ties that bound the empire as it became Commonwealth.

Some authors attempted more ambitious general statements, of which two stand out by both length and grasp. The first of these, H. Duncan Hall's long-awaited, *Commonwealth: A History of the British Commonwealth of Nations* (London, 1971), running to 1,016 pages in a single volume, proved too long and too traditional in its emphasis on constitutional and defense issues to win a wide following, but as the product of a scholar-participant, it contained much useful and fresh information embedded in too much that was conventional. Nicholas Mansergh, in *The Commonwealth Experience* (London, 1969), also wrote at length and turned his analyses rather too much upon the role of individuals, but the book quickly took its place as the standard single-volume treatment of how the Commonwealth came into being. Read with Joe Garner's *The Commonwealth Office, 1925–68* (London, 1978), the thoughtful work of a former permanent undersecretary to the office, the volumes convincingly showed that the Commonwealth, though the product of evolution, was not merely an inheritor of the old British Empire but a new political species worthy of close study in its own right.

Two earlier studies had laid down the legal position of the Commonwealth, the first with clarity and, despite exceptional complexity a sense of intellectual excitement. This had been Kenneth C. Wheare's *The Constitutional Structure of the Commonwealth* (London, 1960). The other, J. E. S. Fawcett's *The British Commonwealth in International Law* (London, 1963), while necessarily technical, quickly became the base point for future departures. A series of volumes issued from the Commonwealth Studies Center at Duke University provided the most useful of these departures, though like all series they were a bit of a curate's egg. Especially helpful was W. B. Hamilton, Kenneth Robinson, and C. D. W. Goodwin, editors' *A Decade of the Commonwealth, 1955–1964* (Durham, N.C., 1966), with particularly perceptive essays on the manner of birth for new states and on intra-Commonwealth relations. M. Margaret Ball, in *The "Open" Commonwealth* (Durham, N.C., 1971), asked a series of valuable questions about how political consultation and economic and social cooperation work, or might work. Less successful, because too sprawling and uneven, were two other volumes, Ralph Braibanti, editor's *Asian Bureaucratic Systems Emergent from the British Imperial Tradition* (Durham, N.C., 1966) and the earlier *Economic Systems of the Commonwealth* (Durham, N.C., 1962), edited by Calvin B. Hoover.

Questions of imperial ascendancy were embedded in broader European issues in a number of books which, unlike Fieldhouse's inquiry, could not be said to be comparative, though not without their merits. One of the most provocative was M. S. Anderson's *The Ascendancy of Europe: Aspects of European History 1815–1914*, (London, 1972), which sought to account for the process of expansion by examining the economic and political balance of power in Europe, rather in the classic manner of W. L. Langer, and with a proper regard for the position of the Eastern European question in the matter. Heinz Gollwitzer, in *Europe in the Age of Imperialism, 1880–1914* (London, 1969), provided a succinct statement on the social structure of Europe in "the age of imperialism," while Marcus Cunliffe, in *The Age of Expansion, 1848–1917* (London, 1974) integrated the United States into the general story of expansionism. For an earlier period,

J. H. Parry provided his fullest statement of a subject he has made uniquely his own, in *Trade and Dominion: The European Oversea Empires in the Eighteenth Century* (London, 1971).

Two other forms of synthesis emerged from the period under review. One consisted of a wide variety of inquiries into the economics of imperialism, most beginning from a Marxist position; the other consisted of historiographies, finding aids, and lists of various sorts. The first proved valuable for undergraduate teaching, though none moved the central argument to a new arena, except to the measure that they admitted of what has been described here as the dimensions of intellectual history, while the second was chiefly of use to the professional scholar and researcher.

With a gentle sense of irony, A. P. Thornton had written of the *Doctrines of Imperialism* in 1965 (New York). He saw three "doctrines" at work, those of power, of profit, and of civilization. He also showed that the term *imperialism* remained valuable if it was used in a functional rather than a doctrinaire way, and while he did not seek to refute the odd congeries of self-fulfilling prophecies, premises, and premises mistaken for conclusions that comprise much of the Marxist literature, he also saw the value in such approaches to analysis. With the same sense of irony, though with a somewhat inexact style which made it difficult to be certain of precisely what was being said, Ronald Hyam also examined the foundations of power in similar terms, in *Britain's Imperial Century, 1815–1914: A Study of Empire and Expansion* (London, 1976). Both Thornton and Hyam wrote an elliptical prose filled with allusive asides for the literate, which meant that some political scientists and sociologists seemed unclear as to what they were saying; and indeed their oblique prose, with its clear joy in the ambiguities of empire, sometimes seemed supportive of quite different positions. Their subtle, heavily nuanced style was extended best, perhaps, in a book of rare brilliance, *Lion Rampant: Essays in the Study of British Imperialism* (London, 1973), which brought together the powerful analyses of D. A. Low, who also saw the economic issues as embedded in a complex overlay of perceptions of authority, thrusts toward social engineering (Low was particularly acute on India), and the problems of demission of power.

Irony, nuance, ambiguity were not the instruments for analysis chosen by a second group of general inquiries. Robin Jenkins, in *Exploitation: The World Power Structure and the Inequality of Nations* (London, 1970) cast his net most widely, while Teresa Hayter, in *Aid as Imperialism* (London, 1971) made a convincing though shrill case for her title. Martin Carnoy, in *Education as Cultural Imperialism* (New York, 1974), wrote angrily, yet perceptively, of the connection between educational systems and colonialism. The obviously combative nature of these three books probably led to their too-ready dismissal by traditional historians, for stripped of their rhetoric, they still had much to say that was true about those traditional subjects of imperial administration: education, sanitation (through aid, and health), and communication systems.

Among the welter of overtly Marxist literature on the history of imperialism (as opposed to current events), two writers stood out by the end of the 1970s: Harry Magdoff and V. G. Kiernan. Magdoff, an American, had written a number of angry, sometimes rather careless works, of which *The Age of Imperialism* (New York, 1969) was his best known. He responded to his critics with a series of carefully argued essays which, granted their premises, and allowing for the fact that his interest, though expressed historically, was more in contemporary relations with the Third World, were perhaps the best Marxist statement to put before the undergraduate: *Imperialism: From the Colonial Age to the Present* (New York, 1978). The fact that Magdoff always integrated American imperialism into his general examination of expansion since 1763 enriched his book, despite his continued penchant for somewhat selective use of statistics. V. G. Kiernan, a Marxist at the University of Edinburgh, contributed a more readable book, *Marxism and Imperialism* (London, 1974), which contained a particularly pungent examination of some recent requiems of empire.[15]

A number of books sought to present objective, or non-Marxist, analyses of the economics of imperialism (the title of Michael Barratt Brown's book, London, 1974). These ranged from straightforward collections of essays drawn largely from other sources and intended primarily for student use, of which Roger Owen and Bob Sutcliffe's *Studies in the Theory of Imperialism* (London, 1972) and Kenneth E. Boulding and Tapan Mukerjee's *Economic Imperialism* (Ann Arbor, Mich., 1972) were much the best, to close inquiries into *The Theory of Capitalist Imperialism* (this also a book of "readings," edited by David K. Fieldhouse, London, 1967), of which perhaps the most useful was an extended essay by Alan Hodgart, *The Economics of European Imperialism* (London, 1977), which traced the linkage, in theory, between the declining tendency of the rate of profit in modern capitalism from Adam Smith to modern dependency studies. Less sophisticated but helpfully clear was Benjamin J. Cohen's *The Question of Imperialism: The Political Economy of Dominance and Dependence* (New York, 1973). George Lichtheim's *Imperialism* (New York, 1971), also an extended essay, more ambitiously sought to review the several questions about cause which both Marxist and anti-Marxist writers had posed.

Some students of the British Empire might well argue that the study of Marxism was not what they thought they were at; if so, they were putting their heads in the sand; for while arguments about an American imperialism tended, as war in Vietnam entered its apocalyptic stage, to crowd out studies and even polemics on British imperialism, the style and tone of debate, as well as the posturing of the less thoughtful combatants on the darkling plain, continued to invoke the British as a model. This was all the more so when British capitalism seemed so patently in decline, as the Marxist-Leninist view held that it ought to be, imperialism being, Lenin said, the highest stage of capitalism. Dozens of books on Marx and Marxism (of which, for the imperial historian, the most useful was David McLellan's short *Karl Marx*, London, 1975); dozens more on whether capitalism was to be viewed as "open" or "closed," with Samir Amin's *Accumulation on a World Scale*, translated by Brian Pearce (New York, 1974) and Emmanuel Wallerstein's *The Modern World System* (New York, 1974) possibly the most influential; and a fascination with psychohistory in relation to the "homeless left," showed an easy relevance to the questions British imperial historians ought to have been asking. Of this last category, two books on Frantz Fanon, both of that title, the one by David Caute (1970) and the other by Irene L. Gendzier (New York, 1973), together with the popularization of the work of Albert Memmi through English translations of *The Colonizer and the Colonized* (Boston, 1967) and *Dominated Man* (Boston, 1969), were most directly influential on scholars at the School of Oriental and African Studies and in African, Canadian, and American universities.

While all such studies may be fitted to the procrustean bed of the trends suggested earlier in this essay, most do not really fit: further proof that the field, despite discernible trends, remains fragmented. As with all modern scholarship, there is the frequent odor of the lamp about many of the works in the field, and all too frequently a "new" study of an "old" problem proves merely to have restated the old conclusions in more fashionable language, or in language borrowed from a more fashionable discipline. Article literature, in particular, often so hedges earlier conclusions with the minutiae of small change as to leave the reader asking, ever more frequently, "So what?" of much that is said.

Yet, in the traditional language of historical scholarship, many "gaps remain to be filled." Equally, some gaps have been filled already. But "gaps" must be perceived in relation to larger questions: it is not true that we are in equal need of a biography of every colonial administrator or of every instance of gunboat diplomacy. Too often imperial historians seem to have been neglecting the first charge of all historians: to trace cause-and-effect relationships with an eye to the primacy of specific causes. Those who have sought to do so have too frequently fallen into the tendentious, the ideological, or even the despairing schools of thought, the last appearing to conclude that history is simply one damn thing after another. Where superb studies arise to plug a gap, as with David K. Fieldhouse's *Economics and Empire, 1830–1914* (London, 1973), or Ralph Davis's *English Overseas Trade, 1500–1700* (London, 1972), or even A. D. Francis's more limited *The Wine Trade* (London, 1972), critics have at once shown, or argued that given enough time and space they can show, that these are mere fingers in the dike. Davis's useful tables, his comprehensive survey of a complex problem, his analysis of the relationship between trade and agriculture, his inquiry into the nature of shipbuilding, all are greeted as "traditional" and therefore insufficient. Field-house's detailed analysis, based on empirical data, concluded that economic factors were not predominant causes for the expansion of formal empire and guided the reader toward a closer attention to those developments on the periphery of empire over which the nation-states of Europe had no control. The conclusion of such studies—that no universal theory may be applied to account for modern imperialism—therefore either is rejected by those who are convinced that such a single-cause analysis remains, or ought to remain, possible or is too quickly taken up by those in search of anti-Marxist ammunition. A gap that has been filled may thus, by a simple act of definition, continue to be seen as unfilled.

Perhaps it is for this reason, as much as any, that there has been a growth in lists, finding aids, bibliographies, and historiographies: a retreat into stocktaking before one begins to consider what the goods on the shelf really "mean." For certainly recent years have brought a number of useful (in the proper sense of the term) such books. In 1966 there appeared *The Historiography of the British Empire-Commonwealth: Trends, Interpretations, and Resources* (Durham, N.C.), edited by Robin W. Winks, which sought to trace the already vast body of literature, to show why it had taken the shape it had, and to suggest future needs. Organized along Whiggish lines that now seem less appropriate than at the time, the volume sought to bring upward of a thousand titles under control for the scholar in the field. In 1974 John P. Halstead and Serafino Porcari published their giant work, *Modern European Imperialism: A Bibliography* (Boston) in two volumes. In 1969 Luke Trainor began his *Colonial History Newsletter* at the University of Canterbury in New Zealand, so that fellow scholars might know of works in progress. Donald H. Simpson edited an invaluable *Manuscript Catalogue of the Library of the Royal Commonwealth Society* (London, 1975), while Trevor R. Reese wrote *The History of the Royal Commonwealth Society, 1868–1968* (London, 1968) itself. A variety of new guides to the Public Record Office, and to the manuscript collections pouring into Rhodes House, Oxford, alerted scholars to dozens of new projects they might undertake. David P. Henige compiled *A Comprehensive List of Colonial Governors from the Fifteenth Century to the Present* (Madison, Wis., 1970), while Robin Bidwell provided a third volume to his *Guide to Government Ministers*, this one on *The British Empire and Successor States, 1900–1972* (London, 1974). Not all such assistance was truly helpful: one might find the value in a reissue of Grover Clark's volumes of statistical tables, *The Balance Sheets of Imperialism: Facts and Figures on Colonies* (New York, 1967, originally issued in 1936), but there was little value in such shoddy compilations as *Commonwealth Political Facts*, by Chris Cook and John Paxton (New York, 1979). More useful, if more immediately limited, were inventories which focused on groups of manageable areas, as in Thomas P. Birnberg and Stephen A. Resnick's *Colonial Development: An Econometric Study* (New Haven, Conn., 1975), of ten societies.

In quantity and diversity of inquiry, then, as well as the clear note of preparation for the larger battles that the inventories cast into the air, the field appeared healthy. It had, for a time, appeared at risk, as though national, regional, and ethnic studies might engulf it, but by 1980 there still was a clear body of literature, and a clear set of questions, which were properly labled "British Empire history." Every year since 1966, just on sixty doctoral dissertations were written in Britain alone on subjects clearly imperial in major thrust; an equal number, at the least, came from the United States, and again a similar number from universities in the old Commonwealth. The Royal Commonwealth Society, in its extremely useful *Library Notes*, continued to prod scholars into new areas, while attesting almost monthly to the publication of eighty titles considered relevant to the field. One could, by simply reading the accessions lists for the society's library from 1961 to 1979, see the overall growth and chart the particularly dramatic surge in works on Africa, with only "Canada and North America" retaining a major position. Perhaps no inventory so well demonstrated the problems this child of British history brought to the scholar and the librarian, for time and again one was moved to challenge the simple placement of a seminal study under the history of a single unit of Empire or Commonwealth. Eric Stokes's *The Peasant and the Raj: Studies in Agrarian Society and Peasant Rebellion in Colonial India* (Cambridge, 1978), while about Uttar Pradesh, was also a long-awaited series of case studies in resistance movements which elaborated upon Stokes's much-quoted typology, "Traditional Resistance Movements and Afro-Asian Nationalism: The Context of the 1857 Mutiny Rebellion in India" no. 48, 1970: 100–118), which itself had been an extended commentary on the notions of primary, secondary, and tertiary resistance stages first elaborated with respect to East Africa by such scholars as T. O. Ranger. Stokes may have written on Uttar Pradesh, but no student of Samoa, of the Maori wars, of land legislation in East Africa or Rhodesia, indeed no student of twentieth-century Malta could afford to ignore his findings. The walls were down, even though for reasons of tidiness they appeared yet to be in place. Formal empire and informal empire merged, as yet another article in *Past and Present*, (no. 73, 1976: 100–126) this by Peter Winn, on "British Informal Empire in Uruguay in the Nineteenth Century," made clear. A trend in one area was felt in another. Was F. S. L. Lyons's *Charles Stewart Parnell* (London, 1977) to be regarded simply as Irish history? Clearly Christopher Hibberts's *The Great Mutiny: India 1857* (London, 1978), though placed solidly in India, is not exclusively about India, for it is a superb examination of how imperial administrations go wrong. The only answer an imperial historian could give was to be an imperialist and embrace all.

Perhaps no set of inquiries so well illustrates the fact that all questions had come to overlap with virtually all other questions as do those histories which sought to be discrete studies of the history of race relations. Distinct from the studies of slavery cited earlier, these works had originally been interested in the impact of white settlers on natives, as in A. Grenfell Price's important comparative statement in 1950 on the United States, Canada, Australia, and New Zealand: *White Settlers and Native Peoples* (Melbourne). The questions he asked continued to be put, but with growing sophistication. Using ethnographic evidence as well as the traditional methods of the historian, Robin Fisher told a complex story of *Contact and Conflict: Indian–European Relations in British Columbia, 1774–1890* (Vancouver, 1977). V. G. Kiernan used many forms of evidence to reveal the nature of European attitudes "to the Outside World in the Imperial Age" in *The Lords of Human Kind* (London, 1969), while Philip Mason traced the origins of *Patterns of Dominance* (London, 1970) in several societies, most within the British Empire, though not all, since Spanish America and Brazil were included. Robert A. Huttenback wrote of *Racism and Empire: White Settlers and Colored Immigrants in the British Self-governing Colonies, 1830–1910* (Ithaca, N.Y., 1976), while S. H. Alatas, a professor of Malay studies at the University of Singapore, brought *The Myth of the Lazy Native* front and center in a telling, if overwritten, study of the impact of the Malay, Filipino, and Javanese in the ideology of colonialism (London, 1977). A work bound to have substantial impact on the field, Robert F. Berkhofer, Jr.'s *The White Man's Indian* (New York, 1978), combined the several approaches to the study of race relations to get at "the idea of the Indian."

What set these works apart from Tinker's two volumes on Indian labor, or from studies of scientific racism, or from the work of the art historians, is that they were less interested in demonstrating a trend or in promoting a new way of looking at a problem than in providing a study taken as a whole: they were syntheses which would strike one historian as being primarily intellectual, another historian as being essentially economic, or ideological, or sociological, in approach. They represented as much as any subbody of literature the tenth trend I have traced: the presence of diverse historiographies at last coming together into holistic studies outside the confines of a prejudged ideology, though as yet a subject.

Even so, there were numerous contributions to the history of the British Empire which, even at second glance, were largely a history of a unit within it. This had always been so for Australian or Canadian history, of course, and it had been Canadian historians at home or Australian and New Zealand historians working in Britain who had contributed the most in the beginning, for example: *The British Overseas* by New Zealander C. E. Carrington (London, 1950) or Canadian Robert MacGregor Dawson's *The Development of Dominion Status* (London, 1937) or Canadian Alexander Brady's *Democracy in the Dominions* (London, 1947). *Empire of the North Atlantic* (Toronto, 1958), by Gerald S. Graham, a leading generalist as well as a historian of the British in the Indian Ocean, and a Canadian, is one of the best short histories of the Dominion. One still needed to read a good bit of what passed at first glance for national history, just as one once read a good bit of what passed for imperial history, to discover where the line might be drawn between the two. My survey is best concluded, therefore, with a swing around the circuit.

The circuit begins, in 1980, not with Australia or Canada, but with Africa, and with the question How may one find the dividing line between "imperial history" and "African history"? The customary answer rests upon the perception of a point of view: African history is written at the village level, draws heavily upon oral tradition, and most probably begins its account, at least, in the precolonial phase of the traditional society. A history of the building of a railway is clearly imperial history. Yet what does one do with a book such as Richard Elphick's *Kraal and Castle: Khoikhoi and the Founding of White South Africa* (New Haven, Conn., 1977), which is *about* the Khoikhoi, draws upon oral tradition, and is rich in material on the ecological cycle of hunting and herding before the arrival of the European, but which also traces the processes of Western Cape Khoikhoi decline in the face of the European? Clearly the book is of importance to both African and imperial historians, and while its author almost certainly would see himself as an Africanist first, imperial historians interested in the dynamics of racial contact will find the book essential to their queries.

Perhaps the dividing line is best seen in a work which seeks to avoid the line: Monica Wilson and Leonard Thompson's two volumes of *The Oxford History of South Africa* (London, 1969–1971), of which the first half of the first volume is precolonial. The editors assert that "the central theme in South African history is interaction between people of diverse origins, languages, technologies, ideologies, and social systems"—which might well be the central theme of imperial history as a whole. That the best one-volume *History of South Africa* nonetheless remains C. W. de Kiewiet's work of 1957, with a succinct subtitle *Social and Economic* (London), suggests that the central issues have not in fact changed. While race relations preoccupy the front rank of literature, the meat and potatoes of the traditional history—Zulu wars, gold mining, manipulating of labor supplies, and a developing Afrikaner garrison mentality—remain important. The debate over the "liberal-radical controversy" in southern African history has been summarized, perhaps too neatly, by Harrison M. Wright in *The Burden of the Present* (London, 1977). The historian of empire must be struck by the extent to which the debate continues to be restricted to article literature, or is internalized in ways that close rather than open doors to the empire as a whole. Some few do not: Shula Marks, in *Reluctant Rebellion: The 1906–8 Disturbances in Natal* (Oxford, 1970), or Anthony Atmore, in his article written with Marks, "The Imperial Factor in South Africa in the Nineteenth Century: Towards a Reassessment" (*Journal of Imperial and Commonwealth History* 3, 1974: 105–139), did not lose site of the subject of this essay; but many writers do, and for legitimate reasons, since the modern history of southern Africa is also a contribution to current events. One cannot read T. R. H. Davenport's *The Afrikaner Bond: The History of a South African Political Party, 1880–1911* (Cape Town, 1966) except in the light of the headlines, just as one reads Edwin S. Munger's *Afrikaner and African Nationalism: South African Parallels and Parameters* (London, 1967) with an eye to the future.

Some books on southern Africa are significant contributions to imperial history, of course.[16] C. F. Goodfellow's *Great Britain and South African Confederation, 1870–1881* (London, 1966) is one such; David Welsh's *The Roots of Segregation: Native Policy in Natal, 1845–1910* (Cape Town, 1971) is another. Leonard Thompson's *Survival in Two Worlds: Moshoeshoe of Lesotho, 1786–1870* (London, 1975) is an important biography of the father of modern-day Lesotho, while Donald R. Morris's *The Washing of the Spears: The Rise and Fall of the Zulu Nation* (New York, 1965) and J. D. Omer-Cooper's *The Zulu Aftermath: A Nineteenth-century Revolution in Bantu Africa* (London, 1966) are about indigenous politics as written from Western sources. John S. Galbraith, in *Crown and Charter: The Early Years of the British South Africa Company* (Berkeley, 1974), examined the prime imperialist Cecil Rhodes through the Company and concluded that the Jameson Raid flowed naturally from Rhodes's needs. Jeffry Butler, in *The Liberal Party and the Jameson Raid* (London, 1968), showed how the party approached the scandal of the raid, while John Flint, in *Cecil Rhodes* (New York, 1974), provided the best short biography of that prime figure. But weaknesses remain: Oliver Ransford's *The Great Trek* (London, 1972) is not so good as Eric A. Walker's book of the same title (London, 1934), and neither will now do. Rayne Kruger's *Good-bye Dolly Gray: The Story of the Boer War* (Philadelphia, 1960), though highly readable, requires replacement. The same may be said of Stanley Jackson's *The Great Barnato* (London, 1970), which did not sufficiently explain Barnett Isaacs's fascination. Kruger is not displaced, though significantly supplemented, by the massive work of Thomas Pakenham, *The Boer War* (New York, 1979), which represents prodigious research (though not quite so prodigious as appears at first glance) directed toward telling well the story of the war in a way that entertainingly avoids the hard questions. Sir Keith Hancock has served J. C. Smuts well in his two-volume biography *Smuts: The Sanguine Years, 1870–1919* and *Smuts: The Fields of Force, 1919–1950* (London, 1962–1968), but the list of figures who await biographies is great. Even Joseph Chamberlain, central to so many subhistoriographies within the empire, appears unclearly through Peter Fraser's biography subtitled *Radicalism and Empire, 1868–1914* (London, 1966) or Denis Judd's *Radical Joe* (London, 1977).

Southern Africa is of course embedded in the volumes edited by L. H. Gann and Peter Duignan, *Colonialism in Africa, 1870–1960* (London, 1969–1975, 4 vols. of a projected 5), and in the *Cambridge History of Africa* (5 vols. of 8 published to date, London, 1975–1979), edited by J. A. Fage and Roland Oliver. Two remarkable, and massive, sets of essays edited by Prosser Gifford and Wm. Roger Louis dealt with *Britain and Germany in Africa: Imperial Rivalry and Colonial Rule* (London, 1967) and *France and Britain in Africa* (London and New Haven, 1971), with the same subtitle (a third volume, on decolonization, is in press). Gann and Duignan have also written *Burden of Empire: An Appraisal of Western Colonialism in Africa South of the Sahara* (New York, 1967) and *The Rulers of British Africa, 1870–1914* (Stanford, Calif., 1978), both clearly about power and its uses, and the latter the fullest statement we have of just how colonial governance worked at the level of the district officer and below. Viewed as conservative, their work is offset by the heatedly argumentative, yet frequently perceptive, statement by Walter Rodney on *How Europe Underdeveloped Africa* (Dar es Salaam, 1972) and by the cool prose of G. N. Uzoigwe's *Britain and the Conquest of Africa: The Age of Salisbury* (Ann Arbor, Mich., 1974).

West Africa has always been a "special case," of course; it has also given rise to the best use of oral tradition to change conventional views of imperial, as opposed to precolonial, history.[17] There have been numerous glosses on two books which remain the basic statements on their subjects: John D. Hargreaves's *Prelude to the Partition of West Africa* (London, 1963), the first systematic canvass of European developments and interests along the West African coast, and Ronald Wraith and Edgar Simpkins's *Corruption in Developing Countries* (London, 1963), which challenged the idea of "corrupt native governments," in part by viewing Britain as a developing country itself until the 1880s. An excellent general investigation of *West Africa under Colonial Rule* was conducted by Michael Crowder (London, 1968), while Margaret Priestley wrote a detailed case history of the Brew family of Fanti, in southern Ghana, a family of mixed descent that played a vital role in *West African Trade and Coast Society* (London, 1969). In *The Lion and the Unicorn in Africa: A History of the Origins of the United Africa Company, 1787–1931* (London, 1974), Sir Frederick Pedler saw the company somewhat uncritically and from inside.[18]

But even for West Africa, the field, at least temporarily, appeared to have been occupied by those who wrote of a single society, or individual, in the context of an emerging modern national identity. Perhaps this was inevitable, for except in the universities of Nigeria, and even often there, scholars were preoccupied with recounting the histories of their own modern nations. Good short histories of each appeared in the 1960s: John E. Flint's *Nigeria and Ghana* (Englewood Cliffs, N.J., 1966), Harry A. Gailey's *A History of the Gambia* (New York, 1965), and John Peterson's *Province of Freedom: A History of Sierra Leone, 1787–1870* (London, 1969). A variety of relatively traditional imperial histories also appeared, representative of newly accessible archival materials: John E. Flint's *Sir George Goldie and the Making of Nigeria* (London, 1960) was only the first of a number of by-now- "standard" biographies, of which Dame Margery Perham's two volumes on *Lugard* (London, 1956–1960) were the most important. R. E. Wraith wrote of *Guggisberg* (London, 1967); Anthony P. Haydon, of *Sir Matthew Nathan* (St. Lucia, 1976); and Robert Heussler, collectively of *The British in Northern Nigeria* (London, 1968). "Gap-filling"—more setting out of standard statements largely in narrative form—produced numerous useful books, of which Kannan K. Nair's *Politics and Society in South Eastern Nigeria, 1841– 1906: A Study of Power, Diplomacy and Commerce in Old Calabar* (London, 1972) and I. F. Nicolson's *The Administration of Nigeria, 1900 to 1960: Men, Methods, and Myths* (London, 1969) were the most evidently "imperial." But the field was taken increasingly by scholars who could write both from within the societies they examined and with the assistance of ever more sophisticated use of oral tradition to supplement and sometimes to supplant the written record: Francis Agbodeka, *African Politics and British Policy in the Gold Coast, 1868–1900: A Study in the Forms and Force of Protest* (London, 1971); S. A. Akintoye, *Revolution and Power Politics in Yorubaland, 1840–1893* (London, 1971); A. I. Asiwaju, *Western Yorubaland under European Rule, 1889–1945: A Comparative Analysis of French and British Colonialism* (London, 1976); J. A. Atanda, *The New Oyo Empire: Indirect Rule and Change in Western Nigeria, 1894–1934* (London, 1973); or A. E. Afigbo, *The Warrant Chiefs: Indirect Rule in Southeastern Nigeria, 1891–1929* (London, 1972). Particularly valuable to the historian interested in empire were Robin Law's *The Oyo Empire, c. 1600–c. 1836: A West African Imperialism in the Era of the Atlantic Slave Trade* (London, 1977) and Elizabeth A. Isichei's *The Ibo People and the European: The Genesis of a Relationship to 1906* (London, 1973). Michael Crowder, as editor, drew together several essays of mixed quality on a vital subject in *West African Resistance: The Military Response to Colonial Occupation* (London, 1971), a contribution to a subgenre, "resistance studies."

That oral tradition and indigenous scholarship had greater impact on the study of former British West Africa than on former British East Africa can be seen by comparing the now-standard multivolume histories. *The History of West Africa*, in two volumes (London, 1971–1974), was edited by two historians at Nigerian universities, J. F. A. Ajayi and Michael Crowder. Nineteen of the thirty-three contributors were from African universities. The *History of East Africa*, also in two volumes (London, 1963–1965), had been edited by Roland Oliver and Gervase Mathew (vol. 1) and Vincent Harlow and E. M. Chilver (vol. 2), all at British universities, and the twenty-nine essays were all by Europeans. By 1976 the situation in East Africa was more nearly like that in West Africa: nine of twelve essayists in Bethwell A. Ogot's *History and Social Change in East Africa* (Nairobi, 1976) were from East Africa. Histories based on oral tradition were appearing, as with Samwiri Rubaraza Karugiri's short *Nuwa Mbaguta and the Establishment of British Rule in Ankole* (Nairobi, 1973); traditionally constructed histories were being written by local scholars, as in Semakula Kiwanuka's *A History of Buganda: From the Foundation of the Kingdom to 1900* (London, 1972) or A. I. Salim's *Swahili-speaking Peoples of Kenya's Coast, 1895–1965* (Nairobi, 1973); and again, significant gaps were being filled, as in M. P. K. Sorrenson's very able *Origins of European Settlement in Kenya* (Nairobi, 1968); A. T. Matson's *Nandi Resistance to British Rule, 1890–1906* (Nairobi, 1972); or John W. Cell's edition of the correspondence of two significant formulators of the terms for policy debate, Norman Leys and J. H. Oldham, in *By Kenya Possessed* (Chicago, 1976). East Africa, like West, also continued to be the battleground on which economic historians and others fought out their positions on larger issues, as in Richard D. Wolff's *The Economics of Colonialism: Britain and Kenya, 1870–1930* (New Haven, Conn., 1974) or E. A. Brett's *Colonialism and Underdevelopment in East Africa: The Politics of Economic Change, 1919–1939* (New York, 1973). Perhaps most important of all was Colin Leys's *Underdevelopment in Kenya: The Political Economy of Neo-colonialism, 1964–1971* (London, 1975).[19]

Literature on the Crown Jewel of empire is no less extensive, of course, and yet much of the recent outpouring on and from India has been focused so intensively inward as to be less relevant to imperial considerations. This is not because the empire in India has slipped from consciousness, so much as because the mastery of the range of Indian languages necessary to write the "newer" type of imperial history requires a longer maturation period. There was rather less self-conscious use of oral tradition, and perhaps less need to work in local languages, when writing of India, Malaya, or the Pacific Islands, though there were also notable exceptions. But the number of titles of central importance to the historian who preferred the adjective "imperial" to his name was, in proportion to the literature as a whole, less for Asia than for Africa. Indeed, one might argue that one could best grasp the imperial dimension to the history of the subcontinent through the novels of Paul Scott rather than through formal history.[20] A particularly able review of the literature on India, by Robin J. Moore, showed over two hundred titles published between 1960 and 1975, with which the serious student of Indian history must deal; happily that article relieves this writer from the need to survey the literature.[21] The trends most clearly pursued were marked out in 1965 and

1966: deeper cuts into the old battlements of British imperial concerns, as in Peter J. Marshall's *The Impeachment of Warren Hastings* (London, 1965); close pursuit of specific policymakers, as in Robin J. Moore's own *Sir Charles Wood's Indian Policy, 1853–66* (Manchester, 1966); strategic reconnaissance of policies as developed from London, as in Sarvepalli Gopal's *British Policy in India, 1858–1905* (London, 1965); and as in Africa, close studies of the impact of British policy at the village level, as in Robert Eric Frykenberg's *Guntur District, 1788–1848: A History of Local Influence and Central Authority in South India* (London, 1965). To those trends may be added four others of interest to imperial historians: the application to Indian studies of theoretical statements initially devised for use elsewhere, as in Anil Seal's use of Robinson and Gallagher's collaborator motif in *The Emergence of Indian Nationalism: Competition and Collaboration in the Later Eighteenth Century* (London, 1968); "village level" studies of the British community, as in Suresh Chandra Ghosh's *The Social Condition of the British Community in Bengal, 1757–1800* (Leiden, 1970); biographies of significant Indian leaders prior to Tilak, Gokhale, Gandhi, and Nehru, as in Bawa Satinder Singh's *The Jammu Fox* (Carbondale, Pa., 1974), a biography of Maharaja Gulab Singh of Kashmir; and studies of how the Indian question was embedded in larger strategic issues, as in David Gillard's *The Struggle for Asia, 1828–1914: A Study in British and Russian Imperialism* (London, 1977). Most persistently imperial of all, of course, were the many books on decolonization, in India always referred to as "the transfer of power" question, which spawned a large literature, of which H. V. Hodson's *The Great Divide: Britain— India—Pakistan* (London, 1969) was, in strengths and weaknesses, the most representative.

The sweep of British imperial interests across the Indian Ocean and into the China Sea was traced in two thorough and imaginative volumes by Gerald S. Graham, first in *Great Britain in the Indian Ocean, 1810–1850* (Oxford, 1967), then in *The China Station: War and Diplomacy, 1830–1860* (London, 1979). While Ceylon and Hong Kong invited, as two anchors to that sweep, closer attention, they received far less than Malaya, which in the 1960s experienced the same developments as did African and Indian imperial histories. The traditional literature was massively excerpted and represented in John Bastin and Robin W. Winks's *Malaysia* (London, 1966), which looked backward. While subsequent traditionally organized titles of importance would appear, of which the new edition of Nicholas Tarling's *British Policy in the Malay Peninsula and Archipelago, 1824–1871* (London, 1969), C. Mary Turnbull's *The Straits Settlements, 1826– 67: Indian Presidency to Crown Colony* (London, 1972), and Robert Pringle's *Rajahs and Rebels: The Ibans of Sarawak under Brooke Rule, 1841–1941* (Ithaca, N.Y., 1970) were the most valuable, the trend was toward studies of the indigenous peoples and the impact upon them of the British presence. The breakthrough, as it were, had been achieved in 1958 by J. M. Gullick in his *Indigenous Political Systems of Western Malaya* (London). Now followed many titles with more than local significance, for they revealed with greater clarity than similar studies for African society had yet done, especially for the imperial historian, what the dimensions of that impact were. The most important of these was William R. Roff's fine *The Origins of Malay Nationalism* (New Haven, Conn., 1967), based on equal knowledge of Malay and British cultures. There then followed such key works as Emily Sadka's *The Protected Malay States, 1874–1895* (Kuala Lumpur, 1968), Philip Loh Fook Seng's *The Malay States, 1877–1895: Political Change and Social Policy* (Singapore, 1969), Eunice Thio's *British Policy in the Malay Peninsula, 1880–1910* (Singapore, 1969), R. Bonney's *Kedah, 1771–1821: The Search for Security and Independence* (London, 1971), and Khoo Kay Kim's *The Western Malay States, 1850–1873: The Effects of Commercial Development on Malay Politics* (London, 1972). Drawing in apparently equal measure on the methodologies represented by Gullick, Roff, and Chai Hon-Chan in *The Development of British Malaya, 1896–1909* (London, 1964), these and subsequent studies of the rubber and tin industries, of agency houses, the Emergency, and the creation of the Malayan Union provided for a rich historical underpinning to future imperial and Malaysian studies.

The empire in the East, always a staple of imperial history, was served by a lifeline through the Mediterranean and via the Suez Canal or the Persian Gulf to India. This lifeline was reflected in the literature, with diplomatic history blending almost imperceptibly with imperial history. The classic works, such as Sir John A. R. Marriott's *The Eastern Question* (London), first published in 1917, or Winston F. Monk's terse *Britain in the Western Mediterranean* (London, 1953), correctly reflected a subfield that grew less rapidly than any other. The literature on the Mediterranean remains sparse: there is Edith Dobie on *Malta's Road to Independence* (Norman, Okla., 1967) and Dennis Austin on *Malta and the End of Empire* (London, 1971), and a close study of *Party Politics in a Fortress Colony* (Valletta, 1979). But there is markedly little of value on Cyprus, or new on Gibraltar. Michael Pratt has written elegantly but superficially of *Britain's Greek Empire* (London, 1978), and David Walder of *The Chanak Affair* (London, 1969), and there a truly short list ends.

The literature on Suez is richer and growing, often embedded in general studies of "the Near Eastern Question" or of Anglo-Egyptian relations. Elizabeth Monroe's *Britain's Moment in the Middle East, 1914–1956* (London, 1963) remains the most balanced, but Ann Williams's *Britain and France in the Middle East and North Africa* (London, 1968) is also excellent, and M. A. Fitzsimons's *Empire by Treaty: Britain and the Middle East in the Twentieth Century* (London, 1965), though operating largely on the surface, is succinct. Richard Allen's *Imperialism and Nationalism in the Fertile Crescent* (New York, 1974) explores the

British contribution to the Arab-Israeli conflict, as does Aaron S. Klieman's *Foundations of British Policy in the Arab World: The Cairo Conference of 1921* (Baltimore, 1970). While the books of John Marlowe remain useful, three in particular have altered their angle of vision considerably: Afaf Lutfi al-Sayyid's *Egypt and Cromer* (London, 1968), Peter Mansfield's *The British in Egypt* (London, 1971), and Alexander Schölch's *Ägypten den Agyptern!: Die politische und gesellschaftliche Krise der Jahre 1878–1882 in Ägypten* (Zurich, 1972), as of course has Robinson and Gallagher. Robert O. Collins has continued to make the Sudan his own, following *The Southern Sudan, 1883–1898: The Struggle for Control* (New Haven, Conn., 1962) with *King Leopold, England, and the Upper Nile, 1899–1909* (New Haven, Conn., 1968) and *Land Beyond the Rivers: The Southern Sudan, 1898–1918* (New Haven, Conn., 1971). "Chinese" Gordon still eludes even subtle minds, as shown by the latest biography, *Charles Gordon: An Eminent Victorian Reassessed* (London, 1978) by Charles P. Chenevix Trench. J. B. Kelly's *Britain and the Persian Gulf, 1795–1880* (London, 1968) remains the essential volume, though Sir Denis Wright's *The English Amongst the Persians* (London, 1977) is more fun. And Briton Cooper Busch maintains his hold on the post-Kelly years, with *Britain and the Persian Gulf, 1894–1914* (Berkeley, Calif., 1967), *Britain, India, and the Arabs, 1914–1921* (Berkeley, Calif., 1971), and *Mudros to Lausanne: Britain's Frontier in West Asia, 1918–1923* (Albany, N.Y., 1976).

While the lifeline was manned for the sake of India, it was Australia and New Zealand that lay at the uttermost end of it. While New Zealand long remained a true dependency of Britain, both the reality and the historiography of Australia were to pursue a different road, and even more than for Canada one may say that most writing on this "white Dominion" can stand alone, outside the imperial mainstream. The empire is hardly present in Russel Ward's fine *The History of Australia: The Twentieth Century* (New York, 1977), and though the four majestic, idiosyncratic, utterly irreplaceable volumes of C. M. H. Clark's *A History of Australia* (Melbourne, 1962–1978) were aware enough of the empire, the preoccupations, like the tone of voice, were distinctly Australian. There were important books, of course, which tied Britain and Australia thoroughly to each other, as did Peter Burrough's *Britain and Australia 1831–55: A Study in Imperial Relations and Crown Lands Administration* (Oxford, 1967). Any study of Australia as an "open space" contributed to imperial studies, and the long debate engendered by Russel Ward's *The Australian Legend* (Melbourne, 1958) continued.[22] Geoffrey Blainey's *Tyranny of Distance*, discussed earlier, showed, through its subtitle, an imperial theme: *How Distance Shaped Australia's History*. A provocative look at "the creative spirit in Australia from 1788 to 1972," by Geoffrey Serle, in *From Deserts the Prophets Come* (Melbourne, 1973), raised many colonial and imperial questions. So, too, of course, did such a title as

A. C. Palfreeman's *The Administration of the White Australiaa Policy* (Melbourne, 1967). Perhaps most obviously, the spate of studies on convict settlers, such as *The Convict Settlers of Australia* by I. L. Robson (London, 1965) continued to tie the empire together, both A. G. L. Shaw and George Rudé exploring the connection carefully in their respective books, *Convicts and the Colonies: A Study of Penal Transportation from Great Britain and Ireland to Australia and Other Parts of the British Empire* (London, 1966) and *Protest and Punishment: The Story of the Social and Political Protestors Transported to Australia, 1788–1868* (London, 1979).[23]

"Last, loneliest, loveliest": thus Kipling on New Zealand. It continued to enjoy the best short history of any of the Dominions, *A History of New Zealand* (Harmondsworth, 1959, and London, 1961) by Keith Sinclair, first published in 1959 and now oddly out of print. Sinclair had not only staked out the main claim to the Maori Wars; he had written charming biography of *William Pember Reeves, New Zealand Fabian* (London, 1965) and a fascinating, careful account of New Zealand's last, significant, British-born prime minister, *Walter Nash* (Auckland, 1976). But the Maori Wars in particular attracted much further attention, being a genuinely imperial series of wars. In *Race Conflict in New Zealand, 1814–1865* (Auckland, 1966), Harold Miller set out the facts. B. J. Dalton, in *War and Politics in New Zealand, 1855–1870* (Sydney, 1967), provided a greatly altered view of Governor Gore Browne. Alan Ward, in *A Show of Justice: Racial "Amalgamation" in Nineteenth Century New Zealand* (Toronto, 1973), vigorously attacked the notion that Maori-*pakeha* relations had been, on the whole, relatively benign. Peter Adams, in *Fatal Necessity: British Intervention in New Zealand, 1830–1847* (Auckland, 1977), shifted the focus back to Britain and its needs.

With the development of Maori studies in New Zealand universities, much the same trends one encountered in Africa could be seen. *The Journal of the Polynesian Society* and the new *Journal of Pacific History*, begun at the Australian National University in 1966, published more and more articles based on oral tradition. Major Maori figures were examined, as in J. B. Condliffe's *Te Rangi Hiroa: The Life of Sir Peter Buck* (Christchurch, 1971); the dynamics of Maori society in reaction to the European was investigated, as in John A. Williams's *Politics of the New Zealand Maori: Protest and Cooperation, 1891–1909* (Seattle, 1969); and the impact of the Maori on observant whites was probed, as in Judith Binney's *The Legacy of Guilt: A Life of Thomas Kendall* (Christchurch, 1968). Most interesting of all, Maori scholars began to recount the history of their own people, as in Maharaia Winiata's *The Changing Role of the Leader in Maori Society* (Auckland, 1967) or P. W. Hohepa's *A Maori Community in Northland* (Auckland, 1964), on Waima, a Hokianga community.

Out beyond lay the islands, each acquiring a small literature of its own. Towering above all else arose the mountain built by J. C. Beaglehole in his life's work,

The Life of Captain James Cook (London, 1974). Francis West wrote of *Hubert Murray: The Australian Pro-consul* (Melbourne, 1968), who administered Papua for thirty-three years. Noel Rutherford looked to a renegade missionary who became the most important force in Tonga, in *Shirley Baker and the King of Tonga* (Melbourne, 1971), while H. E. Maude roamed the Pacific much in the manner of the *Annales* school, in *Of Islands and Men: Studies in Pacific History* (Melbourne, 1968). Paul M. Kennedy provided a fresh look at *The Samoan Tangle: A Study in Anglo-German-American Relations, 1878–1900* (New York, 1974), and J. W. Davidson wrote on "the emergence of the independent state of Western Samoa" in *Samoa mo Samoa* (Melbourne, 1967). Across the far Pacific, Barry M. Gough brought the empire up against the Canadian shores in *The Royal Navy and the Northwest Coast of North America, 1810–1914: A Study of the British Maritime Ascendancy* (Vancouver, 1971).

Thus by a devious path imperial history once again came to the Mother Dominion, the First Dominion, the linchpin of empire, the first of those historiographies once summarized in the phrase "from colony to nationhood," though no longer. Canadian history had, of course, developed quite independently of British imperial or even Commonwealth history. Rather, it tended to be mixed into diplomatic history, especially of the Anglo-American relationship, in a way that invariably brought a third guest to the dinner table. When Deryck Scarr wrote his *Fragments of Empire: A History of the Western Pacific High Commission, 1877–1914* (Canberra, 1968), he had to give relatively little attention to the United States even as the Pacific was becoming an American lake. Canadians, whether writing of their constitution or of their most imperially oriented leaders, had always to be aware of the continental dimension to their work. As a result, Canadian writing is best set apart from imperial historiography and, with few exceptions, should be examined elsewhere.[24]

Yet, Canada is central to the story of the British Empire. One cannot truly comprehend the process of decolonization without understanding the "first decolonization." So many of the precedents by which colonies did evolve to nationhood as constitutionally defined arose from Canadian circumstances as to put a little bit of Canadian history into the mainstream of Nigerian, or Sri Lankan, or Malaysian history. So many governors who rose to prominence elsewhere began their administrative careers in one of the Canadian colonies. So many decisions made by the British government with respect to foreign policy arose from an awareness of Canada as an Achilles heel, a hostage to the United States, as to make Anglo-Japanese relations, for example, inexplicable without a Canadian component. Paradoxically, Canada stands most central of all the Dominions to the imperial story; and yet, because it has developed its own complex historiography— rendered doubly complex because of the theme of the "two cultures"—it also stands apart from the mainstream in many ways. Obviously a book such as Kenneth Bourne's *Britain and the Balance of Power in North America, 1815–1908* (London, 1967) is about the empire in a way that Mason Wade's massive study *The French Canadians, 1760–1967* (rev. ed. 2 vols., Toronto, 1968) is not. Yet the persistent theme of French-Canadian loyalty to the British Crown through the nineteenth century certainly makes Wade's first volume essential reading even for the scholar who thinks that a title such as Roger Hyam's *Elgin and Churchill at the Colonial Office: The Watershed of the Empire-Commonwealth, 1905–1908* (London, 1968) best encapsulates the central intent of imperial history.

The Canadian historian who has most persistently kept one eye cocked to the empire and its meaning for Canada has been Donald Creighton. The very title of *The Forked Road: Canada, 1939–1957* (Toronto, 1976) reveals its bias and its strength, for many (perhaps most) historians would have thought Canada reached the fork in the road in 1919. Creighton's thoughtful collection of essays, *Towards the Discovery of Canada* (Toronto, 1972), not only reminds one that the co-creator, as it were, of the Laurentian thesis (together with H. A. Innis) has always seen Canada within the larger imperial context, but in such an essay as "The Victorians and the Empire," lavishes an intelligent affection upon that connection.

Clearly three types of Canadian studies above others are integrated into imperial history. These are biographies of essentially imperial figures, such as Janet Adam Smith's *John Buchan* (1965), with its closing invocation of a stoic whose "boy's dreams were still bright" even as he wrote *Sick Heart River* as Lord Tweedsmuir; or studies of Canada within the problem of imperial defense, as in Richard A. Preston's *The Defence of the Undefended Border: Planning for War in North America, 1867–1939* (Montreal, 1977) or the first volume of C. P. Stacey's *Canada and the Age of Conflict: A History of Canadian External Policies* (Toronto, 1977), which runs from confederation to 1921 and integrates imperial with foreign policy issues; or studies of how Canada was, in the words of its premier novelist, Hugh Maclennan, content for a while to "set out in the wet" and "do its duty by the English as long as there was an England left." Canadians were not, of course, ever so docile as Maclennan's remark about Haligonians suggests, but studies like Arthur R. M. Lower's *Great Britain's Woodyard: British America and the Timber Trade, 1763–1867* (Montreal, 1973) do attest to the link that staple dependency created, a link not yet sufficiently studied in the context of *dependencia* theory. Finally, such a close study as Philip G. Wigley's *Canada and the Transition to Commonwealth: British-Canadian Relations, 1917–1926* (Cambridge, 1977) reminds one, in the grand tradition of R. MacGregor Dawson, of Canada's pivotal role in Commonwealth developments.

Yet so much remains undone. There is a new biography of *Curzon in India* by David Dilks (2 vols., London, 1969–1970) but none for Curzon's entire career, nor for Kitchener, nor Raffles, nor Mountbatten. The state of inquiry into the history of the Christian missions, despite ever more accessible primary materials, remains desperately poor, for the work is either excessively Western (if now less pietistic than heretofore), as in Stephen Neill's *Colonialism and Christian Missions* (London, 1966); excessively journalistic and skeptical, as in Geoffrey Moorhouse's *The Missionaries* (London, 1973); or excessively narrow and unimaginative, as in Harris W. Mobley's *The Ghanaian's Image of the Missionary* (Leiden, 1970), which is all too faithfully revealed through its subtitle, *An Analysis of the Published Critiques of Christian Missionaries by Ghanaians, 1897–1865*. There are exceptions, of course: three such are Ake Holmberg's *African Tribes and European Agencies: Colonialism and Humanitarianism in British South and East Africa, 1870–1895* (Goteborg, 1966); E. A. Ayandele's *The Missionary Impact on Modern Nigeria, 1842–1914: A Political and Social Analysis* (London, 1966); and J. F. A. Ajayi's *Christian Missions in Nigeria 1841–1891* (London, 1965).

The state of the art is equally dismal when one looks to so important a question as the impact and transfer of technologies. Indeed, if one may, for the moment, accept one definition of imperialism as "the impact of high technology societies on lesser technologies,"[25] one must conclude that very few of the central questions have even been asked, much less answered. Daniel R. Headrick, in "The Tools of Imperialism: Technology and the Expansion of European Colonial Empires in the Nineteenth Century" (*JMH* 51 1979: 231–263), argues persuasively that the tools of imperialism have yet to be examined by historians of science or technology. Suggestions appear here and there, of course, in the history of exploration and discovery—Harrison on malaria, Curtin on disease and the perception of it; Woodruff and Mendelssohn, all previously cited, approach the subject. Most military and naval histories are more explicitly aware of technology, as are histories of railway building; and there are books (or unpublished dissertations) on such subjects for most British dependencies. Yet the literature remains remarkably thin, even on the obvious choices on which Headrick focused his attention: the river steamboat, the use of quinine, the development of the quick-firing rifle. John Ellis, in *The Social History of the Machine Gun* (New York, 1975), was very good on industrialized war; Carlo M. Cipolla in several books, most notably *Guns, Sails and Empires: Technological Innovation and the Early Phases of European Expansion, 1400–1700* (New York, 1975), was provocative and brief, yet superficial; Thomas R. de Gregori, in *Technology and the Economic Development of the Tropical African Frontier* (Cleveland, 1969), wrote as economist rather than historian. Amazingly, a volume entitled *Britain Pre-eminent: Studies in British World Influence in the Nineteenth Century*, edited by C. J. Bartlett (London, 1969) contains eight essays, with not one on technology.

The sociology of knowledge differs from field to field, time to time, country to country, and certainly from discipline to discipline. One may at best guess why a field takes a certain shape at a specific time. Today missionaries are neither romantic nor believed by many to be of central importance; economic factors are placed well above the desire to Christianize in the litany of "causes of imperialism." Certainly the angry author, the scholar who is aligned to a cause, even the scholar who merely seeks to reflect the headlines in a sensitive way, will find "resistance studies" more attractive than missiology. Certainly the body of literature on empire in Africa will continue to outstrip that on empire in Asia, especially since American scholarship has turned to the field; for the practical implications for current political and social understanding are clearer, the language barriers are less formidable, and the costs of research are less. Some subjects—important ones—are treated with the kind of wild justice Bacon spoke of when defining revenge. We badly need a multiplicity of biographies of mid-level administrators, of "the men-on-the-spot"; we need to examine empire from the bottom up as well as the top down; we need to understand how the introduction of new grasses, new crops, new diseases, influenced man.[26] These are exciting subjects, but perhaps less so than accounts of political intrigue, economic exploitation, and military and diplomatic confrontation.[27]

Perhaps the field has not changed so much after all, since 1966 or even 1946. Between 1974 and 1977 the University of Minnesota Press published eight volumes of a projected ten-volume history of *Europe and the World in the Age of Expansion* (Minneapolis). The project itself was traditional in title and conception. Thoroughly well-established scholars were chosen for each volume, scholars with the expertise of Holden Furber, K. G. Davies, Ernest Dodge, and W. David McIntyre. Yet with the exception of some passages in the volumes by Raymond F. Betts and A. P. Thornton (the last in press),[28] the entire series might well have been written, aside from the growing density of data, two decades ago. Even the considerable growth in Victorian studies generally seems to have had little impact. The problem child remains as Philip Curtin found it in 1966, only larger: intractable, unduly regionalized, yet ever open to daring and original thinking, exciting, attractive, frustrating, depressing—indeed, a reflection of the very empire it seeks to record.

NOTES

1. Vincent Harlow, "The Historiography of the British Empire and Commonwealth since 1945," *Rapports*, vol. 5, *Histoire Contemporaine*, International Committee of Historical Sciences, Stockholm, August 21–28, 1960, Uppsala, 1960, 11; Robin W. Winks, ed., *The Historiography of the British Empire-Commonwealth*, Durham, N.C., 1966, 3–22.

2. David K. Fieldhouse, "'Imperialism': An Historiographical Revision," *Economic History Review*, 2d ser., 14, 1961: 187–209.

3. See C. Vann Woodward, ed., *The Comparative Approach to American History*, New York,

1968, and Marcus Cunliffe and Robin W. Winks, ed., *Pastmasters: Some Essays on American Historians*, New York, 1969.

4. Now being translated by John Williamson.

5. These issues are presented in Laura Foner and Eugene D. Genovese, eds., *Slavery in the New World: A Reader in Comparative History*, Englewood Cliffs, N.J., 1969, and Robin W. Winks, ed., *Slavery: A Comparative Perspective*, New York, 1972.

6. There is a large literature on this subject, though one may still best begin with Hannah Arendt's conceptualization in *The Origins of Totalitarianism*, New York, 1951.

7. This general question is frequently the subject of articles in the *Journal of Commonwealth and Comparative Politics*, the successor to the *Journal of Commonwealth Political Studies*.

8. We seriously need studies of the writings and public impact of G. A. Henty, Gordon Staples, Dornford Yates, Richard Harding Davis, Joseph Altsheler, and (even yet) H. Rider Haggard, despite much literature on the last.

9. One might best begin with Jan Vansina, "Once upon a Time: Oral Traditions as History in Africa," *Daedalus* 100, 1971: 442–468; Ruth Finnegan, *Oral Literature in Africa*, London, 1970; and Joseph C. Miller, "The Dynamics of Oral Tradition, in Africa" in Bernardo Bernardi, ed., *Fonti Orali: Antropologia e storia*, Milan, 1978, 75–101.

10. Henri Baudet, *Paradise on Earth*, New Haven, Conn., 1965, 75.

11. In H. L. Wesseling, ed., *Expansion and Reaction*, Leiden, 1978, 141–163.

12. The central work has now been summarized in Joseph A. Kahl, *Modernization, Exploitation and Dependency in Latin America: Germani, González Casanova and Cardoso*, New Brunswick, N.J., 1976. A. G. Hopkins has warned against "On Importing André Gunder Frank into Africa" too readily, in the *African Economic History Review* 2, 1975: 13–21.

13. The *Journal of British Studies*, begun in 1961, also contains many relevant articles. See Vincent Harlow, *The Founding of the Second British Empire, 1763–1793*, 2 vols., London, 1952–1964; C. A. Bodelsen, *Studies in Mid-Victorian Imperialism*, London, 1960; Helen Taft Manning, *British Colonial Government after the American Revolution, 1782–1820*, Hamden, Conn., 1966.

14. I have written at greater length on the problem of formulating theory in "On Decolonization and Informal Empire," *AH Review* 81, 1976: 540–556.

15. On Kiernan, see Owen Dudley Edwards, ed., "History and Humanism: Essays in Honour of V. G. Kiernan," whole no. of *New Edinburgh Review*, nos. 38–39, 1977; and idem, *America: The New Imperialism: From White Settlement to World Hegemony*, London, 1978. Though one of our most imaginative and least shrill Marxist historians of imperialism, Kiernan nonetheless presents problems of strict factual accuracy. Compare, where relevant, his *The Lords of Human Kind*, London, 1969, with H. A. C. Cairns, *Prelude to Imperialism: British Reactions to Central African Society, 1840–1890*, London, 1965, also not without fault, in the way they deal with image and perception.

16. And some are not. See, for example, the tone of unreconstructed imperialism in Robert Blake's *A History of Rhodesia*, New York, 1978, and compare it with T. O. Ranger, *The African Voice in Southern Rhodesia, 1898–1930*, London, 1970.

17. See, *seriatim*, the *Journal of African History*, among many.

18. We particularly await a biography of Lord Hailey, whom Sir Frederick served and of whom he wrote an "appreciation" for the *Journal of the Royal Society of Arts* 118, 1970: 484–492.

19. The entire problem of "underdevelopment" requires much fuller study, and here, too, African and Latin American scholarship must be read together. Two places to begin are Celso Furtado, *Economic Development of Latin America: A Survey from Colonial Times to the Cuban Revolution* London, 1970, and Dan Nabudere, *The Political Economy of Imperialism: Its Theoretical and Polemical Treatment from Mercantilist to Multilateral Imperialism* London, 1977.

20. Especially Paul Scott, "Raj Quartet": *The Jewel in the Crown, The Day of the Scorpion, The Towers of Silence, A Division of the Spoils*, 1966–1975.

21. Robin J. Moore, "Recent Historical Writing on the Modern British Empire and Commonwealth: Later Imperial India," *Journal of Imperial and Commonwealth History* 4, 1975: 55–76.

22. This book was the subject of a retrospective issue of *Historical Studies* (18, 1978): "The Australian Legend Re-visited."

23. Equally obviously, biographies of certain figures, however Australian they may be, inevitably contribute to imperial history. An example is L. F. Fitzhardinge's two volumes on William Morris Hughes, especially the second, *The Little Digger, 1914–1952* (Sydney, 1979). Another example of a very different sort is A. T. Yarwood's *Samuel Marsden: The Great Survivor* (Melbourne, 1977) which of necessity ties Britain, New Zealand, and Australia together in the fabric of a single life.

24. I have had my say on this subject at length in Winks, *Historiography*, 69–136, and subsequently in *The Relevance of Canadian History* (Toronto, 1979), and will not repeat myself here. The reader should also go to Carl Berger, *The Writing of Canadian History: Aspects of English-Canadian Historical Writing, 1900 to 1970* (Toronto, 1976); Lewis H. Thomas, *The Renaissance of Canadian History: A Biography of A. L. Burt* (Toronto, 1975); and on the manner in which a separate French-Canadian historiography reacts to English-Canadian writing, to the several works of Ramsay Cook.

25. This is an operative definition employed, in different words, in this writer's essay "Imperialism" in the *Encyclopedia Americana*, 1972, 14:820–824.

26. Still useful is "The Moving Frontiers of Disease" in A. Grenfell Price, *The Western Invasions of the Pacific and Its Continents: A Study of Moving Frontiers and Changing Landscapes, 1513–1958*, London, 1963, and Alfred W. Crosby, Jr., has written a fascinating account of *The Columbian Exchange: Biological and Cultural Consequences of 1492*, Westport, Conn., 1972. While usefully suggestive, William H. McNeill's *Plagues and Peoples*, London, 1976, operates at too high a level of generalization.

27. Yet, one wonders: the idea of the collaborator is full of notions of political and economic intrigue, but there are markedly few case studies of the matrix of relations suggested by the term. The Asian equivalent, the comprador, has been studied somewhat, but not much, more. Examples of use to British imperial historians include Yen-P'ing Hao, *The Comprador in Nineteenth Century China: Bridge between East and West*, Cambridge, Mass., 1970, and Norman G. Owen, ed., *Compadre Colonialism: Studies on the Philippines under American Rule*, Michigan Papers on South and Southeast Asia, no. 3, Ann Arbor, 1971.

28. Several new books are in press at the time of writing, and I have been able to read many of them in manuscript and include them as supportive of my generalizations here, but none are cited.

Index of Authors

493

Authors of the Essays

Stephen B. Baxter is Professor of History at the University of North Carolina.

L. P. Curtis, Jr., is Professor of History at Brown University.

Barbara A. Hanawalt is Professor of History at Indiana University.

Maurice Lee, Jr., is Professor of History at Rutgers University.

Bryce Lyon is the Barnaby C. and Mary Critchfield Keeney Professor of Medieval History at Brown University.

Wallace MacCaffrey is Professor of History at Harvard University.

D. C. Moore is a Research Associate of the Center for European Studies at Harvard University.

Robert A. Smith is Professor of History at Emory University.

Henry L. Snyder is Dean of the College of Arts and Sciences at Louisiana State University.

Peter Stansky is Professor of History at Stanford University.

David Underdown is Professor of History at Brown University.

Henry R. Winkler is President of the University of Cincinnati.

Robin W. Winks is Professor of History and Master of Berkeley College at Yale University.

DATE DUE